Political Economy: Institutions, Competition, and Representation presents some of the recent developments in political economy and political science formal theory, along with recent applications of the two closely related areas of theoretical research. Advances in the interface between economics and political science have rendered this area of research very productive in recent years.

The contents of this volume comprise the proceedings of the seventh conference in a series entitled International Symposia in Economic Theory and Econometrics, under the general editorship of William Barnett. This conference was held at Washington University in St. Louis on May 22–25, 1991. The symposia in the series are sponsored by the IC² Institute at the University of Texas at Austin and are cosponsored by the RGK Foundation. This seventh conference was also cosponsored by the Faculty of Arts and Sciences, the Center in Political Economy and the Center for the Study of American Business at Washington University in St. Louis, and the Department of Economics and the Graduate School of Business at the University of Texas at Austin.

The co-organizers of the seventh symposium, which produced the current proceedings volume, were William Barnett, Melvin Hinich, Douglass North, Howard Rosenthal, and Norman Schofield. The co-editors of this proceedings volume are William Barnett, Melvin Hinich, and Norman Schofield.

Political economy: Institutions, competition, and representation

International Symposia in Economic Theory and Econometrics

Editor
William A. Barnett, *Washington University in St. Louis*

Other books in the series

William A. Barnett and A. Ronald Gallant
New approaches to modeling, specification selection, and econometric inference

William A. Barnett and Kenneth J. Singleton
New approaches to monetary economics

William A. Barnett, Ernst R. Berndt, and Halbert White
Dynamic econometric modeling

William A. Barnett, John Geweke, and Karl Shell
Economic complexity

William A. Barnett, James Powell, and George E. Tauchen
Nonparametric and semiparametric methods in econometrics and statistics

William A. Barnett, Bernard Cornet, Claude D'Aspremont,
Jean Gabszewicz, and Andreu Mas-Colell
Equilibrium theory and applications

Political economy: Institutions, competition, and representation

Proceedings of the Seventh International Symposium
in Economic Theory and Econometrics

Edited by

WILLIAM A. BARNETT
Washington University in St. Louis

MELVIN J. HINICH
University of Texas

NORMAN J. SCHOFIELD
Washington University in St. Louis

CAMBRIDGE
UNIVERSITY PRESS

CAMBRIDGE
UNIVERSITY PRESS

32 Avenue of the Americas, New York NY 10013-2473, USA

Cambridge University Press is part of the University of Cambridge.

It furthers the University's mission by disseminating knowledge in the pursuit of
education, learning and research at the highest international levels of excellence.

www.cambridge.org
Information on this title: www.cambridge.org/9780521417815

© Cambridge University Press 1993

This publication is in copyright. Subject to statutory exception
and to the provisions of relevant collective licensing agreements,
no reproduction of any part may take place without the written
permission of Cambridge University Press.

First published 1993

A catalogue record for this publication is available from the British Library

Library of Congress Cataloguing in Publication data

International Symposium in Economic Theory and Econometrics (7th :
1991 : Washington University)

Political economy : Institutions, competition, and representation :
proceedings of the Seventh International Symposium in Economic
Theory and Econometrics / edited by William A. Barnett, Melvin J.
Hinich, Norman J. Schofield.

p.   cm. – (International symposia in economic theory and
econometrics)

Includes index.

ISBN 0-521-41781-3 – ISBN 0-521-42831-9 (pbk.)

1. Political science – Congresses.   2. Economics – Congresses.
I. Barnett, William A.   II. Hinich, Melvin J.   III. Schofield,
Norman J., 1944–   . IV. Title. V. Series.
JA77.I58   1991
338.9 – dc20   92–43595
                                                         CIP

ISBN 978-0-521-41781-5 Hardback

Cambridge University Press has no responsibility for the persistence or accuracy
of URLs for external or third-party internet websites referred to in this publication,
and does not guarantee that any content on such websites is, or will remain,
accurate or appropriate.

Contents

Series editor's preface

The contents of this volume comprise the proceedings of the conference, "Political Economy: Institutions, Competition, and Representation," held at Washington University in St. Louis on May 22–25, 1991. The objective was to present some of the recent developments in political economy and political science formal theory, along with recent applications of the two closely related areas of theoretical research. Advances in the interface between economics and political science have rendered this area of research very productive in recent years. An introductory overview of the papers in the volume was contributed by Norman Schofield, who is one of the co-editors of the volume and one of the co-organizers of the symposium. The overview includes his personal perspective regarding the conference papers and symposium topics.

Two interesting themes are especially evident in this volume. One is the important role in political economy of research on conflict and communication between government and voters; the other is the possible importance of mathematical chaos in modeling political economy. In economic theory, it is now well known that chaos can appear for some parameter settings in even the most classical dynamic models of growth with continuously cleared perfect markets, rational expectations, and Pareto-optimal solution paths.[1] At present, the only confirmed empirical discovery of chaos in economic data is with Barnett's Divisia monetary aggregate data (Barnett and Chen 1986, 1988a,b).[2] The chapter by Barnett in this volume provides theoretical speculations in political economy that may explain

[1] In the case of overlapping-generations modeling, see e.g. Grandmont (1985). In the framework of a Ramsey-type optimal-growth model with infinite lifetimes, see e.g. Boldrin (1989).

[2] Also see Barnett and Choi (1989). The Barnett and Chen discovery was produced by applying nonparametric algorithms used in the experimental physics literature. Those results have been replicated and confirmed by DeCoster and Mitchell (1991). The findings have been further confirmed with conventional statistical testing methods by Barnett and Hinich (1992a,b), using bispectral methods in the frequency domain. Additional tests by

the source of that chaos. In particular, it is found that dynamic gaming between the central bank and the private sector may be relevant to understanding Barnett and Chen's empirical discovery. Further speculations regarding the relevancy of chaos to political economy in general can be found in Schofield's introductory overview and in Ordeshook's Chapter 4 of this volume.

Part I contains overviews of relevant research in the field and general insights into that literature. The rest of the volume is divided into four parts, spanning the scope of the technical papers presented in the conference. Part II concerns representation and voting; Part III, political institutions; Part IV, political competition; Part V, information acquisition by government; and Part VI, government behavior.

Thanks are due to Barry Nalebuff (Yale University), Barry Weingast (Hoover Institution), Howard Rosenthal (Carnegie-Mellon University), Ian Shapiro (Yale University), Kenneth Shepsle (Harvard University), Mary Olson, John Nachbar, Murray Weidenbaum, Anne Sholz, Paul Rothstein, Gary Miller, Robert Parks, Krisha Ladha (Washington University in St. Louis), John Ledyard (California Institute of Technology), and Rebecca Morton (Texas A & M University) for their participation in the conference. I am particularly grateful to Howard Rosenthal and Douglass North, who substantially assisted the editors in the organization of the conference, and to Annette Milford of the Center in Political Economy for her assistance in running the conference and for help in preparing the manuscript.

The conference that produced this proceedings volume is the seventh in a conference series entitled *International Symposia in Economic Theory and Econometrics*. The proceedings series is under the general editorship of William Barnett. Individual volumes in the series generally have co-editors, and the series has a permanent Board of Advisory Editors. The symposia in the series are sponsored by the IC^2 Institute at the University of Texas at Austin and are cosponsored by the RGK Foundation.[3] This seventh conference was also cosponsored by the Faculty of Arts and Sciences of Washington University in St. Louis along with the Center in Political Economy and the Center for the Study of American Business at that university, as well as the Department of Economics and the Graduate School of Business at the University of Texas at Austin.

The first conference in the series was co-organized by William Barnett and Ronald Gallant, who also co-edited the proceedings volume. That

---

Barnett, Gallant, Hinich, and Jensen (1992), including the use of recent neural net methods, have narrowed down the number of monetary aggregates passing the chaos tests.

[3] IC^2 stands for Innovation, Creativity, and Capital.

volume has appeared as the volume 30, October/November 1985 edition of the *Journal of Econometrics* and has been reprinted as a volume in this Cambridge University Press monograph series. The topic was "New Approaches to Modeling, Specification Selection, and Econometric Inference."

Beginning with the second symposium in the series, the proceedings of the symposia appear exclusively as volumes in this Cambridge University Press monograph series. The co-organizers of the second symposium and co-editors of its proceedings volume were William Barnett and Kenneth Singleton. The topic was "New Approaches to Monetary Economics." The co-organizers of the third symposium, which was on "Dynamic Econometric Modeling," were William Barnett and Ernst Berndt; and the co-editors of that proceedings volume were William Barnett, Ernst Berndt, and Halbert White. The co-organizers of the fourth symposium and co-editors of its proceedings volume, which was on "Economic Complexity: Chaos, Sunspots, Bubbles, and Nonlinearity," were William Barnett, John Geweke, and Karl Shell. The co-organizers of the fifth symposium and co-editors of its proceedings volume, which was on "Nonparametric and Semiparametric Methods in Econometrics and Statistics," were William Barnett, James Powell, and George Tauchen. The co-organizers and proceedings co-editors of the sixth symposium, which was on "Equilibrium Theory and Applications," were William Barnett, Bernard Cornet, Claude d'Aspremont, Jean Gabszewicz, and Andreu Mas-Colell.

The co-organizers of the seventh symposium, which produced the current proceedings volume, were William Barnett, Melvin Hinich, Douglass North, Howard Rosenthal, and Norman Schofield. The co-editors of this proceedings volume are William Barnett, Melvin Hinich, and Norman Schofield. The eighth symposium in the series was part of a large-scale conference on "Social Choice, Welfare, and Ethics." That conference was held in Caen, France on June 9–12, 1993. The co-editors of that proceedings volume will be William Barnett, Maurice Salles, Norman Schofield, and Hervé Moulin.

The intention of the volumes in the proceedings series is to provide refereed journal–quality collections of research papers of unusual importance in areas of currently highly visible activity within the economics profession. Because of the refereeing requirements associated with the editing of the proceedings, the volumes in the series will not necessarily contain all of the papers presented at the corresponding symposia.

William A. Barnett
Washington University in St. Louis

REFERENCES

Barnett, William A., and Ping Chen (1986), "Economic Theory as a Generator of Measurable Attractors," *Mondes en Developpement* 14: 209–24. Reprinted in I. Prigogine and M. Sanglier (eds.), *Laws of Nature and Human Conduct: Specificities and Unifying Themes*. Brussels: G.O.R.D.E.S.

(1988a), "The Aggregation-Theoretic Monetary Aggregates are Chaotic and Have Strange Attractors: An Econometric Application of Mathematical Chaos," in W. Barnett, E. Berndt, and H. White (eds.), *Dynamic Econometric Modeling*, Proceedings of the Third International Symposium in Economic Theory and Econometrics. Cambridge: Cambridge University Press.

(1988b), "Deterministic Chaos and Fractal Attractors as Tools for Nonparametric Dynamical Econometric Inference," *Mathematical Computer Modeling* 10: 275–96.

Barnett, William A., and Seungmook S. Choi (1989), "A Comparison between the Conventional Econometric Approach to Structural Inference and the Nonparametric Chaotic Attractor Approach," in W. Barnett, J. Geweke, and K. Shell (eds.), *Economic Complexity: Chaos, Sunspots, Bubbles, and Nonlinearity*, Proceedings of the Fourth International Symposium in Economic Theory and Econometrics. Cambridge: Cambridge University Press.

Barnett, William A., A. Ronald Gallant, Melvin J. Hinich, and Mark J. Jensen (1992), "Robustness of Nonlinearity and Chaos Tests to Measurement Error, Inference Method, and Sample Size," Working Paper no. 167, Department of Economics, Washington University in St. Louis.

Barnett, William, and Melvin J. Hinich (1992a), "Empirical Chaotic Dynamics in Economics," *Annals of Operations Research* 37: 1–15.

(1992b), "Has Chaos Been Discovered with Economic Data?" in P. Chen and R. Day (eds.), *Evolutionary Dynamics and Nonlinear Economics*. Oxford: Oxford University Press.

Boldrin, Michele (1989), "Paths of Optimal Accumulation in Two-Sector Models," in W. Barnett, J. Geweke, and K. Shell (eds.), *Economic Complexity: Chaos, Sunspots, Bubbles, and Nonlinearity*, Proceedings of the Fourth International Symposium in Economic Theory and Econometrics. Cambridge: Cambridge University Press.

DeCoster, Gregory P., and Douglas W. Mitchell (1991), "Nonlinear Monetary Dynamics," *Journal of Business and Economic Statistics* 9: 455–62.

Grandmont, J. M. (1985), "On Endogenous Competitive Business Cycles," *Econometrica* 53: 995–1096.

Contributors

David Austen-Smith
Department of Political Science
University of Rochester

Jeffrey S. Banks
Department of Economics
University of Rochester

William A. Barnett
Department of Economics
Washington University in St. Louis

David P. Baron
Graduate School of Business
Stanford University

Randall L. Calvert
Department of Political Science
University of Rochester

John N. Drobak
School of Law
Washington University in St. Louis

Eric Drissen
Faculty of Economics and Econometrics
University of Amsterdam

Tim Groseclose
Social and Decision Sciences
Carnegie Mellon University

Melvin J. Hinich
Department of Government
University of Texas at Austin

Leonid Hurwicz
Department of Economics
University of Minnesota

Keith Krehbiel
Graduate School of Business
Stanford University

Susanne Lohmann
Graduate School of Business
Stanford University

John Londregan
Woodrow Wilson School of
    Public and International Affairs
Princeton University

Arthur Lupia
Department of Political Science
University of California – San Diego

Richard D. McKelvey
Division of Humanities and Social Sciences
California Institute of Technology

Jongryn Mo
Department of Government
University of Texas at Austin

Michael C. Munger
Department of Political Science
University of North Carolina

Roger B. Myerson
Kellogg Graduate School of Management
Northwestern University

Douglass C. North
Center in Political Economy
Washington University in St. Louis

Peter C. Ordeshook
Division of Humanities and
   Social Sciences
California Institute of Technology

Raymond Riezman
Department of Economics
University of Iowa

Thomas Romer
Woodrow Wilson School of
   Public and International Affairs
Princeton University

Norman J. Schofield
Center in Political Economy
Washington University in St. Louis

Rangarajan K. Sundaram
Department of Economics
University of Rochester

Craig A. Tovey
School of Industrial and Systems
   Engineering
College of Computing
Georgia Institute of Technology

Frans van Winden
Faculty of Economics and Econometrics
University of Amsterdam

Political economy: A personal interpretation and an overview

Norman J. Schofield

1   Political economy: A personal interpretation

It is very natural to think of dynamical systems as *structurally stable,* where this means that small changes in the initial conditions or in the laws of motion will have no qualitative effect on the process. Of course not all processes can be structurally stable, since it is very easy to construct a process that is unstable (in terms of qualitative transformation after perturbation). Until 1966 it was conjectured that structurally stable systems were *generic.* Here generic is a technical term meaning typical in a strong sense. Roughly speaking, a property of a class of models is generic if (i) the property is true of a dense collection of the models (with respect to an appropriate topology on the models), and (ii) any model with the property when perturbed to a small enough degree still has the property. Peixoto (1962) had generically classified all dynamical systems in two dimensions, showing they could be described by sinks, sources, orbits, and so on, thus demonstrating that structurally stable systems were generic in two dimensions. However Smale (1966) constructed a dynamical system with the feature that small changes lead to an infinite variety of qualitatively different systems. At the heart of this construction was the *chaotic strange attractor,* versions of which have been found in simulations of complex systems in meteorology (the Lorenz attractor) and in many other fields (Stewart 1989). Smale's result showed that structurally stable systems could not, in general, be generic.[1]

Some of the ideas presented here were developed while undertaking research sponsored by NSF Grant SES-88-20845. Thanks are due to William Barnett and Donald Saari for helpful comments. Errors in interpretation are my responsibility. I owe a great debt of gratitude to Annette Milford of the Center in Political Economy at Washington University who assisted in the organization of the conference and in the preparation of the book manuscript.

[1] Notice that the Peixoto–Smale result demonstrated that three dimensions were necessary to produce chaos for a dynamical (smooth) system. However, it was later shown (Li and

For social scientists it is equally natural, perhaps, to view the world as essentially deterministic or at least, in principle, predictable. In economic theory, for example, there is a powerful vision of constructing a general equilibrium model of human behavior. It would be arrogant to presume that such a model could even incorporate all aspects of human economic behavior, but it might be reasonable to suppose that it captures the essence of economic production and trade. However, if the true model of human interaction were chaotic, then it would appear very difficult indeed to justify its predictions about human behavior.

The mathematical results on dynamical systems just mentioned show that perfectly reasonable dynamical systems may either be structurally stable (and based on global sinks, sources, limit cycles, etc.) or chaotic (based on strange attractors with fractal dimensions).[2] A priori, there is no reason to suppose that human behavioral systems happen to be of one kind or another. However it is now possible to devise complex statistical tests to check whether chaos exists in real economic or other aggregate data. Recent analyses have conclusively demonstrated the existence of chaos in such data (see Barnett and Chen 1988; Barnett, Gallant, Hinich, and Jensen 1992; Barnett and Hinich 1992) and have estimated the fractal dimension of the strange attractor.

A possible explanation for the occurrence of chaos in economic data is the demonstration by Saari (1991) that a nonlinear difference equation $p_{t+1} = f(p_t)$ (which governs the price changes implied by tâtonnement) can be chaotic. Saari's result depends, in turn, on the existence of an exchange economy whose aggregate excess demand function satisfies the appropriate nonlinear properties.

It is one thing to show the theoretical possibility of chaos in a tâtonnement process, but a much deeper problem, it seems to me, is to model the pattern of human interaction that generates the dynamic process. If such a model could be shown to exhibit a globally stable attractor then we could argue that the process was structurally stable, and make inferences with respect to its predictability. On the other hand, if the properties of the process appear to be deeply susceptible to, say, the structure of beliefs and expectations of the agents being modeled, then chaos may be a real possibility.

Yorke 1976) that chaos can be produced with a 1-dimensional variable x if the change of state rule is discrete, i.e., given by a nonlinear difference equation $x_{t+1} = f(x_t)$. See, for example, May (1975), Rand (1978), and the discussion in Schofield (1980).

[2] It should be mentioned that a dynamical system can be both structurally unstable and nonchaotic. A perturbation of such a system can result in systems of qualitatively different types, either structurally stable or chaotic. Typically, systems of this kind are nowhere dense, and lie on the boundary of classes of chaotic or structurally stable systems.

Arrow's theorem (1951) was extraordinarily prescient in this respect. The focus of his analysis, as I understand it, was the construction of a social welfare function incorporating information concerning all individual preferences. Arrow permitted arbitrary preferences on a finite set of alternatives and showed that the requirement of strong rationality in the social welfare function, together with the usual Pareto (or unanimity) principle, effectively implied dictatorship.

The proof of Arrow's result depended on the demonstration that, for each nondictatorial and Paretian aggregation method, there exists at least one preference profile which gives a social preference violating the rationality rule. However, one may rephrase the Arrow problem for the differentiable category in the following way. Suppose the set of alternatives W has a differentiable structure, and suppose further that f is a simple (or first-order) aggregation procedure that maps a profile $u = (u_1, ..., u_n)$ of preferences or utilities (in a space U), and a list $s = (s_1, ..., s_n)$ of individual characteristics (such as resources) in a space S, into a "social" behavioral rule $f(u, s)$, namely a state transition function or correspondence, on the space W. The strong rationality principle considered by Arrow can be interpreted as the requirement that f be a gradient process, defined in terms of, say, a maximizing principle. If this process exhibits a globally stable attractor, then the process cannot be chaotic. Arrow's result suggests that when f is a gradient system then it is based on a single individual, namely a dictator. For a nondictatorial process f, the relationship between u, s, and the behavior of $f(u, s)$ can be extremely difficult to analyze.

The Peixoto–Smale analysis suggests one way to classify f. Let *Chaos* be the domain in the space $U \times S$ where the dynamical system $f(u, s)$ is chaotic. Similarly, let *Stability* be the domain in $U \times S$ where $f(u, s)$ is structurally stable.[3] Smale's result suggests that, for an interesting (nondictatorial) aggregational rule, the domain *Stability* cannot be a dense set, at least when the state space has high enough dimension.

One possibility is that chaos itself is generic for f. In this case the geometric structure of *Chaos* and *Instability* can be extremely complex. To illustrate the possible degree of complexity, consider the set of irrationals in a compact interval. This set is a *residual* set (namely a countable intersection of open dense sets) which is thus dense. The complement of this set consists of the irrationals. When chaos is generic, then the domains *Chaos* and *Stability* are analogous to the irrationals and rationals, respectively. Generic chaos can occur, for example, if the aggregation rule

---

[3] As implied by note 2, there is also a domain (*Instability*) in $U \times S$ where $f(u, s)$ is structurally unstable.

is based on a voting mechanism of a certain type.[4] A second possibility is that both *Chaos* and *Stability* contain open subsets (and so have non-empty interiors) but neither one is dense.

One research program that has developed from Arrow's result has implications for an understanding of economic processes and suggests that a particular kind of chaos resulting from "manipulation" can be associated with an open class of economies. Gibbard (1973) and Satterthwaite (1975) both gave a significant interpretation of Arrow's theorem when they showed that, with a nondictatorial social choice rule $f(u)$ (that specified a chosen state), individuals may misrepresent their preferences in an attempt to achieve a more preferred outcome. Hurwicz (1972) noted the connection of Arrow's theorem to the analysis of economic systems by demonstrating that exchange economies were susceptible to formal manipulation of this kind. Many authors since then have examined manipulation in preference, or in endowments (Aumann and Peleg 1974; Gale 1974; Guesnerie and Laffont 1978). An important result by Safra (1983) showed that the set of economies that are susceptible to preference manipulation (and therefore resource manipulation) are "rich." More precisely, if we consider the set of all economies, parameterized in some fashion and endowed with an appropriate topology, then there exist open sets of both manipulable and nonmanipulable economies. In a manipulable economy, at least one individual (or agent) is capable of misrepresenting preferencs or resources (perhaps by treating prices nonparametrically) to affect the way the economy behaves in an attempt to bring about a more preferred outcome. Common sense might tell us that the impact of one individual on an economy must be negligible, so that the practical consequences of these results are unimportant. Such an inference is not entirely self-evident. At the time of this writing (September 1992), it is possible that foreign exchange markets – now being described by such terms as "mayhem" and "disorder" – are out of equilibrium, but it is also likely that the markets are engaged in intense speculative manipulation, triggered by political uncertainty in Europe and the United States. A plausible inference is that a manipulable economy will exhibit chaos in its development path. (See a number of the chapters in the volume edited by Barnett, Geweke, and Shell 1989 for theoretical and empirical analyses of speculative bubbles, sunspot equilibria, and complex dynamics.)

---

[4] For a voting procedure, we may ignore the space S. The appropriate parameter space U of smooth profiles is endowed with the Whitney topology. With this topology U is a Baire space. For a voting rule f, the domain *Chaos*, under some conditions, can be shown to be residual and thus dense (McKelvey and Schofield 1986). A *generic property* is one that is satisfied on a dense, residual set.

The results briefly mentioned here on economic and political manipulation are strictly valid only for a simple aggregation procedure, defined by first-order variables such as the profile u and parameter s. To make the social behavioral rule f more realistic, one may add second-order characteristics by modeling in more detail the calculus and behavior of the individuals. While the natural vehicle for any such modeling attempt is game theory, there are a number of ways in which game theory and social choice theory can be combined to give a more complex account of individual behavior.

One way of dealing with the problem of manipulation is through the concept of *implementation*. Given an aggregation procedure f, can a social planner construct a compatible game form (namely, a list of strategy sets for the individuals and a system of regulations or rules) that "oblige" rational individuals to reveal, in some sense, their true preferences and characteristics? As Groves and Ledyard (1980) showed, it is possible to construct a game form that requires individuals to truly reveal their characteristics in Nash equilibrium. As Hurwicz (Chapter 2 in this volume) observes, however, why should individuals restrict themselves to the strategy sets specified by the game form? It may be necessary to add enforcers to monitor behavior. These become agents within the game itself, who themselves require monitoring.

A second possibility with regard to the addition of structure to f is to incorporate beliefs of the individuals. In the manipulation literature the focus is on the existence of an individual i, say, who may lie about u_i or s_i to change the outcome. However, it is clear that there must be an information requirement governing the belief, by i, that such a switch would be beneficial. Suppose i has information that a second individual, j, may also manipulate and bring about an outcome which is worse for both agents. This situation has the structure of a two-person Prisoner's Dilemma. In the single-shot game, each agent has a dominant strategy of noncooperation, so the resulting Hobbesian outcome is non-Paretian. If both cooperate, they can attain a Pareto-optimal outcome. If we consider the extended game, involving n participants, as a simple aggregation procedure, then almost anything can happen (Schofield 1977). Although cooperative coalitions can come into being, they can just as easily collapse. Reiterating the game in time does little to diminish the degree of chaos: Although cooperative coalitions can occur in equilibrium (Taylor 1976), their maintenance depends on knife-edge calculations that ultimately are based on individual beliefs concerning other individuals' behavior. As Calvert shows (Chapter 8), it is possible to sustain cooperation in the two-person game under certain "belief scenarios." However, these beliefs fundamentally depend on foundations in common knowledge (A believes

B believes A . . . will cooperate). As Kreps et al. (1982) have demonstrated, these belief structures may become unstable if the game nears a point of termination.

A more general procedure is to combine these two approaches by adding institutional structure to the aggregation procedure f. That is, we may incorporate complex rules to restrict the behavior and beliefs that individuals use to make sense of their choices. Even institutional enforcement cannot completely maintain institutional rules and regulations, so these will change with time. The beliefs of members will also slowly change to accommodate changing behavior and environment. Underlying the institutional approach is the deep problem that game theory, social choice, and political economy are all obliged to face in attempting to model rational behavior. How exactly do individuals form beliefs about the world and about the behavior of others? Is the process of belief formation (and the consequent individual action) structurally stable? If it is not, then imperceptible perturbations in the structure of any institution can lead to dramatic changes in behavior. This gives a justification for North's view (Chapter 3) that institutional evolution is likely to be "path-dependent." On the other hand, if beliefs were solely based on the operation of the natural world, then one might expect convergence to consensus (McKelvey and Page 1986), at least when communication is rich enough (Weyers 1992). However, if beliefs are held not only about the natural world but also about human rights and responsibilities (as we must expect), then ideological differences could be irreconcilable (see Hinich and Munger, Chapter 1) and human behavior fundamentally chaotic.

The debate concerning the possibility of chaos has been quite vigorous in formal political theory (see the discussion in Ordeshook, Chapter 4). It seems more or less self-evident that political systems can break down unexpectedly into a state of chaos or near-chaos. Aside from noting the examples of the Soviet Union, Eastern Europe, Yugoslavia, and Lebanon, one may wonder about the degree of political stability (as of September 1992) in Italy, for example, or with regard to the process of European integration.

In the analysis of voting models, Arrow's theorem (1951) is often construed in terms of the possibility of constructing a voting cycle (x is socially preferred to y is socially preferred to z . . . is socially preferred to x). Although existence of such a cycle by no means implies chaos, it does suggest that the social choice rule is not "first-order," but rather must be based on additional features of the decision-making institution. Early attempts to circumvent Arrow's theorem showed that cycles could be eliminated if the preference profile were restricted in some fashion (Sen 1970), or if the number of alternatives were sufficiently limited (Ferejohn and

Grether 1974; Nakamura 1979). If the set of alternatives W is geometric in form and restricted to one dimension (and compact), then it was shown that a *core* (or unbeaten point) exists under majority rule (Black 1958; Downs 1957). Interpreting this result in terms of committee decision making or direct democracy implies that the process is structurally stable, since this core acts as a stable global attractor.

There are problems with the direct application of this result to two-party representative democracy. If the parties are uninterested in policy per se, but only concerned with winning, then they should converge on the core point in choosing policies or manifestos to present to the electorate. However, it seems unlikely that this is an appropriate model for political competition; candidates in a two-party system generally do not converge. It was suggested by Wittman (1977, 1983) that if parties had their own preferred policy points then they would not converge in their declared positions. There are two difficulties with this proposition. First of all, if candidates are certain about the electoral response to the competing candidate positions, then any candidate who adopts a compromise (noncore) position will be beaten by an opponent who chooses the core. As a means of implementing a preferred policy point, such a strategy is irrational (at least on the face of it). To maintain divergent positions of the candidates, it is necessary to modify the model in some way. The usual procedure is to smooth the electoral response by assigning probabilities, say ρ_1, ρ_2, that candidates 1 or 2 win when their positions are z_1, z_2, and to show existence of a Nash equilibrium in these positions (Cox 1984, for example). A second difficulty arises in this case. Having won with a position z_i, there is no reason for party i to implement this declared position rather than its true position (Wittman 1990).

This problem of credible commitment by parties to their declared positions is essentially one of a "belief equilibrium" by both parties and voters. If parties (or candidates) can be punished, in some way, for violating their promises, then it is intuitively obvious that the candidates can be bound to their promises. A number of the chapters in Section IV of this volume show the existence of belief and behavioral equilibria in two-party models of competition. Although the models are based on a 1-dimensional space, they show, in the terminology introduced herein, that the aggregation mechanism will be structurally stable when it incorporates second-order phenomena of this kind.

In contrast to the 1-dimensional case, a simple, first-order aggregation procedure based on majority voting in two dimensions can be chaotic. More precisely, McKelvey (1976) showed that if the core is empty then, under *simple* majority rule $f(u)$, it is possible to construct discontinuous voting trajectories that go almost everywhere in the policy space W. Extensive experimental work (reviewed in McKelvey and Orde-shook 1990) indicated that voting mechanisms in two dimensions were generally Paretian and thus not completely chaotic.

A possible explanation is obtained by requiring $f(u)$ to be *continuous*, in the sense that only continuous voting trajectories defined by $f(u)$ are considered. Then the cycles that are generated must be restricted to the Pareto set in two dimensions (Schofield 1978). However, the *voting classification theorem* (Schofield 1984; McKelvey and Schofield 1986) essentially showed that continuous voting trajectories under majority rule, $f(u)$, can certainly wander almost anywhere in four dimensions. The full result classifies any nondictatorial and continuous voting method f by two integers: the stability dimension $v(f)$ and the instability dimension $w(f)$. If the dimension w of the space W is no greater than $v(f)$, then a core exists for any profile of convex preferences. If w is at least $w(f)$ then the core is generically empty, while if $w > w(f)$ then f is generically chaotic.[5] For majority decision making, $v(f) = 1$ whereas $w(f) = 2$ or 3, depending on whether the size of the electorate is odd or even.[6]

A response to this classification result is to infer that direct democracy can almost never define a social welfare function of the Arrovian kind and to seek instead those conditions that are likely to enhance or restrict the degree of political manipulation (Riker 1982, 1986). As we have noted, one way to proceed is by incorporating second-order institutional features that constrain political choice (Shepsle 1979; Shepsle and Weingast 1981) and create equilibrium. A related idea is to construct a "prediction set" – such as the *uncovered set* (Miller 1980) or *yolk* (McKelvey 1986) – which is defined by the second-order characteristics of the simple voting mechanism $f(u)$ and which lies inside the Pareto set. Particular kinds of institutional rules, called amendment procedures, can lead sophisticated voters to behave in ways that give outcomes in the uncovered set. Indeed, such procedures can force voters to truthfully reveal their preferences (Groseclose and Krehbiel, Chapter 10).

Underlying the classification theorem is an Arrovian-like unrestricted domain assumption that all smooth profiles are permitted. One can modify

---

[5] For a smooth profile u and rule f, we say $f(u)$ is *chaotic* if a continuous voting trajectory can be constructed between almost all points in the space W. As observed in note 4, a generic property of f is one that holds for all u in a residual subset of U. Such a subset will be dense and, in the case of a compact space W, also open. Thus *Chaos* for a voting rule can be even more pervasive than for a dynamical system or exchange economy.

[6] Thus chaos is generic for majority rule in three dimensions (for n odd) or four dimensions (for n even). For any democratic voting rule f, it is possible to compute $w(f)$, at least in principle.

this assumption and examine the connecton between symmetry assumptions on the distribution of voter preferences and $v(f)$. For example, if the distribution is log-concave and the voting rule requires a 64-percent majority, then the rule possesses a core (i.e., an α-core) irrespective of the dimension (Caplin and Nalebuff 1988). Schofield and Tovey (1992) have analyzed the connection between the classification theorem and these results on the α-core, and Tovey (Chapter 7) explores a number of consistency and computational problems associated with such social choice estimators as the α-core and yolk.

The classification theorem is certainly valid for a simple voting mechanism f, such as a direct democracy without second-order institutional features. For a representative democracy, chaos, in some sense, can occur if (i) there are only two parties or candidates; (ii) there is certainty in electoral response to candidate messages or positions; and (iii) the dimension of the policy space is at least $w(f)$. Even if candidates have policy objectives, for any position z_i by candidate i there is a position z_j by j that beats z_i and which i prefers. However, a *Nash* equilibrium in candidate positions will exist under general conditions (Cox 1987, 1989; Coughlin and Nitzan 1981; Enelow and Hinich 1984) as long as there is electoral uncertainty, no matter what the dimension. The problem of credible commitment remains, however, and may be difficult to solve.

Models of *multiparty* competition (i.e., with at least three parties), with or without electoral uncertainty, are much more difficult to construct than two-party models. If the candidates attempt to maximize the number of seats they control, then – as Eaton and Lipsey (1975) conjectured and Shaked (1975) showed – there is no equilibrium in the choice of positions. Incorporating policy preferences for parties brings in the problem of credible commitment again. Moreover, the motivational basis for a pure vote-maximization model is obscure. If parties are concerned with policy, then it makes more sense to model the effect of their strategy on the eventual policy outcome.

Schofield (Chapter 6) constructs an equilibrium model in arbitrary dimension where many parties calculate what policy to declare to the electorate by reference both to electoral concerns and final government policy. To do this, however, it is assumed that parties have consistent beliefs concerning the nature of interparty negotiation. It is possible that many of the results (in section IV of this volume) on two-party political competition and the underlying structure of party–voter beliefs can be extended to the general case of many parties and arbitrary dimension. Some insights into how governments may acquire expert or voter information relevant to decision making in multiple dimensions are given in Section V.

2   An overview of the essays

The previous section provided a general framework for interpreting recent work in political economy presented in this volume. In organizing the various contributions, the aim has been to bring out certain themes that run throughout the earlier discussion. Part I, "Perspectives in Political Economy," focuses on some of the general themes: the nature of ideology, institutions, incentives, and the balance between theoretical and empirical work in this relatively new discipline. Part II, "Representation and Voting," deals first with the axiomatic foundation of representation; the next two chapters discuss general voting procedures as methods of preference aggregation on a policy space of unrestricted dimension.

Part III, "Political Institutions," considers the different characteristics that govern the behavior of an institution, conceived in general terms. Three of the chapters focus on communication, formal procedural rules in voting, and on seniority, while a fourth chapter uses the concept of credible commitment to interpret the events leading up to the Civil War in the United States. Part IV is devoted to modeling political competition in a 1-dimensional policy space. The models incorporate candidate abilities, incomplete information, expenditures, and so forth. Part V is concerned with the way in which government may acquire or aggregate information held by voters or advisers. Part VI, comprising the final two chapters of the volume, deals with government choice on monetary policy and taxation.

2.1   Part I: Perspectives on political economy

In "Political Ideology, Communication, and Community," Hinich and Munger address the related concepts of *community* and *ideology*. Although the authors do not spell out the meaning of ideology quite so generally, one can think of ideology as a general system of beliefs about the way the world works, and by inference, the way other people think as well. Implicit is the conception of rights of individuals and collectivities. Hinich and Munger are aware of the difficulties of the origin of ideology, but argue that ideology itself is stable. An immediate consequence of their argument is a change in the way we might study political competition. As they say, "it is wiser to find out what a candidate believes on all issues than it is to decide whether to believe what she says issue by issue."

Another key concept in political economy is the idea of *implementation:* the construction of a game form which has the effect of forcing rational individual choices to lead to an outcome that satisfies a normative criterion or goal. In the chapter on "Implementation and Enforcement," Hurwicz discusses a general form of the manipulation problem. Suppose that a game form is constructed so as to implement a social goal as long as individuals choose from legal strategy domains. How are these legal domains to be enforced? This is a formal way of describing a problem faced by every institution, polity, and economy. Once the enforcers are joined to the game, who is to enforce the rules for the enforcers? In some sense much of current political economy considers a variant of this problem: Is it reasonable to suppose that, in a democracy, the electorate can enforce rules of behavior on the politicians – in order to enforce "satisfactory" rules on civil authorities, in order to maintain "civil order"?

For many years, Douglass North has studied the nature of political and economic institutions. As we must all appreciate after observing recent events in Eastern Europe and the Soviet Union, an institution can be highly inefficient (in some economic sense), persist for years, yet suddenly collapse like a punctured balloon. Among the many insights in North's chapter, "Toward a Theory of Institutional Change," is the emphasis on the importance of beliefs and ideology within an institution in maintaining the institution itself.

The fourth chapter in this section is an overview by Peter Ordeshook, "The Development of Contemporary Political Theory." Ordeshook rapidly reviews the principal results of the spatial voting model, the "new institutionalism," and applications of game theory. He examines the degree to which these theoretical constructs permit a deeper understanding of real-world political phenomenon. Although he seems to suggest at times that there is insufficient empirical work motivated by formal political economy models, he also provides an extensive list of empirical work by many scholars whose work is primarily theoretical.

2.2   *Part II: Representation and voting*

Almost everyone accepts that democracy requires some form of political representation. Either because of the fear of the possible chaos of direct democracy, or because of the impossibility of persuading millions of voters to pay attention to the minutiae of decision making, the electorate must choose political agents to act on their behalf.

In the Westminster model of government, the strength of a party is determined by using plurality rule ("first past the post") over a large number of constituencies. Under such a system it is usual for two parties to dominate, and for one of these to obtain a majority of the seats. In the multiparty systems, with at least three parties, of most of the European countries, proportional representation is used at the electoral level to determine party strengths. Typically, no party obtains a majority and government coalitions are necessary.

Extensive debate on the relative merits of these two systems has proved inconclusive. The Westminster model has appeared unrepresentative to some observers, since a situation can occur where the majority party has the support of no more than 40 percent of the voters.

Myerson, in his chapter on "Proportional Representation," presents an axiomatic analysis of electoral systems in terms of their incentive characteristics. For example, the property of coalitional straightforwardness of an electoral system essentially means that voters may simply vote for the party they most prefer, without being obliged to vote for less preferred parties because of strategic reasons. Myerson shows that any electoral system that satisfies natural representation and incentive axioms must be either approval voting or proportional representation.

In "Party Competition in a Spatial Model of Coalition Formation," Schofield extends the two-party model of political competition to the case of multiparty systems, where coalitions are necessary to the formation of government. In this model it is assumed that parties have true preferences on a space W (of arbitrary dimension w) representing policy options or ideological positions. These true preferences may be generated by elites or activists within the party. Parties transmit messages (in the form of manifestos or platforms) to the electorate. Under an electoral system, such as proportional representation, the allocation of parliamentary seats is dependent on the full list of party manifestos. It is assumed in this model that the message chosen by each party also restricts the party in its negotiations with other parties over coalition government. Consequently, each party is assumed to optimize its choice over electoral consequences and the post-election results of negotiation. When parties have consistent beliefs concerning the outcome of coalition bargaining, it is shown that there exists a Nash equilibrium in the choice of party manifestos. In general, the declared positions will not coincide with true positions. However, because of the structure of this political game, parties will be committed in the post-election negotiation phase to act as though their declared positions were their true positions. Furthermore, the declared positions exhibit a type of weak convergence: the analysis suggests that the expected outcome of coalition negotiation will be close to the "electoral center."

Tovey, in his chapter on "Empirical Study in the Euclidean Spatial Model," focuses on the general aggregation problem when voters have Euclidean preferences on an underlying policy space. An election is conceived by Tovey to be a sample (generally large) of election data of some kind from a population distribution of true preferred points. He shows that estimating voter preferred points from voter responses is computationally difficult; formally, the problem is NP-complete or "exponential." In the previous discussion, mention was made of recent equilibrium results in the analysis of direct democracy, where the underlying problem is the existence of an α-core requiring majorities with at least a proportion ($\alpha > \frac{1}{2}$) of the voting population. Tovey discusses various computational problems associated with the notion of an α-core.

Under certain assumptions on the structure of voting games, outcomes will lie in the *uncovered set* (McKelvey 1986). Tovey argues that the computation of the uncovered set, though polynomial in time, is extremely difficult in all but the simplest cases. However, there are available simple algorithms to determine the yolk – a region in the policy space, centrally located with regard to the voter preferred points, and relevant to the computation of the uncovered set. Tovey also examines the asymptotic consistency of a number of "sample estimates" associated with these concepts. He shows, for example, that the empirical estimate of the yolk radius obtained from a voter sample of size n will approach the underlying yolk radius of the population distribution as the sample size increases. The general inference from these results is that the recent attempts to formulate predictions that are relevant to the behavior of direct democracy are well founded: conclusions that are based on small voter samples will be consistent with results in the whole population.

2.3   *Part III: Political institutions*

In many ways an institution is a mechanism of the kind considered by Hurwicz in his chapter on implementation. The environment of the mechanism includes the preferences of the members of the institution and the channels of communication available to them. The mechanism itself will include a specification of the strategy sets available to the members (and possibly coalitions of members), the formal rules that specify the relationship between behavior and outcomes, and a solution or equilibrium concept that is deemed appropriate for the definition of the mechanism. Whereas implementation theory is concerned with the *design* of a mechanism to implement a particular goal, the formal theory of institutions is more concerned with the properties that a particular institutional mechanism may satisfy.

The repeated Prisoner's Dilemma (PD) is one game form that has exercised theorists for many years. Calvert, in his chapter on "Communication in Institutions," considers a variant of the two-person PD where each player may choose to cooperate or defect at each repetition of the game.

The cost of cooperating is not a constant, but can take high or low values with known probabilities. Benefits and costs are chosen so that the ex ante efficient strategies involve coordination by the players: a low-cost player should cooperate while a high-cost player should defect.

Even in the one-shot game, defection is a dominant strategy. Calvert's analysis focuses on the effects of permitting communication among the players. Communication is cheap talk, thus costless and involving nonbinding promises and unverifiable information. Calvert shows that truthful communication is in equilibrium and obtains a bound on the expected equilibrium payoffs to the players. The results also suggest that permitting cheap talk is sufficient to allow the players to attain a payoff level equal to that resulting from mediated coordination, thus resolving to some degree the problems of cooperation and coordination.

Drobak's chapter, "Courts and Slavery in the United States: Property Rights and Credible Commitment," is a close analysis by a legal scholar of the courts' role in the commitment of the federal government to the preservation of slavery in the first half of the nineteenth century. As Drobak observes, the last major federal decision supporting the freedom of slaves was rendered in 1845. After that, fugitives in free states had no protection. The 1857 opinion of the Supreme Court in the famous Dred Scott case seemed to imply that the Missouri Compromise of 1820 and a related, previous act of Congress were unconstitutional. A conclusion of this opinion was that "as a black, whether slave or free, Scott had no rights under the Constitution." The fear of many was that the Court could in some way extend property rights over slaves so as to restrict the free states' rights to prohibit slavery. The effective veto by the fifteen slave states against the required three-fourths majority for a constitutional amendment abolishing slavery, together with the Court opinion on Dred Scott, made the Civil War inevitable.

An important feature of a representative political institution is the formal set of rules that govern the voting procedure. Typically, representatives will propose alternatives and amendments to alternatives, voting in a well-defined fashion on the proposals. Certain types of voting rules, known as amendment procedures, will result in outcomes that belong to the uncovered set determined by the collection of proposals. Groseclose and Krehbiel, in their chapter "On the Pervasiveness of Sophisticated Sincerity," analyze the behavior of rational representatives who may propose alternatives, under given amendment procedures, and vote sophisticatedly using the information they have on other representatives' preferences. Sophisticated insincerity occurs when a representative appears to vote for an alternative that he does not prefer, when so voting results in a later vote for a more preferred alternative. The converse, sophisticated sincerity, simply means voting in a fashion that appears honest, or at least transparent. The authors obtain conditions on amendment procedures that are necessary and sufficient for sophisticated sincerity. However, they also argue that congressional voting procedures do not satisfy the formal properties of amendment procedures, so that "the normative ideal of designing institutions in which truthful revelation (honesty) is the optimal (best) policy appears to be very difficult to attain in voting situations."

A second phenomenon apparent in the U.S. Congress is the existence of a seniority system. Senior senators chair powerful committees and can influence the presentation of proposals to the House. McKelvey and Riezman present a model of "Legislative Seniority Systems," where representatives vote on a seniority system. If this is accepted, then senior representatives have a higher probability of being selected to propose a motion, essentially a payoff to all congressional districts. Since representatives face re-election, there is an incentive for them to maximize their district's payoff. The authors analyze the nature of equilibrium in this version of pork-barrel politics.

2.4   *Part IV: Political competition*

All four chapters in this part analyze competition between political representatives when one part of their strategy is to select a policy point in a 1-dimensional space. The classical result (Black 1958; Downs 1957), mentioned previously, concerns the simple case when parties are interested only in winning a majority of the votes, voters have preferred points on a compact subset of the real line, there is no noise in the signals from parties to voters, and voters choose the party with the nearest declared position. Under these circumstances, the parties converge to the position of the median voter.

Even if we assume the policy space to be 1-dimensional, this classical model can be extended in many ways: Parties (or candidates) may have preferred policy positions that they wish to implement, and which are unknown to the electorate; candidates' abilities to implement socially preferred policy positions may be quite different and unknown or obscure to the electorate; candidates may make promises to sections of the electorate in return for campaign contributions which they can employ to increase their visibility; candidates' credibility vis-à-vis their declared policies may be in doubt.

In "Adverse Selection and Moral Hazard in a Repeated Election Model," Banks and Sundaram use the concept of sequential equilibrium to formally model a restrospective voting rule in a sequence of elections. The authors note that voter choice includes aspects of moral hazard (the problem of providing incentives for candidates to exert themselves) and adverse selection (the problem of choosing the most able and willing candidates). Candidates once selected can work hard, though this is costly for them, while more able candidates find the task less onerous. Although candidates know their true type (or ability), voters do not. Voters update their beliefs concerning the types of candidates who succeed in obtaining office, and will discard an incumbent if the expected reward from the challenger is higher. An incumbent, once discarded, is never, in equilibrium, returned to office. On the other hand, "if high enough rewards are observed from the incumbent, then the voter would forgive an occasional lower reward and continue to employ the incumbent."

In "Campaign Contributions and Party–Candidate Competition," Baron and Mo present a complex model involving parties, candidates, interest groups, and voters. Interest groups have specific services in mind from winning candidates, and make contributions to candidates to elicit promises with regard to these services. Candidates are committed to honoring their promises (so shirking is not permitted). This can be justified, as in the results by Banks and Sundaram, in terms of an equilibrium in repeated play. The two parties initially choose positions for their candidates in the 1-dimensional policy space. By separating the policy choices of the candidates, thus distinguishing between them, the parties can increase the bargaining power of their candidates vis-à-vis interest groups, thus increasing contributions, campaign expenditures, and the likelihood of election. The authors analyze two situations: when parties are interested only in winning elections, and when they are concerned with implementing policy positions near true preferred positions. They obtain equilibrium conditions involving both candidate incentives and the pattern of interest group preferences in the two cases, showing when candidates will converge or diverge.

In their chapter on "Polarization, Incumbency, and the Personal Vote," Londregan and Romer examine the case where candidates' abilities are relevant to the voter calculus. They suggest that when greater weight is placed by voters on the ability of the candidates to provide constituency services, then the greater will be the divergence between the parties. Empirical evidence for their inference is presented.

One important point referred to in this chapter, and indeed relevant for all models of party competition, is the degree of commitment of the parties in the post-election period. Lupia deals with the question in his chapter, "Credibility and the Responsiveness of Direct Legislation," in a different way from Banks and Sundaram. A simple 1-dimensional model is constructed where the incumbent is represented by a single status-quo point. The challenger's most preferred point x is chosen from a known distribution and the voters' most preferred points are selected from a different known distribution. The cost of challenging is also known. The challenger transmits an incomplete message to the electorate, and the electorate makes appropriate inferences about the benefits of voting for the status quo or challenger. When the challenger is perfectly credible (meaning unable to lie), then only accurate information (in terms of the location of x with respect to the status quo) can be transmitted. The challenger can compute the probability of winning and thus the expected value of challenging. If the incumbent is challenged, then the voters obtain further information concerning the position of x. Problems resulting from rational disbelief, by voters, of noncredible challengers can be avoided by imposing penalties of some kind on challengers who show themselves to have lied.

2.5   *Part V: Information acquisition by government*

The chapters in the previous part modeled the strategic interaction between voters, with their own preferences, and competing candidates for political office. The chapters in this part concentrate on the ways in which government may acquire information.

In "Information Acquisition and Orthogonal Argument," David Austen-Smith uses the concept of sequential equilibrium to model the process by which government selects information made available by two advisers. Because the decision space is 2-dimensional, each adviser can choose to specialize in obtaining information in one or the other of the two dimensions. One feature of the analysis is the fundamental trade-off to the advisers between being better informed and being influential.

The starting point for Lohmann's chapter, "Welfare Analysis of Political Action," is that any government decision is made under uncertainty concerning the true state of the world. Information concerning the state of the world is held by members of the electorate. Voters are requested to make a choice between two alternatives (A and a status quo Q). As in the Condorcet jury theorem (Schofield 1972; Ladha 1991) there is reason to believe that a majority (or supra-majority) may make a decision superior to a single decision maker. Indeed, Lohmann shows that, given knowledge about the dispersion of information in the electorate, "an appropriately chosen optimal decision rule can ensure that the private information dispersed in the population is costlessly utilized in the individuals' collective decisions."

However, voters have their own policy preferences, as well as information, and perform individual calculations on whether to vote – thus revealing the information they hold. Lohmann also uses the concept of sequential equilibrium to show, in the presence of voting costs, that the outcome can be socially suboptimal. For example, individuals who hold information relevant to the government choice may be deterred from voting because of beliefs concerning the costs and consequences of voting.

2.6 *Part VI: Government behavior*

In the chapters on political competition in Part IV, the full consequences of government choice were not specified except through indirect utility functions representing voter preference. The two chapters in Part VI model in greater detail the relationship between government choice, individual actions, and economic behavior.

In his chapter on "Monetary Policy and Credibility," Barnett examines an inconsistency in the calculation of optimal intertemporal behavior by government and a representative consumer. Barnett follows Calvo (1978) in assuming that both government and the consumer have the same intertemporal utility function, but he extends the Calvo dynamic game to include multiple monetary assets. He imposes the necessary weak separability condition for the existence of an exact monetary aggregate over those assets.

Government is assumed to treat total government spending (g at time t) as exogenous and to choose the nominal money balance M_t and tax t. The consumer acts as a Nash–Cournot follower and responds to government choice at time t by maximizing intertemporal utility, thus effectively choosing real money balances. Knowing the decision problem facing the consumer, the government acts as a Stackelberg leader to make its decisions. Barnett argues that there is a problem concerning the government's commitment to its solution to the decision problem, since it has an incentive to use a forward-looking solution on the grounds that what is past is past. As Barnett observes: "In Leonid Hurwicz's terminology, the consumer views the government's commitment to the true intertemporally optimal solution to be incentive incompatible." If the consumer forms expectations that government will succumb to the temptation of discretionary replanning, then the optimal solution becomes impossible to attain. The problem of credible commitment, which has permeated so many of the chapters in this book, is of concern even in a model where government and consumers/voters have identical preferences.

Barnett finds that the problems associated with the attainment of a reputational equilibrium are greatly complicated by the introduction of multiple monetary assets into the model. Under exact aggregation, he finds that three monetary aggregates appear: the exact aggregate measuring the monetary service flow received by demanders of monetary services, the monetary base controlling the "seigniorage" tax received by the government, and the simple sum aggregate used by the central bank as an intermediate target of policy. Under this realistic representation of monetary policy, the time-inconsistency problem becomes very difficult to solve, and hence optimal dynamic policy effectively becomes impossible to attain.

This theoretical result may help to explain why it is Barnett's Divisia monetary aggregates that have produced the empirical discovery of chaos in economic data (Barnett and Chen 1988), as described at the beginning of this overview.

A long-standing problem in political economy has been to construct a "General Equilibrium Model with Endogenous Government Behavior" that fully endogenizes government behavior (Slutsky 1977; Denzau and Parks 1983). Drissen and van Winden, in their chapter on this topic, use a generalized Nash product to represent the way government responds to electoral demands. Implicit in this formulation are the probabilistic models of voting proposed by Coughlin (1986) and Coughlin and Nitzan (1981). It is assumed that there are two social groups: capital owners and workers. Government choice involves a uniform tax rate and group-specific transfers. Tax revenues are used to finance a public consumption good. Given government choices, a general equilibrium model is used to compute production of the private and public goods, prices, and thus consumption. The equilibrium analysis, resulting from an increase in, say, the influence of labor, clearly illustrates the impact of the relative preferences for public and private goods between the two groups. In an interesting observation, the authors note that "an increase in the political influence of a social group may lead to a decrease in utility of members of that group," since the government neglects the (long-run) effects of changes in relative prices on utility.

3   Concluding remarks

The general theme presented in this overview is that economic and political processes, viewed as simple aggregation mechanisms, may very well be chaotic. However, mature political economies have additional structure: institutions, communication networks, common beliefs, and so on. Analysis of models characterized by such structures gives insight into the nature of political and economic behavior. From one point of view, the very possibility of chaos in political economies means that their developmental or evolutionary path is always unexpected and interesting.

REFERENCES

Arrow, K. J. (1951), *Social Choice and Individual Values.* New York: Wiley.
Aumann, R. J., and B. Peleg (1974), "A Note on Gale's Example," *Journal of Mathematical Economics* 1: 209-11.

Barnett, W., and P. Chen (1988), "The Aggregation-Theoretic Monetary Aggregates are Chaotic and Have Strange Attractors: An Econometric Application of Mathematical Chaos," in W. A. Barnett, E. Berndt, and A. White (eds.), *Dynamic Econometric Modeling*, Proceedings of the Third International Symposium in Economic Theory and Econometrics. Cambridge: Cambridge University Press.

Barnett, W., R. Gallant, M. Hinich, and M. Jensen (1992), "Robustness of Nonlinearity and Chaos Tests to Measurement Error, Inference Method, and Sample Size," Working Paper no. 167, Washington University in St. Louis.

Barnett, W., J. Geweke, and K. Shell, eds. (1989), *Economic Complexity: Chaos, Sunspots, Bubbles and Nonlinearity*, Proceedings of the Fourth International Symposium in Economic Theory and Econometrics. Cambridge: Cambridge University Press.

Barnett, W., and M. Hinich (1992), "Has Chaos Been Discovered with Economic Data?" in R. Day and P. Chen (eds.), *Evolutionary Dynamics and Nonlinear Economics*. Oxford: Oxford University Press.

Black, D. (1958), *The Theory of Committees and Elections*. Cambridge: Cambridge University Press.

Calvo, G. A. (1978), "On the Time Consistency of Optimal Policy in a Monetary Economy," *Econometrica* 46: 1411-28.

Caplin, A., and B. Nalebuff (1988), "On 64% Majority Rule," *Econometrica* 56: 787-814.

Coughlin, P. (1986), "Elections and Income Distribution," *Public Choice* 50: 27-91.

Coughlin, P., and S. Nitzan (1981), "Electoral Outcomes with Probabilistic Voting and Nash Social Welfare Maxima," *Journal of Public Economics* 15: 113-21.

Cox, G. W. (1984), "An Expected-Utility Model of Electoral Competition," *Quality and Quantity* 18: 337-49.

(1987), "Electoral Equilibrium under Alternative Voting Institutions," *American Journal of Political Science* 31: 82-108.

(1989), "Undominated Candidate Strategies under Alternative Voting Rules," *Mathematical and Computer Modelling* 12: 451-60.

Denzau, A., and R. Parks (1983), "Existence of Voting Market Equilibria," *Journal of Economic Theory* 30: 243-65.

Downs, A. (1957), *Economic Theory of Democracy*. New York: Harper and Row.

Eaton, B. C., and R. Lipsey (1975), "The Principle of Minimum Differentiation Reconsidered: Some New Developments in the Theory of Spatial Competition," *Review of Economic Studies* 42: 27-50.

Enelow, J., and M. Hinich (1984), *The Spatial Theory of Voting: An Introduction*. Cambridge: Cambridge University Press.

Ferejohn, J., and D. M. Grether (1974), "On a Class of Rational Social Decision Procedures," *Journal of Economic Theory* 8: 471-82.

Gale, D. (1974), "Exchange Equilibrium and Coalitions: An Example," *Journal of Mathematical Economics* 1: 63-6.

Gibbard, A. (1973), "Manipulation of Voting Schemes: A General Result," *Econometrica* 41: 587-601.

Groves, T., and J. Ledyard (1980), "The Existence of Efficient and Incentive Compatible Equilibria with Public Goods," *Econometrica* 48: 1487-1506.

Guesnerie, R., and J. J. Laffont (1978), "Advantageous Reallocations of Initial Resources," *Econometrica* 46: 835-41.

Hurwicz, L. (1972), "On Informationally Decentralized Systems," in R. Radner and C. McGuire (eds.), *Decision and Organization*. Amsterdam: North-Holland.

Kreps, D. M., P. Milgrom, J. Roberts, and R. Wilson (1982), "Rational Cooperation in the Finitely Repeated Prisoners' Dilemma," *Journal of Economic Theory* 27: 245-52.

Ladha, K. (1991), "Information Pooling through Majority-Rule Voting: Condorcet's Jury Theorem with Correlated Votes," Typescript, Center in Political Economy, Washington University in St. Louis.

Li, T., and J. Yorke (1976), "Period Three Implies Chaos," *American Mathematical Monthly* 82: 985-92.

May, R. D. (1975), "Biological Populations Obeying Difference Equations: Stable Points, Stable Cycles and Chaos," *Journal of Theoretical Biology* 51: 511-24.

McKelvey, R. D. (1976), "Intransitivities in Multidimensional Voting Bodies and Some Implications for Agenda Control," *Journal of Economic Theory* 12: 472-82.

(1986), "Covering, Dominance and Institution Free Properties of Social Choice," *American Journal of Political Science* 30: 283-314.

McKelvey, R. D., and P. C. Ordeshook (1990), "A Decade of Experimental Research on Spatial Models of Elections and Committees," in J. Enelow and M. Hinich (eds.), *Advances in the Spatial Theory of Voting*. Cambridge: Cambridge University Press.

McKelvey, R. D., and T. Page (1986), "Common Knowledge, Consensus and Aggregate Information," *Econometrica* 54: 109-27.

McKelvey, R. D., and N. Schofield (1986), "Structural Instability of the Core," *Journal of Mathematical Economics* 15: 179-98.

Miller, N. (1980), "A New Solution Set for Tournaments and Majority Voting: Further Graph Theoretical Approaches to the Theory of Voting," *American Journal of Political Science* 24: 68-96.

Nakamura, K. (1979), "The Vetoers in a Simple Game with Ordinal Preference," *International Journal of Game Theory* 8: 55-61.

Peixoto, M. (1962), "Structural Stability on Two-Dimensional Manifolds," *Topology* 1: 101-20.

Rand, D. (1978), "Exotic Phenomena in Games and Duopology Models," *Journal of Mathematical Economics* 5: 173-84.

Riker, W. (1982), *Liberalism against Populism: A Confrontation between the Theory of Democracy and the Theory of Social Choice*. San Francisco: Freeman.

(1986), *The Art of Political Manipulation*. New Haven, CT: Yale University Press.

Saari, D. (1991), "Erratic Behavior in Economic Models," *Journal of Economic Behavior and Organization* 16: 3-35.

Safra, Z. (1983), "Manipulation by Reallocating Initial Endowments," *Journal of Mathematical Economics* 12: 1-17.

Satterthwaite, M. A. (1975), "Strategy-Proofness and Arrow's Conditions: Existence and Correspondence Theorems for Voting Procedures and Social Welfare Functions," *Journal of Economic Theory* 10: 187-217.

Schofield, N. (1972), "Ethical Decision Rules for Uncertain Voters," *British Journal of Political Science* 2: 193-207.

(1977), "Dynamic Games of Collective Action," *Public Choice* 30: 77-105.

(1978), "The Theory of Dynamic Games," in P. Ordeshook (ed.), *Game Theory and Political Science*. New York: New York University Press.

(1980), "Catastrophe Theory and Dynamic Games," *Quality and Quantity* 14: 519–45.

(1984), "Social Equilibrium and Cycles on Compact Sets," *Journal of Economic Theory* 33: 59–71.

Schofield, N., and C. Tovey (1992), "Probability and Convergence for Supra-Majority Rules with Euclidean Preferences," *Mathematical and Computer Modelling* 16: 41–58.

Sen, A. K. (1970), *Collective Choice and Social Welfare*. London: Oliver and Boyd.

Shaked, A. (1975), "Non-Existence of Equilibrium for the Two-Dimensional Three Firms Location Problem," *Review of Economic Studies* 42: 51–6.

Shepsle, K. A. (1979), "Institutional Arrangements and Equilibrium in Multidimensional Voting Models," *American Journal of Political Science* 23: 27–60.

Shepsle, K. A., and B. R. Weingast (1981), "Structure Induced Equilibrium and Legislative Choice," *Public Choice* 36: 221–37.

Slutsky, S. (1977), "A Voting Model for the Allocation of Public Goods: Existence of an Equilibrium," *Journal of Economic Theory* 14: 299–325.

Smale, S. (1966), "Structurally Stable Systems Are Not Dense," *American Journal of Mathematics* 88: 491–6.

Stewart, I. (1989), *Does God Play Dice?* London: Basil Blackwell.

Taylor, M. (1976), *Anarchy and Cooperation*. London: Wiley.

Weyers, S. (1992), "Three Results on Communication, Information and Common Knowledge," Typescript, CORE, Université Catholique de Louvain.

Wittman, D. (1977), "Candidates with Policy Preferences: A Dynamic Model," *Journal of Economic Theory* 14: 180–9.

(1983), "Candidate Motivation: A Synthesis of Alternative Theories," *American Political Science Review* 77: 142–57.

(1990), "Spatial Strategies When Candidates Have Policy Preferences," in J. Enelow and M. Hinich (eds.), *Advances in the Spatial Theory of Voting*. Cambridge: Cambridge University Press.

PART I

Perspectives on political economy

CHAPTER 1

Political ideology, communication, and community

Melvin J. Hinich and Michael C. Munger

community – 1. Common possession or enjoyment. 2. A society of people having common rights and privileges, or common interests, civil,
political, etc., or living under the same laws and regulations. 3. Common
character; similarity, likeness. (*Webster's New Universal Unabridged
Dictionary,* 2nd ed., 1983)

1   Introduction

A tempest of change is sweeping over the landscape of formal theories of
purposive human behavior. The force behind these scolding winds is the
increasing recognition that existing work is wrong or inadequate in its
account of culture, ideology, and the importance of community and communication. Fortunately, political economy is at last turning its attention
to the challenge of explaining and incorporating these phenomena into
its models.

The origins of this change in direction are obscure, arising from a dis-
satisfaction with existing theories of purposive choice. We review in the
following pages a number of apparently disparate approaches to the problem of communicating and achieving cooperation. In the study of markets, of politics, and of the historical evolution of societies, we have come
to recognize that the most important and interesting institutions are those
whose existence derives from internalizing and routinizing what would
otherwise be decentralized "market" processes. The goal of this chapter

Paper prepared for presentation at the "Conference on Political Economy: Institutions,
Information, Competition, and Representation" at Washington University, St. Louis, May
1991. The authors wish to thank David Austen-Smith, Douglass North, Peter Ordeshook,
Paul Rothstein, A. Raoul Rutten, and Norman Schofield for helpful comments and criti-
cisms. Particular thanks are owed to William Keech, who made numerous suggestions for
improvements in an earlier version. We acknowledge the research assistance of Victoria
Heid. The usual caveat applies.

is to point out that unexpected commonalities in results being obtained in the study of markets, politics, and societies are the consequence of unrecognized similarities in the problems being addressed.

Ultimately, we hope to persuade social scientists of the importance of a single unifying concept: ideology. Ideology solves problems of communication and cooperation when they are solved; ideology causes the failures when communication and cooperation breaks down. In short, ideology provides the means by which credible communication is made possible, and allows the transformation of collections of individuals into communities. In earlier work (Hinich and Munger 1992), we built on Downs's (1957) theory of ideology in *An Economic Theory of Democracy* to suggest a means by which the classical spatial voting model might be reconstituted. We consider now the question of ideology more broadly, and try to give credit to the scholars who have recognized the problem of commitment to cooperation in several of its various guises.

In the following section we review a number of recent works that discuss the problem of political communication, competition, and cooperation. Section 3 defines and discusses a concept that gathers all the other controversies within it: ideology. Section 4 discusses some conjectures on the origin, creation, and popularization of ideologies. The fifth and final section summarizes our conclusions.

2   Setting up the problem

What are the implications for the organization of societies of the interplay between (1) social and economic forces for institutional change and (2) institutional forces for social and economic stasis? The answer to this question does not clearly lie within the intellectual jurisdiction or the methodological compass of any established discipline, but many scholars have given it a go.[1] We choose (probably quite unfairly) to emphasize the importance of just three different approaches to the problem, North (1981, 1990a, 1990b), Schofield (1985), and Kreps (1990). Each of these is distinguished by both the fundamental insight it contains and by the incompleteness of its conclusions.

2.1   *Institutions and organizations*

North (1981) makes a controversial claim about institutions, by which he means the humanly devised constraints or rules that shape human interactions. That claim is that institutions are not necessarily efficient, in the

---

[1] At a minimum, these would include Downs (1957), Higgs (1987), Olson (1965, 1982), Sartori (1969, 1976), and Seliger (1976).

sense of satisfying the Pareto criterion of collective rationality. The puzzle North wants to solve is why some societies and their economies flourish and others, similar at first glance in resources and population, simply stagnate. The lagniappe is that even such stagnant economies do not wither and die, or change. Instead, they may persist in exactly this attenuated, vegetative form for centuries, even though there appear to be feasible Pareto-preferred alternatives.

North (1990a) offers two explanations, path dependence and initial conditions, each of which depends on the existence both of economies of scale (particularly large fixed costs) in establishing institutions and of transactions costs in modifying them. Institutions in any society reduce uncertainty by imparting to human affairs some predictability and stability. As in the simple one-shot Prisoner's Dilemma, a particular outcome may be an equilibrium (i.e., be locally stable) but not a Pareto optimum.[2]

But why would we believe that such an inefficient outcome could be an equilibrium of the societal supergame where this process is iterated indefinitely? Even if inefficient institutional arrangements might not be supplanted by conscious design, surely they would succumb in time to the evolutionary forces outlined by Alchian (1950). There are, after all, at least two sources for the impetus for such change: emulation by political entrepreneurs, or replacement by military hostile takeover of the institutionally inferior society.

North disagrees. His argument turns on the difference, in his view, between institutions and organizations. Institutions create the web of rules, opportunities, and constraints that face all members of a society. Organizational arrangements, some of them very creative and innovative, are responses to these opportunities and constraints. As organizations evolve, they alter institutions in ways that may have been impossible to predict. The path of recursive institutional change–organizational response–institutional change is for North composed of two crucial ingredients: (a) *lock-in,* or a strong resistance to change, created by the symbiotic relationship between institutions and the organizations evolved from the incentive structure provided by exactly those institutions; and (b) *feedback,* the process by which humans react to changes in incentives and opportunities that result from what institutional changes do occur.

The first of these, lock-in, is fairly obvious. Suppose a certain subset of a society finds itself advantaged by a particular institutional arrangement,

---

[2] North (1990a) does not use the game theory metaphor directly, though it clearly is consistent with the logic of his argument. Explicit discussions of collective action as an *n*-person iterated game can be found in Hardin (1971) and Taylor (1976), among others. A review can be found in Schofield (1985), on which more anon.

such as a family that can claim monarchy by divine right because of the tenets of that society's state religion. The advantaged group will use whatever resources are available (up to the rent created by the advantage over their opportunity employment) to defend these rights. In the case of our example, the family would be willing to expend all the resources of the society, since their monarchy gives them such a claim and their opportunity employment is most likely ritual public execution designed to confer legitimacy on the new royal family.

This leaves us with feedback, the second axiom of North's theory. It is here his explanation must stand or fall. He concedes that if political and economic markets were efficient then actors would act only on the "true" models, or else be quickly persuaded toward the accurate predictions of the consequences of complex rearrangements of institutions. But the central claim of his analysis is that information about, and enforcing of, agreements to modify existing institutions are both prohibitively expensive. This claim is repeated by the other authors we discuss herein, but it seems to us that North is the first to make the argument in this explicit context.[3]

North claims the basic human problem is achieving cooperation, and societies prosper based in large measure on the incentives their historically peculiar institutions provide for cooperation. Transactions costs in economic and political exchange lead to inefficient distributions of property rights; the subjective and confused understanding citizens have of the implications of institutional change lead to the persistence of such rights. North does not claim that such persistence constitutes an equilibrium. Rather, if equilibrium is defined by the zero–transactions cost world of flexible, Pareto-efficient institutions, this situation is a persistent, long-run disequilibrium.

2.2   Conventions, community, and cooperation

The second important contribution is a precise notion of "community" and its implications for the technical condition of common knowledge. Schofield (1985) purports to be a review, but it might better be called a

---

[3] To be fair, it must be pointed out that the importance of transactions costs in determining the form of institutional arrangements in private organizations dates back at least to Coase (1937), and is applied to the optimal form of public-sector institutions dealing with externalities in Coase (1960). Further, Olson's (1965) work is based on an understanding of the costs of contracting to forestall the incentives to cheat on agreements, and of the irreducible expense of making agreements in the first place. North was simply the first to focus on the interplay between institutions and organizations, and to link this interplay to the problem of transactions costs.

report. Schofield integrates a number of lines of research and explores the implications of this work for the possibilities of collective action.[4]

The fundamental theoretical problem underlying the question of cooperation is the manner by which individuals attain knowledge of each others' preferences and likely behavior. Moreover, the problem is one of common knowledge, since each individual, i, is required not only to have information about others' preferences, but also to know that the others have knowledge about i's own preferences and strategies. (p. 218)

The question is how this common knowledge is achieved. A simple paraphrasing of his thesis might be that community requires credible communication. We must rely here on a precise definition of community that Schofield adapts from Taylor (1976, 1982):

The key features of community are: (i) shared common beliefs or norms, (ii) direct and complex relations among members, (iii) reciprocity. Communications is not a key aspect since people may communicate while sharing hardly any norms. On the other hand, of course, shared norms may be reinforced through communication. (Schofield 1985, p. 217)

In other words, communication is clearly not sufficient for the existence of community, but it is quite likely necessary. In fact, if we are to expand the focus of inquiry to include the origin of community rather than just its existence, communication about the beliefs and norms that are to be shared is of paramount importance. Given this definition of community, we can conclude that the common-knowledge requirement for cooperation may be satisfied in small groups. Taylor's thesis is that societies will consequently break into small groups, the size of which will be (optimally) determined by the largest community that can be achieved and maintained.

Schofield is rather more circumspect in his willingness to conclude that only through community can cooperation be achieved. If it is *only* through community that the common-knowledge basis of cooperation can be achieved, then the state, which seeks to replace community and voluntary action with hierarchy and coercion, is the enemy of community, altruism, and cooperation. The concentration of force that the state (by definition) represents reduces the need for trust among individuals who share common knowledge, and reduces the possibility of achieving trust and collective goals.

In short, Taylor's argument is that community is necessary for cooperation; Schofield answers that it is sufficient, but that more work needs

---

[4] Since Schofield's piece is in fact a review of the literature, we will not try to review this work here. The clearest antecedents to these conclusions are Hardin (1971, 1982), Margolis (1982), Olson (1965), Schofield (1975), and Taylor (1976, 1982).

to be done before we can conclude it is necessary. How can we be certain that there exist no other means of achieving the level of common knowledge required for some kind of cooperation? And just what is that level?

Schofield concludes with a provocative and, for our purposes, very important observation:

> In the restricted context of a community, Taylor's argument makes good sense: social norms will be well understood and will provide the basis for common knowledge, and this knowledge will be maintained by mechanisms designed to make acts intelligible. In more general social situations, however, individuals will be less able to make reasonable guesses about other individuals' beliefs. The theoretical problem underlying cooperation can be stated thus: what is the minimal amount that one agent must know in a given milieu about the beliefs and wants of other agents, to be able to form coherent notions about their behavior, and for this knowledge to be communicable to the others. It seems to me that this problem is at the heart of any analysis of community, convention, and cooperation. (p. 219)

2.3   The culture of organizations

A possible answer to the problem that Schofield poses (how do groups of individuals communicate credibly without community?), as well as the problem posed by North (why do we observe apparently non-Pareto institutions over long periods?) is given by Kreps (1990). He addresses the question of "corporate culture" and the apparent paradox that, though such a concept is quite outside the orthodox world view of neoclassical economic theory, the culture of corporations is something taken very seriously by corporations themselves. The explanation Kreps offers is extraordinarily insightful, and worth reproducing here at length.

Kreps's theory is founded on the observation that transactions (by which he actually means a broad category of human interaction) are characterized by three crucial attributes: (1) hierarchical relationships, (2) ongoing or repeated dealings, and (3) fundamental and irreducible uncertainty, implying unforeseen contingencies.

> Many transactions will potentially be too costly to undertake if the participants cannot rely on efficient and equitable adaptation to those unforeseen contingencies. Note that such reliance will necessarily involve blind faith; if we cannot foresee a contingency, we cannot know in advance that we can efficiently and equitably meet it. (p. 92)

The implication of hierarchical relationships is, if anything, even more potent when applied to government than it is to the firm or corporation:

> [S]ome transactions will be hierarchical in that one party will have much more authority in saying what adaptation will take place. . . . When I am employed by

a firm, I accept within broad limits the firm's right, as expressed by my superior, to specify how my time will be spent as contingencies arise. Or, to take another example, when students attend a university, they accept the university's right, through administrators, to spell out the terms of the commodity students have bought.

If employees or students are to grant such authority to a firm or a university, they must believe that it will be used fairly. What is the source of this faith? It is that the firm and university are characterized by their reputations. The way an organization adapts to an unforeseen contingency can add to or detract from that reputation, with consequences for the amount of faith future employees or students will have.... The organization, or, more precisely, those in the organization who have decision-making authority, will have an interest in preserving or even promoting a good reputation. (pp. 92–3)

With these three essential elements, Kreps goes on to offer an explanation of "corporate culture" that emphasizes the importance of long-run reputation over more immediate concerns, even when this seems "irrational" from the perspective of the neoclassical model.

In order for a reputation to have an effect, both sides involved in a transaction must *ex ante* have some idea of the meaning of appropriate or equitable fulfillment of the contract. Potential future trading partners must be able to observe fulfillment (or lack of) by the hierarchically superior party. These things are necessary; otherwise the hierarchically superior party's reputation turns on nothing. (p. 93)

So long as the fulfillment of even implicit promises can be monitored, we are in the bailiwick of the neoclassical principal–agent model. But now we must turn to situations where the premise of unforeseeable contingencies is invoked. It is here that Kreps makes the key point, at least for our purposes:

When we speak of adaptation to unforeseen contingencies, however, we cannot specify *ex ante* how those contingencies will be met. We can at best give *some sort of principle or rule that has wide (preferably universal) applicability and that is simple enough to be interpreted by all concerned.... The organization will be characterized by the principle it selects....* In order to protect its reputation for applying the principle in all cases, it will apply the principle even when its application might not be optimal in the short run. It will apply the principle even in areas where it serves no direct organization objective if doing so helps preserve or clarify the principle. (p. 93, emphasis added)

Finally, Kreps observes that both the quality of the principle (in terms of the results that it creates in the organization), and the level of commitment that the organization shows to the principle, together determine the extent to which the organization will prosper, or fail, in competition with other organizations.

Because decision-making in a firm is diffuse, those who make decisions in the firm's name will be judged by their diligence in applying and embracing the principle. In this light I interpret corporate culture as partly the principle itself (or more realistically, the interrelated principles that the organization employs) and partly the means by which the principle is communicated to hierarchical inferiors. . . . Because it will be designed through time to meet unforeseen contingencies as they arise, it will be the product of evolution inside the organization and will be influenced by the organization's history. (pp. 93–4)

There are a number of important differences between "corporate culture," the phenomenon that Kreps is investigating, and the political ideologies that are our subject in the next sections. The most important differences are (1) the nature of competition in a political system, (2) the importance of the universality of the organizing principle, and (3) the nature of the hierarchical relation between government and voters. The essential point Kreps makes – the importance of an organizational reputation in solving problems of unforeseeable contingencies – is exactly analogous to the ideological reputations of parties, however.

The nature of competition in political systems is quite different from that in economics, because for the firm it is possible to judge ex post the quality of the firm's response even to unforeseen contingencies. It is not possible, as Kreps points out, to compare the outcome to any ex ante commitment, but it is possible to judge profits, output, employment, and other measurable results of the firm's decisions. There is in most cases some reasonably well-defined output that the firm produces. Even if the firm is a conglomerate, its success in a particular industry (say, textiles or apparel) may be quite independent of its success in others (producing microprocessors).

In some measure, the extent of the firm's diversification into other industries will be determined by the universality of the applicability of the "cultural" organizing principle. If the principle is equally applicable to textiles and microprocessors, the firm may profitably produce both. If not, the firm that tries to produce both will go bankrupt. The point is that *the firm will optimally expand across industries according to the universality of the cultural organizing principle;* the firm is under no organizational or competitive imperative for such diversification.

This is not true of the ideology of the political party. The nature of political competition requires that ideologies be applicable to all activities. An ideology that is universally applicable has a much bigger advantage over its competitors than a corporate culture with equally broad applicability, because the competitive imperative in politics is to control all of the government, or none.

Finally, the hierarchical relation in politics is unique. Kreps's description of the hierarchy is quite accurate, but we already have an apt description of this problem in the work of an earlier scholar: Thomas Hobbes in

Leviathan (1651). Hobbes does not describe political competition; *Leviathan* contains no hint of democratic theory. His contribution is his recognition of the *abjectness of the hierarchical relation of the governed to the government.* There is a paucity of alternatives, except in temporal sequence, to the current government. The only alternatives, even in a democratic system, are immediate revolution or tossing the malfeasors out in the next election. The path of continuous revolt holds little promise:

> The condition of man . . . is a condition of war of everyone against everyone. . . . [In a state of nature] no arts; no letters; no society; and which is worst of all, continual fear and danger of violent death; and the life of man, solitary, poor, nasty, brutish, and short. (part I, chapters 4 and 13)

The only recourse, then, is to rely on the threat of replacement of the current government by an alternative whose commitment to its organizing ideology is largely unknown. Two firms compete by both producing output, and simultaneously displaying commitment to their cultural organizing principles in their daily activities. By definition, a party out of power has no daily activities in government by which it could show commitment to an ideology. Power in the market is shared, whereas power in government is exclusive.

Combining these points, we see we are dealing with a very different phenomenon in political ideologies. Competition of ideologies for the control of government means competition for universal control, which requires universal applicability of the ideology. The hierarchical relation of government to voter places more power in the hands of the hierarchical superior than the analogous relation in the market. Finally, the party (or better, ideology) out of power faces a problem of commitment, since any claims it makes about commitment could quite plausibly be dismissed as cheap talk.

We believe that ideological messages contain sensible meanings on whose content different citizens can on average agree, and that a commitment to winning is not an ideology that has any chance of winning real elections. Consequently, we propose to reformulate Downs's fundamental insights on the importance of uncertainty in political positions and homiletics in a more complete theory of ideology.

3   Defining and understanding ideology

3.1   *Definitions*

Before we can discuss the concept of ideology we must settle on a definition, but this is no mean task. Dozens of different definitions exist, each with some claim to primacy. Here we review three of the more prominent interpretations:[5]

> Ideologies are collections of ideas with intellectually derivable normative implications for behavior and for how society should be organized (Higgs and Twight 1987; Reichley 1981; North 1981; Lodge 1976).
> Ideologies are economizing devices by which individuals understand, and communicate about, politics (Higgs 1987; Enelow and Hinich 1984a, 1984b; North 1981; Macridis 1980; Downs 1957).
> Ideologies are complex, dogmatic belief systems by which individuals interpret, rationalize, and justify behavior and institutions (Higgs 1987; Domhoff 1983; Jovrasky 1970; Sartori 1969).

These terse summaries represent what we believe are the three major aspects of ideology emphasized by scholars. Higgs (1987) emphasizes four separate aspects (cognitive, affective, programmatic, and solidary), but we will use only three, choosing to merge the affective and solidary functions. Higgs notes:

Ideologies perform an important psychological service because without them people cannot know, assess, and respond to much of the vast world of social relations. Ideology simplifies a reality too huge and complicated to be comprehended, evaluated, and dealt with in any purely factual scientific, or other disinterested way. (pp. 37-8)

All notions of ideology exhibit an inherent tension between an anthropomorphic conception of ideologies as collections of ideas and the application of these ideas one finds in an individual's belief system. We discuss this problem later, but for now will resolve this tension by fiat: ideologies are disembodied ideas. Individual belief systems may mimic some or all parts of a particular ideology, but these "schema" are distinct from what we intend. Following is what we mean by ideology.

> Ideology: an internally consistent set of propositions that makes both proscriptive and prescriptive demands on human behavior. All ideologies have implications for (a) what is ethically good, and therefore what is bad; (b) how society's resources should be distributed; and (c) where power appropriately resides.

More simply, an ideology tells us what is good, who gets what, and who rules. Given the generality of this definition, many ideas that are not

---

[5] The definitions we advance are reviewed by Higgs (1987, pp. 35-56). For another excellent (though lengthy) definition, see Seliger (1976).

obviously political are still (in our terms) "ideologies." It is no accident that these powerful ideas – including religion, seemingly simple moral precepts such as Kant's (1785) "categorical imperative,"[6] formal familial relations, and traditional obligations – are included. They all potentially shape the universe of political elocution and the conceptual framework individuals use to understand and debate politics.

In fact, this definition is so general and encompassing that it is important to distinguish some ideologies and nonideologies. Instinctual, genetically programmed, or sexual reactions are not ideological, for ideologies are always intellectual. Often an ideology (such as Islam, Marxism, or feminism) is partly composed of ideas that serve to control or divert basic human behavior by asserting its baseness or unworthiness. This may lead to some rather subtle distinctions, of course. Are a group of men who beat and rob a lone traveler alone in a forest behaving ideologically? One might answer no, they are simply thugs trying not to starve. Yet if we asked them what motivates their behavior, we would likely hear some justification (they are oppressed politically, the man they robbed is a rich-tax collector-Jew-South African-sociologist) that implies their action is not "bad," and may even be moral. Though their actions hurt the man they robbed, there exists a conception of "society" that might dictate (under the terms of the robber-revolutionaries' ideology) that society is better off after the robbery than before.

Imagine two examples, one of an ideology no one now believes, and another that no one believes yet. For the first, consider the "divine right of kings." A simple description of this ideology is "the supposedly God-given right to rule formerly attributed to monarchs."[7] In using "supposedly" and "formerly," the definition clearly considers the divine right of kings to be an anachronism.

Surely, however, this is not accurate; some minority of elderly Japanese no doubt still believed in Emperor Hirohito's divine right to rule, or even his outright divinity, until the time of his death in 1988. Numerous African and South Pacific island nations retain some vestige of a divine imprimatur on the mandate to rule. Still, by our definition, the divine right of kings is an ideology even if literally no one believes it. The set of ideas that together make up the ideology (the king rules with a divine mandate, revolution is blasphemy, fealty to king is fealty to God) exist independently of whether anyone finds them persuasive.

The second example, an ideology no one believes *yet,* is both more amorphous and more interesting. Imagine a world, or in Plato's sense an

---

[6] "There is, therefore, only one categorical imperative. It is: Act only according to that maxim by which you at the same time will that it should become a universal law" (Kant 1785, p. 39).

[7] *Webster's New Universal Unabridged Dictionary,* 2nd edition, 1983.

order of being, in which all potential ideologies – or internally consistent sets of ideas with implications for "right" human action – are arrayed before us. Any individual or group could begin to comprehend fully only a fraction of these. The number she actually is persuaded by, believes in, or accepts as correct must be a set of measure zero in the space of potential ideologies. Yet it is possible to conceive of conceiving a new set of ideas with implications for political behavior. We are led to look to ideology's origin.

3.2   Origins

How can we explain the origin of ideologies? The most basic human disputes are over property rights, rights to food, shelter, and protection of the family from aggression. At their roots these disputes are not ideological, but any such contention possesses an ideological aspect. In the earlier example of robbers in the forest, the wealthy traveler might assert he was attacked by unprincipled thugs, but the "thugs" themselves are likely to assert, and even believe, their right to redistribute income from the rich to the poor.[8]

This tendency to use ideas to justify some action that one wants to take in any case might be considered strategic. But we must be careful lest we attribute too much intellectual power, bordering on foresightedness, to people justifying what are essentially primitive urges. Imagine you are hungry and that an obviously well-fed passerby has a cartload of food. You tell yourself he won't miss the food you will take, and it will save your life. So you take it, by force if necessary.

---

[8] A more extended, and far richer, example of the evolution of ideology and its relation to the institutions by which resources are owned and allocated in societies are two recent studies of the development of markets in Kenya. The first, Bates (1989), takes a mostly economic perspective; the second, Ensminger and Rutten (1990), is more anthropological. In both cases the analysis looks at the development and maintenance of common property rights by rural Kenyan farmers. Ensminger and Rutten point out:

> Ideology is particularly important for those property rights that are determined politically. Indeed, there is good reason to believe that politics does not simply mimic the market, even when people are narrowly self-interested. To the extent that this is the case, political considerations will affect the choice of property rights. The result may be property rights that decrease economic performance. (p. 9)

The general point pervading the neoinstitutional economic literature (particularly Bates 1989 and North 1990a, 1990b) is that institutions shape outcomes, citizens are aware of this influence, and the structure of institutions is sensitive to this awareness. Although we cannot nearly do justice to this point, we do wish to emphasize the extent to which ideologies constrain and redirect attempts to modify institutions for reasons of self-interest. Ideologies are the reason that institutions respond far more slowly to economic forces than would appear rational according to a model that ignores ideology.

How far would you go? Would you injure the person if he tries to resist? Does it matter that the food is for him alone, or is he taking it to an orphanage? If he dies in the ensuing struggle, how would you act the next time you are similarly hungry and see someone better off than yourself? The answers to these questions become more useful as "you" are part of a society of similar people and these confrontations become routine. Over time, an ideology or set of ideas dictating appropriate behavior will evolve. It will not be "created" in the usual sense of a strategic choice by a rational actor, but rather will be tested by whether it works.

At the outset, "working" may well be defined simply as providing a justification for doing what was desired anyway. Very soon, however, much more is demanded, for long-term success involves consistency of two types:

(1) *Logical consistency.* An ideology must justify the same action in all similar situations, rather than implying that an action is both right and wrong.

(2) *Temporal consistency.* As the ideology evolves over time and becomes more sophisticated, it must avoid ruling out actions it once approved, and vice versa.

Repeated, unexplainable failure of either type of consistency can make the ideology wither away. This is not to say that *perfect* consistency is required since, as Higgs (1987) points out, this is impossible. Still, there exists a threshold above which contradictions in an ideology weaken its foundations of legitimacy and cause it to lose adherents rapidly.

To summarize, the origin of ideology is the legitimation and justification of acts the citizens wanted first to perform for other reasons. As the acts or processes become regular and routinized, the justification becomes accepted by repetition and by its utility in consistently resolving disputes.[9] It becomes orthodox, and is widely believed so long as the group or individual whose power is given legitimacy does not contradict the ideology by word or deed. This orthodoxy creates, or at least suggests, an opposition or heterodox position. Such an observation is hardly novel, having been discussed at length by Hegel, Marx, Habermas, Hayek, and others.[10] What is interesting is the extent to which the orthodox ideology provides the organizing principle – quite analogously to Kreps's "culture," but if anything even more pervasive and important.

[9] This is not to say that all attempts to create ideologies are successful; some attempts to legitimate actions will fail to be persuasive. In this case the explanation or justification never becomes routine, and it never becomes an ideology.

[10] A thorough exploration of the links between various neo-Marxist theories of ideology and institutions is beyond the scope of the present chapter. For an interesting and provocative review, see Bates (1983) and North (1986).

3.3   Ideology sets the terms of debate

Dissidents are often those least advantaged by the orthodoxy. Their opposition may be motivated either by this strategic objection or by a genuine moral and emotional outrage against the inequities of "the system." The rhetorical requirements of a successful polemic ensure that any heterodox ideology *must* oppose the orthodox by suggesting intellectual or emotional reasons why the status quo is wrong or insupportable. This tension between exactly two opposing sets of ideas creates a relevant policy space of a single dimension, as two points determine a line. Though the orthodox and the heterodox ideologies may differ on numerous issues, the basis for such differences derives from this unidimensional (though perhaps very complex) opposition.

As a result, the latitude for genuine political strategizing of the sort routinely assumed by formal game theory is severely circumscribed. The political process, depending as it must on the evolution of ideas, their emotional and moral appeal, and the credibility of participants on both sides, just won't allow it. Political arguments will always be made in terms of ideologies with contradictory normative implications. That is, the argument will take the form of a debate over how the dispute *should* be resolved, and rarely or never in terms of the naked self-interest of the disputants.

3.4   The tendency to centralize

The creation and popularization of an ideology is not a simple strategic matter of choosing a set of ideas with the desired implications and then reaping the benefits. Rather, it is an enormously expensive and complex process. No single person, no matter how intelligent or charismatic, could create an established ideology alone. A more likely development is slow expansion, with an evolution and growth of the ideology that in turn persuades more people to join. Neither is it likely that the originator could be successful unless she genuinely and fervently believes in what she preaches.

This distinction between instrumental or strategic choices and success due to purely evolutionary forces is made far too rarely in rational choice theory. Analogous to Alchian's (1950) famous piece, we cannot infer that all those who create an ideology actually set out to do so; we know only that successful ideologies persuade enough people to make a commitment to persuade others. The reason may vary from firm personal conviction to purely cynical support based on naked self-interest, but the effect is the same.

This effect can be thought of as a kind of economy scale. The importance of ideologies in the practice of politics rewards the large-scale organization, either creating a tendency to centralize or rewarding those that centralize for other reasons. A number of small-scale disputes might individually come to myriad different resolutions. In fact, we would expect this to happen because of variations in local conditions and the differential abilities of the disputants. But if some entrepreneur can identify a single issue that unites the apparently disparate disputes into a single cause, the situation is ripe for the creation of a successful ideology.

A second reason exists for the tendency toward centralization. Either in the creation of the original ideology or in the heterodox response, it is clearly advantageous to gain the cooperation of (and hopefully to control entirely) higher levels of government, so that local disputes do not remain local. Provided some organizing principle can be found to exist for state or national government, these disputes can be resolved both quickly and in a way citizens accept as legitimate. Even if there is conflict over the proposed solution, each side will appeal to ideology rather than self-interest in order to render the claim legitimate and encourage potential supporters to participate.

For example, consider the role of the constitutional Parliament of England of the mid-seventeenth century, particularly in the Civil War (1642–46).[11] Two aspects of our conception of ideology are clearly illustrated by the events of the war and the conflict leading up to them. First, there were two "sides," divided by economics but separately united over ideas. The Puritans (or Parliamentarians) were united by a complex set of religious and political beliefs. Their opponents, the Royalists, coalesced around little else than their desire to oust the Puritans. This split came to cleave along several important dimensions:

First, there was a geographical division. . . . [M]ost of the east and south-east of England was Parliamentarian, and most of the north and west of England (and almost the whole of Wales) Royalist. That is, by and large the areas of the country which at this date were the more populous, the economically more advanced were for the Parliament; the economically more backward, the less populous were for the King.

Secondly, there was a religious division which partly corresponded with this geographical one. . . . Most strong Puritans were Parliamentarians; very few active ones supported the King. Nor can many strong Anglicans, who had no Puritan leanings, be found on Parliament's side.

There were also significant social and economic divisions. Up to a point it was a war of town against country; London, most of the larger market and cloth-manufacturing towns and almost all the seaports . . . were for the Parliament. The

---

[11] For a useful and in-depth examination of the evolution of institutions of government in England over this period, see North and Weingast (1989).

larger part of the rural areas . . . were for the King. . . . [U]p to a point this corresponded to a class division.

Another division suggested recently, is that between the "ins" and "outs," or court and country. . . . According to this view, the Civil War was a conflict between people who were office-holders and had some connection with royal court or shared in the benefits of the previous regime, and those who were excluded from these advantages. (Aylmer 1963, pp. 126-8)

The war had everything to do with economics, and nothing, for it was about two opposing ideologies. The ideologies existed because of the disputes over economics, but the war occurred only because the ideologies transported these disputes into the realm of ideas. Men were persuaded by the language of duty, and by emotion. Economics can send men to battle, but only ideology can give spring to their step and give them any hope of winning.

Second, the ideas in conflict united apparently disparate interests into organic units:

There is a sense in which the war consisted of a large number of local and even personal conflicts coming together on a national scale. It involved the settling of many private and family feuds. . . . [I]t is difficult to single out one factor among so many, to explain why people took sides as they did. But at least within the upper social groups (the gentry in particular), differences of political, or constitutional outlook were perhaps decisive. . . . [M]any members of the upper classes who thought of the King as the upholder of the traditional system in church and state, rallied to him out of instinctive loyalty, while those who thought more rationally about it and recognized the need for further changes, tended to be Parliamentarians. With some this may have been a matter of temperament, with others of material interest or what they believed to be their interest; but it was also at least in men's conscious minds a matter of outlook and beliefs. (Aylmer 1963, p. 129)

Both the influences we seek to emphasize – the usefulness of translating disputes over economic interests into ideological causes, and the tendency to centralize and proselytize – are clearly visible in these passages. We now turn to a question that takes us to the opposite pole of the analysis: If in fact ideologies are so important, why do we not see more of them, and why is it that those that do exist (particularly in the United States) seem so ephemeral?

3.5   Excellent ideologies are rare; new ones are difficult

All excellent things are as difficult as they are rare – Benedict B. Spinoza, *Ethics*, 1677 (book IV, prop. 42, note)

A new, or nascent but hopeful, political party faces an almost insurmountable problem of entry. The difficulty is not one of choosing among a variety of available and well-understood ideologies and then adopting the set of positions associated with that ideology. It is generally impossible to carve out some new position in the space of ideologies, and then run campaigns against existing parties on that basis. No new ideologies exist!

The reasons are not obvious, particularly from a theoretical perspective. Consider the "space of ideologies" just alluded to. We might imagine a collection of all functional relations, or mappings, between some set of ideas and an exhaustive list of implied policies. These mappings exist, to the extent that they imply – through some logical and aggregative mechanism we must leave abstract – a set of policies, broadly conceived. Imagining this entire space of mappings, or "functionals," in any intuitive sense is extraordinarily difficult. We as humans can imagine a collection of ideologies we know (socialism, communism, ritual cannibalism, free-market capitalism, Christianity, or Islam), but the larger set of ideologies that *could* exist, from which the examples we know are chosen, is quite beyond our comprehension. The act of creation of an ideology requires an intellectual step, a spark of recognition, of thinking of something no one else has ever conceived. We can with difficulty conceive of the abstraction of an insensible space containing correspondences between sets of ideas and the policies they imply. The question is: How large is the set of potential, or as yet unconceived of, ideologies? There are two restrictions on the number of ideologies we might count as genuine elements of this set of sets of ideas, and the correspondences to policy they represent.

The first set of restrictions comes from the rules of logical and temporal consistency, only now we look from the perspective of identifying what ideas can serve as ideologies rather than circumscribing behavior once a particular ideology is settled on. The rules of consistency dramatically restrict the set of correspondences that qualify as ideologies. We cannot simply take a set of ideas at random and examine the set of policies implied: most sets of ideas have no implication or else imply everything.

The second problem harks back to our earlier discussion of the origin of opposition. Even if there exists a latent universe of rhetorical understanding in the space of potential ideologies, the act of creation, if successful, also creates its opposition. Heterodox ideologies are restricted to those ideas that provide a justification for gainsaying the prevailing ideology, or (what amounts to the same thing) attacking the justification the prevailing ideology offers.

We can conclude that the set of feasible "new" ideologies at any given point is severely restricted, even before one encounters the problems of popularizing and persuading. Any aspirant, in order even to qualify for consideration, must answer or contradict the prevailing ideology, and must do so in a way that is both logically coherent and emotionally appealing. This barrier to the entry of new parties is not remotely fungible. Groups that would certainly otherwise organize can be permanently thwarted by this barrier alone.[12]

4   Ideology creates community and stability

Ideology is useful to the extent that it transmits information to, and excites enthusiasm in, the listener. These attributes would suffice to render ideology a powerful competitive advantage in political discourse and in electoral politics. But ideology also solves the problem of ex post reneging by politicians by making it difficult or impossible to move. By preventing politicians from changing their positions, even to increase their vote share, it allows candidates to make credible commitments. Let us investigate why this is true.

Campaigns must accomplish two things. One is to establish a candidate's position in the policy space. The other is to persuade citizens that, once in office, the candidate will pursue those same policies. Elections reflect the aggregation of individual voters' assessments of the candidate's (or party's) success in *both* those endeavors. Spatial theory has focused on the former function (choice of optimal platform), but the latter function of campaigns (establishing credibility and commitment) is the more important.

There is another reason why the political debates we actually observe center on ideology rather than policy. Most voters know little of a candidate's actual policy stands, whereas establishing an ideological position is fairly easily accomplished. Citizens recognize that the decisions elected officials must make are hard to predict, because they involve unknowable future events; in the classic distinction of Knight (1921), they represent uncertain, rather than risky, choices. Consequently, voters depend on ideology and commitment for comparing candidates.

As noted above, political science has focused primarily on the first function of campaigns, choosing a position, under the assumption of a fixed and known set of voter preferences. The game is to choose the vector of policies that maximizes the candidate's expected vote share, given the expected response of the opponent. When the expected response of

[12] Also necessary, of course, are the political resources to bring the idea to the attention of the public. Neither idea nor money is alone sufficient for success; each is necessary. The best ideology, in terms of internal logical consistency and emotional appeal, is as nothing without committed apostles to spread it and financial resources to make their efforts effective. Neither is an enormous quantity of money, used to advertise an ideology in every conceivable forum, of any use unless the message is effective.

the opponent implies as a best response the position the candidate has already chosen, an equilibrium is established and the analysis is over, just when the real campaign is just beginning.

Compare this analysis with an actual election. Incumbents run on, and challengers against, the record the incumbent has established. Even in open-seat elections there are party cues, endorsements by political elites, or prior experience with the candidates to give voters some means of guessing what the candidates will do, separate from what they claim. Candidates spend enormous amounts of time taking positions. The question is, why would anyone believe them? That is what campaigns are primarily about, and spatial theory ignores campaigns. If campaigns really were just cheap talk, we wouldn't observe them. That doesn't mean that the task is easy, or that the messages are persuasive. Most of the time, candidates and parties are simply unable to solve the problem of commitment and communication; they are unable to achieve community with the voters and win their trust. Still, if (as we have argued) the primary goal of campaigns is to persuade voters that the candidate or party will *not* move, this analytical approach of modeling strategy as movement seems paradoxical.

These problems indicate why we have yet to develop a very useful equilibrium theory of politics, even at the microanalytic level. Voters evaluate candidates based on their reputations for probity, commitment, and consistency. Movement devalues these reputations: a candidate who claims to believe simultaneously two contradictory things achieves only the appearance of believing neither.

Finally, the importance of ideology in campaigns restricts movement at a higher level of aggregation as well. The party of the candidate in power is restricted to the set of issues that legitimize their power. Opponents attack the incumbents on these issues, and along the dimensions established by this struggle for legitimacy. The policy space may be enormous and of very high dimensionality. But the ideological space in which the political debate of the campaign takes place is of low dimensionality, and "positions" in this space (i.e., distinct ideologies) are extremely sparse.[13]

To summarize all these influences together, politicians can't move without hurting their chances, couldn't move far because the effective space is small and simple, and can't move anyway because there aren't many places to go. If true, this conclusion is important from two quite distinct theoretical perspectives: It answers Gordon Tullock's famous question,

---

[13] For an excellent empirical analysis from a comparative politics perspective, see Schofield (1992).

"Why so much Stability?"; and it forces a reexamination of the equilibrium theorems we have received from game-theoretic models of politics. We consider each of these perspectives in turn.

Tullock (1981) challenged scholars in public choice and political science to reconcile a contradiction. On the one hand, all the best models of voting predict the absence of equilibrium because of the demonstrable nonexistence of a Condorcet winner, or single alternative that defeats all others in pairwise comparisons.[14] On the other hand, instability in real politics is the exception rather than the rule. Riker's (1980) concept of strategic use of institutions, and "heresthetics" (the process of realignment or shifting of the support coalitions of the parties), would indicate that these strategies are what disequilibrium in politics is all about.

This may be true, but such events are rare. The typical progression of political choices is stable, almost changeless. This is not to say voters may not want change, or that political leaders, particularly those who oppose the status quo, might not be eager to provide it. Something about the nature of the political process itself dictates this stability.

Of the answers that have been offered to Tullock's question, including logrolling (Tullock 1981) and legislative institutions (Shepsle and Weingast 1981), none seem to address the question in any fundamental way. Their focus is on legislative voting, when in fact voting on referenda exhibits the same general stability. To be successful, an answer must account for something in the very nature of political discourse. Our answer, as will no doubt by now be clear, is that the importance of ideology dictates this stability. "Moving" from one position to *any* other means that neither position is credible. Changing position in the policy space requires changing position along the ideological dimensions, saying in effect, "I no longer believe what I once asserted and tried hard to persuade you was moral and good. You were a fool to believe me."[15]

---

[14] These models (e.g., Cox 1987; McKelvey 1979, 1986; McKelvey and Ordeshook 1976, 1985) place few restrictions on preference profiles or feasible policies, and tend to imply an endless wandering among all feasible policies or among some proper subset such as the "top-cycle set" or the "uncovered set."

[15] This formulation of ideology in a spatial model is not the only attempt to simplify the concept of issues and reduce the informational requirements facing voters. An important variant on the standard spatial model that addresses and solves many of the problems we raise is the "directional" theory of voting in MacDonald and Rabinowitz (1987, 1990) and Rabinowitz and MacDonald (1989). The emphasis in this work is not on ideology but rather on symbolic politics, which implies a different modeling approach:

> If we attempt to represent this type of symbolic response in a formal way, we can imagine two qualities that are evoked by the symbol. First, there is a *direction* to the response. Does the person feel favorable or unfavorable toward

Let us now turn to consider the nature of game-theoretic models of the political process. This approach to modeling is extremely convenient, and can be used to motivate experiments in which participants choose policy positions to maximize their payoffs. Such an approach is most interesting from a scientific perspective but is of little direct, descriptive use in studying the process of political interaction. The assumption is that a candidate who chooses a position is somehow forced to deliver that position, or at least that voters believe she will, in spite of constant evidence to the contrary. Movement makes all claims incredible since voters realize that the candidate is committed only to winning, possessing no policy preferences of her own.

This is not to say equilibrium results from game theory are incorrect or useless. They are clearly correct on their own terms because they are proved correct in a rigorous fashion. The utility of the game-theoretic approach derives from the restrictions it places on possible outcomes. These restrictions are just as applicable and just as useful in real politics as they are in the stylized world of game theory. It matters little how an outcome in the top-cycle set is chosen, but we know that any outcome outside this set cannot be sustained, and it is unsustainable for precisely the reasons game theorists claim. Game theory allows us to place an additional restriction on the set of ideological positions we expect to observe. But it is important to distinguish the value of the results from the misleading strategic premise of unfettered movement by candidates.

Ultimately, a gap exists between what we know about information in politics and what we can predict as outcomes of democratic processes. One approach is to model voters' use of information on *all* issues. Recent work by Austen-Smith (1990), Austen-Smith and Banks (1990), Banks (1990), Banks and Sobel (1987), and Ledyard (1990) places rather strict limitations on how voters might rationally process information they receive from candidates with incentives to misrepresent their likely behavior in office. These highly sophisticated models challenge the ability of the

> the symbol? Second, there is a magnitude or an *intensity* to the response. How strongly does the person feel about the issue? (Rabinowitz and MacDonald 1989, p. 94)

The directional model emphasizes the diffuse, rather than coherent, response to individual issues by voters, and highlights the very low levels of information under which voters appear to make important political decisions. Although there are similarities in our approaches, there is one crucial difference: we assert the existence of a higher order of coherence across issues, in that there is a basic understanding by voters of the relation between issues and ideology. The linkages among issues, though tenuous and diffuse for any single issue, are still the basis for voter choice among candidates. The directional model would deny these linkages.

classical spatial model to represent political competition in any useful fashion. Banks (1990) states this challenge most clearly:

[The] strong assumption implicit in the Hotelling–Downs model is that the positions the candidates announce prior to an election will be the positions they subsequently enact once in office. Since voters typically have preferences defined over policy outcomes and not over electoral announcements per se, but their only information at the time of voting consists of these announcements, the equivalence of announced position and policy outcome appears to be one of analytical tractability at the expense of realism.

This work is important, for it highlights the shortcomings in previous work in spatial models. The Banks (1990) piece, and the review in Banks (1991), are easily the best work yet produced on the subject. Unfortunately, it substitutes a new, impossibly complex, set of informational requirements for the old, impossibly unrealistic, model of the campaign. Voters are assumed to know exactly what they want on each of a large number of policy dimensions, and to know exactly what candidates claim they aim to do. On this account, the only problem voters face is whether to believe the messages candidates send out.

The approach relying on ideology is radically different. Our perspective is that before voters can decide whether to believe, they must first hear and understand. It is wiser to find out what a candidate believes on all issues at once than it is to decide whether to believe what she says issue by issue.

5   Conclusion

In this chapter we have set out an overview of the need for a theory of purposive, strategic political interaction that accounts for three major problems in formal analysis. The first (North 1990a, 1990b) is the long-run nonoptimality of institutions. The second (Schofield 1985) is the relation among community, communication, and cooperation. The third (Kreps 1990) is the use of simplifying principles to contract around unforeseeable contingencies. The thesis of this chapter is that only a formal theory of ideology is capable of solving these problems simultaneously.

Ideology exists in politics because it answers the needs of actors forced to make important decisions with very little information, either about their own specific policy preferences or the likely activities of elected representatives once they take office. In order to succeed, the enterprise of creating a formal theory of ideology must accomplish three things.

First, it must offer substantive reasons why it is "ideology" (a more or less coherent set of ideas about what constitutes good public policy), rather than some other institution, that has evolved to answer the needs of political actors. A competing paradigm is orthodox spatial theory, which claims that voters evaluate politicians based on the expected utility of their promised platforms. We point out several problems with this approach, including the assumption of two types of irrationality on the part of voters: (a) Why would voters believe such claims? (b) Why would voters acquire sufficient information to evaluate such claims, when the acquisition of such information is a public good? There are other approaches that answer objection (a), such as the recent elegant work by Banks and others on games of asymmetric information, but they cannot answer (b). We argue that only a theory accounting for ideology can solve both these problems and still maintain a theory of purposive action by political actors.

Second, our enterprise must offer a more comprehensive theory of ideology than has heretofore been available. What must an ideology possess, and why do some ideologies prosper and others fail? Our answer on the necessary content of an ideology has four parts: Ideologies must make both proscriptive and prescriptive demands on human behavior, with implications for what is good, who gets what, and who rules. Further, we distinguish between individual belief systems (or schema) and ideologies, which we conceive as disembodied ideas. The success of an ideology can be measured partly by how many individuals claim they are adherents, and with what intensity. But it also can be measured by the correspondence between the logical implications of the ideas and the understanding of the implications in individuals' personal beliefs.

Third, a successful theory must describe accurately the political interactions we actually observe. The orthodox spatial model would appear to imply endless cycles and constant instability in electoral politics, because of the general nonexistence of Condorcet-winning platforms in multidimensional policy settings. A variety of alternative theories have been offered to account for the (apparently) contradictory reality of relative stability. These include structure-induced equilibrium, logrolling, or a variety of complex norms. Each of these may appear to offer partial answers, but they suffer from two flaws relative to our approach. (a) These theories focus on legislatures, but the same stability (at least) is observed in electoral politics. Rather than rely on multiple theories to account for the same phenomenon in different settings, a unified theory would be preferable (if one is possible). (b) These theories impose enormous informational requirements on participants. Such requirements, as Black (1958) argued, make sense for legislators but strain credulity for citizens. A theory with the same implications but a more realistic description of information-acquisition activities for citizens has an advantage.

REFERENCES

Alchian, A. (1950), "Uncertainty, Evolution, and Economic Theory," *Journal of Political Economy* 58: 211–21.

Austen-Smith, D. (1990), "Information Transmission in Debate," *American Journal of Political Science* 34: 124–52.

Austen-Smith, D., and J. Banks (1990), "Electoral Accountability and Incumbency," in P. Ordeshook (ed.), *Models of Strategic Choice in Politics*. New York: Cambridge University Press.

Aylmer, G. E. (1963), *A Short History of 17th Century England: 1603–1689*. London: Blandford.

Banks, J. (1990), "A Model of Electoral Competition with Incomplete Information," *Journal of Economic Theory* 50: 309–26.

Banks, J. (1991), *Signalling Games in Political Science*. Chur, Switzerland: Harwood.

Banks, J., and J. Sobel (1987), "Equilibrium Selection in Signalling Games," *Econometrica* 55: 647–61.

Bates, R. (1983), *Essays on the Political Economy of Rural Africa*. New York: Cambridge University Press.

——— (1989), *Beyond the Miracle of the Market: The Political Economy of Agricultural Development in Kenya*. New York: Cambridge University Press.

Black, D. (1958), *The Theory of Committees and Elections*. Cambridge: Cambridge University Press.

Coase, R. H. (1937), "The Nature of the Firm," *Economica* 4: 386–405.

——— (1960), "The Problem of Social Cost," *Journal of Law and Economics* 3: 1–44.

Cox, G. W. (1987), "Electoral Equilibrium under Alternative Voting Institutions," *American Journal of Political Science* 31: 82–108.

Domhoff, William. (1983), *Who Rules America Now?* Englewood Cliffs, NJ: Prentice-Hall.

Downs, A. (1957), *An Economic Theory of Democracy*. New York: Harper and Row.

Enelow, J., and M. Hinich (1984a), *The Spatial Theory of Voting*. New York: Cambridge University Press.

——— (1984b), "Probabilistic Voting and the Importance of Centrist Ideologies in Democratic Elections," *Journal of Politics* 46: 459–78.

Ensminger, Jean, and A. Raoul Rutten (1990), "The Political Economy of Changing Property Rights: Dismantling a Kenyan Commons," Political Economy Working Paper, Washington University, St. Louis.

Hardin, R. (1971), "Collective Action as an Agreeable *n*-Person Prisoner's Dilemma," *Behavioral Science* 16: 472–81.

——— (1982), *Collective Action*. Baltimore: Johns Hopkins.

Higgs, R. (1987), *Crisis and Leviathan: Critical Episodes in the Growth of American Government*. New York: Oxford University Press.

Higgs, R., and C. Twight (1987), "National Emergency and the Erosion of Private Property Rights," *Cato Journal* 6: 747–73.

Hinich, M., and M. Munger (1992), "A Spatial Theory of Ideology," *Journal of Theoretical Politics* 4: 5–31.

Hinich, M., and W. Pollard (1981), "A New Approach to the Spatial Theory of Electoral Competition," *American Journal of Political Science* 25: 323–41.

Hobbes, T. (1979), *Leviathan*. New York: Penguin (originally printed in England in 1651).

Jovrasky, D. (1970), *The Lysenko Affair*. Cambridge, MA: Harvard University Press.

Kant, I. (1976), *Foundations of the Metaphysics of Morals* (translated from original German, 1785). Indianapolis, IN: Bobbs-Merrill.

Knight, F. (1921), *Risk, Uncertainty, and Profit*. New York: Harper and Row.

Kreps, D. (1990), "Corporate Culture and Economic Theory," in J. Alt and K. Shepsle (eds.), *Perspectives on Positive Political Economy*. New York: Cambridge University Press.

Ledyard, J. (1990), "Information Aggregation in Two-Candidate Elections," in P. Ordeshook (ed.), *Models of Strategic Choice in Politics*. New York: Cambridge University Press.

Lodge, G. C. (1976), *The New American Ideology*. New York: Knopf.

MacDonald, S., and G. Rabinowitz (1987), "The Dynamics of Structural Realignment," *American Political Science Review* 81: 775-96.

(1990), "Direction and Uncertainty in a Model of Issue Voting." Paper presented at the 1990 meetings of the American Political Science Association, San Francisco, CA.

Macridis, R. C. (1980), *Contemporary Political Ideologies: Movements and Regimes*. Cambridge, MA: Winthrop.

Margolis, H. (1982), *Selfishness, Altruism, and Rationality: A Theory of Social Choice*. New York: Cambridge University Press.

McKelvey, R. (1979), "General Conditions for Global Intransitivities in Formal Voting Models," *Econometrica* 47: 1085-1111.

(1986), "Covering, Dominance, and Institution-free Properties of Public Choice," *American Journal of Political Science* 30: 283-314.

McKelvey, R., and P. Ordeshook (1976), "Symmetric Spatial Games Without Majority Rule Equilibria," *American Political Science Review* 70: 1172-84.

(1985), "Elections with Limited Information: A Fulfilled Expectations Model Using Contemporaneous Poll and Endorsement Data as Information Sources," *Journal of Economic Theory* 36: 55-85.

North, D. (1981), *Structure and Change in Economic History*. New York: Norton.

(1986), "Is It Worth Making Sense of Marx?" *Inquiry* 29: 57-63.

(1990a), *Institutions, Institutional Change and Economic Performance*. New York: Cambridge University Press.

(1990b), "A Transactions Cost Theory of Politics," *Journal of Theoretical Politics* 2: 355-67.

North, D., and B. Weingast (1989), "The Evolution of Institutions Governing Public Choice in 17th Century England," *Journal of Economic History* 49: 803-32.

Olson, M. (1965), *The Logic of Collective Action*. Cambridge, MA: Harvard University Press.

(1982), *The Rise and Decline of Nations: Economic Growth, Stagflation, and Social Rigidities*. New Haven, CT: Yale University Press.

Rabinowitz, G., and S. MacDonald (1989), "A Directional Theory of Voting," *American Political Science Review* 83: 93-121.

Reichley, J. A. (1981), *Conservatives in an Age of Change: The Nixon and Ford Administrations*. Washington, DC: Brookings.

50   Melvin J. Hinich and Michael C. Munger

Riker, W. (1980), "Implications from the Disequilibrium of Majority Rule for the Study of Institutions," *American Political Science Review* 74: 432–46.

Sartori, G. (1969), "Politics, Ideology, and Belief Systems," *American Political Science Review* 63: 398–420.

(1976), *Parties and Party Systems: A Framework for Analysis.* New York: Cambridge University Press.

Schofield, N. (1975), "A Game Theoretic Analysis of Olson's Game of Collective Action," *Journal of Conflict Resolution* 19: 441–61.

(1985), "Anarchy, Altruism, and Cooperation," *Social Choice and Welfare* 2: 207–19.

(1992), "Political Competition in Multiparty Coalition Governments," Working Paper no. 164, Center in Political Economy, Washington University, St. Louis.

Seliger, M. (1976), *Ideology and Politics.* New York: Cambridge University Press.

Shepsle, K., and B. Weingast (1981), "Structure-Induced Equilibrium and Legislative Choice," *Public Choice* 37: 503–19.

Taylor, M. (1976), *Anarchy and Cooperation.* London: Wiley.

(1982), *Community, Anarchy, and Liberty.* New York: Cambridge University Press.

Tullock, G. (1981), "Why So Much Stability?" *Public Choice* 37: 189–202.

CHAPTER 2

Implementation and enforcement in institutional modeling

Leonid Hurwicz

The aim of this chapter is to explore certain relationships between the theory of implementation of social choice rules[1] and concepts originating in the study of institutional arrangements.[2] What follows is only a brief outline of the basic ideas.

To begin with, by way of background, we look at some classical theorems of welfare economics. The first theorem of welfare economics states that in a certain class of environments,[3] perfectly competitive (Walrasian) allocations are Pareto-optimal. Existence theorems (which come in many varieties) guarantee the existence of Walrasian equilibria for certain classes of environments having, among others, properties of convexity and continuity. A space of environments for which the conclusions of both theorems hold may be called *classical*. The Walrasian equilibria may be thought of as stationary points of a dynamic process, called by Walras the *tâtonnement*. If Pareto optimality is a desideratum, then tâtonnement may be viewed as a mechanism constituting the means of achieving this goal.

Although these results still occupy a place of pride in microeconomic theory, they are inadequate in some important respects. First, even if Pareto optimality is our only concern, we may be interested in mechanisms that work in nonclassical environments – for example, in the presence of externalities or economies of scale. (In fact, much of the literature on mechanism design originates in attempts to cope with two important categories of nonclassical environments: those with public goods, and those

---

[1] The term *social choice rules* is somewhat ambiguous in that it might seem to refer to means (rules of the implementing mechanism) rather than to the ends. For this reason I often use the term *goal correspondence* or *goal function*.

[2] I use here the term *institutional arrangements* to distinguish this meaning of the term *institution* from the other one, that of an artificial person, entity, or organization.

[3] Those with preferences that are selfish and locally nonsatiated. A point e in the space E of environments is defined by the initial endowments, preferences of the agents, and the technologies of firms.

with increasing returns to scale.) But, second, there are social goal criteria other than Pareto optimality – for example, fairness or minimum consumption standards for everyone – that are not, in general, satisfied by Walrasian allocations. So here again it is natural to search for alternative mechanisms. (Just what precisely is meant by a mechanism will be discussed shortly. For the moment let us only agree that a mechanism generates equilibrium positions for the economy, even though the term equilibrium also has different meanings.)

To formulate with some generality the type of problem these considerations lead to, let us first note that goal criteria such as optimality or fairness are relative to the prevailing economic environment, both because of feasibility and preferences. Hence we define the goal criteria as correspondences that associate with every point in the space of environments a set in the space Z of outcomes. Thus Pareto optimality is an example of such a goal correspondence, while fairness is another. Let there be given a class E of environments and a goal correspondence F defined on E (or, possibly, on a superset of E). Our (analytical) objective is to look for a mechanism χ with the following two properties:

(a)   for every environment e in E, every equilibrium outcome $z \in \chi(e)$ of that mechanism (where $\chi(e)$ denotes the equilibrium outcome set of the mechanism χ) is consistent with the goal F (i.e., $z \in F(e)$);

(b)   for every environment e in E, the set $\chi(e)$ of equilibrium outcomes generated by the mechanism χ is nonempty.

If such a mechanism χ can be (analytically) defined, we could (modestly) say that if χ could be made effective, then (outcomes consistent with) F could be attained (at equilibrium) within the class E. However, in the accepted terminology, it is customary to say that χ *implements F* over E, and hence that F is implementable on E.[4] Thus, if Walrasian tâtonnement were to qualify as a mechanism, we could say that it implements Pareto optimality over classical environments. But in the implementation literature the notion of a mechanism is restricted to game forms[5] of

---

[4] I believe that both the generalization beyond Pareto optimality as the goal correspondence and the implementation terminology are due to Eric Maskin. The concept of implementation comes in several flavors. That used in the text is weaker than what is called *full* implementation.

[5] A game form for a set N of n players is defined by the n strategy domains S^i, $i = 1, \ldots, n$, and the outcome function $h: S \to Z$, where S is the Cartesian product of the S^is, and Z is the outcome space. Assuming (for the sake of simplicity) that the ith player's preferences are representable by a utility function u^i, we define this player's payoff function by $\pi^i(s) = u^i(h(s))$. The Nash equilibria under consideration are those of the game with the same strategy domains S^i and the payoff functions π^i.

noncooperative games. We shall limit ourselves here even further and consider only Nash equilibria[6] associated with such forms. Walrasian tâtonnement does not define a game form (because it does not specify feasible outcomes for nonequilibrium strategies) and hence does not qualify as a mechanism in this restricted sense. However, the Walrasian correspondence viewed as a goal correspondence has been shown to be implementable on classical environments, although by mechanisms that Walras would probably disavow. Analogous examples involving voting mechanisms could also be given.

Let us now look at the meaning of such implementability. Let $\gamma = (S^1, \ldots, S^n; h)$ be the game form implementing the goal correspondence F on the class E of environments. This tells us that outcomes consistent with F will be achieved (1) if each player stays within his or her strategy domain and, furthermore, (2) if the prescribed outcome $h(s)$ occurs when the n-tuple of strategies s has been chosen by the players. Consider the first requirement. Ordinarily, the range of behaviors feasible for the ith player (to be called the ith *natural*[7] *strategy domain*) includes actions not permissible within the prescribed domain S^i. Examples include kicking a bridge partner under the table, price-fixing agreements prohibited by the antitrust laws, and so forth. There may also exist strategies within the prescribed domain that are only possible because of the structure of the outcome function, hence not contained in the natural domain. What prevents the players from going outside of their prescribed domains? In some cases the restrictions of S^i may have been internalized, but in many there is need for an enforcement system.

The preceding statement (about the need for an enforcement system) may seem to go against the often quoted assertion that a Nash equilibrium is self-enforcing. But, in my opinion, that assertion is only valid if it means that no one has an incentive to depart unilaterally from a Nash equilibrium strategy *when all players stay within their prescribed strategy domains and the prescribed outcome function is effective.* There is nothing to imply that the players would stay within these domains, nor to clarify how the outcome function would be made effective. For the observance of the limits of strategy domains, it is natural to think of some enforcement machinery. This machinery would typically involve additional agents (e.g., courts, police, administrative agencies) and some system of sanctions – punishments for transgressions or perhaps rewards for obeying the rules. To model this, we must introduce the new players

---

[6] See note 5.
[7] The "natural" strategy domain is meant to exclude behaviors that are either physically or psychologically infeasible, but to include everything else. Hence in particular any prohibitions that have been internalized are not in the natural domain.

involved in the enforcement process and construct a game form where the original players' strategy domains are the natural rather than the prescribed ones. But the enforcement of the prescribed domains is only one problem. The other is making the prescribed (desired) outcome function effective.

Consider the relatively simple and typical case where, depending on the strategy n-tuple chosen, some players must make payments (say taxes) to be distributed to others, perhaps in the form of subsidies or social insurance. Clearly, this requires personal information processing, and (as is usual with taxes) some enforcement apparatus. Again, additional players (whether live persons or, say, agencies) must be introduced into the model to carry out all such functions. The new agents, in turn, will be endowed with their own action domains and preferences. (The case of artificial persons is more complex.) The game form must thus be expanded in several ways: by the addition of players, and by specification of their strategy domains as well as of the entries in the outcome function corresponding to strategic choices made by both the original and the new players. We thus obtain an *augmented game form* for, say $n + m$ players (there being m new players), where the strategy domains are the "natural" ones, and (if the design is successful) the original desired game form is a *subform* of this augmented form (i.e., where the desired outcome function is a restriction to S of the augmented outcome function).

Formally, let S^* be the natural joint domain and h^* the outcome function of the augmented game form, while (S, h) is the desired (prescribed) game form. As before, we abbreviate by using the Cartesian product S to represent the n-tuple $(S^1, \ldots, S^n)$. Similarly, S^* is the Cartesian product of the $n + m$ strategy domains S^{j*}. To simplify, we assume here that, for the original players $i = 1, \ldots, n$, the prescribed domains are subsets of the natural domains; hence S is a subset of S^*. Finally, for any s in S, we have $h^*(s) = h(s)$. It is in this situation that we call (S, h) a subform of (S^*, h^*).

If the design is successful, we would want the Nash equilibria of the augmented game to have the original n players using the Nash equilibrium strategies of the original game. Here, the augmented game whose payoff function π^* is a composition of the augmented outcome function h^* with the utility functions u^j of the $n + m$ players, defined on the range $h^*(S^*)$ of the augmented outcome function. Let s^* be an equilibrium strategy in the augmented game. Write $s^* = (s^*, s'^*)$ where s' is the n-tuple of equilibrium strategies of the additional m players. What we want of any such equilibrium of an $(n + m)$-tuple of strategies is for the first component s^* to be an equilibrium strategy for the original game defined by (S, h); hence, in particular, we want s^* to be an element of S.

If such a result were achieved it would seem to be in the spirit of everyday language to say that "the augmented game form (N^*, S^*, h^*) implements the original game form (S, h)." But since the term implementation has been preempted to describe the relationship of equilibria generated by the original form (N, S, h) to the desired goal function f outcomes, we shall say instead that "the augmented game form (N^*, S^*, h^*) *makes the original game form (N, S, h) effective.*"[8] Note that we are now using a more complete notation for game forms, indicating the set of participants: N denotes the original n players, while N^* stands for the expanded set of $n + m$ players. Thus N is a subset of N^*. Furthermore, if there exists a game form (N, S, h) implementing (in the Maskin sense) the goal correspondence F on the space E of environments, and if there exists an augmentation (N^*, S^*, h^*) that makes (N, S, h) effective, we shall say that F is *achievable* on E.[9]

We know that not every goal correspondence is Nash-implementable (in the weak sense used in this chapter), because monotonicity of a subcorrespondence is a necessary condition and there are correspondences lacking this property.[10] Hence not all goal correspondences are achievable. But a goal (correspondence) might be implementable without being achievable. To see why, let us first look at the case where achievability is plausible.

Consider a situation where the set N is a relatively small subset of the total population and where there exists a well-functioning enforcement system with some excess capacity operated by a set M of efficient and incorruptible persons. Let the social goal require that the behavior of the

---

[8] It might be more precise to say that it is the *difference* of the two game forms that makes the original game form effective.

[9] Recall that S^* is the Cartesian product of "natural" strategy domains, hence a given constant of the problem and not subject to the designer's choice. Similarly N and E, as well as F, are given to the designer who can only choose the original game form (N, S, h), the set $M = N^* \setminus N$ of additional players, and to some extent the augmented outcome function h^*.

Formally one could regard achievability as a very special case of implementability, where $N^* = N$, $S^* = S$, and $h^* = h$. But in most if not all cases of interest, S^* is much broader than S.

[10] The Walrasian correspondence with boundary competitive equilibria is an example. To be fully implementable, F itself must be monotonic. For other types of equilibria (e.g., undominated Nash), implementability may be easier to satisfy. But the achievability problem will remain. Remember that F is *monotonic* if and only if it is the case that $z \in F(e)$ implies $z \in F(e')$ for any environment e' in which preferences for z are maintained. More formally, if $z \in F(e)$ and $u_i(z) \geq u_i(y)$ implies $u_i'(z) \geq u_i'(y)$ for any y, then $z \in F(e')$. See Maskin (1977) and Ferejohn, Grether, and McKelvey (1982).

*i*th member of N be limited to the proper subset S^* of the "natural" domain S^{j*}. The augmented game form would then call for punishment strategies to be used by the members of M (assumed to have or be able to acquire adequate information concerning the activities of members of N), severe enough to discourage the members of N from venturing outside of S.[11] Assume that the law-abiding members of N would not have to contribute any resources to support the activities of the members of M. Then, if the game form (N, S, h) implements F, the augmented game form (N^*, S^*, h^*), where S^{j*} (for j in M) contains the punishment strategies and h^* the consequences of these strategies, would make (N, S, h) effective, and hence F achievable.

Even in the situation just described, which is intended to be maximally favorable to achievability, one can observe potential sources of difficulty. There might be problems in observing the transgressions. Also, the augmented outcome function h^* can only be chosen subject to physical, resource, and psychological constraints. But this example is of a partial-equilibrium nature. When the initial set of players N includes most of the society's members, it is no longer permissible to assume that they will not have to contribute any resources for either information processing or enforcement aspects of operating the system. Also, one can no longer ignore the possibility of strategic interactions between members of the two sets M and N. Indeed, it might be the case that M is a subset of N (so that $N^* = N$).

Consider for example an economy with N as the set of agents who are potential workers able to produce commodities that enter into their utility functions (e.g., food, shelter, clothing, etc.). A point e in the environment space E is a description of the agents' endowments ω^i, their utility functions u^i, and the production possibility sets Y_j. In particular, the endowments include the agents' time and skills available as labor input in producing the goods entering the utility functions by utilizing some appropriate Y_j. Let P denote the Pareto correspondence. The usual approach is to ask whether P is implementable, that is, whether a mechanism (a game form (N, S, h)) exists that has some Nash equilibria and all of whose Nash equilibrium allocations are Pareto-optimal. For classical E spaces such mechanisms have been designed. They require that the participants be confined to sending messages of a particular form – for example, of the form (p, q, r), where p is a proposed price vector, q a proposed net

---

[11] For the sake of simplicity we have considered game forms and games in normal (strategy) forms. A formulation in extensive form would be more informative. In particular, the punishments and rewards involved in the enforcement process occur not just at the end of the game but also while the game is going on.

trade vector, and r a real number or integer.[12] In other mechanisms the message may include the agent's statement about the profile of preferences, for example, the n-tuple of the form $(u^1(\cdot), ..., u^n(\cdot))$, again followed by a number. So the permissible strategy space excludes a variety of other means of communication and/or physical actions. There is no reason to expect that these requirements would be obeyed without an enforcement system. But that means that some members of the set N will be diverted from producing commodities entering the utility functions to enforcement and information processing activities, and other resources will have to be used in connection with these activities. Now Pareto optimality with respect to E implies the full utilization of human and other resources for the production of goods entering the utility functions. Hence the diversion for enforcement and information processing purposes is roughly equivalent to operating in an environment E' with a lower resource endowment than that in E. However efficient they are with respect to E', they will not be Pareto-optimal with respect to E. Hence the goal correspondence P, although implementable, is not achievable. In fact, it will not be possible to find an augmented form (N^*, S^*, h^*), with $N^* = N$ in the example, such that h is a restriction of h^* to S. (Recall that here (N, S, h) is a game form that does implement P.)

The first conclusion from this type of example is that first-best Pareto optimality is not achievable in general. This poses the problem of how to formulate a second-best version of the goal, taking into account the resources needed for "operating the system" (information processing and enforcement). An obvious answer is a second-best Pareto-optimality result with respect to initial resources that considers both alternative ways of operating the system – that is, the alternative game form (N^*, S^*, h^*) as one of the unknowns of the problem – and that takes into account the resource costs associated with the various operating alternatives.

But a more serious problem, and one of which we are well aware in practice, is that those charged with enforcement or information processing responsibilities will collaborate with those whose behavior they are supposed to regulate in a manner that is variously described as collusion, corruption, or being co-opted. Another possibility to be taken into account is that those responsible for enforcement are out of sympathy with the rules or regulations they are supposed to enforce. Either of these phenomena may be observed, whether the set M of those operating

[12] The (p, q, r) example, as well as the following one with profiles of preferences, is appropriate for pure exchange games. Where production is involved there are additional components. These illustrations are adequate for our purposes here and help avoid involvement in the excessive detail necessary to describe a more complete model.

the system is disjoint from N or whether, for instance, each member of N has enforcement duties in addition to other roles in society (while $N^* = N$).

Such phenomena can be modeled as the presence of Nash equilibria characterized by slack or nonexistent enforcement, with or without a material quid pro quo. Such equilibria might conceivably coexist with other "goods" whose outcomes are consistent with the goals defined by a given F. This might mean that the society falls into a "good" or "bad" pattern of behavior, depending perhaps on initial conditions and other factors (e.g., internalization induced by education). But the question remains under what circumstances the chances of equilibria with effective enforcement are likely to prevail. One possibility that deserves consideration is the existence of a subset N' of players who have a strong interest in seeing the rules enforced and also possess some "assets" (not necessarily financial or even material) that can be used to influence the behavior of those charged with enforcement. I have used the (perhaps ill-chosen) term *intervenors* for members of N'. To explain why the intervenors might want to use their assets to ensure that the enforcement system works, one may either suppose that the institutional framework enters directly into their utility functions, or that they maximize utility functions that are nonselfish and calculate the expected values over a very long run, rather than focusing on their own short-run consumption components. (The former alternative might be regarded as an analytical proxy for the latter.) It should be made clear that N' need not (and perhaps cannot) be a singleton consisting of a "good king" or (if there is such a thing) a "benevolent dictator," with charisma as the chief asset. The set N' may, for instance, be exemplified by a majority of citizens voting to "throw the rascals out" or risking their lives in demonstrations for democracy. Of course, there are also intermediate possibilities with N' consisting of significant but not numerically large groups with resources, power, or influence. Their role, whether through carrot or stick, is to create incentives for those operating the system to do so in an appropriate manner.

It must be kept in mind, however, that intervenors with assets but hostile to the system (perhaps because they favor an alternative system) may also be present. This suggests a model with a cascade of games, where the first game has as its outcome space "rules about rules" in the next game, and so on with increasing specificity, until the last game where substantive outcomes (e.g., resource allocations) are determined. The first game might be that played in a constitutional convention, the second in the nation's legislature, the third in an agency drafting (say) price-control regulations, and so on, while the last game would be played out in firms, households, and markets.[13]

Beyond modeling issues there is an interesting substantive question. To what extent is the presence of intervenors essential for the achievement of social goals when enforcement is necessary? Although I am not familiar with the literature of political science, I believe that the issue has been discussed there.[14] I hope to learn more about this in the near future.

REFERENCES

Ferejohn, J., D. M. Grether, and R. D. McKelvey (1982), "Implementation of Democratic Social Choice Functions," *Review of Economic Studies* 49: 439–46.

Maskin, E. (1977), "Nash Equilibrium and Welfare Optimality," Mimeo, Department of Economics, Massachusetts Institute of Technology, Cambridge.

Milgrom, P., D. North, and B. Weingast (1990), "The Role of Institutions in the Revival of Trade," *Economics and Politics* 2: 1–23.

Reiter, S., and J. Hughes (1981), "A Preface on Modeling the Regulated United States Economy," *Hofstra Law Review* 9: 1381–1421.

---

[13] See the article by Reiter and Hughes (1981), which uses a sequence of games akin in spirit to that suggested here.

[14] I am grateful to Roger Myerson for mentioning the article by Milgrom, North, and Weingast (1990), which is relevant to this concern.

Observe that even where no third party is brought in, members of society may play the role of intervenors vis-à-vis one another.

CHAPTER 3

Toward a theory of institutional change

Douglass C. North

Modeling institutions and the way they change is important for further progress in economic theory. In this chapter I specify what institutions and organizations are; how they change; and then explore the implications of this analysis for economic theory – a tall order for a brief essay, and it will certainly be incomplete, but I hope to whet your appetite.[1]

Why model institutions? The short answer is that they are the incentive structure of an economy and therefore fundamentally influence individual choices.

Let me give you a more complete answer from neoclassical growth theory. In a recent article entitled "A Contribution to the Empirics of Economic Growth," Mankiw, Romer, and Weil (1991) summarize and extend the earlier models of Romer (1986, 1987, 1990) and Lucas (1988), concluding that 80 percent of the variation in income per capita in 98 countries can be explained by population growth, savings, and schooling. Thus a one-percent increase in the fraction of output saved or devoted to education leads to about a one-percent increase in the level of GDP per worker. Population growth operates the other way. So all that countries need do is follow the prescription implied by that information and they will all be rich. Why don't they, if there is such a high payoff? Because the institutional framework determines the payoffs. Poor countries are poor because the payoffs do not reward productive activity. All but the most myopic economists agree that institutions are important. What is missing is a way to integrate institutional analysis into economic theory.

In the following pages, I sketch out a framework for analyzing institutions. This framework builds on the basic assumption of scarcity

An earlier version of this paper was given as the C. Woody Thompson lecture at the Midwest Economic Association Meetings in April 1991, and published in the journal of the association under the title "Towards a Theory of Institutional Change."

[1] This essay is drawn from a recently published book by the author (1990) entitled *Institutions, Institutional Change and Economic Performance.*

and hence competition and therefore of choice, subject to constraints of economic theory. However, it incorporates new assumptions about both the constraints that individuals face and about the process by which they make choices within those constraints. Among the traditional neoclassical assumptions that are relaxed are those of costless exchange, perfect information, and unlimited cognitive capabilities.

Too many gaps still remain in our understanding of this new approach to call it a theory. What I do provide is a set of definitions and principles and a structure, which provide much of the scaffolding necessary to develop a theory of institutional change.

1   Institutions and organizations

Institutions are the humanly devised constraints imposed on human interaction. They consist of formal rules, informal constraints (norms of behavior, conventions, and self-imposed codes of conduct), and their enforcement characteristics. In short, they consist of the structure that humans impose in their dealing with each other. The degree to which there is an identity between the objectives of the constraints institutions impose and the choices individuals make in that institutional setting depends on the effectiveness of enforcement. Enforcement is carried out by the first party (self-imposed codes of conduct), by the second party (retaliation), and/or by a third party (societal sanctions or coercive enforcement by the state). Institutions affect economic performance by determining (together with the technology employed) transaction and transformation (production) costs.

If institutions are the rules of the game, organizations are the players. They are made up of groups of individuals engaged in purposive activity. The constraints imposed by the institutional framework (together with the other constraints) define the opportunity set and therefore the kinds of organizations that will come into existence. Given the objective function of the organization – profit maximization, winning elections, regulating businesses, educating students – the firm, the political party, the regulatory agency, and the school or college will engage in acquiring skills and knowledge that will enhance its survival possibilities in the context of ubiquitous competition. The kinds of skills and knowledge that will pay off will be a function of the incentive structure inherent in the institutional matrix. If the highest rates of return in a society are piracy then organizations will invest in knowledge and skills that will make them better pirates; if the payoffs are highest for firms and other organizations to increase productivity then they will invest in skills and knowledge to achieve that objective. Organizations not only will directly invest in acquiring skills and knowledge but will indirectly (via the political process) induce public investment in those kinds of knowledge that they believe will en-hance their survival prospects.

The new (or neo) institutional economics has produced a substantial literature dealing with institutions and organizations. The property-rights literature (Alchian 1965; Demsetz 1967), for example, analyzes the impli-cations of institutions and organizations for performance, but their for-mation and evolution remain exogenous to the analysis. Another part of the growing literature pioneered by Oliver Williamson (1975, 1985) treats the institutional framework as exogenous and explores the transaction and transformation costs of various organizational forms. The objective of my work and specifically of this chapter is to put forth an explanation of institutional and organizational change as endogenous, an essential step (in my view) to further progress in economic history and economic development.

2 Institutional change

Modeling institutional change requires identifying the agent, source, pro-cess, and path of institutional change. Let me take each in turn.

The agent of change is the entrepreneur, the decision maker(s) in orga-nizations. The subjective perceptions (mental models) of entrepreneurs determine the choices they make.

The sources of change are the opportunities perceived by entrepre-neurs. They will stem from either external changes in the environment or from the acquisition of learning and skills which, given the mental con-structs of the actors, will suggest new opportunities. Changes in relative prices have been the most commonly observed external sources of institu-tional change in history, but changes in taste have also been important. The acquisition of learning and skills will lead to the construction of new mental models by entrepreneurs to decipher the environment; these models will in turn alter perceived relative prices of potential choices. In fact, it has usually been some mixture of external change and internal learning that triggers the choices that lead to institutional change.

Deliberate institutional change will therefore come about as a result of the demands of entrepreneurs in the context of the perceived costs of altering the institutional framework at various margins. The entrepreneur will assess the gains to be derived from recontracting within the existing institutional framework compared to the gains from devoting resources to altering that framework. Necessarily, bargaining strength and the inci-dence of transaction costs are not the same in the polity as in the econ-omy, otherwise it would not be worthwhile for groups to shift the issues to the political arena. Thus entrepreneurs who perceive themselves and their organizations as relative (or absolute) losers in economic exchange as a consequence of the existing structure of relative prices can turn to the political process to right their perceived wrongs by altering that relative price structure. In any case, it is the perceptions of the entrepreneur – correct or incorrect – that are the sources of action.

Changes in the formal rules may come about as a result of legislative changes such as the passage of a new statute; judicial changes stemming from court decisions that alter the common law; regulatory rule changes enacted by regulatory agencies; and constitutional rule changes that alter the rules by which other rules are made.

Institutional change resulting from changes in informal constraints – norms, conventions, or personal standards of honesty, for example – will have the same sources of change as learning or relative price changes but will occur far more gradually and sometimes quite subconsciously, as individuals evolve alternative patterns of behavior consistent with their newly perceived evaluation of costs and benefits.

The process of change is overwhelmingly incremental (although I shall deal with revolutionary change shortly). The reason is that the economies of scope, the complementarities, and the network externalities that arise from a given institutional matrix of formal rules, informal constraints, and enforcement characteristics will typically bias costs and benefits in favor of choices consistent with the existing framework. The larger the number of rule changes, ceteris paribus, the greater the number of losers and hence opposition. Therefore, except in the case of gridlock (described in what follows), institutional change will occur at those margins considered most pliable in the context of the bargaining power of interested parties. Incremental change will come from a change in the rules via statute or legal change. Alternatively, changes in informal constraints will be a very gradual withering away of an accepted norm or social convention, or the gradual adoption of a new one as the nature of the political, social, or economic exchange gradually changes.

The direction of change is characterized by path dependence. The political and economic organizations that have come into existence in consequence of the institutional matrix typically have a stake in perpetuating the existing framework. The complementarities, economies of scope, and network externalities mentioned herein bias change in favor of the interests of the existing organizations. Both the interests of the existing organizations that produce path dependence and the mental models of the actors – the entrepreneurs – that produce ideologies "rationalize" the existing institutional matrix, and therefore bias the perception of the actors in favor of policies conceived to be in the interests of existing organizations.

Altering or reversing paths is a result of external sources of change which weaken the power of existing organizations and strengthen or give rise to organizations with different interests. Such changes may also result from unanticipated consequences of the policies of the existing organizations. That is, the mental models of the entrepreneurs that determine the choices they make produce consequences at variance with their desired outcomes; this variance leads to the weakening of the power of existing organizations and the rise of organizations with different interests. The critical actor(s) in such situations will be political entrepreneurs whose degrees of freedom will increase in such situations and, on the basis of their perception of the issues, give them the ability to induce the growth of (or strengthen existing) organizations and groups with different interests.

Revolutionary change will occur as a result of gridlock arising from a lack of mediating institutions that enable conflicting parties to reach compromises and bargains that capture some of the gains from potential trades. The key to the existence of such mediating political (and economic) institutions is not only formal rules and organizations but also informal constraints that can foster dialogue between conflicting parties. The inability to achieve compromise solutions may reflect a lack of mediating institutions, as well as limited degrees of freedom of the entrepreneurs to bargain and still maintain the loyalty of their constituent groups. Thus the real choice set of the conflicting parties may have no intersection, so that even though there are potentially large gains from resolving disagreements, the combination of the limited bargaining freedom of the entrepreneurs and a lack of facilitating institutions makes it impossible to do so.

However, revolutionary change is never as revolutionary as its rhetoric would have us believe. It is not just that the power of ideological rhetoric fades as the mental models of the constituents confront their utopian ideals with the harsh realities of postrevolutionary existence. Rather, it is that the formal rules may change overnight but the informal constraints do not. Inconsistency between the formal rules and the informal constraints (which may be the result of a deep-seated cultural inheritance because such constraints have traditionally resolved basic exchange problems) results in tensions that are typically resolved by some restructuring of the overall constraints – in both directions – to produce a new equilibrium that is far less revolutionary.

3   Transaction costs

Information processing by the actors as a result of the costliness of transacting underlies the formation of institutions. At issue are both the meaning of rationality and the characteristics of transacting that prevent the actors from achieving the joint maximization result of the zero-transaction cost model.

The instrumental rationality postulate of neoclassical theory assumes that the actors possess information necessary to evaluate correctly the alternatives and in consequence will make choices that achieve the desired ends. In fact, such a postulate implicitly assumes the existence of a particular set of institutions and costless information. If institutions play a purely passive role, so that they do not constrain the choices of the players and the players are in possession of the information necessary to make correct choices, then the instrumental rationality postulate is the correct building block. If, on the other hand, the players are incompletely informed, devise subjective models as guides to choices, and can only imperfectly correct their models with information feedback, then a procedural rationality postulate is the essential building block to theorizing. Such a postulate not only can account for the incomplete and imperfect markets that characterize much of the present and the past world, but also leads the researcher to the key issues of just what it is that makes markets imperfect – the cost of transacting.

The cost of transacting arises because information is costly and asymmetrically held by the parties to exchange. In consequence, any way that the players develop institutions to structure human interaction results in some degree of market imperfection. In effect, the incentive consequences of institutions provide mixed signals to the participants, so that even in those cases where the institutional framework is more conducive to capturing the gains from trade (as compared to an earlier institutional framework), there will still be incentives to cheat, free ride, and so forth that will contribute to market imperfections. The success stories of economic history describe institutional innovations that have lowered the costs of transacting and permitted capturing more of the gains from trade, hence permitting the expansion of markets. But such innovations, for the most part, have not created the conditions necessary for the efficient markets of the neoclassical model. The polity specifies and enforces the property rights of the economic marketplace, and the characteristics of the political market are the essential key to understanding the imperfections of markets.

Just as the efficiency of an economic market can be measured by the degree to which the competitive structure – via arbitrage and efficient information feedback – mimics or approximates the conditions of a zero-transaction cost framework, so an efficient political market would be one in which constituents accurately evaluated the policies pursued by competing candidates in terms of the net effect on their well-being; only legislation (or regulation) that maximized the aggregate income of the affected parties to the exchange would be enacted, and compensation to those adversely affected would ensure that no party was injured by the action.

To achieve such results, constituents and legislators would need to possess true models that allowed them to accurately evaluate the gains and losses of alternative policies. Legislators would vote their constituents' interests – that is, the vote of each legislator would be weighted by the net gains or losses of the constituents, and losers would be compensated so as to make the exchange worthwhile to them. All this would occur at a transaction cost that still resulted in the highest net aggregate gain.

I do not wish to imply that the political process in democracies does not sometimes approach such a nirvana, just as economic markets sometimes approximate the zero-transaction cost model implicit in much economic theory. But such instances are rare and exceptional. Voter ignorance, incomplete information, and in consequence the prevalence of ideological stereotypes (as the underpinnings of the subjective models individuals develop to explain their environment and make choices) result in political markets that can and do perpetuate unproductive institutions and organizations.[2] The implications for economic theory of institutions and imperfect (or procedural) rationality are as follows.

1. Economic (and political) models are specific to particular constellations of institutional constraints that vary radically, both through time and cross-sectionally in different economies. The models are institution-specific and in many cases highly sensitive to altered institutional constraints.

Even more important is that the specific institutional constraints dictate the margins at which organizations operate, and hence make intelligible the interplay between the rules of the game and the behavior of the actors. If organizations devote their efforts to unproductive activity, the institutional constraints have provided the incentive structure for such activity. Third world countries are poor because the institutional constraints define a set of payoffs to political and economic activity that do not encourage productive behavior. Socialist economies are beginning to learn the hard lesson that the underlying institutional framework is the source of the current poor performance, and are attempting to grapple with ways of restructuring the institutional framework to redirect incentives that in turn will direct organizations along paths of increased productivity. As for the first world, we need to not only appreciate the importance of the overall institutional framework responsible for economic growth, but also be self-conscious about the consequences of the marginal changes that are continually occurring. We have long been aware that

---

[2] See North (1991), "A Transaction Cost Theory of Politics."

taxes, regulations, judicial decisions, and statute laws shape the policies of organizations, but such awareness has not led to the focusing of economic theory on modeling the political-economic process that produces these results.

2. A self-conscious incorporation of institutions will force social scientists in general and economists in particular to question the behavioral assumptions that underlie their disciplines and, in consequence, to explore much more systematically than we have done so far the implications of the costly and imperfect processing of information for the consequent behavior of the actors. Social scientists have incorporated the costliness of information in their models, but have not (for the most part) come to grips with the subjective mental constructs by which individuals process information and arrive at conclusions that shape their choices.

3. Ideas and ideologies matter, and institutions play a major role in determining just how much they matter. Ideas and ideologies shape the mental constructs that individuals use to interpret the world around them and make choices. Moreover, by structuring the interaction of human beings in certain ways, formal institutions (deliberately or accidentally) lower the price of acting on one's ideas and therefore increase the role of mental constructs and ideological stereotypes in choices. Voting systems, lifetime tenure for judges - indeed, the institutional framework of hierarchies in general - all provide a setting that alters the price one pays for expressing and acting on one's ideas, convictions, dogmas, or insights.

4. The polity and the economy are inextricably linked in any understanding of the performance of an economy; we must therefore develop a true political economy discipline. A set of institutional constraints and consequent organizations define the exchange relationships between the two and therefore determine the way a political-economic system works. Not only do polities specify and enforce property rights that shape the basic incentive structure of an economy; in the modern world, the share of gross national product going through government - and the ubiquitous and ever-changing regulations imposed by it - are the keys to economic performance.

Let me conclude by summing up the key features of this analytical framework of institutional change.

1. The continuous interaction between institutions and organizations in the competitive economic setting of scarcity is the key to institutional change.

2. Competition forces organizations to continually invest in knowledge in order to survive.

3. The institutional framework dictates the kind of knowledge perceived as yielding the maximum payoff.

4. The mental constructs of the players – given their inherited cultural conditioning, the complexity of the environment, and the limited information feedback on the consequences of actions – determine perceptions.

5. Economies of scope, complementarities, and the network externalities of an institutional matrix render institutional change overwhelmingly incremental and path-dependent.

REFERENCES

Alchian, Armen (1965), "Some Economics of Property Rights," *Il Politico* 30: 816–29. Reprinted in A. Alchian, *Economic Forces at Work* (Indianapolis: Liberty Press, 1977).

Demsetz, Harold (1967), "Toward a Theory of Property Rights," *American Economic Review* 57: 347–59.

Lucas, Robert (1988), "On the Mechanics of Economic Development," *Journal of Monetary Economics* 22: 3–42.

Mankiw, Gregory, David Romer, and David Weil (1992), "A Contribution to the Empirics of Economic Growth," NBER Working Paper no. 3541, New York.

North, Douglass C. (1990), *Institutions, Institutional Change and Economic Performance.* Cambridge: Cambridge University Press.

(1991), "A Transaction Cost Theory of Politics," *Journal of Theoretical Politics* 2: 355–68.

Romer, Paul (1986), "Increasing Returns and Long-Run Growth," *Journal of Political Economy* 94: 1002–37.

(1987), "Growth Based on Increasing Returns Due to Specialization," *American Economic Review* 77: 56–82.

(1990), "Endogenous Technological Change," *Journal of Political Economy* 98: S71–S102.

Williamson, Oliver (1975), *Markets and Hierarchies: Analysis and Antitrust Implications.* New York: The Free Press.

(1985), *The Economic Institutions of Capitalism.* New York: The Free Press.

CHAPTER 4

The development of contemporary
political theory

Peter C. Ordeshook

In his notes on the Federal Convention, James Madison (1898, pp. 108-9) reports the following comments by Benjamin Franklin with respect to the manner in which judges ought to be chosen:

Doctor Franklin observed, that the two modes of choosing Judges had been mentioned, to wit, by the Legislature and by the Executive. He wished such other modes to be suggested as might occur to other gentlemen; it being a point of great moment. He would mention one which he had understood was practised in Scotland. He then, in a brief and entertaining manner, related a Scotch mode, in which the nomination proceeded from the lawyers, who always selected the ablest of the profession, in order to get rid of him, and share his practice among themselves. It was here, he said, the interest of the electors to make the best choice, which would always be made the case if possible.

Thus, with a particular problem in hand, Franklin identifies the components of rational self-interest and suggests an incentive-compatible mechanism for making the desired social choice. The question that we address here is whether we have advanced the science of politics in an appreciable way in the 200+ years since Franklin spoke.

To render a judgment about contemporary political theory, we should return to the decade immediately following World War II, because it was then that the research regarded by political scientists as path-breaking was not an outgrowth of economics or the rationalism of the eighteenth century, but rather of the "behavioral revolution." In response to the purely institutional descriptive mode of inquiry that was previously dominant, this revolution sensitized us to the importance of sociopsychological variables and statistical methodologies, and to the relevance of public opinion and its measurement. But much of that research followed a path in which scholarship was judged by the size of one's data set and by the

Prepared for delivery at the Eighth International Symposium in Economic Theory and Econometrics, Washington University, St. Louis, May 22-25, 1991.

novelty of the statistical tools employed, rather than by its contribution to the development of a coherent, parsimonious, and deductive theory of political action. Correlation piled upon correlation, and political scientists felt compelled to become familiar with a plethora of ill-defined ideas such as anomie, alienation, cognitive dissonance, and attitude, as well as innumerable concepts defined by ad hoc measurements rather than theoretical constructs.

Of course, behavioralism was not the only contender for the political scientist's soul. But paralleling events of an earlier time in which the radical empiricism of the sixteenth and seventeenth centuries gave way to the rationalism of Hobbes, Locke, and Rousseau in the eighteenth century, a series of books inaugurated a second revolution in the study of politics at approximately the time of behavioralism's ascendancy – a revolution that would draw our attention back to the institutional context of political activity, that would sharpen the distinction between normative and descriptive analysis, and that would reinvigorate the development of a deductive theory of political processes. The centerpieces of that revolution are Arrow's (1951) *Social Choice and Individual Values,* Downs's (1957) *Economic Theory of Democracy,* Black's (1958) *Theory of Committees and Elections,* Buchanan and Tullock's (1962) *Calculus of Consent,* Riker's (1962) *Theory of Political Coalitions,* and Olson's (1965) *Logic of Collective Action.* These volumes brought order to political analysis and set the direction for future research so that it could begin to uncover first principles of political action in such areas as social choice theory, voting in committees, coalition formation, majority-rule elections, and interest-group action.

Three other books also contributed importantly to this second revolution: Luce and Raiffa's (1957) *Games and Decisions,* Key's (1966) *The Responsible Electorate,* and Farquharson's (1969) *Theory of Voting.* Although von Neumann and Morgenstern's (1945) *Theory of Games and Economic Behavior* is the seminal volume of game theory, Luce and Raiffa's interpretative survey trained a generation of scholars to think in game-theoretic (strategic) terms. Through their effort, ideas such as Nash equilibria; strategy; extensive, normal, and characteristic function form; the core; and V-sets became familiar to those who saw themselves as replacing pure empiricism with formal, deductive thinking. And today, game theory is the primary theoretical structure that anchors and integrates the most recent developments in political theory.

Farquharson makes no direct mention of game theory, but he made coherent the idea that voting procedures are strategic environments and that the outcomes they produce can be ascertained only by evaluating how voters respond to the anticipated actions of other voters, where all responses are mediated by the prevailing electoral institution. Farquharson, then, anticipated not only the development of ideas such as subgame perfection, and the necessity for understanding how procedural details can be used by those who design and implement those procedures to manipulate outcomes; he also anticipated the hallmark of contemporary political theory – that all political–economic action takes place in contexts in which people's fates are interdependent and in which they must make decisions with the understanding that others about them are oftentimes acting so as to anticipate their actions.

Unlike these other volumes, Key's does not offer any formal structure; nor does he consider any game-theoretic ideas. But this last contribution by the leading scholar of American politics of his generation legitimized the application of rational choice models in a context – voting – that most researchers assumed was reserved for psychosociological analysis. Although few would dispute the assertion that election candidates, interest-group leaders, and bureaucrats acted in accordance with a well-defined self-interest, such an hypothesis seemed more difficult to sustain for mass political action. Individual perceptions were blurred, motivations unclear, and habit and socialization seemed the principle explanatory constructs. Key challenged such views and the subsidiary assertion that the rational-choice paradigm was too crude a tool with which to approach the study of mass political behavior, and he argued that this paradigm must, of necessity, become the centerpiece of all political analysis.

A series of seminal papers followed the publication of these volumes and inaugurated more mathematically rigorous developments. Gibbard (1973) and Satterthwaite (1975) demonstrated that no democratic institution is immune from manipulation, and they thereby placed the study of strategic maneuver and institutions at the heart of formal political analysis. Kramer's (1972) analysis of the influence of parliamentary procedures established the ways in which such procedures may or may not induce stability in political outcomes, while simultaneously providing a set of results about voting that today are the foundation of models of legislative process. Plott (1967) and Davis and Hinich's (1967) extensions of Black and Downs's analyses of committees and elections offered a representation of political preferences that paralleled in importance the indifference-curve representation of consumer preferences in economics, and demonstrated the fragility of stability in even the simplest of political processes – two-candidate elections and majority-rule committees. Building on Plott and Davis and Hinich's construction, McKelvey (1976, 1979) and Schofield (1980) demonstrated the extent of instability under majority rule and the opportunities to influence outcomes via manipulation of voting agendas. Schwartz (1977) clarified the intimate connection between opportunities for vote trading in legislatures and the Condorcet paradox; and, building on Farquharson's insights, innumerable papers on incentive compatibility and manipulability made us sensitive to the possibilities (or impossibility) of designing political-economic institutions that realize normative ends (cf. Clarke 1971; Groves and Ledyard 1977; Maskin 1977).

To this list we should also append those contributions that did not offer any startling theoretical conclusion, but showed instead how the paradigm and its associated analytic perspectives could be applied to a wide range of political matters. We have in mind here Niskanen's (1971) analysis of bureaucracy that paralleled Downs's treatment of political parties and candidates; Mayhew (1974) and Fiorina's (1977) analyses of the members of the U.S. Congress in the same terms, as goal-directed utility maximizers; Popkin's (1979) analysis of peasants in Viet Nam; and Schelling's (1960) seminal discussion of the application of game theory to the study of deception and deterrence.

From such surveys, then, we have the impression of impressive advances. Our journals are replete with game-theoretic models of elections, committees, and war and deterrence; and press editors eagerly pursue half-completed manuscripts by practitioners in the field. But a less sanguine view argues that our understanding of politics has improved only slightly; that much of this research, like a giant ingrown toenail, is wholly literature-driven and directed in inconsequential matters; and that success at finding publication outlets owes more to an intoxication with notation than to substantive significance. With some justification, people have wearied of a field that seems preoccupied with technical results about majority-rule instability and sufficient conditions for the existence of Condorcet winners. They have become intolerant of research monographs that toil through a seemingly endless array of notation and manipulation of Bayesian probabilities in order to establish that a particular conjunction of strategies constitutes an esoteric type of equilibrium for a game that ostensibly describes a three-person legislature or a two-country international system. They have learned to avoid papers whose abstracts begin with "we explore a model . . ." or "we show that an equilibrium exists under which. . . ." They despair because, although much is known about simple forms of majority rule, very little is known about those rules and procedures that actually characterize political institutions. And they find insufferable the hubris of colleagues whose reputations are based on a familiarity with the current fad in game-theoretic technology, and for whom empirical research consists of reading the latest issues of *JET,* the *APSR, Social Choice and Welfare,* the *AJPS,* and *Econometrica.*

We cannot dismiss such criticism out of hand. Contemporary political theory identifies a wide range of circumstances under which majority rule yields equilibrium and disequilibrium, but can we argue that simple majority rule characterizes anything more than a tiny proportion of political institutions? Countless articles have been written about the infinitely repeated two-person Prisoner's Dilemma, but can we identify any circumstance in which identically the same game between the same two people repeats itself even twice? We see the "new institutionalism" heralded as though it were equivalent to the discovery of the atom, but aren't these ideas new only because we have accepted a straw-man characterization of our intellectual predecessors? We have witnessed the skill with which our colleagues manipulate equations pertaining to Bayesian beliefs and sequential equilibria, but what is the technology for measuring such beliefs and how do we contend with the experimental evidence that suggests that that model cannot characterize subjective probability? And we have seen the impressive growth of models of legislative processes, but has our willingness to accept abstraction been extended too far by special characterizations of issues and preferences and by highly restrictive assumptions about information and institutional structure?

Overviews of the field can also be discouraging. Even after four decades, practitioners in the field do not agree even among themselves about the ultimate implications of their research. Riker (1983) and Coleman and Ferejohn (1986), for example, disagree over whether contemporary social choice theory and, in particular, the "chaos" theorems of McKelvey and Schofield imply anything about the relative value and stability of populist versus liberal democracy. Similarly, McKelvey and Ordeshook (1984) and Shepsle and Weingast (1984b) disagree over whether the "new institutionalism" in fact offers anything other than the proposition that institutions deflect majority preferences only to the extent that transaction costs are high.

Finally, moving into the inner recesses of the most advanced papers on political theory is often a disappointment. Paper abstracts lead us to believe that advances are being made at a rapid pace, but the essays themselves often reveal a different story. To render matters well-defined, ad hoc extensive or strategic forms, which everyone is presumed to see with perfect clarity, constitute the core formulation. We see legislatures consisting of one or three members, models of intergenerational transfers in which all of society dies after two periods, models of elections in which the victorious candidate is dictator over all social policy, and analyses of international affairs in which country A but not B can make the first threat. To render the analysis tractable and consistent with the dictates of contemporary game theory, the *as if* principle is extended without limit so that common knowledge is assumed to apply to complex strategic representations and probability densities with which even the analyst has difficulty contending. And of course, nearly everyone is willing to accept "the well documented empirical fact" that all utility functions are separable, strictly concave, and twice differentiable.

So what is it, then, that has been accomplished this past forty years? Is our understanding of politics deeper, or is it merely our understanding of our colleagues' papers – along with our ability to manipulate notation and to string together abstract definitions – that has grown?

This chapter will argue that both views are essentially correct. Although our understanding of politics (and of economics) remains in such a primitive state that we cannot ignore the practical necessity for considering other, less formal modes of inquiry, something has been accomplished. In particular, contemporary political theory has isolated important "first principles" and has provided a core theoretical structure for integrating these principles and generalizing their domain. However, we also argue that many of the critiques of that theory hit their target, primarily because practitioners in the field fail to appreciate something that was apparent to arguably the most successful set of political engineers in history – the Founders of the American republic – namely, the distinction between science and engineering, between model and theory, and between proper and improper use of empirical methodologies.

1   The spatial election model

In the space of a single chapter it is, of course, impossible to review critically the vast literature that constitutes "contemporary political theory." However, regardless of our starting point, and regardless of our demarcation of "important contributions," it is evident that of all the asserted accomplishments of that theory, none is more important than that it has led to a reintegration of politics and economics under a common paradigm and deductive structure.

Both the evidence and source of this integration is generally taken to be the increasingly widespread acceptance of Key's argument that the rationality hypothesis has broad if not universal application in politics. Indeed, those scholars who critique this enterprise as either too limited in its application or too narrow in its normative implications focus typically on the meaning and generality of the assumption of self-interested action (cf. Monroe 1990). However, the mere acceptance of this postulate does not account for theoretical developments. Indeed, we can easily imagine a scenario in which its acceptance leads to little more than a reformulation of the behavioralist agenda, with political scientists focusing their attention on the sociological determinants of tastes and perceptions.

The second ingredient of this integration – supplied by each of the seminal volumes in the field – is a concern with political institutions. If economics and politics are to be understood in the same terms, it is imperative that we incorporate into our research agendas the fact that these disciplines, if they differ at all, differ only to the extent that the study of politics and economics is little more than a preoccupation with the performance of different institutions.

The focus of economics, of course, is the market and the ways in which governmental decisions impact on it. For political scientists, the focus is elections, constitutional design, parliaments, and, in the case of international politics, coordination in anarchic systems. This distinction is not sharp, as when taxation and trade policy are the subject of inquiry, but to be certain that we are studying matters that allow for interdisciplinary research, the institutional context of that research must be explicit. That is, studying the relative performance of alternative institutions of social choice and determining how they interact is the primary task of those who seek to develop a wholly integrated, scientifically correct field of political economy.

1.1   *The representation of preferences*

It is, however, too self-congratulatory to argue that the previously cited research holds a monopoly on appreciating the roles of self-interest and institutions. Morgenthau's (1948) text on international politics, Hoag and Hallett's (1926) study of voting procedures, or Bentley's (1935) analysis of interest groups should convince us that the perspectives of Franklin, Madison, and their contemporaries had not somehow been banished from the landscape, only to be resurrected in 1957 or 1962. And although acceptance of the rationality postulate necessarily leads to game theory, merely studying alternative institutions with a plethora of game-theoretic formulations yields a dizzying selection of models in which synthesis is not assured. Even though game theory provides a unifying theoretical base, it alone cannot produce substantively meaningful integrative theory, because of necessity it remains little more than a set of mathematically abstract ideas (outcome sets, actions, topological trees, strategies) held together by ad hoc notions of equilibrium.

In addition to abiding by the rationality paradigm, exhibiting a concern with institutions, and employing game theoretic tools, what was required for the development of true theory was a unifying representation of preferences allowing for comparisons of the relative performance of those institutions and the determination of how they evolve and interact. And in this respect the key contribution is the spatial preference structure first described by Black and Newing (1951) and formalized by Plott and by Davis and Hinich in terms of convex preference sets and Euclidean loss functions.

To illustrate this idea's importance, consider the early research on Condorcet's paradox. Without applying a particular topology to outcomes and preferences, assessing the importance of that paradox relied on a simple counting of possibilities under empirically vacuous null assumptions of equiprobability. On the other hand, once provided with a spatial topology, Plott, Davis and Hinich, and Sloss (1971) could convince us of the fragility of Condorcet winners, and McKelvey and Schofield could establish the potential severity of cycles in democratic systems. Specifically, only by accepting the spatial representation can we see that Condorcet winners are rare and that "top-cycle" sets can readily encompass the entire set of feasible outcomes.

More generally, the spatial idea unifies the treatment of the primary actors in markets and elections – consumers and voters – in such a way that they can be viewed as the same individuals operating in different institutional contexts. At the heart of economic theory is the idea that if people's preferences over alternative states of the world satisfy only two assumptions (transitivity and completeness), then we can begin to describe abstractly the basic activities of barter and production. Moreover, if we add a few technical assumptions about preference and outcomes (e.g., continuity), then we can represent preferences by indifference curves and we can apply the tools of calculus and algebra to characterize barter and production in compact and wholly general ways that allow for the formulation of that most important idea in social science – the characterization of efficient markets.

So powerful are these ideas about preferences that their initial acceptance in economics largely accounts for the unfortunate separation of political economy into two disciplines. However, in principle at least, the spatial model allows us to formally reconnect economic and political theory. The mechanism whereby this reconnection occurs stems from the fact that spatial preferences can be derived from economic preferences. Briefly, if we imagine a two-good model in which both goods are to be publicly provided, then Black's notion of a single peaked preference corresponds to the preference of an individual over a budget constraint that models a government's feasible spending policies with respect to those two goods. By extension, the spatial preference representation generalizes Black's idea to preferences over a budget simplex involving n goods, or $n-1$ goods plus a tax rate that determines the government's budget and the consumer/voter's ability to purchase other commodities in the market (cf. Coughlin and Hinich 1984; Ordeshook 1986). Thus, the idea of a spatial preference allows us to analyze processes in which people can simultaneously be consumers and voters (cf. Klevorick and Kramer 1973; Meltzer and Richard 1981; Romer and Rosenthal 1979), and it thereby moves us closer to the goal of integrating the analysis of political and economic institutions.

1.2   The median voter theorem

Perhaps no result captured as much attention as Black's median voter theorem, especially after Downs breathed substantive life into it. The theorem, which illuminates the strong centralizing tendency of simple majority-rule electoral institutions, is perhaps intuitive and obvious – especially to politicians whose livelihoods depend on understanding the basic forces of the political system with which they must deal. However, people have been designing and overturning political institutions for millennia, and we should not be surprised to find that a great deal of what we learn about them through game theory, axiomatic analysis, or the application of new empirical methodologies merely reconfirms or restates ideas that are otherwise obvious or well understood. The fundamental contribution of theoretical inquiry is not always the production of the counterintuitive result; rather, it is the expanded ability to relate seemingly diverse phenomena via a unified deductive structure.

The median voter theorem was the first step toward understanding a variety of phenomena using such a structure. First, in exploring this idea's generality, we establish a venue for bringing mathematical argument to politics, for injecting game-theoretic reasoning into our discourse in a serious way, and for developing a standard whereby we can descriptively and normatively evaluate the performance of alternative political institutions. Second, that model plays the same role in political theory as does the neoclassical model of markets. Although few empirical examples of markets match the mathematics that introductory economics texts describe, the neoclassical model of perfectly competitive markets has served as a focus for most of the theoretical advances in economics this past forty or so years. Treatment of externalities and public goods, the initial development of the rational-expectations hypothesis, and the incorporation of game-theoretic reasoning, for example, all occurred under the impetus of generalizing and extending that model.

Following a similar path of development, early variants of election models abstracted greatly from reality with assumptions about perfectly informed voters and candidates, two-candidate competition, and perfect spatial mobility. But political scientists have extended that model so that today it accommodates a diverse array of considerations. Although most spatial analyses focus on a two-candidate scenario, the spatial model has been used to show how political parties can protect themselves from third-party entry either by nominating candidates that deviate from the median preference (Brams and Straffin 1982; Palfrey 1984) or – appealing to some recent research that has formalized Duverger's (1954) hypothesis that simple majority rule fosters the development of a two-party system (Cox 1987b; Fedderson, Sened, and Wright 1990; Palfrey 1989) – by manipulating election procedures so that they more closely match simple majority rule (Bartholdi, Tovey, and Trick 1989). And paralleling the economist's research into the sources of market failure and the development of the idea of rational expectations, we know that the median voter theorem is robust to some weakening of the assumption of complete information. Thus, we can assert with greater confidence than our intellectual predecessors that democratic institutions do not necessarily operate imperfectly in less than ideal circumstances (Austen-Smith and Banks 1988; Banks 1989; Ledyard 1989; McKelvey and Ordeshook 1985).

We learned early, of course, that the median voter theorem is not robust to the dimensionality of the policy space, and this fact generated nearly as much turmoil as constructive research. Political theorists became mesmerized by the fact that even the slightest perturbation in preferences away from perfect symmetry destroyed the existence of a Condorcet winner, and McKelvey's (1976, 1979) and Schofield's (1980) results convinced some researchers of the inherent unpredictability of political outcomes (but see Coleman and Ferejohn 1986). Indeed, at least one prominent contributor to contemporary political theory came perilously close to asserting that the instability of majority rule precluded a science of politics (Riker 1980).

At approximately the same time, though, there emerged more general hypotheses about equilibria and candidate platforms, such as the uncovered set (Miller 1980). Thus, we now know that if people vote deterministically, the domain of undominated spatial strategies is limited to a subset of the policy space with an identifiable structure that can be viewed as a generalization of a multidimensional median, and that even without a multidimensional median, candidates will not wander far from the "center" of the policy space (McKelvey and Ordeshook 1976; McKelvey 1986).

2   Committees

Mass elections are not the only venue for applying the spatial preference structure. Indeed, Black and Newing's early monograph, as well as Black's subsequent presentation of the median voter theorem, assume that the same model of preferences applies to committees as to electorates; thus both volumes are seminal with respect to the contemporary study of legislatures, committees, and the integration of models of political institutions.

2.1 The "new institutionalism"

Of the several extensions of Black and Newing, perhaps none is more important that Kramer's (1972) analysis of issue-by-issue voting. Begun initially as a search for variants of majority rule that would guarantee stability in an otherwise unstable environment, Kramer incorporated Farquharson's perspectives and formalized Black and Newing's spatial analysis of committees so as to offer a set of theorems about sophisticated voting showing that the existence of a stable point under issue-by-issue voting depends critically on the assumption that preferences on the issues are separable. Although frequently ignored or misrepresented (but see Denzau and Mackay 1981, Enelow and Hinich 1983, and Epple and Kadane 1990 for a correct interpretation), this result is profoundly important. Specifically, owing to the evident restrictiveness of the separability assumption, we can infer that procedural details such as dividing the question or assigning substantive jurisdictions to subcommittee need not resolve the instabilities inherent in simple majority rule processes, unless voters are naive or stupid.

This is not to say, however, that Kramer's analysis establishes the irrelevance of institutions and committee procedures, because it is also true that issue-by-issue voting occasions a stable point with strategically sophisticated voters in the special case of separable preferences. Thus, Kramer enriches our understanding of institutions and procedures by showing that their performance depends not only on their character, but also on the structure of preferences and the sophistication of decision makers. That is, we cannot appeal – as early twentieth-century institutionalists were wont to do – to mere descriptions of institutions, however carefully crafted, to infer final outcomes; nor can we look, as naive behavioralists, only at the structure of preferences. Instead, we must look at all factors simultaneously before definitive conclusions can be uttered, and in this way, we have moved closer to achieving a truly causal explanation of political outcomes.

More generally, by refocusing attention on procedural details, we have not only gained a deeper appreciation of the role of those details in facilitating stability (Hammond and Miller 1987, 1989; Riker 1983; Shepsle 1979; Shepsle and Weingast 1981), but we have also begun to understand how institutions mediate the perceptions and beliefs that the behavioralist seeks to measure. At the same time, we have also learned how to identify circumstances under which institutional structures make little difference in the final determination of outcomes, or least to appreciate the limits of their influence on outcomes. We now know, for example, that final outcomes in two-candidate elections are constrained to the same subset of the policy space as are the outcomes that are predicted (via the V-solution, bargaining set, or competitive solution) to arise in simple majority-rule committees (McKelvey 1986).

This fact is profoundly important for democratic theory. Specifically, we are no longer required to rationalize the use of elections solely on the basis of simple majoritarian principles or vague appeals to legitimacy. In addition, we now have a well-founded theoretical basis for viewing two-party, mass elections as a reasonable substitute for the ideal of democracy, the "New England town meeting," whenever the number of potential participants in such a meeting exceeds the limits of practicality.

2.2   Agendas

Aside from establishing some results about a particular procedural detail, Black and Newing showed how the spatial model can be applied usefully to a wide range of political institutions, and the research that followed contributed to a clearer understanding of the influences of various rules and institutional structures in legislatures (Denzau and Mackay 1983; Shepsle and Weingast 1984a), of the historical trends in the ideological basis of American politics (Poole and Rosenthal 1985, 1991), and of coalition formation in parliaments (Ordeshook and Winer 1980; Rosenthal 1970).

But in addition to learning that "institutions matter," we also gained a deeper appreciation for how specific procedural details might be manipulated to influence outcomes. Research on voting agendas provides the best example. Farquharson's familiar discussion of the example of Pliny the Younger reveals that students of politics have long been acquainted with the opportunity to manipulate outcomes by manipulating the ways in which voting and majority rule are implemented in committees. And Levine and Plott's (1977) study of a Southern California flying club also convinced us in contemporary terms of the importance of agendas.

The particular difficulty with such examples, however, matches that of determining the consequences of electoral disequilibrium. Although people can manipulate outcomes by manipulating agendas, this fact alone does not allow us to measure an agenda setter's power. But the spatial model provides the structure required to evaluate that power. The seminal essay here is McKelvey's (1976) proof that if there is no Condorcet winner, cycles encompass the entire issue space. Although this result has mistakenly been interpreted (not by McKelvey) to mean that an agenda setter's power is absolute and that majority rule processes in general are chaotic, McKelvey's analysis spurred attempts to measure the influence of agendas and a setter's power. The critical contribution in this instance is Miller's (1980) formulation of the uncovered set and his proof that, with strategic voters, amendment agendas cannot produce outcomes that are covered by any outcome on the agenda. Shepsle and Weingast's (1984a) subsequent extension of Miller's analysis to spatial preferences, then, moves us closer to completing a research agenda that parallels the one set for two-candidate elections – determining the range of outcomes that can arise in committees that use some type of agenda to give order and coherence to their deliberations (see also Ferejohn, McKelvey, and Packel 1984 for a different institutional analysis that nevertheless yields an equivalent conclusion – namely, that even if cycles are ubiquitous, final outcomes have a limited domain).

A number of subsidiary results followed quickly. In particular, Ordeshook and Schwartz (1987) noted that, except for those instances in which only three motions (including the status quo) are considered, Congressional agendas do not correspond necessarily to amendment agendas, and that an agenda setter's power is increased considerably if we allow the full range of agendas that might be formed. On the other hand, Austen-Smith (1987) modeled a particular endogenous agenda-formation process and gave us reasons for supposing that members of Congress can construct amendment agendas so as to secure the outcomes they want while simultaneously voting sincerely. Banks (1989) shows how earlier results can be extended to one type of agenda, the two-stage agenda, that can arise in Congress.

Admittedly, though, this research has two weaknesses. First, it assumes complete information on the part of all participants, whereas Ordeshook and Palfrey (1988) give examples of how incomplete information can upset even the most basic conclusions – namely, that sophistication and binary agendas are sufficient to produce Condorcet winners as final outcomes – and how events such as nonbinding straw polls that precede the implementation of an agenda can influence outcomes. As with previous research, however, Ordeshook and Palfrey present only a possibility result by way of example, whereas Jung (1989) shows how these conclusions about the impact of informational asymmetries – especially those concerning the ability of agendas to produce Condorcet winners – must be modified if preferences are spatially structured. Specifically, if it is common knowledge that all voters have single-peaked preferences, then the Condorcet winner once again reappears as the final outcome of amendment agendas if committees are "sufficiently large."

More problematical is the issue of endogenous agendas, the process whereby agendas are formed via the sequential introduction and labeling of alternatives to be voted on. Although Banks and Gasmi (1987) offer a limited analysis in a spatial context, we can also infer from their analysis that studying the processes whereby agendas arise in "large" committees (i.e., $n > 3$) will pose severe analytic difficulties. The general difficulty, of course, is that the processes whereby agendas are formed in committees are not well-defined, in the sense that those processes do not correspond to any self-evident game form. Thus, models like Austen-Smith's (1987) are driven more by the demands of tractability and available technology than they are by the substantive context of choice. At present, then, there is no successful model of endogenous agenda formation that allows for any meaningful interpretation of events.

The particular problem is that to apply game theory we must provide a game form that specifies precisely the identity of decision makers, the sequence with which they make decisions, and the information at their disposal when they act. And although agenda voting, like simple descriptions of elections, lends itself readily to the construction of such a form, the processes whereby agendas are formed is far less structured and, thereby, less amenable to unambiguous game-theoretic analysis. Thus, before we can achieve meaningful results about endogenous agenda processes, greater attention must be paid to the real-world processes that characterize their construction.

Despite these limitations, we have learned a great deal about agendas, including that they cannot lead anywhere if voters are sophisticated, that final outcomes are sensitive to information structure, and (perhaps most important) that even with sophisticated voters, agenda voting confers considerable power on those who design them or who otherwise control their construction. Thus, although many things must be measured and understood before we can predict outcomes, we have learned the factors that mediate the influence of procedures as well as how those factors combine. And, in addition, we have learned and can now formally document something that was self-evident to the Founders of the American republic – namely, that not only does the broad character of institutions matter, but so do procedural details, and that gaining control of those details is often the critical political event.

3   Game theory

The literature on two-candidate elections and agendas reveals not only the extent of game theory's impact; it reveals also the increasing sophistication with which political scientists make use of that theory. With the exceptions of spatial election models that relied on zero-sum games, Riker's (1962) development of the size principle, Kramer's (1972) analysis of issue-by-issue voting, and Klevorick and Kramer's (1973) study of pollution control in Germany, the application of game theory throughout the 1960s and most of the 1970s consisted mainly of simple stories about and adaptations of 2×2 games – if a political process did not correspond to a Prisoner's Dilemma, then it must have been a Game of Chicken or a Battle of the Sexes; if a coalitional process could not be analyzed using some descriptively meaningless "power index," then a simple majority game with transferable utility was assumed to apply. These analyses illustrated and illuminated the forces that are common to a wide range of political phenomena, but they are little more than examples to be appended to more serious empirical research.

The more sophisticated applications of game theory began in two areas. Unsurprisingly, one of these areas pertained to spatial games, while the other concerned the analysis of voting procedures. In the first area, McKelvey, Ordeshook, and Winer (1978) observed that, although much of the profession was transfixed by the generic instability of majority rule, it had been evident to von Neumann and Morgenstern (1945) that such instability characterized nearly all cooperative processes. But rather than conclude that generic instability implied "chaos," McKelvey et al. instead provided a solution hypothesis – the V-set – to deal with such matters. Unfortunately, the application of these ideas to spatial majority-rule games revealed their general inadequacy: they either made no predicton at all or they made predictions that were patently silly. Consequently, McKelvey, Ordeshook, and Winer developed the "competitive solution," and applied it to the study of parliamentary coalitions and to Congressional vote trading (McKelvey and Ordeshook 1980, Ordeshook and Winer 1980). At about the same time, Schofield (1980, 1982) developed various extensions of solution theory that also treated parliamentary coalitions. Neither the competitive solution nor Schofield's extensions have proven to be wholly satisfactory, and research in this area languished as people became concerned with the endogenous sources of cooperation and with the "Nash agenda" for studying cooperation. Nevertheless, research has continued, even though a wholly satisfactory cooperative solution hypothesis has not yet appeared (cf. Bennett and Zame 1988; Greenberg 1991; Sharkey 1990).

The second venue for the sophisticated application of game theory concerned agendas, and began with McKelvey and Niemi's (1978) and Moulin's (1979) demonstration of the correspondence between the analysis of sophisticated voting and subgame perfection, together with their subsidiary results about agenda outcomes. These essays, of course, are the immediate predecessors of the research reviewed in the previous section.

Today the applications of game theory to politics encompass nearly all areas and all forms of analysis. In addition to the applications to elections cited previously, the technology of incomplete information games has allowed us to extend and generalize Schelling's (1960) treatment of threats and deception and has thereby revolutionized the analysis of strategic deterrence in international affairs (cf. Bueno de Mesquita and Lalman 1991; Kilgore and Zagare 1990; O'Neill 1989a,b; Powell 1990). Similarly, recursive games have been applied to formulate hypotheses about the sources of seniority rule in Congress (McKelvey and Riezman 1991) and the nature of Congressional redistributive politics (Baron and Ferejohn 1989). The concept of evolutionary stable strategies (Maynard Smith 1982) is slowly creeping into our research, and promises to offer a better understanding of equilibrium selection and the evolution of institutions. And applying the repeated Prisoner's Dilemma to explain endogenously enforced cooperation has advanced from Taylor's (1976, 1987) and Axelrod's (1984) treatments to include the study of monitoring and decentralization (Bendor and Mookherjee 1987), reciprocity (Calvert 1989), and leadership (Bianco and Bates 1990). Indeed, political scientists have been nearly as quick as their colleagues in economics to realize that contemporary developments in game theory allow them to theorize about the fundamental question of institutions – namely, how those institutions emerge and are maintained in otherwise anarchic systems.

Game-theoretic reasoning has also escaped the boundaries set by the topics of war, elections, and committees. The application of the repeated Prisoner's Dilemma is no longer relegated to simple stories about the sources of cooperation, but is used instead to model, for example, the endogenous development of institutions to accommodate the provision of public goods and the management of common property resources (Ostrom 1990, Ostrom and Walker 1991). In at least one instance, games of incomplete information have been applied to study a specific policy matter: the consequences of alternative forms and levels of punishment on criminal behavior (Cox 1992). Thus, in addition to facilitating the analysis of existing institutions, we are now beginning to see game theory applied to their design.

Attention to the "Nash agenda" with respect to cooperation has also led to some initial success at addressing a classic problem of political theory, namely, the sources of cooperation and stability in anarchic international affairs. We have previously noted Morgenthau's (1948) general acceptance of the rationality postulate. But without the tools of contemporary theory, and game theory in particular, students of international politics had to contend with a confusing array of concepts and definitions – alliance, collective security, power, stability, and balance of power – and seemed unable to achieve the fundamental objective of international political theory: determining the sources of stability in anarchic systems and the viability of alternative prescriptions for foreign policy.

Admittedly, with the exception of recent research in deterrence and the applications of various 2×2 games, the development of international relations theory has lagged behind the study of elections and committees, and students of international relations continue to debate such basic matters as the goals that ought to be assigned to states, the role of domestic politics in international affairs, or whether states themselves should be treated as the primary decision makers in their theories. This lag is due, doubtless, to the structural character of various committees and election processes being well defined – or at least better defined than that of international politics. (Indeed, as we have already noted, when dealing with ill-defined committee processes such as endogenous agenda formation, our advances are no more striking than those we attribute to international relations theorists.) Wagner (1986), however, pointed the way toward the application of recursive games, and Niou and Ordeshook (1990, 1991a,b), building on Wagner's framework, have established that a balance of power (corresponding to an equilibrium of stationary strategies) and collective security (corresponding to an equilibrium of simple punishment strategies) can simultaneously exist in an otherwise anarchic system, and that alliances that correspond to limited collective security arrangements can survive as well.

More generally, game theory has contributed to a deeper appreciation of the imperative of strategic interaction in politics. Outside of the traditions of formal analysis, different types of political actors, as well as the institutions in which they operate, are frequently treated in isolation and without full regard for the strategic complexity of their environments. If other decision makers are relevant to the actions of those under investigation, then their motives are largely treated as exogenous to the analysis, and their actions are treated as contingent in some simple way on the actions of the class of decision makers under investigation. Thus, voters are studied in contexts in which the strategic responses of candidates and parties are ignored in favor of understanding the sociological and psychological determinants of attitudes and the influence of attitudes on party or candidate choice. Legislators, although assumed to be primarily interested in maximizing their chances of re-election, are assumed to act in an environment in which voters and interest groups either approve or disapprove of their actions or in which bureaucrats either shirk or respond to congressional initiatives. Similarly, in evaluating, say, a particular election reform, it is not uncommon to see past voting data "plugged into" an alternative procedure for tabulating votes in order to "see what would have happened had this procedure been in effect," despite the fact that the voting behavior, as well as the behavior of other relevant decision makers (e.g., candidates), might have been influenced by a change in procedures. In contrast, owing to its reliance on game theory, contemporary theory requires a full strategic view in which, given the institutional context of choice, candidates and voters choose best responses to each others' strategies, and in which the actions of constituents, legislators, and government bureaucrats are simultaneously viewed as maximizing their objectives under the assumption that all other actors are seeking to do the same thing.

4   Science, engineering, and mathematics

Game theory forms the core of contemporary political theory, and those who wish to remain on the frontiers of research must continually learn new concepts and results as they appear. However, it is also fair to say that within certain intellectual circles there is greater interest in displaying newly learned technology and mathematical skills than in understanding politics. Too often an analysis is judged by its mathematical sophistication rather than by its substantive significance, with the authors of essays seemingly more intent to mimic mathematicians than social scientists. Indeed, with more than a handful of essays appearing to be little more than formal extensions of previously published abstract and irrelevant research, it is reasonable to ask: Are the components of this research anything more than a forgettable series of essays that the demands of tractability render irrelevant to the real world?

The first fact that we should confront is that no one pursues a research agenda in which all potentially relevant strategic interaction is studied in the same model. Thus, there is no spatial elections model, for example, that accommodates the strategic decision of voters, candidates, party leaders, and campaign contributors, operating under complex but realistic elections rules, while simultaneously taking into account the fact that the election will be followed by a period of legislative–executive interaction, which will be followed by another election, and so on.

Consider the ostensible contributions of spatial election models, which include: demonstrating the profound difference between uni- and multidimensional election contests (Downs versus Plott and Davis and Hinich); demonstrating the possibility of placing bounds on the strategies that candidates adopt in multidimensional two-candidate contests (McKelvey 1986; McKelvey and Ordeshook 1976); establishing the possibility of complete information revelation in incomplete information elections (Ledyard 1989; McKelvey and Ordeshook 1985); developing statistical procedures for measuring spatial preferences and candidate locations, and for determining how voters map their concerns into a general policy space (Enelow and Hinich 1984); ascertaining the theoretical basis of Duverger's hypothesis (Cox 1987b; Fedderson et al. 1990; Palfrey 1989); showing how the spatial analysis of two-candidate elections can be extended to multicandidate contests and to the analysis of alternative voting institutions (Cox 1987a, 1990; Greenberg and Weber 1985); showing how probabilistic voting can "smooth" candidate responses and generate stability (Coughlin 1984; Hinich, Ledyard, and Ordeshook 1972); and showing that even if all of the other assumptions of the median voter theorem are satisfied, probabilistic voting can yield outcomes other than the median (Hinich 1977).

By themselves, however, these contributions do not constitute a complete model of any election, and this fact seems to diminish their usefulness. Consider, for example, the following practical matter: Under authoritarian control since 1949, Taiwan seeks to democratize. This commitment to reform occasions a series of design issues such as determining whether representatives should be elected in single- or multimember districts, and, if multimember, whether districts should be large or small, and whether a single nontransferable vote scheme should be implemented. A related issue concerns the selection of a presidential versus a parliamentary system. The specific concern here is ascertaining the consequences of alternative reforms for political stability, party factionalism, and relative Kuomintang influence, as well as determining the impact of these alternatives on the relative political power of native Taiwanese versus mainlanders.

This is not an unimportant matter, but merely being told of the centralizing tendency of two-candidate plurality-rule elections is unlikely to win many converts in Taiwan to a more theoretical perspective. We can say that multimember districts induce party factionalism (Cox 1990) – a fact already widely understood on the basis of Japan's experience – or that bicameralism facilitates stability (Hammond and Miller 1987), but there are only a few attempts at understanding the relationship between electoral and parliamentary processes (Austen-Smith and Banks 1988; Rosenthal 1970), and we have made almost no progress at all in determining the implications for minority rights of alternative electoral systems except in the most abstract way. Indeed, despite thirty years of modeling efforts, we know relatively little about multiparty electoral competition (cf. Cox 1990, and Shepsle 1990 for a review) and competition in those electoral systems that more generally characterize reality.

For another example, consider what is arguably the most exciting and extensive political institutional design opportunity of this century – the construction of democratic institutions for Eastern Europe and the successor states of the former Soviet empire. Each of these states requires constitutional structures that must contend with an enormous diversity of circumstances, encompassing such matters as ethnic conflict, hostile neighbors, bankrupt economies, and an almost complete lack of experience with democratic processes. The question, though, is whether formal theory has anything to say about such matters. Certainly, the theorist's contribution cannot be found in any theorem about some esoteric equilibria derived for some model of a nonexistent political process. It should, in fact, be a salutary lesson that few if any practitioners of contemporary political theory, including those who label themselves the new institutionalists, are centrally involved in any of the constitutional design efforts currently underway. And our discomfort should be increased by the additional fact that the issues under consideration are precisely those that have been or ought to have been the subject of the formal theorist's inquiries – federalism, election procedures, the choice of presidential versus parliamentary systems, the sources of political stability, and the nature of self-enforcing constitutional provisions.

This critique of contemporary theory can engender at least two responses. First, we can continue on the path of incrementally exploring alternative models that are driven largely by the availability of new analytic technologies and the demands of mathematical tractability – arguing with our more substantively oriented colleagues that theory construction proceeds incrementally and requires patience. Doubtless, in a hundred years or so we might have something more specific to report to the residents of Taiwan, Russia, Ukraine, Bulgaria, and so on. However, there is a reasonably good chance that we will at that time have merely replicated our current inability to "derive" effective economic reform policies using any part of the hundreds of essays appearing in *Econometrica* or *Jet,* despite their mathematical sophistication.

Alternatively, we might respond by trying to construct wholly integrated models that add as many features of reality as possible, including simultaneous assessments of elections, legislatures, and regional governments along with a consideration of the macroeconomic forces that impinge on the performance of political institutions. The difficulty here, however, is that such models are unlikely to yield the sort of punchy analytic results that guarantee success in the ultimate objective of lengthening our vitae. And should such results be sought, the necessity for maintaining rigor and tractability would require compromises of Herculean proportions.

There is, however, a third response, which requires that we distinguish between the *scientific* enterprise of uncovering fundamental principles of political action that operate universally and the *engineering* enterprise of using those principles, in combination with common sense and experience, to model and to think about actual or proposed political–economic institutions and processes.

To appreciate this distinction, we note that spatial analysis, coupled with the logical structure of game theory, constitutes the beginnings of a mathematically rigorous and parsimonious theory of political–economic processes. Within its domain we find new first principles of politics and restatements of old ones. For the Founders of the American republic, such principles took the form of ideas about the permanence of factions, the necessity for a tripartite balance of forces, the inhibiting influence of a bicameral legislature, and the fact that institutions can regulate but cannot eliminate the forces of self-interest. To these ideas contemporary political theory adds the median voter theorem, Gibbard (1973) and Satterthwaite's (1975) manipulability result, McKelvey and Schofield's (1987) research into the necessary and sufficient conditions for the existence of cores, Miller's (1980) development of the uncovered set, Plott (1967) and Davis and Hinich's (1967) proof of the relevance of issue dimensionality, Kramer's (1973) analysis of issue-by-issue voting, and McKelvey and Ordeshook's (1985) demonstration of the possibility of rational expectations in elections.

It is a mistake to suppose, however, that we can derive a model of some ongoing political process directly from these results, any more than we can deduce the characteristics of specific markets from the contemporary theory of competitive economies and the representation of that theory in, say, Debreu's *Theory of Value*. Instead, it is better to conceptualize contemporary theory in terms of a "hard" core of first principles and a "soft" outer layer of applications and operational definitions of theoretical constructs. The core, which we want to be general and thus mathematically elegant, is the knowledge to which we appeal when we check the logical consistency of arguments and when we judge whether we have considered all potentially relevant factors.

The core itself will consist of primitive constructs and purely abstract relations that we are temporarily unwilling to subject to direct empirical refutation – such as the assumption that preferences are transitive, that people are Bayesians, that utility functions are continuous, or that notions of noncooperative equilibria are our primary predictive tools. This core, however, will assume substantive significance only through derivative ideas such as the previously mentioned first principles – principles that are in theory, but not necessarily in any practical way, testable.

It is these derivative ideas that we use to guide our more specific empirical research. For example, then, in modeling any election process, we can appeal to our theoretical core to assert that issue dimensionality is a potentially relevant parameter; in turn, we can appeal to ideas such as the uncovered set to illustrate that it is unnecessary to presuppose that a simple equilibrium prevails before useful predictions can be uttered. We also know that we should be cognizant of the possibility that voters and candidates will gather information about relevant parameters in indirect ways. In evaluating any existing or proposed electoral system, we should take careful measurements of preferences and perceptions, with the understanding that the general character of competition will be molded by the underlying structure of preferences and the ways in which voters combine substantive issues in order to produce a coherent spatial map for themselves. And in assessing any electoral reform, we have learned not only to consider the possibility that new parties will form, but also to anticipate the responses of pre-existing parties.

Similarly, with respect to the general problem of constitutional design, contemporary game theory tells us that although cooperation can emerge in anarchic systems, the multiplicity of equilibria in essentially every ongoing social process creates a serious coordination problem. Although the myriad of essays on equilibrium selection, folk theorems, and the like are unlikely to evolve into a "theory of constitutions," the general principles such essays establish about equilibria and about the outcomes that can be sustained as equilibria do tell us something general about a constitution's role as a social coordinating mechanism, about how constitutions are self-enforcing, and about how we can best design a stable constitution (Ordeshook 1992). With this perspective in hand, we can then begin to examine the component parts of a constitution – its specification of rights, of the jurisdiction afforded to different branches of government, of the interplay between electoral institutions and the institutions of federalism – with models of specific possibilities.

Thus, in fitting the theoretical pieces together in order to model a particular situation, we cannot anticipate models that will generate readily interpretable analytic results. Indeed, we may be able to determine outcomes and various analytic relationships only through the application of such techniques as laboratory experimentation and computer simulation (cf. Downs and Rocke 1990). At times, of course, we may get lucky and be presented with a design problem that lends itself to wholly abstract analysis. Klevorick and Kramer's (1973) path-breaking analysis of pollution control in Germany illustrates such an effort – an effort that, unfortunately, has had few imitators. However, just as neither the scientist nor the engineer attempts to derive theorems about bridge design or to establish equations in closed analytic form about the point at which fluid moving through a pipe changes from laminar to turbulent flow, we should not anticipate theorems here. Instead, this research, which will make heavy use of experience and common sense, will form the soft outer layer of our understanding of politics. Put simply, application of first principles will be as much an art as it is a science, with perhaps the greater emphasis placed on art.

Of course, if our theoretical core is poorly developed, the components of the outer layer can move far apart, with the result that discussion of substantive matters will become dictated more by ideology and prejudice than by anything else. On the other hand, by being forced to appeal to the first principles and to relate our empirical concepts to those that form the language of the core, research into specific substantive matters expands that core and maintains a connection with other seemingly unrelated substantive studies. In this way, Fiorina and Mayhew's analysis of Congress, Olson's arguments about interest groups, Popkin's study of rural peasants, and Horowitz's (1991) analysis of South Africa – none of which contain any exciting mathematical formulation – are profoundly important because of the way they expand the core's reach.

We see from this description of contemporary political theory, then, that political analysis consists of two enterprises. The first concerns the discovery of basic laws and forces. It is this part that identifies general empirical phenomena that warrant explanation, that formalizes and generalizes ideas previously understood only imperfectly, and that explores the logical relationships of theoretical constructs. The second enterprise, political engineering, tries via a variety of formal and informal means to apply components of our theory to an understanding of specific processes and phenomena. (Notice that our use of the word "engineering" includes, but is not limited to, the design of political institutions. Thus, engineering also includes the explanation of historical data as well as of ongoing political processes.) This second part, then, in addition to mathematical argument, relies on a variety of tools, including experience and common sense, and part of its art consists of understanding those phenomena that are guided by first principles alone versus those that must be approached with a more complex interplay of theory and data.

One final point warrants emphasis. Specifically, our characterization of contemporary theory does not justify deriving with skill that next cute theorem in the context of an otherwise silly model. Those who prefer to play with theorems in a purely abstract environment can, of course, argue that it is legitimate to explore the logical relationships of the inner core of a theory without the necessity of establishing empirical relevance. Indeed, postulating Bayesian beliefs or abstract forms of utility functions that cannot be measured does not invalidate the potential import of an analysis if general propositions can be derived from the exercise. However, the theorist should better appreciate the interplay between theory and data. Physicists may postulate unobservable or unmeasurable entities, but they do so in order to explain empirical phenomena. The political theorist should be subject to the same restriction.

5   Empirical research

Too frequently the path to critiquing contemporary political theory is opened by the failure of its advocates to understand the distinctions between science and engineering and between the characteristics of the inner core of theory and its softer, applied component. Owing perhaps to the felt necessity for immediate empirical relevance, it is not uncommon to see a purely abstract analysis dressed up as an absurd caricature of some political process ("assume that voters confront an infinite stream of alternative candidates drawn from the distribution"; "suppose that public goods provision corresponds to an infinite sequence of two-person Prisoner's Dilemmas"; "we model legislative–bureaucratic interaction as a game among one decision maker and two agents"; "suppose that all players in our legislature share common priors on . . . given by the Beta distribution with parameters . . ."; etc.). If the theorist wishes to thus portray an analysis as a model, then that person had better be prepared for immediate rejection on the basis of "reality checks."

With this in mind, we should turn next to an evaluation of empirical applications. It is certainly true that although theoretical advances (both useful and otherwise) continue to be made at a fast pace, direct empirical applications of theory proceed with considerably greater difficulty. There are far too few parallels, for example, to Sawyer and MacRae's (1962) analysis of cumulative voting in Illinois; Romer and Rosenthal's (1979) study of Oregon referenda; Rosenthal and Sen's (1973, 1977) empirical testing of alternative hypotheses about nonvoting; Poole and Rosenthal's (1985, 1991) historical study of issue cleavages in the U.S. Congress; Enelow and Hinich's (1984) estimation of the correspondence between actionable issues and generalized policy spaces; McCubbins and Kiewiet's (1988) analysis of presidential vetoes; Cain's (1978) analysis of strategic voting in Britain; Cox's (1987c) study of political party development in England; Roberts's (1990) validation of the rational-expectations hypothesis in politics (see also Forsythe et al. 1991); Plott and Levine's (1978), Enelow's (1981), and Enelow and Koehler's (1980) examples of agenda manipulation; and Riker's (1983, 1984, 1988) applications of social choice theory to macrohistorical data.

Each of these studies gives us confidence that the theorist's preoccupation is more than a pleasant hobby. However, the actual contribution of the majority of empirical research to theory is difficult to evaluate, because it is often difficult to determine its purpose. We are amused, for example, by those essays that ostensibly test even today the hypothesis that voters are rational. Is it possible that practitioners in the field are prepared to accept the hypothesis that the rationality paradigm is bunkum? Or consider those analyses that "test" models that are grossly false a priori. Of what value is it, for example, to explain patterns of nuclear deterrence with a model that assumes that one country but not the other can make the first threat, or to explore some time series of macro political–economic data with a model that assumes that party policy positions are set in concrete over decades or that candidates care only about public policy but not about whether they win or lose elections?

Even if such models fit the data up to an acceptable level of statistical accuracy, we must contend with the fact that we can establish nearly any reasonable outcome as an equilibrium to some model, provided only that that model is sufficiently complex. One might attempt to defend such research with appeals to the *as if* principle – after all, there is only an imperfectly defined barrier between acceptable and unacceptable applications of this principle. However, the necessity for abstraction is not an excuse for employing patently absurd assumptions in a model designed explicitly for empirical analysis. Designing assumptions so that a model's predictions fit the data is, in fact, little more than an exercise in curve fitting, albeit of a slightly more complicated sort than the type we generally hold in disrepute.

Despite this critique, there are some trends in the empirical application of contemporary political theory that hold considerable promise – most notably, but not exclusively, experimental research. First, we should understand that empirical research that is intended to develop political theory ought to have one of four objectives: (1) identifiying or otherwise demonstrating the existence of empirical generalities that require explanation; (2) demonstrating the universality of some first principle by way of empirical (historical or experimental) example; (3) estimating a model's parameter values; and (4) testing the design of political mechanisms.

Nearly all empirical research matches one of these categories, but examples of research that correspond cleanly to categories (1) and (2) can be found in a growing experimental literature. For example, Berl et al.'s (1976) and Fiorina and Plott's (1978) studies of the core establish this idea as more than a mere mathematical invention – it is a solution hypothesis that is at least as robust to a variety of socio-psychological variables as any other available idea. Augmenting the Congressional studies cited earlier, experimental work by McKelvey and Ordeshook (1984), Wilson (1986), Salant and Goodstein (1987), Herzberg and Wilson (1991), and Rapoport, Felsenthal, and Maoz (1991) gives us confidence that theoretical research into the effects of institutions and procedures is not without substantive foundation. McKelvey and Ordeshook's (1985) incomplete-information election experiments draw attention to broader definitions of equilibrium and to the notion of rational expectations. And Miller and Oppenheimer's (1982) and Eavey and Miller's (1984) research on fairness serves as a warning about the existence of motivating factors other than a myopic concern with the maximization of wealth, and suggests that people consider fairness in systematic ways.

Of course, political scientists will quibble over whether their empirical research matches one particular category and whether experimental or field data are best suited for a particular purpose. This is due in part to the fact that the notion of a first principle is itself not rigorously defined. Such a principle can refer to some "micro" idea about, say, how people process information or the validity of a specific equilibrium notion, or it can refer to a more "macro" idea, such as the median voter theorem or an hypothesis about the sources of governmental growth and inefficiency. However, regardless of how we interpret "first principle," little research matches the third or fourth categories, which are those corresponding most closely to "engineering" as that word is most commonly understood. As a consequence, contemporary theory has not yet achieved its potential.

6   Conclusion

We began this essay by observing that those preeminent political engineers, the Founders of the American republic, anticipated at least some of the ideas that lie at the core of contemporary political theory. More-over, we would argue that they achieved their success by understanding the arguments about science versus engineering and the role of empirical research that the previous sections offer. First, they proceeded in much the same way as theorists operate today, in that they

relied mainly on deducing descriptive and prescriptive truths . . . from First Principles. . . . Historical and contemporary experience were considered not the sole source of truth but merely a quarry from which illustrations could be mined to clarify and lend persuasive force to the truths revealed by Right Reason from First Principles. (Ranney 1976, p. 144)

But the Founders were also experimentalists in that they understood that neither historical experience nor deductive logic could definitely answer all questions (cf. the debate between Schwartz 1989 and Cain and Jones 1989). Of course, they lacked the tools of laboratory experimentation or econometrics, but they struck an imaginative alternative approach – designing a political system that would be an experiment capable of self-correction as seemed warranted by the data. Even though they understood fully the importance of institutions, they designed a constitution that was itself open-ended and capable of revision in light of experience. And rather than proscribe specific procedures for the branch of government – the legislative – they regarded as most important, they allowed that branch to choose its own rules of organization and voting.

Today, of course, far too little use is made of historical data as a source of new ideas and as a test of existing ones. Nevertheless, one of the most encouraging features of contemporary political theory is that it appears to be accommodating itself slowly to an engineering–experimental agenda. Ostrom and Walker's (1991) research on common pool resource issues, Isaac and Walker's (1988) study of public goods provision and group size, Boylan et al.'s (1991) analysis of the influence of electoral mechanisms on government investment, and Plott's (1991) analysis of the influence of polls on election results all illustrate research that moves us closer to understanding the behavior of complex systems. Far more studies of this sort, however, are required before we can assert that the practical value of contemporary political theory has equaled or surpassed the level achieved in 1787.

REFERENCES

Arrow, Kenneth J. (1951), *Social Choice and Individual Values.* New York: Wiley.
Austen-Smith, David (1987), "Sophisticated Sincerity: Voting over Endogenous Agendas," *American Political Science Review* 81: 1323-9.
Austen-Smith, David, and Jeffrey S. Banks (1988), "Elections, Coalitions, and Legislative Outcomes," *American Political Science Review* 82: 405-22.
Axelrod, Robert (1984), *The Evolution of Cooperation.* New York: Basic Books.
Banks, Jeffrey S. (1989), "Equilibrium Outcomes in Two Stage Amendment Procedures," *American Journal of Political Science* 33: 25-43.
Banks, Jeffrey S., and Farid Gasmi (1987), "Endogenous Agenda Formation in Three-Person Committees," *Social Choice and Welfare* 4: 133-52.
Baron, David P., and John Ferejohn (1989), "Bargaining in Legislatures," *American Political Science Review* 83: 1181-1206.
Bartholdi, John J., Craig A. Tovey, and Michael A. Trick (1989), "The Computational Difficulty of Controlling an Election," *Social Choice and Welfare* 6: 227-41.
Bendor, Jonathan, and Dilip Mookherjee (1987), "Institutional Structure and the Logic of Ongoing Collective Action," *American Political Science Review,* 81: 129-54.
Bennett, Elaine, and W. E. Zame (1988), "Bargaining in Cooperative Games," *International Journal of Game Theory* 17: 279-300.
Bentley, Arthur F. (1935), *The Process of Government.* Evanston, IL: Principia Press.
Berl, Janet, Richard D. McKelvey, Peter C. Ordeshook, and Mark Winer (1976), "An Experimental Test of the Core in a Simple *N*-Person Cooperative Non-sidepayment Game," *Journal of Conflict Resolution,* 30: 453-79.

Bianco, William T., and Robert H. Bates (1990), "Cooperation by Design: Leadership, Structure, and Collective Dilemmas," *American Political Science Review*, 84: 133–47.

Black, Duncan (1958), *The Theory of Committees and Elections*. Cambridge: Cambridge University Press.

Black, Duncan, and R. A. Newing (1951), *Committee Decisions and Complementary Valuation*. London: Hodge.

Boylan, Richard, John O. Ledyard, Arthur Lupia, Richard D. McKelvey, and P. C. Ordeshook (1991), "Political Competition and a Model of Economic Growth: Some Experimental Results," in T. Palfrey (ed.), *Contemporary Laboratory Research in Political Economy*. Ann Arbor: University of Michigan Press.

Brams, Steven J., and Philip D. Straffin (1982), "The Entry Problem in a Political Race," in P. C. Ordeshook and K. A. Shepsle (eds.), *Political Equilibrium*. Boston: Kluwer-Nijhoff.

Buchanan, James M., and Gordon Tullock (1962), *The Calculus of Consent*. Ann Arbor: University of Michigan Press.

Bueno de Mesquita, Bruce, and David Lalman (1991), *War and Reason*. New Haven, CT: Yale University Press.

Cain, Bruce E. (1978), "Strategic Voting in Britain," *American Journal of Political Science*, 22: 639–55.

Cain, Bruce E., and W. T. Jones (1989), "Madison's Theory of Representation," in B. Grofman and D. Wittman (eds.), *The Federalist Papers and the New Institutionalism*. New York: Agathon.

Calvert, Randall L. (1989), "Reciprocity among Self-Interested Actors: Uncertainty, Asymmetry, and Distribution," in P. C. Ordeshook (ed.), *Models of Strategic Choice in Politics*. Ann Arbor: University of Michigan Press.

Clarke, E. H. (1971), "Multipart Pricing of Public Goods," *Public Choice* 11: 17–33.

Coleman, Jules, and John Ferejohn (1986), "Democracy and Social Choice," *Ethics* 97: 6–25.

Coughlin, Peter (1984), "Probabilistic Voting Models," in S. Kotz, N. Johnson, and C. Read (eds.), *Encyclopedia of the Statistical Sciences*, v. 6. New York: Wiley.

Coughlin, Peter, and Melvin J. Hinich (1984), "Necessary and Sufficient Conditions for Single-Peakedness in Public Economic Models," *Journal of Public Economics* 25: 323–41.

Cox, Gary W. (1987a), "Electoral Equilibrium under Alternative Voting Institutions," *American Journal of Political Science* 31: 82–108.

(1987b), "Duverger's Law and Strategic Voting," Mimeo, Department of Political Science, University of California at San Diego.

(1987c), *The Efficient Secret*. New York: Cambridge University Press.

(1990), "Multicandidate Spatial Competition," in J. Enelow and M. J. Hinich (eds.), *Advances in the Spatial Theory of Voting*. New York: Cambridge University Press.

(1992), "A Note on Crime and Punishment," *Public Choice* (forthcoming).

Davis, Otto A., and Melvin J. Hinich (1967), "A Mathematical Model of Policy Formation in a Democratic Society," in J. L. Bernd (ed.), *Math Applications in Political Science*, v. 2. Dallas: Southern Methodist University Press.

Denzau, Arthur, and Robert J. Mackay (1981), "Structure Induced Equilibrium and Perfect Foresight Expectations," *American Journal of Political Science* 25: 762-79.

(1983), "Gatekeeping and Monopoly Power in Committees: An Analysis of Sincere and Sophisticated Behavior," *American Journal of Political Science* 27: 740-61.

Downs, Anthony (1957), *An Economic Theory of Democracy*. New York: Harper.

Downs, George W., and David M. Rocke (1990), *Tacit Bargaining, Arms Races, and Arms Control*. Ann Arbor: University of Michigan Press.

Duverger, Maurice (1954), *Political Parties*. New York: Wiley.

Eavey, Cheryl, and Gary Miller (1984), "Experimental Evidence on the Fallibility of the Core," *American Journal of Political Science* 28: 570-86.

Enelow, James (1981), "Saving Amendments, Killer Amendments, and an Expected Utility Theory of Sophisticated Voting," *Journal of Politics* 43: 1062-89.

Enelow, James, and Melvin J. Hinich (1983), "Voting One Issue at a Time: The Question of Voter Forecasts," *American Political Science Review* 77: 435-45.

(1984), *The Spatial Theory of Voting*. New York: Cambridge University Press.

Enelow, James, and David H. Koehler (1980), "The Amendment in Legislative Strategy: Sophisticated Voting in the U.S. Congress," *Journal of Politics* 42: 396-413.

Epple, Dennis, and Joseph B. Kadane (1990), "Sequential Voting with Endogenous Voter Forecasts," *American Political Science Review* 84: 165-75.

Farquharson, Robin (1969), *Theory of Voting*. New Haven, CT: Yale University Press.

Fedderson, Timothy J., Itai Sened, and Stephen G. Wright (1990), "Rational Voting and Candidate Entry under Plurality Rule," *American Journal of Political Science,* 34: 1005-16.

Ferejohn, John, Richard D. McKelvey, and Edward Packel (1984), "Limiting Distributions for Continuous State Markov Voting Models," *Social Choice and Welfare* 1: 45-68.

Fiorina, Morris P. (1977), *Congress: Keystone of the Washington Establishment*. New Haven, CT: Yale University Press.

Fiorina, Morris P., and Charles R. Plott (1978), "Committee Decisions Under Majority Rule," *American Political Science Review* 72: 575-98.

Forsythe, Robert, Forrest Nelson, George Neumann, and Jack Wright (1991), "The Explanation and Prediction of Presidential Elections: A Market Alternative to Polls," in T. Palfrey (ed.), *Contemporary Laboratory Research in Political Economy*. Ann Arbor: University of Michigan Press.

Gibbard, Allen (1973), "Manipulation of Voting Schemes: A General Result," *Econometrica* 41: 587-601.

Greenberg, Joseph (1991), *The Theory of Social Situations*. Cambridge: Cambridge University Press.

Greenberg, Joseph, and Shlomo Weber (1985), "Multiparty Equilibria Under Proportional Representation," *American Political Science Review* 81: 525-38.

Groves, Theodore, and John O. Ledyard (1977), "Optimal Allocation of Public Goods: A Solution to the 'Free Rider' Problem," *Econometrica* 45: 783-809.

Hammond, Thomas H., and Gary J. Miller (1987), "The Core of the Constitution," *American Political Science Review* 81: 1155-74.

   (1989), "Stability and Efficiency in a Separation of Powers Constitutional System," in B. Grofman and D. Wittman (eds.), *The Federalist Papers and the New Institutionalism.* New York: Agathon.

Herzberg, Roberta, and Rick Wilson (1991), "Costly Agendas and Spatial Voting Games: Theory and Experiments on Agenda Access Costs," in T. Palfrey (ed.), *Contemporary Laboratory Research in Political Economy.* Ann Arbor: University of Michigan Press.

Hinich, Melvin J. (1977), "Equilibrium in Spatial Voting: The Median Voter Result is an Artifact," *Journal of Economic Theory* 16: 208-19.

Hinich, Melvin J., John O. Ledyard, and Peter C. Ordeshook (1972), "Nonvoting and the Existence of Equilibrium under Majority Rule," *Journal of Economic Theory* 4: 144-53.

Hoag, C. G., and G. H. Hallet (1926), *Proportional Representation.* New York: Macmillan.

Horowitz, Donald (1991), *A Democratic South Africa?* Berkeley: University of California Press.

Isaac, Mark, and James Walker (1988), "Group Size Effects in Public Goods Provision: The Voluntary Contributions Mechanism," *Quarterly Journal of Economics* 102: 179-200.

Jung, Joon Pyo (1989), "Condorcet Consistent Binary Agendas Under Incomplete Information," in P. C. Ordeshook (ed.), *Models of Strategic Choice in Politics.* Ann Arbor: University of Michigan Press.

Key, V. O. (1966), *The Responsible Electorate.* New York: Vintage.

Kilgore, D. Marc, and Frank C. Zagare (1990), "Uncertainty and Deterrence," *American Journal of Political Science* 35: 305-34.

Klevorick, Alvin K., and Gerald H. Kramer (1973), "Social Choice on Pollution Management," Cowles Foundation Paper no. 387, Yale University, New Haven, CT.

Kramer, Gerald H. (1972), "Sophisticated Voting Over Multidimensional Choice Spaces," *Journal of Mathematical Sociology* 2: 165-80.

Ledyard, John (1989), "Information Aggregation in Two-Candidate Elections," in P. C. Ordeshook (ed.), *Model of Strategic Choice in Politics.* Ann Arbor: University of Michigan Press.

Levine, Michael E., and Charles Plott (1977), "Agenda Influence and Its Implications," *Virginia Law Review* 63: 561-604.

Luce, R. Duncan, and Howard Raiffa (1957), *Games and Decisions.* New York: Wiley.

Madison, James (1989), *Journal of the Federal Convention,* ed. by E. H. Scott. Chicago: Scott, Foresman (originally published in 1898).

Maskin, E. (1977), "Nash Equilibrium and Welfare Optimality," unpublished manuscript.

Mayhew, David (1974), *Congress: The Electoral Connection.* New Haven, CT: Yale University Press.

Maynard Smith, John (1982), *Evolution and the Theory of Games.* Cambridge: Cambridge University Press.

McCubbins, Matthew D., and Roderick Kiewiet (1988), "Presidential Influence on Congressional Appropriations Decisions," *American Journal of Political Science* 32: 713-36.

McKelvey, Richard D. (1976), "Intransitivities in Multidimensional Voting Models and Some Implications for Agenda Control," *Journal of Economic Theory* 12: 472–82.

(1979), "General Conditions for Intransitivities in Formal Voting Models," *Econometrica* 47: 1085–1111.

(1986), "Covering, Dominance, and the Institution Free Properties of Social Choice," *American Journal of Political Science* 30: 283–314.

McKelvey, Richard D., and Richard Niemi (1978), "A Multistage Representation of Sophisticated Voting for Binary Procedures," *Journal of Economic Theory* 18: 1–22.

McKelvey, Richard D., and Peter C. Ordeshook (1976), "Symmetric Spatial Games without Majority Rule Equilibria," *American Political Science Review* 70: 1172–84.

(1980), "Vote Trading: An Experimental Study," *Public Choice* 35: 151–84.

(1984), "An Experimental Study of the Effects of Procedural Rules on Committee Behavior," *Journal of Politics* 46: 182–205.

(1985), "Elections with Limited Information: A Fulfilled Expectations Model Using Contemporaneous Poll and Endorsement Data as Information Sources," *Journal of Economic Theory* 36: 55–85.

McKelvey, Richard D., Peter C. Ordeshook, and Mark Winer (1978), "The Competitive Solution for *n*-Person Games without Transferable Utility," *American Political Science Review* 72: 599–615.

McKelvey, Richard D., and Raymond Riezman (1991), "Seniority in Legislatures," Mimeo, Division of Humanities and Social Sciences, California Institute of Technology, Pasadena.

McKelvey, Richard D., and Norman Schofield (1987), "Generalized Symmetry Conditions at a Core Point," *Econometrica* 55: 923–33.

Meltzer, Allan H., and Scott F. Richard (1981), "A Rational Theory of the Size of Government," *Journal of Political Economy* 89: 914–27.

Miller, Gary, and Joe A. Oppenheimer (1982), "Universalism in Experimental Committees," *American Political Science Review* 76: 561–74.

Miller, Nicholas R. (1980), "A New Solution Set for Tournaments and Majority Voting," *American Journal of Political Science* 24: 68–96.

Monroe, Kristen R. (1990), *The Economic Approach to Politics*. New York: Harper-Collins.

Morgenthau, Hans (1948), *Politics Among Nations*. New York: Knopf.

Moulin, Hervé (1979), "Dominance Solvable Voting Schemes," *Econometrica* 47: 1337–51.

Niou, Emerson M. S., and Peter C. Ordeshook (1990), "Stability in Anarchic Systems," *American Political Science Review* 84: 1208–34.

(1991a), "Realism versus Neoliberalism: A Formulation," *American Journal of Political Science* 35: 481–511.

(1991b), "Alliances in Anarchic International Systems," Mimeo, Division of Humanities and Social Sciences, California Institute of Technology, Pasadena.

Niskanen, William (1971), *Bureaucracy and Representative Government*. Chicago: Aldine.

Olson, Mancur (1965), *The Logic of Collective Action*. Cambridge, MA: Harvard University Press.

O'Neill, Barry (1989a), "International Escalation and the Dollar Auction," *Journal of Conflict Resolution* 30: 33–50.

(1989b), "Game Theory and the Study of Deterrence and War," in P. C. Stern et al. (eds.), *Perspectives on Deterrence and War.* New York: Oxford University Press.

Ordeshook, Peter C. (1986), *Game Theory and Political Theory.* New York: Cambridge University Press.

(1992), "Constitutional Stability," *Constitutional Political Economy* 3: 137-76.

Ordeshook, Peter C., and Thomas Palfrey (1988), "Agendas, Strategic Voting, and Signalling with Incomplete Information," *American Journal of Political Science* 32: 441-66.

Ordeshook, Peter C., and Thomas Schwartz (1987), "Agendas and the Control of Political Outcomes," *American Political Science Review* 81: 180-99.

Ordeshook, Peter C., and Mark Winer (1980), "Coalitions and Spatial Policy Outcomes in Parliamentary Systems: Some Experimental Results," *American Journal of Political Science* 24: 730-52.

Ostrom, Elinor (1990), *Governing the Commons.* New York: Cambridge University Press.

Ostrom, Elinor, and James Walker (1991), "Communication in a Commons: Cooperation without External Enforcement," in T. Palfrey (ed.), *Contemporary Laboratory Research in Political Economy.* Ann Arbor: University of Michigan Press.

Palfrey, Thomas R. (1984), "Spatial Equilibrium with Entry," *Review of Economic Studies* 51: 139-56.

(1989), "A Mathematical Proof of Duverger's Law," in P. C. Ordeshook (ed.), *Models of Strategic Choice in Politics.* Ann Arbor: University of Michigan Press.

Plott, Charles R. (1967), "A Notion of Equilibrium and its Possibility Under Majority Rule," *American Economic Review* 57: 787-806.

(1991), "A Comparative Analysis of Direct Democracy, Two-Candidate Elections, and Three-Candidate Elections in an Experimental Environment," in T. Palfrey (ed.), *Contemporary Laboratory Research in Political Economy.* Ann Arbor: University of Michigan Press.

Plott, Charles R., and Michael E. Levine (1978), "A Model of Agenda Influence on Committee Decisions," *American Economic Review* 68: 146-60.

Poole, Keith T., and Howard Rosenthal (1985), "A Spatial Model for Legislative Roll Call Analysis," *American Journal of Political Science* 29: 357-84.

(1991), "Patterns of Congressional Voting," *American Journal of Political Science* 35: 228-78.

Popkin, Samuel (1979), *The Rational Peasant.* Berkeley: University of California Press.

Powell, Robert (1990), *Nuclear Deterrence Theory: The Search for Credibility.* New York: Cambridge University Press.

Ranney, Austin (1976), "The Divine Science: Political Engineering in American Culture," *American Political Science Review* 70: 140-8.

Rapoport, Amnon, Dan Felsenthal, and Zeev Maoz (1991), "Sincere vs. Strategic Behavior in Small Groups," in T. Palfrey (ed.), *Contemporary Laboratory Research in Political Economy.* Ann Arbor: University of Michigan Press.

Riker, William H. (1962), *The Theory of Political Coalitions.* New Haven, CT: Yale University Press.

(1980), "Implications from the Disequilibrium of Majority Rule for the Study of Institutions," *American Political Science Review* 74: 432-46.

(1983), *Liberalism Against Populism.* San Francisco: Freeman.

(1984), "The Heresthetics of Constitution-Making: The Presidency in 1787, with Comments on Determinism and Rational Choice," *American Political Science Review* 78: 1-16.

(1988), *The Art of Political Manipulation.* New Haven, CT: Yale University Press.

Roberts, Brian E. (1990), "Political Institutions, Policy Expectations, and the 1980 Election: A Financial Market Perspective," *American Journal of Political Science* 34: 289-310.

Romer, Thomas, and Howard Rosenthal (1979), "Bureaucrats vs. Voters: On the Political Economy of Resource Allocation in a Direct Democracy," *Quarterly Journal of Economics* 93: 563-87.

Rosenthal, Howard (1970), "The Size of Coalitions and Electoral Outcomes in the French Fourth Republic," in S. Groennings et al. (eds.), *The Study of Political Coalitions.* New York: Holt, Rinehart & Winston.

Rosenthal, Howard, and Subrata Sen (1973), "Electoral Participation in the French Fifth Republic," *American Political Science Review* 67: 29-54.

(1977), "Spatial Voting Models for the French Fifth Republic," *American Political Science Review* 71: 1447-66.

Salant, Steven, and Eban Goodstein (1987), "Committee Voting Under Alternative Procedures and Preferences: An Experimental Analysis," Mimeo, Department of Economics, University of Michigan, Ann Arbor.

Satterthwaite, Mark (1975), "Strategy-Proofness and Arrow's Conditions: Existence and Correspondence Theorems for Voting Procedures and Social Welfare Functions," *Journal of Economic Theory* 10: 187-217.

Sawyer, Jack, and Duncan MacRae (1962), "Game Theory and Cumulative Voting in Illinois 1902-1954," *American Political Science Review* 56: 936-46.

Schelling, Thomas C. (1960), *Strategy and Conflict.* New York: Oxford University Press.

Schofield, Norman (1980), "The Bargaining Set in Voting Games," *Behavioral Science* 25: 120-9.

(1982), "Bargaining Set Theory and Stability in Coalition Governments," *Mathematical Social Sciences* 3: 9-31.

Schwartz, Thomas (1977), "Collective Choice, Separation of Issues, and Vote Trading," *American Political Science Review* 71: 999-1010.

(1989), "Publius and Public Choice," in B. Grofman and D. Wittman (eds.), *The Federalist Papers and the New Institutionalism.* New York: Agathon.

Sharkey, W. W. (1990), "A Model of Competition Among Political Interest Groups," Mimeo, Bellcore, Morristown, NJ.

Shepsle, Kenneth (1979), "Institutional Arrangements and Equilibrium in Multidimensional Voting Models," *American Journal of Political Science* 23: 27-59.

(1990), *Models of Multiparty Competition.* London: Harwood.

Shepsle, Kenneth, and Barry Weingast (1981), "Structure Induced Equilibrium and Legislative Choice," *Public Choice* 37: 503-19.

(1984a), "Uncovered Sets and Sophisticated Voting Outcomes with Implications for Agenda Institutions," *American Journal of Political Science* 28: 49-74.

(1984b), "When Do Rules of Procedure Matter," *Journal of Politics* 46: 182-205.

Sloss, Judith (1971), "Stable Outcomes in Majority Voting Games," *Public Choice* 15: 19-48.

Taylor, Michael (1976), *Anarchy and Cooperation*. New York: Wiley.

—— (1987), *The Possibility of Cooperation*. Cambridge: Cambridge University Press.

von Neumann, John, and Oskar Morgenstern (1945), *The Theory of Games and Economic Behavior*. Princeton: Princeton University Press.

Wagner, R. Harrison (1986), "The Theory of Games and the Balance of Power," *World Politics* 8: 546-76.

Wilson, Rick (1986), "Foreword and Backward Agenda Procedures: Committee Experiments on Structurally Induced Equilibrium," *Journal of Politics* 48: 390-409.

PART II

Representation and voting

Proportional representation, approval voting, and coalitionally straightforward elections

Roger B. Myerson

1   Introduction

The ability of organizations to exploit the broader public is limited by potential competition from other similar organizations. For these purposes, however, the absolute number of such competing organizations that exist at any time is not necessarily the definitive structural parameter, because the leaders of a small number of organizations could reach a collusive agreement to jointly exploit the public and then divide the profits. Instead, the critical parameter may be the ease with which new competing organizations could be created if the leaders of existing organizations did collude to exploit the public. Structural variables that increase the costs of creating new competing organizations are called barriers to entry. Hence lowering barriers to entry may be the most effective way of preventing organizations from exploiting the public. In economic theory, where the organizations in question are oligopolistic firms, the significance of barriers to entry has been the subject of much analysis (see Baumol, Panzar, and Willig 1986). However, the analysis of barriers to entry may be equally important in political science for the study of parties and other political organizations.

The need of voters in a block or interest group to coordinate their votes on election day can create barriers to entry against new political parties. For example, suppose that 60 percent of the electorate are leftist voters, 40 percent are rightist voters, and there are two leftist candidates and one rightist candidate running for an office. Under plurality voting, if the leftist voters divide their votes evenly among the two leftist candidates, then the rightist candidate will win. So, before the election, the leftist voters need some leadership to coordinate them behind one leftist candidate. Thus, the outcome of the election may be determined by those whom the voters accept as leaders or political arbiters before the election. This power of pre-election leaders can create a barrier to entry against new political organizations that attempt to challenge the old leaders. Thus, barriers to entry can be created by voters' incentive to coordinate their votes.

To put it another way, a bandwagon effect may be created by voters' fear of wasting votes on parties whose expected support from other voters is small. (In general, we may say that there is a *bandwagon* effect if predictions that a candidate has a greater chance of winning would make individual voters increase their support for this candidate. See Simon 1954.) Such a bandwagon effect is a barrier to entry against minor parties that do not have a bandwagon rolling for them.

However, bandwagon effects and other incentives for voters to coordinate may be different under different electoral systems. In this chapter, we search for procedures for electing a legislature that can minimize such barriers to entry. We consider electoral systems that satisfy a *coalitional straightforwardness* property which asserts that, at least among a class of voters who have a particularly simple kind of preference over electoral outcomes, there should be no need for coordination and pre-election leadership. A formal definition of this property is developed in Section 3.

Some electoral systems may also create underdog effects and may effectively reward blocks that divide their support among many small parties. (In general, we may say that there is an *underdog* effect if predictions that a candidate has a smaller chance of winning would make individual voters increase their support for this candidate. See Simon 1954.) Such incentives to divide support among candidates who have small chance of winning create barriers to consolidation for parties. For an extreme example, consider negative plurality voting, in which each voter names one candidate, and the winner is the candidate who is named by the smallest number of voters. In this case, if 60 percent of the voters are leftists and 40 percent are rightists, and one leftist candidate is running against two rightist candidates, then a rightist candidate is sure to win, because the negative leftist votes will be split.

In a game-theoretic model designed to evaluate the effectiveness of electoral systems for reducing government corruption, Myerson (1993) found that, like barriers to entry, barriers to consolidation can also reduce the incentives against political corruption. Barriers to entry can prevent new parties from challenging large corrupt parties, but barriers to consolidation can protect corrupt parties from being fully displaced by less corrupt competitors. Furthermore, there is an integrative function of politics that would be badly served if a block of voters would be penalized for consolidating its support behind one party. Thus, we should seek electoral systems that are nondivisive, in the sense that they create no barriers to consolidation for parties. A nondivisiveness axiom is formulated in Section 4.

In Section 5, we formulate several other properties of legislative electoral systems that may be desirable: neutrality with respect to party labels, responsiveness, and homogeneity (or coalitional autonomy). The main result of this chapter, presented in Section 6, is that only two classes of electoral systems satisfy the axiomatic properties from Sections 3, 4, and 5: single-vote proportional-representation systems, and approval-vote winner-take-all systems. Thus, proportional representation and approval voting are seen to be uniquely compatible in terms of the incentives for party structure that they create. Other factors that may influence barriers to entry are discussed in Section 7. The proof of the main result is given in Section 9.

Riker (1982a) has distinguished two kinds of criteria for evaluating electoral systems. Criteria of the first kind, which Riker calls *populist,* evaluate electoral systems by the way that they determine governmental policy positions as a function of voters' preferences. Criteria of the second kind, which Riker calls *liberal,* evaluate electoral systems by the extent to which they restrain the power of government leaders by forcing them to compete for votes. When we seek electoral systems with low barriers to entry, we are applying a criterion that is purely liberal, in this sense. Our concern is this: whatever governmental policy position might ultimately result from the political process, the electoral system should not deter several independent political parties from advocating essentially the same policy position and competing with each other for public offices and power.

Although proportional representation and approval voting share important properties from this liberal viewpoint, they may seem quite different by populist criteria. Analysis suggests that approval voting would encourage parties to advocate centrist positions (see Brams and Fishburn 1983; Cox 1985, 1987; and Myerson and Weber 1993), whereas proportional representation can encourage parties to take widely divergent positions (see Austen-Smith and Banks 1988 and Cox 1990). Possible use of proportional representation and approval voting together in a bicameral legislature is discussed in Section 8.

2   A general model of legislative elections

When electoral systems are compared by empirical analysis, it is only possible to compare systems that have actually been used. But we may naturally ask whether some other electoral system that has never been used might satisfy all of our criteria (whatever they may be) better than the systems that have been used in the past. In addressing this question, this chapter follows an axiomatic approach to the design of electoral systems. We begin, in this section, by considering a very general class of systems for electing legislative representatives. Then, in Sections 3–6, we develop a list of formal properties that such electoral systems might be asked to satisfy, and characterize the electoral systems that satisfy these properties.

Let us consider an election in which voters in a given district elect legislative representatives. The "district" here could be an entire nation, or a smaller geographical region. We assume that the district has a fixed number of legislative seats, which will be allocated among various competing parties in a way that depends on the results of the voting. We allow the possibility that "seats" may be divisible, and so a party could be allocated any fraction of the district's seats in the legislature.

Let K denote the set of parties that are competing for seats. We assume that K is a finite set including at least three parties, so

$$|K| \geq 3.$$

Let L denote the set of all nonempty proper subsets of the set of parties, so

$$L = \{S \mid S \subset K, S \neq \emptyset, S \neq K\}.$$

We may refer to any set S in L as a (possible) *coalition* of parties.

Electoral systems like plurality voting and proportional representation often stipulate that each voter must write on the ballot the name of one party for which he or she is voting. However, there exist strategically equivalent versions of plurality voting and proportional representation in which each voter has a single divisible vote, which can be divided equally among any set of parties. That is, the set of permissible ballots in proportional representation or plurality voting can include all of L if, for each set S in L, we interpret a ballot S to mean the same thing as giving $1/|S|$ votes to each of the parties in the set S. (Here, for any set S of parties, we let $|S|$ denote the number of parties in S.) Thus, in such an electoral system, if all the voters in some block or group submitted the ballot $\{1, 2\}$, the effect would be the same as if half of the block voted for party 1 and the other half voted for party 2; so adding the possibility of naming both parties 1 and 2 on the ballot does not increase the range of strategic options that are available to the block. (See Brams and Fishburn 1990 for a discussion of other ways to use coalitional voting in proportional representation systems.)

In general, we let V denote the set of permissible ballots that an individual voter can submit in the election, as specified by the rules of the electoral system. In this chapter, we assume that V is a nonempty finite set that includes all of the possible coalitions in L, and so

$$V \supseteq L.$$

That is, we assume that the rules of the election allow the possibility that a voter may submit a ballot which simply lists a set of parties. By itself, the assumption that V includes L can have no restrictive content, because we have not yet made any assumptions about how specific ballots are to be interpreted. (For instance, a ballot that lists two or more parties could be treated like an abstention in some electoral systems. Notice also that V may include any number of other permissible ballots that are not in the set L.) We are making this assumption here only to simplify the notation in Sections 3–5, where restrictive assumptions will be introduced.

For any finite set A, we let $\Delta(A)$ denote the set of all distributions on A. Thus, the set of possible distributions of ballots in the election is $\Delta(V)$, where

$$\Delta(V) = \{\mu \in \mathbb{R}^V \mid \sum_{v \in V} \mu(v) = 1, \mu(w) \geq 0, \forall w \in V\}.$$

The set of possible distributions of seats to the various parties is $\Delta(K)$, where

$$\Delta(K) = \{r \in \mathbb{R}^K \mid \sum_{i \in K} r_i = 1, r_j \geq 0, \forall j \in K\}.$$

(Here, for any finite set A, we let $\mathbb{R}^A$ denote the set of functions from A into the real numbers $\mathbb{R}$. Mathematically, $\mathbb{R}^A$ is a vector space with $|A|$ dimensions.) For any permissible ballot w in V, we let $[w]$ denote the ballot distribution in which everyone is submitting the ballot w. That is,

$$[w] \in \Delta(V), \quad [w](v) = 0 \text{ if } v \neq w, \quad \text{and} \quad [w](w) = 1.$$

For any distribution μ in $\Delta(V)$, we may then write

$$\mu = \sum_{w \in V} \mu(w)[w].$$

We assume that the outcome of the election will depend only on the relative numbers of voters who submit each of the possible ballots. Thus, the rule for determining the outcome of the election can be represented by a function from $\Delta(V)$, the set of ballot distributions, into $\Delta(K)$, the set of parties' seat distributions. We may denote this electoral outcome function by $F: \Delta(V) \to \Delta(K)$. Suppose that μ denotes the distribution of ballots submitted in the election, in the sense that, for each w in V, $\mu(w)$ is the fraction of the electorate that submitted the ballot w. Then $F(\mu) =$

$(F_i(\mu))_{i \in K}$ denotes the distribution of legislature seats to the parties, according to the rules of the electoral system (V, F). That is, for each party i in K, $F_i(\mu)$ denotes the fraction of the district's seats that will be allocated to party i, when μ is the distribution of ballots submitted by the voters. Notice that

$$\Sigma_{i \in K} F_i(\mu) = 1 \quad \text{and} \quad F_j(\mu) \geq 0, \; \forall j \in K, \; \forall \mu \in \Delta(V),$$

because a party cannot get a negative allocation of seats, and the parties in K will divide among themselves 100 percent of the available seats. The set of permissible ballots V and the outcome function $F: \Delta(V) \to \Delta(K)$ together completely characterize the electoral system.

(This assumption, that the relative distribution of seats depends only on the relative distribution of ballots, can itself be derived from two more basic assumptions. First, we may suppose that voters submit their ballots anonymously. This first assumption implies that the distribution of seats can only depend on the numbers of voters who submit each kind of ballot. Second, we may suppose that the relative distribution of seats would not change if this district were enlarged by merging it with other districts in which the absolute numbers of voters submitting each ballot were identical with the original district. This second assumption implies that the outcome can only depend on the relative distribution of ballots, and not on the absolute numbers in the electorate. See also Young 1974 and Smith 1973.)

Consider, for example, the version of plurality voting in which each voter has a single vote that can be divided equally among any set of parties. Let $N(\mu)$ denote the set of parties that get the most votes when μ is the ballot distribution; that is,

$$N(\mu) = \{i \in K \mid \Sigma_{S \supseteq \{i\}} \mu(S)/|S| = \max_{j \in K} \Sigma_{S \supseteq \{j\}} \mu(S)/|S|\}.$$

Suppose that seats are divided among the winning parties equally, in case of a tie. Then the distribution of seats depends on the distribution of ballots according to the function F, where

$$F_i(\mu) = \begin{cases} 1/|N(\mu)| & \text{if } i \in N(\mu), \\ 0 & \text{if } i \notin N(\mu). \end{cases}$$

We may say that an electoral system is a proportional representation system if, when each voter names a single party on the ballot, the legislative seats are allocated to each party in proportion to the number of voters who named the party. When r is a distribution over the set of parties (that is, when $r \in \Delta(K)$), we may let $F_i(r)$ denote the fraction of the district's seats that will be allocated to party i if every voter in the district names a single party on the ballot and, for each party j, r_j is the fraction of voters who name party j. That is, in terms of the notation just developed, we may write

$$F_i(r) = F_i(\sum_{j \in K} r_j[\{j\}]), \quad \forall i \in K, \ \forall r \in \Delta(K).$$

With this notation, we may say that (V, F) is a *proportional representation* (PR) system if and only if

$$F_i(r) = r_i, \quad \forall i \in K, \ \forall r \in \Delta(K). \tag{1}$$

There are a variety of ways that proportional representation systems can be extended to the case where voters can also submit ballots that name two or more parties. As we have seen, the simplest way is to suppose that a voter who lists any set S of parties is giving $1/|S|$ votes to each of the parties in the set S. Then the rule of allocating seats to parties in proportion to their vote totals gives us the outcome function F such that

$$F_i(\mu) = \sum_{S \supseteq \{i\}} \mu(S)/|S|, \quad \forall i \in K, \ \forall \mu \in \Delta(L). \tag{2}$$

In approval voting, each voter can give a whole approval vote to each of as many parties as desired, and the district's legislative seats are all allocated to the party or parties that receive the most approval votes. For any ballot distribution μ in $\Delta(L)$, let $M(\mu)$ denote the set of the parties that get the most approval votes when μ is the distribution of ballots; that is,

$$M(\mu) = \{i \in K \mid \sum_{S \supseteq \{i\}} \mu(S) = \max_{h \in K} \sum_{S \supseteq \{h\}} \mu(S)\}.$$

(The condition that μ is in $\Delta(L)$ means that, if $V \neq L$, then μ is a distribution in which no voters are choosing ballots outside of L. In the distribution μ, $\sum_{S \supseteq \{i\}} \mu(S)$ is the fraction of voters who are including party i among the set of parties to which they give approval votes.) Then, in general, we may say that an electoral system (V, F) is an *approval voting* (AV) system if and only if

$$\sum_{i \in M(\mu)} F_i(\mu) = 1, \quad \forall \mu \in \Delta(L). \tag{3}$$

There are several ways to define approval-voting outcomes in the case of ties and so complete the definition of the outcome function F. The simplest way is to let $V = L$ and specify that seats would be divided equally among the winning parties; hence,

$$F_i(\mu) = \begin{cases} 1/|M(\mu)| & \text{if } i \in M(\mu), \\ 0 & \text{if } i \notin M(\mu). \end{cases} \tag{4}$$

3 Coalitional straightforwardness

In Section 1, we argued that barriers to entry can be created by voters' need to find pre-election leadership to coordinate their votes. Pre-election leadership is, by definition, not chosen in the election itself, and unelected leadership makes political change more difficult. Thus, we should seek electoral systems that minimize the need for such unelected leadership. In this section, we consider one way to formalize this goal of minimizing the need for coordinating leadership.

The theorem of Gibbard (1973) and Satterthwaite (1975) implies that, if voters can have arbitrary preferences over legislative seat allocations, it is essentially impossible to design an electoral system in which voters can always identify their optimal voting strategies without any information about each other. So no electoral system can eliminate the incentive for voters to share information and coordinate in all situations. Thus, we focus here on the incentive to coordinate in a block of voters who have a very simple class of dichotomous preferences. That is, we consider here a block of voters who like all the parties in some set S, and who dislike all the other parties, and who simply want to maximize the fraction of the legislature that is allocated to the parties that they like.

To understand why we should focus on dichotomous preferences, consider first the situation in which a voter has completely identified his or her interests with some party j, and so simply wants to maximize the number of seats that party j gets. If any voters do not need pre-election leadership then surely such a voter should not, because the leaders of party j are that voter's leaders. Just knowing that he is for party j should be all the voter needs to know on election day. There should be no need for a higher-level leader to tell such supporters of party j how to vote.

We are seeking electoral systems that minimize the deterrents against new parties that would adopt the same position as an existing party, because such deterrents would constitute barriers to entry that protect the politicians in the existing party. So suppose now that some other parties do adopt exactly the same position as party j, and let S denote the set of parties that adopt this position. That is, S is a set of parties that includes j, and a representative from any party in S would behave identically in the legislature. Then the voters who formerly identified with party j should now have the objective of maximizing the total number of legislative seats that are allocated to the parties in S. To minimize barriers to entry, there should be no need for these voters to follow a leader who transcends the party structure and tells them whether to continue supporting party j or transfer support to other parties. Simply knowing that they are for the parties in S should be all that these voters need to know to identify their optimal ballots.

So consider a block (or set) of voters who constitute some fraction p of the total electorate, where $0 < p < 1$. Let μ denote the distribution of ballots submitted by the voters who are not in this block. If the distribution of ballots from the voters within the block is λ, then the distribution of ballots in the whole district will be $(1-p)\mu+p\lambda$, and so the fraction of the legislative seats that are won by the parties in S will be

$$\Sigma_{i \in S} F_i((1-p)\mu+p\lambda).$$

We may say that a ballot w is a *dominant vote for S* if and only if setting λ equal to $[w]$ maximizes this sum independently of μ and p. That is, w is a dominant vote for S if and only if

$$\Sigma_{i \in S} F_i((1-p)\mu+p[w]) \geq \Sigma_{i \in S} F_i((1-p)\mu+p\lambda),$$

$$\forall p \in [0,1], \quad \forall \mu \in \Delta(V), \quad \forall \lambda \in \Delta(V).$$

(Recall that $[w]$ is the ballot distribution in which everyone submits w. So $(1-p)\mu+p[w]$ is the ballot distribution that results if everyone in the block of size p submits the ballot w, while μ is the distribution of ballots from the other voters.)

Thus, our search for electoral systems that minimize the need for coordinating leadership brings us to look for electoral systems in which dominant votes exist. Relabeling the ballot set if necessary, we can assume without loss of generality that, if any ballot in V is a dominant vote for S, then the ballot "S" itself is a dominant vote for S. That is, if there is a voting strategy that is always optimal for supporters of the parties in S, then one such voting strategy should be to simply write on the ballot the names of the parties in S.

So let us say that a voting system (V, F) is *coalitionally straightforward* if and only if $V \supseteq L$ and, for every S in L,

$$\Sigma_{i \in S} F_i((1-p)\mu+p[S]) \geq \Sigma_{i \in S} F_i((1-p)\mu+p\lambda),$$

$$\forall p \in [0,1], \quad \forall \mu \in \Delta(V), \quad \forall \lambda \in \Delta(V).$$

That is, an electoral system is coalitionally straightforward if and only if, for any coalition S such that $S \subseteq K$ and $\emptyset \neq S \neq K$, the ballot "S" is a dominant vote for S. (There is no need to worry about dominant votes for K, the set of all parties, because $\Sigma_{i \in K} F_i(\mu)$ always equals 1.)

To reinterpret coalitional straightforwardness, suppose that there is a block of voters who care only about some simple yes-or-no question of government policy (e.g., should our nation go to war?), and who simply want to maximize the number of seats occupied by legislators who will vote Yes on this question. If the electoral system is coalitionally straightforward then, no matter how many independent parties may advocate the Yes position and seek to represent this block of voters, the voters in this block will not need any pre-election leadership to help them coordinate their votes with each other or the rest of the electorate (see also

Myerson 1993). All they need to know is the names of the Yes parties, because it is always optimal for them to simply list all these parties on their ballots. Thus, when several groups of political leaders are competing to represent a block of voters, this competition would not create a need for a higher level of leadership to tell the block how to vote, at least in this case where the voters in the block have the simplest possible preferences about government policy.

4   Nondivisiveness

A basic goal of the political process is to form a unifying government for a diverse electorate. This integrative function would be badly served if the electoral system positively encouraged schisms and discouraged consolidation of political organizations. Furthermore, Myerson (1993) has found that divisiveness and underdog effects can also decrease the effectiveness of electoral systems for reducing government corruption. This is so because, if a block of voters is positively rewarded for dividing its support among a set of parties, then the block may continue to support all of these parties even when some of them have been shown to be relatively more corrupt. Thus, to characterize good electoral systems, we also need an axiom of nondivisiveness. That is, in addition to asking that an electoral system minimize barriers to entry against new political parties, we also want an electoral system that minimizes barriers to consolidation of existing political parties.

Given an electoral system (V, F), for any ballot distribution μ in $\Delta(V)$ and any number p between 0 and 1, let $C(\mu, p)$ denote the convex hull of the legislative seat allocations that a block could implement by putting all its support behind one party, when p is the fraction of the electorate in the block and μ is the ballot distribution submitted by the voters who are not in the block. That is, let

$$C(\mu, p) = \{\textstyle\sum_{i \in K} r_i F((1 - p)\mu + p[\{i\}]) \mid r \in \Delta(K)\}.$$

Here $F((1 - p)\mu + p[\{i\}])$ denotes the distribution of seats that would occur when the voters in the block of size p give their votes only to party i (that is, they all vote for the coalition $\{i\}$) and μ is the ballot distribution from the other voters. So when $r = (r_i)_{i \in K}$ is in $\Delta(K)$,

$$\textstyle\sum_{i \in K} r_i F((1 - p)\mu + p[\{i\}])$$

is a weighted average of seat distributions that the block could achieve by allocating their support to a single party.

We say that an electoral system is *nondivisive* if and only if the seat distribution that a block of voters could achieve by voting for any coalition of parties is always a weighted average of the seat distributions that a slightly larger block could achieve by consolidating its support behind a single party, when the ballot distribution from the voters outside the block remains constant. That is, (V, F) is nondivisive if and only if, for every block size p and every number ϵ such that $0 < p < p + \epsilon < 1$,

$$F((1-p)\mu + p[S]) \in C(\mu, p+\epsilon), \quad \forall \mu \in \Delta(V), \quad \forall S \in L.$$

According to this definition, if the electoral system is nondivisive then, in any direction that one might want to move the distribution of seats, a block of voters that spreads its support among many parties should not be able to move the seat distribution any further than a slightly larger block that gives all its support to one well-chosen party. Hence nondivisiveness asserts that the only essential reasons for a block to vote for a coalition of several parties must be uncertainty (about the distribution of votes outside the block, or about the size of the block itself) or nonlinearity of preferences on $\Delta(K)$ (e.g., a desire to not let any one party get too big).

Proportional representation satisfies both the coalitional straightforwardness and the nondivisiveness properties as formulated here, whereas plurality voting satisfies nondivisiveness but violates coalitional straightforwardness. Thus, we may infer that proportional representation has both low barriers to entry and low barriers to consolidation, but plurality voting has high barriers to entry with low barriers to consolidation. We may expect that an electoral system with low barriers to both entry and consolidation would be essentially neutral with respect to the number of political parties that form; thus the number of political parties could be large or small, in response to the social and cultural needs of the society. In contrast, an electoral system with high barriers to entry but low barriers to consolidation would tend to generate small numbers of political parties. Analysis of empirical data (see Rae 1971 and Lijphardt 1990) tends to confirm these predictions for proportional representation and plurality voting. Countries with proportional representation have widely varying numbers of political parties, but countries with plurality voting rarely have more than three parties. The observed fact that plurality voting (in single-member districts) generally leads to the formation of just two political parties is known as Duverger's law (see Riker 1982b).

Approval voting also satisfies these coalitional straightforwardness and nondivisiveness conditions. However, approval voting would violate nondivisiveness if we altered the definition of nondivisiveness by eliminating the ϵ parameter or by allowing it to equal zero. To see why, consider a three-party example with $K = \{1, 2, 3\}$, and consider the simple symmetric tie-breaking rule discussed at the end of Section 2. (Actually, any version of approval voting that satisfies the axioms of this chapter will do.) Suppose that ⅓ of the electorate votes for the set {1, 2}, ⅓ of the electorate votes for {1, 3}, and ⅓ of the electorate votes for {2, 3}. Then each party is getting approval votes from ⅔ of the voters, and so the three parties divide the seats equally in the seat distribution (⅓, ⅓, ⅓). But if the block of voters who are voting {1, 2} changed their votes to support only party 1, then the seat distribution would change to (½, 0, ½), because only parties 1 and 3 would be tied for most approval votes. Similarly, if the block of voters who are voting {1, 2} changed their votes to support only party 2 then the seat distribution would change to (0, ½, ½); and if this block changed their votes to support only party 3 then the seat distribution would change to (0, 0, 1). Thus, when this block consolidates their support behind just one party, they cannot reduce party 3's seat allocation below ½, but they can reduce party 3's seat allocation to ⅓ by supporting both parties 1 and 2. Thus, this block may seem to derive some advantage from dividing its support among two different parties.

However, this advantage is not robust to even tiny changes in the size of the block. If the block were enlarged by even one voter, keeping the number and ballots of the other voters fixed, then the members of this block could generate the allocation (1, 0, 0) by voting for party 1, and they could generate the allocation (0, 1, 0) by voting for party 2. Thus, the advantage that this block derives from having two parties to support is not more than the advantage that the block could derive from recruiting just one more voter to join them.

Although proportional representation in its ideal form satisfies both coalitional straightforwardness and nondivisiveness, these properties are not jointly satisfied by the finite approximations to proportional representation that are used in districts with a finite number of indivisible seats. For example, consider a district with two indivisible legislative seats, and suppose that, if each voter endorsed a single party, then these two seats would be allocated according to the greatest-divisor method of Jefferson and d'Hondt. (See Balinski and Young 1982.) Consider a situation in which 30 percent of the electorate is expected to vote for party 1, 25 percent is expected to vote for party 2, 25 percent is expected to vote for party 3, and the remaining 20 percent of the electorate is a block of voters who want to maximize the total number of seats for parties 2 and 3. If this 20 percent block concentrated all their support on any single party, then party 1 would get at least one of the two seats. For example, if everyone in the block voted for party 2, then party 2 would earn a seat with 45 percent of the votes, party 1 would earn a seat with 30 percent of the votes, and party 3 with 25 percent would get no seats. (Notice also that increasing the block slightly would not change this result.) However, if the block divided its support equally between parties 2 and 3, then parties 2 and 3 would each earn a seat with 35 percent of the votes, while party 1 with 30 percent would not get a seat.

This example shows that our nondivisiveness property is stronger than the property of "encouraging coalitions" that has been discussed by Balinski and Young (1982) as a motivation for the greatest-divisor method. For an electoral system to be nondivisive in our sense, it is not enough that a set of parties would not lose seats if the leaders of these parties decided to merge them. We require here that any small block of voters who favor these parties should be able to initiate the consolidation process, by concentrating their support behind one party, without reducing the total number of seats that these parties get.

5 Neutrality, responsiveness, and homogeneity

In free democracies, the rules of the electoral system should not intrinsically favor any one party. So the outcome of the election should not depend on party labels. A *relabeling* of parties is any function $\pi\colon K \to K$ that is one-to-one and onto (i.e., $\pi(i) \neq \pi(j)$ if $i \neq j$). For any relabeling π and any set of parties S, let

$$\pi(S) = \{\pi(i) \mid i \in S\}.$$

Then we may say that an electoral system (V, F) is *neutral* if and only if, for each relabeling $\pi\colon K \to K$, for each distribution of coalitional ballots $r = (r_S)_{S \in L}$ in $\Delta(L)$, and for each party i in K,

$$F_i(\textstyle\sum_{S \in L} r_S[S]) = F_{\pi(i)}(\textstyle\sum_{S \in L} r_S[\pi(S)]).$$

That is, an electoral system is neutral if the outcome would not be changed by permuting the names of the parties, at least in the case when voters all cast coalitional ballots.

None of our assumptions has as yet ruled out the possibility that the electoral system simply divides the seats equally among the parties no matter how people vote. To rule out this system, we need some assumption that says that control of the seat distribution really does belong to the voters. One natural axiom of this form is to assert that, if all voters unanimously vote for one unique party, then that party should get all the seats. In our notation, $\{i\}$ denotes the simple vote for party i, and $[\{i\}]$ denotes the ballot distribution in which everyone submits a simple vote for party i. So we may say that an electoral system (V, F) is *responsive* if and only if

$$F_i([\{i\}]) = 1, \quad \forall i \in K.$$

Approval voting and proportional representation satisfy all the conditions that we have developed so far: coalitional straightforwardness, nondivisiveness, neutrality, and responsiveness. Other electoral systems that satisfy these four conditions can be constructed by dividing the seats into two groups, of which one group is allocated by approval voting and the other group by proportional representation. At the time of this writing, I do not know of any electoral systems that satisfy these four conditions other than mixtures of PR and AV, but I also cannot disprove the existence of other electoral systems that satisfy these conditions. The characterization that I do have requires one more condition, one which is motivated by a political interpretation that may be less compelling than neutrality and responsiveness.

Suppose, for example, that the parties in S are leftist parties, and the other parties (in $K \setminus S$) are rightist parties. Adding a block of leftist voters who vote for S obviously might decrease the share of seats that are allocated to the rightist parties. But we may want to stipulate that, when voters in some block choose to give maximal support to the leftist parties, they should not have any say about how the rightist parties proportionally divide among themselves the seats (if any) that they win in this district. That is, to provide some autonomy for the rightist faction, we may ask that the relative importance of the various rightist parties should be determined only by the rightist voters themselves, not by the leftist voters.

Adding a block of votes for S would change a ballot distribution μ to a distribution of the form $(1-p)\mu + p[S]$, where p is between 0 and 1. To assert that the parties outside of S would not change their relative strengths when such a block of votes for S is added, we may want to write

$$\frac{F_i((1-p)\mu + p[S])}{F_j((1-p)\mu + p[S])} = \frac{F_i(\mu)}{F_j(\mu)}, \quad \forall i \in K \setminus S, \; \forall j \in K \setminus S.$$

Unfortunately, this homogeneity equation is not well-defined if the denominators are zero. However, we can equivalently (but less intuitively) rewrite this condition by multiplying both sides by the product of the denominators. Thus, we may say that an electoral system (V, F) is *homogeneous* (or *coalitionally autonomous*) if and only if

$$F_i((1-p)\mu + p[S])F_j(\mu) = F_j((1-p)\mu + p[S])F_i(\mu),$$

$$\forall S \in L, \; \forall p \in [0,1], \; \forall \mu \in \Delta(V), \; \forall i \in K \setminus S, \; \forall j \in K \setminus S.$$

(Equivalently, we may say that (V, F) is homogeneous if and only if, for any S in L, for any p between 0 and 1, and for any μ in $\Delta(V)$, there exists some number q such that, for every party i that is not in S,

$$F_i((1-p)\mu + p[S]) = qF_i(\mu).$$

Here q may depend on μ, p, and S, but q does not depend on $i \in K \setminus S$.)

6 Proportional representation and approval voting

It is not difficult to verify that simple examples of approval voting and proportional representation, formulated in equations (2) and (4) with $V = L$, satisfy all five conditions developed in Sections 3–5. In fact, all other electoral systems that satisfy these five conditions are just generalizations of these two examples. This result is stated in the following theorem, which is proven in Section 9.

Theorem. *Suppose that (V, F) is coalitionally straightforward, nondivisive, neutral, responsive, and homogeneous. Then (V, F) is either an approval voting system or a proportional representation system (as defined by equations (1) and (3) in Section 2).*

To appreciate the power of this theorem, it may be helpful to consider some other electoral systems that do not satisfy all five of the conditions. Plurality voting violates only coalitional straightforwardness. Mixed systems, in which some fraction of the seats are allocated by AV and some by PR, violate only the homogeneity condition.

The term *approval voting* is used here to mean "multiple approval votes, winner take all," whereas the term *proportional representation* is used here to mean "single divisible vote, proportional seat allocation." In contrast, we might consider a "multiple approval votes, proportional seat allocation" electoral system, in which each voter can give approval votes to as many parties as desired, and legislative seats are allocated in proportion to the number of approval votes that each party receives. To formalize such an electoral system, let $V = L$ and suppose

$$F_i(\mu) = \frac{\sum_{S \supseteq \{i\}} \mu(S)}{\sum_{j \in K} \sum_{T \supseteq \{j\}} \mu(T)}, \quad \forall \mu \in \Delta(L), \ \forall i \in K.$$

This system satisfies four of our five conditions, but it violates nondivisiveness. This violation of nondivisiveness is indeed very problematic, and makes this system a bad way to elect a legislature. For example, suppose that 60 percent of the electorate are leftists and 40 percent are rightists, but there are two rightist parties competing with only one leftist party. Then the single leftist party would get $\frac{6}{14}$ of the seats whereas each rightist party would get $\frac{4}{14}$ of the seats, giving the rightists an overall $\frac{8}{14}$ majority. More generally, this "multiple approval votes, proportional seat allocation" electoral system creates an incentive for any party to split into a large set of identical parties, so that their followers can vote for all of them and thus increase the total seats allocated to this set of cloned parties.

The conclusion of the theorem is weakened by the fact that our definitions of AV systems and PR systems (in Section 2) say nothing about the outcomes that may occur when some voters submit ballots that do not simply list a coalition of parties (which may occur when V is strictly larger than L). However, the coalitional straightforwardness axiom imposes significant restrictions on the effect of noncoalitional votes – because non-coalitional votes cannot be better than coalitional votes for voters with dichotomous preferences – and these restrictions have not been formulated in the theorem. So there seems to be a need for future research to find a stronger conclusion in this theorem.

Of course, other ways to formulate the ideas of "low barriers to entry" and "low barriers to consolidation" (different from our coalitional straightforwardness and nondivisiveness conditions) should also be considered in future research. It seems reasonable to expect that other axiomatic formulations of these ideas may be found that lead similarly to approval voting and proportional representation systems. One might, for example, consider axioms that pertain to changes in equilibrium outcomes when parties merge or split. Such axioms have been avoided in this chapter because they require an agreed-upon equilibrium concept for elections, and because changing the set of parties K means changing the range of the outcome function $F: \Delta(V) \to \Delta(K)$ that is used here as the basic model of an electoral system. Thus, axioms about the effects of splitting and merging parties would require a more complicated model of an electoral system than we have used here. (See also the work of Gibbard 1978 on random social-choice mechanisms, which can be reinterpreted as an axiomatization of proportional representation. The main theorem of Gibbard 1978 implies that, if an electoral system is responsive and is straightforward for every voter whose objective is to maximize a linear function of the seat distribution, then this electoral system must be a proportional representation system.)

7   Other factors affecting barriers to entry

The main focus in this chapter is on the barriers to entry that may be created by the rules of the electoral system. We must note, however, that barriers to entry in political systems depend on much more than just the rules of the electoral system itself.

Freedom of speech is clearly the first essential prerequisite for lowering barriers to entry in politics. Conversely, under any electoral system, economies of scale in the mass media can raise barriers to entry, and voters' limited ability to assimilate political information may put an upper bound on the number of parties that can effectively compete for voters' support.

The process of fundraising to finance electoral campaigns can also create barriers to entry, regardless of the voting system, if voters can be influenced by campaign spending. When campaign contributions are offered in return for the prospect of future favors from a winning candidate, then donors will prefer to contribute money only to the campaigns of candidates who are likely to win. Thus, the perception that a new challenger has little chance of winning may hinder that candidate's fundraising ability, and so may become a self-fulfilling prophecy.

Regional autonomy in government is another general factor that can help reduce barriers to entry. Locally and regionally elected offices create opportunities for politicians to develop independent local power bases, which can allow them to challenge established national leaders. Local and regional administrative offices (if they are not subservient to centrally appointed prefects) create opportunities for local politicians to prove their ability to govern, and to develop the credentials they need to offer themselves as alternatives for national leadership.

The concept of barriers to entry into national leadership can also help us to understand why regional districts may be important even in PR elections of a national legislature. If the entire country is one PR district, then each party must nominate a single national list, which may be controlled by the party's central committee. So a legislator who wants to be renominated cannot seriously challenge the party leadership without being prepared to leave it and create an independent party. On the other hand, when the PR election is broken up into regional districts, then regional party organizations can take some control over the nomination process. With regionally decentralized nomination, legislators who have strong support in their regions gain some independence to challenge the national party leadership. Similarly, an open-list PR system (in which the voters who endorse a party can also vote to determine which of the party's candidates will have the highest priority to get the seats that the party wins) can give politicians more freedom to compete individually for voters' support.

8   Constitutional implications

The main conclusion of this chapter is that proportional representation and approval voting are uniquely compatible, in the sense that they share some important properties. In particular, PR and AV both reduce barriers to entry for new parties without being divisive, and thus they both allow flexible party configurations that respond to social and political needs. This result suggests that, in the broader questions of constitutional design, we should consider structures that mix these two systems. Because such mixtures have not been seriously considered in the past, it may be worthwhile here to introduce some (admittedly speculative) specific ideas about how approval voting and proportional representation could be combined in a constitutional system, in order to take advantage of the best features of each system.

With respect to incentives for party positioning, proportional representation and approval voting have very different and complementary properties. Theoretical analysis suggests that parties advocating centrist positions would be rewarded under approval voting, perhaps even more than under plurality voting. (For example, see Brams and Fishburn 1983; Cox 1985, 1987; and Myerson and Weber 1993.) In contrast, proportional representation encourages parties to adopt a broad range of positions (see Austen-Smith and Banks 1988 and Cox 1990, for example).

The relative desirability of centrism and breadth in a legislature should be discussed with reference to two rival theories of where government policy should be determined: in the general election, or in legislative bargaining. Of course, details of policy determination must be left to bargaining among elected representatives, because general public debate on every detail is impossible. However, the extreme multiplicity of equilibria in many natural bargaining models (see Myerson 1991, chapter 8) suggests that trying to resolve everything by bargaining among representatives who perfectly reflect the whole spectrum of public opinion may lead to a legislature that is unpredictable, arbitrary, or deadlocked. The problem is that, because legislators do not act anonymously, their actions may be distorted by a desire to cultivate a reputation for intransigence which may be helpful in future bargaining. That is, a legislative leader may fear that, if she offers concessions and agrees to support a bill that is less than her ideal but is (actually) acceptable, then she may be expected to offer many more costly concessions in future legislative bargaining. On the other hand, voters in a general election submit their ballots anonymously and so have fewer such reputational incentives. This distinction may be an important reason to encourage electoral policy determination before legislative policy determination, whenever possible. (For similar reasons, economists generally recommend that prices should be determined by anonymous market forces, rather than by bargaining between representatives of a buyers' organization and a sellers' cartel.)

In comparisons between political systems, we may say that electoral policy determination increases as the variance of policy positions that are advocated by the elected representatives decreases, while the distribution of voters' policy preferences is held fixed. Thus, the goal of maximizing electoral policy determination implies that an electoral system should be *centrist,* in the sense that it tends to give the most legislative seats to the parties that advocate compromise positions which can get wide support among voters.

On the other hand, one might also ask that a legislature should be *broad,* in the sense that it should include representatives of all major ideological and geographical factions. If a legislature is not broad, then significant segments of public opinion may feel left out of policy debates. Conversely, when a national consensus is needed to cope with a major crisis, this consensus can be expressed in the legislature only if it is sufficiently broad.

Breadth and centrism are not necessarily incompatible, because inclusion of all major factions does not necessarily imply that these factions all get seats in proportion to their support in the electorate. One way to create a legislature that is both broad and centrist is by combining PR and AV in a bicameral legislature, thus making use of both their compatibility and their differences. For example, let us consider a legislature in which the lower house is elected by proportional representation, and the upper house consists of representatives from single-member districts who are elected by approval voting. In such a legislature, we may expect to find breadth in the PR house, and strong centrism in the AV house.

Having two such different houses could make it hard to pass legislation, especially because the formation of a coherent majority is often difficult in a broadly representative PR house, which may include a wide range of idiosyncratic and ideological parties. One way to avoid such indecisiveness is to lower the quota for passing bills through the PR house. That is, the constitution could specify that, to become law, a bill needs to be approved by more than *half* of the upper AV house but only by more than a third of the lower PR house. A one-third quota is the lowest quota such that at most two disjoint coalitions can pass bills out of the lower house. Notice that, to prevent the legislature from passing laws that contradict each other without any legislator changing his or her mind, a majority quota is really only needed in one house. With its lower quota, the broad lower house could take a leading role in formulating bills, while the centrist upper house with its higher quota would have the more important role of ratifying bills. Because two disjoint coalitions could pass bills out of the lower house, these legislative rules would allow an opposition coalition to create a tangible record of their versions of all major legislation. Even if the lower house became divided into extreme leftist and extreme rightist coalitions, however, competition between these two coalitions to get their versions ratified by the centrist upper house would give them an incentive to propose bills closer to the centrists' ideal point.

(People have relatively little experience with procedural rules for a less-than-majority quota, so some possible procedural rules for such a legislature might be worth discussing here. Suppose that bills ordinarily start in the lower house. When a bill is proposed in the lower house, it can be brought up, together with all the alternative versions that have been sponsored by some required number of representatives, for a primary lower-house vote in which each representative can give an approval vote to as many versions of the bill as he or she wishes. All the versions of the bill that get the $\frac{1}{3}+$ quota in this approval-voting primary are then considered in a second lower-house vote, in which each representative can vote for at most one version. Any versions that get the $\frac{1}{3}+$ quota in this second vote are then sent to the upper house; notice that at most two such versions can be sent. If two versions are sent to the upper house, then there is a primary upper-house vote in which a majority of those voting determines which version goes to the final upper-house vote. In the final upper-house vote, a majority is needed to pass the bill, in its one remaining version, into law.)

Constitutional debates in some countries have recently focused on proposals to combine a unicameral PR legislature with a directly elected president or chief executive (see Susser 1989). Our results suggest that, in such a constitution, approval voting can be recommended as a procedure for electing the president; this would make the presidential elections compatible with the party structure that is induced by PR in the legislative elections.

Other ways to combine approval voting and proportional representation in constitutional design may be worth considering. For example, even within a unicameral legislature, we should consider the possible advantages of an electoral system in which some fraction of the seats are allocated by approval voting, while the other seats are allocated by proportional representation.

Of course, the formal properties that we have studied here are only imperfect and incomplete formulations of the criteria by which a political scientist might try to identify better constitutional structures. We may anticipate that further axiomatic analysis of electoral systems and other constitutional provisions may be a rich source of new and practical ideas about how to design political institutions that can improve the chances for a successful functioning democracy.

9   Proof of the theorem

Throughout this proof, we assume that $F: \Delta(V) \to \Delta(K)$ is coalitionally straightforward, nondivisive, neutral, responsive, and homogeneous. Recall also that we assume $|K| \geq 3$ and $V \supseteq L$, where L is the set of all proper subsets of K.

Homogeneity and neutrality imply that, if each voter names a single party on the ballot, then the ratio of seats that two parties get should depend only on the ratio of the number of votes that these parties get. That is, there must exist some function $\phi: [0,1] \rightarrow [0,1]$ such that, for any r in $\Delta(K)$ and for any two parties h and j, if $0 \leq r_h \leq r_j$ and $0 < r_j$ then

$$F_h(r) = \phi(r_h/r_j) F_j(r).$$

(Here, $[0,1]$ is the set of all numbers between 0 and 1.) To prove this, given any two different parties h and j, let

$$\phi(q) = \frac{F_h((q/(1+q))[\{h\}] + (1/(1+q))[\{j\}])}{F_j((q/(1+q))[\{h\}] + (1/(1+q))[\{j\}])}.$$

By neutrality, this function is independent of which two parties h and j are considered. Homogeneity implies that mixing in any distribution of votes for parties other than h and j cannot affect the ratio of the numbers of seats that go to parties h and j.

Neutrality and responsiveness also imply that $\phi(1) = 1$ and $\phi(0) = 0$. By coalitional straightforwardness, the function ϕ must be nondecreasing. The assumption that K includes at least three parties implies that ϕ must also satisfy the equation $\phi(pq) = \phi(p)\phi(q)$, for all numbers p and q in $[0,1]$. A nondecreasing function ϕ can satisfy these conditions only if there exists some number α, which we may call the *scoring exponent,* such that

$$0 \leq \alpha \leq +\infty \quad \text{and} \quad \phi(p) = p^\alpha \ \forall p \in [0,1].$$

(Here we let $p^{+\infty} = 0$ if $0 \leq p < 1$, $1^{+\infty} = 1$, and $0^0 = 0$.) To prove this claim, let α be such that $\phi(0.5) = 0.5^\alpha$. Let n and m be any integers. Because $\phi(0.5^{n/m})^m = \phi(0.5^n) = \phi(0.5)^n = 0.5^{\alpha n}$, we must have $\phi(0.5^{n/m}) = (0.5^{n/m})^\alpha$. That is, $\phi(p) = p^\alpha$ for any number p that is a nonnegative rational power of 0.5. Then the formula $\phi(p) = p^\alpha$ can be extended to all p in $[0,1]$ because ϕ is nondecreasing.

Thus, when each voter supports one party, the seats must be allocated in proportion to the α-power of the number of supporters. That is, if $\alpha < +\infty$ then, for any r in $\Delta(K)$,

$$F_j(r) = (r_j)^\alpha / (\textstyle\sum_{i \in K}(r_i)^\alpha).$$

If $\alpha = +\infty$ (which occurs when $\phi(0.5) = 0$) then, for any r in $\Delta(K)$,

$$\{j \mid F_j(r) > 0\} \subseteq \operatorname{argmax}_{j \in K} r_j.$$

That is, when α is infinite, all seats go to the parties with most support.

If α were less than 1, then support for parties would give decreasing returns, which implies a violation of nondivisiveness. For example, let $K = \{1,2,3\}$. Then $\alpha < 1$ would imply that

$$\textstyle\sum_{j \in \{1,2\}} F_j(0.25[\{1\}] + 0.25[\{2\}] + 0.5[\{3\}])$$

would be strictly greater than ½ and strictly greater than $\sum_{j \in \{1,2\}} F_j([\{3\}])$ and $\sum_{j \in \{1,2\}} F_j((0.5+\epsilon)[\{i\}] + (0.5-\epsilon)[\{3\}])$, for all i in $\{1, 2\}$ and all sufficiently small positive ϵ. But $F(0.5[\{1, 2\}] + 0.5[\{3\}])$ is in the convex hull of

$$\{F([\{3\}]), F((0.5+\epsilon)[\{1\}] + (0.5-\epsilon)[\{3\}]),$$
$$F((0.5+\epsilon)[\{2\}] + (0.5-\epsilon)[\{3\}])\},$$

by nondivisiveness, and

$$\sum_{j \in \{1,2\}} F_j(0.5[\{1, 2\}] + 0.5[\{3\}])$$
$$\geq \sum_{j \in \{1,2\}} F_j(0.25[\{1\}] + 0.25[\{2\}] + 0.5[\{3\}]),$$

by coalitional straightforwardness. Thus, the scoring exponent α must satisfy $1 \leq \alpha \leq +\infty$.

Lemma. *Given any μ in $\Delta(V)$, any S in L, and any p in $[0,1]$, suppose that there exists some h in K such that*

$$\sum_{i \in S} F_i((1-p)\mu + p[\{h\}]) > \sum_{i \in S} F_i((1-p)\mu + p[\{j\}]), \quad \forall j \in K \setminus \{h\},$$

and, for every j in K, $F((1-p-\epsilon)\mu + (p+\epsilon)[\{j\}])$ is a continuous function of ϵ in some interval $[0, e]$, where $0 < e < 1$. Then

$$F((1-p)\mu + p[S]) = F((1-p)\mu + p[\{h\}]).$$

The proof of this lemma follows immediately from nondivisiveness and coalitional straightforwardness. Nondivisiveness implies that

$$F((1-p)\mu + p[S])$$

is in $C(\mu, p+\epsilon)$ for every positive ϵ. The continuity condition in the theorem implies that any sequence of points in $C(\mu, p+\epsilon)$ must approach $C(\mu, p)$ as $\epsilon \to 0$. So $F((1-p)\mu + p[S]) \in C(\mu, p)$. Coalitional straightforwardness implies that

$$\sum_{i \in S} F_i((1-p)\mu + p[S]) \geq \sum_{i \in S} F_i((1-p)\mu + p[\{h\}]).$$

But the assumptions in the lemma specify that $F((1-p)\mu + p[\{h\}])$ uniquely maximizes the total allocation of seats to parties in S, among all allocations in $C(\mu, p)$. So the conclusion of the lemma follows.

By analyzing a specific example, we now show that α must be either 1 or $+\infty$. So suppose now (contrary to this claim) that $1 < \alpha < +\infty$. Using neutrality and the existence of at least three parties, we may without loss of generality assume that $K \supseteq \{1, 2, 3\}$. When α is finite,

$$F(r_1[\{1\}] + r_2[\{2\}] + r_3[\{3\}])$$

is a continuous function of (r_1, r_2, r_3) in $\Delta(\{1, 2, 3\})$. When $\alpha > 1$,

$\Sigma_{i \in \{1, 2\}} F_i(0.52[\{1\}] + 0.48[\{3\}])$

$> \Sigma_{i \in \{1, 2\}} F_i(0.50[\{1\}] + 0.02[\{2\}] + 0.48[\{3\}])$

$> \Sigma_{i \in \{1, 2\}} F_i(0.50[\{1\}] + 0.5[\{3\}])$.

That is, $\alpha > 1$ implies that a block of size 0.02 that wants to maximize the total number of seats allocated to parties 1 and 2 can maximize its impact by voting for party 1 if, among the other voters, there are more votes for party 1 than for party 2. In effect, $\alpha > 1$ implies that there are increasing returns to joining other voters in support of a party. So, by the lemma,

$$F(0.50[\{1\}] + 0.02[\{1, 2\}] + 0.48[\{3\}]) = F(0.52[\{1\}] + 0.48[\{3\}]).$$

Similarly,

$\Sigma_{i \in \{1, 2\}} F_i(0.52[\{1\}] + 0.47[\{2\}] + 0.01[\{3\}])$

$> \Sigma_{i \in \{1, 2\}} F_i(0.50[\{1\}] + 0.49[\{2\}] + 0.01[\{3\}])$

$> \Sigma_{i \in \{1, 2\}} F_i(0.50[\{1\}] + 0.47[\{2\}] + 0.03[\{3\}])$,

and so

$$F(0.50[\{1\}] + 0.02[\{1, 2\}] + 0.47[\{2\}] + 0.01[\{3\}])$$
$$= F(0.52[\{1\}] + 0.47[\{2\}] + 0.01[\{3\}]).$$

Furthermore, when $\alpha > 1$,

$\Sigma_{j \in \{2, 3\}} F_j(0.52[\{1\}] + 0.48[\{3\}])$

$> \Sigma_{j \in \{2, 3\}} F_j(0.52[\{1\}] + 0.47[\{2\}] + 0.01[\{3\}])$

$> \Sigma_{j \in \{2, 3\}} F_j(0.99[\{1\}] + 0.01[\{3\}])$

$= \Sigma_{j \in \{2, 3\}} F_j(0.97[\{1\}] + 0.02[\{1, 2\}] + 0.01[\{3\}])$.

These results imply that

$$F(0.50[\{1\}] + 0.02[\{1, 2\}] + 0.47[\{2, 3\}] + 0.01[\{3\}])$$
$$= F(0.52[\{1\}] + 0.48[\{3\}]).$$

On the other hand,

$\Sigma_{j \in \{2, 3\}} F_j(0.50[\{1\}] + 0.49[\{2\}] + 0.01[\{3\}])$

$> \Sigma_{j \in \{2, 3\}} F_j(0.50[\{1\}] + 0.02[\{2\}] + 0.48[\{3\}])$

$> \Sigma_{j \in \{2, 3\}} F_j(0.97[\{1\}] + 0.02[\{2\}] + 0.01[\{3\}])$,

and so

$$F(0.50[\{1\}] + 0.02[\{2\}] + 0.47[\{2, 3\}] + 0.01[\{3\}])$$
$$= F(0.50[\{1\}] + 0.49[\{2\}] + 0.01[\{3\}]).$$

Then, using coalitional straightforwardness, we conclude that

$$\sum_{i \in \{1, 2\}} F_i(0.52[\{1\}] + 0.48[\{3\}])$$

$$= \sum_{i \in \{1, 2\}} F_i(0.50[\{1\}] + 0.02[\{1, 2\}] + 0.47[\{2, 3\}] + 0.01[\{3\}])$$

$$\geq \sum_{i \in \{1, 2\}} F_i(0.50[\{1\}] + 0.02[\{2\}] + 0.47[\{2, 3\}] + 0.01[\{3\}])$$

$$= \sum_{i \in \{1, 2\}} F_i(0.50[\{1\}] + 0.49[\{2\}] + 0.01[\{3\}]).$$

That is, we must have

$$0.52^\alpha/(0.52^\alpha + 0.48^\alpha) \geq (0.50^\alpha + 0.49^\alpha)/(0.50^\alpha + 0.49^\alpha + 0.01^\alpha).$$

But this inequality does not hold for any α such that $1 < \alpha < +\infty$. (It would hold only if $(52/48)^\alpha \geq 50^\alpha + 49^\alpha$, which is certainly not true for any finite positive α.)

Thus, the scoring exponent α cannot be strictly between 1 and $+\infty$. That is, we must have either $\alpha = 1$ or $\alpha = +\infty$. When $\alpha = 1$, we have a proportional representation system, as defined in Section 2. So let us henceforth consider the case of $\alpha = +\infty$.

Given any μ in $\Delta(L)$, let $M(\mu) = \text{argmax}_{i \in K} \sum_{T \supseteq \{i\}} \mu(T)$. By induction in m we can show that, for any vote distribution μ in $\Delta(L)$ such that m is the number of coalitions containing two or more parties that are endorsed by a positive fraction of the voters, the only parties that get seats are those in the set $M(\mu)$. For $m = 0$, the claim holds because $\alpha = +\infty$. Now suppose inductively that $m \geq 1$ and the claim holds for $m - 1$.

Let μ be any vote distribution such that exactly m coalitions containing two or more parties are endorsed by a positive fraction of the voters. Let S be any coalition in L such that $\mu(S) > 0$ and S contains two or more parties. If $\mu(S) = 1$ then responsiveness and coalitional straightforwardness would together imply that $\sum_{i \in S} F_i(\mu) = 1$, which would prove the claim (because $S = M(\mu)$ when $\mu(S) = 1$). So we may suppose that $\mu(S) < 1$. Let η denote the distribution of votes among the voters who do not vote for S. That is,

$$\eta(S) = 0 \quad \text{and} \quad \mu = (1 - \mu(S))\eta + \mu(S)[S].$$

There would be only $m - 1$ coalitions of two or more parties that are endorsed by a positive fraction of the voters if the S supporters in μ switched to endorse a single party. Let

$$M^*(\mu, S) = \bigcup_{i \in K} M((1 - \mu(S))\eta + \mu(S)[\{i\}])).$$

Notice that $i \in M^*(\mu, S)$ if and only if $i \in M((1 - \mu(S))\eta + \mu(S)[\{i\}])$. A sufficiently small increase in $\mu(S)$ (with small proportional decrease in the other elements of μ) would not change $M^*(\mu, S)$, so nondivisiveness and the induction hypothesis imply that

$$\sum_{i \in M^*(\mu, S)} F_i(\mu) = 1.$$

To complete the proof, we consider two cases which together include all possibilities.

Case 1: First suppose that $M(\mu)\setminus S \neq \emptyset$. Then

$$M^*(\mu, S)\setminus M(\mu) \subseteq K \setminus S,$$

because the S supporters cannot make a party in S get more approval votes than a party in $M(\mu)\setminus S$ by reassigning their votes from all of S to any single party. Furthermore, $M(\eta) = M(\mu)\setminus S$, so removing the S supporters altogether would leave a vote distribution in which the parties in $M(\mu)\setminus S$ would get all the seats. That is, by the induction hypothesis for $m-1$,

$$\sum_{i \in M(\mu)\setminus S} F_i(\eta) = 1.$$

By homogeneity, going from η to μ cannot change the relative distribution of seats among the parties in $K \setminus S$, so

$$F_j(\mu) = 0, \quad \forall j \in (K \setminus S)\setminus M(\mu).$$

But $(K \setminus S)\setminus M(\mu) \supseteq M^*(\mu, S)\setminus M(\mu)$, so we can conclude that

$$\sum_{i \in M(\mu)} F_i(\mu) = 1.$$

Case 2: Now suppose instead that $M(\mu) \subseteq S$. By switching to support any one party in $M(\mu)$, the supporters of S could create a vote distribution in which, by the induction hypothesis, this party would get all the seats. Thus, by coalitional straightforwardness,

$$\sum_{i \in S} F_i(\mu) = 1.$$

If the theorem fails, then there must exist some party j such that $j \in S \setminus M(\mu)$ but $F_j(\mu) > 0$. Let h be any party that is not in S. (Here is the only place where we use the assumption that the set of all parties K is not in L.) Let

$$\mu' = (1-p)\mu + p[\{h\}],$$

where the number p is chosen so that

$$\max_{i \in M(\mu)} \sum_{T \supseteq \{i\}} \mu'(T) > \sum_{T \supseteq \{h\}} \mu'(T) > \sum_{T \supseteq \{j\}} \mu'(T).$$

Then $M(\mu') = M(\mu)$, and so the same argument implies that

$$\sum_{i \in S} F_i(\mu') = 1.$$

However, if we changed μ' by having the voters who support S in μ' switch to support only j or any other single party, we could not create a vote distribution in which party j would have the most approval votes. That is, $j \notin M^*(\mu', S)$. This property would hold even if we perturbed μ' by a sufficiently small increase in the size of the block supporting S and correspondingly small proportional decreases in the sizes of all other voting blocks. Thus, by nondivisiveness and the induction hypothesis for $m-1$, $F_j(\mu') = 0$. By homogeneity, the change from μ to μ' cannot transfer seats from j to other parties in S, because $\mu' = (1-p)\mu + p[\{h\}]$ and $h \notin S$. So $F_j(\mu) = 0$. This contradiction of the way that we chose j implies that

$$\Sigma_{i \in M(\mu)} F_i(\mu) = 1. \qquad \square$$

REFERENCES

Austen-Smith, D., and J. Banks (1988), "Elections, Coalitions, and Legislative Outcomes," *American Political Science Review* 82: 405-22.
Balinski, M. L., and H. P. Young (1982), *Fair Representation*. New Haven, CT: Yale University Press.
Baumol, W. J., J. C. Panzar, and R. D. Willig (1986), "On the Theory of Perfectly-Contestable Markets," in J. E. Stiglitz and G. F. Mathewson (eds.), *New Developments in the Analysis of Market Structure*. Cambridge: MIT Press.
Brams, S. J., and P. C. Fishburn (1983), *Approval Voting*. Boston: Birkhauser.
(1990), "Coalition Voting," Discussion Paper, Department of Politics, New York University.
Cox, G. W. (1985), "Electoral Equilibrium under Approval Voting," *American Journal of Political Science* 29: 112-18.
(1987), "Electoral Equilibrium under Alternative Voting Institutions," *American Journal of Political Science* 31: 82-108.
(1990), "Centripetal and Centrifugal Incentives in Electoral Systems," *American Journal of Political Science* 34: 903-35.
Gibbard, A. (1973), "Manipulation of Voting Schemes: A General Result," *Econometrica* 41: 587-601.
(1978), "Straightforwardness of Game Forms with Lotteries as Outcomes," *Econometrica* 46: 595-614.
Lijphardt, A. (1990), "The Political Consequences of Electoral Laws, 1945-85," *American Political Science Review* 84: 481-96.
Myerson, R. B. (1991), *Game Theory: Analysis of Conflict*. Cambridge, MA: Harvard University Press.
(1993), "Effectiveness of Electoral Systems for Reducing Government Corruption: A Game-Theoretic Analysis," *Games and Economic Behavior* 5: 118-32.
Myerson, R. B., and R. J. Weber (1993), "A Theory of Voting Equilibria," *American Political Science Review* 87: 102-14.
Rae, D. W. (1971), *The Political Consequences of Electoral Laws*. New Haven, CT: Yale University Press.
Riker, W. H. (1982a), *Liberalism Against Populism*. San Francisco: Freeman.
(1982b), "The Two-Party System and Duverger's Law," *American Political Science Review* 76: 753-66.

Satterthwaite, M. A. (1975), "Strategy-Proofness and Arrow's Conditions: Existence and Correspondence Theorems for Voting Procedures and Social Welfare Functions," *Journal of Economic Theory* 10: 187–217.

Simon, H. A. (1954), "Bandwagon and Underdog Effects and the Possibility of Equilibrium Predictions," *Public Opinion Quarterly* 18: 245–53.

Smith, J. (1973), "Aggregation of Preferences with a Variable Electorate," *Econometrica* 41: 1027–41.

Susser, B. (1989), "'Parliadential' Politics: A Proposed Constitution for Israel," *Parliamentary Affairs* 42: 112–22.

Young, H. P. (1974), "Social Choice Scoring Functions," *SIAM Journal of Applied Mathematics* 28: 824–38.

CHAPTER 6

Party competition in a spatial model of coalition formation

Norman J. Schofield

1   Introduction

Proportional representation generally results in a political system with three or more parties, where governments comprise coalitions of some of the parties. Such an electoral system in principle has the virtue of permitting representation of a wide range of electoral preferences. However, earlier empirical work (Dodd 1974; Schofield 1987; Taylor and Herman 1971; Warwick 1979) all seemed to suggest that multiparty governments were relatively unstable (in terms of average duration of government).

On the other hand, in what we may term the "Westminster" model of government, where party strength is determined by some form of plurality rule in single-member districts or constituencies, it is usually the case that one party attains a majority and can therefore implement a relatively long-lived government. That this need not necessarily occur was the subject of intense pre-election debate in Britain in 1992. The general conclusion of that debate was that the incomplete representation of the Westminster model was preferable to the instability associated with proportional representation and multiparty coalition politics.

In attempting to judge the relative advantages of proportional representation against the Westminster model, it would be useful to have a general model of political competition which could be applied to both cases. In the past decade there has been extensive modeling of two-party competition in a spatial context. In such models the two parties (labeled i and j) adopt policy positions (z_i, z_j, say) that determine the probabilities $\alpha_i(z_i, z_j)$, $\alpha_j(z_i, z_j)$ that the respective party wins the election. (See for example Cox 1984; Enelow and Hinich 1984; Wittman 1983.) Until recently,

This material is based upon work supported by NSF Grant SES-88-20845. I thank David Austen-Smith, Jeffrey Banks, Robert Parks, and the anonymous referees for many helpful comments.

135

however, there has been very little research on modeling party behavior in a situation where coalition governments are typical. However, Austen-Smith (1986), Austen-Smith and Banks (1988), and Baron (1989, 1991) have all proposed useful theoretical models of coalition behavior.

The focus of this chapter is on the application of the spatial model of voting to multiparty coalition governments. That is, we assume that parties have some policy preferences that are entirely private and that are unknown to the other parties and the electorate. Parties choose policy declarations that jointly determine the parties' electoral strength and are used as negotiating stances in coalition bargaining. The choice of these declarations has an impact on the eventual outcome. Consequently, it is important to model the connection between the pre-election game of declaration choice and the post-election game of coalition formation.

Recent empirical work (Laver and Schofield 1990) strongly suggests that a 1-dimensional model of coalition bargaining is unsatisfactory. For that reason we assume, as does Baron, that the policy space is 2-dimensional. However, Baron (1991) considers only three-party negotiation in two dimensions, in the post-election situation when the set of winning coalitions is known. In contrast to Baron's work, we assume here that the policy positions of the parties, and thus their electoral strength, are determined by strategic calculation by the parties. In this sense the model proposed here is related to that of Austen-Smith and Banks (1988). However, a fundamental assumption of their model is that the three parties are engaged in a 1-dimensional policy game. Moreover, the parties in their model are not directly interested in policy per se, but instead view their declarations as means to attaining political power.

In the next section of the paper we construct a post-election cooperative model of coalition bargaining in a policy space of two or more dimensions. That is, we assume that a fixed set $N = \{1, \ldots, n\}$ of parties have made their policy declarations and that each party acts in the coalition game as though its declared policy were its true preferred policy, with the trade-offs implicit in coalition bargaining determined by an induced Euclidean utility function. We assume in this section that the election has already occurred, so that the party strengths, and thus the decisive structure (or set of majority coalitions), are already known.

At this point it is necessary to deal with the well-known results on majority-rule instability in the spatial model. Earlier results by Plott (1967), Kramer (1973), McKelvey (1976, 1979), and Schofield (1983) showed that instability was likely in a simple majority rule game in two or more dimensions. Later results by McKelvey and Schofield (1986, 1987) showed that weighted majority rule systems, where parties are endowed with different strengths, have quite subtle features. In two dimensions, *a core* (or unbeaten policy point) can occur "with positive probability." When there is no core, then there has been extensive debate over the possibility of complete voting chaos. In recent work Miller (1980), Shepsle and Weingast (1984), McKelvey (1986), and Cox (1987) have argued that instead of voting chaos, the outcomes of a majority-rule process will lie in a restricted set of points known as the *uncovered set*. However, the application of this notion to legislatures has greatest relevance in bodies, such as the U.S. Senate, where each member has one vote.

For the case of a multiparty legislature, this chapter proposes a set of outcomes known as the *heart*. In the case that the core is empty, and parties have Euclidean preferences, the heart is simply the set of points bounded by median lines associated with majority coalitions. It is known from earlier work (Schofield 1985) that in two dimensions the heart belongs to the convex set generated by the declared positions. (Appendix 2 presents a formal definition of the heart, and shows why the heart has this Pareto property in arbitrary dimension.)

The justification of the heart rests on empirical analysis of coalition governments. First of all, the core (when nonempty) is the heart. The core can only occur at the declared position of the "largest" party in the Parliament. Empirically it is the case that only large parties form minority governments when they are at the core position. Second, when the core is empty the boundary of the heart is associated with a small number of "bounding" coalitions. Estimates of the location of party declarations support the inference that these bounding coalitions play a significant role in the coalition game. For example, in the three-party case each of the two-party winning coalitions bounds the heart. In a country such as Germany, where there are essentially three parties, one or the other of these two-party winning coalitions generally forms.

Section 3 considers the pre-election game where three parties choose policy declarations but the decisive structure is fixed, rather than being determined by the policy declarations. For example, in Germany the parties can generally assume that no single party can gain a majority, and so every government must contain at least two of the parties. The model developed in this section assumes that each two-party coalition, if it forms, adopts the mean policy point of the two declared policies of the coalition members. The probability associated with the coalition is inversely proportional to the variance of the declared positions of its members.

The outcome f is thus a lottery across three possible coalition outcomes, with specific probabilities associated with these outcomes. The relationship between the list of party choices and the lottery outcome is common knowledge to all. The parties strategically choose their declared positions so as to obtain the best possible lottery outcome, while aware that all parties do the same. Assuming that the parties have true preferences that are represented by utility functions that are Euclidean in position and linear in probability, Theorem 1B shows that there exists a Nash equilibrium in the choice of declared positions. For this reason it is argued that it is rational within the terms of this model for each party to act in post-election coalition negotiations as though its declared position were its true preferred policy position. A general version of this model with n parties is also considered. Because the optimality equation has an identical form to the three-party case, it is conjectured that a local Nash equilibrium also exists in the general case.

Section 4 extends the game to analyze the situation in which policy declarations affect the electoral outcome and thus the decisive structure. The model in this section supposes that the relationship between the profile of party declarations and the electoral outcome is known with certainty and is common knowledge to the parties. It is assumed that, for each profile of declarations z, the lottery outcome belongs to the heart of the coalition game as determined by the predictable electoral outcome. Because the heart correspondence is continuous, the lottery outcome can be taken to be a continuous selection from the heart correspondence. If the preferences of the parties induced by this outcome function satisfy certain continuity and convexity properties, then there will again exist a Nash equilibrium. In this model, the election confers no information. Thus parties will attempt to implement their declared positions in coalition negotiations.

The final model developed in Section 4 can be regarded as a direct generalization to the multiparty case of the standard model of two-party competition incorporating electoral uncertainty (Cox 1984). Instead of assuming that, for each profile z of party declarations, the resulting decisive structure is predictable, we suppose instead that z defines a list of probabilities $\{\alpha_\sigma(z)\}$, one for each possible decisive structure, $\mathfrak{D}_\sigma$. The outcome $f(z)$ is now a lottery across outcomes $\{f_\sigma(z)\}$, each one of which is associated with the decisive structure $\mathfrak{D}_\sigma$. Suppose there is a Nash equilibrium $(z_1^*, \ldots, z_n^*)$ in the pre-election game. The election now provides information about the decisive structure. In the post-election coalition game it need not be rational for the parties to remain committed to their Nash declarations. Indeed, it is intuitively obvious that the greater the electoral uncertainty, the weaker this commitment. One strategy that might appeal to parties is to present an ambiguous policy declaration, effectively a mixed strategy across policy declarations that are optimal with regard to various likely decisive structures.

Note that there is a pronounced difference between this generalized multiparty model and the two-party model. In the latter case, once the election has occurred and one party has attained a majority, there is nothing (formally) to prevent it implementing its true policy position. Thus convergence to an electoral center, in the pre-election game, may not be realized in the post-election situation. In the multiparty case, however, the analytical results of Section 3 suggest that some sort of convergence of party positions will occur even in the post-election period. It is therefore possible that the Westminster model of government and the European coalitional polities are very different in the way they translate electoral preferences into policy outcomes. In the former model, although governments tend to be long-lived, dramatic policy shifts may occur once a party has been defeated. In coalition systems, policies do change with governments, but these policies tend to be determined by parties that have become committed to nonextreme positions.

The concluding section draws out some intuitive inferences based on the general results of the models that have been proposed. Though the models are quite complex, the empirical patterns that can be observed in European multiparty polities are compatible with these inferences.

2   Post-election coalition bargaining in multiparty systems

The basic assumption we make is that there is an underlying policy space W that includes all possible policy choices that each party can make. W is a compact, convex subset of $\mathbb{R}^w$. Each party i is concerned with policy, in the sense that it has a well-defined utility function $u_i: W \to \mathbb{R}$. For purposes of exposition we shall assume that each u_i is Euclidean and has the form $u_i(x) = -\frac{1}{2}\|x - x_i\|^2$, where $x_i \in W$ is the *bliss point* of party i and $x \in W$ is the outcome. We assume the set of parties $N = \{1, ..., i,, ..., n\}$ is exogenously determined.

Modeling multiparty systems is extremely difficult because party behavior necessarily involves both competitive and cooperative features. On the one hand, parties must compete with one another vis-à-vis the electorate to gain parliamentary seats. One way to model this competition is to analyze the choice of a declaration or manifesto, $z_i \in W$, by party i. We can assume that the list of policy declarations (the manifesto profile) $z = (z_i, ..., z_n)$ gives rise to a vector of seat allocations $e(z) = (e_1(z), ..., e_n(z))$, where $e_i(z)$ is the proportion of seats controlled by party i.

In the two-party case it is appropriate to seek a Nash equilibrium where the parties attempt to gain a majority of the seats. However in the multiparty case (with $n > 2$) we assume that parties are concerned with the final policy outcome, and it is not appropriate to assume that parties simply attempt to maximize the number of seats they control. In any case it is known that no Nash equilibrium need exist in the seat maximization game (Eaton and Lipsey 1975).

Instead, it is crucial to the modeling that we explore the cooperative aspect of the coalition game by looking at the relationship between the profile of declarations z and the eventual coalition outcomes. We attempt to build a model where the choice of declared policies derives from a competitive process, where parties compute the electoral consequences of the declarations and attempt to estimate the constraints these declarations impose on coalition bargaining. We shall set up the model essentially by way of examples, while presenting technical proofs in the appendixes.

Suppose that the parties have made their policy declarations, and that, as a result of an election their seat allocations have been made. Assume further that each party acts in the game of government formation as though its declared position were its true bliss point. (We shall discuss this assumption later.) Given the declaration $z_i \in W$ by party i, we assume that the induced utility function for this party is $u_i'(x) = -\frac{1}{2}\|x - z_i\|^2$.

Any coalition M that controls more than half the seats is winning. Let $\mathfrak{D}(z)$ be the family of winning (or decisive) coalitions defined by the manifesto profile z. We call $\mathfrak{D}(z)$ the *decisive structure* at z. Let $W(M)$ be the compromise set of coalition M (namely, the convex hull of the declared positions of the members of M).

The *core*, or choice $CH(\mathfrak{D}(z))$, is the intersection across all $W(M)$ for M in $\mathfrak{D}(z)$. Earlier results by Schofield (1984) and McKelvey and Schofield (1987) allow us to determine when the core exists. More precisely, core existence is characterized by two integers, the Nakamura number $v(\mathfrak{D}(z))$ and the instability dimension $w(\mathfrak{D}(z))$. Assuming that there is no veto party (i.e., that no party belongs to every winning coalition), then $v(\mathfrak{D}(z))$ is the cardinality of the smallest subfamily of $\mathfrak{D}(z)$ with no vetoer. If the dimension w is no greater than $v(\mathfrak{D}(z)) - 2$ then a core must exist. On the other hand, if the dimension w is at least $w(\mathfrak{D}(z))$ then a core can almost never exist.

Example 1. To illustrate, consider Table 1, which presents the seats controlled by the eight parties in the Dutch Parliament in 1952. There are three minimal majority coalitions $\{PvdA, KVP\}$, $\{PvdA, ARP, CHU\}$, $\{KVP, ARP, CHU\}$ with no intersection, so $v(\mathfrak{D}(z)) = 3$. As usual, in one dimension there must be a core. For example if the parties, as in Table 1, are ranked from left to right (i.e., CPN on the left to SGP on the right) then the CHU would be the core party (alternatively one can say that the CHU is at the median).

In two dimensions there is no guarantee that a core exists. However, as Figure 1 shows, a core can exist. As long as the declared position of the

Table 1. *The election of June 1952 in the Netherlands*

Party name	Symbol	Seats
Communists	*CPN*	6
Labor Party	*PvdA*	30
Anti-Revolutionary Party	*ARP*	12
Christian Historical Union	*CHU*	9
Catholic People's Party	*KVP*	30
Liberals	*VVD*	9
Political Reform Party	*SGP*	2
Other		2
Total		100

TRADITIONALISM

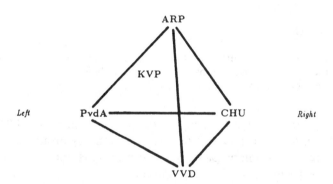

MODERNIZATION

Figure 1. A structurally stable core at the *KVP* position in 2-dimensional policy space after the election in the Netherlands in 1952.

KVP is within the compromise set of the {*PvdA*, *ARP*, *VVD*} and {*PvdA*, *ARP*, *CHU*} coalitions, then that position is the core of the coalition game.

McKelvey and Schofield (1987) obtained certain symmetry conditions which characterize core positions. Using these it is possible to show that the *KVP* position in Figure 1 is *structurally stable*. That is to say, the *KVP* position is a core even after small perturbations in the positions of

TRADITIONALISM

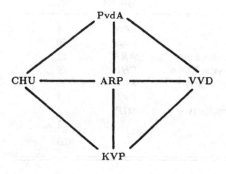

Left   *Right*

MODERNIZATION

Figure 2. A structurally unstable core at the *ARP* position for a hypothetical configuration of party positions in 2-dimensional policy space in
the Netherlands.

the other parties. Figure 2 shows a core configuration at the *ARP* position. Note, however, that this feature is structurally unstable, since a
small change in position by (say) the *PvdA* means that the *ARP* position
is not in every winning coalition compromise set.

The symmetry results can be used to show that only the larger parties
(namely the *KVP* and *PvdA*) can occupy a structurally stable core position (Schofield 1989). In three dimensions the *KVP* "generally" cannot
lie in the plane generated by the coalition {*PvdA, ARP, CHU*} and so a
structurally stable core cannot occur. Thus the instability dimension associated with Table 1 is given by $w(\mathfrak{D}(z)) = 3$.

A fundamental assumption here is that when a party occupies the core
position then it is capable, in principle, of forming a minority (or non-
majority) government and enforcing a policy outcome that coincides with
its declared core policy. On the other hand, if the party has declared a
policy which is not a core position, then it cannot form a minority government to implement this position.

This reasonable assumption allows us to make a strong empirical inference concerning the nature of the policy space in the various European

multiparty democracies. In the postwar era, minority governments have occurred in at least a third of the occasions in Norway, Sweden, Denmark, Finland, Ireland, and Italy (Schofield 1993), and have occurred infrequently in Belgium, Iceland, and the Netherlands. In every case the minority government has been based on the "largest" party (the party capable of controlling the structurally stable core position in a 2-dimensional policy space). If the policy space were actually 1-dimensional, then by chance the core position could be occupied by a smaller party (such as the *CHU* in the example from the Netherlands). Since smaller parties never form minority governments, we infer that there must be more than one underlying dimension of policy or ideology in these countries. In the first group of six countries, it is reasonable to assume that the underlying policy space is 2-dimensional. In Belgium, Iceland, and the Netherlands, the policy space is unlikely to be 1-dimensional but may be 3-dimensional. For example, factor analysis of the party manifestos by Hearl (1987) suggests that a 2-dimensional policy space (comprising economic left/right and a clerical/anticlerical dimension) was augmented by a third dimension associated with language and autonomy in the late 1960s in Belgium.

In three of the other European countries (Austria, Germany, and Luxembourg) there are essentially three parties. In such triadic systems the instability dimension is two, and so a core can only occur in two dimensions at the declared position of a party with an effective majority of the seats. In Germany and Luxembourg, minority governments have never occurred in the postwar period, and in Austria a single minority government did form, but the minority party had formal support from one other party. In these three triadic systems, the norm is in fact a two-party minimal winning coalition.

The empirical evidence, then, is that the underlying policy space is 2-dimensional in at least six of the twelve European countries that have been examined. When a minority government forms in these countries it is reasonable to infer that it is based on the "largest" party taking up a core position. In three countries (Belgium, Iceland, and the Netherlands), minority governments, and thus core parties, appear to be rare, while in the triadic systems a core only occurs when one party attains a blocking majority.

Implicit in this reasoning is the inference that controlling the core policy position is highly desirable for a party. However, since the core position is by definition centrally located with respect to the declared positions of the other parties, the attainment of such a position by a party may involve the party in unattractive policy compromises. To analyze the required compromises we need to evaluate the situation when the core is empty.

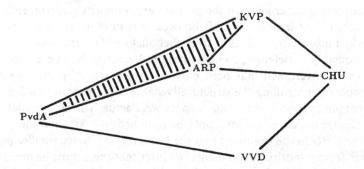

Figure 3. An empty core and nonempty cycle set (shaded) for a hypothetical configuration of party positions in 2-dimensional policy space in the Netherlands.

Figure 3 shows a configuration of declared policy positions for the situation described in Table 1, where no party belongs to every winning compromise set. To analyze this situation, we introduce the notion of a *median line*. Consider the median line through the $\{KVP, ARP\}$ positions. On the line and to its right lies a majority coalition $\{KVP, ARP, CHU, VVD\}$, while on the line and to its left lies another majority $\{KVP, ARP, PvdA\}$. The three medians – namely, $\{KVP, ARP\}$, $\{ARP, PvdA\}$, and $\{PvdA, KVP\}$ – span a convex set, with vertices $\{KVP, ARP, PvdA\}$. Earlier work (Schofield 1985) has shown that the shaded set in Figure 3 is a *cycle set*. We shall label this set $CY(\mathfrak{D}(z))$. At any point x in the interior of $CY(\mathfrak{D}(z))$, there exist three nearby points $\{y_1, y_2, y_3\}$ such that each point y_i is preferred to x by one of the bounding coalitions (either $\{KVP, ARP, CHU\}$, or $\{PvdA, ARP, CHU\}$, or $\{KVP, PvdA\}$). Moreover, there exists a majority cycle from y_1 to y_2 to y_3 back to y_1. Another way of characterizing the point x is that there exist points $\{y_1, y_2, y_3\}$, each preferred by distinct winning coalitions to x, such that x belongs to the convex hull of the three points. $CY(\mathfrak{D}(z))$ is the closed set bounded by median lines. If d is a point outside $CY(\mathfrak{D}(z))$ then there exists some point g, closer to $CY(\mathfrak{D}(z))$ than d, which is preferred to d by a majority coalition. Appendix 2 gives a more abstract definition of $CY((\mathfrak{D})(z))$ and presents a process of negotiation between the parties which leads into this cycle set. Note that the cycle set $CY(\mathfrak{D}(z))$ belongs to the convex hull of the declared positions of the five parties shown in Figure 3. This property is shown in Appendix 2 to be generally true for the generalized cycle set in arbitrary dimension.

To present a unified interpretation of Figures 1-3, define the *political heart* $H(\mathfrak{D}(z))$ associated with the manifesto profile $z = (z_1, \ldots, z_n)$ to be the union of the core and cycle set; that is,

$H(\mathfrak{D}(z)) = CH(\mathfrak{D}(z)) \cup CY(\mathfrak{D}(z))$.

The emphasis on the cycle set $CY(\mathfrak{D}(z))$ in Figure 3 suggests that the three bounding coalitions $\{PvdA, KVP\}$, $\{PvdA, ARP\}$, and $\{KVP, ARP\}$ are natural candidates for government. If a majority coalition such as $\{KVP, ARP, CHU\}$ forms, then every point in the interior of this coalition compromise set is beaten by some point on the line joining the KVP and ARP positions. We suggest therefore that each of the bounding coalitions propose a single point on the appropriate part of the boundary of the cycle set.

Suppose further that each of the three bounding coalitions forms with some probability. Then the lottery across the three possible outcomes has expectation some point f within the cycle set. Thus the profile $z = (z_1, \ldots, z_n)$ of declared positions gives rise to a lottery outcome $f(z)$, which is functionally dependent on the profile z. This allows us to determine conditions under which there exists a Nash equilibrium in the choice of declared positions.

3 Nash equilibrium in the choice of manifestos with three parties and fixed decisive structure

In this section we discuss a model of manifesto choices by three parties $\{1, 2, 3\}$. We shall for the moment ignore the electoral consequences of the declared positions, and assume that each of the two-party coalitions is decisive.

Example 2. To analyze a simple symmetric version of the model, consider Figure 4, where two parties (a central party labeled CEN and a liberal party labeled LIB) have declared positions at $(0, r/2)$ and $(0, -r/2)$, respectively.

A Conservative party (CON) has a true preferred position at $(L, 0)$, with $L \gg 0$. By symmetry we may suppose that the Conservative party declares a position $(x, 0)$, $x > 0$. We shall also suppose that if parties i and j declare positions z_i and z_j then they implement the mean position $\frac{1}{2}(z_i + z_j)$ if they form a government. We also suppose that the coalition $\{i, j\}$ forms with probability inversely proportional to $\|z_i - z_j\|^2$.

To maintain symmetry, let

$$\|CEN, LIB\| = r \quad \text{and} \quad \|CON - CEN\| = \|CON - LIB\| = s.$$

By assumption, the probabilities of coalition formation are

$$\text{prob}\{CEN, CON\} = \text{prob}\{LIB, CON\} = \frac{r^2}{s^2 + 2r^2} \quad (= \rho_1).$$

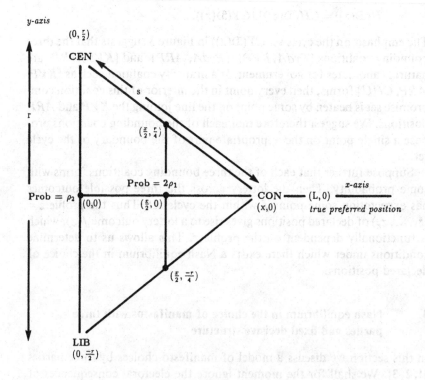

Figure 4. Three-party coalition negotiation.

Also,

$$\text{prob}\{CEN, LIB\} = \frac{s^2}{s^2 + 2r^2} \quad (= \rho_2).$$

Since *CON* chooses a position $(x, 0)$, it calculates that it will form a government with *CEN* with probability ρ_1, choosing a point $(x/2, r/4)$, or a government with *LIB*, again with probability ρ_1 but choosing the point $(x/2, -r/4)$.

The outcome is therefore a lottery:

outcome $(0, 0)$ with probability ρ_2;
outcome $(x/2, r/4)$ with probability ρ_1;
outcome $(x/2, -r/4)$ with probability ρ_1.

In order to evaluate this lottery, we must make some assumptions about the way the Conservative party evaluates lotteries. For purposes of exposition let us suppose that the party treats this lottery as though it were identical to the point in $\mathbb{R}^2$ given by

$$\rho_2(0,0)+(x/2,r/4)\rho_1+(x/2,-r/4)\rho_1.$$

(Variants on this assumption are discussed later.) Then the lottery across the two governments $\{CON, CEN\}$ and $\{CON, LIB\}$ is identified with the point $(x/2,0)$ with probability $2\rho_1$.

The lottery between the $\{CEN, LIB\}$ government with probability ρ_2 at the point $(0,0)$ and the CON governments at $(x/2,0)$ with probability $2\rho_1$ is thus identified with a point $(t,0)$, where

$$t=2\left(\frac{r^2}{s^2+2r^2}\right)\left(\frac{x}{2}\right).$$

Notice that increasing x affects t in two ways: $x/2$ clearly increases, so that the coalition compromises involving CEN and LIB move to the right (in CON's favor), but the probability associated with these coalitions decreases (because s increases as x does). Since we have assumed that the true preferred position for CON is far to the right, CON should choose x so as to maximize t. This is easily seen to be at $x^*=\frac{3}{2}r$, where $s=\sqrt{\frac{5}{2}}r$, $t=r/3$, and $\rho_1=\frac{2}{9}$.

Thus when the two parties CEN and LIB respectively choose positions $(0,r/2)$ and $(0,-r/2)$, there is a best response, $(3r/2,0)$, by CON under the conditions specified. Note also that, when CON responds by the manifesto declaration $(3r/2,0)$, it is in its best interests to act in the ensuing coalition negotiations as though its true preferred policy position were its declared policy position. To see this, note that if CON attempts to implement a position $(x,0)$ with $x>x^*$ then the coalition $\{CEN, LIB\}$ can retaliate by increasing the probability ρ_2 that it forms. The lottery equivalent outcome then moves to the left, which is not in the interests of CON. It is therefore rational for CON to assume that, whatever its declared policy position, it is committed to acting as though this declared position were its true preferred position. This phenomenon can be called *equilibrium commitment*.

The second point to notice is that the lottery equivalent point $(r/3,0)$ is in the convex hull of the declared positions of the three parties. Indeed, because of the assumption of a fixed decisive structure $\mathfrak{D}$, the lottery equivalent point belongs to the heart $H(\mathfrak{D})$, which in this particular case is simply the convex hull of $\{z_1,z_2,z_3\}$.

The third point is that the best response declaration by CON is much less extreme than its true preferred position. Although we have not mentioned the true preferred positions of the two center parties, CEN and LIB, it is reasonable to infer that the lottery equivalent point (under best response) belongs to the convex hull of the true positions of the parties. To justify this, however, we need to examine the existence of a Nash equilibrium in this model.

We now set up the general form of our model. For the typical multi-party coalition game involving the set $N = \{1, \ldots, n\}$ of parties on the space W, each party i has a true preference correspondence $P_i \colon W \to W$, where $P_i(x)$ is the convex set of outcomes strictly preferred to x. Any point x_i such that $P_i(x_i) = \emptyset$ is a bliss point for party i.

Let $\tilde{W}$ refer to the space of finite lotteries over W, and similarly, for any $A \subset W$, let $\tilde{A}$ be the subspace of lotteries over points in A. Preference correspondences are extended over $\tilde{W}$ and also written $P_i \colon \tilde{W} \to \tilde{W}$. The lottery outcome function $f \colon W^N \to \tilde{W}$ maps a profile $z = (z_1, \ldots, z_n) \in W^N$ to a lottery $f(z)$ in $\tilde{Z}$, where $Z = \{z_1, \ldots, z_n\}$.

Definition 1. For each i, the outcome function defines an induced preference correspondence $f^{-1}(P_i) \colon W \times W^{N-\{i\}} \to W$ by

$$z_i' \in f^{-1}(P_i)(z_i, (z_{N-i})) \quad \text{if and only if} \quad f(z_i', (z_{N-i})) \in P_i(f(z_i, (z_{N-i}))).$$

Here $z_{N-i} = (z_1, \ldots, z_{i-1}, z_{i+1}, \ldots, z_n) \in W^{N-\{i\}}$. A best response by i to z_{N-i} is the set $\{z_i^* \colon f^{-1}(P_i)(z_i^*, z_{N-i}) = \emptyset\}$. A *Nash equilibrium* for f is a manifesto profile $z^* = (z_1^*, \ldots, z_n^*)$ such that, for all i, $f^{-1}(P_i(z_i^*, z_{N-i}^*)) = \emptyset$.

In proving existence of a Nash equilibrium, it is usual to use the Fan (1961)–Bergstrom (1975, 1992) theorem, making use of the compactness of W and continuity of the outcome function, and assuming that the induced preference correspondences are continuous and convex-valued. In the models presented here the outcome function and induced preference correspondences will be continuous, but under some conditions the latter need not be convex-valued. Consequently, we introduce the notion of a local Nash equilibrium.

Definition 2. A *local Nash equilibrium* for f is a manifesto profile z^* such that, for all i, there exists a neighborhood $U(z_i^*)$ of z_i^* in W with $f^{-1}(P_i)(z_i^*, z_{N-i}^*) \cap U(z_i^*) = \emptyset$.

We now set up the first model and show existence of a Nash equilibrium.

Model 1

There are three parties $N = \{1, 2, 3\}$ and a fixed decisive structure $\mathfrak{D} = \{\{1, 2\}, \{1, 3\}, \{2, 3\}\}$. Each party i has a Euclidean utility function u_i, based on a bliss point x_i, with domain W (a convex, compact subset of $\mathbb{R}^2$), containing the convex hull of $\{x_1, x_2, x_3\}$.

For a profile $z = (z_1, z_2, z_3)$ of declared positions, the outcome is the lottery

$$f(z) = \sum_{\mathfrak{D}} \rho_M z_M.$$

That is, for coalition $M = \{i, j\}$, $z_M = (z_i + z_j)/2$ is the coalition outcome, and the probability of occurrence ρ_M is inversely proportional to $\|z_i - z_j\|^2$.

It is usual to assume that when preference on W is induced from a utility function $u_i : W \to \mathbb{R}$, u_i can be extended to a von Neumann-Morgenstern utility function $U_i : \tilde{W} \to \mathbb{R}$, where for any lottery $f(z) = \sum \rho_M z_M$, U_i is defined by

$$U_i(f(z)) = E(u_i(f(z))) = \sum \rho_M u_i(z_M).$$

Here E is the expectation operator.

In the case of a Euclidean function u_i, it is clear that u_i is *concave*. That is, for any $z_1, z_2 \in W$ and $\lambda \in [0, 1]$,

$$u_i(\lambda z_1 + (1-\lambda)z_2) \geq \lambda u_i(z_1) + (1-\lambda) u_i(z_2).$$

Consequently, the von Neumann–Morgenstern assumption requires that i be *risk averse;* namely, that

$$u_i(E(f(z))) \geq U_i(f(z)).$$

Again $E : \tilde{W} \to W$ is the expectation operator mapping the lottery $f(z) = \sum \rho_M z_M$ to the point in W defined by interpreting the probabilities simply as coefficients. It is useful to modify the implicit assumption of risk aversion without changing the definition of utility function u_i on W. One way to do this is to extend u_i over $\tilde{W}$ by defining the extension $\bar{u}_i$ on a lottery $f(z)$ to be the value of the expectation of the outcomes. That is, let $\bar{u}_i : \tilde{W} \to \mathbb{R}$ be given by $\bar{u}_i(f(z)) = u_i(E(f(z)))$. By definition this requires that u_i be risk neutral. Such an assumption makes sense if the events being considered have extended duration. To determine the effects of attitude to risk, we distinguish between these two assumptions.

Assumption A (expected outcome). Each individual has a Euclidean utility function $u_i : W \to \mathbb{R}$ which is extended to $\bar{u}_i : \tilde{W} \to \mathbb{R}$ by defining the value of $\bar{u}$ on the lottery $f(z) = \sum \rho_M z_M$ to be $u_i(E(f(z)))$. The preference correspondence $P_i : \tilde{W} \to \tilde{W}$ is induced from $\bar{u}_i$ in the usual way. When this assumption is utilized we shall simply write $f(z)$ for $E(f(z))$ and u_i for $\bar{u}_i$.

Assumption B (expected utility). For each i, the preference correspondence $P_i : \tilde{W} \to \tilde{W}$ is induced from a von Neumann-Morgenstern utility function $U_i : \tilde{W} \to \mathbb{R}$ defined as before by $U_i(f(z)) = Eu_i(f(z))$, where u_i is a Euclidean utility function on W. The lottery equivalent for party i is the equivalence class $[f(z)]_i$ of points satisfying $u_i([f(z)]_i) = U_i(f(z))$.

Theorem 1A. *There exists a local Nash equilibrium in Model 1, under Assumption A.*

The proof of Theorem 1A is given in Appendix 1. To interpret the proof of this theorem, suppose that parties j, k have chosen positions z_j, z_k. The decision problem for party i is to choose a position $z_i = (x, y) \in W$ such that the outcome f, which can be written as a function of (x, y), results in a local maximum of the utility u_i. Then

$$f(x, y) = (f_1(x, y), f_2(x, y))$$

$$= \rho_j(x, y)\left[\frac{z_i + z_j}{2}\right] + \rho_k(x, y)\left[\frac{z_i + z_k}{2}\right] + (1 - \rho_j - \rho_k)\left[\frac{z_j + z_k}{2}\right] \in \mathbb{R}^2.$$

Here $\rho_j = \rho_j(x, y)$ and $\rho_k = \rho_k(x, y)$ are the probabilities associated with coalitions $\{i, j\}$ and $\{i, k\}$, respectively.

We show that the best response is given by the Jacobian equation

$$\begin{pmatrix} \dfrac{\partial u_i}{\partial x} \\ \dfrac{\partial u_i}{\partial y} \end{pmatrix} = \begin{pmatrix} \dfrac{\partial f_1}{\partial x} & \dfrac{\partial f_2}{\partial x} \\ \dfrac{\partial f_1}{\partial y} & \dfrac{\partial f_2}{\partial y} \end{pmatrix} \begin{pmatrix} \dfrac{\partial u_i}{\partial f_1} \\ \dfrac{\partial u_i}{\partial f_2} \end{pmatrix} = J_i(du) = 0.$$

Here J_i is the Jacobian of the coordinate transformation taking gradients with respect to outcomes (f_1, f_2) to gradients with respect to the strategic variables (x, y). It is further shown that J_i is essentially a quadratic form given by

$$J_i = \tfrac{1}{2}(\rho_j + \rho_k)I + \Lambda J_0 \Lambda'.$$

Here Λ and Λ' are linear coordinate transformations involving the positions z_j, z_k and the strategic variable $z_i = (x, y)$, while J_0 is a two-by-two matrix whose entries involve the probabilities ρ_j, ρ_k and distances $\|z_i - z_j\|, \|z_i - z_k\|$, and whose diagonal entries are negative. It is because of this structure that the Jacobian equation has a solution, giving a local maximum for u_i.

The simple version of the model presented earlier in this section can also be used to illustrate one important feature of the model. We showed in Example 2 that if CON had a bliss point at $(L, 0)$ with $L \gg 0$ then there was a best response $(x^*, 0) = (\tfrac{3}{2}r, 0)$ giving an outcome $(f_1, f_2) = (\tfrac{2}{9} \cdot \tfrac{3}{2}r, 0)$. We show in the proof of Theorem 1A that if $L = r/3 - \delta$ for some $\delta > 0$, then the best response of CON is to set $x^* = \tfrac{3}{2}r + \delta'$ or $x^* = \tfrac{3}{2} - \delta''$, where δ' and δ'' are functionally dependent on δ. By choosing x^* in this way, it is possible for CON to force the lottery outcome (f_1^*, f_2^*) to be equal to its preferred position $(L, 0)$.

Note, however, that for $L < r/3$ the induced preference is not convex-valued, so that the critical response correspondence is not single-valued. Determining the local Nash equilibria is difficult. However, the earlier discussion of the symmetric case shows that for $L > r/3$ a best response is to choose x so that $s > r$. In this case, *divergence* of declared positions occurs, and the Nash equilibrium declarations lie on the boundary of the (compact) domain W. Computer simulation indicates that the expectation of the lottery outcome lies within the convex hull of the true preferred positions of the parties.

Theorem 1B.   *There exists a Nash equilibrium in Model 1, under Assumption B.*

Appendix 1 sets out the problem of maximizing the von Neumann–Morgenstern utility function $U_i(x, y) = \sum \rho_M u_i(z_M)$, where $(x, y) \in \mathbb{R}^2$ is the party declaration.

In the symmetric case $r = r_1 = r_2$, it is shown that the von Neumann–Morgenstern utility is concave along the x-axis, so a global maximum for U_i exists at a point $(x^*, y^*) = (\alpha(L), 0)$, where $\alpha(L)$ is functionally dependent on L. When the three parties' bliss points are equidistant, the Nash equilibrium z^* is symmetric in the sense that $\|z_1^* - z_2^*\| = \|z_2^* - z_3^*\| = \|z_1^* - z_3^*\|$. These symmetric equilibrium positions need not, in general, lie inside the Pareto set (the convex hull of the bliss points) of the parties. Note however that the expectation $E(f(z^*))$ of the lottery lies within this Pareto set. See Parks and Schofield (in preparation) for full analysis.

Model 2

To extend Model 1 in two dimensions to the case with $n > 3$ parties, we first consider a fixed decisive structure $\mathfrak{D}$. Suppose each party i has a true Euclidean utility function $u_i(x) = -\frac{1}{2}\|x - x_i\|^2$ which can be extended linearly over lotteries on W. Let $z = (z_1, \ldots, z_n)$ be a profile of strategy choices, and for each $M \in \mathfrak{D}$ let $z_M = (1/|M|)\sum_{i \in M} z_i$ be the coalition outcome. The probability ρ_M that coalition M forms the government is inversely proportional to the variance $\sigma^2(z_M) = (1/|M|)\sum_{i \in M}\|z_i - z_M\|^2$. The lottery outcome $f = (f_1, f_2)$ is $f = \sum_{M \in \mathfrak{D}} \rho_M z_M$. To determine the optimal choice z_i for player i given that $\{z_k : z_k \neq i\}$ are chosen, we may express f as the sum of two components, one of which involves z_i directly. That is, let $\{M_1, \ldots, M_\beta\}$ be those coalitions in $\mathfrak{D}(z)$ that contain i, and let $\{M_{\beta+1}, \ldots, M_v\}$ be those that do not. Then

$$f(z) = \sum_{j=1}^{\beta} \rho_j(z_i) \frac{z_i}{|M_j|} + \sum_{j=1}^{\beta} \rho_j(z_i)(\text{terms in } z_k : k \neq i)$$

$$+ \sum_{j=\beta+1}^{v} \rho_j(z_i)(\text{terms in } z_k : k \neq i).$$

Under Assumption A, the Jacobian equation for party i in Model 2 will therefore have the identical structural form as in Model 1; namely,

$$J_i = \left(\sum_{j=1}^{\beta} \frac{\rho_j(z_i)}{|M_j|} \right) I + \Lambda J_0 \Lambda'.$$

In this case J_0 will be a $(v-1) \times (v-1)$ matrix whose entries capture the relationships between coalition probabilities and the distances between parties.

It is evident that the vector equation $J_i(du) = 0$ has a solution just as in Model 1. Since this equation is a generalized quadratic form, its solution gives existence of a local maximum of u_i, and thus a local best response.

The results of Model 1 suggest that a (local) Nash equilibrium exists in Model 2 under both Assumptions A and B. When many coalitions are possible it is evident that the optimization problem is quite difficult, and it may be theoretically more tractable to examine the possibility of mixed-strategy equilibria, where parties may randomize across declarations.

The previous models have not considered the possibility that the membership of a coalition also rewards the party in a nonpolicy fashion with ministries or portfolios (see Austen-Smith and Banks 1988; Laver and Schofield 1990).

Appendix 1 considers Model 1 under the expected utility hypothesis, when the private reward is of order σr^2. It is shown in the symmetric case ($r = r_1 = r_2$) that if $\sigma \simeq 1$ then the optimal response $(x^*, 0)$ by the party satisfies $x^* < L$ for all $L > 0$. In particular, if $\sigma = 1$ and $L = r\sqrt{3}$ then $x^* = r(\sqrt{3}/2)$. Thus a symmetric Nash equilibrium exists such that each equilibrium declaration z_i^* belongs to the convex hull of the bliss points. Call this phenomenon *weak convergence* of declarations. This suggests the following conjecture (Parks and Schofield, in preparation).

Conjecture. In the general n-party model with fixed decisive structure and with Assumption B, if private coalition rewards are sufficiently high then there exists a Nash equilibrium $\{z_i^* : i \in N\}$ such that each z_i^* belongs to the convex hull of bliss points of the parties. Moreover, each pattern of private rewards is associated with a unique Nash equilibrium.

A few remarks can be made on possible generalizations of these models. A key assumption is that the lottery outcome is a smooth function of party declarations. This would still be satisfied if the coalition probabilities were weighted by the number of seats held by coalition members. We could assume, as we have in this section, that the seats are fixed or, as we do in the following section, that the proportion of seats held by each party is smoothly dependent on the profile of declarations.

We have also assumed that, once coalition M forms, it adopts the specific policy point z_M on the compromise set induced by the declarations z_i, $i \in M$. This is equivalent to adopting the assumption that in coalition negotiations each party acts as though it had induced Euclidean preferences. It is more plausible to suppose that there is uncertainty about intra-coalition negotiation. Then, instead of assuming that z_M occurs, party i in M could evaluate the coalition in terms of some linear combination $\{u_i(z_j): j \in M\}$. Risk aversion would imply that

$$u_i(E(\{z_j: z_j \in M\})) \geq U_i(\text{lottery on } z_j: j \in M).$$

Greater convergence in such a model would thus be expected.

In principle, it is possible to examine models where the declarations (or messages) transmitted by the parties to the electorate comprise a list of utility functions $\{u_1^0, \ldots, u_n^0\}$ rather than simply positions. There is no theoretical reason why the policy space must be restricted to two dimensions.

In the empirical work (Budge, Robertson, and Hearl 1987) that stimulated the work on this model, the underlying policy space involved many dimensions. However, factor analysis of the underlying data (Schofield 1993) suggested that only two dimensions were fundamentally important in most cases. Hinich and Munger (Chapter 1, this volume) suggest that these fundamental dimensions should be viewed as *ideological* rather than policy-oriented. If we assume that ideological compromise is much more difficult to attain than policy compromise, then it would be appropriate to modify the assumptions made on the treatment of lotteries. With an ideological interpretation, however, it is still plausible that parties are obliged to accept compromise in order to construct government.

In the models presented in the next section, we consider a more general outcome function that must again be substantiated by the beliefs of the parties concerning the nature of the post-election coalition game. An additional purpose is to model beliefs that the parties have concerning the relationship between the profile of declared positions and their electoral consequences.

4   Nash equilibrium with electoral response

To clarify the nature of the calculations that a party might make in choosing its policy declaration, let us first consider an extended example.

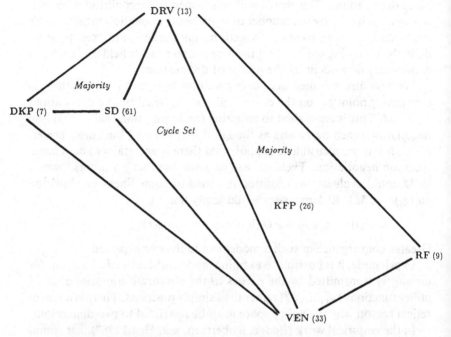

Figure 5. Configuration of party manifestos in Denmark in 1953. The left-right dimension is economic; the north-south dimension concerns social justice and welfare. Note that the *DRV* is the median on the first dimension.

Example 3. Figure 5 presents a typical example from Denmark in 1953. The picture represents the party declarations before the election, and also shows the number of seats obtained by the six parties after the election. Consider this situation from the point of view of the Social Democrat Party (*SD*). After the election it faces a coalition of four bourgeois parties controlling a majority (Radical Venstre, *DRV*; Venstre, *VEN*; Conservatives, *KFP*; Justice Party, *RF*). Let us assume that whatever the party declarations, each party acts as though its utility function were Euclidean and based on its declared position. The post-election heart is the convex set spanned by {*SD, DRV, VEN*}, with bounding coalitions {*SD, DRV*}, {*SD, VEN*} and {*DRV, VEN*}. Instead of considering negotiations between the full set of winning coalitions, we shall follow the arguments set out in Section 2 and assume that negotiations only take place between the three bounding coalitions. Clearly the situation is identical to the one presented in Model 1. Assuming that the conditions of Model 1 hold, and that the party positions are in Nash equilibrium, then the probability associated with the coalition $\{SD, DRV\}$ is high, and the lottery outcome f would be equivalent to a point close to the SD declared position.

It would also be reasonable to suppose that the true preferred position of SD is to the left of its declared position. If we assume that the electoral distribution is unimodal, then it might be the case that the SD would gain seats if before the election it moved its declared position further to the right. A majority of the Parliament is 75, and thus the SD would need to gain 7 more seats to destroy the bourgeois majority. Then the Social Democrats face the difficult problem of deciding whether to move to the right so as to attain a core policy position. The problem, of course, is that the point at which it attains a core position could be less attractive for it than the lottery outcome associated with the three-party negotiation.

Notice, in particular, that if the Social Democrat party does move to the right then there may be a discontinuity in the outcome as the switch from a bourgeois majority to a Social Democrat core occurs. This is not a purely theoretical problem. Danish politics are characterized by alternations between SD minority (core) governments and bourgeois majority governments.

In focusing on the heart in Figure 5, we have implicitly neglected the role played by parties lying outside the heart, such as the Conservatives and the Justice party. To fully analyze the game, we must therefore incorporate the full range of electoral and coalitional possibilities. In constructing our third model, we assume that electoral outcomes are continuous and known with certainty by the parties.

Model 3 (Choice of party declarations with electoral certainty)

We observed in an earlier section that for any selection of policy declarations $z = (z_1, ..., z_n)$ the electorate responds by allocating seats in the ratios $e_1(z) : ... : e_n(z)$. Without loss of generality we shall assume $\sum_{i=1}^{n} e_i(z) = 1$, so that $e(z) = (e_1(z), ..., e_n(z))$ can be identified with a point on the $(n-1)$-dimensional simplex Δ_n. We also assume that W is a compact, convex subset of $\mathbb{R}^w$.

Assumption 1. The electoral map $e: W^N \to \Delta_n$ is continuous and common knowledge to all parties.

We now propose that the choice of party positions z and the post-election seat allocations induce a class of decisive coalitions $\mathfrak{D}(z)$ whose (political) heart $H(\mathfrak{D}(z))$ contains the outcome of political bargaining.

Assumption 2. For each profile $z = (z_1, ..., z_n)$ of declared positions, it is common knowledge to all parties that the lottery outcome $f(z)$ will belong to the (political) heart $\tilde{H}\mathfrak{D}(z)$, where $\tilde{H}\mathfrak{D}(z)$ is defined in terms of the relative seat strengths $\{e_1(z), ..., e_n(z)\}$ and the declared positions of the parties. $\tilde{H}\mathfrak{D}(z)$ is the set of lotteries over $H\mathfrak{D}(z)$.

In Appendix 2, the abstract definition of the heart is given for general utility functions. Under Assumption 2 we propose that each party i acts in negotiation with the other parties as though its policy preferences were defined in terms of a utility function $u_i(z) = -\frac{1}{2}\|x - z_i\|^2$, where z_i is its declared policy. The justification for this assumption is consistency with the choice of Nash equilibrium policies to which each party is committed.

For each profile z of declarations the vector of seat proportions $e(z)$ and thus the decisive structure $\mathfrak{D}(z)$ of winning coalitions is known to the parties. That is, $M \in \mathfrak{D}(z)$ if and only if $\sum_{i \in M} e_i(z) > \frac{1}{2}$. Thus the (political) heart $H\mathfrak{D}(z)$ can be computed. Appendix 2 shows that the heart is well behaved. For example, with Assumption 2, the heart is a subset of the convex hull of the declared positions of the parties. The idea behind the model being proposed is that the full political game can be thought of as comprising a union of games defined on various domains in W^N. For each fixed decisive structure $\mathfrak{D}_\sigma$, say, let $W^N(\mathfrak{D}_\sigma)$ be the subset of W^N that gives rise to the fixed decisive structure $\mathfrak{D}_\sigma$ under the electoral map. The technique of Section 3 then gives a lottery outcome function f_σ defined on $W^N(\mathfrak{D}_\sigma)$. As we have noted, however, there may be discontinuities involved in moving from one domain to another. Since continuity of the outcome function is important in proving existence of Nash equilibrium, we need to construct an outcome function f which approximates f_σ on each domain $W^N(\mathfrak{D}_\sigma)$. As a first step we propose that the outcome function simply be a selection from the full heart correspondence. As we now show, the heart correspondence does admit a continuous selection.

Definition 3. A correspondence h between topological spaces X, Y is

(i) *lower hemicontinuous* if and only if, for any open set $V \subset Y$, the set $\{z \in X : h(z) \cap V \neq \emptyset\}$ is open;

(ii) *upper hemicontinuous* if and only if, for any open set $V \subset Y$, the set $\{z \in X : h(x) \subset V\}$ is open;

(iii) *continuous* if and only if it is both lower and upper hemicontinuous.

Theorem 2. *Under Assumptions 1 and 2, the heart correspondence* $H\mathfrak{D}: W^N \to W$

(a) *is lower hemicontinuous;*

(b) *admits a continuous selection* $f: W^N \to W$ *in the sense that, for all* $z \in W^N$, $f(z) \in \mathrm{Con}(H\mathfrak{D}(z))$, *where* $\mathrm{Con}(H\mathfrak{D}(z))$ *is the convex hull of* $H\mathfrak{D}(z)$;

(c) *is a subcorrespondence of* $\mathrm{Con}: W^N \to W$, *in the sense that* $H\mathfrak{D}(z) \subset \mathrm{Con}\{z_1, \ldots, z_n\}$ *for any* $z = (z_1, \ldots, z_n)$.

Parts (a) and (c) are proved formally in Appendix 2. Part (b) follows from Michael's (1956) selection theorem: any lower hemicontinuous correspondence $h: X \to Y$ admits a selection, namely a continuous function $f: X \to Y$ such that $f(x) \in \mathrm{Con}\, h(x)$. An insight into part (a) can be given in terms of Example 1. Perturbing the KVP position (in Figure 1) a small amount would not change the decisive structure but would simply move the core position. This is continuous. Moving the ARP position in the structurally unstable core of Figure 2 may destroy the core and create a cycle set, with the ARP position on its boundary. The transformation from the unstable core point to the cycle set is lower hemicontinuous. In Figure 3, with a cycle set, if the changes in the party positions are sufficiently small then the decisive structure is unchanged, so the resulting transformation will be continuous.

Assumption 3.

(i)   The lottery outcome function $f: W^N \to \tilde{W}$ resulting from the profile of party declarations is a continuous selection from the heart correspondence $\tilde{H}\mathfrak{D}$. Moreover, f is common knowledge to all parties.

(ii) The true preference correspondence for each party i, $P_i: W \to W$, and the induced preference correspondence, $f^{-1}(P_i): W^N \to W$, are both continuous.

For convenience, in the next definition we write the domain of $f^{-1}(P_i)$ as $W^N = W^i \times W^{n-i} = \{z_i, (z_1, \ldots, z_{i-1}, z_{i+1}, \ldots, z_n)\}$, where W^i is a copy of W representing the strategy space of party i.

Definition 4.   The induced preference correspondence

$$f^{-1}(P_i): W^i \times W^{N-i} \to W$$

is *semiconvex* if and only if, for any $z = (z_1, \ldots, z_n)$, z_i does not belong to the convex hull of $f^{-1}(P_i)(z_i, (z_1, \ldots, z_{i-1}, z_{i+1}, \ldots, z_n))$.

Theorem 3.   *In Model 3 (when Assumptions 1, 2, and 3 are satisfied), if the induced preference correspondences are semiconvex then there exists a Nash equilibrium* $z^* = (z_1^*, \ldots, z_n^*)$.

The proof is by standard application of the Fan–Bergstrom theorem.

Note that if the selection f is constructed, as suggested previously, by piecing together lottery outcomes defined as in Model 2 for different decisive structures, then it might be possible to show that the expectation of the lottery outcome $f(z^*)$ belongs to the convex hull of true preferred positions $\{x_1, \ldots, x_n\}$.

A possible extension of Model 3 would be the case when parties jointly declare a profile $u = (u_1, \ldots, u_n)$ of utility functions that describe, for bargaining purposes, their policy preferences. In this case the heart correspondence has as its domain a function space of utility functions, but will still be lower hemicontinuous (Schofield 1989). In principle, the Fan theorem can still be employed to prove existence of equilibrium.

Model 4 (Electoral risk)

In Model 3, as we have noted, we constructed a continuous outcome function that can be interpreted as a continuous piecing together of lottery outcomes defined over different domains. Underlying this model is the assumption of electoral certainty by the parties. It is perhaps more realistic, and indeed conceptually more elegant, to suppose instead that each profile of declarations determines a probability distribution over the seat allocations. Write Prob(Δ_n) for the set of continuous probability distributions over the simplex Δ_n.

Assumption 4. The electoral map is a continuous function $e: W^N \to$ Prob(Δ_n) and is common knowledge to all parties.

Clearly any seat allocation $e(z) \in \Delta_n$ defines some decisive structure $\mathfrak{D}(z)$, where $M \in \mathfrak{D}(z)$ if and only if $\sum_{i \in M} e_i(z) > \frac{1}{2}$. We can therefore interpret Assumption 4 in the following way. Let $\{\mathfrak{D}_\sigma: \sigma = 1, \ldots, T\}$ be the collection of all decisive structures defined on the set $\{1, \ldots, n\}$ of parties. For each σ and each $z \in W^N$, let $\alpha_\sigma(z)$ be the probability that the decisive structure $\mathfrak{D}_\sigma$ results when parties choose the profile z of declarations. Clearly $\sum_{\sigma=1}^{T} \alpha_\sigma(z) = 1$ for fixed z, so we may write $\alpha(z) = (\alpha_1(z), \ldots, \alpha_T(z)) \in \Delta_T$, where Δ_T is the $(T-1)$-dimensional simplex. The following assumption is more convenient to use.

Assumption 5. The map $\alpha: W^N \to \Delta_T$ is continuous and common knowledge to all parties.

Note that the case of electoral certainty described in Assumption 1 does not satisfy Assumption 5, since all the probability weight can switch discontinuously from α_i to α_j as z changes. For each fixed decisive structure $\mathfrak{D}_\sigma$ and profile z of declarations, we can compute the heart $H\mathfrak{D}_\sigma(z)$, based on induced Euclidean preferences with bliss points $\{z_1, \ldots, z_n\}$. The outcome is now a piecing together of the different selections via the probability weights $\{\alpha_\sigma\}$.

Assumption 6.   The lottery outcome is a continuous function $f: W^N \to \tilde{W}$ defined from the electoral map by

$$f(z) = \sum_{\sigma=1}^{T} \alpha_\sigma(z) f_\sigma(z).$$

Here each $f_\sigma: W^N \to \tilde{W}$ is a continuous selection from the heart correspondence $\tilde{H}\mathfrak{D}_\sigma: W^N \to \tilde{W}$ associated with the fixed decisive structure $\mathfrak{D}_\sigma$.

Theorem 4.   *In Model 4 (when Assumptions 5 and 6 are satisfied), if induced preferences are continuous and semiconvex then a Nash equilibrium exists.*

The proof is identical to the proof of Theorem 3.

Note that Model 4 is a direct generalization of the model of two-party competition presented by Cox (1984). In Cox's model, if one of the two parties (labeled i or j) wins the election then the decisive structure is simply $\mathfrak{D}_i = \{i\}$ or $\mathfrak{D}_j = \{j\}$, so the outcome is simply $f_i(z) = z_i$ or $f_j(z) = z_j$. Thus the lottery outcome is simply

$$f(z) = \alpha_i(z) f_i(z) + \alpha_j(z) f_j(z).$$

Although we have not emphasized this feature, Model 4 can in principle deal with situations where one party or the other has a chance of gaining an outright majority.

Example 4.   Perhaps the general idea underlying Theorem 4 can be given in terms of the Danish case presented as Example 3. For purposes of exposition, let us concentrate on the *SD* and keep the other party positions fixed. Suppose that, in the *SD* position in Figure 5, the pre-election probability that the Social Democrats gain enough seats to block the bourgeois majority (thus making the *SD* a core) is zero. Let us also suppose that the probability of this event at some position *SD'*, closer to the electoral center, is unity. Depending on the probability estimates, the best response for *SD* may be to choose a position between *SD* and *SD'*. Once the election has occurred, the best position for coalition bargaining might be either *SD* or *SD'*, depending on the precise election results. An appropriate way for the party to appear credible to the electorate would be to employ a degree of ambiguity, using mixed strategies in the pre-election game.

However, it is intuitively plausible that even the Social Democrat Party will be rationally committed in coalition bargaining to positions that are less extreme than its true preferred position.

5   Conclusions

The models of political competition presented in Section 3 have the virtue of analytical precision. Making detailed assumptions about the nature of the outcome function (via coalition outcomes and probabilities) permits computation, in principle at least, of the Nash equilibrium. The theorems in Section 4 are more general in one sense, but they do require the assumption that the induced preference correspondences are semiconvex. This assumption is unduly strong. Indeed, it is evident from the analysis of Model 1 that very reasonable models will violate the assumption.

In Models 3 and 4 there is emphasis on the possibility of a centrally located party choosing a policy position that is likely to be a core among the declared positions of the other parties. This feature is not built into Model 2, and suggests that the outcome function constructed in Model 2 be modified somewhat to account for this strategic possibility. A more general model of this kind would give additional insight into the nature of the political trade-offs between electoral and coalitional advantage.

If we accept for the moment the overall plausibility of the models presented here then we can draw some general conclusions, all of which can in principle be shown to be valid under appropriate conditions, and many of which seem to be reasonable inferences from the empirical analyses of coalition behavior.

Conclusion 1: Credible commitment to policy declarations
In Models 1, 2, and 3 it is assumed that, once the profile of declared positions is known, the decisive coalition structure is also known. If a profile z is in Nash equilibrium (and no party has a majority), then it is in the interest of each party to act as though its declared position were its true position. As we saw in Example 1, other parties have the ability to punish any party that deviates from the Nash position.

In Model 4, however, parties choose their positions under some electoral risk. Once the election has occurred they may well move to a different Nash equilibrium policy, defined in terms of the post-election decisive structure. This need not affect the parties' ex ante policy choice. However, it is reasonable to expect post-election policy change in situations of high electoral uncertainty, or after electoral surprises. (It would be interesting to pursue this further with respect to the 1992 Italian election.)

Conclusion 2: Induced Euclidean preferences
For purposes of exposition, we have implicitly assumed that parties act in coalition bargaining as though they had Euclidean utility functions based

on their declared policy positions. This is possibly unwarranted. However, in Model 1 the induced utility gradients (in terms of the strategic variables) are calculated. The Nash equilibrium is shown to be stable, since the gradients point toward the critical point. This suggests, in fact, that the induced preferences can be assumed to be a linear transformation of the true preferences. Even if the induced preferences are non-Euclidean, the results of Models 3 and 4 remain valid if the heart is redefined in terms of profiles of declared utility functions.

Conclusion 3: Pareto property

In Model 1 it is shown that not only is the expectation of the lottery outcome in the convex hull of the declared positions, but that it belongs also to the convex hull of the true preferred positions of the parties and thus lies inside the political Pareto set. A related question concerns the relationship between the lottery outcome and the distribution of electoral preferences. In the case that electoral preferences are Euclidean, recent results have suggested that the electoral heart will comprise an extremely small subset of the policy space (Schofield and Tovey 1992). It is reasonable to regard this electoral heart as the center of the electoral distribution. An interesting theoretical problem is whether the political lottery outcome, resulting from Nash equilibrium policy declarations, belongs to the electoral heart.

Conclusion 4: Core parties

There seem to be two general and conflicting strategies available to parties with true preferred points near the electoral heart. If such a party computes that by choosing a centrally located point there is a high probability that it will be in a core position, then it will do just that. On the other hand, if the probability of such an event is low then the party will choose a more extreme point, hoping to move the outcome nearer to its preferred point. We saw this phenomenon in the proof of Theorem 1.

Conclusion 5: Extreme parties

In terms of Models 3 and 4, a party with an extreme preferred policy point may reason that no equilibrium policy point available to it is likely to put the party in the (political) heart. Since its policy declaration will then have no direct impact on the lottery outcome, its best policy declaration might be its true preferred point. For example, it has been noticed that the Communist party in Italy has appeared unwilling to participate in government coalitions. In the recent Italian election in 1992 this party split in two, with the more "moderate" faction declaring a policy that implied a possible compromise with the Center parties.

A second possibility is the situation in which an extreme party calculates that the center party can attain a core position with high probability. A strategy in this case would be to declare a policy position which has some chance of destroying the core property. In Belgium, for example, small parties such as the Francophone Democratic Front seem to have adopted such a strategy (Schofield 1993).

Conclusion 6: Moderate parties

Moderate parties unlikely to be at a core position, but with a high probability of belonging to coalitions that bound the heart, are likely to adopt policy positions that make them attractive coalition partners to other moderate parties, or (in some circumstances) to parties with centrally located preferred positions.

Some of these conclusions are borne out by the empirical work on European coalition politics (Laver and Schofield 1990). A very general observation, that fits with the general structure of the model, is that in many of the European countries the typical pattern of policy declarations and party strengths is fairly stable over many years. If electoral uncertainty is low, then the equilibrium position of the parties becomes well known. We may even characterize these equilibria as party *niches*. However, dramatic change does occur, particularly when radically different policy concerns become relevant. In general this occurs when new parties, concerned about these issues, come into being. This phenomenon was obvious in Belgium in the late 1960s with respect to the issue of language, and more recently in Italy regarding the issue of corruption.

Multiparty political games of the kind modeled here are extremely complex, and the reader may feel that it is impossible for political elites to calculate in the way described by these models. It is plausible, however, that the real political game is as complex as the one described here but that elites use various heuristics to solve the equilibrium problem. When new parties and new policy dimensions appear, it is usually the case that increased uncertainty exacerbates the difficulty of the problem. When this happens the heuristics do not work, and the situation is usually described as a political crisis.

Even so, the competitive nature of the game might well endow multiparty political systems with considerable adaptability. Of course this conclusion depends on the degree to which new issues become politically relevant, and this in turn will depend on the ability of new parties to form and enter the political arena. It is hoped that later work, based on the models presented here, will address this question.

Appendix 1

Proof of Theorem 1A

We seek to show that if the choices of the first two parties (z_1, z_2) are known then there is a local best response by party 3. Without loss of generality, choose coordinates so that $z_1 = (0, r_1/2)$, $z_2 = (0, -r_2/2)$, and the bliss point of party 3 is $(L, 0)$. That is, define the y-axis in terms of the line joining z_1 and z_2 and define the x-axis in terms of the perpendicular from the bliss point of party 3 onto this y-axis. Assume further that r_1, r_2, and L are positive. Let $z_3 = (x, y) \in \mathbb{R}^2$ be the choice of party 3. Since z_1, z_2 are assumed fixed, the outcome may be written as a function of (x, y). That is,

$$(f_1(x, y), f_2(x, y))$$

$$= f(x, y)$$

$$= \rho_1(x, y)\left[\frac{z_1 + z_3}{2}\right] + \rho_2(x, y)\left[\frac{z_2 + z_3}{2}\right] + (1 - \rho_1 - \rho_2)\left[\frac{z_1 + z_2}{2}\right] \in \mathbb{R}^2,$$

where ρ_1, ρ_2 are the probabilities associated with coalitions $\{1, 3\}$ and $\{2, 3\}$, respectively. Let $(\partial u/\partial x, \partial u/\partial y)$ be the direction gradient of party 3, expressed in terms of the strategic variables, and let $du = (\partial u/\partial f_1, \partial u/\partial f_2)$ be the direction gradient in terms of the outcome (f_1, f_2). Note that du is the true direction gradient of the party. We obtain

$$\begin{bmatrix} \dfrac{\partial u}{\partial x} \\[2ex] \dfrac{\partial u}{\partial y} \end{bmatrix} = \begin{bmatrix} \dfrac{\partial f_1}{\partial x} & \dfrac{\partial f_2}{\partial x} \\[2ex] \dfrac{\partial f_1}{\partial y} & \dfrac{\partial f_2}{\partial y} \end{bmatrix} \begin{bmatrix} \dfrac{\partial u}{\partial f_1} \\[2ex] \dfrac{\partial u}{\partial f_2} \end{bmatrix} = J(du). \tag{1}$$

The Jacobian J expresses the transformation from true preferences to induced preferences via the outcome function f. Because of the coordinate choice, the coalition outcomes take the simple term

$$\frac{z_1 + z_3}{2} = \left(\frac{x}{2}, \frac{y}{2} + \frac{r_1}{4}\right),$$

$$\frac{z_2 + z_3}{2} = \left(\frac{x}{2}, \frac{y}{2} - \frac{r_1}{4}\right), \quad \text{and}$$

$$\frac{z_1 + z_2}{2} = \left(0, \frac{r_1 - r_2}{2}\right).$$

Because f is assumed linear in probability, J takes the form

$$J = \begin{bmatrix} \frac{1}{2}(\rho_1+\rho_2) & 0 \\ 0 & \frac{1}{2}(\rho_1+\rho_2) \end{bmatrix} + (d\rho) \begin{bmatrix} \frac{x}{2} & \left[\left(\frac{y}{2}+\frac{r_1}{4}\right)-\frac{r_1-r_2}{4}\right] \\ \frac{x}{2} & \left[\left(\frac{y}{2}-\frac{r_2}{4}\right)-\frac{r_1-r_2}{4}\right] \end{bmatrix}.$$

Note that the matrix

$$d\rho = \begin{bmatrix} \dfrac{\partial \rho_1}{\partial x} & \dfrac{\partial \rho_2}{\partial x} \\ \dfrac{\partial \rho_1}{\partial y} & \dfrac{\partial \rho_2}{\partial y} \end{bmatrix}$$

captures the changes in the probabilities ρ_1, ρ_2 as a result of changing (x, y). Now $\|z_1 - z_2\| = (r_1 + r_2)/2$, while $s_i = \|z_3 - z_i\|$ for $i = 1, 2$. Since we assume ρ_i is inversely proportional to s_i^2, we may write

$$\rho_i = \left(\frac{1}{s_i^2} + \frac{1}{s_j^2} + \left(\frac{2}{r_1+r_2}\right)^2\right)^{-1}\left(\frac{1}{s_i^2}\right).$$

Then

$$\frac{\partial \rho_i}{\partial s_i} = -\frac{2}{s_i}(\rho_i - \rho_i^2) \quad \text{and} \quad \frac{\partial \rho_i}{\partial s_j} = \frac{2\rho_i\rho_j}{s_j}.$$

Since $s_1^2 = x^2 + (r_1/2 - y)^2$ and $s_2^2 = x^2 + (r_2/2 + y)^2$, we find that

$$\frac{\partial s_i}{\partial x} = \frac{x}{s_i} \quad \text{and} \quad \frac{\partial s_i}{\partial y} = \left(y + (-1)^i\left(\frac{r_i}{2}\right)\left(\frac{1}{s_i}\right)\right).$$

Hence $(d\rho)$ can be written in terms of $\partial \rho_i/\partial x$, $\partial \rho_i/\partial y$, $\partial s_i/\partial x$, and $\partial s_i/\partial y$ as

$$d\rho = \begin{bmatrix} \dfrac{\partial s_1}{\partial x} & \dfrac{\partial s_2}{\partial x} \\ \dfrac{\partial s_1}{\partial y} & \dfrac{\partial s_2}{\partial y} \end{bmatrix} \begin{bmatrix} \dfrac{\partial \rho_1}{\partial s_1} & \dfrac{\partial \rho_2}{\partial s_1} \\ \dfrac{\partial \rho_1}{\partial s_2} & \dfrac{\partial \rho_2}{\partial s_2} \end{bmatrix}.$$

Consequently, the Jacobian can be written in generalized quadratic form as follows:

$$J = \frac{1}{2}(\rho_1+\rho_2)I$$

$$+ \begin{bmatrix} x & x \\ y-\dfrac{r_1}{2} & y+\dfrac{r_2}{2} \end{bmatrix} \begin{bmatrix} -\dfrac{\rho_1(1-\rho_1)}{s_1^2} & \dfrac{\rho_1\rho_2}{s_1^2} \\ \dfrac{\rho_1\rho_2}{s_2^2} & -\dfrac{\rho_2(1-\rho_2)}{s_2^2} \end{bmatrix} \begin{bmatrix} x & y+\dfrac{r_2}{2} \\ x & y-\dfrac{r_1}{2} \end{bmatrix}.$$

The key to solving the equation is that the diagonal probability entries on the right are negative. Although J is not symmetric, the eigenvalues will be real and negative.

(i) To illustrate the solution, in the case of a Euclidean utility function with bliss point $(L, 0)$, the true direction gradient will be $du = (L - f_1, -f_2)$. If we suppose that $L > f_1$ and $|L - f_1| \gg |f_2|$, then a first-order approximation to the solution of equation (1) is found by setting $(\partial f_1 / \partial x, \partial f_1 / \partial y) = (0, 0)$. This gives

$$\frac{\partial f_1}{\partial x} = \frac{\rho_1 + \rho_2}{2} - x^2 \left(\frac{\rho_1}{s_1^2} + \frac{\rho_2}{s_2^2} \right) (1 - \rho_1 - \rho_2) = 0.$$

When $r_1 = r_2$ there is, as we have seen, an easy solution to this equation. We obtain

$$\frac{\partial f_1}{\partial y} = x(\rho_1 + \rho_2 - 1) \left\{ y \left(\frac{\rho_1}{s_1^2} + \frac{\rho_2}{s_2^2} \right) + \frac{r}{2} \left(\frac{\rho_2}{s_2^2} - \frac{\rho_1}{s_1^2} \right) \right\} = 0,$$

which has the exact solution $y^* = 0$ when $s_1 = s_2$. When $s_1 = s_2$ then $\rho_1 = \rho_2 = \rho$, so $\partial f_1 / \partial x = 0$ gives the equation $\rho - (2x^2/s^2)(\rho - 2\rho^2) = 0$, which has the solution $x^* = \frac{3}{2} r$ as before.

The case when $r_1 \neq r_2$ is more difficult to solve analytically. Setting $\partial f_1 / \partial y = 0$ gives

$$y^* = \left(\frac{r_1}{2} \frac{\rho_1}{s_1^2} - \frac{r_2}{2} \frac{\rho_2}{s_2^2} \right) \left(\frac{\rho_1}{s_1^2} + \frac{\rho_2}{s_2^2} \right)^{-1},$$

which is close to 0 when $r_1 \simeq r_2$. From the inverse function theorem the solution for $x^* \simeq \alpha r_1 + \beta r_2$, where $\alpha + \beta \simeq \frac{3}{2}$ for $r_1 \simeq r_2$.

If we perturb the solution (x^*, y^*) to $(x^* + dx, y^* + dy)$ then we obtain

$$\frac{\partial u}{\partial x} \simeq -2\rho x^* \frac{(1 - 2\rho)}{s^2} [2(L - \rho x^*) \, dx - \rho \, dy^2]$$

$$\frac{\partial u}{\partial y} \simeq -2\rho x^* \frac{(1 - 2\rho)}{s^2} [L - \rho x^*] \, dy - \left(1 - \frac{r^2}{4s^2} \right) \rho^2 \, dy.$$

When $L > \rho x^*$ and $L \gg dy$, then $\partial u / \partial x$ and $\partial u / \partial y \lesseqgtr 0$ as dx and $dy \gtreqless 0$. Thus the solution (x^*, y^*) is a local maximum.

(ii) The second possibility that must be considered is when $L < f_1(x^*, y^*)$, where x^*, y^* are the solutions obtained in (i). In this case we must solve the equation

$$\begin{bmatrix} \dfrac{\partial u}{\partial x} \\[2mm] \dfrac{\partial u}{\partial y} \end{bmatrix} = J \begin{pmatrix} L - f_1(x, y) \\ -f_2(x, y) \end{pmatrix} = \begin{pmatrix} 0 \\ 0 \end{pmatrix}.$$

When $r_1 = r_2$, it is easy to see that choosing $y^* = 0$ gives $f_2(x, y) = 0$. The solution for x is obtained by setting

$$L = \rho(x, 0)x = \frac{r^2}{(2r^2 + s^2)} x,$$

where by the assumption $L < r/3$. Solving the expression, we obtain $x^* = (r^2 \pm \sqrt{r^4 - 9L^2r^2})/2L$. Clearly, if $L = r/3 - \delta$ for $\delta > 0$ but close to zero, then there will be local maxima at $x^* = \frac{3}{2}r + \delta'$, $\frac{3}{2}r - \delta''$ for δ', δ'' positive and close to zero.

A third solution is obtained by setting $x^* = \frac{3}{2}r$ as in (i). Since $L < r/3$ by assumption, this third solution corresponds to a local minimum in the x-coordinate; hence $(\frac{3}{2}r, 0)$ is a saddlepoint. Thus party 3 can bring about the outcome $L = f_1(x^*, 0)$ either by choosing $x^* = \frac{3}{2}r - \delta''$, thereby moving the coalition outcome nearer its desired point, or by choosing $x^* = \frac{3}{2}r + \delta'$, reducing slightly the probability of the coalition outcome.

In both cases (i) and (ii) there exists a strategic choice (x^*, y^*) which locally maximizes the utility of player 3. Note that for (i) and (ii), in the asymmetric case when $r_1 \neq r_2$, the solution to the Jacobian involves quadratic equations which thus give both local maxima and minima. Even so, because the diagonal entries in the Jacobian are negative, a stable, locally best response can always be found for the generic positions considered here. The only case that has not been considered is when the bliss point of player 3 is collinear with the declared positions of the other player. It is evident that a best response can easily be found in this case.

We have now shown that for every choice (z_1, z_2) of parties {1, 2} there are solutions to equation (1), which we write as the set of critical responses $R(z_1, z_2)$ by {3} in W. As we have noted, however, the response correspondence $R: W^2 \rightarrow W$ for player 3 is not single-valued; but as a solution to a differential equation it *is* lower hemicontinuous. Indeed, there is a continuous selection b_3 of R such that the response $b_3(z_1, z_2)$ is always a local maximum of u_3. The same argument can be made to show that for each individual i there is a locally best response by i which is continuous in the choice z_j, z_k of the other two parties. Consequently a local Nash equilibrium exists. □

As an illustration of the general concavity of the induced utility function, even under Assumption A, Figure 6 illustrates the function in the case $r_1 = r_2 = 10$ and $L = 5$.

Von Neumann–Morgenstern utilities and Proof of Theorem 1B

It is useful to give an indication of the proof of Theorem 1 under Assumption B (expected utility).

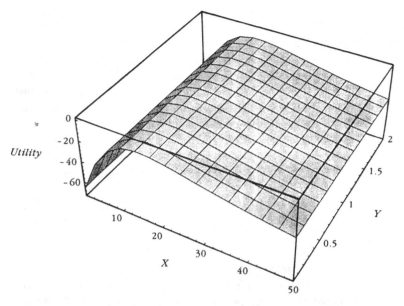

Figure 6. Representation of the induced utility function with true bliss point $(5, 0)$ in the symmetric case $r_1 = r_2 = 10$, in the domain $x \in [0, 50]$, $y \in [0, 2]$, showing a global maximum at $y^* = 0$.

The Von Neumann–Morgenstern utility function can be written as

$$U(x, y) = \rho_1 u\left(\frac{z_1 + z_3}{2}\right) + \rho_2 u\left(\frac{z_2 + z_3}{2}\right) + (1 - \rho_1 - \rho_2) u\left(\frac{z_1 + z_2}{2}\right).$$

Assuming as before that u is maximized at $(L, 0)$, we obtain

$$\begin{bmatrix} \dfrac{\partial U}{\partial x} \\[2ex] \dfrac{\partial U}{\partial y} \end{bmatrix} = \begin{bmatrix} \dfrac{\rho_1 + \rho_2}{2}\left(L - \dfrac{x}{2}\right) \\[2ex] -\rho_1\left(\dfrac{y}{2} + \dfrac{r_1}{4}\right) - \rho_2\left(\dfrac{y}{2} - \dfrac{r_2}{4}\right) \end{bmatrix}$$

$$+ (d\rho) \begin{bmatrix} u\left(\dfrac{x}{2}, \dfrac{y}{2} + \dfrac{r_1}{4}\right) - u\left(0, \dfrac{r_1 - r_2}{4}\right) \\[2ex] u\left(\dfrac{x}{2}, \dfrac{y}{2} - \dfrac{r_2}{4}\right) - u\left(0, \dfrac{r_1 - r_2}{4}\right) \end{bmatrix}. \qquad (2)$$

In the symmetric case $(r_1 = r_2)$, it is obvious that $y^* = 0$, so $\partial U/\partial x = 0$ gives

$$\rho\left(L - \frac{x}{2}\right) + \left(Lx - \frac{x^2}{4} - \frac{r^2}{16}\right)(2\rho^2 - \rho)\frac{2x}{s^2} = 0.$$

An analytic solution is hard to find, but if $L \gg r$ then this equation reduces, as one would expect, to the optimality equation obtained in the proof of Theorem 1A.

For example, suppose we let $x = \alpha r$ and $L = \beta r$ for $\alpha, \beta > 0$. Then the optimality equation relates x to L by $\alpha = \frac{1}{2}(-1/\beta \pm \sqrt{9 + 1/\beta^2})$. Clearly, if $L \gg r$ so $\beta \gg 1$, then $\alpha = \frac{3}{2}$ as before. Since in general there is only one positive root and this corresponds to a maximum, the von Neumann-Morgenstern utility function is concave on the x-axis. Note that $x^* = L$ when $\alpha = \frac{1}{2}\sqrt{5}$. In the range $L \in [\frac{1}{2}\sqrt{5}r, \infty)$ we can deduce that $x^* \in [\frac{1}{2}\sqrt{5}r, \frac{3}{2}r]$, whereas if $L \in (0, \frac{1}{2}\sqrt{5}r)$ then $x^* \in (L, \frac{1}{2}\sqrt{5})$. In particular, if $\beta = 1/\sqrt{3}$ then $\alpha = \sqrt{3}/2$, so if $L = r/\sqrt{3}$ we obtain $x = (\sqrt{3}/2)r$, which gives $s = r$.

Consequently, there exists a symmetric Nash equilibrium z^* with z_i^* outside the convex hull of the bliss points but $\|z_1^* - z_2^*\| = \|z_2^* - z_3^*\| = \|z_1^* - z_3^*\|$. □

Private gains from government

To make the model more realistic, let us suppose that when the party joins the coalition it also receives a nonpolicy side payment (Wittman 1983). To simplify the computation, suppose this side payment is σr^2 for some $\sigma > 0$. Then it can easily be shown that the optimality equation becomes

$$\alpha = \frac{1}{2}\left(-\frac{1}{\beta}(1 + 2\sigma) \pm \sqrt{\frac{(1 + 2\sigma)^2}{\beta^2} + 9}\right).$$

This can be shown to have only one positive root when $\sigma \geq \frac{5}{8}$. For any σ satisfying this constraint, any solution x^* must satisfy $x^* < L$. For example, if $\sigma = 1$ and $\beta = \sqrt{3}$ then $\alpha = \sqrt{3}/2$. Thus a symmetric Nash equilibrium can exist with each z_i^* lying inside the convex hull of the bliss points.

Dynamic computer simulation of this game (Parks and Schofield, in preparation) shows that convergence to the Nash equilibrium is extremely rapid even from initial positions of the parties far from Nash positions.

Appendix 2

To give a formal definition of the choice and cycle sets, we assume that each party i declares to the electorate that it has a smooth utility function $u_i : W \to \mathbb{R}$. At point x, the gradient is defined by

$$du_i(x) = \left(\frac{\partial u_i}{\partial x_i}\bigg|_x, \ldots, \frac{\partial u_i}{\partial x_w}\bigg|_x\right) \in \mathbb{R}^w.$$

This defines the gradient cone

$$p_i(x) = \{\lambda \cdot du_i(x) \subset \mathbb{R}^w : \lambda > 0\}.$$

The *preference cone* of party i is

$$h_i(x) = \{v \in \mathbb{R}^w : v \cdot y > 0 \; \forall y \in p_i(x)\}.$$

For coalition M, $h_M(x) = \bigcap_{i \in M} h_i(x)$, and for a decisive structure $\mathfrak{D}$,

$$h_{\mathfrak{D}}(x) = \bigcup_{M \in \mathfrak{D}} h_M(x).$$

The choice, or *core,* is

$$CH(\mathfrak{D}) = \{x \in W : h_{\mathfrak{D}}(x) = \emptyset\}.$$

Notice that this choice is, of course, dependent on the profile $u = (u_1, \ldots, u_n)$, but that we have suppressed this in the notation. A condition guaranteeing existence of $CH(\mathfrak{D})$ is that for all x, $h_{\mathfrak{D}}(x)$ lies in an open half-space of $\mathbb{R}^w$. In general this cannot be assumed.

We can interpret this condition in another way. For coalition M, let $p_M(x)$ be the cone defined as the convex hull of the cones $\{p_i(x) : i \in M\}$. If $0 \in p_M(x)$ then $h_M(x) = \emptyset$.

Let $p_{\mathfrak{D}}(x) = \bigcap_{M \in \mathfrak{D}} p_M(x)$. Then x belongs to the choice set if and only if $0 \in p_{\mathfrak{D}}(x)$. Now $h_{\mathfrak{D}}(x)$ lies in an open half-space if and only if $p_{\mathfrak{D}}(x) \neq \emptyset$. So this latter condition at every $x \in W$ is necessary and sufficient for existence of a choice. In this case the cone $p_{\mathfrak{D}}(x)$ is nonempty and defines a gradient or dynamic process that approaches $CH(\mathfrak{D})$.

Suppose now that $CH(\mathfrak{D})$ is empty. We seek to define a gradient process whose sink belongs to the Pareto set defined by $\{u_i : i \in N\}$.

For each M, define $hp_M(x) = h_M(x) \cap p_M(x)$. Note in particular that if $0 \in p_M(x)$ then $hp_M(x) = \emptyset$. Any vector $v \in hp_M(x)$ has the property that, for all $i \in M$,

$$v \cdot \left. \frac{\partial u_i}{\partial x} \right|_x > 0.$$

Moreover, for any other vector v' with this property but not in $hp_M(x)$, we have

$$v \cdot \left. \frac{\partial u_i}{\partial x} \right|_x \geq v' \cdot \left. \frac{\partial u_i}{\partial x} \right|_x,$$

with strict inequality for some i. For this reason we call $hp_M(x)$ the cone of *efficient* coalition vectors of change for coalition M.

Definition 5.

(i) The efficient gradient process for $\mathfrak{D}$ is $hp_{\mathfrak{D}}(x) = \bigcup_{M \in \mathfrak{D}} hp_M(x)$.

(ii) The cycle set $CY(\mathfrak{D})$ of this process is the closure of the set

$$\{x \in W : hp_{\mathfrak{D}}(x) \text{ does not belong to a half-space}\}.$$

(iii) The heart $H(\mathfrak{D})$ is defined by $H(\mathfrak{D}) = CH(\mathfrak{D}) \cup CY(\mathfrak{D})$.

If $CY(\mathfrak{D})$ is empty then $CH(\mathfrak{D})$ must be nonempty. (See Schofield 1984 for the proof when W is compact and convex.)

In this case the efficient gradient process $hp_{\mathfrak{D}}: W \to W$ will lead to changes in the outcome which approach $CH(\mathfrak{D})$. On the other hand, if $CY(\mathfrak{D})$ is nonempty and $CH(\mathfrak{D})$ is empty, then the efficient gradient process will approach $CY(\mathfrak{D})$ from outside this set; this process will therefore result in outcomes in the heart. A previous paper (Schofield 1991) argued that negotiation among a small number of agents can be modeled by such a mechanism. We term it "efficient" because under a standard convexity assumption the heart belongs to the Pareto set, as the following lemma shows.

We shall now say that the declared profile $u = (u_1, \ldots, u_n)$ is *admissible* if each u_i is smooth and satisfies the following convexity property:

for all $x \in W$, $\{y \in W: u_i(y) \geq u_i(x)\}$ is a convex set.

Lemma. *If W is compact and convex and the profile u is admissible, then the heart (as defined previously) is a nonempty subset of the Pareto set for u.*

Proof: Suppose that x does not belong to the Pareto set. From standard results (Schofield 1985, for example) this means there exists $v \in \mathbb{R}^w$ such that

$$v \cdot \frac{\partial u_i}{\partial x}\bigg|_x > 0 \quad \forall i.$$

Hence the cones $\{p_i(x): i \in N\}$ must lie in a half-space, and so for every M, $p_M(x)$ lies in the same half-space. Hence so does $hp_{\mathfrak{D}}(x)$. Thus, if $CY(\mathfrak{D})$ is nonempty, it must belong to the Pareto set. If $CY(\mathfrak{D})$ is empty, then $CH(\mathfrak{D})$ is nonempty and by definition this set lies inside the Pareto set. $\qquad \square$

Proof of Theorem 2(c)
Consider now a profile of declarations $z = (z_1, \ldots, z_n)$. That is, each party i implicitly transmits to the electorate the message that its utility function is $u_i(x) = -\frac{1}{2}\|x - z_i\|^2$. Then $du_i(x) = z_i - x$, a vector pointing from x to z_i. Let $\mathfrak{D}$ be the fixed decisive structure defined by z.

Under these conditions, any point x in the Pareto set for N satisfies the condition

$$\sum_{i=1}^{n} \lambda_i(z_i - x) = 0, \quad \text{where} \quad \sum_{i=1}^{n} \lambda_i = 1. \tag{3}$$

Thus $x \in \mathrm{Con}\{z_1, \ldots, z_n\}$. The proof then follows from the previous lemma. $\square$

To give some of the intuition underlying this result, note that if x belongs to the interior of $CY(\mathfrak{D})$ then there exists a family of vectors $v_1, \ldots, v_t$ such that $v_j \in p_{M_j}(x)$, some $M_j \in \mathfrak{D}$, and $0 \in \mathrm{Con}\{v_1, \ldots, v_t\}$. Another way of saying this is that there is a semipositive solution $\{\lambda_1, \ldots, \lambda_t\}$ to the equation $\sum \lambda_j v_j = 0$. Moreover, each $v_j = \sum_{i \in M_j} k_i(z_i - x)$ with $\sum_{i \in M_j} k_i = 1$.

Hence $\sum_j \lambda_j(\sum_i k_i(z_i - x)) = 0$ with $\sum_j \lambda_j = 1$, so x belongs to the convex hull of $\{z_i : i \in N\}$. In particular, a boundary point of $CY(\mathfrak{D})$ can be found by taking the limiting condition $\lambda_j \to 1$, $\lambda_l \to 0$ (for some particular j and all $l \neq j$). Thus $CY(\mathfrak{D})$ is a star-shaped figure within the Pareto set, whose boundary components can be identified with certain winning coalitions in $\mathfrak{D}$. In general $CY(\mathfrak{D})$ need not be convex.

Proof of Theorem 2(a)
The strategy of proof is to consider the choice and cycle components of the heart at z and then to perturb z to a point z', with $z' \in W^N$ close to z. In the natural way, we say $H\mathfrak{D}$ is lower hemicontinuous (lhc) at $z \in W^N$ if there is a neighborhood $U(z)$ of z such that the correspondence $H\mathfrak{D}: W^N \to W$ (defined as in the proof of Theorem 2(c)) is lhc on $U(z)$.

(i) Suppose $H(\mathfrak{D}(z))$ comprises a single structurally stable core component. Then, from the previous results, we know that $z_i \in H(\mathfrak{D}(z))$ for a point z_i declared by the largest party i. In particular, for each $M_j \in \mathfrak{D}(z)$ we have $z_i \in \mathrm{Con}\{z_k : k \in M_j\}$. Since $e: W^N \to \Delta_n$ is continuous, there exists a neighborhood $U(z)$ of z in W^N such that every decisive coalition in $\mathfrak{D}(z)$ is also decisive in $\mathfrak{D}(z')$ for all $z' \in U(z)$. Because of structural stability, there exists $U'(z) \subset U(z)$ such that $z_i' \in \mathrm{Con}(z_k' : k \in M_j)$ for all $z' \in U'(z)$. Hence $H\mathfrak{D}$ is lower hemicontinuous at z.

(ii) Suppose $H(\mathfrak{D}(z)) = CY(\mathfrak{D}(z))$, with $CH(\mathfrak{D}(z)) = \emptyset$. If x belongs to the interior of the cycle set $CY(\mathfrak{D}(z))$, then as before, there exists a solution to the equation

$$\sum_j \lambda_j \left(\sum_{i \in M_j} k_i(z_i - x) \right) = 0, \quad \sum \lambda_j = 1, \quad \sum k_i = 1,$$

where j indexes the coalitions in $\mathfrak{D}(z)$. Clearly there exists a neighborhood V of x and a neighborhood U of z such that, for any $z' \in U$, the equation has a solution for all $x' \in V$. Thus $x' \in CY(\mathfrak{D}(z'))$ and so $CY(\mathfrak{D}) = H(\mathfrak{D})$ is lhc at z.

(iii) The proof of lower hemicontinuity at a structurally unstable core point is somewhat more difficult. Suppose that $H\mathfrak{D}(z) = CH(\mathfrak{D}(z)) =$

$\{z_i\}$ is structurally unstable. Then there exists a neighborhood $U(z)$ of z such that:

(i) $\mathfrak{D}(z)$ is fixed for all $z' \in U(z)$.
(ii) $U_0(z) = \{z' \in U(z) : CH(\mathfrak{D}(z')) = \emptyset\}$ is open.
(iii) $U_1(z) = \{z' \in U(z) : CH(\mathfrak{D}(z')) = z_i'\}$ is nowhere dense in $U(z)$.
(iv) $U_0(z) \cup U_1(z) = U(z)$.

At a profile $z' \in U_1(z)$ there exists a solution to the semipositive equations

$$z_i' = \sum_{t \in M_j} k_t z_t', \quad \text{for each } M_j \in \mathfrak{D}(z).$$

A perturbation can destroy some of these solutions. Thus there exists a neighborhood V of z_i such that, for any perturbation z' of z with $z' \in U_0(z)$, there exists a solution to the semipositive equation

$$\sum_{M_j} \lambda_j \left(\sum_{t \in M_j} k_t(z_t' - x) \right) = 0$$

for some $x \in V$. That is, $x \in CY(\mathfrak{D}(z')) \cap V$. Thus V can be chosen so that $H\mathfrak{D}(z') \cap V \neq \emptyset$ for all $z' \in U(z)$. Consequently $H\mathfrak{D}$ is lhc at z. $\square$

REFERENCES

Austen-Smith, D. (1986), "Legislative Coalitions and Electoral Equilibrium," *Public Choice* 50: 185-210.
Austen-Smith, D., and J. Banks (1988), "Elections, Coalitions and Legislative Outcomes," *American Political Science Review* 82: 405-22.
Baron, D. (1989), "A Non-Cooperative Theory of Legislative Coalitions," *American Journal of Political Science* 33: 1048-84.
   (1991), "A Spatial Bargaining Model of Government Formation in Parliamentary Systems," *American Political Science Review* 85: 137-64.
Bergstrom, T. (1975), "The Existence of Maximal Elements and Equilibria in the Absence of Transitivity," Typescript, Department of Economics, University of Michigan, Ann Arbor.
   (1992), "When Non-Transitive Relations Take Maxima and Competitive Equilibrium Can't Be Beat," in W. Neuefeind and R. Riezman (eds.), *Economic Theory and International Trade: Essays in Memoriam J. Trout Rader*. Heidelberg: Springer.
Budge I., D. Robertson, and D. J. Hearl, eds. (1987), *Ideology, Strategy and Party Change: A Spatial Analysis of Post-War Election Programmes in Nineteen Democracies*. Cambridge: Cambridge University Press.
Cox, G. (1984), "An Expected-Utility Model of Electoral Competition," *Quality and Quantity* 18: 337-49.
   (1987), "The Uncovered Set and the Core," *American Journal of Political Science* 31: 408-22.
Dodd, L. C. (1974), "Party Coalitions in Multiparty Parliaments: A Game Theoretic Analysis," *American Political Science Review* 68: 1093-1117.

Eaton, C., and R. Lipsey (1975), "The Principle of Minimum Differentiation Reconsidered: Some New Developments in the Theory of Spatial Competition," *Review of Economic Studies* 42: 27-50.

Enelow, J. M., and M. J. Hinich (1984), *The Spatial Theory of Voting: An Introduction.* Cambridge: Cambridge University Press.

Fan, K. (1961), "A Generalization of Tychonoff's Fixed Point Theorem," *Mathematische Annalen* 42: 305-10.

Hearl, D. J. (1987), "Belgium: 1946-1981," in I. Budge, D. Robertson, and D. J. Hearl (eds.), *Ideology, Strategy and Party Change: A Spatial Analysis of Post-War Election Programmes in Nineteen Democracies.* Cambridge: Cambridge University Press.

Kramer, G. H. (1973), "On a Class of Equilibrium Conditions for Majority Rule," *Econometrica* 41: 285-97.

Laver, M., and N. Schofield (1990), *Multiparty Government: The Politics of Coalition in Europe.* Oxford: Oxford University Press.

McKelvey, R. (1976), "Intransitivities in Multidimensional Voting Models and Some Implications for Agenda Control," *Journal of Economic Theory* 12: 472-82.

(1979), "General Conditions for Global Intransitivities in Formal Voting Models," *Econometrica* 47: 1085-1111.

(1986), "Covering, Dominance and Institution-Free Properties of Social Choice," *American Journal of Political Science* 30: 283-314.

McKelvey, R., and N. Schofield (1986), "Structural Instability of the Core," *Journal of Mathematical Economics* 15: 179-98.

(1987), "Generalized Symmetry Conditions at a Core Point," *Econometrica* 55: 923-33.

Michael, E. (1956), "Continuous Selections I," *Annals of Mathematics* 63: 361-82.

Miller, N. (1980), "A New Solution Set for Tournaments and Majority Voting," *American Journal of Political Science* 24: 68-96.

Parks, R., and N. Schofield (in preparation), "Computation of Nash Equilibria in a Spatial Model of N-Party Competition."

Plott, C. (1967), "A Notion of Equilibrium and its Possibility under Majority Rule," *American Economic Review* 57: 787-806.

Schofield, N. (1983), "Generic Instability of Majority Rule," *Review of Economic Studies* 50: 695-705.

(1984), "Social Equilibrium and Cycles on Compact Sets," *Journal of Economic Theory* 33: 59-71.

(1985), *Social Choice and Democracy.* Heidelberg: Springer.

(1987), "Stability of Coalition Governments in Western Europe: 1945-1986," *European Journal of Political Economy* 3: 555-91.

(1989), "Strategy of Party Competition," Typescript, Center in Political Economy, Washington University in St. Louis.

(1991), "A Theory of Coalition Government in a Spatial Model of Voting," Typescript, Center in Political Economy, Washington University in St. Louis.

(1993), "Political Competition in Multiparty Coalition Governments," *European Journal of Political Research* 23: 1-33.

Schofield, N., and C. Tovey (1992), "Probability and Convergence for Supra-Majority Rule with Euclidean Preferences," *Mathematical and Computer Modelling* 16: 41-58.

Shepsle, K., and B. Weingast (1984), "Uncovered Sets and Sophisticated Voting Outcomes with Implications for Agenda Institutions," *American Journal of Political Science* 28: 49-74.

Taylor, M., and V. M. Herman (1971), "Party Systems and Government Stability," *American Political Science Review* 65: 28-37.

Warwick, P. (1979), "The Durability of Coalition Governments in Parliamentary Democracies," *Comparative Political Studies* 11: 464-98.

Wittman, D. (1983), "Candidate Motivation: A Synthesis of Alternative Theories," *American Political Science Review* 77: 142-57.

CHAPTER 7

Some foundations for empirical study in the Euclidean spatial model of social choice

Craig A. Tovey

1 Introduction

Experiments and historical data analysis with the spatial model of voting call for underpinning theoretical work. Two categories of results needed to support empirical research, categories that have only recently begun to receive attention, are computational methods and statistical convergence.

This chapter surveys results of these types, contributes some new results, and states open problems for further research. We can attempt to give a fairly complete picture of the current status of this research area, because of its newness. We hope that the work surveyed here will aid in the empirical study of the spatial model and stimulate additional advances and applications. In the remainder of the introduction we explain the motivation for each of the two categories of results, and state the principal new results given here.

Computational methods
Use of the spatial model often requires methods of computing ideal points from preference and voting data. As we show in Section 2, it is quite a challenging problem to find the best "fit" to the data, even in one dimension.

In addition, methods are needed to compute solution sets from ideal-point data. A typical scenario that requires such a computational method arises as follows: a researcher has numerical data giving the locations of voter ideal points and of the resulting group choice. The researcher wants to determine whether the outcome lies in a particular solution set, in order

Presented at the Seventh International Symposium in Economic Theory and Econometrics, St. Louis, May 1991. Research supported by a Presidential Young Investigator Award from the National Science Foundation (ECS-8451032) and a Senior Research Associateship from the National Research Council.

to test the predictive power of the solution concept. This requires that the solution set be computed with respect to the numerical data. If the number of voters is small, this computation can ordinarily be performed by hand. But as the number of voters grows, the difficulty of the computation may increase enormously.

We temporarily depart from our scenario to introduce informally some notions of computational complexity. In the field of computer science, computational requirements are generally measured as a function of the size of the problem (in this case, the number of voters) (see [17]). Larger-size problems require more computer time; the key question is, at what rate of increase? Roughly speaking, a computational procedure, or *algorithm,* is considered "fast" if it requires computer time growing as a polynomial function of the problem size. An algorithm is considered "slow" if it requires time growing as an exponential function of the problem size. For example, a procedure that examined all pairs of voters would require time quadratic in problem size, and would be fast; a procedure that examined all subsets of voters would require about 2^n time, where $n =$ the number of voters, and would be slow. There is a corresponding taxonomy of problems: a problem is considered "easy" if there is a fast algorithm known to solve it; a problem is considered "hard" if no fast algorithm is known that solves it. The "NP-complete" problems are a prominent class of hard problems.

Returning to our scenario, we have the unfortunate situation that almost any solution concept worth its salt is hard. This is a consequence of an observation and a theorem. The observation is: most good solution concepts coincide precisely with the Condorcet winner, when the latter exists. The theorem is: it is hard to determine if there is a Condorcet winner [1; 15]. Therefore, most good solution concepts implicitly check to see if a Condorcet winner exists, and so computing them must be hard as well.[1]

This does not mean that the researcher in our scenario is doomed to failure. But this does mean that our scenario demands genuine expertise in computational methods. As researchers begin to work with data from committees comprised of more than a handful of voters (e.g. legislative

---

[1] Fast algorithmic tools are a practical possibility, despite the theoretical "hardness" just explained. The whole field of heuristics in operations research is devoted to practical means of overcoming computational difficulty. One reason this is possible is that the taxonomy given is "worst-case" – many or most numerical cases of a problem may be easy to solve, even if the problem is hard. For spatial data in particular, the theorem cited ([1]) is true only when the dimension is permitted to be large. If the dimension is fixed at a small level (e.g. two in most current empirical studies) then the problem, though not trivial, is technically "easy."

assemblies), we must pay some serious attention to computational methods to support this work. Good algorithmic tools are needed to compute cores, win-sets, and critical levels for various solution concepts, as well as to fit spatial locations to voting data.

The principal new results in the area of computational methods are: NP-completeness of 1-dimensional recovery of spatial locations from historical voting data; improvements in heuristics for multidimensional spatial location recovery; fast algorithms to compute Simpson–Kramer points and α-majority cores in fixed (low) dimension; and fast algorithms to compute membership and critical levels of epsilon cores in two dimensions.

Statistical accuracy of population samples

Empirical studies with the spatial model will almost inevitably involve some degree of randomness, due to variations in individual behavior, imprecision in measurements, use of sample data (e.g. survey or poll data), and other uncertainties of information. As discussed in [31], we would like to extract data on the ideal points of committee members or a population, and make a prediction regarding the outcome based on a solution concept. Can we be confident that a prediction based on polls taken one day will be close to the actual results the next day, given the random factors mentioned (individual variability, incomplete survey information, etc.)?

One approach to this problem is to think of the population's views as having a probability distribution. When a person responds to a survey or votes, it is on the basis of a random sample from this distribution. The problem is then to establish the stability of a solution concept under these conditions.

In the language of probability and statistics, a finite sample of n points from a probability distribution μ corresponds to an empirical measure μ_n. This measure puts mass $1/n$ at each of the n sample points. A solution concept is a function f operating on probability measures, mapping to sets in $\mathbb{R}^d$. If we could establish that

$$\lim_{n \to \infty} f(\mu_n) \to f(\mu) \text{ a.e.,}$$

then the sample statistic $f(\mu_n)$ would be an asymptotically consistent estimator for $f(\mu)$, and we would be confident of the limiting behavior of the sample solution concept.

Thus the second category of results consists of proofs of consistency of sample estimators for various solution concepts. The new results include the consistency of the sample core under supermajority voting, the yolk center, and the epsilon core and critical level.

2   Recovery of spatial locations

In this section we address the problem of "recovering" spatial locations from voting data. From a different point of view, we can define the problem as that of *fitting* the spatial model to data. The idea is that we have data such as roll call votes on how each member of a population voted on a set of issues. We want to determine locations for the voter ideal points or issue locations (or both) that best fit the data.

Let us be precise. In the recovery problem, we are given the following data: a list of voters indexed $1, \ldots, n$; a list of proposals $1, \ldots, m$; a dimension d; and voting data in the form of an $n \times m$ matrix A, where

$A_{ij} = 1$ if voter i voted for proposal j,

$A_{ij} = -1$ if voter i voted against proposal j,

$A_{ij} = 0$ if voter i did not vote on j or the information is not available.

The recovery problem is to specify locations in $\mathbb{R}^d$ for the voter ideal points and for the "yea" and "nay" of the proposals that best fit the data A_{ij}, according to some criterion. The simplest criterion would be to minimize the number of errors – that is, conflicts between the data and the model predictions. When this criterion is used the problem will be referred to as the *simple recovery problem*. More sophisticated weighted-error measures are also possible. For example, one could base the measure on a probabilistic model of individual choice as in [8] or [9] (see also [23; 25]).

Some researchers locate ideal points by an analysis of the content of the proposals (e.g. [18]). This method has both potential advantages (use of expert knowledge, predictive power) and drawbacks (judgment-based, not easily replicable). The recovery problem defined here may not arise when this method is used. However, a constrained version of the recovery problem might arise if proposal content were used to locate the proposals and then voting data were used to recover the voter ideal points. This constrained version can be solved optimally by methods presented later in this section. (The content-based method also seems related to the recovery problem, in that the study of good solutions to the recovery problem could help clarify the understanding of content; see e.g. [24].)

The principal results of this section are:

It is NP-complete (i.e., computationally hard in the worst case) to solve the simple recovery problem, even in one dimension.

In low dimension (i.e., three or less), for the simple recovery problem there are computationally fast algorithms to optimally recover ideal points given fixed proposal locations, and vice versa (recover proposal locations given fixed ideal points). Improved heuristic algorithms can then be developed for both simple and general recovery in low dimension.

The complexity result provides theoretical justification for employing heuristic methods to solve the recovery problem, such as the alternating heuristic of Poole and Rosenthal [23]. The algorithms here lead to some refinements of this heuristic.

2.1   *Complexity of the simple recovery problem*

Surprisingly, the simple recovery problem is not simple, even in one dimension.

Theorem 1.   *The simple recovery problem is NP-complete in one dimension. If the orientation of each proposal is fixed, the problem remains NP-complete.*

Proof: This type of proof is called a "reduction." We start with a different problem, already known to be hard, and show how to transform it into an equivalent version of our problem, the simple recovery problem. The known hard problem is then said to *reduce* to our problem. The idea is that if there were a fast method to solve our problem then we could use it to solve the other (hard) problem quickly, by transforming it to our problem first and then applying the hypothesized method. However, the other problem is known to be hard, so this would contradict established fact, from which we conclude that our problem must be hard too (the interested reader is referred to [12] for details on reduction proofs.)

Our proof will begin with a known NP-complete problem called "feedback arc set," defined as follows. Given a directed graph $G = (V, E)$,[2] one can think of each arc $(i, j) \in E$ as pointing from vertex i to vertex j. Now suppose the vertices V are arranged in a vertical ordering: each arc (i, j) will point upward or downward, depending on whether i is placed lower or higher than j in the ordering. The feedback–arc set problem is to find an ordering of V that minimizes the number of downward-pointing arcs.

To show that the simple recovery problem is hard, we start with an arbitrary instance of feedback arc set (namely, a directed graph G), and show how to concoct from it a corresponding instance of our simple recovery problem (namely, a matrix A as defined earlier in this section). Then we verify that if one solved the recovery problem for A, one would have solved the feedback–arc set problem for G.

---

[2] A directed graph is defined as a structure consisting of a finite set V of elements, called *vertices*, and a set $E \subseteq V \times V$ of ordered pairs of vertices, called *arcs*.

Given an arbitrary directed graph G, insert a vertex into each arc. Each arc becomes a path of length 2, and the modified graph $\tilde{G}$ is bipartite. That is, the vertices of $\tilde{G}$ can be separated into two parts such that all arcs contain one vertex from each part. Associate a voter with each vertex in the first part of $\tilde{G}$ and a proposal with each vertex in the second part. An arc from a voter i to a proposal j will mean a yes vote, $A_{ij} = 1$; an arc from proposal j to voter i will mean a no vote, $A_{ij} = -1$; otherwise $A_{ij} = 0$. Pad the voter set with K "yes" voters, who vote in favor of every proposal, and an equal number of "no" voters, who vote against every proposal. For large K these extra voters force the orientation of each proposal. In particular, K is large enough if $K =$ the number of arcs in $\tilde{G}$. Without loss of generality, suppose the yes voters will be placed at the bottom of the ordering and the no voters will be at the top. (This padding ensures that the problem remains hard even if the proposal orientations are fixed.) Then arranging the voter ideal points and proposal centers to minimize the number of errors is equivalent to arranging the vertices of $\tilde{G}$ to minimize the number of downward-pointing arcs. This is the feedback–arc set problem on $\tilde{G}$.

The last step of the proof is to show this is also the feedback–arc set problem on G. Now, minimizing the number of downward-pointing arcs is equivalent to determining a minimum cardinality subset $\tilde{S}$ of arcs in $\tilde{G}$ such that every directed cycle in $\tilde{G}$ contains at least one member of $\tilde{S}$. Similarly, let S denote the minimum feedback arc set of graph G. Suppose arc (u, v) in G corresponds to arcs (u, j), (j, v) in $\tilde{G}$; that is, suppose j was the vertex inserted into arc (u, v). The two arcs (u, j) and (j, v) intersect the same cycles in $\tilde{G}$, so the minimum cardinality $\tilde{S}$ does not contain both. Hence there exists a 1–1 correspondence between members of $\tilde{S}$ and members of S, and minimizing $|\tilde{S}|$ minimizes $|S|$ as well.

Finally we observe that the reduction is legitimate, because the matrix A has size polynomial in $|G|$. $\square$

The reduction shows that the recovery problem is similar to the problem of scoring a Kemeny election [16][3] and is hard for related reasons [2]. The key similarity is this: in both cases we are attempting to summarize highly multidimensional information from many voters into a single permutation, and we measure the quality of the summary by counting the disagreements between it and the original multivoter data. Intuitively, this is why both NP-completeness reductions are from the feedback–arc set problem, where arcs pointing the wrong way are the disagreements. Of

---

[3] The Kemeny voting procedure, an extension of the Condorcet principle, selects that preference order that minimizes the sum of "distances" to the preferences of the voters.

course all NP-complete problems are equivalent in a formal sense; the similarity described here is meant to be illuminating, though informal.

2.2   Optimal recovery of ideal points with respect to fixed proposals

Suppose the proposal locations are fixed. This could arise if they are exogenously determined, or during a step of a heuristic procedure for the recovery problem as in [25]. The recovery problem then reduces to n independent voter location problems. Conversely, if ideal points are fixed then the proposal-location recovery problem reduces to m independent location problems. We note that proposal location in the dual or polar space is identical to voter location in the usual space. Thus all results in this section apply to both problems.

Theorem 2.   *The simple recovery problem with fixed proposals is NP-complete in arbitrary dimension, and polynomially solvable in any fixed dimension. The corresponding proposal-location recovery problem with fixed ideal points has the same complexity.*

Proof: Each proposal location can be taken as a hyperplane in $\mathbb{R}^d$ with orientation (indicating the "yes" half-space). If a voter is placed in the wrong half-space, an error results. The recovery problem therefore is equivalent to the following: given a collection of linear inequalities, find a location in $\mathbb{R}^d$ that minimizes the number of violated inequalities. This is NP-complete [12, p. 267].

In fixed dimension, a well-known combinatorial formula (see e.g. [3]) states that m hyperplanes partition $\mathbb{R}^d$ into $\sum_{i=0}^{d}\binom{m}{i}$ distinct regions (or fewer if they are not in general position). Thus the voter must be placed in one of $O(m^d)$ possible regions. Obviously the error count is the same for all points within any particular region. The region with the least error count is the optimal solution, and can be found in polynomial time.   □

The Poole–Rosenthal recovery heuristic [23] selects the coordinates of the locations one dimension at a time. For each dimension, the heuristic alternates between fixing the ideal points and fixing the proposal locations, until a locally optimal solution is reached (i.e., until the method ceases to improve the solution). When the coordinates for a dimension have been selected in this way, the heuristic seeks a locally optimal solution for the next dimension, and so on until all are selected [24; 25]. When the simple error count is to be minimized, or the random factor is small, Theorem 2 suggests an alternate version of this heuristic, in which all

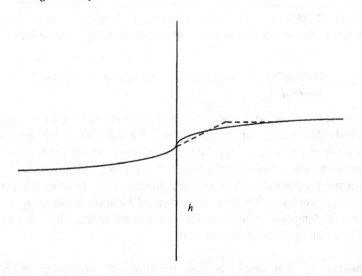

h

Figure 1. Piecewise linear approximation of nonconvex penalty function.

dimensions are considered simultaneously. The more powerful neighborhood structure provided by Theorem 2 suggests that the alternate version would perform better. Of course, given Theorem 1, it is unlikely that the alternate version will *always* dominate the other in numerical performance. To be sure of dominance, one could apply the alternate version to the solution generated by the original heuristic: this hybrid heuristic would be guaranteed always to perform at least as well as the original heuristic.

Theorem 2 holds promise for weighted recovery problems, as well. In the unweighted recovery problem, the penalty is constant within each polyhedral region, so one simply has to pick the best region. In the more general weighted recovery problem, the penalty will vary within each region. If the penalty function behaves tractably (e.g. is convex) on each side of the proposal hyperplane, then one need only solve a convex minimization problem for each region (the sum of convex functions is convex). This would be computationally feasible in two or three dimensions.

Unfortunately, the most widely used penalty functions are not convex. Rather, they tend to flatten out far away from the proposal hyperplane. That is, the penalty for being on the wrong side of the hyperplane is nearly the same at distance 100 or 101; similarly it isn't much better to be on the right side at distance 101 than to be on the right side at distance 100. But there is a big difference between being distance 0 (i.e. on the hyperplane) and distance 1.

For these penalty functions we modify the construction of regions given in the proof of Theorem 2 (see Figure 1). The penalty function is convex on the correct side of the hyperplane, but not on the wrong side. Approximate the penalty on the wrong side by a piecewise linear function. (Note that the piecewise function is concave.) For simplicity suppose there is only one breakpoint. Now place a hyperplane parallel to the proposal hyperplane, at distance corresponding to the breakpoint. If this is done for each proposal, there will be $2m$ hyperplanes in $\mathbb{R}^d$, and still only $O(m^d)$ regions. (The upper bound will increase by roughly 2^d, a modest amount for $d = 2$ or 3. Actually, for $d = 2$ the number of regions increases by a little less than a factor of three.) Within each of these regions, the penalty function will be a sum of linear and convex functions. Now one simply solves the convex program for each region. If linear programs are desired, approximate the penalty function on the correct side by a piecewise linear function as well. If a better fit is desired, one can use piecewise convex instead of piecewise linear functions, or one can increase the number of breakpoints.

3   Computational methods for α-majority cores

In this and the next two sections, we consider algorithmic procedures for computing solution concepts and associated values. The first solution concept we address involves supermajority or α-majority voting.

We let V denote the set of voter ideal points. For any $1/2 \le \alpha \le 1$ let $A(\alpha, V)$ denote the α-majority core, the set of points that would be unbeaten with respect to supermajority rule at level α. Let $\alpha^*(x, V)$ denote the smallest supermajority level at which x is undominated (in the α core), $\inf_\alpha \{\alpha : x \in A(\alpha, V)\}$. Let $\alpha^*(V)$ denote $\min_x \alpha^*(x, V)$, the smallest level at which the α core is nonempty. Thus $A(\alpha^*(V), V)$ is the Simpson–Kramer minimax point. These supermajority cores have very interesting and powerful properties; see [4; 5; 13; 19]. In this section we develop computational methods for these concepts.

There are several related algorithmic problems.

(1) *Membership:* given V, x, and α, is $x \in A(\alpha, V)$? (Is x undominated with respect to α-majority rule?)

(2) *Critical level:* given V and x, find $\alpha^*(x, V)$. (What is the smallest supermajority level α at which x is undominated?)

(3) *Alpha core:* given V and α, find the set $A(\alpha, V)$ or determine that it is empty. That is, find some "good" representation of the α core for the given value of α.

(4) *Minimax level and point:* given V, find $\alpha^*(V)$ and $A(\alpha'(V), V)$. (Find the Simpson–Kramer minimax point and its associated α level.)

As stated in the introduction, all these problems are NP-hard in arbitrary dimension (this follows from the co-NP-completeness of determining if $x \in A(1/2, V)$ [1; 15]). Fortunately, all these problems may be solved fairly easily in low dimension.

(1)   *Algorithm for membership*
The point x is undominated with respect to α-majority rule if and only if no open half-space defined by a hyperplane through x contains more than $\alpha |V|$ ideal points. Therefore we can determine membership by finding the "densest" open halfspace – the open half-space containing the most points of V – and counting the number of points it contains. Johnson and Preparata [15] provide polynomial algorithms to find the densest closed and open half-spaces with respect to a set of points in fixed dimension. This resolves membership in fixed dimension.

One drawback to the algorithm of [15] is that it is moderately complicated to implement. Here we suggest an alternate algorithm that is conceptually simple, and has the same order of speed on nondegenerate cases. The algorithm should be easy to implement, particularly as it requires computations similar to those for the yolk. The principal disadvantage to our algorithm is its relatively poor performance on degenerate configurations, although it is still "fast" (polynomial time) for any fixed dimension. In four or more dimensions, the algorithm of [15] would be much faster on highly degenerate cases.

Construct all the extremal or limiting hyperplanes through x, and count the number of ideal points in each half-space. (A *limiting hyperplane* passes through d affinedly independent ideal points in $\mathbb{R}^d$. The point x is counted as an ideal point, whether or not $x \in V$.) This finds the densest closed half-space, with the same time complexity as [15]. The search for a densest closed half-space is restricted to the limiting hyperplanes, even for degenerate configurations, because any hyperplane through x can be tilted so as to touch d ideal points while keeping at least as many ideal points in each closed half-space defined by the hyperplane [27, Lemma 5]. Let h denote the hyperplane defining this half-space, and let V_h denote the points of V on h, excluding x. If the configuration is nondegenerate, it is possible to perturb h to a new hyperplane $\tilde{h}$, which passes through x and leaves all the points V_h on its dense side. This perturbation is possible because $|V_h| = d - 1$ when the configuration is nondegenerate.

Note that the fundamental operations involved are: (i) finding the limiting hyperplanes, and (ii) counting the number of points in the half-spaces so defined. These operations comprise part of the fundamental operations in yolk computations, which should be an advantage to implementors. In addition, one must count the number of points on h to verify $|V_h| = d - 1$, but this is trivial given (ii). In two (or more) dimensions, the algorithm can be sped up by a factor of $n/\log n$ by the preprocessing

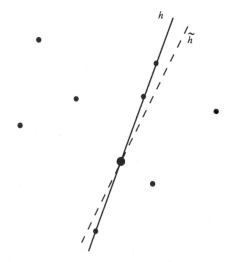

Figure 2. Finding $\tilde{h}$ in two dimensions.

of V [7], just as with yolk computations [33]. The algorithm requires time $O(n^{d-1}\log n)$ in the nondegenerate case (or for the general case, if a densest closed half-space is desired), the same as the algorithm of [15].

It remains to modify the algorithm in the case of degeneracy. If configurations are degenerate, it may not be possible to perturb h to get all the points of V_h on the same side. (Indeed, the densest open half-space might not be a perturbation of the densest closed half-space. However, the densest open half-space is defined by a perturbation of some limiting hyperplane.) Fortunately, the problem of finding the best perturbation of h, that which gets as many points as possible on the dense side, is precisely the densest-hemisphere problem in a lower-dimensional space. This simplifies implementation considerably.

To be precise, we must find all limiting hyperplanes h, and for each h find its best perturbation $\tilde{h}$. If $|V_h| = d - 1$ this requires no additional computation. If there are more points on h, we recursively solve the densest-open hemisphere problem at x for the point set V_h in the $(d-1)$-dimensional subspace h. The base case of the recursion is two dimensions: when $d = 2$ (see Figure 2), h is a line through x passing through two or more (other) points of V. This line is divided into two half-lines emanating from x. Select the half-line with the greater number of points.

Both algorithms extend immediately to the case of weighted voters.

(2)   *Algorithm for critical level*

This could be accomplished with binary search on α using (1). However, examination of either algorithm for (1) shows that they actually compute $\alpha^*(x, V)$ directly, since they find the densest open half-space.

(3)   *Algorithm for alpha core*

Find all the limiting hyperplanes h (those passing through d ideal points). Form a list E of all closed half-spaces defined by these h. Extract a list L of closed half-spaces h^+ containing $\alpha n + 1$ or more ideal points. If a point is to be in $A(\alpha, V)$ it must be in each of these closed half-spaces, for otherwise some other point could get $\alpha n + 1$ or more supporters to defeat it. Therefore the α-majority core is the set of feasible solutions to the linear program that constrains points to be in each closed half-space on the list L.

As a corollary, we find that the α-majority core is a polyhedral set. (This was established for the special case $\alpha = \alpha^*$ by Kramer [19].)

(4)   *Algorithm for minimax level*

This can be found, in principle, by binary search with (3). A direct implementation would proceed as follows: Sort the list E from (3) (there are $O(n^d)$ in this list) in order from largest to smallest number of ideal points contained (descending order of $|V \cap h^+|$). Perform binary search on the cut-off point of E. Each "query" for the binary search solves a feasibility linear program with $O(n^d)$ constraints in d dimensions. (For computational purposes, the dual would probably be faster to solve, since there are far more constraints than variables in the primal.)

If preferences are linear rather than Euclidean (see [5]) all these problems reduce to (2) – critical level. This is because we need to know the densest half-space, the open half-space containing as many preference gradients as possible. As already observed, the densest–half-space problem is solved in [15], or may be solved with the alternative algorithm described herein for (1).

4   **Computational methods for the yolk**

The yolk is another important solution concept, motivated by experimental data and possessed of beautiful theoretical properties [11; 20]. As with the Simpson–Kramer minimax point, it is NP-hard to determine the yolk in arbitrary dimension (as stated in Section 1, any solution concept that coincides with the classical core when the core is nonempty will suffer from this complexity, because it is co-NP-complete to determine if the classical core is nonempty [1]).

For two dimensions, the computational situation is much rosier. Although the extremal median hyperplanes employed in Section 3 are not enough to determine the yolk [29], there is a polynomial algorithm to compute the yolk radius and center, in fixed dimension [33]. In two dimensions, this algorithm requires provably $O(n^{4.5})$ time, and has even better time complexity $o(n^{3+\epsilon})$ for all $\epsilon > 0$ (i.e. nearly cubic) if a conjecture of Erdös et al. [10] is true.

We should also remark that the linear program given in [20] is easily computed and should make an excellent heuristic. It provides a rigorous lower bound on the yolk radius, and when its solution is exact this event can be determined in time $O(n^2)$ [33].

Koehler has proposed extending the yolk to n even. The algorithm just cited also works in this case, with the same time complexity. The algorithm also works for "supermajority rule" yolks (see [18; 30]).

For the 3-dimensional case, the algorithm of [33] has time complexity $O(n^{10})$ and would not be practical for more than a handful of points. This case needs more development but appears to be within reach – either through effective heuristics or an improved optimizing procedure, perhaps making strong use of the convexity of the yolk radius function.

5   Computational methods for other solution concepts

5.1   *The uncovered set*

The uncovered set is another solution concept with powerful theoretical properties. It is defined as follows: alternative x *covers* alternative y if and only if x defeats (is majority preferred to) y, and for all z which y defeats, x defeats z. An alternative x is *uncovered* if and only if there is no other alternative that covers x [21; 22].

The computational picture with respect to the uncovered set is bleak at present. Hartley and Kilgour [14] show how to find the uncovered set in two dimensions when $n = 3$, and their method is not simple. To the author's knowledge, no efficient general procedure is available even for two dimensions, although no forbidding complexity levels (e.g. NP-completeness) have been established for the fixed-dimensional case, either. This remains a challenging open problem.

To get an idea of why the problem is not simple, consider the presumably easier question of determining whether a given alternative x covers another given alternative y, in two dimensions. For any point $z \in \mathbb{R}^2$ and any $0 \le \theta \le 2\pi$, let $f(z, \theta) \ge 0$ denote the distance from z along the ray at angle θ to the first point that z defeats. (Technically f is defined as an infimum to allow $f = 0$.) It is obvious that z will defeat all points on the ray past this first point. It is fairly straightforward to see that for any z, $f(z, \theta)$ takes the form of a piecewise trigonometric function with polynomially many breakpoints. Then the question of whether x covers y is essentially the question of whether the exterior region in the plane of one such function about x contains the exterior region of another such function about y. This could be checked in polynomial time, because each pair of the trigonometric functions will intersect a small number of times, but the procedure would be tedious to say the least.

Therefore, to determine whether x covers y is polynomially solvable, but seems near the limit of computational practicality. Fast methods for determining the uncovered set in two dimensions may be difficult to attain. On the brighter side, McKelvey [20] provides bounds on the uncovered set in terms of the yolk, which can be computed by the algorithm cited in Section 4.

5.2   The epsilon core

Another solution concept of interest is the epsilon core: A point x is considered undominated if there is no point y which is more than ϵ closer to a majority of the voters. This concept was introduced by Shapley and Shubick [28]; promising empirical results are given in [26]; some motivations and properties of the epsilon core for the spatial model are given in [32].

The epsilon core presents the same four algorithmic problems as supermajority voting.

(1) *Membership:* given ϵ and x, is x in the epsilon core?
(2) *Critical level:* for given x, find the least value of ϵ for which x is undominated.
(3) *Epsilon core:* for given ϵ, find the epsilon core.
(4) *Minimum level:* find the least value of ϵ for which the epsilon core is nonempty.

Here we give fast computational methods to solve the first two problems, membership and critical level, in two dimensions. At present I know of no computationally efficient methods to solve the other problems, epsilon core and minimum level.

(1)   *Algorithm for membership*
For given ϵ, the point x is in the epsilon core if none of the hyperbolic regions, with one focus at x and parameter ϵ, contain more than half the

voter ideal points. These regions are all congruent and are found by ro-
tating a hyperbolic curve around x. The number of points in the region
inside the curve changes only when the curve passes over an ideal point.
Therefore we can restrict our attention to the $2(n-1) = O(n)$ curves that
intersect an ideal point. If none of these contain more than half the voter
ideal points, then x is undominated. The membership algorithm is therefore $O(n^2)$. (The same idea works in higher, fixed dimensions, except one
must be careful if the ideal points are sparse; when n is much larger than
d the method extends easily.)

(2)   *Algorithm for critical level*
This is solved by binary search on ϵ, using the membership algorithm as
the query subprocedure.

As an approximate method for epsilon core and minimum level, the crit-
ical-level algorithm could be invoked for each point of a grid. Decreasing
the spacing of the grid would give as fine an approximation as desired.

6   Convergence and asymptotic consistency of sample estimators

In this section we survey convergence results for several solution concepts, as motivated in the introduction.

6.1 α-majority (*Simpson-Kramer*) cores

There are several related convergence questions here, just as there are several related algorithmic questions in Section 3. Corresponding to "membership" we could define a (0–1)-valued random variable that indicates
whether x is an α-majority winner or not. Unfortunately, the sample statistic would not be consistent. In fact we could have the sample statistic
converge to 0 a.s., while the distribution value equals 1 (see [31]). The
other convergence questions have nicer answers.
    Recall from Section 1 that a random sample of n points from a proba-
bility measure μ is represented as a (random) empirical measure μ_n. We
employ the notation of Section 3, using μ_n or μ in place of V as needed.
For example, $A(\alpha^*(\mu_n), \mu_n)$ denotes the minimax set of a set of n points
sampled randomly from μ. We have the following problems.

Minimax value: Does $\alpha^*(\mu_n) \to \alpha^*(\mu)$?
Minimax set: Does $A(\alpha^*(\mu_n), \mu_n) \to A(\alpha^*(\mu), \mu)$?
Critical level: Does $\alpha(x, \mu_n) \to \alpha(x, \mu)$?
α *core:* Does $A(\alpha, \mu_n) \to A(\alpha, \mu)$ in some suitable topology?

Demange [6] considers a sequence of probability measures μ_n converging to μ and shows convergence of minimax value and minimax set. The proof appears to assume continuity of μ_n, and does not appear to apply to the question considered here, where μ_n is a discrete (empirical) measure. Caplin and Nalebuff [4] establish a.s. convergence of minimax value under stated assumptions that μ is concave and has compact support. As they comment, however, their proof applies equally well to the more general case of continuous densities μ with compact support. Moreover, their proof also shows convergence of critical level. Convergence of minimax value for arbitrary μ is proved in [31].

Minimax set and α-majority core are a little different and appear to require stronger assumtions on μ. These questions ask if the location of the solution set converges, rather than if the necessary parameter level for the nonemptiness of the solution set converges. In [31], convergence of minimax set is proved, under the assumption that μ is continuous and has unique minimax point. Convergence of the α-majority core is proved in Theorem 4, under the assumption that μ is continuous and has compact support (see Section 6.3).

6.2   The yolk

There are two related convergence questions for the yolk, pertaining to its size and location. Let $r(\mu)$ and $c(\mu)$ denote, respectively, the radius and center of the yolk with respect to a distribution μ. Convergence of $r(\mu_n)$ to $r(\mu)$ (with probability 1) is proved in [32], assuming μ is continuous and strictly positive in its region of support. If no restrictions are placed on μ, the sample radius $r(\mu_n)$ may not have a limit. I conjecture, moreover, that in sufficiently high dimension, it can happen that $\limsup_n r(\mu_n) < r(\mu)$.

Here we prove the convergence of the yolk center.

Theorem 3.   *If μ is positive-continuous on $\mathbb{R}^d$ and has compact support, then $\lim_{n \to \infty} c(\mu_n) \to c(\mu)$ a.s.*

Proof: We will need two lemmata, as follows.

Lemma 1.   *Let $r(z, \mu)$ denote the radius of the z-centered yolk. Then $\lim_{n \to \infty} r(z, \mu_n) \to r(z, \mu)$ a.s. uniformly over all z.* (This is proved in [32].)

Lemma 2.   *The function $r(z, \mu)$ is continuous and convex in z.* (The proof is easy and found in [33].)

Let c denote $c(\mu)$, the center of the distributional yolk. Then $r(c, \mu_n) \to r(\mu)$ a.s. by Lemma 1. Now let $\epsilon > 0$ be arbitrary. We will show that for all $z \in \mathbb{R}^d$ more than distance ϵ from c, eventually $z \notin c(\mu_n)$ with probability 1. This will imply that $c(\mu_n)$ must almost surely converge to points within c.

Let D denote the set of points in the support of μ, at distance ϵ or more from c. D is compact and so, by Lemma 2, $r(z, \mu)$ attains a minimum value r_D when z ranges over D. By assumption, D does not intersect c. Hence $r_D > r(\mu)$.

Let $\delta = r_D - r(\mu) > 0$. By Lemma 1, eventually as $n \to \infty$,

$$\sup_z |r(z, \mu_n) - r(z, \mu)| < \delta/3 \text{ a.s.}$$

Thus, eventually for all $z \in D$ and all points p in c, we have $r(z, \mu_n) \geq r_D - \delta/3 > r_D - 2\delta/3 \geq r(p, \mu_n)$ a.s. Hence eventually $z \notin c(\mu_n)$ a.s., since there is another point p with smaller p-centered radius. $\qquad \square$

Lemma 3 in [33] gives a related result: If V is any finite configuration of ideal points and $\tilde{V}$ is an arbitrarily slight nondegenerate perturbation of V, then the yolk radius and center of $\tilde{V}$ can be made arbitrarily close to the yolk radius and center of V. In case $|V|$ is even, the center of V may not be unique. In this case, the yolk center of $\tilde{V}$ can be made arbitrarily close to some (but not any) yolk center of V. This result, too, guarantees a certain robustness of the yolk solution concept.

6.3   The epsilon core

In this section we show convergence properties related to the epsilon core. This solution concept and the α-majority concept have similar properties.

Let $\epsilon(x, \mu)$ denote the smallest value of ϵ that makes x undominated; let $\epsilon^*(\mu)$ denote the smallest value of ϵ for which the epsilon core is nonempty; let $EC(\epsilon, \mu)$ denote the epsilon-core at value ϵ; and let $EC^*(\mu)$ denote the epsilon core at value $\epsilon^*(\mu)$.

Theorem 4. *If μ is continuous on $\mathbb{R}^d$ and has compact support, then with probability 1:*

(1) $\epsilon(x, \mu_n) \to \epsilon(x, \mu)$.
(2) $\epsilon^*(\mu_n) \to \epsilon^*(\mu)$.
(3) $\forall \epsilon > 0$, $EC(\epsilon, \mu_n) \to EC(\epsilon, \mu)$. *In particular, if $\epsilon^*(\mu) > 0$, then* $EC^*(\mu_n) \to EC^*(\mu)$.
(4) $\forall \alpha$, $A(\alpha, \mu_n) \to A(\alpha, \mu)$.

Proof: The key property we rely on is that the probability measure of the region defined by a hyperbolic hypersurface changes continuously as the surface is translated continuously through $\mathbb{R}^d$. This follows immediately from the assumptions. Now apply the uniform convergence of the empirical measure μ_n to μ over all these hyperboloid regions [32, Lemma 2] to get convergence of the critical level $\epsilon(x, \mu)$ and the minimum level ϵ^*.

To prove convergence of the epsilon cores $EC(\epsilon)$, we use the same argument as for the convergence of the yolk center in Section 6.2. That is, once we know that critical level and minimum level converge, the continuity of the probability measure and the compactness of its support imply that, for all $\eta > 0$, eventually all points more than η from the epsilon core $EC(\epsilon, \mu)$ will have critical level greater than ϵ. The same proof works for convergence of $A(\alpha, \mu_n)$, the α-majority core, as well. $\square$

7   Computations for large data sets and directions for further research

7.1   Computing solution sets for very large populations

If a population is very large, even the relatively fast algorithms of Section 2 may be too slow for practical purposes. For these situations we may combine the two categories of results in this chapter to obtain fast, accurate computations.[4] Suppose two random samples of n points are drawn from a distribution μ, leading to empirical measures μ_n and μ'_n. Suppose further we are interested in $f(\mu)$, where the a.s. asymptotic consistency of the sample estimates $f(\mu_n)$ is established. Then, since both $f(\mu_n)$ and $f(\mu'_n)$ converge to $f(\mu)$ a.s., it must be that $\lim_{n \to \infty} f(\mu_n) = \lim_{n \to \infty} f(\mu'_n)$ a.s.

Now suppose we have data for a large population P. The data may be thought of as a very large sample from some continuous distribution μ. By the asymptotic equivalence between sampling with and without replacement, we can approximate a sample from μ by a sample from P. Think of P as μ_n. To estimate $f(P)$, we draw samples μ'_m from P and compute $f(\mu'_m)$. The equality of limits in the preceding paragraph assures us that (for large enough m) the sample value $f(\mu'_m)$ is a good estimate of the value of $f(\mu_n) = f(P)$. If n is very large, the required sample size m would be much smaller than n, rendering the problem computationally tractable. (Note that if P has multiplicities then this reasoning fails. I think the method would still work well, but have no mathematical justification except in the case of the yolk, where Lemma 3 in [33] would fill in the gap.)

---

[4] The idea described in this section is due to Richard McKelvey.

7.2   Directions for further research

This chapter has assembled a number of computational and convergence results in support of empirical research with the spatial model. As indicated in the text, several computational problems remain open. These include finding good methods for the uncovered set and epsilon core winsets, and also for the yolk in three or more dimensions.

Regarding convergence results, finding *rates* of convergence appears to be an important open research area. If these could be estimated, and the role of the variance of μ clarified, it should then be possible to construct statistical tests (e.g. confidence intervals) for empirically computed values such as the yolk radius and location, or the minimax level.

REFERENCES

[1] Bartholdi, John J., N. Narasimhan, and Craig A. Tovey (1991), "Recognizing Majority-rule Equilibrium in Spatial Voting Games," *Social Choice and Welfare* 8: 183-97.
[2] Bartholdi, John J., Craig A. Tovey, and Michael A. Trick (1989), "Voting Schemes for which It Can Be Difficult to Tell Who Won the Election," *Social Choice and Welfare* 6: 157-65.
[3] Buck, R. C. (1943), "Partition of Space," *American Mathematical Monthly* 50: 541-4.
[4] Caplin, Andrew, and Barry Nalebuff (1988), "On 64% Majority Rule," *Econometrica* 56: 787-814.
[5] Caplin, Andrew, and Barry Nalebuff (1991), "Aggregation and Social Choice: A Mean Voter Theorem," *Econometrica* 59: 1-24.
[6] Demange, Gabrielle (1982), "A Limit Theorem on the Minmax Set," *Journal of Mathematical Economics* 9: 145-64.
[7] Edelsbrunner, H., D. G. Kirkpatrick, and H. A. Maurer (1982), "Polygonal Intersection Searching," *Information Processing Letters* 14: 74-9.
[8] Enelow, James, and Melvin Hinich (1984), *The Spatial Theory of Voting*. Cambridge: Cambridge University Press.
[9] Enelow, James, and Melvin Hinich (1989), "A General Probabilistic Spatial Theory of Elections," *Public Choice* 61: 101-13.
[10] Erdös, P., L. Lovasz, A. Simmons, and E. G. Straus (1973), "Dissection Graphs of Planar Point Sets," in J. N. Srivastava et al. (eds.), *A Survey of Combinatorial Theory*. Amsterdam: North-Holland.
[11] Ferejohn, John A., Richard McKelvey, and Edward Packel (1984), "Limiting Distributions for Continuous State Markov Models," *Social Choice and Welfare* 1: 45-67.
[12] Garey, Michael, and David Johnson (1978), *Computers and Intractability: A Guide to the Theory of NP-Completeness*. San Francisco: Freeman.
[13] Greenberg, Joseph (1979), "Consistent Majority Rules over Compact Sets of Alternatives." *Econometrica* 47: 627-36.
[14] Hartley, Richard, and Marc Kilgour (1987), "The Geometry of the Uncovered Set in the Three-Voter Spatial Model," *Mathematical Social Sciences* 14: 175-83.

[15] Johnson, David S., and F. P. Preparata (1978), "The Densest Hemisphere Problem," *Theoretical Computer Science* 6: 93-107.

[16] Kemeny, J. (1959), "Mathematics without Numbers," *Daedalus* 88: 571-91.

[17] Knuth, Donald E. (1973), *The Art of Computer Programming: Fundamental Algorithms.* Reading, MA: Addison-Wesley.

[18] Koehler, David H. (1990), "The Size of the Yolk: Computations for Odd and Even-numbered Committees," *Social Choice and Welfare* 7: 231-45.

[19] Kramer, Gerald H. (1977), "A Dynamical Model of Political Equilibrium," *Journal of Economic Theory* 16: 310-34.

[20] McKelvey, Richard D. (1986), "Covering, Dominance, and Institution Free Properties of Social Choice," *American Journal of Political Science* 30: 283-314.

[21] Miller, N. R. (1980), "A New Solution Set for Tournaments and Majority Voting," *American Journal of Political Science* 24: 68-96.

[22] Miller, N. R. (1983), "The Covering Relation in Tournaments: Two Corrections," *American Journal of Political Science* 27: 382-5.

[23] Poole, Keith, and Howard Rosenthal (1985), "A Spatial Model for Legislative Roll Call Analysis," *American Journal of Political Science* 29: 357-84.

[24] Poole, Keith, and Howard Rosenthal (1990), "Spatial Realignment and the Mapping of Issues in American History: the Evidence from Roll Call Voting," Technical Report GSIA WP 1990-41, Carnegie Mellon University, Pittsburgh.

[25] Poole, Keith, and Howard Rosenthal (1991), "Patterns of Congressional Voting," *American Journal of Political Science* 35: 228-78.

[26] Salant, Stephen W., and Eban Goodstein (1990), "Predicting Committee Behavior in Majority Rule Voting Experiments," *RAND Journal of Economics* 21: 293-313.

[27] Schofield, Norman J., and Craig A. Tovey (1992), "Probability and Convergence of Supra-majority Rule with Euclidean Preferences," *Mathematical and Computer Modelling* 16: 41-58.

[28] Shapley, Lloyd, and Martin Shubick (1966), "Quasi-cores in a Monetary Economy with Non-convex Preferences," *Econometrica* 34: 805-27.

[29] Stone, Richard E., and Craig A. Tovey (1992), "Limiting Median Lines Do Not Suffice to Determine the Yolk," *Social Choice and Welfare* 9: 33-5.

[30] Tovey, Craig A. (1990), "The Almost Surely Shrinking Yolk," Technical Report 161, Center in Political Economy, Washington University, St. Louis (submitted to *Mathematics of Operations Research*).

[31] Tovey, Craig A. (1991), "A Critique of Distributional Analysis," Technical Report NPSOR-91-16, Department of Operations Research, Naval Postgraduate School, Monterey, CA (forthcoming in *American Political Science Review*).

[32] Tovey, Craig A. (1991), "The Instability of Instability," Technical Report NPSOR-91-15, Department of Operations Research, Naval Postgraduate School, Monterey, CA (forthcoming in *American Political Science Review*).

[33] Tovey, Craig A. (1992), "A Polynomial Algorithm for Computing the Yolk in Fixed Dimension," *Mathematical Programming* 57: 259-77.

Political institutions

Communication in institutions: Efficiency in a repeated Prisoner's Dilemma with hidden information

Randall L. Calvert

1 Introduction

All political behavior occurs in a context of established patterns of inter-action. These patterns may be as informal as a relationship of trust and reciprocity between two career legislators, or as formal as the written rules of an organization. Political scientists refer to such patterns, even sometimes the least formal ones, as "institutions."[1] For analytical pur-poses, we often portray political behavior as though it took place among rational actors against a fixed institutional background, the "rules of the game." Koford (1982), for example, models legislative leadership as a pro-cess of working out vote trades among the rank and file, using a fictional "medium of exchange" to clear the "market." But the model's fictitious medium, and the trades themselves, really stand for the carrying out of promises and the presence of trust; there can really be no medium of ex-change and few spot trades in this market. Other prominent examples are the study of structure-induced equilibrium (beginning with Shepsle and Weingast 1981) and the spatial model of electoral competition (begin-ning with Downs 1957), both of which rest on the existence of fixed rules of procedure and of established expectations about the future perfor-mance of politicians based on institutional prescriptions. Such portrayals

Presented at the Conference on Political Economy, Washington University, St. Louis, May 22-25, 1991. Research and writing of this paper were funded by the National Science Foun-dation through grants SES-8908226 and BNS-9700864, the latter through the Center for Advanced Study in the Behavioral Sciences, which generously supported the author as a Fellow during 1990-91. The author thanks participants in the Hoover Institution Seminar on Collective Choice for comments on an early draft, and John Nachbar and an anony-mous referee for helpful comments.
[1] For a brief survey of various uses of the concept, see Jackson (1990, pp. 10-13).

197

are convenient fictions for analyzing many political phenomena. However, to achieve their analytical leverage they ignore a factor of enormous long-run importance: The trust and rules and institutions that give structure to these political interactions cannot be created arbitrarily, and are constantly subject to controlled and uncontrolled change.

Using this same rational-actor approach, it is possible to analyze institutions at a deeper level. Schotter (1981) suggested that institutions be viewed as equilibrium behavior patterns in some underlying game defined by nature (or, as in the literature just cited, by pre-existing behavior patterns assumed to be stable). This was an apt description of what an institution really is: a persistent pattern of behavior to which all actors adhere because each knows that others will adhere and will expect adherence, in such a way that any individual who deviates is made worse off. Other equilibrium patterns of behavior may be possible, but a society or group, whether by planning or through spontaneous emergence, "institutes" one of them in particular. From Schotter's point of view, then, one understands institutions by understanding the underlying game and the properties of the particular observed equilibrium institution (and how it might have arisen).

Real-life institutions often involve elements of communication: Actors make known to others their willingness to trade, their preferred candidate, their factual findings, or their orders or suggestions for action, and such communication affects other actors' subsequent behavior in a systematic way. One model in which institutions play a communication role portrays institutions as methods of solving coordination problems. In Schelling (1960, p. 144), Farrell (1987), and Calvert (1992a), mediation or leadership institutions perform the function of directing groups of people toward the solution of coordination problems by creating focal points. In those models a leader, player, or mediator suggests actions that other players then find in their interests to follow, simply because the suggestion was made. In such a setting it is clearly in the communicator's interest to provide the needed suggestion,[2] so the whole institution can be portrayed as an equilibrium, as Schotter's view requires. Another approach is the use of communication to overcome problems of imperfect information and extend group members' ability to monitor and react to one another's actions, as in Milgrom, North, and Weingast (1990); Greif, Milgrom, and Weingast (1990); and Calvert (1992b). In those models, central clearinghouses of information pass along records about actors' behavior to other

---

[2] The communicator can be just another player in a pure coordination game, in which case she too benefits from coordinating; or she can be a player in a mixed-motive coordination game, so that her suggestion can create an outcome that is good for all players but especially good for her; or she can be paid to provide the needed suggestion out of the "profits" resulting from successful coordination by the other players.

actors, or announce whether punishment or cooperation is in order. Although the problem of rationally providing the needed information is a sticky one here, all these papers make some attempt to close the models by showing how the overall institution is an equilibrium.

The present chapter explores the nature of another kind of communicative institution. It describes a model in which players must exchange private information to realize gains from cooperation, and shows how an equilibrium in a communication-augmented repeated game can accomplish such an exchange and realize those gains. The model provides some evidence that, in a repeated game with hidden information, communication makes it possible to realize gains that could not otherwise be achieved. In the models cited previously, there are equilibria in which all the gains are achieved without the use of communication, although in some cases those equilibria seem implausible as explanations for successful coordination. In the present model, however, I argue (but cannot quite prove) that certain gains cannot possibly be achieved in equilibrium without the use of communication.

Inasmuch as real-life social interactions involve making distinctions about appropriate actions based on the private circumstances of individuals, this kind of communication must be an important feature of real-life institutions. For example, if members of a group observe a norm in which each member makes a fixed contribution to some public good unless the cost of that contribution would be too high, and if each individual knows more than others about her own true costs of contribution, then the norm must involve an equilibrium exchange of private information. For this reason, and because of the apparent reasonableness of the communication institutions analyzed in the previous literature, I conclude that communication – whether of intentions, suggestions, or private information – is a central function of institutions understood from the viewpoint of rational-actor theory.

The chapter proceeds as follows. Section 2 presents the model and derives the classically efficient payoff level, both with and without correlated strategies. This derivation makes clear the problem posed by a repeated Prisoner's Dilemma (PD) game when incomplete information is present: The players wish not just to achieve cooperation, but to achieve cooperation when appropriate and to allow defection when one player knows that cooperation is inappropriate. Section 3 examines the problem of achieving efficient payoffs when communication is possible, both with and without a mediator. The analysis demonstrates that a particular, high level of expected payoffs is available through communication, although it does not identify the optimal payoff level. Finally, Section 4 discusses the situation when communication is not possible, and derives the payoffs in general for a strategy closely analogous to Tit for Tat for the incomplete-information setting. This analysis demonstrates the shortcoming of Tit for Tat, in a manner analogous to the literature on imperfect monitoring; here, however, the imperfect monitoring is replaced by a richer setting in which players "should," from the standpoint of both individual rationality and Pareto optimality, sometimes defect. Section 5 draws conclusions concerning the nature of institutions that improve social welfare, with particular attention to the likely importance of "review strategies," a feature not dealt with in the present analysis.

2   The basic model and classical efficiency

To accomplish this analysis of communication in institutions, I will concentrate on a situation based on the familiar two-player Prisoner's Dilemma game. The PD nicely captures the general problem of achieving group goals at the expense of atomistic individual rationality, and the repeated PD allows the basic opportunity to achieve cooperation among rational individuals. In addition to this abstract role in addressing problems of institutional maintenance, the simple two-player PD has specific applicability to many political interactions, capturing the problems inherent in reciprocity, promise-keeping, arms races, and other situations of direct importance in politics.

Invariably, however, such real-life political situations include complications not addressed in the simple PD game. One of the most important is the general fact that accidents and special circumstances cause exceptions and violations to any rule. That is, actors in the real world never realize an equilibrium path of perfect cooperation. Even a small possibility of such imperfections can mean significant losses to the players, since equilibrium typically requires one defection to be punished with others. As a means of capturing such complications, game theorists have carried out extensive examinations of repeated PD-type games in which the monitoring of opponents' past actions is imperfect, so that a player's intended act of cooperation may look to others as if it were an act of defection. The first such effort, Porter's (1983) model of cartel trigger-price strategies, demonstrates how some gains could be extracted in equilibrium even though the imperfect monitoring prevents the players from realizing all the theoretically available gains from cooperation. In extolling the virtues of the Tit for Tat strategy in achieving stable cooperation in the repeated PD, Axelrod (1980, 1984) notes that the payoff from Tit for Tat suffers greatly under imperfect monitoring, and conjectures that a somewhat less retaliatory strategy might serve better in an environment of noisy monitoring. Sugden (1986), Bendor (1987), and Segerstrom (1988) analyze further the danger of over-retaliation that a reciprocating strategy such as Tit for Tat presents, and show how more forgiving approaches might yield higher payoffs in this environment.

My approach in the present chapter is similar in spirit to the models of cooperation under imperfect monitoring, but unlike them I create circumstances in which otherwise cooperative players will *purposely* defect under special circumstances. That is, in every equilibrium the rational individual will sometimes be forced to defect; and, in addition, efficient equilibrium will require that players sometimes be *allowed* to defect. This reflects a feature of real political and social life not captured by models of imperfect monitoring. Even in life's "repeated" interactions, circumstances differ from one iteration to the next, often in ways about which the players are asymmetrically informed. As a result, real-world norms and rules fostering social gains should take these variations into account and provide for exceptions and unavoidable violations. Under such institutions, actors actually carry out trade-offs, sometimes obeying rules and sometimes violating them and enduring the consequences. In contrast, in an efficient equilibrium under imperfect monitoring, actors always attempt to cooperate.

The analysis will deal with both single-play and repeated versions of the incomplete-information PD game, because the single-play results are a step toward establishing those for the repeated-play case. In the single-play game, Players 1 and 2 are to play a Prisoner's Dilemma game whose strategy choices are denoted "cooperate" (C) and "defect" (D). Payoffs are computed as follows: Each player receives a benefit of b times the number of players who cooperate (0, 1, or 2), and each player i pays a cost of c_i for cooperating and 0 for defecting. The cost c_i is private information. It takes on the value $\bar{c}$ with probability p and the value $\underline{c}$ with probability $1-p$, where $0 < b < \underline{c} < 2b < \bar{c}$ and $0 < p < 1$. The probability value p is common knowledge. Thus, when the cost for both players is $\underline{c}$, the pattern of payoffs corresponds to that of the standard PD, but when a player draws cost $\bar{c}$ that player actually prefers mutual defection to mutual cooperation.

A *strategy* for player i in the single-play game is a function $s_i(c)$ denoting player i's probability of cooperating when his or her true cost is c. The action $(C$ or $D)$ actually taken by player i is denoted a_i; the outcome of the single-play game is denoted (a_1, a_2). A strategy profile is a pair (s_1, s_2). A strategy profile is *symmetric* if $s_1(c) = s_2(c)$ for all possible cost realizations c. Within this chapter I confine attention to symmetric strategy profiles[3]

---

[3] Every symmetric game has symmetric equilibria, and every asymmetric equilibrium in a symmetric game has a "mirror image" that is also an asymmetric equilibrium. The argument for restricting attention to symmetric equilibria is that, given a symmetric game, there is no criterion that would lead us to predict an asymmetric decision rule over

and (later) symmetric mechanisms, respecting the symmetries of the game itself.

A *decision rule* for the single-play game is any function mapping the actual costs of the players stochastically into an outcome of the game. When the players' true costs are (c_1, c_2), then $d(a_1, a_2; c_1, c_2)$ denotes the probability that decision rule d chooses outcome (a_1, a_2). Any strategy profile determines a decision rule, by setting $d(C, C; c_1, c_2) = s_1(c_1) \cdot s_2(c_2)$, and so on. Other processes, such as the mediation rules to be dealt with in Section 3, also determine decision rules. All possible ways of connecting cost draws with outcomes are decision rules; but not all decision rules can be achieved by rational players in equilibrium (even when using communication mechanisms). A decision rule is symmetric if for all outcomes and cost draws, $d(a_1, a_2; c_1, c_2) = d(a_2, a_1; c_2, c_1)$.

In the repeated version of the game, each player i draws a new cost value c_{it} in iteration t. Neither player ever learns the opponent's true costs on previous plays of the game. Payoffs for the repeated game are the discounted sum of the payoffs from all iterations; both players use discount factor δ.

Since this is not the standard Prisoner's Dilemma game, I begin by specifying the ex ante classically efficient[4] outcomes of these games in order to demonstrate why this version of the PD is of special interest. Suppose first that we are free to designate any symmetric decision rule d, without regard to the motivations or information of the players. What d would yield the highest (symmetric) payoffs to the players?[5]

Proposition 1. *The unique (ex ante) optimal symmetric decision rule sets* $d(C, C; \underline{c}, \underline{c})$, $d(C, D; \underline{c}, \bar{c})$, $d(D, C; \bar{c}, \underline{c})$, *and* $d(D, D; \bar{c}, \bar{c})$ *equal to* 1, *and all other values of d equal to* 0.

Proof: The expected payoff to either player from d is

$$\sum_{a_1, a_2} \sum_{c_1, c_2} d(a_1, a_2; c_1, c_2) \pi(c_1) \pi(c_2) u(a_1, a_2; c_1),$$

where $u(a_1, a_2; c_i)$ represents player i's payoff in the single-play game when i's true type is c_i and the actions actually taken are a_1 and a_2; $\pi(c_j)$

---

its mirror image, and no reason a priori to expect the players to behave asymmetrically. See Farrell (1987, p. 36).

[4] That is, the expected payoff as measured prior to the players learning their true cost values, without regard to whether the payoff can be achieved in any equilibrium. Here and throughout, I use the terminology of Holmstrom and Myerson (1983).

[5] Any decision rule that is Pareto optimal in the set of symmetric decision rules is also Pareto optimal among all decision rules. This follows directly from the convexity in payoff space of the set of all decision rules.

denotes the probability that cost c_j is drawn, so $\pi(\underline{c}) = 1 - p$ and $\pi(\bar{c}) = p$; the first summation is taken over all possible outcomes; and the second summation is taken over all possible pairs of costs drawn by the players. Since the ex ante efficient decision rule must be interim-efficient for each interim state (i.e., for each possible cost draw (c_1, c_2)), we can determine the optimal symmetric d easily by examining the payoffs from all outcomes in each cost draw.

Consider first the case $(c_1, c_2) = (\underline{c}, \underline{c})$. If the outcome is (C, C) then each player receives $2b - \underline{c}$. The payoff from (D, D) is 0, which is less than $2b - \underline{c}$, so certainly $d(D, D; \underline{c}, \underline{c}) = 0$. If the players take different actions, the cooperator receives $b - \underline{c}$ while the defector receives b. Since d is symmetric, the same weight must be placed on both outcomes (C, D) and (D, C). Thus the expected payoff from choosing (C, C) with probability q and (C, D) or (D, C) with the remaining probability is

$$(2b - \underline{c})q + (b - \underline{c})(1 - q)/2 + b(1 - q)/2.$$

The derivative of this with respect to q is positive, so the efficient decision rule puts all weight on (C, C). By a similar calculation, $d(D, D; \bar{c}, \bar{c}) = 1$.

Finally, consider the two cases where the players draw different cost values. By symmetry, we must have $d(C, D; \underline{c}, \bar{c}) = d(D, C; \bar{c}, \underline{c})$ and vice versa; call this value R, and let $S = d(D, C; \underline{c}, \bar{c}) = d(C, D; \bar{c}, \underline{c})$. Also, (C, C) and (D, D) must get the same probability weight under either of the two cost combinations; let these be P and Q. Thus the expected payoff from a particular symmetric decision rule, conditional on the players receiving different cost draws, is

$$\tfrac{1}{2}[P(2b - \underline{c}) + Q \cdot 0 + R(b - \underline{c}) + Sb] + \tfrac{1}{2}[P(2b - \bar{c}) + Q \cdot 0 + Rb + S(b - \bar{c})].$$

After collecting terms on P, Q, R, and S, it is obvious that the derivative of this expected payoff with respect to R is greater than the derivatives with respect to P, Q, and S for all admissible parameter values; hence expected payoff is maximized at $R = 1$, as required. □

In words, the best symmetric decision rule is to always require a low-cost player to cooperate and always allow a high-cost player to defect.[6] If the players could actually implement such a rule before learning their types, this is what they would choose. To maximize ex ante expected payoff is analogous to having individuals choose an institutional form under which they will act, before they know exactly what issues the institution will be dealing with. (Naturally, once the players learn their types it would

---

[6] Notice, therefore, that the optimal rule does not require correlated strategies. It can be implemented by having each player i use the (nonequilibrium) strategy $s_i(\underline{c}) = 1$ and $s_i(\bar{c}) = 0$.

be impossible to get the same agreement.) This approach takes on further importance due to the fact that, in the repeated game, player "types" (the costs) are chosen anew at each iteration. Thus the decision rule that maximizes ex ante expected payoff in the single-play game is also the one that, applied in each iteration, maximizes the expected discounted present value of payoffs in the repeated game.

Unfortunately there is a problem in realizing the classically efficient payoff, whether the game is repeated or not. For the one-shot game, cooperation when cost is low is subject to exactly the same problems as cooperation in the conventional full-information Prisoner's Dilemma: defection is the dominant strategy. In the repeated game, there is the possibility of enforcing cooperative behavior; but since the true costs are private information, there is no direct way to verify whether a player has drawn the high cost and is therefore "entitled" to defect in the interest of overall efficiency. The classically efficient decision rule stands as an ideal, but as we will see it cannot be achieved by rational players under the given information conditions, even if the players can communicate. This ideal expresses a somewhat richer social goal than does either the standard PD game or the PD with imperfect monitoring; optimally, the players would like to require cooperation only when the cost of cooperating is not unreasonably high. The goal might be seen as a formalization of the communist precept, "from each according to his ability"; the sticky problem, as always, lies in determining what others' abilities are.

3   Optimal play when communication is possible

The ultimate goal of this section is to calculate the payoff level that the players in the repeated game can reach if they are able to communicate with one another before playing each iteration of the game. Specifically, I calculate a (reasonably high) lower bound on the highest payoff available under these conditions. Throughout, all communication is in the form of cheap talk.[7] The argument in this section proceeds as follows. First, I compute the maximum payoff in the single-play game when an impartial mediator is available who has the power both to communicate with the players and to unilaterally bind the players to certain actions. Second, for the repeated game, I dispense with the mediator's allocative power to show how the same payoff can be attained (as an expected per-period average taking the discounting into account), provided that the discounting is not too heavy. Finally, I dispense with the mediator entirely

---

[7] That is, communication is costless, promises are not binding, and claims about private information cannot be verified. See Farrell (1987).

and demonstrate how direct communication between the players is sufficient to achieve this payoff.

3.1 *Single-play allocation by a mediator*

In order to construct the more general case, begin by assuming that the game is to be played only once, and that before play there can be any specific form of communication among the two players and a mediator. Following this, the mediator will use the content of the communication to determine the outcome of the game, not subject to any interference from the players.

In this setting, the revelation principle (Myerson 1985) yields a method of computing the maximum payoff that can be achieved. Suppose that communication and choice of outcomes take the form of a direct mechanism. That is, the game consists of the following schedule of events:

(1) each player privately learns his or her true cost c_i;
(2) each player privately reports a cost value r_i to the mediator; the value reported depends on the true cost but need not be truthful;
(3) the mediator determines an outcome (a_1, a_2) depending on the reports;
(4) the players receive the payoffs from (a_1, a_2), and the game ends.

Specifically, player i reports $r_i = \bar{c}$ with probability $\rho(c_i)$ and $r_i = \underline{c}$ with probability $1 - \rho(c_i)$, and the mediator determines the outcome (a_1, a_2) according to a rule μ as follows: $\text{Prob}\{a_1, a_2 | r_1, r_2\} = \mu(a_1, a_2; r_1, r_2)$. The mediator's rule μ is itself sometimes called a direct mechanism, with the understanding that the overall game is as given in (1)-(4). A rule μ is symmetrical if, for all a_1, a_2, r_1, and r_2, it satisfies $\mu(a_1, a_2; r_1, r_2) = \mu(a_2, a_1; r_2, r_1)$. That is, a symmetrical rule treats both players in exactly the same way.

Let $U(r_i; c_i, \mu)$ represent a player's expected payoff if that player's true cost is c_i, the player reports r_i, the mediator uses μ, and the other player reports truthfully. The mediator's rule μ is said to be *incentive compatible* if it satisfies the following constraint:

$$U(c_i; c_i, \mu) \geq U(r_i; c_i, \mu) \quad \text{for all } i, r_i, c_i. \tag{IC}$$

The revelation principle says that the distribution over outcomes generated by any equilibrium in any game preceded by any communication process can be duplicated as an equilibrium in a suitable incentive-compatible direct mechanism (ICDM). In particular, to find the maximum possible equilibrium expected payoff from any process of mediated communication and binding allocation, it is sufficient to solve the following problem:

maximize, over all symmetrical, feasible direct mechanisms μ, the expected payoff $EU(c; c, \mu)$ subject to the incentive compatibility constraint (IC).[8] (The expectation here is taken with respect to the value of c and the outcome of any randomization in μ.)

In the appendix, one ICDM is calculated corresponding to the one-shot PD game with incomplete information. Although that ICDM is not quite optimal, it is sufficient to prove the following result.

Proposition 2. *In the single-play game with mediated communication and binding allocation by the mediator, the players can achieve a symmetric equilibrium expected payoff of at least* $(1 - p)^2 (2b - \underline{c}) b / [b - p(2b - \underline{c})]$.

Remark. This payoff is achieved if the mediator chooses outcome (C, C) when both players report low cost, chooses (D, D) when both report high cost, and – when they report different costs – chooses (C, D) or (D, C) (the high-cost player defecting) with the probability given in the appendix and (D, D) with the complementary probability. This possibility of induced failure is what keeps the players honest. A slightly more complicated calculation than that given in the appendix yields the true maximum payoff. To achieve that, for certain parameter values when the players report different costs the mediator chooses (C, D) with a slightly increased probability over that given here, chooses (C, C) with probability equal to that increase, and chooses (D, D) with the (now smaller) remaining probability.

3.2   Mediated communication in the repeated game

In the repeated game, provided that discounting is not too heavy, the players can achieve the same level of payoffs (as an expected, discounted per-period average) without using the mediator's ability to determine unilaterally the final outcome. Let us assume now that, after receiving the reports of the players in iteration t, the mediator recommends actions $m_{1t}, m_{2t} \in \{C, D\}$ to the players privately, deriving these recommendations from the reports in iteration t and the history of previous reports and previous play. In short, the sequence of events is:

(1)   each player privately learns his or her true cost, c_i;
(2)   each player privately reports a cost value r_i to the mediator; again, r_i depends on c_i but need not equal c_i;

---

[8] Note that, once again, the symmetry assumption does not cause us to miss any Pareto improvements. A mechanism that is Pareto optimal in the set of symmetric mechanisms is also Pareto optimal in the set of all mechanisms. The argument is identical to that used to prove the same fact about decision rules generally. See Banks and Calvert (1992) for details.

(3) the mediator determines an outcome $(m_1, m_2) \in \{C, D\} \times \{C, D\}$ depending on the reports, and privately communicates each m_i as a recommended action to each player i;
(4) the players take actions (a_1, a_2);
(5) the players receive the payoffs from (a_1, a_2), and the whole sequence is repeated.

Suppose that, as long as the players follow the mediator's recommendations, the mediator continues to recommend actions in each iteration that would lead to the same outcomes as in the single-play allocation game (given in the appendix); but if either player ever deviates from these recommendations, the mediator recommends defection by both players in every period thereafter. Since following such a recommendation is equilibrium behavior, this threat will deter each player from deviating, and the outcome in each period will be exactly as if the mediator had made the allocation himself. In short, we can prove the following result.

Proposition 3. *In the repeated-play game with communication in which the mediator uses a symmetric rule for recommending actions, the players can achieve a symmetric equilibrium expected payoff (in discounted present value) of at least* $(1-p)^2 (2b - \underline{c}) b / \{(1 - \delta)[b - p(2b - \underline{c})]\}$, *provided that*

$$\delta > \frac{(\bar{c} - b)[b - p(2b - \underline{c})]}{(\bar{c} - b)[b - p(2b - \underline{c})] + (1 - p)^2 (2b - \underline{c}) b}.$$

Remark. The remark following Proposition 2 applies here as well. Moreover, an even higher payoff level than that guaranteed by repeated application of the single-period optimal mechanism might be attainable, since the repetition of the game could provide the tools to squeeze additional unilateral cooperation out of the players in equilibrium while still forcing them to report truthfully. This issue is taken up in Section 5.

Proof: Formally, let (m_{1t}, m_{2t}) be the mediator's recommendation in each iteration t, and let (a_{1t}, a_{2t}) be the actual outcome of play in iteration t. Let H_t represent the history of play and communication up to but not including period t:

$$H_t \equiv \{(r_{1\tau}, r_{2\tau}), (m_{1\tau}, m_{2\tau}), (a_{1\tau}, a_{2\tau})\}_{\tau=1}^{t-1}$$

for $t = 2, 3, \ldots$, and let H_1 be some constant. The mediator uses a rule μ' to determine each period's recommendation, defined as

$$\text{Prob}\{(m_{1t}, m_{2t}) \mid (r_{1t}, r_{2t}), H_t\} \equiv \mu'(m_{1t}, m_{2t}; r_{1t}, r_{2t}, H_t).$$

Symmetry is defined similarly to the single-play case: μ' is symmetric if for all i, t, m_{it}, r_{it}, and H_t,

$$\mu'(m_{1t}, m_{2t}; r_{1t}, r_{2t}, H_t) = \mu'(m_{2t}, m_{1t}; r_{2t}, r_{1t}, H_t'),$$

where H_t' is formed by reversing the player subscripts in all previous iterations. Construct μ' as follows. Let

$$\mu'(m_{1t}, m_{2t}; r_{1t}, r_{2t}, H_t) = \mu(m_{1t}, m_{2t}; r_{1t}, r_{2t})$$

if $t = 1$ or if $a_{i\tau} = m_{i\tau}$ for all $\tau < t$, where μ is the rule used in the appendix to achieve the single-play maximum payoff. Otherwise, let

$$\mu'(D, D; r_{1t}, r_{2t}, H_t) = 1.^9$$

Notice that μ' is symmetric if and only if μ is symmetric.

It must be demonstrated that the players will always report truthfully and obey the recommendations. By Proposition 2, given that both players will obey the recommendations, it is an equilibrium for both to report truthfully. I first show the reverse: if both players are truthful then it is equilibrium behavior for both to obey. It is then an easy step to show as well that a player will never gain by both lying and disobeying, provided the other player does not lie or disobey.

Suppose that Player 2 always tells the truth and follows the mediator's recommendations, and examine the incentives of Player 1. Suppose that Player 1 reports her true cost, c_1. If told to do C, there are two possibilities: either Player 2 was told to do C or to do D. If Player 2 was told C, Player 1 by obeying will receive $2b - c_1$ and by disobeying will receive b in the current iteration; so disobeying will yield a short-run gain of $b - (2b - c_1) = c_1 - b$. On the other hand, if Player 2 was told D then Player 1 receives $b - c_1$ by obeying and 0 by disobeying; again, disobeying yields a gain of $c_1 - b$ in the present iteration. Thus, in general, when Player 1 is told to do C, the temptation to disobey is the current-period gain of $c_1 - b$. However, disobeying will lead to a payoff of zero in all future periods, whereas the expected payoff from future cooperation under μ' is $(1-p)^2(2b-\underline{c})b/[b-p(2b-\underline{c})]$ in each future period, for a total discounted present value of $\delta(1-p)^2(2b-\underline{c})b/\{(1-\delta)[b-p(2b-\underline{c})]\}$. Therefore Player 1 will follow the suggestion of C provided that the latter loss outweighs the one-period gain of $c_1 - b$. A little algebra then provides the following condition: for $c_1 \in \{\underline{c}, \bar{c}\}$,

$$\delta > \frac{(c_1 - b)[b - p(2b - \underline{c})]}{(c_1 - b)[b - p(2b - \underline{c})] + (1-p)^2(2b - \underline{c})b}.$$

[9] This "grim trigger" approach may not be necessary, especially if the discount factor is high enough; a finite period of noncooperation may suffice instead to deter any noncooperation from occurring. The point here is simply that it is possible to deter deviation from the mediator's recommendations; a less grim punishment scheme may do the trick as well.

Since $\underline{c} < \bar{c}$, a little more algebra shows that the right-hand side of this inequality is larger when $c_1 = \bar{c}$, so the following condition is sufficient for obedience to a recommendation of C, given truthfulness:

$$\delta > \frac{(\bar{c}-b)[b-p(2b-\underline{c})]}{(\bar{c}-b)[b-p(2b-\underline{c})] + (1-p)^2(2b-\underline{c})b}.$$

Finally, if the mediator recommends that Player 1 play D, disobeying yields a loss both in the current iteration and all future play. Therefore recommendations of D will be followed regardless of the discount factor.

It remains to show that Player 1 will also have no incentive to both lie and disobey. Again suppose Player 1's true cost is c_1, and that she reports $r_1 \neq c_1$. If told to play D, again there is never any gain from disobeying. If told to play C, disobedience yields gains according to Player 1's true cost; but this works just as before, a sure gain of $c_1 - b$ in the present iteration and the loss of all cooperation benefits thereafter. Thus the previous condition on δ guarantees that if Player 1 has lied, she will still obey the mediator's recommendation. But the original incentive compatibility condition ensures that, if obedience is forthcoming anyway, there will be no advantage in lying. Thus no matter what the circumstances, Player 1 will report truthfully and, provided δ is sufficiently large, follow any suggestion by the mediator.   □

3.3   Unmediated communication in the repeated game

If the mediator's role is simply to implement the rule described in the proof of Proposition 3, it is easy to see that no mediator is really necessary as long as the players have extensive abilities to communicate with one another. Without the help of the mediator, the players could implement μ' in the following manner. First, the players simultaneously reveal to one another their reports r_{it}. Then, they consult a mutually observable random device to decide upon prescribed actions according to $\mu(m_{1t}, m_{2t}; r_{1t}, r_{2t})$.[10] Finally, as long as neither player has ever deviated from the prescribed actions determined in this manner, they now follow the prescription again in playing the current PD iteration. If either player ever deviates, both players defect in all subsequent turns.[11] If the players use such a system, Propositions 1 and 2 demonstrate that truthful reporting

[10] Strictly speaking, they only need the mediator to perform the randomization. Even this is unnecessary, because the players can arbitrarily closely approximate the outcome probabilities given by μ through a system of independent private randomizations and (incentive-compatible) reports. See Aumann, Maschler, and Stearns (1968) for details.

[11] Again, some sort of finite punishment scheme may work just as well, but the point here is just to show that adherence to the prescription can be enforced.

of costs and universal adherence to the prescribed actions is an equilibrium. In short, none of the privacy in communication, achieved through the use of a mediator, is necessary in order to achieve the solution described in Proposition 3. Thus we have the following corollary.

Corollary. *In the repeated-play game with communication between the players, the players can achieve an expected discounted present value of at least* $(1-p)^2(2b-\underline{c})b/\{(1-\delta)[b-p(2b-\underline{c})]\}$ *in equilibrium, provided that the discount factor meets the condition in Proposition 3.*

The mediator and his powers have thus been a convenient fiction for the calculation of achievable payoffs using communication. A real-life institution serving these purposes may or may not employ a person in the role of the mediator, and may or may not use the particular mechanism derived for these results; other mechanisms could achieve the same results. However, any such mechanism would have to accomplish what the one used here accomplishes: it would have to make a report of high cost sufficiently risky, in terms of failing to elicit cooperation from the other player, that only a truly high-cost player will be willing to behave as a high-cost player is expected to behave. Finally, the mechanism used in this section indicates that a real-life (nearly) optimal mechanism need not be too complicated.

4   Payoffs achievable without communication

If the players are unable to communicate at all, the best they can do is to resort to equilibrium play in the repeated game as originally given. As the calculation (in Section 2) of the classically efficient payoff shows, the possibility of high cost draws complicates this type of play in a way that does not occur in the complete-information or the imperfect-monitoring version of the repeated Prisoner's Dilemma. Ideally the players would like to identify equilibrium strategies in which there is some allowance for a player who draws $\bar{c}$ to defect without badly disturbing the overall pattern of cooperation. The main question, then, is whether equilibrium payoffs without communication can equal those with communication.[12]

---

[12] Game-theoretic models with imperfect monitoring, broadly related to the Prisoner's Dilemma, have answered related questions both "yes" and "no." In Radner's (1985) repeated principal–agent game with discounting, the (iteration-wise Stackelberg) equilibrium payoff can arbitrarily closely approach the classically efficient payoff as the discount rate goes to 1. On the other hand, Radner, Myerson, and Maskin (1986) demonstrate, for a repeated partnership game with discounting and a random noise component in the

A general result of this sort has proven elusive, but there are several indications that the answer is "no." Two general types of strategies immediately suggest themselves as possible methods for achieving the maximum payoff without communication, and they may well exhaust the possibilities. The first type is the "review strategies" of Radner (e.g. 1985). In the present game, a review strategy would take the following form: on certain iterations, each player would look back at a specific set of previous iterations and see how often his opponent had defected. On the principle that defections should occur only when a high cost is drawn, the player would perform a hypothesis test concerning whether the number of defections observed is likely to have been drawn from a binomial distribution with defection probability of at most p. If the opponent's past behavior fails this test, some sort of punishment phase begins. It seems clear that any such strategy would necessarily leave open the possibility of undetected defections by low-cost players, and of punishments occasionally being carried out on the equilibrium path. Both these features lower the payoffs of a review-strategy equilibrium below the classically efficient level, but it is not immediately clear whether such an equilibrium could approach the optimal payoff with communication.[13]

The second likely place to look for optimal strategies without communication is among the "extremal" strategies described by Abreu, Pearce, and Stacchetti (1990) for the case of repeated games with imperfect monitoring (or those with perfect information). An extremal strategy is one that, in every iteration after every possible history, yields a payoff at an extreme point of the set of per-period payoffs achievable in supergame equilibria. In the Abreu et al. setting, extremal strategies have an appealingly simple (and thus tractable) structure. Their results demonstrate, among other things, that optimal equilibrium payoffs can always be achieved using extremal strategies. The present model violates some assumptions of the

outcome, that for certain parameter values the highest (subgame-perfect) equilibrium payoff is bounded away from the classically efficient payoff level, even as $\delta \to 1$. Neither these nor other writers have compared communication and no-communication payoffs in such situations, or addressed any of these issues in the Prisoner's Dilemma game itself.

[13] Of the applications of review strategies I am aware of, all but one assume maximization of long-run average payoff, with no discounting (Dionne 1983; Malueg 1986, 1988; Radner 1981, 1986; Rubinstein 1979). All these apply the "Law of the Iterated Logarithm" (see e.g. Feller 1968, pp. 204–8) to get a review criterion that precludes any cheating in equilibrium. Such a modeling approach is not available when payoffs are discounted. The only paper that does not fit this pattern, Radner (1985), uses a different approach to derive a review strategy equilibrium for a repeated principal-agent game. I have been unsuccessful in attempting to adapt Radner's method to the present problem.

Abreu et al. result, but it may well be possible to prove their result for the present model. The reformulation necessary to do that, however, would probably result in a dynamic programming analog whose states have a complicated structure, so that the extremal strategies themselves would be rather complex in terms of the original formulation of the game. They may, for example, end up looking like review strategies.

If one could get high payoffs from strategies that were simple in terms of the straightforward formulation of the game, then the nearest analogy to an extremal strategy would have to be one in which a player punishes defections without knowing the defector's motivations (high cost or cheating); the outcome of an iteration would determine whether the players continue cooperating or enter some punishment phase. Naturally, the actual use of such punishment episodes would reduce payoffs below the classically efficient level, since in a symmetric strategy profile the expected payoff from all turns on which one is either punishing or being punished (b or 0 in the first case, $b - c_i$ or 0 in the second) averages out to less than one would expect from simply continuing cooperation ($2b - c$ in both cases). Intuitively, it seems likely that the set of efficient symmetric equilibrium strategies in this class would include one that punishes most defections, so that cheating is deterred, but does so with minimal ferocity, so that overall cooperation is maximized.

One obvious candidate for such a strategy would be a variant of Tit for Tat (Rapoport and Chammah 1965; Axelrod 1980, 1984) that allows for some kind of "repentance" to re-establish cooperation following a defection (as in Sugden 1986 and Segerstrom 1988). I will call this variant "Tit for Tat with apologies" (TFTA). To define it, divide the iterations of the game into "cooperation phases" and "punishment phases", with the first iteration being in a cooperation phase. Play then proceeds as follows:

I. In a cooperation phase:

(1)   each player always cooperates when cost is c, and always defects when cost is $\bar{c}$;
(2)   if both players cooperate or both defect during a cooperation phase, the cooperation phase continues in the next iteration; otherwise, a punishment phase begins.

II. In a punishment phase, the player whose defection invoked the phase plays the part of "deviant", while the other is "punisher":

(1)   the punisher always defects, while the deviant cooperates when his cost is c and defects when his cost is $\bar{c}$;
(2)   if the deviant cooperates, a new cooperation phase begins in the next iteration; otherwise the punishment phase continues.

Reasoning similar to that used to prove Tit for Tat an equilibrium (Taylor 1976) makes it clear that the profile in which both players use TFTA is an equilibrium, provided that: (i) δ is sufficiently high, so that a low-cost player wishes to avoid punishment; and (ii) $\bar{c}$ is sufficiently large, so that a player prefers to endure punishment rather than cooperate when the cost is high. Condition (ii) represents the most interesting setting, since in that case the high cost of cooperation really does complicate the problem.[14] For present purposes, then, we assume δ and $\bar{c}$ sufficiently large in order to compare the payoffs from TFTA with those from the optimal communication scheme.

Proposition 4. *For sufficiently large $\bar{c}$ and δ, the payoff from TFTA is strictly less than the equilibrium payoff attainable through communication.*

Proof: Let V represent the expected discounted present value of all payoffs to a player, as seen before any information is revealed in the first iteration. Then V is also the expected payoff for the continuation of play prior to any iteration in a cooperation phase. Let X be the ex ante expected payoff for the remainder of the game to a punisher at the outset of a punishment phase, and Y that to a deviant (again before the cost values in the first punishment iteration are known). Then

$$V = (1-p)^2(2b-\underset{\sim}{c}+\delta V) + p^2\delta V + p(1-p)[2b-\underset{\sim}{c}+\delta(X+Y)]$$

$$X = (1-p)(b+\delta V) + p\delta X = (1-p)(b+\delta V)/(1-p\delta)$$

$$Y = (1-p)(b-\underset{\sim}{c}+\delta V) + p\delta Y = (1-p)(b-\underset{\sim}{c}+\delta V)/(1-p\delta).$$

Substituting X and Y into V and solving for V yields, after some simplification,

$$V = \frac{(1-p)(2b-\underset{\sim}{c})(1-p^2\delta)}{1-[1-p-p\delta(1-2p)]\delta - 2p(1-p)^2\delta^2},$$

which we can compare with the payoff available when communication is possible. From Proposition 3 or its corollary, we know the payoff with communication is at least $(1-p)^2(2b-\underset{\sim}{c})b/\{(1-\delta)[b-p(2b-\underset{\sim}{c})]\}$. Setting the payoff from TFTA to be less than this minimal communication payoff and performing an enormous amount of algebra, Proposition 4 requires that the following inequality hold:

[14] If (ii) does not hold, then the players receive a reasonably high payoff by playing simple Tit for Tat (which is in equilibrium) and just enduring high-cost cooperation, receiving an expected discounted present value of $[2b-(1-p)\underset{\sim}{c}-p\bar{c}]/(1-\delta)$. If $\bar{c}$ is barely larger than $2b$, this payoff may actually be higher than that obtained in the communication mechanism of Proposition 3.

$$p(2p^2\delta - 1)b - [p^2\delta(1-p) + \delta - 1]\underline{c} < [2p^2\delta - 2p\delta + 2\delta - 1]\delta p^2 b.$$

For large δ, this is approximately

$$p(2p^2 - 1)b - p^2(1-p)\underline{c} < [2p^2 - 2p + 1]p^2 b.$$

Setting $\underline{c}$ to be equal to b makes this inequality harder to satisfy than it would be for any legal value of $\underline{c}$; but even then the inequality reduces to

$$2p^3 - 4p^2 + 2p + 1 > 0,$$

which holds for all values of $p \in [0, 1]$. □

This Tit for Tat analogue fails to provide higher payoffs because one punishment per observed defection is too much. On the other hand, it is difficult to design a simple symmetric equilibrium that metes out lighter punishment. If punishment were supposed to be carried out only with some probability less than 1, there would be no incentive for the punisher to refrain from punishing. A strategy letting some defections go unpunished according to a determinate schedule, such as "Tit for Two Tats" (Axelrod 1980), would in general invite each player to take inappropriate advantage of free defections. Thus any strategy of lighter punishment would have to be backed up by some complicated method for assessing (through review of previous actions) whether a player has been systematically defecting or punishing too often, and for punishing such behavior in turn.

This result also speaks to the issue of whether Tit for Tat is a "robust" strategy, prominent in the literature on the repeated Prisoner's Dilemma. Axelrod (1980) notes the "echo effect" that occurs when a strategy that punishes all defections, such as one based on Tit for Tat, defects against an opponent who also punishes all defections. This would of course happen even if the defections were introduced randomly and unintentionally, as long as intentions were unobservable. Axelrod (1984) suggests that the introduction of proportional reciprocity could help dampen the echo effect in situations where noise is present. Bendor (1987) and Segerstrom (1988) explore this problem further and suggest modifications that could restore the ability of Tit for Tat to engender extensive cooperation. The present analysis basically adopts Segerstrom's approach, but applies it in a context in which players actually desire to defect once in a while. Proposition 4 shows that, despite the improvement brought about by adding repentance to the basic Tit for Tat strategy, Tit for Tat still generally falls short of achieving the highest payoffs that can be obtained consistent with rational behavior by the players. Whether any other no-communication strategy can do better than Tit for Tat is a separate question to which I return shortly.

Thus, although it is an open question whether any strategy not using communication could achieve the payoff levels of the best strategies with communication, it is clear that simple communication strategies outperform simple noncommunicative strategies. In institutions that emerge wholly or partly without planning, simpler equilibria would seem to be easier to achieve than complicated ones. In a setting of incomplete information, then, it is easier to achieve the available gains from trade by communicating about private information than by using the indirect signals available through review strategies or other complex punishment schemes. In any event, communication processes provide one tool to support efficient equilibrium, alongside the traditional tool of possibly complex sanctioning mechanisms.

5   Conclusions

The preceding sections have shown that (1) in repeated interaction with asymmetric information, efficiency may require that prescribed behavior take into account private information, which individuals have limited incentive to reveal; (2) a communication process can be used to extract a large proportion of the available gains from cooperation, by imposing a risk on lying about private information; (3) simple strategies that do not use communication do not perform as well, although more complex review strategies may perform better. The communication of private information, and the creation of incentives to do so truthfully, thus can be important in the functioning of social institutions that promote cooperative behavior.

5.1   Communication and social institutions

Most writers on the topic of cooperation through institutions emphasize the enforcement role of institutions, and enforcement is certainly one role of the mechanisms discussed in this chapter. But another function of social institutions, I believe, is to channel communication and use it to prescribe behavior contingent on the special circumstances of situations. Although the incentive-compatible direct mechanism derived here is just an analytical placeholder for messier real-life processes, it does make clear some of the features that must be present in the real thing. When asymmetric information about payoffs is important, an ideal institution should include a method of eliciting from individuals their assessments of whether their cooperation is worthwhile in a given instance. The institution must function in a manner that leads players with different payoffs to behave differently – in effect, to identify "truth" from the assessments. One means of encouraging truth is for the process occasionally to force mutual defection even though only one player has high cost; this is how the mediation rule of Propositions 2 and 3 (as described in the appendix) elicits truthful reporting. Thus a premium is placed on telling the truth; only if a player's cost is truly high will it be worth the risk to report high cost.

5.2   Communication and history

As suggested in the remark following Proposition 3, players in this game have another tool for extracting truthful reporting that I have not yet exploited. In addition to deterring lies through the possibility of cooperation failure due to a unilateral report of high cost, the mediator could himself use a kind of "review mechanism," periodically looking back at previous reports and testing the hypothesis that the observed number of high-cost reports by each player could have occurred given truthfulness under the actual probability distribution on costs. If a player fails the test, the mediator could enter a "failure phase" during which mutual defection is always proposed. Because of the possibility of a bad sequence of cost draws by a player, there will always be a positive probability that such punishment would be mistakenly invoked (or that a high-cost contribution would be forced); and because of the possibility of an unusually good series of cost draws, players may sometimes find it worthwhile to cheat on such a system, profitably reporting high cost when the actual cost is low. Still, a proper choice of the hypothesis test by the mediator ought to balance off these occasional type I and type II errors and allow an increase in the frequency of appropriate unilateral cooperation, and an overall increase in expected payoff. Notice that, as in the corollary to Proposition 3, the players still would require no mediator to carry out such a mechanism, beyond the use of a commonly observed random device.

In short, the truly optimal communication mechanism in the repeated game would have to take into account not just current reports by the players and their past record of performance, but also their records of past reports. It would have to assess the truthfulness of the players by means of their overall reporting behavior – a sort of reputational mechanism. Taking the view that social institutions function, in part, to implement such communication processes, this conclusion suggests that institutions are most effective in providing social welfare if they take into account the reputations of individuals for cooperative behavior and for claimed exemptions from required cooperation. Unfortunately, the methods used in this chapter are insufficient to construct such a mechanism, since it inescapably involves violations of the incentive-compatibility constraint for the one-stage game. It is unclear to what extent the mechanism of Proposition 3 falls short of optimality. Thus it remains unclear how important it is for institutional communication to keep track of reputations in this way, given the payoff and probability parameters.

5.3 The role of communication in institutions

Previous analysts have discerned a number of functions of communication in supporting coordinated or cooperative behavior through social institutions. Communication can be used to signal one's intentions (as in Farrell 1987) or to create a focal point (as in Schelling 1960), either of which helps individuals act in a coordinated fashion. In addition, communication can be used to assist monitoring by alleviating imperfect information about past events (as in Milgrom et al. 1990). The suggestion of this study has been that there is yet another role for communication in institutions: namely, to increase gains from cooperation by revealing private information about the variations in individuals' circumstances. In the model developed here, both players are better off if there is a mechanism that allows both of them, unilaterally and without retribution, to avoid contributions that would, for reasons known best to the potential contributor, be unreasonably costly. Despite this common interest, rational players face a problem in assuring that such information is accurately revealed, and a social institution is in part a mechanism for eliciting and using such communication to create the proper expectation of cooperative behavior.

Appendix: Mediation rule for the single-play game with allocation by the mediator

This appendix calculates a nearly optimal, symmetrical, incentive-compatible direct mechanism or mediation rule for the single-play game, and in so doing proves Proposition 2. The difference between this and the fully optimal mechanism is clarified at the end of the appendix. Let i be either player and let j be the other player. Using the notation presented in Section 2, Player i's payoff given that Player j always reports honestly is

$$U(r_i; c_i, \mu) \equiv \sum_{a_1, a_2} \sum_{c_j \in \{\underline{c}, \bar{c}\}} u(a_1, a_2; c_i) \mu(a_1, a_2; r_1, r_2) \pi(c_j),$$

where $u(a_1, a_2; c_i)$ represents player i's payoff in the original, single-play game when i's true type is c_i and the actions actually taken are a_1 and a_2; $\pi(c_j)$ denotes the probability that cost c_j is drawn, so $\pi(\underline{c}) = 1 - p$ and $\pi(\bar{c}) = p$; and the first summation is taken over all possible outcomes that the mediator could determine (namely $(a_1, a_2) \in \{(C, C), (C, D), (D, C),$ $(D, D)\}$). The problem then is to find a function μ that nearly maximizes Player i's ex ante expected payoff from telling the truth, which (in a readability-enhancing abuse of notation) I will write as

$$U(\mu) \equiv (1 - p) U(\underline{c}; \underline{c}, \mu) + p U(\bar{c}; \bar{c}, \mu),$$

subject to the incentive-compatibility constraint that makes it rational for i to be truthful, given as (IC) in Section 2. Note that (IC) reduces to two specific inequalities: $U(\underline{c}; \underline{c}, \mu) \geq U(\bar{c}; \underline{c}, \mu)$ and $U(\bar{c}; \bar{c}, \mu) \geq U(\underline{c}; \bar{c}, \mu)$.

The first step is to rearrange $U(\mu)$ and (IC) so that some simplifications become clear. By writing out $U(\underline{c}; \underline{c}, \mu)$ and $U(\bar{c}; \bar{c}, \mu)$ in full and then using the symmetry of μ to substitute $\mu(C, C; \underline{c}, \bar{c})$ for $\mu(C, C; \bar{c}, \underline{c})$, $\mu(D, D; \underline{c}, \bar{c})$ for $\mu(D, D; \bar{c}, \underline{c})$, and, for any c and c', $\mu(C, D; c, c')$ for $\mu(D, C; c', c)$, the ex ante expected payoff becomes

$$U(\mu) = \mu(C, C; \underline{c}, \underline{c})(1-p)^2(2b-\underline{c}) + \mu(C, C; \underline{c}, \bar{c})p(1-p)(4b-\underline{c}-\bar{c})$$
$$+ \mu(C, C; \bar{c}, \bar{c})p^2(2b-\bar{c}) + \mu(C, D; \underline{c}, \underline{c})(1-p)^2(2b-\underline{c})$$
$$+ \mu(C, D; \underline{c}, \bar{c})p(1-p)(2b-\underline{c}) + \mu(C, D; \bar{c}, \bar{c})p^2(2b-\bar{c})$$
$$+ \mu(D, C; \underline{c}, \bar{c})p(1-p)(2b-\bar{c}).$$

The incentive-compatibility constraints, (IC), can be rewritten as

$$\sum_{a_1, a_2} \sum_{c_j} u(a_1, a_2; \underline{c}) \pi(c_j) [\mu(a_1, a_2; \underline{c}, c_j) - \mu(a_1, a_2; \bar{c}, c_j)] \geq 0,$$

$$\sum_{a_1, a_2} \sum_{c_j} u(a_1, a_2; \bar{c}) \pi(c_j) [\mu(a_1, a_2; \bar{c}, c_j) - \mu(a_1, a_2; \underline{c}, c_j)] \geq 0,$$

with Player 1 in the role of Player i. Writing these out and again making use of the symmetry of μ gives the first inequality as

$$\mu(C, C; \underline{c}, \underline{c})(1-p)(2b-\underline{c}) + \mu(C, C; \underline{c}, \bar{c})(2p-1)(2b-\underline{c})$$
$$- \mu(C, C; \bar{c}, \bar{c})p(2b-\underline{c})$$
$$+ \mu(C, D; \underline{c}, \underline{c})(1-p)(2b-\underline{c})$$
$$+ \mu(C, D; \underline{c}, \bar{c})[p(b-\underline{c}) - (1-p)b]$$
$$- \mu(C, D; \bar{c}, \bar{c})p(2b-\underline{c})$$
$$+ \mu(D, C; \underline{c}, \bar{c})[pb - (1-p)(b-\underline{c})] \geq 0.$$

Henceforth I refer to this inequality as (IC$\underline{c}$). Through a similar process, we can rewrite the second inequality of (IC) as

$$-\mu(C, C; \underline{c}, \underline{c})(1-p)(2b-\bar{c}) - \mu(C, C; \underline{c}, \bar{c})(2p-1)(2b-\bar{c})$$
$$+ \mu(C, C; \bar{c}, \bar{c})p(2b-\bar{c})$$
$$- \mu(C, D; \underline{c}, \underline{c})(1-p)(2b-\bar{c})$$

$$-\mu(C, D; \underline{c}, \bar{c})[p(b - \bar{c}) - (1 - p)b]$$
$$+\mu(C, D; \bar{c}, \bar{c})p(2b - \bar{c})$$
$$-\mu(D, C; \underline{c}, \bar{c})[pb - (1 - p)(b - \bar{c})] \geq 0.$$

which I henceforth identify as (IC$\bar{c}$). Thus the optimization problem can be expressed as: choose μ to maximize $U(\mu)$ subject to (IC$\underline{c}$) and (IC$\bar{c}$).

From the signs of the coefficients in $U(\mu)$, (IC$\underline{c}$), and (IC$\bar{c}$), we can draw several immediate conclusions about the optimal μ. First notice that, in each of the three expressions, the coefficient of $\mu(C, C; \underline{c}, \underline{c})$ is positive. Thus larger values of $\mu(C, C; \underline{c}, \underline{c})$ both increase the objective function and help satisfy the constraints. Moreover, increasing $\mu(C, D; \underline{c}, \underline{c})$ and $\mu(D, C; \underline{c}, \underline{c})$ increases $U(\mu)$ by half as much and has the same effect on the constraints as $\mu(C, C; \underline{c}, \underline{c})$, whereas increasing $\mu(D, D; \underline{c}, \underline{c})$ has no effect on $U(\mu)$ or the constraints. Thus any optimal μ must have $\mu(C, C; \underline{c}, \underline{c}) = 1$. In words, if both players report low costs, the mediator always chooses mutual cooperation as the outcome.

Second, in all expressions the coefficients of $\mu(C, C; \bar{c}, \bar{c})$, $\mu(C, D; \bar{c}, \bar{c})$, and $\mu(D, C; \bar{c}, \bar{c})$ are negative, hurting both the objective function and the constraints. Thus any optimal μ must have $\mu(D, D; \bar{c}, \bar{c}) = 1$. That is, if both players report high costs then the mediator always chooses mutual defection as the outcome.

Incorporating these conclusions into the (IC$\bar{c}$) constraint allows us to drop that constraint altogether. To see this, use the properties of μ just derived to rewrite (IC$\bar{c}$) as

$$-(1 - p)(2b - \bar{c}) - \mu(C, C; \underline{c}, \bar{c})(2p - 1)(2b - \bar{c})$$
$$-[\mu(C, D; \underline{c}, \bar{c}) + \mu(D, C; \underline{c}, \bar{c})][p(2b - \bar{c}) - b]$$
$$+\mu(D, C; \underline{c}, \bar{c})\bar{c} \geq 0.$$

Moving the second term to the right-hand side and then rearranging the left-hand side yields

$$(\bar{c} - 2b)[1 - p + p\mu(C, D; \underline{c}, \bar{c}) + p\mu(D, C; \underline{c}, \bar{c})]$$
$$+ b[\mu(C, D; \underline{c}, \bar{c}) + \mu(D, C; \underline{c}, \bar{c})]$$
$$+ \bar{c}\mu(D, C; \underline{c}, \bar{c}) \geq \mu(C, C; \underline{c}, \bar{c})(1 - 2p)(\bar{c} - 2b).$$

Now the second and third terms on the left-hand side are nonnegative; further, the $p\mu$ terms inside the brackets in the first term on the left-hand side are nonnegative as well. On the right-hand side, the μ term is of course less than or equal to 1; thus for this constraint to hold it would suffice to have $(\bar{c} - 2b)(1 - p) \geq (\bar{c} - 2b)(1 - 2p)$, which is always true. Hence the (IC$\bar{c}$) constraint is satisfied for any μ that meets the conditions previously derived.

After factoring out a common $p(1-p)$ from the payoff function, the remaining problem is to choose $\mu(\cdot, \cdot; \underline{c}, \bar{c})$ to

$$\max[\mu(C, C; \underline{c}, \bar{c})(4b - \underline{c} - \bar{c}) + \mu(C, D; \underline{c}, \bar{c})(2b - \underline{c})$$
$$+ \mu(D, C; \underline{c}, \bar{c})(2b - \bar{c})]$$

subject to (IC$\underline{c}$), which now takes the form

$$(1 - p)(2b - \underline{c}) + \mu(C, C; \underline{c}, \bar{c})(2p - 1)(2b - \underline{c})$$
$$+ \mu(C, D; \underline{c}, \bar{c})[p(2b - \underline{c}) - b]$$
$$+ \mu(D, C; \underline{c}, \bar{c})[p(2b - \underline{c}) + \underline{c} - b] \geq 0.$$

Notice that $\mu(C, D; \underline{c}, \bar{c})$ has the largest coefficient in the objective function. Clearly (IC$\underline{c}$) would be satisfied by a mechanism setting $\mu(C, D; \underline{c}, \bar{c})$ as large as the constraint will allow and putting the remaining probability weight on (D, D). This may not be the optimal mechanism; for certain parameter values, it is better to put some or all weight on (C, C).[15] Still, the simpler mechanism suggested here would yield the payoff given in Proposition 2: the constraint is satisfied with equality by setting

$$\mu(C, D; \underline{c}, \bar{c}) = \frac{(1 - p)(2b - \underline{c})}{b - p(2b - \underline{c})},$$

and the resulting payoff when $(c_1, c_2) = (\underline{c}, \bar{c})$ is

$$\mu(C, D; \underline{c}, \bar{c}) p(1 - p)(2b - \underline{c}).$$

Plugging this into the overall payoff expression yields an expected payoff of $(1 - p)^2(2b - \underline{c})b/[b - p(2b - \underline{c})]$, as required in Proposition 2.   □

REFERENCES

Abreu, Dilip, David Pearce, and Ennio Stacchetti (1990), "Toward a Theory of Discounted Repeated Games with Imperfect Monitoring," *Econometrica* 58: 1041–63.

Aumann, Robert J., M. Maschler, and R. E. Stearns (1968), "Repeated Games of Incomplete Information: An Approach to the Non-Zero-Sum Case," in *Report to the U.S. Arms Control and Disarmament Agency* (Final Report on Contract S.T. 143). Prepared for the U.S. Arms Control and Disarmament Agency by Mathematica, Inc., Princeton, NJ.

---

[15] The actual optimal mechanism for this problem gives a slightly higher payoff for certain parameter values; specifically, when the "high" cost is not too high but it occurs relatively often, the optimal mechanism puts more weight on (C, D) and positive weight on (C, C) when the players report $(\underline{c}, \bar{c})$. The simpler mechanism reported here is sufficient for the results proved in this chapter. However, the calculation of the true optimal mechanism, as well as algebraic details of the construction reported here, are available from the author on request.

Axelrod, Robert (1980), "Effective Choice in the Prisoner's Dilemma," *Journal of Conflict Resolution* 24: 3-25.

(1984), *The Evolution of Cooperation*. New York: Basic Books.

Banks, Jeffrey S., and Randall L. Calvert (1992), "A Battle of the Sexes Game with Incomplete Information," *Games and Economic Behavior* 4: 347-72.

Bendor, Jonathan (1987), "In Good Times and Bad: Reciprocity in an Uncertain World," *American Journal of Political Science* 31: 531-58.

Calvert, Randall L. (1992a), "Leadership and Its Basis in Problems of Social Coordination," *International Political Science Review* 13: 7-24.

(1992b), "Rational Actors, Equilibrium, and Social Institutions," in J. Knight and I. Sened (eds.), *Explaining Social Institutions*. Cambridge: Cambridge University Press.

Dionne, Georges (1983), "Adverse Selection and Repeated Insurance Contracts," *The Geneva Papers on Risk and Insurance* 8: 316-32.

Downs, Anthony (1957), *An Economic Theory of Democracy*. New York: Harper and Row.

Farrell, Joseph (1987), "Cheap Talk, Coordination, and Entry," *RAND Journal of Economics* 18: 34-9.

Feller, William (1968), *An Introduction to Probability Theory and Its Applications, vol. I*, 3rd ed. New York: Wiley.

Greif, Avner, Paul Milgrom, and Barry Weingast (1990), "The Merchant Guild as a Nexus of Contracts," Working Papers in Political Science P-90-9, Hoover Institution, Stanford University.

Holmstrom, Bengt, and Roger B. Myerson (1983), "Efficient and Durable Decision Rules," *Econometrica* 51: 1799-1819.

Koford, Kenneth J. (1982), "Centralized Vote-Trading," *Public Choice* 39: 245-68.

Jackson, John E. (1990), "Institutions in American Society: An Overview," in John E. Jackson (ed.), *Institutions in American Society*. Ann Arbor: University of Michigan Press.

Malueg, David A. (1986), "Efficient Outcomes in a Repeated Agency Model without Discounting," *Journal of Mathematical Economics* 15: 217-30.

(1988), "Repeated Insurance Contracts with Differential Learning," *Review of Economic Studies* 55: 177-81.

Milgrom, Paul, Douglass C. North, and Barry R. Weingast (1990), "The Role of Institutions in the Revival of Trade: The Law Merchant, Private Judges, and the Champaign Fairs," *Economics and Politics* 2: 1-23.

Myerson, Roger B. (1985), "Bayesian Equilibrium and Incentive Compatibility: An Introduction," in L. Hurwicz et al. (eds.), *Social Goals and Social Organization: Essays in Memory of Elisha Pazner*. Cambridge: Cambridge University Press.

Porter, Robert (1983), "Optimal Cartel Trigger Price Strategies," *Journal of Economic Theory* 29: 313-38.

Radner, Roy (1981), "Monitoring Cooperative Agreements in a Repeated Principal-Agent Relationship," *Econometrica* 49: 1127-48.

(1985), "Repeated Principal-Agent Games with Discounting," *Econometrica* 53: 1173-98.

(1986), "Repeated Partnership Games with Imperfect Monitoring and No Discounting," *Review of Economic Studies* 53: 43-57.

Radner, Roy, Roger Myerson, and Eric Maskin (1986), "An Example of a Repeated Partnership Game with Discounting and with Uniformly Inefficient Equilibria," *Review of Economic Studies* 53: 59-69.

Rapoport, Anatol, and Albert M. Chammah (1965), *Prisoner's Dilemma*. Ann Arbor: University of Michigan Press.

Rubinstein, Ariel (1979), "An Optimal Conviction Policy for Offenses That May Have Been Committed by Accident," *Applied Game Theory:* 406-13.

Schelling, Thomas C. (1960), *The Strategy of Conflict*. Cambridge, MA: Harvard University Press.

Schotter, Andrew (1981), *The Economic Theory of Social Institutions*. Cambridge: Cambridge University Press.

Segerstrom, Paul S. (1988), "Demons and Repentance," *Journal of Economic Theory* 45: 35-52.

Shepsle, Kenneth A., and Barry R. Weingast (1981), "Structure-Induced Equilibrium and Legislative Choice," *Public Choice* 37: 503-19.

Sugden, Robert (1986), *The Economics of Rights, Co-operation, and Welfare*. Oxford: Basil Blackwell.

Taylor, Michael E. (1976), *Anarchy and Cooperation*. New York: Wiley.

CHAPTER 9

The courts and slavery in the United States: Property rights and credible commitment

John N. Drobak

The famous compromises of the first half of the nineteenth century are well-known examples of Congress's attempt to reinforce the credibility of the commitment to the institution of slavery that was written into the Constitution. The compromises allowed the expansion of slavery into some territories and maintained the power of the slave states in the Senate through the balance rule (Weingast 1991, pp. 6–9). Less known, however, is the role played by the federal courts in reaffirming the constitutional commitment to slavery. Beginning in the 1830s, the state courts of the North, through their interpretation of state statutes and their development of the common law, began to rule with increasing hostility to the rights of slaveowners. The state courts in the South responded by giving less deference to these northern rulings and eventually disregarding them. As the chasm grew between the state courts of the North and South, the federal courts, including those in the northern states, worked at maintaining and sometimes strengthening the federal government's commitment to preserve slavery.

The work of the federal courts reached its culmination in *Dred Scott v. Sandford,* the best known of these cases. *Dred Scott,* although resting heavily on principles of states' rights, took a new and powerful approach by constitutionalizing property rights in slaves through the due-process clause. The approach in *Dred Scott,* dramatic and inflammatory to the North, laid the seeds for further constitutional (and therefore federal) limitations on the power of the free states. Lincoln, in his campaign for the presidency, expressed the fear of many northerners that *Dred Scott*

I wish to thank the following people for their helpful comments: Arthur Denzau, John Ferejohn, Stanton Krauss, Douglass C. North, Robert B. Thompson, Andrew Rutten, and Barry Weingast. I am also indebted to the thorough compilation and analysis of state and federal cases concerning slavery and federalism in P. Finkelman, *An Imperfect Union: Slavery, Federalism and Comity* (1981). I hope that my contribution is a worthy complement to his fine book.

could give truth to John C. Calhoun's claim that "slavery is national, freedom sectional" (Finkelman 1984, p. 263). This commitment in *Dred Scott* to the preservation of slavery was so radical to the North that the decision became one of the events that pushed the country into war three years later. Ironically, the decision did little to placate the South. By 1857, when the Supreme Court decided *Dred Scott,* decades of ever-increasing hostility toward slavery had made it too late for the courts to make the federal commitment to slavery credible.

The actions of the courts reflect, of course, both the governing law and the participants in the judicial process. The pro-slavery provisions of the Constitution and the federal statutes carrying them out sometimes gave little choice to a judge, so a judge who was staunchly anti-slave would occasionally end up authoring a pro-slavery opinion.[1] It was also to be expected that federal courts sitting in northern states would render decisions that supported slavery more than their state-court counterparts. Many of the presidents who appointed the federal judges were themselves pro-slavery. And the state judges were less apt to hear controversies that were governed by the pro-slavery federal law. Both the abolitionists and the pro-slavery forces used the courts to develop the law in their favor. Some of the most able advocates of the day took part in many of the slavery suits, intentionally litigating far-reaching principles. Similarly, many of the most powerful slavery opinions were written by highly respected judges on prestigious courts, just as some were authored by pro-slavery Democrats who were ridiculed for letting their personal ideology take precedence over the law. Finally, it is important to remember that courts seldom are the source of social change. The work of the courts reflects changes that are driven by political, economic, ideological, and religious factors. That was truly the case with slavery. The story of the courts in the conflict between North and South is only one chapter in a much larger story, but it is nonetheless an important chapter. The courts shaped some aspects of the slavery crisis, affected the likelihood of successful compromise, and influenced the pace at which the country moved toward war.

This chapter will examine the courts' role in the commitment of the federal government to the preservation of slavery. After describing the constitutional framework for slavery, the chapter will analyze the tension between the courts of the free and slave states and explain the importance of the federal courts' attempts to counteract the decisions of the northern

---

[1] For example, Justice Joseph Story, well known for his anti-slavery views, wrote the opinion in *Prigg v. Pennsylvania,* a case that upheld the constitutionality of the 1793 Fugitive Slave Law and expanded federal authority at the expense of the states (Storing 1988, p. 49).

state courts. The chapter will end by examining the impact of these court decisions on the tension between the North and South on the eve of the Civil War.

1   The Constitution

Any analysis of the role of the courts must start with the Constitution. Even though the Framers were too squeamish to use the words slave or slavery, there is no doubt that the Constitution accommodated the existence of slavery at the time the document was written and established legal principles that would be used to preserve it into the future. Nine clauses of the Constitution dealt with slavery in some way. The best known are the clauses that counted slaves as three-fifths for voting and taxation purposes, the sentence that gave Congress the power to ban the importation of slaves after 1807, and the section that required the return of fugitive slaves. Other clauses empowered Congress to suppress insurrections (which to at least some of the Framers meant slave uprisings), limited amendment of the slave trade and proportionate taxation sections until 1808, and prohibited the taxation of exports (which could have been an indirect tax on slavery through taxation of the products of slave labor).[2]

There has long been great debate on whether the Framers intended to preserve slavery or only accommodated it as a temporary phenomenon, with the expectation of its withering away. Following the views of William Lloyd Garrison that the Constitution united the states by a "covenant with death" and "agreement with Hell," the radical abolitionists saw no hope for universal freedom under the Constitution. Consequently, many radical abolitionists in the 1830s supported secession of the free from the slave states (Potter 1976, p. 45; Wieck 1988, p. 35). But the black abolitionist Frederick Douglass claimed that

the Federal Government was never, in its essence, anything but an anti-slavery government. Abolish slavery tomorrow, and not a sentence or syllable of the Constitution need be altered. It was purposely so framed as to give no claim, no sanction to the claim, of property in man. If in its origin slavery had any relation to the government, it was only as the scaffolding to the magnificent structure, to be removed as soon as the building was completed. (quoted in Jensen 1988, pp. 9–10)

Even today, scholars continue this debate over the Framers' expectations.[3]

---

[2] U.S. Constitution, art. I, §2, cl. 3; art. I, §9, cl. 1; art. IV, §2, cl. 3; art. I, §9, cl. 4; art. I, §8, cl. 15; art. IV, §4, cl. 4; art. V; art. I, §9, cl. 5; and art. I, §10, cl. 2. See Wieck 1988, p. 32.

[3] For example, see the views of Justice Thurgood Marshall in "Reflections on the Bicentennial" (1989) and the response in Jensen (1988). See generally Goldwin & Kaufman (1988).

Regardless of any hopes in 1787 for the gradual demise of slavery, technology made that impossible. The invention of the cotton gin and the birth of the cotton economy in the South at the beginning of the nineteenth century induced a gigantic expansion of slavery, making slavery too profitable to end on its own (Fogel 1989, pp. 29–34). Likewise, regardless of whatever the original intent of the Framers concerning the Constitution's governance of slavery, the uncertainty over the precise terms of the Constitution's accommodation of slavery and the power left to the states in the original federal structure both provided the courts with ways to reinforce the federal government's commitment to slavery.

2   Comity and state sovereignty

2.1   *Commitment to slavery in the South*

Perhaps the aspect of the Constitution that supported slavery to the fullest was the Constitution's silence on the issues of who was a slave and how a slave became free. By leaving these issues untouched, the Constitution continued to leave them to the states. It is ironic that the Bill of Rights – through the tenth amendment's admonition that all powers not delegated to the federal government remain with the states or the people – expressed the notion of limited federal authority, which would result in nearly all issues of slavery remaining within state control. Leaving to the states the issue of who was enslaved or free was also consistent with the common law's treatment of status as a local issue.

The federal government has always left issues of status to the states. Even today, it is state law that determines whether someone is divorced, whether a child is legitimate, whether a particular parent has custody, and whether someone qualifies as an heir. Although it may seem inappropriate today to include slavery with these issues, whether someone is a slave or free is legally an issue of the person's status, historically left to the states until the thirteenth amendment abolished slavery.

State control over the existence of slavery also stemmed from the common-law view that slavery was against "natural law" and thus could not legally exist without "positive" (i.e., statutory) law authorizing its existence. This notion was instilled in the American common law by the famous case of *Somerset v. Stewart,* which greatly curtailed slavery in England in 1772. As Lord Mansfield, the Chief Justice of the Court of the King's Bench, wrote in *Somerset:*

The state of slavery is of such a nature, that it is incapable of being introduced on any reasons, moral or political; but only by positive law, which preserves its force long after the reason, occasion, and time itself from whence it was created, is erased from memory: it's so odious, that nothing can be suffered to support it, but positive law. (p. 510)

These three factors – the Constitution's implicit recognition of a state's authority to determine whether slavery will be legal within its borders, the historical allocation of issues of status to state control, and the need for positive law to legalize slavery – all gave strong legal support for the slave states to maintain the existence of slavery. Throughout the antebellum slavery crisis, there was no real likelihood that slavery would become illegal in the South, although the abolitionists hoped otherwise. President Lincoln and the Republican leaders, who rode to victory on their opposition to any expansion of slavery, tried to avert war by supporting a constitutional amendment to preserve slavery in the slave states (Potter 1976, pp. 550, 565). This proposed constitutional amendment, so astonishing to us today, would have been essentially an express codification of the then-prevailing view of the legality of slavery in the South.

2.2   Slaveowners' rights in the North

The controversy over the expansion of slavery into the territories is well known from a litany of important historical events: the Missouri Compromise in 1820, the Compromise of 1850, the Kansas–Nebraska Act in 1854, the 1857 *Dred Scott* decision, Lincoln's election in 1860, and the failed attempts at the Crittenden compromise on the eve of the Civil War. But at the same time, another dispute over slavery was slowly growing: the ability of the free states to free slaves who came within their borders and the extent to which the Constitution compelled them to support the institution of slavery. This was a dispute over the relative importance of state sovereignty, comity, and federalism in the states themselves, not in the territories. Congress took the lead in the dispute over the territories, while federal and state courts were the key players in the controversy between the states.

Historically, a state's authority to affect the status of someone within its borders depended upon the degree of permanence of that person's connection with the state. There was no doubt that a person's physical presence in the state, coupled with the intention to remain permanently, was enough for a state to use its authority to determine status. So if a slaveowner moved with his slaves to a free state and became a resident of that state, the free states viewed themselves as having the legal authority to free the slaves. On the other hand, if a slaveowner journeyed through a free state with his slaves, at least into the 1840s, the free states would not alter the status of a slave in transit. The more difficult issues involving the requisite connection between the slave and the state arose in the context of a slaveowner's less than permanent presence in a free state with a slave, such as a slaveowner's temporary six-month or even six-week visit to a free state with a slave.

The rights given to visiting slaveowners in Pennsylvania are typical of the rights of slaveowners throughout the North until the mid-1830s. Pennsylvania was a leader among the states in the movement to free the slaves even before the enactment of the Constitution. Philadelphia was the home of the country's first active anti-slave society, whose members zealously worked to free slaves brought into Pennsylvania by their masters and gladly helped fugitive slaves. Bordered by slave states, Pennsylvania was a busy station on the underground railroad and was frequently visited by professional slave catchers. On the other hand, Philadelphia was a leading commercial center and, during the 1790s, the nation's capital. As a result, it was the site of visits and temporary residence by many slaveowners and their slaves (Finkelman 1984, pp. 46-7).

In 1780, Pennsylvania enacted an emancipation statute that attempted to end slavery without hindering economic growth. The statute freed the children of Pennsylvania slaves upon birth but required them to remain apprentices until they turned 18. Members of Congress and diplomats were permitted to retain their domestic slaves. The law freed the slaves of other people if the slaves were kept in Pennsylvania for longer than six months. An amendment in 1788 freed slaves of new Pennsylvania residents the instant they became residents (Finkelman 1984, p. 48).

The emancipation statute led to considerable litigation over the years, much instigated by the Abolition Society, to resolve questions unanswered by the statute.[4] Although the Pennsylvania courts broadly carried out the state's policy toward freedom, the opinions through the mid-1830s show that the courts acted differently toward nonresident slave owners – by assisting with the return of fugitive slaves, by adhering strictly to the six-months rule and by protecting the transit of slaves through the state.[5] This was also typical for the courts in the other free states into the 1830s. By then, however, public sentiment against slavery was growing much stronger. This attitude was soon reflected in the state courts.

[4] These questions included, for example, such issues as what constituted residency, making the six-month period inapplicable, and whether a series of visits to Pennsylvania could aggregate to six months.

[5] For example, the Abolition Society argued in *Respublica v. Richards* that the Pennsylvania statutes gave every black – whether free, slave, or fugitive slave – the right to a judicial hearing before being removed from the state. The Pennsylvania Supreme Court rejected that interpretation, reasoning that it would unduly burden masters who were legally in the state with their slaves. The court concluded that a master not only had a right to remove a slave, but if the slave resisted, "it was the duty of every magistrate to employ all the legitimate means of coercion in his power, for securing and restoring the negro to the services of his owner" (*Respublica*, p. 224). See Finkelman (1984, pp. 63-4, 68-9).

The northern abolition societies and some of the most able lawyers in the North had been striving to get the courts to adopt the principles of *Somerset v. Stewart.* In 1836, the Supreme Judicial Court of Massachusetts rendered an opinion in *Commonwealth v. Aves* that deeply affected the development of slavery law in both the North and South. The case concerned a slaveowner from New Orleans who visited her father in Boston, intending to remain there for a few months. She brought with her a six-year-old slave girl. Shortly after their arrival, the Boston Female Anti-slavery Society sued in the state court to free the girl. Some of the most prestigious members of the Boston bar took up the cause of each side. (One of the lawyers for the slaveowner, Benjamin Curtis, would ultimately rise to the United States Supreme Court and dissent in *Dred Scott,* relying on some of the arguments made by his opponent in *Aves;* Finkelman 1984, p. 103.) In an opinion written by Chief Justice Lemuel Shaw, one of the country's most influential jurists of his time, the court freed the slave and developed a rationale that could have been used to end nearly all the rights of slaveowners in free states.

Shaw acknowledged that slavery was recognized by the Constitution and many of the states, even though it was contrary to natural law. He understood that comity to the interests of the slave states supported a ruling that Massachusetts could not free the slave, but he saw the severe restraint this analysis would impose on Massachusetts' attempts to deal with slavery within its borders. As Shaw explained, "the right of personal property follows the person, and . . . by the comity of nations the same must be deemed his property everywhere." But this approach would impinge on the free states: "[I]f slavery exists anywhere, and if by the laws of any place a property can be acquired in slaves, the law of slavery must extend to every place where such slaves may be carried." This logic would make slavery legal in Massachusetts. So Shaw reasoned that comity should "apply only to those commodities which are everywhere, and by all nations treated and deemed subject of property" (*Aves,* p. 216). This, of course, excluded slaves.

After rejecting the application of comity, Shaw turned to the importance of local law. Noting that slave states considered the relationship between owner and slave to be "a creature of municipal law," Shaw pointed out that everyone entering Massachusetts was subject to all of its laws and "entitled [only] to the privileges which those laws confer." He concluded that slaves entering Massachusetts became free "not so much because any alteration is made in their status or condition," but because the laws of the state, applying to everyone except fugitives, "prohibit their forcible detention or forcible removal" (*Aves,* p. 217).

Although the opinion made *Aves* a broad precedent, Shaw did attempt to limit the reach of *Aves* into certain areas. After noting that *Aves* did not involve a fugitive slave, Shaw pointed out that a slaveowner could pass through a free state with a captured fugitive. He also emphasized that *Aves* did not involve a traveling slaveowner who "necessarily passes through a free State, or where by accident or necessity he is compelled to touch or land therein, remaining no longer than necessary." He gave no opinion about the outcome of that kind of case, but speculated (probably hopefully) that "our geographic position exempts us from the probable necessity of considering such a case" (*Aves*, p. 225).

The importance of the *Aves* decision was obvious to both the South and North. Typical of the concern in the South, the *Augusta Sentinel* asked southerners if they were "willing to sustain forever a confederation with states into which you dare not travel with your property, lest that property becomes by law actually confiscated" (Finkelman 1984, p. 125). Abolitionists applauded the decision and quickly tried to expand the holding of *Aves* to other states. The courts of the free states gradually followed Massachusetts. By 1860 nearly all the free states had embraced some version of *Aves* through the common law, statutes, or state constitutions.[6] This made it impossible for slaveowners to visit many free states with their slaves. Even if the law of a state had not developed to the full extent of *Aves,* it was risky for a slaveowner to send or journey with a slave into the state. Whenever a slave entered a state, there was always the risk that abolitionists would free the slave physically or through a writ of habeas corpus, contending that state law made the slave legally free. This would force the master to sue for return of the slave, with the uncertainty over how the court would rule. Sometimes the slave would have vanished, leaving the owner with only a suit for damages against the abolitionists.

The expansion of the *Aves* principles culminated in a decision in 1860 by the New York Court of Appeals in *Lemmon v. The People.* The case involved husband and wife slaveowners from Virginia who were traveling in late 1852 to Texas via New York City with their eight slaves. The fastest route was to travel from Virginia to New York by ship and then from New York to New Orleans by steamboat. There was no steamboat service to New Orleans from the Virginia area; the overland route took much longer. Although the ship's captain warned the slaveowners not to take the slaves ashore in New York, they disregarded the warning and checked into a hotel with their slaves to wait the three days until the steamboat departed. Within the day, the slaveowners were served with a writ of habeas corpus to free the slaves (Finkelman 1984, p. 296). Early in the nineteenth century, New York State had enacted a statute, similar to Pennsylvania's,

---

[6] All of the free states had embraced some version of *Aves* except California, Illinois, Indiana, New Jersey, and Oregon. Finkelman (1984, p. 127, n. 4).

that freed all slaves who remained in New York more than nine months. The judge in the habeas corpus proceeding in *Lemmon* freed the slaves, concluding that an 1841 repeal of the nine-month provision had the effect of freeing all slaves who entered New York State upon their entry into the state.

This ruling answered the question left open in *Aves* because it dealt with slaveowners in transit with their slaves, not with a slaveowner who entered a state with an intention to remain, however temporarily. And it caused consternation in the South. The *Richmond Daily Dispatch* saw the decision cutting into the roots of the Union:

> If it be true that the inhabitants of one State had not the right to pass with their property through the territory of another, without forfeiting it, then the Union no longer exists. The objects for which it was instituted, and for which the Constitution of the United States was established, have been rendered, in one respect, impossible of attainment. Fifteen States have been declared out of the pale of legal protection, so far as New York can effect it, and the citizens of these states cannot pass through New York with property of a certain kind, without losing it, though it is recognized by the Constitution of the United States. (November 17, 1852, quoted in Finkelman 1984, pp. 298–9)

The slaveowners in *Lemmon,* who had been compensated by the New York business community after the freed slaves fled to Canada, had no interest in appealing the habeas corpus decision. With such an important principle at stake, the Virginia legislature directed the state attorney general to proceed with an appeal in the New York state courts and appropriated funds for the appeal. The governor of Virginia took up the cause against the *Lemmon* decision in his 1853 annual message:

> If it be true that the citizens of the slaveholding States, who, by force of circumstances, or for convenience, seek a passage through the territory of a non-slaveholding State with their slaves, are thereby deprived of their property in them, and the slaves *ipso facto* become emancipated, it is time that we know the law as it is. No court in America has ever announced this to be law. It would be exceedingly strange if it should be. By the comity of nations the personal status of every man is determined by the law of his domicile. . . . This is but the courtesy of nation to nation founded not upon the statute, but is absolutely necessary for the peace and harmony of States and for the enforcement of private justice. A denial of this comity is unheard of among civilized nations, and if deliberately and wantonly persisted in, would be just cause of war. (quoted in Finkelman 1984, p. 300)

After the case had worked its way through the New York appellate system, the Court of Appeals, New York's highest court, finally announced its decision in April 1860. In a five-to-three decision to free the slaves, the court affirmed the trial judge's conclusion that the 1841 statute freed all slaves upon their entry into New York. The majority saw itself bound to follow the direction of the New York legislature rather than common-law principles of comity. It also viewed the case as raising an issue of status, controlled by state law, implicitly rejecting the notion that something more than transitory presence was necessary before a state could regulate status. In rejecting the claim that people in transit were protected by the commerce or privileges-and-immunities clauses of the Constitution, the majority pointed out that if the Constitution were interpreted as allowing the federal government to "rightly interfere in the regulation of the social and civil condition of any description of persons within the territorial limits of the respective States of the Union, it is not difficult to foresee the ultimate result" – federal interference with slavery in the South (*Lemmon, p.* 625). The majority expressly distinguished the problem of transit with fugitive slaves, because the fugitive-slave clause of the Constitution established limits on state power.

The dissent relied on the Constitution's creation of a union between slave and free states. Emphasizing the greater importance of comity between the states in the United States when compared to comity between nations, the dissent claimed that the Constitution prohibited a state from ignoring "the right to property in the labor and service of persons *in transitu* from [slave] States," although a state was free "to abolish or retain slavery in reference to its own inhabitants" (*Lemmon, p.* 643). The dissent also expressed the fear that the majority's rejection of comity to the slave states was playing into the hands of the supporters of secession and could lead to civil war. *Lemmon* was not appealed to the Supreme Court, although opponents of the decision apparently rattled their sabers about getting the Supreme Court that decided *Dred Scott* to also rule on *Lemmon* (Finkelman 1984, p. 313). Other events on the eve of the Civil War dwarfed *Lemmon* in importance, however.

These cases in the courts of the free states, from the mid-1830s to 1860, exacerbated the growing tension between the North and South over slavery. The lawsuits enraged slaveowners, both because the rulings limited their movement out of the South and because the judges' rhetoric insulted their way of life. The slaveowners also feared that these decisions created incentives for slaves to escape and, even worse, to revolt. The fear of violent slave insurrection was a powerful influence in the antebellum South.[7]

---

[7] For example, Jefferson was referring to slave insurrection when he wrote that "we have a wolf by the ears and we can neither hold him, nor safely let him go. Justice is in one scale, and self preservation in the other" (quoted in Storing 1988, p. 56). See also Buchanan's annual message to Congress in December 1860, quoted in Potter (1976, p. 519). This fear was a reason for many of the detailed arcane laws of slavery in the South that treated slaves as property, that tried to rid the South of free blacks, and that did everything possible to limit the education, gathering, power, and other aspects of slaves that could lead to revolt.

2.3   *The response of the southern courts*

Through the early nineteenth century, courts in the South were quite le-
nient in recognizing the freedom of slaves who had gained their freedom
under the law of a free state or territory.[8] This issue arose in various ways.
Sometimes a slave who had spent time in a free state would sue for freedom in his home state in the South and claim his freedom under the law
of the free state. Sometimes the effect of the law of a free state would
be treated when a freed slave was involved in litigation in a southern
court over an inheritance. In reaching these decisions, the southern courts
sometimes expressly relied on comity, respecting the law of the state that
freed the slave. Sometimes the courts, relying on the positive-law theory
of *Somerset,* reasoned that a slave who had become free could not be
re-enslaved without a statute expressly providing for that. A few southern courts also found a common-law preference for freedom.

  Rankin v. Lydia, an 1820 decision by the Kentucky Court of Appeals,
was one of the leading southern court opinions supporting freedom. Lydia, who was born a slave in Kentucky, sued for her freedom following her
return to Kentucky after a seven-year stay in the free Indiana territory.
In ruling for Lydia, the court relied on natural law and comity. Emphasizing the distinction between residence and transit in a free jurisdiction,
the court reasoned that Lydia was free under Indiana law. Then it concluded that it was "not aware of any law of [Kentucky] which can or does
bring into operation the right of slavery when once destroyed" (*Rankin,*
p. 471). The court even declared that "freedom is the natural right of man,
although it may not be his birthright" (p. 476). In its reliance on comity,
the court emphasized the tit-for-tat problem inherent in a rejection of
comity. If Kentucky ignored the laws of Indiana, Indiana could very well
do the same and free transient slaves from Kentucky. This, of course,
implied that the court would re-examine its conclusions if the free states
acted more harshly toward slave owners.

  Although "the Kentucky court remained, with respect to comity, one
of the most consistent and fair-minded of any of the slave-state courts"
in its dealings with slaves who had been freed in other states (Finkelman
1984, p. 205), one Kentucky decision stands out as an example of the
slave states' retreat from comity with the North. In 1847, the Pennsylvania
legislature repealed its six-month clause, attempting to free slaves the instant they touched Pennsylvania soil. The next year a Kentucky slaveowner

---

[8] This was true for border states, such as Kentucky and Missouri, as well as Mississippi and
   Louisiana in the deep South. In fact, until the Missouri Supreme Court declared that Dred
   Scott had remained a slave, the Missouri courts had consistently recognized the freedom
   of a slave who had resided in a free state or territory (Brophy 1990, p. 196, n. 24).

took her slave to Pennsylvania, where a free black promptly sought a writ of habeas corpus to free the slave. A Pennsylvania state judge freed the slave in the habeas corpus proceeding, but the slave returned with her master to Kentucky. Two years later the slave sued for her freedom in Kentucky state court, relying on the 1847 Pennsylvania statute and the Pennsylvania judgment. In *Maria v. Kirby,* the Court of Appeals rejected her claim. Reasoning from the premise that some permanent connection is required before a state can affect status, the court in *Kirby* concluded that Pennsylvania lacked the authority to stamp "a new and permanent condition or *status*" on a nonresident who was in Pennsylvania "on a transient entry or momentary sojourn" so that the new status would "adhere to them and determine their condition on their return to their own domicile" (*Maria v. Kirby,* p. 545). The decision was particularly important because the court not only rejected the effect of the Pennsylvania statute but also rejected the effect of the judgment of the Pennsylvania court. The court refused to apply comity to Pennsylvania judgments that denied "rights of property established by [Kentucky] law," rights that should have been respected in Pennsylvania under those same principles of comity (p. 547).

Louisiana had been more tolerant of free blacks than most southern states and relatively liberal in recognizing the freedom of slaves freed elsewhere, probably as a consequence of its French heritage and legal system (Finkelman 1984, p. 206). As slavery became the divisive issue in the country, the Louisiana courts became much more pro-slavery. In two different cases in the early 1850s, the Louisiana Supreme Court was forced to decide if someone currently in the state remained a slave under the law of Mississippi (where they had been enslaved) or had been freed under the law of Ohio (where the slaves had been manumitted). In each case the court chose slavery because manumission (emancipation) was considered a "fraud" against the laws of Mississippi (*Mary v. Brown; Haynes v. Forno*). In 1846, the Louisiana legislature enacted a statute declaring that "no slave shall be entitled to his or her freedom under the pretense that he or she has been, with or without the consent of his or her owner, in a country where slavery does not exist, or in any of the States where slavery is prohibited" (Act of May 30, 1846). In *Barclay v. Sewell,* a case in which the Louisiana Supreme Court held that an 1839 Ohio emancipation was legal because it occurred before the Louisiana statute went into effect, the court explained that the 1846 statute was enacted "probably in consequence of injudicious and impertinent assaults from without upon an institution thoroughly interwoven with our interior lives" (*Barclay v. Sewell,* p. 263).

As the sectional conflict worsened, even the rhetoric of the southern opinions hardened. In 1859, the Mississippi Supreme Court, in a vitriolic opinion scornful of comity to the North, refused to recognize the manumission in Ohio of a Mississippi slave. As the court put it, "the rights of Mississippi are outraged, when Ohio ministers to emancipation and the abolition of our institution of slavery, by such unkind, disrespectful, lawless interference with our local rights" (*Mitchell v. Wells,* p. 263). This change in attitude of the southern courts toward the freedom of slaves was a response to the growing anti-slave sentiment and activity outside the South. In departing from a long line of precedent recognizing the freedom of slaves freed in free states and territories, the Missouri Supreme Court in its opinion in the *Dred Scott* case explained:

> Times are not as they were when the former decisions on this subject were made. Since then not only individuals but States have been possessed with a dark and fell spirit in relation to slavery, whose gratification is sought in the pursuit of measures, whose inevitable consequence must be the overthrow and destruction of our government. Under such circumstances it does not behoove the State of Missouri to show the least countenance to any measure which might gratify this spirit. (*Scott v. Emerson,* p. 586)

3 The pro-slavery federal courts

As the courts in the free states worked to limit slavery, the federal courts became decidedly pro-slavery and rendered a series of decisions that reaffirmed the federal government's commitment to slavery. Until the mid-1840s, federal decisions were mixed, with some supporting the northern states' attempts to free slaves who entered their territory. In 1845, Supreme Court Justice John McLean, sitting as a circuit judge in Indiana, rendered the last major federal decision supporting the freedom of slaves obtained through transit or residence in a free state (*Vaughn v. Williams;* Finkelman 1984, p. 250). After that, the Supreme Court and lower federal courts generally protected slaveowners. The federal courts could not stem the tide of freedom, but, with their decisions and their opinions, they sure tried.

3.1 Fugitive-slave cases

The early pro-slavery federal decisions carried out the 1793 Fugitive Slave Law, enacted to enforce the fugitive-slave clause of the Constitution. In 1842, Justice Joseph Story, who believed that the federal scheme created by the Constitution gave states the authority to free slaves who entered into their territory (Finkelman 1984, p. 297, n. 30), interpreted the Fugitive Slave Law in *Prigg v. Pennsylvania* to be a constraint on state power. Prigg had been convicted under a Pennsylvania personal liberty law for removing a fugitive slave from the state without an order from a magistrate. In *Prigg,* the Supreme Court held the Pennsylvania law to be an unconstitutional violation of the fugitive-slave clause. Justice Story explained that the 1793 federal law did not compel the states to assist in any way with the federal right to recapture slaves; their rights as sovereigns under the Constitution freed them from any obligation to assist. On the other hand, the states could not interfere with the right to recapture, nor could they interfere with people traveling through their territory with captured fugitive slaves. Thus, there was a constitutional limitation excepting fugitive slaves from the states' attempts to free slaves who entered into their territories.[9]

The harsh Fugitive Slave Law of 1850, an important part of the Compromise of 1850, stirred up widespread protest and resistance to the law in the North, as well as more federal litigation. The Supreme Court dealt with this problem in *Ableman v. Booth,* an appeal from a decision of the Wisconsin Supreme Court freeing an abolitionist who had been convicted of violating the 1850 act. In *Ableman* Chief Justice Taney, writing for a unanimous court, overruled the state court, reaffirmed the supremacy of federal law, and emphasized each state's obligation to support all the provisions of the federal Constitution – even a clause as repugnant to a state as the fugitive slave clause.

3.2   *Federal transit cases*

With fugitives having no protection in the free states, the question of whether a slave was a fugitive or lawfully within a state often became crucial. *Oliver v. Kauffman,* an 1850 decision by a federal circuit court in Pennsylvania, is a good example of the pro-slavery approach of the federal courts on this issue. Two months after Pennsylvania repealed its six-months statute, thereby making slaves free upon their entry into Pennsylvania, a slaveowner crossed Pennsylvania with her slaves while returning home to Maryland. A few months later, the slaves ran back to Pennsylvania, where they were aided by Kauffman. After the slaveowner failed to recover the slaves, she sued Kauffman for their value under the fugitive slave act. Kauffman defended by claiming that the people he helped were not slaves, having become free by Pennsylvania law upon their passage through the state.

The judge told the jury that the law required him, not the jury, to decide which state law applied in determining whether the blacks Kauffman

---

[9] Ten years later, in 1852, the Supreme Court upheld in *Moore v. The People* the constitutionality of an Illinois statute making criminal the harboring of a fugitive slave. The Court ruled that states had the authority to assist the purpose of the fugitive-slave clause.

helped were slaves or free. Since the blacks had resided in Maryland, he concluded that the issue depended upon "the law of Maryland, and not of Pennsylvania. This Court cannot go behind the status of these people where they escaped" (*Oliver v. Kauffman*, p. 660). With this preference for the law of the slave state over that of the free, the judge instructed the jury that the blacks were slaves when they left Maryland and entered Pennsylvania. Consequently, the jury had little choice but to find Kauffman liable.[10]

While the circuit court was deciding *Oliver*, the Supreme Court established a related legal principle in *Strader v. Graham*. The case concerned a slaveowner's suit against an owner of a steamboat on which three slaves escaped from Kentucky to Ohio and then on to Canada. The suit, brought in Kentucky state court under a Kentucky statute, turned on whether the slaves were free blacks when they boarded the steamboat, as a result of their earlier journeys into free states to perform as musicians. The Kentucky court ruled that the slaves had not become free under Kentucky law even though their owner had allowed them to work in Ohio and Indiana. On appeal to the Supreme Court, the steamboat owner claimed that the Kentucky court had erred when it refused to apply the law of the free states. Chief Justice Taney, again writing for a unanimous court, ruled that the Supreme Court lacked the jurisdiction to review this issue of state law. Relying on the "undoubted right" of every state to determine the status of its residents, Taney concluded that "[i]t was exclusively in the power of Kentucky to determine for itself whether [the slaves'] employment in another State should or should not make them free on their return" (*Strader*, p. 94). The Court would not force Kentucky to apply the laws of Ohio and Indiana.

The reasoning of *Dred Scott* has roots in a concurrence in *Groves v. Slaughter*, an 1841 case involving the effect of a provision in the Mississippi constitution that prohibited the importation of slaves purchased outside the state. By ruling that the constitutional provision had no legal effect until the Mississippi legislature implemented it through a statute, the Supreme Court avoided the more difficult issue of whether the provision violated the commerce clause. Nonetheless, three justices wrote concurrences to express their views on the issue.

---

[10] Five year later, another federal court in Pennsylvania considered the effect of the repeal of the six-months statute and concluded that it affected only people who resided or sojourned in Pennsylvania with their slaves. The Constitution, the court concluded, protected the right of passage of both person and property through states. Thus, a free state could not affect the "property" of slaveowners passing through (*U.S. v. Williamson*, pp. 686, 692-3). This case, relying on the constitutional protection of slaves as property, presaged the analysis used by the Supreme Court in *Dred Scott*.

Justice McLean wrote that the commerce clause could not be applicable because slaves were people, not property, under the Constitution. He acknowledged that the laws of some states treated slaves as property, but those laws had no bearing on the reach of the commerce clause (*Groves v. Slaughter*, pp. 506–7). In response, Justice Baldwin asserted that slaves were property under the Constitution: "whenever slavery exists by the laws of a state, slaves are property in every constitutional sense, and for every purpose" (p. 517). As a Democrat from Pennsylvania, Baldwin would have been sensitive to the issue of slave transit (Finkelman 1984, p. 270). So it is not surprising that he developed the slaves-as-property theme in the context of slave transit. Baldwin wrote:

If, however, the owner of slaves in Maryland, in transporting them to Kentucky, or Missouri, should pass through Pennsylvania, or Ohio, no law of either state could take away or affect his right of property; nor, if passing from one slave state to another, accident or distress should compel him to touch at any place within a state, where slavery did not exist. Such transit of property, whether of slaves or bales of goods, is lawful commerce among the several states, which none can prohibit or regulate, which the constitution protects, and Congress may, and ought to preserve from violation. (*Groves v. Slaughter*, p. 516)

These decisions, in the Supreme Court and in the lower federal courts, were part of the federal government's commitment to slavery. The federal courts generally took the side of slavery as the sectional crisis grew, but they came nowhere near approaching Congress in terms of stirring up resentment and controversy in the free states and territories – not until the Supreme Court decided *Dred Scott,* that is.

3.3   *Dred Scott v. Sandford*

Dred Scott was a slave to any army doctor who lived in the Jefferson Barracks in St. Louis. In 1834, the doctor took Scott to Illinois, a free state, and then to the upper Louisiana Territory (now Minnesota), which was also free. In Illinois, Scott married and fathered a baby girl. After Scott and his family returned to Missouri in 1838 with the doctor, Scott sued in state court, claiming he was free by virtue of his four years' residency in a free state and a free territory. He lost in the Missouri state courts, when the Missouri Supreme Court departed from well-established precedent that freed slaves who had lived in free states. Scott then sued in federal court.

The lawsuit was widely known and controversial when it was pending before the Supreme Court. The case was argued twice before the Court rendered its opinion in 1857. It appears that the Court originally planned to dispose of the case with a brief opinion, relying on *Strader v. Graham*. The justices changed their minds, in part because of pressure from some of the pro-slavery justices to write a broader and stronger pro-slavery opinion. The result was a long, rambling, and – even for its day – racist "Opinion of the Court" written by Chief Justice Taney (Fehrenbacher 1978, pp. 428–31). Six other justices concurred with Taney; two dissented. All the justices wrote separate opinions to explain their positions.

Taney wrote that Congress lacked the power under the Constitution to declare slavery illegal in the territories. Thus, he held that the Missouri Compromise of 1820 was unconstitutional, only the second time in the history of the Supreme Court that it declared an act of Congress unconstitutional.[11] Taney rested this conclusion on two grounds. First, with some contorted legal logic and reliance on a Southern constitutional theory advanced by John C. Calhoun, Taney was able to shrink the meaning of the words of the Constitution that give Congress the power to make rules and regulations for the territories. Calhoun had claimed that the Constitution required the federal government to recognize the fundamental rights of all states, including the right of slavery (Brophy 1990, pp. 197–200). In order to treat the slave states on equal terms with those that had abolished slavery, Congress had to permit slavery in the territories.[12]

As a second basis for the holding of unconstitutionality, Taney relied on the protection of property in the due-process clause of the fifth amendment.[13] This was the first use of economic substantive due process by the Supreme Court. The key section of the opinion is brief:

[T]he rights of property are united with the rights of person, and placed on the same ground by the fifth amendment to the Constitution, which provides that no person shall be deprived of life, liberty and property, without due process of law. And an act of Congress which deprives a citizen of the United States of his liberty or property, merely because he came himself or brought his property into a particular territory of the United States, and who had committed no offence against

[11] When the Supreme Court decided *Dred Scott* in 1857, Congress had already repealed the Missouri Compromise by the Kansas–Nebraska Act, which allowed the settlers in the previously free territory to decide for themselves whether they wanted to be free or slave.
[12] *Dred Scott*, pp. 441–52. Since the Missouri Compromise was unconstitutional, Scott no longer had any basis to claim he had become free. Taney also rested the decision on a third conclusion: as a black, whether slave or free, Scott had no rights under the Constitution and hence no standing to sue in federal court. The decision about this issue, the most racist and also the longest part of Taney's opinion, had virtually no support in either legal precedent or history (see Fehrenbacher 1978, pp. 340–66). And the conclusion was devastating for free blacks, since it deprived them of all federal rights, including access to federal court.
[13] For an interpretation of the opinion as limited in its reliance on due process, see Fehrenbacher (1978, pp. 382–4).

the laws, could hardly be dignified with the name of due process of law. (*Dred Scott*, p. 450)

Taney's opinion left no doubt that a slave was property for constitutional purposes and protected by the Constitution as a species of property (*Dred Scott*, p. 451).

Some historians believe that Taney and the majority of the justices had hoped that they could strike a workable national compromise on the slavery issue through the *Dred Scott* opinion, succeeding where Congress had failed for decades. It is virtually impossible that the Supreme Court could have done that in the late 1850s, even with a more palatable outcome and a better-crafted opinion. What the Court gave the country in *Dred Scott* was a source of outrage and fear to the North, a powerful political tool to the growing Republican party, and a wedge that drove the country even further apart. The Court gave the South important pro-slavery legal principles in *Dred Scott,* but that commitment to slavery could not counteract all the anti-slavery sentiment and action in Congress and in the free states and territories. With *Dred Scott,* the Supreme Court threw oil on the kindling fires of sectional conflict (Potter 1976, p. 118).

Before the Supreme Court decided *Dred Scott,* the law provided strong support for the states that chose to abolish slavery. This stemmed from the law of status, historically within state and not federal authority, and the great power given to states in the federal scheme created by the Constitution. At the margin, the battle was over the power of a state to free a nonresident transient slave, as in *Lemmon,* or a slave within the state on a short visit. With those limited exceptions, most people, in both the North and South, accepted the authority of free states to eliminate slavery within their borders. *Dred Scott* changed that. Since slaves were now considered to be property protected by the Constitution, it was possible that the protection of property rights would ultimately outweigh both the historical power of states to control status and the authority to control in-state slavery as an aspect of state sovereignty. Many people feared that the Supreme Court, especially the pro-slavery Court that decided *Dred Scott,* could just as well expand the notion of a constitutional protection of slaves as property to restrict the free states' prohibition of slavery. Even though the fifth amendment restricted only the federal government, not the states, it was possible that the constitutional protection of slavery in the free states could have been buttressed on either the commerce clause or the privileges-and-immunities clause (Finkelman 1984, pp. 326–36). This constitutional theory would reinforce the trend in the federal courts to protect the owners of transient slaves. It could make it impossible for free states to prevent short or perhaps even long visits within their borders by slaves. It is inconceivable that the property rights theory could have been expanded to prevent states from freeing the slaves of their own residents.[14] But up to that limit, states could have lost much control over slavery within their own borders. To the opponents of slavery, the in-state presence of a potentially large number of transient or sojourning slaves would have changed drastically the atmosphere within the state and made the state essentially no longer free.

The decision in *Dred Scott* became a lightning rod for anti-slavery sentiment. Northerners protested, editorials expressed outrage, and politicians used worst-case extensions of the principles of *Dred Scott*. The legislatures of a number of free states passed resolutions condemning the decision (Fehrenbacher 1978, pp. 431–5). Lincoln built much of his campaigns around the prospects of the South attempting to make slavery national. *Dred Scott* was an important part of this argument, at least as early as his House Divided Speech during the 1858 Senate campaign (Fehrenbacher 1978, p. 438; Finkelman 1984, p. 316). Many Republicans believed that the next step for the Supreme Court was to reverse *Lemmon* or a similar case.

Besides its stimulus to the anti-slavery fervor and its political impact, the opinion in *Dred Scott* had other important consequences that limited the potential approaches to the slavery crisis. *Dred Scott* established significant limits on the federal power over slavery. By reinforcing the view that slavery was primarily an issue for the states, and by raising the fifth amendment's protection of property, the Court left Congress with little power over slavery. This limited the ways that Congress could have attempted to broker a compromise to prevent war.

Dred Scott also affected the methods that could have been used to abolish slavery in the South. Three approaches could have been taken. First, adhering to the fifth amendment theme of *Dred Scott,* Congress could have used the eminent-domain power, recognized in the fifth amendment, to condemn the slaves as property. It been calculated that the required "just compensation" would have been one year's GNP for the entire nation in the 1860s – surely too costly to northern politicians and taxpayers (Lee & Passell 1979, chap. 10). In addition, many northerners would have felt that compensation for the slaves was actually ransom, which should not be paid as a matter of principle. A possible way to

---

[14] *Dred Scott* was inconceivable to many in its day. "[I]f the Dred Scott decision had not been rendered, it might have seemed incredible that the Court could deny the power of Congress to regulate slavery in the territories despite the fact that it had been doing so since 1789 under Article IV, Section 3, of the Constitution, which specified that 'the Congress shall have power to . . . make all needful rules and regulations respecting the Territory or other property belonging to the United States'" Potter (1976, p. 351).

avoid compensation would have been to use gradual emancipation, as the northern slave states and some Caribbean countries had. There were two drawbacks to that approach – one legal, one practical. Gradual emancipation would have been analogous legally to the modern approach to eliminating existing uses of property that fail to conform to a changed zoning ordinance. Generally there is no requirement for compensation as long as the property owner is allowed to continue the nonconforming use long enough to realize substantial income from the property and to plan a move to another, conforming location. But this analogy breaks down because slaves could not be moved to produce income later; they would be freed. Further, it is likely that a Supreme Court composed of justices like the ones who decided *Dred Scott* would have found gradual emancipation to be an unconstitutional violation of the fifth amendment. The practical problem stems from the extreme difficulty, perhaps impossibility, of maintaining a large slave system throughout the South in which children became free at an early age and adults remained slaves or became indentured for many years. With the different treatment of some slaves and with the prospects of true freedom in the future for the rest, the system would have been too unstable to last in this form.

A second approach to the abolition of slavery in the South could have been a constitutional amendment either expressly abolishing slavery or giving Congress the power to gradually eliminate it. The fifteen slave states could have blocked any amendment, however, because amendment requires ratification by three-fourths of the states. Furthermore, the constitutional theory of Calhoun, espoused in *Dred Scott,* would prohibit amendment of the Constitution to eliminate such a "fundamental" right, inherent in the original Union, without unanimous consent by all the states.

A third approach could have been for the Supreme Court to change the constitutional law of slavery. The *Dred Scott* Court would not have undone its own handiwork. And it would have taken until the late 1860s or early 1870s for two successive Republican presidents to change the composition of the Court to anti-slavery, had there not been a war (Finkelman 1984, p. 323). There was an even more fundamental problem, however. Although much of the analysis of *Dred Scott* lacked support in precedents, other parts of the opinion were consistent with earlier federal cases. Even if a new Supreme Court could have rejected the holding of *Dred Scott* and ruled that slaves became free when they touched free soil, the Court would have faced a virtually impossible task if it had tried to make inroads against slavery in the South. The Constitution, with its accommodation of slavery and its recognition of the power of the states, would have been a formidable barrier to judicial emancipation. Finally, if a new Supreme Court had later overruled *Dred Scott* and attempted to limit slavery, the South would have resisted just as violently as it actually did – unless the South had changed enough by then to begin to support emancipation on its own.

None of these options for emancipation was feasible. Even if the Supreme Court had stayed out of the national controversy over slavery by avoiding *Dred Scott* and similar cases, it is inconceivable to me that the country would have avoided civil war. If there might have been some chance for peaceful settlement, *Dred Scott* diminished it and made war even more likely as the only way to emancipation. As many historians believe, "the Dred Scott decision bears directly upon the coming of the Civil War."[15]

4 Conclusion

The thirteen colonies would not have become the United States of America but for the Constitution's commitment to slavery. And a constitutional commitment is one of the strongest, most secure promises a government can give. As anti-slavery sentiment grew in the North beginning in the 1830s, the northern state courts began to rule with increasing hostility to slavery. These rulings never threatened the existence of slavery in the South, although they made it risky for slaveowners to travel into free states and led slaveowners to believe that the rulings encouraged slaves to escape and revolt. The anti-slavery actions and rhetoric throughout the North, including the state court decisions, undercut the commitment to slavery. To help hold the line, the federal courts became increasingly pro-slavery, reinforcing the Constitution's and the federal government's commitments to slavery. As public sentiment in the North began to swell against slavery, it became harder and harder for the federal government to maintain its obligations to slavery. The Constitution made the task easier by protecting the existence of slavery in the South. But all other aspects of slavery became more difficult to preserve.

Sometimes commitments can no longer be made credible. By 1857, when the Supreme Court decided *Dred Scott,* the country's attitude toward slavery had changed so much since the ratification of the Constitution that the Supreme Court could do little to make the slavery commitment credible. Words in the Constitution and in court opinions meant little when compared to thirty years of ever-increasing anti-slave activity. The commitment to slavery could never again be credible.

[15] Kutler (1967, p. xviii). See Bestor (1964, pp. 327, 345); Fehrenbacher (1978, p. 3); Finkelman (1984, p. 274); and Potter (1976, pp. 291–3).

TABLE OF CASES

REFERENCES

Bestor, A. E. (1964), "The American Civil War as a Constitutional Crisis," *American Historical Review* 69: 327-52.
Brophy, A. L. (1990), "Note, Let Us Go Back and Stand Upon The Constitution: Federal-State Relations in *Scott v. Sandford*," *Columbia Law Review* 90: 192-224.
Fehrenbacher, D. E. (1978), *The Dred Scott Case: Its Significance in American Law and Politics*. New York: Oxford University Press.
Finkelman, P. (1981), *An Imperfect Union: Slavery, Federalism and Comity*. Chapel Hill: University of North Carolina Press.
Fogel, R. W. (1989), *Without Consent or Contract: The Rise and Fall of American Slavery*. New York: Norton.
Goldwin, R. A., and A. Kaufman, eds. (1988), *Slavery and Its Consequences: The Constitution, Equality, and Race*. Washington, DC: American Enterprise Institute for Public Policy.
Jensen, E. (1988), "Commentary: The Extraordinary Revival of *Dred Scott*," *Washington University Law Quarterly* 66: 1-10.
Kutler, S., ed. (1967), *The Dred Scott Decision: Law or Politics?* Boston: Houghton Mifflin.
Lee, S. P., and P. Passell (1979), *A New Economic View of American History*. New York: Norton.
Marshall, T. (1989), "Reflections on the Bicentennial of the United States Constitution," *Harvard Law Review* 101: 1-5.
Potter, D. M. (1976), *The Impending Crisis, 1848-1861*. New York: Harper & Row.

Storing, H. J. (1988), "Slavery and the Moral Foundations of the American Republic," in R. A. Goldwin and A. Kaufman (eds.), *Slavery and Its Consequences: The Constitution, Equality and Race*. Washington, DC: American Enterprise Institute for Public Policy.

Weingast, B. (1991), "Institutions and Political Commitment: A New Political Economy of the American Civil War Era," unpublished manuscript, Hoover Institution, Stanford University.

Wieck, W. M. (1988), "'The Blessings of Liberty': Slavery in the American Constitutional Order," in R. A. Goldwin and A. Kaufman (eds.), *Slavery and Its Consequences: The Constitution, Equality, and Race*. Washington, DC: American Enterprise Institute for Public Policy.

CHAPTER 10

On the pervasiveness of sophisticated sincerity

Tim Groseclose and Keith Krehbiel

Consider a setting in which members of a collective choice body can choose the rules of collective choice. Once chosen, rules are binding constraints on behavior, at least in the short run. Thus, the setting lies somewhere in the middle of a spectrum whose two endpoints are what might be called *strong Riker* (1980), which is characterized by rampant and instant inheritability, and *strong Shepsle* (1979), which is characterized by rock-solid and immutable institutionalism. Parliamentary rights, therefore, are not inalienable. They may not even be property rights. Nevertheless, they have some bite in terms of constraining behavior during the choice process.

Institutions, rules, or procedures – which, by definition, structure choice settings by assigning parliamentary rights – are potentially valuable not only to individual recipients of special rights but also, perhaps, to the collectivity. As such, intuition suggests that assignors of parliamentary rights will pay close attention to their de facto institutional design choices. For instance, if it were possible under some institutional arrangements to avoid costs associated with members' strategically lying or misrepresenting their preferences, then such institutional arrangements should be pervasive.

Are institutional arrangements such as this pervasive in collective choice settings? An initial attempt to answer this question must focus on institutional possibilities for truthful revelation of preferences that may not be public information. Though stated somewhat differently in recent research by Austen-Smith (1987), such revelation of preferences is the essence of his concept of *sophisticated sincerity.* Following Banks and Gasmi (1987), Austen-Smith proves that when the set of proposals on an agenda is formed endogenously – that is, actors rationally offer proposals prior to the commencement of voting over a known finite agenda – an equilibrium always exists in which voting on the resulting agenda is both sophisticated (utility maximizing) and sincere (truthfully revealing). Truthful revelation is an optimal strategy for all voters with any configuration of preferences. Or, in common parlance, honesty is the best policy.[1]

This theoretical insight and surrounding interpretations have mixed and sometimes murky implications for viewing real voting situations and conducting empirical analysis. If Austen-Smith's model is a reasonable representation of collective choice processes within voting bodies, then the sophisticated voting hypothesis is difficult to test in isolation and impossible to test against the sincere voting hypothesis. However, Ordeshook and Schwartz take issue with the class of voting theory of which Austen-Smith's work is an example. After noting that the preponderance of voting theory presumes *amendment agendas,* Ordeshook and Schwartz present findings that suggest that previous results do not extend to "common type[s] of congressional agenda[s]" (1987, p. 181). As such, the models of Austen-Smith and others are perhaps not reasonable approximations of actual collective choice processes. If so, then we should try to analyze and interpret more realistic models.

This chapter attempts to clarify the relationship between voting theory and voting practices by reassessing theoretically the claims of Austen-Smith and Ordeshook and Schwartz, by qualifying and extending those claims, and by reinterpreting them in a somewhat richer empirical context. Section 1 introduces the model. Section 2 presents results for endogenously constructed amendment agendas, including a stronger version of Austen-Smith's theorem with a relatively short and transparent proof. Section 3 presents results for other types of agendas, culminating in a proposition that under so-called congressional agendas, sophisticated sincerity *never* occurs. Section 4 is a discussion.

1   Assumptions and definitions

A set of alternatives $X = \{x_1, \ldots, x_M\}$ exists over which voters $N = \{1, 2, \ldots, n\}$ have preferences defined by the binary relation P_i, $i = 1, 2, \ldots, n$. P_i is complete, transitive, and asymmetric; hence

$$x_j\, P_i\, x_k \;\Rightarrow\; \neg(x_k\, P_i\, x_j).$$

Social preferences are determined by majority rule and represented by the binary relation P, where

---

[1] To be more precise, honesty is *a* best policy. Obviously, *honesty* here means truthful revelation. See, for example, Black's (1958) discussion of the Borda method and its properties under the assumption of sincere voting. Black (p. 182) quotes Borda: "My scheme is only intended for honest men." Less obviously, *best policy* refers not to the welfare properties of the sophisticated outcome but rather to a set of optimal voting strategies.

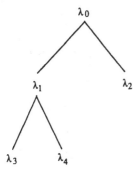

Figure 1.

$$x_j \, P \, x_k \iff |\{i : x_j \, P_i \, x_k\}| > n/2.$$

We assume that n is odd; thus P is complete and asymmetric. In terms of social preferences, this implies no ties.

1.1 Voting trees

There exists a binary voting tree defined by a set of nodes Λ and an asymmetric binary relation Q. We adopt the convention of labeling nodes by λ_i, $i = 1, 2, \ldots$, reserving the symbol λ_0 to indicate the top node of the voting tree. Q represents whether one node immediately follows another node. For instance, consider Figure 1. In this voting tree, the nodes are $\Lambda = \{\lambda_0, \lambda_1, \ldots, \lambda_4\}$, and the following Q relations are true: $(\lambda_0 \, Q \, \lambda_1)$, $(\lambda_0 \, Q \, \lambda_2)$, $(\lambda_1 \, Q \, \lambda_3)$, and $(\lambda_1 \, Q \, \lambda_4)$. All other Q relations are false. For instance, $\neg(\lambda_4 \, Q \, \lambda_0)$, since λ_0 does not follow λ_4. Similarly, $\neg(\lambda_4 \, Q \, \lambda_1)$. This approach allows us to define the following correspondence.

Definition. Let $Q(\lambda_i) = \{\lambda_j : \lambda_i \, Q \, \lambda_j\}$.

For all $\lambda \in \Lambda \setminus \lambda_0$, $Q^{-1}(\cdot)$, the inverse of $Q(\cdot)$, is well defined, single-valued, and thus a function. $Q^{-1}(\cdot)$ maps any nonzero node into its unique, immediately preceding node. For instance, in our example $Q^{-1}(\lambda_3) = Q^{-1}(\lambda_4) = \lambda_1$ and $Q^{-1}(\lambda_1) = Q^{-1}(\lambda_2) = \lambda_0$.[2]

We reserve the symbol Λ_t to represent the *terminal nodes* of the tree. For instance, in Figure 1 $\Lambda_t = \{\lambda_2, \lambda_3, \lambda_4\}$. For all nonterminal nodes, $Q(\lambda_i)$ has exactly two elements. These are the two nodes connected by the left

---

[2] In some instances, the following dummy-variable notation for one node following another is useful: $Q(\lambda_i, \lambda_j) = 1$ if $\lambda_i \, Q \, \lambda_j$, or 0 otherwise.

and right branches emanating from λ_i. Let $Q_L(\lambda_i)$ denote the left node and $Q_R(\lambda_i)$ denote the right node. Thus, for example, in Figure 1 $Q_L(\lambda_1) = \lambda_3$ and $Q_R(\lambda_1) = \lambda_4$.

Next we define the competing node of λ_i and the nodes within the subtree defined by λ_i.

Definition.   The *competing node* of λ_i is $C(\lambda_i) = Q(Q^{-1}(\lambda_i)) \backslash \lambda_i$.

Definition.   The *nodes within the subtree* of λ_i comprise the set

$$\bar{Q}(\lambda_i) = \{\lambda_j : \lambda_i \; Q \; \lambda_j \text{ or } \exists (\lambda_{i_1}, \lambda_{i_2}, ..., \lambda_{i_m}) \text{ such that }$$
$$\lambda_i \; Q \; \lambda_{i_1} \; Q \; \lambda_{i_2} \; Q \cdots Q \; \lambda_{i_m} \; Q \; \lambda_j \}.$$

1.2   The voting game

The game begins with a set of proposers $\{1, 2, ..., T\}$ who name proposals in a specified order. The proposers are a subset of N and therefore have preferences defined by P_i. Their proposals are represented by the ordered set $y = (y_1, y_2, ..., y_T)$. We assume that the order of proposing is specified in advance and known to all proposers.[3]

Proposers are not allowed to repeat any previous proposal, but they are allowed to decline to propose. We represent this decision with the symbol ϕ. Thus if proposer t declines to propose, we write $y_t = \phi$.[4]

Although proposers cannot repeat previously named alternatives, they can always decline to propose, even if a past proposer has declined to propose. This allows us to write the relevant proposal space for proposer t as

$$y_t \in \phi \cup (X \backslash \{y_1, y_2, ..., y_{t-1}\}).$$

We assume that the net cost of proposing is positive unless otherwise noted.[5] Specifically, for any alternative $x \in X$, proposer t prefers having outcome x and not making a proposal to having outcome x and making a proposal. Thus, for any given proposer, if any proposal he makes results in the same outcome for the voting game, then he will decline to propose.

---

[3] We make this assumption primarily for heuristic purposes. As it turns out, the assumption can be relaxed substantially and the propositions still follow. For instance, they still follow if we adopt Austen-Smith's assumption that once a proposer is chosen and has named an alternative, the next proposer is selected from a lottery over proposers not yet chosen.

[4] To avoid ambiguity, we denote the empty set as { }.

[5] In actual legislative situations, of course, benefits as well as costs are associated with proposing amendments. Among the most noteworthy arguments regarding benefits is

There exists a mapping $p^{-1}(\cdot)$ which is a correspondence from the elements in the ordered set of proposals $(y_1, y_2, \ldots, y_T)$ to the non-top nodes of the voting tree $\Lambda \backslash \lambda_0$. This mapping is exogenous and known to the proposers; the correspondence is onto and defined for all y_t. We also assume that $p^{-1}(y_t)$ is nonempty for all y_t, and that

$$\forall y_s, y_t \text{ such that } y_s \neq y_t, \quad p^{-1}(y_s) \cap p^{-1}(y_t) = \{ \}.$$

In other words, two different proposals cannot be mapped to the same node. These facts imply that $p(\cdot)$, the inverse of $p^{-1}(\cdot)$, is a function, is onto, and is defined $\forall \lambda \in \Lambda \backslash \lambda_0$. We shall call $p(\lambda_i)$ the *ostensive alternative* at node λ_i.

If an alternative is placed on the agenda, it must be possible, under some sequence of votes, to adopt that alternative as the final choice. In terms of the agenda tree, this means that, for any given node λ other than the initial node λ_0 and terminal nodes Λ_t, the ostensive alternative at that node $p(\lambda)$ is the ostensive alternative in at least one terminal node in the subtree $\bar{Q}(\lambda)$ defined by that node. Formally:

$$\forall \lambda \in \Lambda \backslash (\lambda_0 \cup \Lambda_t), \quad \exists \bar{\lambda} \in \bar{Q}(\lambda) \cap \Lambda_t \text{ such that } p(\bar{\lambda}) = p(\lambda). \tag{1}$$

Returning to our example from Figure 1, suppose $T = 3$ and $p^{-1}(\cdot)$ is defined by $p^{-1}(y_1) = \{\lambda_4\}$, $p^{-1}(y_2) = \{\lambda_2\}$, and $p^{-1}(y_3) = \{\lambda_1, \lambda_3\}$. Thus, we have $p(\lambda_4) = y_1$, $p(\lambda_2) = y_2$, and $p(\lambda_1) = p(\lambda_3) = y_3$. The voting tree with ostensive alternatives is shown in Figure 2. Voting consists potentially of two rounds. The first is between y_3 and y_2. If y_3 wins, the second round is between y_3 and y_1.

The term *agenda* refers to the voting tree and the mapping from alternatives to nodes. Formally, an agenda is the triple $(\Lambda, Q, p^{-1}(\cdot))$. Although the shape of the potential (maximally filled) voting tree is exogenous, the proposers' right to decline to propose implies that the actual tree on which votes are observed may be different. In Figure 2, for instance, suppose $y_1 = \phi$. Then the resulting voting tree will appear as in Figure 3. That is, nodes λ_3 and λ_4 are eliminated.

Mayhew's (1974) view that position taking plays a significant role in electoral success. This view possesses at least two offsetting or off-putting characteristics, however. First, it leaves unanswered the following important question: If an amendment is doomed to fail, why would a rational electorate reward a legislator for proposing it? Second, floor activity has expanded significantly in recent years (Smith 1989), and restrictive procedures are increasingly common (Bach and Smith 1988). It would seem to follow that, at the margin, the opportunities for proposal making have diminished because floor time is scarce, and likewise the costs of making a given proposal in terms of foregone future opportunities to make such proposals is great.

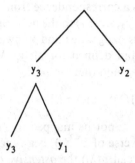

Figure 2.

Figure 3.

If at least one proposer declines, the voting tree changes shape through an elimination of specific nodes. We call the former tree the *potential agenda* and the latter tree the *observed agenda*. The potential and observed agendas are identical if and only if no proposer declines. If, however, one or more proposers declines, the trees differ as follows. Let t be the declining proposer; that is, $y_t = \phi$. The algorithm for constructing the observed agenda has four steps:[6]

1. For all $\lambda \in p^{-1}(y_t)$, eliminate these nodes.
2. Eliminate all subtrees emanating from these nodes.
3. For each of these nodes, eliminate the competing node.
4. Adjust the branches of the tree accordingly.

[6] The algorithm is defined more formally as follows. Let the new branches of the tree be described by Q', which is defined in terms of Q. Specifically,

$$Q'(\lambda_i, \lambda_j) = \begin{cases} 0 & \text{if } p(\lambda_j) = \phi, \\ 0 & \text{if } \lambda_j \in \bar{Q}(\lambda_k) \text{ for some } \lambda_k \text{ such that } p(\lambda_k) = \phi, \\ 0 & \text{if } p(C(\lambda_j)) = \phi, \\ 0 & \text{if } \lambda_j \in Q(\lambda_i) \text{ and } p(C(\lambda_i)) = \phi, \\ 1 & \text{if } Q^{-1}(Q^{-1}(\lambda_j)) = \lambda_i \text{ and } p(C(Q^{-1}(\lambda_j))) = \phi, \\ Q(\lambda_i, \lambda_j) & \text{otherwise.} \end{cases}$$

Finally, define $\Lambda' = \bar{Q}'(\lambda_0) \cup \lambda_0$.

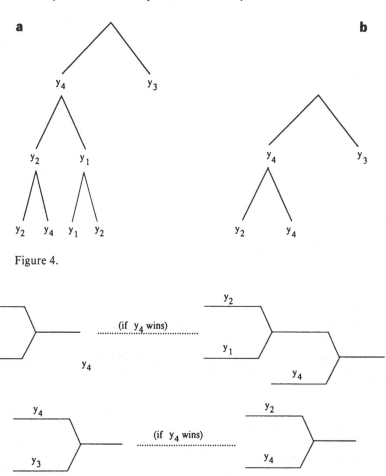

Figure 4.

Figure 4'.

This leaves a new set of nodes and a new Q relation. Define these as Λ' and Q', respectively. The function $p(\cdot)$ remains the same except that it is no longer defined for nodes $\Lambda \backslash \Lambda'$. For example, Figures 4a and 4b represent the potential and observed agendas when $y_1 = \phi$.[7]

[7] This convention may at first seem odd, but it becomes reasonable once we consider the voting trees in their corresponding tournament-style representations. In these representations, the observed agenda can be derived by treating a ϕ proposal as if it were an alternative that was defeated by all non-ϕ proposals. For instance, the tournament-style representation of the voting tree in Figure 4a is as appears in Figure 4'a. If $y_1 = \phi$, we write the new tournament-style representation as in Figure 4'b. Note that the corresponding voting-tree representation is exactly as appears in Figure 4b.

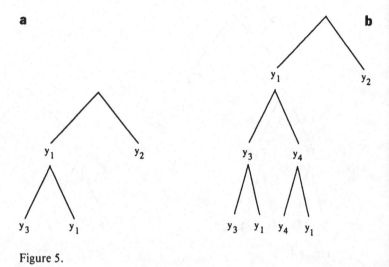

Figure 5.

Ordeshook and Schwartz (1987) present several terms for categorizing agendas. Two that we use are *continuity* and *symmetry*.

Definition.   An agenda is *continuous* if $\forall \lambda \in \Lambda \setminus \Lambda_t$, $p(\lambda) = p(Q_L(\lambda))$ or $p(\lambda) = p(Q_R(\lambda))$.

Definition.   An agenda is *symmetric* if for every node the left and right subtrees following this node are identical, with the exception of the alternatives at the top of the subtrees, which appear at exactly the same locations in the respective subtrees.[8]

The agenda in Figure 5a is continuous, while the agenda in Figure 5b is not. The agenda in Figure 6a is symmetric, while the agenda in Figure 6b is not. As an exercise, the reader may verify that the agenda in 6b is continuous, while Figure 6a is not.

---

[8] To define a symmetric agenda more formally, additional terminology is required. Consider Figure 1, and suppose we wanted to describe the relationship of node λ_0 to node λ_4. One might say λ_4 is the node reached from λ_0, first by traveling down the left branch and then traveling down the right branch. That is, $\lambda_4 = Q_R(Q_L(\lambda_0))$. We call $Q_R(Q_L(\cdot))$ a *compound Q*-function. Define Σ as the space of all such compound Q-functions. These functions describe the series of steps needed to travel from an upper node to a lower node. Let $\sigma(\cdot)$ denote a typical element of Σ. Hence $\sigma(\cdot) = Q_R(Q_L(\cdot))$ and $\sigma(\cdot) = Q_R(Q_L(Q_L(\cdot)))$ are two more examples of functions within Σ. Given this, define a symmetric agenda as one in which $\forall \lambda \in \Lambda \setminus \Lambda_t$, $\forall \sigma(\cdot) \in \Sigma$, $p(\sigma(Q_L(\lambda))) = p(\sigma(Q_R(\lambda)))$ or $[p(\sigma(Q_L(\lambda))) = p(Q_L(\lambda))$ and $p(\sigma(Q_R(\lambda))) = p(Q_R(\lambda))]$.

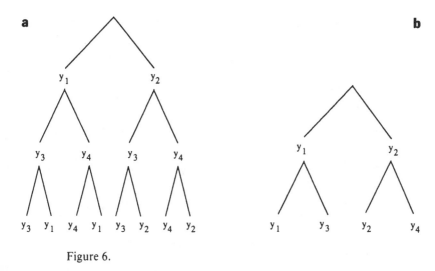

Figure 6.

Finally, we modify slightly Ordeshook and Schwartz's definition of an amendment agenda.

Definition. An *amendment agenda* is an agenda equivalent to $A(x_1, \ldots, x_m)$ for some $x_1, \ldots, x_m$, where $A(x_1, \ldots, x_m)$ is defined by the following recursion: $A(x_1)$ is the one-node tree with x_1 as the ostensive alternative at that node. $A(x_1, \ldots, x_{k+1})$ is the tree in which x_1 occupies the top node; the left subtree from this node is described by $A(x_1, x_3, x_4, \ldots, x_{k+1})$, the right subtree by $A(x_2, x_3, \ldots, x_{k+1})$.

By Ordeshook and Schwartz's definition, the top node of each amendment agenda has an associated ostensive alternative. In this chapter, the top node remains unlabeled. Figures 7a and 7b are examples of amendment agendas.

2 Sophisticated sincerity and amendment agendas

With these assumptions and definitions we can relate the following propositions.[9]

Proposition 1 (Ordeshook and Schwartz 1987, Theorem 2). *An agenda is an amendment agenda if and only if it is symmetric and continuous.*

[9] We use the term *proposition* to refer to any result that we prove or has been proven elsewhere. For lack of a better word, we use the term *fact* to refer to any result that is neither proven here nor introduced elsewhere but that is sufficiently obvious that proofs would only clutter the broader argument.

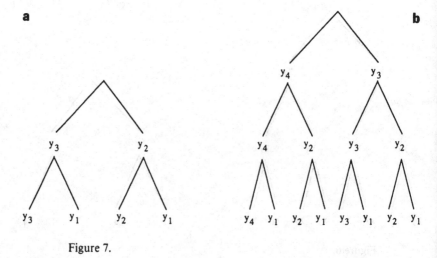

Figure 7.

Because of the symmetry and continuity of amendment agendas and the algorithm for truncating the voting tree if and when a proposer declines to propose, the following holds.

Fact 1. *If a potential agenda is an amendment agenda, then its observed agenda will be an amendment agenda.*

This holds no matter how many proposers decline. For example, the agenda represented by Figure 7a is the resulting observed agenda when Figure 7b is the potential agenda and $y_4 = \phi$. Consistent with Fact 1, Figure 7a is an amendment agenda. When the potential agenda is an amendment agenda, we can rewrite the ordered set of proposals as $y' = (y_1', y_2', ..., y_{T'}')$, where y_1' is the first non-ϕ proposal, y_2' is the second non-ϕ proposal, and so on. Thus, $T' \leq T$.

Another concern is whether an amendment agenda is backward built.

Definition. An amendment agenda is *backward built* if its representation
$$A(x_1, x_2, ..., x_m) \text{ has } x_1 = y_{T'}', x_2 = y_{T'-1}', ..., x_m = y_1'.$$

This means that alternatives proposed later appear higher in the voting tree. The amendment agenda in Figure 8a is backward built; the amendment agenda in Figure 8b is not.

The construction of a backward-built amendment agenda has an implication that is central to our proof of Austen-Smith's theorem.

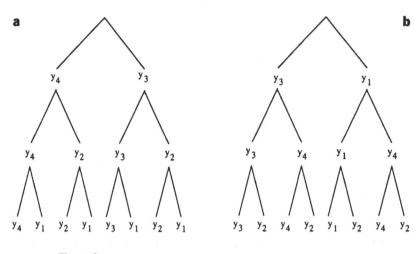

Figure 8.

Fact 2. *Let* $(y_1', y_2', ..., y_{T'}')$ *be the ordered set of non-ϕ proposals for a backward-built amendment agenda with corresponding observed voting tree* (Λ', Q'). *Let* λ *be an arbitrary node in* $\Lambda' \backslash \lambda_0$. *Let* $\bar{\lambda}$ *be an arbitrary node in* $\bar{Q}'(\lambda) \cap \Lambda_t'$, *and define* $y_s' = p(\lambda)$ *and* $y_t' = p(\bar{\lambda})$. *Then* $t \leq s$.

In other words, let y_s' be the ostensive alternative of any node of a backward-built amendment agenda, and consider the alternatives at the terminal nodes of this subtree. All such alternatives will have subscripts less than or equal to s. Likewise, none of these alternatives will have been proposed after y_s'.

After proposals are offered, voters are assumed to be *sophisticated* in the sense of Farquharson (1969), McKelvey and Niemi (1978), and others. It suffices to quote Banks (1989, p. 29) as follows.

Definition. We assume that individuals adopt *sophisticated voting* strategies, so that (1) at the final decision nodes (i.e., those followed only by terminal decision nodes), they vote for the preferred alternative from those associated with the subsequent terminal nodes; (2) at the penultimate decision nodes, they vote for the preferred alternative from those derived from the optimizing behavior of the voters at the final decision nodes; and so on, back up the tree. Thus, at each decision node we can associate an alternative that will be the ultimate outcome if that decision node is reached; label this outcome $s(\lambda)$.

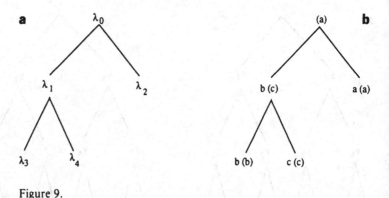

Figure 9.

The assumption of sophisticated voting in turn allows us to define recursively sophisticated equivalents at a given node and the sophisticated outcome of a voting game.

Definition. *Sophisticated equivalents* for an agenda are determined as follows:

$$\forall \lambda \in \Lambda'_t, \quad s(\lambda) = p(\lambda)$$

$$\forall \lambda \notin \Lambda'_t, \quad s(\lambda) = \begin{cases} s(Q_L(\lambda)) & \text{if } s(Q_L(\lambda)) \, P \, s(Q_R(\lambda)), \\ s(Q_R(\lambda)) & \text{otherwise.} \end{cases} \qquad (2)$$

Call $s(\lambda_0)$ the *sophisticated outcome* of the voting game.

For example, consider the voting tree of Figure 9a with corresponding agenda represented by Figure 9b, where ostensive alternatives are not in parentheses. Suppose the following social preferences hold: $a \, P \, c \, P \, b \, P \, a$. Then the sophisticated equivalents are given in parentheses beside the ostensive alternatives.

Given the definition of sophisticated equivalents, it follows that, for any given node and its corresponding subtree, if there is a Condorcet winner among alternatives at the terminal nodes of this subtree then this alternative, as a sophisticated equivalent, will figuratively rise to the top of the subtree. This is presented formally in the following proposition.

Proposition 2 (McKelvey and Niemi 1978, Corollary 1). *Let λ be any node in $\Lambda' \backslash \Lambda'_t$, and suppose that $\exists \bar{\lambda} \in \bar{Q}'(\lambda) \cap \Lambda'_t$ such that $\forall \lambda \in \bar{Q}'(\lambda) \cap \Lambda'_t$, $p(\bar{\lambda}) \, P \, p(\tilde{\lambda})$ or $p(\bar{\lambda})$. Then $s(\lambda) = p(\bar{\lambda})$.*

2.1 Sophisticated sincerity

During the first round of voting in Figure 9b, the vote is ostensibly between b and a. However, since c defeats b, voters know that a win for b in the first round ensures c as the eventual outcome. Consequently, in the first round, sophisticated voters treat this vote as a choice between c and a. In the voting literature such a case has sometimes been called *insincere* voting, since a voter who prefers c to a will ostensibly vote for b, even though he really may prefer a to this choice. The reason such a choice occurs is because, at node λ_1, the sophisticated equivalent is not the same as the ostensive alternative; that is, $s(\lambda_1) \neq p(\lambda_1)$. If such a case never occurs we say the agenda exhibits sophisticated sincerity.[10]

Definition. An agenda exhibits *sophisticated sincerity* if

$$\forall \lambda \in \Lambda' \setminus \lambda_0, \quad s(\lambda) = p(\lambda).$$

This definition is slightly stronger than what may commonly be thought of as sophisticated sincerity. We require not only that all realized votes have identical ostensive alternatives and sophisticated equivalents, but also that this condition holds for all unrealized votes as well. In other words, $p(\lambda) = s(\lambda)$ must hold even for nodes off the equilibrium path.[11]

In the rest of this section we show that sophisticated sincerity results for all backward-built agendas with endogenous agenda formation and costly proposing. First, however, we relate a simple method for determining winners of an amendment agenda. This is a slightly revised version of the method proposed by Shepsle and Weingast (1984), extended to allow for the case of proposers declining to propose.

---

[10] The analytic perspective we take here is akin to assuming Arrow's unrestricted domain. Specifically, for sophisticated sincerity to be guaranteed, we mean that for a given agenda process *and for all possible preferences over feasible alternatives*, sophisticated sincerity over the optimally constructed agenda is guaranteed.

[11] Our definition of sophisticated sincerity is also slightly stronger than Austen-Smith's. That is, any agenda exhibiting sophisticated sincerity by our definition will exhibit sophisticated sincerity by Austen-Smith's. Formally, Austen-Smith's definition, using our terminology, can be written as follows. An agenda exhibits (Austen-Smith) sophisticated sincerity if $\forall \lambda \in \Lambda' \setminus \Lambda'_i$, $s(Q_L(\lambda)) P_i s(Q_R(\lambda)) \Leftrightarrow p(Q_L(\lambda)) P_i p(Q_R(\lambda))$, $\forall i \in N$. Informally, Austen-Smith's definition only requires that ostensive alternatives and sophisticated equivalents be observationally equivalent to being identical, where here *observations* means votes by individual voters – both actual votes at nodes along the equilibrium path and potential votes off the equilibrium path. See Appendix II for a fuller explanation and an example of how our definitions differ.

Definition.   To identify *sophisticated winners on an amendment agenda*, let:

$$y_1^* = y_1;$$

$$y_{t+1}^* = \begin{cases} y_{t+1} & \text{if } y_{t+1} \ne \phi \text{ and } \forall s \le t, (y_s^* = \phi \text{ or } y_{t+1} P y_s^*), \\ y_t^* & \text{otherwise.} \end{cases}$$

Proposition 3 (Shepsle and Weingast 1984, Theorem 1).   *Let* $(\Lambda, Q,$ $p^{-1}(\cdot))$ *be a backward-built* (*potential*) *amendment agenda. Then* $s(\lambda_0) =$ y_T^*.

This definition and proposition give proposers a method for determining the set of alternatives that are not destined to fail – that is, proposals that are viable.

Definition.   A proposal is *viable* if it belongs to the set

$$W_t^* = \{x \in X : \forall s < t, \ y_s^* = \phi \text{ or } x P y_s^*\}.$$

Shepsle and Weingast call W_t^* the set of "non-innocuous alternatives." It is the set of proposals such that if all future proposers were to decline, the last-offered proposal would be the sophisticated outcome. Thus, if proposer t offered a proposal outside the set, it surely would not be the sophisticated outcome of the voting game. This establishes the following.

Fact 3.   *In an amendment agenda that is backward built under costly proposing,* $\forall t \le T, \ y_t = \phi \text{ or } y_t \in W_t^*$.[12]

Fact 4 follows straightforwardly from Fact 3.

Fact 4.   *In an amendment agenda that is backward built under costly proposing,*

$$\forall s, t \le T', \ y_s' P y_t' \Leftrightarrow s > t.$$

----

[12] A proof would show that naming a proposal y_t outside of W_t^* results in the same outcome of the voting game, $s(\lambda_0)$, as would the proposal $y_t = \phi$. Fact 3 would then follow from costly proposing. The difficult part of the proof is showing that a future proposer's optimal response is independent of whether $y_t = \phi$ or $y_t = x$, where $x \notin W_t^*$. In an earlier draft of this chapter we give such a proof. It begins by showing that T's optimal proposal is independent of t's choice of $y_t = \phi$ or $y_t = x$. Next one assumes that the same is true for all proposers $T, T-1, \ldots, T-j$, and shows that this implies it is true for $T-j-1$. By induction, it then follows that the optimal responses of all future proposers are invariant with respect to t's choice of $y_t = \phi$ or $y_t = x$.

Fact 4 says that, in the observed agenda, all proposals with greater subscripts are socially preferred to those with smaller subscripts. That is, $y'_{T'} P y'_{T'-1} P \cdots P y'_2 P y'_1$. In other words, the set of alternatives in the observed agenda do not cycle, and furthermore they satisfy the notion of a *chain* in Banks (1985).

With these facts, we can prove – in a much simplified fashion – Austen-Smith's theorem.

Proposition 4 (Austen-Smith 1987, Theorem and Corollary). *Any potential amendment agenda that is backward built under costly proposing exhibits sophisticated sincerity.*

Proof: Let λ be an arbitrary node in $\Lambda' \backslash \lambda_0$. We must show $p(\lambda) = s(\lambda)$. Define y'_s as the ostensive alternative at this node; that is, $y'_s = p(\lambda)$. Consider the set of ostensive alternatives at the terminal nodes of the subtree defined by λ: formally, the set $\{p(\bar{\lambda}): \bar{\lambda} \in \bar{Q}'(\lambda) \cap \Lambda'_t\}$. By Fact 2, all of these alternatives have subscripts less than or equal to s, and by (1) at least one of these alternatives is y'_s. By Fact 4, y'_s is the Condorcet winner of these alternatives. Hence by Proposition 2, $s(\lambda) = y'_s = p(\lambda)$. Since λ is an arbitrary element of $\Lambda' \backslash \lambda_0$, it follows that $\forall \lambda \in \Lambda' \backslash \lambda_0$, $p(\lambda) = s(\lambda)$; that is, the agenda exhibits sophisticated sincerity.   □

In the game we analyze, *all* equilibrium sets of proposals produce an agenda that exhibits sophisticated sincerity. Because this game is slightly different from Austen-Smith's, this result is slightly different from Austen-Smith's. Unlike our game, Austen-Smith's only ensures that *at least one* set of equilibrium proposals produces sophisticated sincerity. (However, like our game, all equilibria give the same sophisticated outcome.) The key difference between our game and Austen-Smith's is our assumption of costly proposing. As the next section shows, without costly proposing there can exist equilibria that do not generate sophisticated sincerity.

2.2   *Example 1: costless proposing and sophisticated sincerity*

Let $X = \{a, b, c\}$ and $N = \{1, 2, 3, 4, 5\}$. The preferences in Table 1 yield the following social preference ordering: $a P b P c P a$. The potential agenda is a three-element, backward-built amendment agenda with costless proposing. Voter 1 names the first proposal y_1, voter 2 names y_2, and voter 3 names y_3. This agenda is given in Figure 10.

As is usual in problems of this sort, we seek a solution by working backwards, first identifying optimal strategies in proposal period 3, then in 2, then in 1. Thus, we first consider the optimal choice of voter 3 for

Table 1. *Example: No sophisticated sincerity under costless proposing*

Voter	Proposer	Preference ordering
1	1	c, a, b
2	2	c, a, b
3	3	b, c, a
4	—	b, c, a
5	—	a, b, c

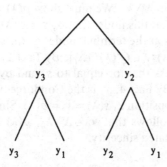

Figure 10.

every combination of choices that voters 1 and 2 may propose. For instance, suppose $y_1 = a$ and $y_2 = b$. Voter 3 would then be allowed to propose $y_3 = \phi$ or $y_3 = c$. The former choice causes the sophisticated outcome of the voting game to be a, while the latter choice causes it to be c. Since 3 prefers c to a, he would propose $y_3 = c$. Similarly, suppose $y_1 = a$ and $y_2 = c$. In this case, both $y_3 = \phi$ and $y_3 = b$ cause the outcome of the voting game to be c. Since proposing is costless, 3 is indifferent between the two choices. To compute equilibria for this game we continue this method, determining 3's optimal response for every possible combination of y_1 and y_2. We then examine 2's optimal behavior, given 1's decision and the conditional decisions of 3 computed above. Then, finally, we compute the optimal decision of 1, given the computed conditional decisions of 2 and 3.

For this example, there are many equilibria. It can be verified that one such equilibrium is $(y_1, y_2, y_3) = (a, c, b)$ in which sophisticated sincerity does *not* result. Figure 11 lists the ostensive alternatives along with the sophisticated equivalents in parentheses. Note that one node does not

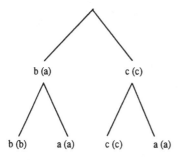

Figure 11.

have an ostensive alternative equal to its sophisticated equivalent; hence the agenda does not exhibit sophisticated sincerity. Thus, without costly proposing we cannot be assured of sophisticated sincerity in a backward-built amendment agenda.

3   Sophisticated sincerity and nonamendment agendas

How common is sophisticated sincerity in agendas other than amendment agendas? After proving his sophisticated sincerity result for amendment agendas, Austen-Smith (1987) conjectures that the same result will generalize to all binary agendas:

> The key to the result is that sophisticated voting over an agenda induces legislators to confine their proposals to alternatives that can beat – under *sincere* voting – the proposals offered earlier in the agenda-setting process. Since the formal structure of sophisticated voting is invariant across the class of binary agendas (McKelvey and Niemi 1978), this suggests that the theorem holds not only for the amendment procedure, but also for any binary agenda and (binary) agenda-setting mechanism. (pp. 1328–9)

However, this section presents results showing that this conjecture is not true. The first step is to show that with discontinuous observed agendas, sophisticated sincerity *never* occurs.

Proposition 5.   *If an observed agenda exhibits sophisticated sincerity, then it is continuous.*

Proof: Let $(\Lambda', Q', p^{-1}(\cdot))$ be any observed agenda that exhibits sophisticated sincerity. This implies:

$$\forall \lambda \in \Lambda' \setminus \lambda_0, \quad p(\lambda) = s(\lambda). \tag{3}$$

We show that this, in turn, implies that the agenda is continuous. To do so, suppose the contrary; that is, suppose

$$\exists \bar{\lambda} \text{ such that } p(\bar{\lambda}) \neq p(Q_L(\bar{\lambda})) \text{ and } p(\bar{\lambda}) \neq p(Q_R(\bar{\lambda})). \tag{4}$$

By (3),

$$s(Q_L(\bar{\lambda})) = p(Q_L(\bar{\lambda})) \quad \text{and} \quad s(Q_R(\bar{\lambda})) = p(Q_R(\bar{\lambda})).$$

By (2) (the definition of $s(\cdot)$), this implies:

$$s(\bar{\lambda}) = p(Q_L(\bar{\lambda})) \quad \text{or} \quad s(\bar{\lambda}) = p(Q_R(\bar{\lambda})). \tag{5}$$

But (3) also implies $p(\bar{\lambda}) = s(\bar{\lambda})$. Substituting this into (5) gives

$$p(\bar{\lambda}) = p(Q_L(\bar{\lambda})) \quad \text{or} \quad p(\bar{\lambda}) = p(Q_R(\bar{\lambda})). \tag{6}$$

But (6) contradicts (4). It follows that the observed agenda must be continuous.   □

The proposition reveals that, for observed agendas, continuity is necessary for sophisticated sincerity. In other words, sophisticated sincerity implies continuity. Next we show that the converse is false; that is, continuity does *not* imply sophisticated sincerity.

3.1   Example 2: Continuity and sophisticated sincerity

Let $X = \{a, b, c, d\}$, over which the social preference ordering is:

$$a P b P c P d P a; \quad c P a; \quad \text{and} \quad d P b.$$

(The individual voter-preference combinations in Table 2, for example, yield these social preferences.)

The potential agenda is a three-element agenda described by Figure 12. Note that it is continuous but not symmetric. Voter 1 names the first proposal, voter 2 the second, and voter 3 the third. Although we assume costly proposing, we further stipulate for this example that proposing is never so costly as to make a proposer decline when proposing ensures an outcome that he would prefer to the outcome had he not proposed. For instance, if by proposing voter 3 can cause c to be the outcome but by declining causes d to be the outcome, we assume that costs are not large enough to make 3 choose not to propose.

To solve the game, we proceed as before, first calculating 3's optimal proposal given every combination of 1's and 2's proposals, then likewise calculating 2's optimal proposal, and finally 1's optimal proposal. In this game there are exactly three equilibrium values for (y_1, y_2, y_3). They are (a, b, d), (b, d, ϕ), and (d, b, a). All produce the same outcome to the

Table 2. *Example: No sophisticated sincerity in a continuous agenda*

Voter type	N	Proposer	Preference ordering
I	1	1	c, b, d, a
II	1	2	d, a, b, c
III	1	3	a, c, d, b
IV	5	—	a, d, b, c
V	5	—	c, d, a, b
VI	5	—	b, c, d, a
VII	1	—	a, b, d, c

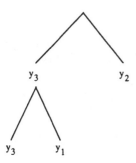

Figure 12.

voting game, but the third differs from the others in that it does not produce an observed agenda with sophisticated sincerity. For this equilibrium, Figure 13 lists the ostensive alternatives with sophisticated equivalents in parentheses. Note that one node has $p(\lambda) \neq s(\lambda)$. The potential and observed agendas are the same in this example, since no one declined to propose. Accordingly, we can conclude that for both potential and observed agendas, continuity is not sufficient for sophisticated sincerity.

This example is especially enlightening in regard to Austen-Smith's conclusion, which can be restated as two conjectures: (i) with endogenous proposal making, actors propose only alternatives that can defeat all previously named alternatives; and (ii) when each proposal defeats all previously named alternatives, sophisticated sincerity is guaranteed. These two conjectures together imply that sophisticated sincerity occurs with all binary agendas.

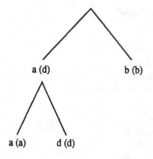

Figure 13.

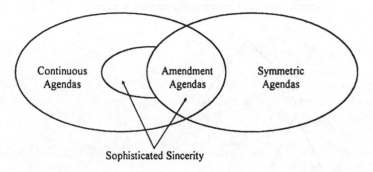

Sophisticated Sincerity

Figure 14.

Note that the example of this section shows that this latter statement is not true (i.e., sophisticated sincerity does *not* always occur with all binary agendas). Note also that the example contradicts conjecture (i). Specifically, in this example the third alternative proposed, *a*, does not defeat the first alternative proposed, *d*. However the example still leaves room for conjecture (ii) to be true. That is, it may be that for any binary agenda sophisticated sincerity occurs whenever each proposal defeats all previously named alternatives.

Finally, if we confine ourselves to potential agendas whose corresponding observed agenda maintains the same properties regarding symmetry and continuity,[13] then we can relate continuity, symmetry, amendment agendas, and sophisticated sincerity as in Figure 14. In brief, sophisticated sincerity is certain to hold for amendment agendas (continuous and symmetric), is certain not to hold for discontinuous agendas, and may hold but is not guaranteed for nonsymmetric agendas.

---

[13] An equilibrium in which no one declines to propose is sufficient to ensure this.

3.2   "Congressional agendas"

Our final stage of theoretical analysis begins with an empirical diversion. Since ultimately we are interested in the prevalence of sophisticated sincerity in actual parliamentary settings, it is necessary to analyze agendas that more closely approximate standard parliamentary procedure than do amendment agendas. Unfortunately, this is not easy for two reasons overlooked in the sophisticated-voting literature.

The first and relatively minor problem is that, in parliamentary voting situations, nominal votes may differ from actual votes. The most straightforward example is a parliamentary situation in which there is a bill, an amendment to the bill, and a substitute to the amendment. These are voted on in reverse order, but it is not quite that simple. Suppose, for instance, that the substitute passes in the first vote. The next vote nominally is on the amendment. Substantively, however, it is not. Passage of the substitute effectively replaces the amendment, so the next vote is really on the amendment as substituted – in other words, on the substitute again. In this respect, the second vote is redundant.[14]

A response to this claim about redundant voting leads to another, deeper source of confusion in the formal sophisticated-voting literature. Namely, it can be argued that such repeated votes are not really redundant, since the consequences of voting nay are different in stage two than in stage one. In this example, a nay vote at stage one means that the amendment is still alive, whereas a nay vote at stage two means that neither the amendment (killed previously in our scenario) nor the substitute are alive. Only the bill and (implicitly) the status quo remain as viable options.

This illustrates the second problem. The meaning of nay votes is fundamentally ambiguous. In this case, is a nay at the first vote really a yea vote for the amendment? If we listen only to the parliamentarian, we absolutely cannot tell: he never says (as do voting theorists) "The vote is on the amendment as substituted (y_3) *versus the bill* (y_1)." In other words, when as theorists we label the nay nodes of a binary tree, we in effect supply information about the voting situation that parliamentarians over the ages have not seen fit to supply. This has a variety of interpretations ranging from benign to offensive. In the best case, we are supplying obvious and correct information about the meaning of nay votes. In the moderate case, we impute some form of behavior to voters that is reasonably accurate. In the worst case, we impute some form of behavior to voters that, while theoretically convenient, has no empirical basis. Whichever

---

[14]   As a consequence, in legislative situations this second (arguably redundant) vote is often a voice vote, while the first is a roll-call vote.

of these interpretations holds, it seems clear that we need to inspect more carefully the conventions for labeling the nay branches of binary trees.

Ordeshook and Schwartz's study of sophisticated voting serves as a useful point of departure since it is a concerted attempt to bridge the gap between sophisticated-voting theory and what they regard as common types of congressional agendas. For present purposes, their chief argument is that the confinement of existing voting theory to amendment agendas is inappropriate and misleading. It is inappropriate because empirically common agendas are not of this form. It is misleading because empirically common agendas, when analyzed with more or less orthodox theoretical techniques, have drastically different properties in terms of the range of outcomes a strategic agenda setter can achieve and in terms of the stability of equilibrium outcomes. Specifically, under agenda institutions in the class that Ordeshook and Schwartz analyze, agenda setters can obtain more favorable outcomes than under amendment agendas. Also, majority rule is less well behaved under what Ordeshook and Schwartz regard as realistic agendas than under "the unrealistic assumption that feasible agendas are all of a special type called *amendment agendas*" (1987, p. 179).

The focus here is on whether, in the voting situation that Ordeshook and Schwartz call a "congressional agenda" (1987, p. 180, fig. 2),[15] the deviation from amendment agendas facilitates or undermines the prospects for sophisticated sincerity. Six alternatives that make up the agenda are a status quo q, a bill b, a first-degree amendment a, a second-degree amendment to the amendment aa, a first-degree substitute s, and a second-degree amendment to the substitute as. The corresponding agenda Ordeshook and Schwartz present is reproduced in Figure 15. Notice first that the agenda is *not* continuous; in particular, nodes λ_1 and λ_2 violate the continuity definition. Thus, using Ordeshook and Schwartz's convention for labeling nay nodes, Proposition 5 tells us that sophisticated sincerity cannot occur.[16]

---

[15] Ordeshook and Schwartz write "Rule XIV of the House *requires* that members perfect the amendment" (emphasis added). However, the House's standing rules (Rule XIX, actually) do not require any specific forms of agendas; they merely provide opportunities for such agendas. It is therefore misleading to call any kind of agenda "a congressional agenda" as if a particular form is the norm. Granted, some empirical corner cutting of this sort is essential in this field, and therefore it is worthwhile to analyze Ordeshook and Schwartz's "common type of congressional agenda" (1987, p. 181). But we do so as a sort of upper bound in terms of agenda complexity. Since it proscribes the maximum number of motions that can fill a parliamentarian's tree, Rule XIX roughly defines what we are calling a potential agenda under the normal procedure in the House.

[16] More precisely, sophisticated sincerity cannot occur unless someone declines to make a proposal and thus causes the observed agenda to be different from the potential agenda.

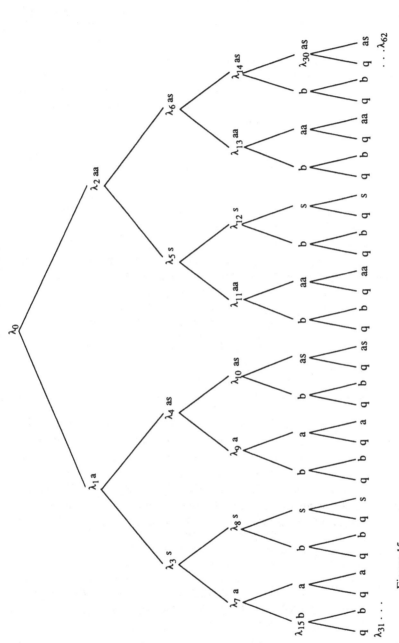

Figure 15.

Although this labeling convention for an observed agenda guarantees that sophisticated sincerity will not occur, the idea we develop and illustrate in Appendix I is that this – indeed any – labeling convention is ad hoc. Rather than attempt to resolve the question of which of the conventions discussed in the appendix is most appropriate, we turn instead to a related but broader analytic question. Does there exist *any* way to label nay nodes such that sophisticated sincerity occurs? The answer is no. The following proposition shows that for observed agendas that are "congressional" (in the sense of Ordeshook and Schwartz), regardless of the convention adopted and the social preference relation P, such agendas can never produce sophisticated sincerity.

Proposition 6.   *For any convention of labeling nay nodes, the observed "congressional agenda" does not exhibit sophisticated sincerity.*

Proof: Adopt an agnostic labeling convention for the alternatives of a "congressional agenda" as in Figure 16. That is, leave the nay nodes unlabeled. To show that the agenda cannot ever exhibit sophisticated sincerity, we assume that there exists a set of social preferences P on $\{q, b, a, s, aa, as\}$ that produces sophisticated sincerity. First, since sophisticated sincerity implies $s(\lambda) = p(\lambda)$ $\forall\lambda$, it must be true that

$$s(\lambda_2) = aa, \quad s(\lambda_6) = as, \quad s(\lambda_{12}) = s,$$

$$s(\lambda_{14}) = as, \quad s(\lambda_{24}) = aa, \quad \text{and} \quad s(\lambda_{28}) = aa.$$

By (2) (the definition of $s(\cdot)$), $s(\lambda_2) = s(\lambda_5)$ or $s(\lambda_2) = s(\lambda_6)$. Given the values of $s(\lambda_2)$ and $s(\lambda_6)$, we must have $s(\lambda_5) = s(\lambda_2) = aa$. This implies

$$aa\, P\, as. \tag{7}$$

By the same logic, we must have $s(\lambda_{11}) = s(\lambda_5) = aa$. This implies aa defeats $s(\lambda_{23})$, the winner of q and b in a pairwise vote. In turn, this implies that aa defeats $s(\lambda_{27})$, also the winner of q and b in a pairwise vote. This implies that $s(\lambda_{13}) = aa$. By (7) this implies $s(\lambda_6) = aa$, a contradiction. The proposition follows. $\square$

Corollary.   *There does not exist a labeling convention of the "congressional agenda" that makes it continuous and symmetric.*

Proof: Assume the converse. Then, by Propositions 1 and 4, the agenda would exhibit sophisticated sincerity and hence would contradict Proposition 6. $\square$

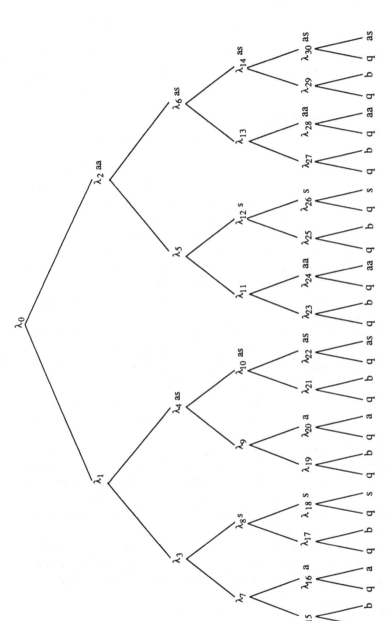

Figure 16.

4   Discussion

The bulk of the theoretical analysis is contrary to empirical intuitions that sophisticated sincerity is pervasive. As summarized in Figure 14, sophisticated sincerity is confined to the following regions. First, sophisticated sincerity is assured within the "lens," which represents Austen-Smith's result for amendment agendas (see Proposition 4). However, this result is qualified by the added necessary condition of costly proposing (Example 1). Second, sophisticated sincerity may exist for some agendas that are continuous but not symmetric, but it does not exist for all such agendas (Example 2). Thus, the "tumor" of sophisticated sincerity grows on only one side of the lens, and does not fill the space of continuous agendas.

Several informal arguments may be added to these results to try to resurrect or bolster intuitions that sophisticated sincerity is pervasive. First, the tumor of unknown size seems to be large inasmuch as it is difficult to find counterexamples based on what seem to be realistic agendas. Second, in legislative settings with endogenous agenda formation, leaders or bill managers often retain control over proposal making, and have both incentives and abilities not to let complex, nonsophisticated sincerity agendas emerge.[17] Third, perhaps sophisticated sincerity is not all that important in light of empirical accounts of "explaining Washington activity" (Fenno 1978, chap. 5). If, as Fenno argues, members have substantial leeway when explaining votes, then sophisticated voting in settings without sophisticated sincerity would not be so costly after all.[18]

Perhaps readers will find these informal arguments plausible; perhaps not. Either way, the fact is they are informal arguments, not results. To the extent that the analytic tools of voting theory can be applied to somewhat more realistic settings (as has been attempted here), the results are clear relative to the informal arguments. As more realistic agenda settings are considered, more refined findings emerge. For amendment agendas, costly proposing helps ensure sophisticated sincerity (Proposition 2 and Example 1). However, in so-called congressional agendas, sophisticated sincerity does not occur (Proposition 6).

The broadest conclusion that emerges from these findings relates to the adage that honesty is the best policy or – more specifically – its interpretation in social settings where rational actors can design institutions

---

[17] See Krehbiel and Rivers (1990) for a more detailed argument to this effect.

[18] In light of this reading of Fenno, the "Fenno and Farquharson" dichotomy that guides the interpretation in Denzau, Riker, and Shepsle's (1985) analysis seems misleading, if not false. Fenno says, in effect, that a legislator can have it both ways: vote sophisticatedly and be able to explain it to his constituents. See Austen-Smith (1992) for a signaling model of "explaining the vote" that subjects these intuitions to a logical test and finds them to be sustainable, in part.

Table 3. *Advantages and disadvantages of labeling conventions*

Convention	Advantages	Disadvantages
1. No labels	True to parliamentary situation Not arbitrary	No theory
2. Next branch	Fills nodes Theory applies	Arbitrary Elevates nonviable proposals
3. Next yes	Fills nodes Theory applies	Arbitrary Elevates nonviable proposals
4. Sophisticated equivalent	Fills nodes	Arbitrary Theory applies but is presumed Investigator must know preferences
5. Last-passed (or status quo)	Fills nodes Theory applies No elevation of nonviable proposal Relatively behaviorally agnostic	Arbitrary

or procedures that shape individuals' incentives for truthfully revealing their preferences to broader publics, such as constituents, journalists, or researchers. Based on this analysis, the normative ideal of designing institutions in which truthful revelation (honesty) is the optimal (best) policy appears to be very difficult to attain in voting situations with endogenous agenda formation.

Appendix I: Conventions for labeling nay nodes

This appendix presents five conventions for labeling nay nodes in an Ordeshook and Schwartz "congressional agenda." Table 3 summarizes them (see also Figure 15 in the main text).

Convention 1 is not to label nay nodes. The main advantage of this approach is that, unlike all others, it is strictly true to the parliamentary situation and the parliamentarian's (actually, presiding officer's) words. When a member votes nay, he votes against that which he could vote for by voting aye – nothing more, nothing less. The disadvantage from a theoretical standpoint is that we end up with a binary tree many of whose nodes are blank – to be precise, fifteen in the case of Ordeshook and Schwartz's "common type of congressional agenda." Consequently, our theory does not apply; we cannot talk in any meaningful fashion about sincere voting.

Convention 2, the *next-branch* approach, is defined with reference to the parliamentary tree. The presumption is that a nay vote on a given branch (alternative) is a yea vote for whatever that branch is attached to. For instance, when voting nay on the amendment to an amendment, one is voting yea on the amendment itself, because the amendment to the amendment is attached to, and seeks to modify, the amendment. This is the convention that Ordeshook and Schwartz adopt. The advantages are that, like all remaining conventions and unlike convention 1, it solves the empty-node problem and allows voting theory to be applied. The disadvantage is that, like all remaining conventions and unlike convention 1, it is arbitrary. It implicitly embeds an extreme form of myopia by elevating even preposterous alternatives to the nay node.

Convention 3, the *next-yes* approach, is slightly different from convention 2 in that, instead of nay on motion *y* meaning yea on that motion to which *y* is attached in the parliamentary tree, it means yea on the next alternative to be voted on (in the words of the parliamentarian or presiding officer). This may seem like a very subtle distinction; however, it leads to a different binary tree than convention 2. The advantages and disadvantages of this approach are the same as with convention 2. It is different, but not indisputably better or worse.

Convention 4, the *sophisticated equivalent* approach, is a mirror image of convention 2. Instead of embedding extreme myopia, it embeds extreme foresight. A nay vote is labeled as a vote for the alternative that will emerge as winner if a majority indeed votes nay. Its advantages are that it leaves no empty nodes, enables application of a well-defined theory, and – unlike conventions 2 and 3 – does not elevate bogus alternatives. Instead, alternatives must earn their positions on nay nodes. So far so good. Unfortunately, the unique disadvantage of this labeling convention is crippling: It is impossible to use without information about voters' preferences. That is, labels are functions not just of the set of alternatives but also of voters' preferences over those alternatives.

Convention 5, the *last-passed-motion* approach, seeks and obtains a balance between conventions 2 and 3 on the one hand and convention 4 on the other. The presumption now is that a nay vote is implicitly a vote on whatever motion most recently received a majority (or, if none, for the status quo, which by definition is the last policy to pass). The intuition is that at any given node a voter either votes yea for the nominal alternative (true to the parliamentary situation) or, by voting nay, prefers to reject the nominal alternative in favor of the proposal that has most recently received majority support and, as such, remains viable. Notice that this convention does not elevate blatantly nonviable alternatives as do conventions 2 and 3, and thus it does not impute myopia to voters. Rather, in effect it characterizes nay votes in terms of something that has just been affirmed empirically. Thus, it is relatively agnostic with respect to the implied behavior. Finally, this convention does not yield a discontinuous agenda – the feature on which Ordeshook and Schwartz's critique of amendment agendas fundamentally rests.

Although convention 5 seems to us to be most reasonable, we must conclude with several caveats. First, like all other conventions, it is somewhat arbitrary. Second, as Proposition 6 demonstrates, when it comes to sophisticated sincerity the convention does not matter in the final analysis – the result is general with respect to labeling conventions for so-called congressional agendas. Finally, we caution against over-interpreting these results. Our model of this relatively complex situation is still quite a simplification of the agenda-formation processes in Congress (and other legislatures). Probably the most flagrant simplification of our model (and others) is its not allowing proposers to rebuild the tree after some proposals are disposed of. It is not clear how this pervasive real-world feature would affect existing results.

Appendix II: Definitions of sophisticated sincerity

Two debatable conditions come into play when defining sophisticated sincerity: (i) Does the definition apply to nodes off the equilibrium path? (ii) Does the definition require ostensive alternatives to equal sophisticated equivalents, or only that each agent merely vote *as if* this were true?

The second question is more subtle than the first, so we begin by illustrating it. Suppose the voting tree appears as in Figure 11, with sophisticated equivalents in parentheses. For this figure the answer to the second question is no: the top left node has an ostensive alternative b that is not equal to its sophisticated equivalent a. But this does not imply that an agent adopting a sophisticated strategy will vote against his sincere position. For such an agent to exist, his preferences for a, b, and c must have a special form. In particular, they must be ranked acb (in which case he would vote for b since he prefers a to c) or bca (in which case he would vote for c since he prefers c to a). In both cases his vote differs from his sincere preference. No other preference orderings, however, give this result. For instance, if the sophisticated agent ranks the alternatives abc, his sophisticated strategy "vote for b" (since he prefers a to c) is the same as his sincere strategy "vote for b" (since he prefers b to c). Note that in this example, if no voter has preferences ranked acb or bca, then the votes will be as if all ostensive alternatives were equivalent to their sophisticated equivalents when all voters are sophisticated.

Let us define sophisticated sincerity as *strong* if all ostensive alternatives are equal to their sophisticated equivalents. Define sophisticated sincerity as *weak* if it is merely the case that preferences are arranged such that all sophisticated votes occur as if ostensive alternatives were equal to sophisticated equivalents. Next, define as *equilibrium-path sophisticated sincerity* those instances of sincere voting that apply only to votes along the equilibrium path; *everywhere sophisticated sincerity* occurs when sincere voting applies to all votes, even those off the equilibrium path. These two conditions (strong vs. weak and everywhere vs. equilibrium-path) are logically independent. This allows four possible notions of sophisticated sincerity: *equilibrium-path weak sophisticated sincerity, equilibrium-path strong sophisticated sincerity, everywhere weak sophisticated sincerity,* and *everywhere strong sophisticated sincerity.* The notion of sophisticated sincerity that this chapter adopts is everywhere strong. The notion Austen-Smith's paper adopts is everywhere weak. Austen-Smith's definition is not equilibrium-path strong, as some readers have mistakenly inferred.

Given these definitions, an important fact follows: if every possible preference ordering is represented by at least one voter, then an agenda exhibits everywhere weak sophisticated sincerity (Austen-Smith's) if and only if it exhibits everywhere strong sophisticated sincerity (ours). (Furthermore, an agenda exhibits equilibrium-path weak sophisticated sincerity if and only if it exhibits equilibrium-path strong sophisticated sincerity.)

To see the intuition behind this fact, recall the example of Figure 11. This example violates everywhere strong sophisticated sincerity but does not necessarily violate everywhere weak sophisticated sincerity; however, if there is an *acb* voter or a *bca* voter, then it does. The condition that every possible preference ordering is represented, of course, implies that both of these types of voters exist, and hence that everywhere weak sophisticated sincerity is violated. This makes the definition in this chapter only trivially different from Austen-Smith's. The main reasons for the difference are analytic tractability and intuitiveness.

Of course, since our definition is stronger than Austen-Smith's, Propositions 5 and 6 do not necessarily apply to Austen-Smith's definition. However, they do apply as long as all preference orderings are represented. Also, because our definition of sophisticated sincerity is stronger than Austen-Smith's, the examples showing a violation of our notion of sophisticated sincerity do not necessarily show a violation of Austen-Smith's notion. However, both of our counterexamples do in fact show a violation of Austen-Smith's notion of sophisticated sincerity. For instance, in Example 1 note that the first vote ostensibly is between *b* and *c*. All type-3 voters prefer *b* to *c*, but they vote for the latter alternative because they prefer this to *a*, the competing sophisticated equivalent to *c*. Since there is at least one voter with these preferences, Austen-Smith's notion is violated. (Note also that since this vote is on the equilibrium path, this example also violates equilibrium-path weak sophisticated sincerity.)

In fact, both examples in the main text violate equilibrium-path weak sophisticated sincerity, the weakest of all four definitions discussed. It therefore follows that not only is everywhere strong sophisticated sincerity (our notion) violated, but so too are everywhere weak (Austen-Smith's notion) and equilibrium-path strong sophisticated sincerity violated.

REFERENCES

Austen-Smith, David (1987), "Sophisticated Sincerity: Voting over Endogenous Agendas," *American Political Science Review* 81: 1323-9.
— (1992), "Explaining the Vote: Homestyle Constraints on Legislative Strategy," *American Journal of Political Science* (forthcoming).
Bach, Stanley, and Steven Smith (1988), *Managing Uncertainty in the House of Representatives: Adaptation and Innovation in Special Rules.* Washington, DC: Brookings.
Banks, Jeffrey S. (1985), "Sophisticated Voting Outcomes and Agenda Control," *Social Choice and Welfare* 1: 295-306.
— (1989), "Equilibrium Outcomes in Two Stage Amendment Procedures," *American Journal of Political Science* 32: 25-43.
Banks, Jeffrey S., and Farid Gasmi (1987), "Endogenous Agenda Formation in Three-Person Committees," *Social Choice and Welfare* 4: 133-52.
Black, Duncan (1958), *The Theory of Committees and Elections.* London: Cambridge University Press.
Denzau, Arthur, William Riker, and Kenneth Shepsle (1985), "Farquharson and Fenno: Sophisticated Voting and Home Style," *American Political Science Review* 79: 1117-34.
Farquharson, Robin (1969), *Theory of Voting.* London: Hodge.
Fenno, Richard F. (1978), *Home Style: Representatives in their Districts.* Boston: Little, Brown.
Krehbiel, Keith, and Douglas Rivers (1990), "Sophisticated Voting in Congress: A Reconsideration," *Journal of Politics* 52: 548-78.
Mayhew, David (1974), *Congress: The Electoral Connection.* New Haven, CT: Yale University Press.
McKelvey, Richard D., and Richard G. Niemi (1978), "A Multistage Game Representation of Sophisticated Voting for Binary Procedures," *Journal of Economic Theory* 18: 1-22.
Ordeshook, Peter C., and Thomas Schwartz (1987), "Agendas and the Control of Political Outcomes," *American Political Science Review* 81: 179-200.
Riker, William H. (1980), "Implications from the Disequilibrium of Majority Rule for the Study of Institutions," *American Political Science Review* 74: 432-46.
Shepsle, Kenneth A. (1979), "Institutional Arrangements and Equilibrium in Multidimensional Voting Models," *American Journal of Political Science* 23: 27-60.
Shepsle, Kenneth A., and Barry R. Weingast (1984), "Uncovered Sets and Sophisticated Voting Outcomes with Implications for Agenda Institutions," *American Journal of Political Science* 28: 49-74.
Smith, Steven (1989), *Call to Order: Floor Politics in the House and Senate.* Washington, DC: Brookings.

CHAPTER 11

Initial versus continuing proposal power in legislative seniority systems

Richard D. McKelvey and Raymond Riezman

1   Introduction

In this chapter we compare two different systems of legislative seniority. In the first, senior legislators are given disproportionate power to make initial proposals, but once the proposal is brought before the legislative body the senior members lose their power. In the second system, senior legislators have disproportionate proposal power throughout the legislative session. Although it might seem at first glance that the latter system would give more power to senior members, we show that – in any equilibrium that sustains an incumbency effect and a seniority system – senior members actually have less power under the second system than under the first. In fact, under the second system they have no more power than the junior members.

Our analysis takes place in the same formal model of the legislative and electoral system developed in McKelvey and Riezman (1992). We model the representative process as an $(\mathcal{L} + n)$-player stochastic game, where $\mathcal{L}$ is the number of legislators and n is the number of voters, partitioned into $\mathcal{L}$ distinct legislative districts. The game alternates back and forth between an election and a legislative session. The election is modeled as a game (called the Voter Game) in which all the voters in each of the $\mathcal{L}$ legislative districts vote to determine who will be their representative for the next legislative session. In the legislative session the legislators first decide whether or not to have a seniority system for the current session and then proceed to select a policy. The policy selected is a decision on a distribution

This chapter was prepared for the conference on Political Economy, Washington University, St. Louis, May 22–25, 1991. The research reported here was funded in part by NSF Grants #SES-9022932 to the California Institute of Technology, and #SES-9023056 to the University of Iowa. We are grateful to Ken Shepsle for comments on an earlier paper which led to this research.

of a fixed amount of money among the legislative districts. We model the policy-making process in the legislative session using the approach of Baron and Ferejohn (1989), who consider the legislature as a form of a Rubinstein bargaining game: There is a random recognition rule, which depends on seniority, that determines which legislator makes a proposal. The legislators then vote, by majority rule, whether to accept or reject the proposal. The process continues until the legislature accepts a proposal, at which time the legislature adjourns and new elections are held (i.e., we return to the voter game) and the process begins all over again.

The difference between the two systems we examine concerns what happens if the legislature rejects the proposal once it comes to the floor. Under continuing proposal power, in the second and subsequent considerations by the legislative body the seniority system is the same as in the first proposal. Under initial proposal power, the seniority system is only in effect for the initial proposal; in the second and all subsequent proposals, all members have equal probability of recognition.

In our previous work (McKelvey and Riezman 1992) we show that, under initial proposal power, an equilibrium exists in which the legislature always votes to impose on itself a nontrivial seniority system. In the proposal stage, the proposer selects a minimum winning coalition, retaining $(\mathfrak{L}+1)/2\mathfrak{L}$ for its own district and allocating $1/\mathfrak{L}$ to the districts of the remaining coalition members. Districts that are not part of the winning coalition get nothing. This proposal passes and the game proceeds to the voter game. Voters always re-elect incumbents. The intuition behind the results is that voters, understanding the incentives in the legislative session, realize that their representative will be disadvantaged without seniority; hence voters always choose to re-elect their representatives. The next three sections draw heavily on McKelvey and Riezman (1992).

2   General framework

Before introducing the model, we develop some general notation for stochastic games. Our model will be a special case of such a general model.

Assume that there is a set N of *players*, a set X of *alternatives*, and for each player $i \in N$, a von Neumann–Morgenstern *utility function* $u_i : X \to \mathbb{R}$ over the set of alternatives. We assume that X contains a *null outcome* x_0, with $u_i(x_0) = 0$ for all $i \in N$. Let T be a finite set of *states*. We now define a *stochastic game* $\Gamma = \{\Gamma^t : t \in T\}$ to be a collection of *game elements* $\Gamma^t = (S^t, \pi^t, \psi^t)$. Here $S^t = \prod_{i \in N} S_i^t$ is an n-tuple of *pure strategy sets*. Next, $\pi^t : S^t \to \mathfrak{M}(T) = \Delta^{|T|}$ is a *transition function* specifying, for each $s^t \in S^t$, a probability distribution $\pi^t(s^t)$ on T which determines, for each $s^t \in S^t$ and $y \in T$, the probability $\pi^t(s^t)(y)$ of proceeding to game element Γ^y.

Finally, $\psi^t: S^t \to X$ is an *outcome function* that specifies for each $s^t \in S^t$ an outcome $\psi^t(s^t) \in X$. We let $S = \prod_{t \in T} S^t$ be the collection of pure strategy n-tuples, one for each game element. We write $\Sigma_i^t = \mathfrak{M}(S_i^t)$, where $\mathfrak{M}(S_i^t)$ is the set of probability distributions over S_i^t, and then define $\Sigma_i = \prod_{t \in T} \Sigma_i^t$ to be the set of *stationary strategies* for player i and $\Sigma = \prod_{i \in N} \Sigma_i$. Elements of Σ are written in the form $\sigma = (\sigma_1, \sigma_2, \ldots, \sigma_n)$. We also use the abusive notation $\sigma^t(s^t) = \prod_{i \in N} \sigma_i^t(s_i^t)$ and $\sigma(s) = \prod_{t \in T} \sigma^t(s^t)$ to represent the probability under σ of choosing the pure strategy profile $s^t \in S^t$ and $s \in S$, respectively.

For stationary strategies, we can define the payoff function $M^t: \Sigma \to \mathbb{R}^n$ by

$$M_i^t(\sigma) = \sum_{\tau=1}^{\infty} \sum_{r \in T} \pi_\tau^t(\sigma)(r) \cdot u_i(\psi^r(\sigma^r)), \qquad (2.1)$$

where $\pi_\tau^t(\sigma)(r)$ is defined inductively by

$$\pi_1^t(\sigma)(r) = \pi^t(\sigma^t)(r) = \sum_{s^t \in S^t} \sigma^t(s^t) \cdot \pi^t(s^t)(r),$$

$$\pi_\tau^y(\sigma)(r) = \sum_{y \in Y} \pi_{\tau-1}^y(\sigma)(y) \cdot \pi_1^y(\sigma^t)(r),$$

and $u_i(\psi^t(\sigma^t))$ is defined by

$$u_i(\psi^t(\sigma^t)) = \sum_{s^t \in S^t} \sigma^t(s^t) \cdot u_i(\psi^t(s^t)).$$

Note that the payoff function is well defined only if the sum in (2.1) converges for all σ, t, and i.

A strategy n-tuple $\sigma \in \Sigma$ is said to be a *Nash equilibrium* if

$$M_i(\sigma_i', \sigma_{-i}) \leq M_i(\sigma) \quad \text{for all } \sigma_i' \in \Sigma_i.$$

It follows from standard results of stochastic games that any stationary Nash equilibrium can be characterized by a collection $\{v^t\}_{t \in T} \subseteq \mathbb{R}^n$ of values for each game element Γ^t, and a strategy profile $\sigma \in \Sigma$ satisfying:

(a) for all $t \in T$, σ^t is a Nash equilibrium to the game with payoff function $G^t: \Sigma^t \to \mathbb{R}^n$ defined by

$$G^t(\sigma^t) = u(\psi^t(\sigma^t)) + \sum_{y \in T} \pi^t(\sigma^t)(y) \cdot v^y$$

$$= E_{\sigma^t}\left[u(\psi^t(s^t)) + \sum_{y \in T} \pi^t(s^t)(y) \cdot v^y \right]$$

$$= \sum_{s^t \in S^t} \sigma^t(s^t) \cdot \left[u(\psi^t(s^t)) + \sum_{y \in T} \pi^t(s^t)(y) \cdot v^y \right];$$

(b) for all $t \in T$, $v^t = G^t(\sigma^t)$.

We will use this result to characterize equilibria in the stochastic game under consideration. Finally, it also follows from results in Sobel (1971) that a Nash equilibrium in the set of stationary strategies is also a Nash equilibrium in the larger class of nonstationary strategies.

3   The game with initial proposal power

We consider an infinitely repeated game between legislators and their constituents. The game alternates back and forth between a legislative session, in which legislators decide on a division of a fixed pie among the legislative districts, and an election, in which the voters decide whether or not to re-elect their legislators.

The legislative session consists of three parts: a vote on the seniority structure, a proposal by a randomly selected member, and a vote on the proposal. The legislative session starts with a vote on the seniority structure. If a majority of the legislators vote for a seniority system then it passes; otherwise, there is no seniority system. Next, a random recognition rule (like that of Baron and Ferejohn 1989) is used to select a legislator as a proposer. If no seniority system was passed, all legislators have equal probability of being selected. On the other hand, if a seniority system was passed then the probability of recognition is an increasing function of the legislator's relative seniority. The proposer proposes a division of the pie among the $\mathcal{L}$ legislative districts. The legislature then votes on the proposal. If the proposal is defeated, a new proposer is selected and the game continues as before. Under continuing proposal power, the next proposer is selected in the same manner as in the first round. Under initial proposal power, seniority is ignored in selecting the second and all subsequent proposers. Once a proposal passes, the legislative session ends.

After each legislative session there is an election. The voters can choose to re-elect their incumbent legislator, in which case the legislator has seniority in the next session and receives a salary of c, or the voters can vote not to re-elect the incumbent, in which case their legislator receives no salary and goes to the next session with no seniority. Although this is not completely realistic, it at least captures the idea that voters can punish their representatives if they feel that those representatives are not acting in the voters' best interests. Our formulation allows more limited punishments than would be the case if voters could remove the legislator from office permanently. After each election the legislative session begins again with the new seniority structure. All agents have utility functions that are the discounted present value of their lifetime stream of utility. For the legislators, payoffs in each period consist of a salary, which depends on whether they are re-elected, and a percentage $(1 - \theta)$ of what they secure for their district. Thus, they skim some exogenously given portion of their district's payoff. For the voters, in each period they get θ times their share of what their legislator is able to secure for the district.

We now define the legislative seniority game more formally as a special kind of stochastic game. We let the set of players be $N = L \cup V$, where L is the set of legislators with $\mathcal{L} = |L| \geq 3$ odd, and V is the set of voters. We assume that there is a function $\phi: V \to L$ identifying the legislative districts, such that voter v is in legislator l's district if $\phi(v) = l$. We assume that $n_l = |\phi^{-1}(l)|$ is odd for all $l \in L$. We assume that the set of outcomes is $X = X' \cup \{x_0\}$, where $X' = \Delta^{\mathcal{L}} \times \{0, 1\}^{\mathcal{L}}$ and x_0 is the null outcome. Elements of X' are written in the form $x = (z, q)$, where $z \in Z = \Delta^{\mathcal{L}}$ and $q \in Q = \{0, 1\}^{\mathcal{L}}$. So $z = (z_1, \ldots, z_{\mathcal{L}}) \in Z = \Delta^{\mathcal{L}}$ represents a division of the resources between the $\mathcal{L}$ districts and $q = (q_1, \ldots, q_{\mathcal{L}}) \in Q = \{0, 1\}^{\mathcal{L}}$ represents the seniority structure of the legislature, with $q_i = 1$ indicating that legislator i has seniority and $q_i = 0$ indicating i does not have seniority. We assume that utility functions over X' are of the form $u_i(x) = (1 - \theta)z_i + cq_i$ for $i \in L$ and $u_i(x) = (\theta/n_{\phi(i)})z_{\phi(i)}$ for $i \in V$. Further, for the null outcome, it is assumed that $u_i(x_0) = 0$ for all $i \in N$.

Let $0 < \delta < 1$ be a fixed discount rate, and let q^* be the element of Q satisfying $q_i^* = 1$ for all i. Let $p: Q \to \Delta^{\mathcal{L}}$ be a function indicating the proposal power of each legislator as a function of his or her seniority. We assume p is strictly monotonic in each component: for all $q \in Q$ and $i \in L$, $q_i > q_i' \Rightarrow p_i(q) > p_i(q_i', q_{-i})$, and $q_i = q_j \Rightarrow p_i(q) = p_j(q)$. Thus, more seniority means a higher probability that a legislator is selected as the proposer, and legislators with the same seniority have equal probability of being selected.

We assume that there are two basic phases of the game, called the Legislative Session and the Election, plus an ending state, called the Termination Game. The Election consists of a single component, called the Voting Game, but the Legislative Session is further divided into four stages, called the Legislative Seniority Game, the Legislative Recognition Game, the Legislative Proposal Game, and the Legislative Voting Game. This yields a total of six basic game elements, represented by the set $\{LS, LR, LP, LV, V, T\}$. Each of these is further indexed by the current state variable. Let

$$\mathfrak{I} = (\{LS\} \times Q) \cup (\{LR\} \times Q) \cup (\{LP\} \times Q \times L) \cup (\{LV\} \times Q \times Z)$$

$$\cup (\{V\} \times Z) \cup (\{T\})$$

be the set of states.

The strategy sets and transition functions for the game elements are defined as follows.

LS: *Legislative Seniority Game*

For $t \in \{LS\} \times Q$:

$$S_i^t = \begin{cases} \{0,1\} & \text{if } i \in L, \\ \{0\} & \text{if } i \in N-L; \end{cases}$$

$$\pi^t(s^t)(LR, t_1) = 1 \quad \text{if } \sum_{i \in L} s_i^t > \frac{\mathcal{L}}{2};$$

$$\pi^t(s^t)(LR, q^*) = 1 \quad \text{if } \sum_{i \in L} s_i^t \leq \frac{\mathcal{L}}{2};$$

$$\psi^t(s^t) = x_0 \quad \text{for all } s^t \in S^t.$$

The first decision the legislature makes is whether or not to have seniority for the current session. This game is indexed by $t = (LS, t_1)$, where $t_0 = LS$ indicates that we are in the Legislative Seniority Game and t_1 is the current seniority vector. The vote determines if seniority is used in the Legislative Recognition Game that follows. If a majority of the legislators vote for seniority, then the current seniority vector t_1 is used in the Legislative Recognition Game. If there is not a strict majority voting for seniority then the seniority vector q^*, which assigns equal weight to all legislators, is used in the Legislative Recognition Game.

LR: *Legislative Recognition Game*

For $t \in \{LR\} \times Q$:

$$S_i^t = \{0\} \quad \text{if } i \in N;$$

$$\pi^t(s^t)(LP, t_1, y) = p_y(t_1) \quad \text{if } y \in L;$$

$$\psi^t(s^t) = x_0 \quad \text{for all } s_t \in S_t.$$

The Legislative Recognition Game is the second stage of the legislative session. This game is indexed by $t = (LR, t_1)$, where $t_0 = LR$ indicates we are in the Legislative Recognition Game and t_1 is the current seniority vector. If seniority passed in the Legislative Seniority Game, the seniority vector t_1 is the same as that in the Legislative Seniority Game. If seniority failed then q^* is used for the seniority vector. A legislator is selected by a random recognition rule to make a proposal for consideration by the legislature. This rule is similar to the Baron–Ferejohn recognition rule, except we let the recognition rule be a function of seniority. Our assumptions guarantee that higher seniority leads to higher probability of being selected as the proposer.

LP: Legislative Proposal Game
For $t \in \{LP\} \times Q \times L$:

$$S_i^t = \begin{cases} Z & \text{if } i = t, \\ \{0\} & \text{if } i \in N - \{t\}; \end{cases}$$

$$\pi^t(s^t)(LV, t_1, s_t^t) = 1;$$

$$\psi^t(s^t) = x_0 \quad \text{for all } s^t \in S^t.$$

The Legislative Proposal Game is the third stage of the legislative session. This game is indexed by $t = (LP, t_1, t_2)$, where $t_0 = LP$ indicates that we are in the proposal game, t_1 is the current seniority vector, and $t_2 \in L$ is the legislator who has been selected to make a proposal. This legislator, who has been selected as the proposer in the Legislative Recognition Game, makes a proposal for a division of the dollar between the legislative districts. If the legislator proposes the division z, then we proceed to the Legislative Voting Game (LV, t_1, z).

LV: Legislative Voting Game
For $t \in \{LV\} \times Q \times Z$:

$$S_i^t = \begin{cases} \{0, 1\} & \text{if } i \in L, \\ \{0\} & \text{if } i \in V; \end{cases}$$

$$\pi^t(s^t)(V, t_2) = 1 \quad \text{if } \sum_{i \in L} s_i^t > \frac{\mathcal{L}}{2};$$

$$\pi^t(s^t)(LR, q^*) = 1 \quad \text{if } \sum_{i \in L} s_i^t \leq \frac{\mathcal{L}}{2};$$

$$\psi^t(s^t) = x_0 \quad \text{for all } s^t \in S^t.$$

The Legislative Voting Game is the fourth state of the legislative session. This game is indexed by $t = (LV, t_1, t_2)$, where $t_0 = LV$ indicates that we are in the Legislative Voting Game, t_1 is the current seniority vector, and $t_2 \in Z$ indicates the proposal for division of the dollar that was selected by the proposer in the Legislative Proposal Game. In this game, the proposal t_2 is before the legislature, and the legislators must vote whether to accept it or reject it. If the legislators vote to accept the proposal, the legislative session ends, and we proceed to the Voter Game. If the legislators reject the proposal we return to the Legislative Recognition Game; however, with initial proposal power seniority is ignored in selecting the proposer. Note that the Legislative Proposal and Legislative Voting Games together are similar to the closed-rule version of the Baron–Ferejohn model.

V: Voter Game

For $t \in \{V\} \times Z$:

$$S_i^t = \begin{cases} \{0, 1\} & \text{if } i \in V, \\ \{0\} & \text{if } i \in L; \end{cases}$$

$$\pi^t(s^t)(LS, q(s^t)) = \delta;$$

$$\pi^t(s^t)(T) = 1 - \delta;$$

$$\psi^t(s^t) = (t_1, q(s^t));$$

where $q(s^t) = (q_1(s^t), q_2(s^t), \ldots, q_{\mathcal{L}}(s^t)) \in Q$ is defined by

$$q_i(s^t) = \begin{cases} 1 & \text{if } \sum_{j \in \phi^{-1}(i)} s_j^t > n_i/2, \\ 0 & \text{if } \sum_{j \in \phi^{-1}(i)} s_j^t \leq n_i/2, \end{cases}$$

and where $0 < \theta < 1$ and $0 < c$ are constants.

The Voter Game consists of a set of simultaneous elections in all of the legislative districts. This game is indexed by $t = (V, t_1)$, where $t_0 = V$ indicates that we are in the Voter Game and $t_1 \in Z$ represents the outcome of the Legislative Voting Game. In each legislative district, the voters of that district vote whether or not to re-elect their legislator. In the version of the game presented here, there is only one legislator in each district and no challenger. So the effect of a negative vote in a given district is that the legislator from that district does not get a salary for the next period and loses seniority.

The Voter Game also determines the termination conditions of the game. With probability δ, the game proceeds to the Legislative Seniority Game; with probability $1 - \delta$ the game proceeds to the Termination Game. This is a formal way of introducing discounting into the model. It is assumed that there is a probability $1 - \delta$ of termination after each round of the game. Note that the entire game terminates when this occurs. This is equivalent to assuming that players discount future payoffs by an amount δ. The Termination Game is an absorbing state with zero payoffs forever.

T: Termination Game

For $t \in \{T\}$:

$$S_i^t = \{0\} \quad \text{if } i \in N;$$

$$\pi^t(s^t)(0) = 1;$$

$$\psi^t(s^t) = x_0 \quad \text{for all } s^t \in S^t.$$

This completes the description of the stochastic game. Note that there are no payoffs except in the Voter Game. At that point, policy $x = (\tau_1, q(s^t))$

is implemented. Thus, the pie is divided up among the districts according to $z = t_1 \in \Delta^{\mathcal{L}}$, and $q(s') \in Q$ determines which legislators are re-elected and which are not. Given the utility functions we have specified, it follows that the output t_{1l} to district l is first divided up, with θt_{1l} actually delivered to the voters and $(1 - \theta) t_{1l}$ being skimmed off by legislator l. The voters each receive an even share of the delivered output. The lesiglators, in addition to their share of the output, get a salary that is dependent on whether or not they are re-elected.

4 Equilibrium with initial proposal power

The following proposition is proven in McKelvey and Riezman (1992).

Proposition 1. *The following is a stationary equilibrium to the Legislative Seniority Game defined in Section 3.*

(a) *For $t \in \{LS\} \times Q$ and $i \in L$, $\sigma_i^t(t_{1i}) = 1$.*

(b) *For $t \in \{LP\} \times Q \times L$,*

$$\sigma_t^l = \frac{1}{|\Omega_t|} \sum_{w \in \Omega_t} \delta_{z_t(w)},$$

where $\Omega_t = \{\omega \in \{0, 1\}^{\mathcal{L}} : \sum_i \omega_i = (\mathcal{L} + 1)/2, \ \omega_t = 1\}$, δ_x is the Dirac delta at x, and $z_t : \Omega_t \to \mathbb{R}^{\mathcal{L}}$ is defined by

$$z_{ti}(\omega) = \begin{cases} (\mathcal{L} + 1)/2\mathcal{L} & \text{if } i = t; \\ 1/\mathcal{L} & \text{if } i \neq t, \ \omega_i = 1; \\ 0 & \text{otherwise.} \end{cases}$$

(c) *For $t \in \{LV\} \times Q \times Z$ and $i \in L$,*

$$\sigma_i^t(1) = \begin{cases} 1 & \text{if } t_{1i} \geq 1/\mathcal{L}, \\ 0 & \text{if } t_{1i} < 1/\mathcal{L}. \end{cases}$$

(d) *For $t \in \{V\} \times Z$ and $i \in V$, $\sigma_i^t(1) = 1$ for all i.*

Proposition 1 gives equilibrium strategies for both legislators and voters in the game with initial proposal power. In the Legislative Seniority Game all legislators with seniority vote in favor of the seniority system; those who do not have seniority vote against the seniority system. In this equilibrium, since all legislators get re-elected the seniority system always passes.

In the Legislative Proposal Game, the proposer selects a minimal winning coalition of legislators which includes herself. The proposer retains $(\mathcal{L} + 1)/2\mathcal{L}$ for her own district, leaving $1/\mathcal{L}$ to be allocated to the districts of each of the remaining members of the coalition. Districts whose legislators are not a part of the winning coalition are allocated zero. Thus the proposer obtains a premium of $(\mathcal{L}+1)/2\mathcal{L} - 1/\mathcal{L} = (\mathcal{L}-1)/2\mathcal{L}$ due to her proposal power. As $\mathcal{L} \to \infty$ this premium goes to one half.

In the Legislative Voting Game, a legislator votes for a proposal if and only if he receives at least $1/\mathcal{L}$. Thus, in equilibrium all proposals receive $(\mathcal{L}+1)/2$ votes and pass.

Finally, in the Voter Game the voters always re-elect their legislators. It should be noted that although the proof shows only that this is a Nash equilibrium for the voters, in fact the strategy of voting for the incumbent is a dominant strategy for the voters in any given legislative district.

The intuition behind Proposition 1 is straightforward: Voters know that in equilibrium the seniority system will pass; hence it is in their best interest to re-elect the incumbent, since a senior legislator will better serve the constituency than a junior legislator. Note that voters do not know that there will be a seniority system in the next session, but rather know that – in the steady-state equilibrium – seniority will be voted in each session. In the next section we show that the results change if legislatures use continuing proposal power rather than initial proposal power.

5   Equilibrium with continuing proposal power

In our model the seniority system works through the Legislative Proposal stage by influencing the probability that legislators get chosen to be the proposer. We assumed that seniority only is used for selecting the proposer in the first round of any legislative session; hence, if a proposal is turned down in the legislature, seniority is no longer used to select the proposer during that legislative session. The alternative we now analyze is the case in which seniority is in effect throughout the legislative session. One might think that this system, which on its face gives more power to the senior members, would make them better off and hence would be selected by them. However, we show that the opposite is true. When seniority is in effect for the entire session, the only equilibrium is one in which legislators with and without seniority have the same continuation values. In other words, any equilibria will have the property that seniority has no benefits for legislators. Thus legislators would be indifferent between having and not having such a seniority system, and hence would prefer a system in which seniority is used for only the first proposal in each legislative session. Thus we obtain the rather paradoxical result that legislators with seniority will choose a system that would seem to give less power to senior members.

It is worth pointing out that a seniority system which gives only initial proposal power is a realistic description of the seniority system for the

U.S. Congress, in the sense that seniority is embodied in the committee system. Committees make proposals by sending bills to the floor. Once bills go to the floor, the committees lose most of their power, since bills that are amended or defeated generally do not go back to committee in that session. Hence our model might explain certain features about the way in which seniority systems are set up – in particular, the importance of initial proposal power.

We now turn to consideration of the Legislative Voting Game when seniority is used for selection of the proposer in every round. The rest of the stochastic game is as before. We change the Legislative Voting Game so that when a proposal is rejected the subsequent Legislative Recognition Game will use the original seniority vector.

LV': Revised Legislative Voting Game
For $t \in \{LV'\} \times Q \times Z$:

$$S_i^t = \begin{cases} \{0, 1\} & \text{if } i \in L, \\ \{0\} & \text{if } i \in V; \end{cases}$$

$$\pi^t(s^t)(V, t_2) = 1 \quad \text{if } \sum_{i \in L} s_i^t > \frac{\mathcal{L}}{2};$$

$$\pi^t(s^t)(LR, t_1) = 1 \quad \text{if } \sum_{i \in L} s_i^t \leq \frac{\mathcal{L}}{2};$$

$$\psi^t(s^t) = x_0 \quad \text{for all } s^t \in S^t.$$

Consider the stochastic game of Section 3, substituting LV' for the previous Legislative Voting Game; we call this the Revised Game.

Proposition 2. *In the Revised Game there is no symmetric stationary equilibrium with the following two properties.*

(a)   *Voters always re-elect incumbents: for $t \in \{V\} \times Z$ and $i \in V$, $\sigma_i^t(1) = 1$.*

(b)   *The value of senior and nonsenior members in the Legislative Seniority Game is different.*

Proof: Let $v_i^{LR,q}$ be the value to $i \in L$ in the Legislative Recognition Game, given seniority vector $q \in Q$. Assume, without loss of generality, that $v_1^{LR,q} \leq v_2^{LR,q} \leq \cdots \leq v_{\mathcal{L}}^{LR,q}$. Let K be the largest integer for which $v_1^{LR,q} = v_K^{LR,q}$. We will first show that either $K = \mathcal{L}$ or the legislators vote against seniority in the Legislative Seniority Game. We deal first with the case when pure strategies are adopted in the Legislative Proposal Game, and then discuss the case of mixed strategies. So assume $K < \mathcal{L}$. There are two cases.

Case 1: $K \leq (\mathfrak{L}-1)/2$. First, write $v_i^* = v_i^{LR,q^*}$. By parts (a) and (b) of the proposition and by using symmetry, it follows that $v_i^* = v_j^*$ for all $i \neq j$. So write $v^* = v_i^*$. Now, since legislators adopt an undominated Nash equilibrium in the Revised Legislative Voting Game, it follows that legislator i will vote for t_2 (i.e. $s_i^I = 1$) if $v_i^{V,t_2} \geq v_i^{LR,t_1}$. But by parts (a) and (b), writing $z = t_2$,

$$v_i^{V,z} = v_i^{V,t_2} = (1-\theta)z_i + c + \delta v^*$$

and

$$v_i^{LR,q} = v_i^{LR,t_1}.$$

Hence $s_i^I = 1$ if

$$(1-\theta)z_i + c + \delta v^* \geq v_i^{LR,q}.$$

It follows that in the Legislative Proposal Game, Nash equilibrium implies $t_2 = j$ will choose z^j to maximize z_j^j subject to z^j being approved by a majority in the Revised Legislative Voting Game. Hence voter j will select a coalition $C_j \subseteq L - \{j\}$ of size $(\mathfrak{L}-1)/2$ for which $\sum_{i \in C_j} v_i^{LR,q}$ is minimized, and set

$$z_i^j = \frac{1}{1-\theta}(v_i^{LR,q} - c - \delta v^*) \quad \text{for } i \in C_j, \tag{1}$$

$$z_j^j = 1 - \sum_{i \in C_j} z_i^j, \quad \text{and}$$

$$z_i^j = 0 \quad \text{for } i \notin C_j, \; i \neq j.$$

Since $v_1^{LR,q}$ is minimal and $|\{i \in L : v_i^{LR,q} = v_1^{LR,q}\}| \leq (\mathfrak{L}-1)/2$, it follows that for all $j \neq 1$,

$$z_1^j = \frac{1}{1-\theta}(v_1^{LR,q} - c - \delta v^*) = z_1.$$

This may be rewritten as

$$(1-\theta)z_1^j + c + \delta v^* = v_1^{LR,q}.$$

But

$$v_1^{LR,q} = \sum_{i \in L} p_i(q)v_1^{LP,q,i},$$

where

$$v_1^{LP,q,i} = v_1^{LV,q,z^i} = (1-\theta)z_1^i + c + \delta v^*.$$

So

$$(1-\theta)z_1^j + c + \delta v^* = \sum_{i \in L} p_i(q)[(1-\theta)z_1^i + c + \delta v^*]$$

$$\Rightarrow (1-\theta)z_1^j = (1-\theta) \sum_{i \in L} p_i(q)z_1^i$$

$$\Rightarrow z_1^j = p_1(q)z_1^1 + (1-p_1(q))z_1^j$$

$$\Rightarrow z_1^1 = z_1^j.$$

But we have shown that $z_1^i = z_1^1$ for all $i \in L$; hence

$$v_1^{LR,q} = \sum_{i \in L} p_i(q) v_1^{LP,q,i}$$

$$= \sum_{i \in L} p_i(q)[(1-\theta)z_1^i + c + \delta v^*] = (1-\theta)z_1^1 + c + \delta v^*.$$

Further, from equation (1) it follows that for all $j \in C_1$,

$$v_j^{LR,q} = (1-\theta)z_j^1 + c + \delta v^*.$$

Hence, setting $C = C_1 \cup \{1\}$,

$$\sum_{j \in C} v_j^{LR,q} = \sum_{j \in C} [(1-\theta)z_j^1 + c + \delta v^*] = (1-\theta) + \frac{\mathcal{L}+1}{2}(c + \delta v^*).$$

But

$$\sum_{j \in L} v_j^{LR,q} = \sum_{j \in L} \sum_{i \in L} p_i(q) v_j^{LP,q,i} = \sum_{j \in L} \sum_{i \in L} p_i(q)[(1-\theta)z_j^i + c + \delta v^*]$$

$$= \sum_{i \in L} p_i(q) \sum_{j \in L} [(1-\theta)z_j^i + c + \delta v^*]$$

$$= \sum_{i \in L} p_i(q)[(1-\theta) + \mathcal{L}(c + \delta v^*)]$$

$$= (1-\theta) + \mathcal{L}(c + \delta v^*).$$

Combining the last two equations, it follows that

$$\sum_{j \in L-C} v_j^{LR,q} = \left[\mathcal{L} - \frac{\mathcal{L}+1}{2}\right](c + \delta v^*) = \frac{\mathcal{L}-1}{2}(c + \delta v^*).$$

Since we also have that for each $j \in L$, $v_j^{LR,q} \geq c + \delta v^*$, it follows that for all $j \in L-C$, $v_j^{LR,q} = c + \delta v^*$. But since $\mathcal{L} \notin C$ and since, for some $j \in C$, we must have $z_j^1 > 0$, it follows that $v_{\mathcal{L}}^{LR,q} < v_j^{LR,q}$ – a contradiction.

Case 2: $(\mathcal{L} - 1)/2 < K < \mathcal{L}$. In this case, in the Legislative Seniority Game, it follows that individual i will only vote for seniority (i.e. $s_i^i = 1$) if $v_i^{LR,q} \geq v^*$, where (as in Case 1) $v^* = v_i^* = v_i^{LR,q^*}$ for all $i \in L$. By the same argument as in Case 1,

$$\mathcal{L}v^* = \sum_{j \in L} v_j^* = \sum_{j \in L} v_j^{LR,q^*} = (1-\theta) + \mathcal{L}(c + \delta v^*). \tag{2}$$

So

$$v^* = (1/\mathcal{L})(1-\theta) + (c + \delta v^*).$$

Now, it must be the case that $v_1^{LR,q} < v^*$. To see this, assume to the contrary that $v_1^{LR,q} \geq v^*$. Then using $v_1^{LR,q} \leq v_j^{LR,q}$ for all $j \in L$ and $v_1^{LR,q} < v_j^{LR,q}$ for $j > K$, it follows that

$$\sum_{j \in L} v_j^{LR,q^*} > \sum_{j \in L} v_1^* = \mathcal{L}v^*,$$

which contradicts (2). But now, since $v_j^{LR,q} = v_1^{LR,q}$ for all $j \leq K$, it follows that $v_j^{LR,q} < v^*$ for all $j \leq K$. Hence, in the Legislative Seniority Game,

$s_i^j = 1$ for all $i \leq K$. But by assumption, $(\mathfrak{L}-1)/2 < K$; or, equivalently, $(\mathfrak{L}+1)/2 \leq K$. Thus a majority vote against seniority in the Legislative Seniority Game.

We have thus shown that either $K = \mathfrak{L}$ or a majority vote against seniority in the Legislative Seniority Game. But if a majority vote against seniority in the Legislative Seniority Game, it follows that

$$v_i^{LS,q} = v_i^{LR,q^*} = v^* \quad \text{for all } i \in L.$$

On the other hand, if $K = \mathfrak{L}$ it follows that

$$v_i^{LR,q} = v_j^{LR,q} \quad \text{for all } i,j \in L.$$

So regardless of the vote in the Legislative Seniority Game, we have

$$v_i^{LS,q} = v_j^{LS,q} \quad \text{for all } i,j \in L.$$

Hence, in both cases, we have shown that

$$v_i^{LS,q} = v_j^{LS,q} \quad \text{for all } i,j \in L,$$

which violates part (b) of the proposition.

This argument has assumed that pure strategies are adopted in the Legislative Proposal Game. However, if mixed strategies are adopted, then any mixed strategy for legislator j must mix between pure strategies which satisfy the condition that j will select a coalition $C_j \subseteq L - \{j\}$ of size $(\mathfrak{L}-1)/2$ for which $\sum_{i \in C_j} v_i^{LR,q}$ is minimized. Thus the same argument as before can be applied.   □

The intuition behind this result has to do with how proposers choose coalition partners. Once chosen, proposers want to include in the coalition those with the lowest continuation values, because they can be given less and will still vote for the proposal. It follows that, when seniority is used throughout the legislative session, if seniority benefits senior members then they will be less likely to be included in coalitions. What Proposition 2 shows is that for senior members the effect of being less often included in coalitions swamps the advantage of being more often chosen as proposer when seniority is used throughout the session. Thus, once the proposer is chosen, senior members want to look like nonsenior members so that they will be as likely to be included in the coalition.

REFERENCES

Baron, D., and J. Ferejohn (1989), "Bargaining in Legislatures," *American Political Science Review* 83: 1181–1206.
McKelvey, R. D., and R. Riezman (1992), "Seniority in Legislatures," *American Political Science Review* 86: 951–65.
Sobel, Matthew J. (1971), "Noncooperative Stochastic Games," *Annals of Mathematical Statistics* 42: 1930–5.

Political competition

CHAPTER 12

Adverse selection and moral hazard in a repeated elections model

Jeffrey S. Banks and Rangarajan K. Sundaram

1 Introduction

In this chapter we consider the problem faced by a (median) voter in an electorate who must, in each period of an infinite horizon, select a candidate for the performance of some task, where we refer to the candidate selected in period t as the period-t incumbent. Rewards accrue to the voter as a consequence of her choice, where we can think of these rewards as government-controlled benefits secured by the incumbent, and the voter's objective is to maximize the discounted sum of rewards over the infinite horizon. However, a factor determining the distribution of rewards in any given period – namely, the incumbent's action that period – is unobservable to the voter. Actions preferable to the voter are associated with higher costs for the incumbent. Moreover, the voter is uncertain about a parameter describing these costs to a candidate, where this is labeled a candidate's *type*. Although the voter does not care about a candidate's type per se, learning this information will assist the voter in ascertaining the desirability of a candidate, since different types will take different actions. There are an infinite number of candidates available to the voter (so, in particular, at every point in time there is at least one untried candidate); candidates are all ex ante identical and are infinitely lived, and there are no restrictions on how often a candidate can be in office. Finally, each candidate attempts to maximize his own discounted sum of payoffs over the infinite horizon through his action choices while in office.

The voter's choice problem thus includes aspects of *moral hazard,* in that she must provide incentives for a candidate to take costly actions, as well as *adverse selection,* in that the voter would like to choose only those candidates who take the higher actions. Thus, to a considerable degree,

Financial support to the first author from the National Science Foundation and Sloan Foundation is gratefully acknowledged.

the moving parts of this model are the same as those that arise frequently in the principal–agent literature and in other contracting models of economic theory. On the other hand, there are substantial differences as well, the foremost being the presumed inability of the voter and the candidates to sign contracts determining payments to a candidate as a function of the rewards the latter generates, thereby ruling out equilibria of the form that are standard in economic models. Rather, the voter must rely on the only policy instrument at her disposal – the control of re-election rules – to provide candidate incentives that mitigate the voter's moral-hazard and adverse-selection problems. Indeed, since re-election rules offer the elected candidates the only incentives to take desired actions, repetition of the voter–candidate relationship is the sine qua non for providing such incentives, in contrast to principal–agent models.

Most previous research on repeated elections in the presence of informational asymmetries has studied the voter's decision problem from either the moral-hazard or the adverse-selection perspective; examples of the former include Barro (1973), Ferejohn (1986), and Austen-Smith and Banks (1989), and of the latter Rogoff (1990), Reed (1991), and Banks and Sundaram (1990).[1] For example, in Ferejohn (1986) the voter knows the preferences of the candidates with certainty, but only observes the action choice by the incumbent with noise. The incumbent observes this noise term prior to taking his action, and the voter selects a re-election rule to provide incentives for incumbents to take costly actions. Conversely, Rogoff's (1990) model of political budget cycles is more in the adverse-selection vein, where candidate "types" denote competency at delivering public goods to the voters.[2] In contrast to our model, the actions taken by candidates while in office are observable by the voter, and hence act as a signal of candidate competency. In addition, a candidate's competency varies over time, so in particular competency is uncorrelated across electoral cycles. Thus the issue of the voter learning about candidates through their performance, which forms a crux of the current model, is avoided.

We analyze the interaction between the voter and candidates as a (stochastic) game of incomplete information, and characterize a particular class of sequential equilibria. In these, the voter employs a simple *retrospective voting rule* (Fiorina 1981): retain the current incumbent as long as rewards remain above a certain level. Faced with this re-election rule, incumbents adopt time-invariant actions as functions of their true type,

---

[1] Other game-theoretic models of repeated elections include Alesina (1988) and Alesina and Spear (1988) on credible policy pronouncements, Ledyard (1989) on the transmission of information between candidates regarding voter preferences, and McKelvey and Reizman (1992) on the observance of seniority norms in legislatures.

[2] See also Rogoff and Sibert (1988).

where lower cost types take higher actions, and are consequently re-elected more often. Thus, as an incumbent's tenure increases, the voter is more confident she has selected a (relatively) hard-working type, since the voter's belief about the incumbent is placing greater weight on higher types after every re-election of the incumbent. This behavior also implies that, from the voter's perspective, an incumbent's probability of re-election is a strictly increasing function of his tenure in office.

2   The model

An individual, whom we refer to as the *voter,* has a task to be performed in time periods $t = 1, 2, \ldots$. In each period the voter selects a single candidate for the performance of this task, where we let $N = \{1, 2, \ldots\}$ denote the (infinite) set of available candidates. The chosen candidate, whom we refer to as the period-t *incumbent,* selects an action $a \in A \equiv [\underline{a}, \bar{a}] \subset \mathbb{R}$, where this action is unobserved by the voter, and (stochastically) determines the voter's reward for that period. Specifically, the voter's per-period reward is a realization from a continuous density $f(\cdot; a)$, where for any $a \in A$, supp $f(\cdot; a) := \{r \mid f(r; a) > 0\}$ denotes the support of the density $f(\cdot; a)$, $\bar{r}(a) = \int r f(r; a) \, dr$ denotes the expected reward, and $F(\cdot; a)$ is the associated distribution. We make the following assumptions on $f(\cdot; \cdot)$:

A1   for all $a \in A$, supp $f(\cdot; a) = R \subseteq \mathbb{R}$;
A2   for all $a_1, a_2 \in A$, if $a_1 > a_2$ then $\bar{r}(a_1) > \bar{r}(a_2)$; and
A3   there exists $\hat{r} \in \text{int } R$ such that for all $r \in R$ and $r \geq \hat{r}$,
        $f(r; a_1) > f(r; a_2)$ if $a_1 > a_2$, where $a_1, a_2 \in A$.

Assumptions A1 and A2 are self-explanatory. A3 requires that the family of reward densities parameterized by the actions $a \in A$ are "stacked" beyond some point. Such a condition is met if, for example, the realized reward is given by $(a + \epsilon)$, where ϵ has a unimodal density (say, normal) on the real line.

The per-period payoff for the voter is simply equal to her realized reward, whereas the incumbent's payoff is a function of the action chosen as well as his "type" $\omega \in \{\omega_1, \ldots, \omega_n\} \equiv \Omega$. Let $u(a, \omega)$ denote this payoff, where $u(\underline{a}, \omega) > 0$ for all $\omega \in \Omega$, and $u(\cdot)$ is continuously differentiable in a, with $u_1 \equiv \partial u / \partial a < 0$. Thus taking higher actions, which are preferred by the voter, is more costly for an incumbent. We further add Inada-type conditions to guarantee interior action choices by incumbents: For all $\omega \in \Omega$, $u_1(a, \omega) \to 0$ as $a \to \underline{a}$ and $u_1(a, \omega) \to -\infty$ as $a \to \bar{a}$. We assume without loss of generality that for all $a \in A$, $u(a, \omega_1) < \cdots < u(a, \omega_n)$, so for any fixed action higher types receive higher per-period rewards; we also assume that $u_1(a, \omega)$ is nondecreasing in ω – that is, the marginal disutility from taking any action is lower for higher types.[3] All nonchosen candidates receive a per-period payoff of zero, regardless of type. The voter (resp. each candidate) discounts future payoffs by a factor $\delta \in [0, 1)$ (resp. $\rho \in [0, 1)$).

Candidate types are drawn independently from Ω according to $b^0 = (b_1^0, \ldots, b_n^0)$, where $b_j^0 > 0$, $j = 1, \ldots, n$. Each candidate knows his own type, but does not know any other candidate's type, and the voter does not know any candidate's type. Let $P(\Omega)$ denote the set of probability measures on Ω, and set $\Pi(\Omega) = \times_{i=1}^{\infty} P(\Omega)$. Thus the voter's prior belief on candidate types is given by $b_{\infty}^0 \equiv (b^0(1), \ldots, b^0(i), \ldots) \in \Pi(\Omega)$, while candidate i's prior belief differs from the voter's only in that $b^0(i)$ has a 1 on his true type and 0 and all other types.

A *history* of length t, denoted h^t, is a specification of all public events through period t: namely, the candidates chosen each period and the rewards realized. Let H^t denote the set of all possible histories of length t, and set $H^0 = \emptyset$. For a generic candidate i, this history is augmented by the actions taken by i in the periods (if any) where i was the incumbent. We will refer to the set of i's augmented histories by H_i^t, with common element h_i^t. Of course, if i has not figured in the history h^t then $h_i^t = h^t$.

A *strategy* σ for the voter is a sequence of functions $\sigma = \{\sigma^t\}_{t=1}^{\infty}$, where for each t, $\sigma^t : H^{t-1} \to N$ is a measurable map defining the candidate to be chosen in period t as a function of the history through period $t-1$. Let Σ denote the set of all possible strategies for the voter. A strategy γ_i for candidate i is a sequence of functions $\gamma_i = \{\gamma_i^t\}_{t=1}^{\infty}$, where for each t, $\gamma_i^t : H_i^{t-1} \times \Omega \to A$ is a measurable map specifying the action to be taken if i is the period-t incumbent, as a function of the history h_i^{t-1} through period $t-1$ as well as of candidate i's type. Thus i's choice of action in any period can in principle depend on i's previous actions while in office. However, since candidate i's actions are not observable by anybody but i, and do not affect i's payoffs in subsequent periods, we can without loss of generality restrict attention to candidate strategies that condition only on the voter's selections and the subsequent rewards. Thus for all t, $h^{t-1} \in H^{t-1}$, let $\gamma_i^t(h^{t-1}, \omega)$ denote the action taken by candidate i if i is the period-t incumbent, conditional on the (public) history h^{t-1} and i's type. The set of all such strategies for a candidate is evidently the same as that for any other candidate; denote this common set by Γ. A *strategy profile* is then a list of strategies, one for the voter and one each for the candidates; a generic strategy profile will be denoted (σ, γ), where $\gamma = (\gamma_i)_{i \in N}$.

A *belief system* for the voter is a sequence of measurable maps $\mu = \{\mu^t\}_{t=1}^{\infty}$, where for each t, $\mu^t : H^{t-1} \to \Pi(\Omega)$. Thus, $\mu^t(h^{t-1})$ gives the voter's

---

[3] For example, we could have $u(a, \omega) = \omega - c(a)$, where $\partial c / \partial a > 0$; these are the incumbent preferences in Ferejohn (1986) and Austen-Smith and Banks (1989).

beliefs about the candidates' types after observing a history h^{t-1}. A belief system for candidate i is similarly a sequence of maps $\varphi_i = \{\varphi_i^t\}$ describing i's beliefs about candidate types; of course, for all t, $\varphi_i^t(\cdot)$ will assign probability 1 to i's true type. A *belief profile* is then (μ, φ), where $\varphi = \{\varphi_i\}_{i \in N}$.

Given a strategy profile (σ, γ) and a belief $\mu^t(h^{t-1})$ at history h^{t-1}, the voter can compute her expected payoff conditional on being at h^{t-1}; denote this by $W(\sigma, \gamma, \mu; h^{t-1})$. Similarly, for candidate i we have $C_i(\sigma, \gamma, \varphi_i; h^{t-1})$. A *sequential equilibrium* (Kreps and Wilson 1982) consists of a strategy profile (σ, γ) and a belief profile (μ, φ), such that (1) the strategies are sequentially rational given the beliefs, and (2) the beliefs are consistent with the strategies. Sequential rationality requires, for all t and h^{t-1},

(i) $W(\sigma, \gamma, \mu; h^{t-1}) \geq W(\sigma', \gamma, \mu; h^{t-1})$ for all $\sigma' \in \Sigma$, and
(ii) for all $i \in N$, $C_i(\sigma, \gamma, \varphi_i; h^{t-1}) \geq C_i(\sigma, \gamma_i', \gamma_{-i}, \varphi_i; h^{t-1})$ for all $\gamma_i' \in \Gamma$.

Consistency requires at a minimum that, for all histories h^{t-1} that are "reached" by the strategy profile (σ, γ), $\mu^t(h^{t-1})$ and $\{\varphi_i^t(h^{t-1})\}$ be derived via Bayes's rule from the strategies (σ, γ) and the prior b_∞^0.[4] So suppose h^{t-1} is reached by (σ, γ), and let candidate $i = \sigma^t(h^{t-1})$; that is, candidate i is the period-t incumbent. Given a current belief about candidate i with $b^t(i) = (b_1^t(i), \ldots, b_n^t(i))$, and given an observed reward r and a conjectured action rule $a(\omega) \equiv \gamma_i^t(h^{t-1}, \omega)$ (stochastically) generating r, in equilibrium the voter (as well as the nonincumbent candidates) updates her belief about candidate i in a Bayesian fashion:

$$b_j^{t+1}(i) = \beta_j(b^t(i), r; a(\omega)) \equiv \frac{b_j^t(i) f(r; a(\omega_j))}{\sum_{k=1}^n b_k^t(i) f(r; a(\omega_k))}.$$

On the other hand, by the independence assumption on candidate types, the voter learns only about the incumbent's type; therefore, for all nonincumbents $m \in N$, $b^{t+1}(m) = b^t(m)$.

With respect to out-of-equilibrium beliefs – that is, beliefs at histories not reached by the profile (σ, γ) – consistency requires such beliefs to be the limit of beliefs formed from completely mixed strategies by the players, where these completely mixed strategies converge to the candidate equilibrium strategies (σ, γ). However, since the reward densities have the same support regardless of a candidate's strategy or his true type (from A1), such histories occur only when the voter selects the wrong (according to σ) candidate. Therefore it is sufficient to assume that only the voter "trembles" away from σ. But then out-of-equilibrium beliefs are completely specified by the candidates' equilibrium strategies, since even if

---

[4] Indeed, this is a requirement of the Nash equilibrium concept itself.

$i \neq \sigma^{t}(h^{t-1})$, i's strategy dictates what i would have done if selected; therefore the "consistent" belief upon observing the subsequent reward is precisely that derived via Bayes's rule if i were in fact equal to $\sigma^{t}(h^{t-1})$ – that is, if i were *supposed* to have been selected. Therefore, out-of-equilibrium beliefs are derived from (σ, γ), in particular from γ, in exactly the same fashion as equilibrium-path beliefs. Thus in what follows we suppress belief profiles in the characterization of sequential equilibria, since they follow immediately from the description of the strategy profile.

3   Simple equilibria

Clearly, the repeated nature of the elections, plus the ability of the voter to potentially "learn" about the true types of candidates through the realized rewards, foreshadows a possibly large and complex set of sequential equilibria for this game. This being so, in what follows we focus attention on a particularly manageable class of equilibria with the following characteristics:

(i)   candidate i's strategy is only a function of his "personal" history with the voter, that is, the rewards i has generated and the voter's response of either retaining or replacing i as the incumbent;

(ii) all candidates adopt identical strategies (as functions of their personal histories and types), and the voter's strategy treats all candidates symmetrically; and

(iii) the voter adopts a *no-recall* strategy, in which previously selected and discarded candidates are never again chosen.

One can also make a selection argument for examining only such equilibria, based on the structure of the interaction between the voter and the candidates. For instance, condition (i) asserts that the only relevant information for a candidate is his own relationship with the voter; condition (ii) seems natural given the symmetry of the game from the candidate's perspective and from the independence of candidate types; and similarly condition (iii) seems natural given the infinite set of candidates, the independence of candidate types, and the (assumed) symmetry of the candidates' strategies. At any time, the voter can "start over" with an untried candidate, and if starting over is preferred to the period-t incumbent at the beginning of period $t+1$ then it should be still preferred in any subsequent period.

We can describe such behavior in a more compact notation than that given in Section 2. Let $(r, I)^{t} \equiv ((r_{1}, I_{1}), \ldots, (r_{t}, I_{t})) \in [\mathbb{R} \times \{0, 1\}]^{t}$ denote a t-period personal history of rewards and subsequent decisions to retain ($I = 1$) or replace ($I = 0$) the incumbent. Let $\alpha_{i} = \{\alpha_{i}^{t}\}$ be a measurable sequence of functions, where $\alpha_{i}^{0}(\omega) \in A$ for all $\omega \in \Omega$ and

$\alpha_i^t \colon [\mathbb{R} \times \{0, 1\}]^{t-1} \times \Omega \to A$ for $t \geq 1$.

The strategy $\gamma_i^{\alpha_i}(\omega)$ for candidate i is defined as follows: If i is selected as the period-t incumbent after the public history h^{t-1} then, given h^{t-1}, i can compute his personal history $(r, I)^\tau$, where $\tau \leq t - 1$. If i is of type $\omega \in \Omega$, he takes action $\alpha_i^{\tau+1}((r, I)^\tau, \omega)$. Thus, $\gamma_i^{\alpha_i}$ depends only on the personal history of rewards and responses generated by i, and not on the personal histories generated by other candidates. The symmetry requirement on the candidates is that $\alpha_i = \alpha_m = \alpha$ for some α and for all $i, m \in N$.

We can likewise describe the no-recall condition for the voter's strategy in terms of personal histories: For each $i \in N$, there is a candidate-specific re-election rule $\nu_i = \{\nu_i^t\}$, where $\nu_i^{t+1} \colon [\mathbb{R} \times \{0, 1\}]^{t-1} \times \mathbb{R} \to \{0, 1\}$ for all $t \geq 1$. The interpretation is that $\nu_i^{t+1}((r, I)^{t-1}, r)$ denotes the voter's decision to retain or replace candidate i with a previously untried candidate as a function of i's personal history prior to the last period $(r, I)^{t-1}$, the voter having selected i in the previous period and i having generated a reward $r \in \mathbb{R}$. If the voter treats the candidates symmetrically, we have $\nu_i = \nu_m \equiv \nu$ for some ν and for all $i, m \in N$. The voter's strategy σ^ν is then defined as follows. Given a public history h^{t-1}, suppose candidate i is the period-$(t-1)$ incumbent, where (according to h^{t-1}) i has also been selected in τ previous periods. The voter retains i for period t if i's personal history is such that $\nu^{\tau+2}((r, I)^\tau, r) = 1$, and replaces i with an untried (according to h^{t-1}) candidate otherwise. Hence σ^ν (in equilibrium) never recalls a previously selected and discarded candidate, and decides whether to retain or replace an incumbent based solely on the incumbent's personal history.

So we can characterize such equilibria by the pair (α, ν), where $\alpha(\cdot)$ is the (common) candidate strategy describing the actions taken as a function of the candidate type and personal history, and $\nu(\cdot)$ is the voter strategy specifying when the voter replaces an incumbent with an untried candidate as a function of the incumbent's personal history.[5] Within this class of equilibria there exist some of a quite Spartan form – namely, ones where (along the equilibrium path) the voter's replacement rule is a function only of the last reward generated by the incumbent, and is the same rule regardless of how long the incumbent has been in office. This will give a candidate of type ω an incentive to adopt the same action in every period in office, regardless of personal history (again, along the equilibrium path). These we label *simple* equilibria.

One type of simple equilibrium is the following. All candidates of all types adopt the lowest action $\underline{q}$ in every period in office, and the voter always replaces the incumbent with an untried candidate. Thus, if the voter is going to replace the incumbent with probability 1 regardless of

---

[5] Note that we are not restricting the strategies available to the players in any way; we are merely focusing on a class of equilibria with a particular structure.

the realized reward, an incumbent has no incentive to take any but the lowest-cost action; and if all incumbents take the lowest-cost action then the voter might as well simply throw out all incumbents. Note that such behavior would also constitute an equilibrium if the game had but a finite time horizon, since in the last period the incumbent will certainly choose $a = \underline{a}$ regardless of type or history, leaving the voter indifferent over all candidates: if she selects from the untried candidates, then the incumbent in the penultimate period will certainly choose $a = \underline{a}$; and so on.[6] We can therefore think of such behavior as being analogous to one-shot Nash behavior in repeated games. On the other hand, the model also generates simple equilibria of a more interesting nature. These we characterize in the following result.

Proposition.   *There exist sequential equilibria with the following structure:*

$$\nu^{t+1}((r, I)^{t-1}, r_t) = \begin{cases} 1 & \text{if } r_\tau \geq r^* \ \forall \tau \leq t \text{ and } I_\tau = 1 \ \forall \tau \leq t-1, \\ 0 & \text{otherwise;} \end{cases}$$

$$\alpha^t((r, I)^{t-1}, \omega) = \begin{cases} a^*(\omega) & \text{if } r_\tau \geq r^* \text{ and } I_\tau = 1 \ \forall \tau \leq t-1, \\ \underline{a} & \text{otherwise;} \end{cases}$$

where $a^*(\omega)$ is strictly increasing in ω and depends on ρ, but where $a^*(\cdot)$ and r^* do not depend on δ.

Proof: We begin by showing that, along the equilibrium path, a candidate's choice of best response to $\nu(\cdot)$ may be modeled as a two-state dynamic programming problem. Fix a candidate $i \in N$ and a type $\omega \in \Omega$. Define $G = \bigcup_{t=1}^{\infty} R^t$ with generic element g, let $|g|$ denote the length of g, and let e_n denote the n-vector each of whose elements is unity. Define

$$G_1 = \{g \in G \mid g \geq r^* \cdot e_{|g|}\} \quad \text{and}$$

$$G_2 = G \setminus G_1.$$

In this notation, the voter's strategy may be written $\nu: G \to \{0, 1\}$, where $\nu(g) = 1$ if and only if $g \in G_1$.

Let $S = \{0, 1\}$, where $s = 0$ signifies that i's history to date satisfies $g \in G_2$ and $s = 1$ signifies either $g \in G_1$ or $g = \emptyset$. If $s = 1$, the probability that i will continue in state $s = 1$ after taking action $a \in A$ is evidently just the probability the action will generate a reward of at least r^*, which is $1 - F(r^*, a)$. On the other hand, $s = 0$ is an absorbing state, no matter what action is taken. Consequently, we may define transition probabilities $Q(\cdot \mid \cdot, \cdot)$ from $S \times A$ to S by

---

[6] However, this will not be the only equilibrium in the finite-horizon game: due to the voter's indifference over candidates in the final period of such a game, she can make her selection a nontrivial function of realized rewards (cf. Austen-Smith and Banks 1989).

$$Q(1\,|\,1,a) = 1 - F(r^*,a) = 1 - Q(0\,|\,1,a) \quad \text{and} \quad Q(0\,|\,0,a) = 1$$

for all $a \in A$. Next, recall that i receives a time-invariant payoff while in office and a zero payoff otherwise. This may be represented by $r: S \times A \to \mathbb{R}$, where, for all $a \in A$,

$$r(1,a) = u(a,\omega) \quad \text{and} \quad r(0,a) = 0.$$

The tuple $\{S, A, Q, r\}$ now represents a standard dynamic programming problem. All the conditions of Maitra (1968) are seen to be met (in particular, A is compact), and the solution to this problem may be obtained via the Bellman equation

$$V(s) = \max_{a \in A}\left\{r(s,a) + \rho \int V(s')Q(ds'\,|\,s,a)\right\}. \tag{1}$$

Substituting for $r(\cdot)$ and $Q(\cdot)$, we finally obtain

$$V(1) = \max_{a \in A}\{u(a,\omega) + \rho[1 - F(r^*,a)]V(1)\} \quad \text{and}$$

$$V(0) = 0. \tag{2}$$

Evidently, if $s = 1$ then the constant action that maximizes (2) is optimal for candidate i, while any action is optimal at $s = 0$; denote the former by $a^*(\omega)$. We can therefore suppress the dependence of V on the state, and highlight the dependence of V on the parameter ω, by rewriting (2) as

$$V(\omega) = \max_{a \in A}\{u(a,\omega) + \rho[1 - F(r^*,a)V(\omega)]\}. \tag{3}$$

By (3), the solution $a^*(\omega)$ solves

$$u_1(a^*,\omega) - \rho F_2(r^*,a^*)V(\omega) = 0. \tag{4}$$

Also, $V(\omega) > 0$ for all ω, and is strictly increasing in ω, since (by $u(a,\omega)$ increasing in ω) higher types can emulate the behavior of lower types and receive a strictly higher payoff in every period in office. To see that $a^*(\omega)$ is increasing in ω, let $a_j = a^*(\omega_j)$ for $j = 1, \ldots, n$, and let $k > j$ (so $\omega_k > \omega_j$). Clearly we must have $a_k \neq a_j$, since if (4) holds at a_j for ω_j then, by $V(\cdot)$ increasing in ω and $u_1(a,\omega)$ nondecreasing in ω, (4) does not hold at a_j for ω_k. For all $a \in A$ let $p(a) = 1 - F(r^*,a)$, and note that $p(\cdot)$ is strictly increasing on A and $p(a) > 0$ for all $a \in A$. By incentive compatibility,

$$u(a_k,\omega_k) + p(a_k)V(\omega_k) \geq u(a_j,\omega_k) + p(a_j)V(\omega_k); \tag{5}$$

$$u(a_j,\omega_j) + p(a_j)V(\omega_j) \geq u(a_k,\omega_j) + p(a_k)V(\omega_j). \tag{6}$$

Subtracting the RHS of (6) from the LHS of (5), and the LHS of (6) from the RHS of (5), and then rearranging terms, we obtain

$$[p(a_k) - p(a_j)][V(\omega_k) - V(\omega_j)]$$
$$\geq [u(a_j,\omega_k) - u(a_k,\omega_k)] - [u(a_j,\omega_j) - u(a_k,\omega_j)]. \tag{7}$$

If $a_j > a_k$, then both terms on the RHS of (7) are negative, yet by $u_1(a, \omega)$ nondecreasing in ω the first of these is (in absolute-value terms) less than or equal to the second. Therefore, if $a_j > a_k$ we would have

$$[p(a_k) - p(a_j)][V(\omega_k) - V(\omega_j)] \geq 0, \tag{8}$$

which contradicts $V(\cdot)$ increasing in ω and $p(\cdot)$ increasing in a. Therefore $a_j > a_k$ is ruled out, and since we've already shown $a_k \neq a_j$, we now have $a_k > a_j$, thus proving $a^*(\omega)$ strictly increasing.

Out of equilibrium – that is, if the voter has retained candidate i after observing a reward $r < r^*$ or if the voter returns to i after previously replacing him – it is clear that $\alpha(\cdot)$ is optimal since, according to $\nu(\cdot)$, the voter will (with probability 1) replace i in the next period and never select i again; thus, choosing the lowest-cost action of $a = \underline{a}$ is optimal. A similar reasoning holds if the voter ever recalls candidate i when i has (sometime in the past) generated a reward $r < r^*$. Therefore $\alpha(\cdot)$ is a best response to $\nu(\cdot)$ for any possible history.

Alternatively, if the voter has ever observed a reward of $r < r^*$ from candidate i, or has previously replaced i, then the voter will never select i again regardless of her beliefs, since according to $\alpha(\cdot)$ i would now take action $a = \underline{a}$ if selected regardless of type, implying that any untried candidate is strictly better for the voter. Thus, it remains to be shown that the voter prefers to retain an incumbent who continually generates rewards greater than r^*, independent of the value of $\delta \in [0, 1)$.

For notational ease, let $a_i = a^*(\omega_i)$, $i = 1, \ldots, n$. Since $a_1 < \cdots < a_n$, by A3 we know that there exists $\hat{r} \in \text{int } R$ such that for all $r \geq \hat{r}$, $f(r; a_1) < \cdots < f(r; a_n)$. Next, note that our arguments concerning a candidate's optimal strategy did not depend on the *value* of r^*; we merely claimed that the voter was adopting r^* as a cut-off rule. Thus, choose r^* so that $r^* \geq \hat{r}$; we will show that such a cut-off rule is consistent with an equilibrium.

Given the candidates' common strategy $\alpha(\cdot)$, we pose the voter's problem of identifying a best response to $\alpha(\cdot)$ as a stationary dynamic programming problem. Associate with candidate i a state $(b(i), s(i)) \in P(\Omega) \times \{0, 1\}$, where as before the indicator s describes whether all previous rewards by a candidate have been above r^* ($s = 1$) or if some previous reward was below r^* ($s = 0$), and let the set of actions available to the voter be $N = \{1, \ldots, i, \ldots\}$. We can simplify notation by noting that $\alpha(\cdot)$ is played by all candidates, and is a function only of personal history; therefore the voter's decision problem is isomorphic to one with a single candidate. There are two actions available to the voter, $A = \{0, 1\}$, where $a = 1$ denotes retaining the candidate as the incumbent and $a = 0$ denotes starting the process over at the "initial" state $(\pi, 1)$, where $\pi = b^0$.

So let $Z = P(\Omega) \times \{0, 1\}$ denote the state space, and for $(b, s) \in Z$ and $r \in R$, if $a = 1$ then define the new state by $(b, s)(r) = (\beta(b, r; a^*), \mu(s, r))$, where $\beta(\cdot)$ denotes Bayes's rule and

$$\mu(s, r) = \begin{cases} 1 & \text{if } s = 1 \text{ and } r \geq r^*, \\ 0 & \text{otherwise.} \end{cases}$$

On the other hand, if $a = 0$ then the new state is $(\pi, 1)$. In state $(b, s) \in Z$ the expected reward to the voter from the action $a = 1$ is given by

$$\lambda(b, s, 1) = \begin{cases} \bar{r}(\underline{q}) & \text{if } s = 0, \\ E(b) & \text{if } s = 1, \end{cases}$$

where $E(b) = \sum_{j=1}^{n} b_j \cdot \bar{r}(a_j)$ for any $b \in P(\Omega)$; if $a = 0$ then $\lambda(b, s, 0) = E(\pi)$.

Let $V(\cdot)$ be the unique fixed point of the appropriately defined contraction which satisfies

$$V(b, s) = \max\{V(\pi, 1), LV(b, s)\}, \tag{9}$$

where

$$LV(b, s) = \lambda(b, s, 1) + \delta \int V[\beta(b, r), \mu(s, r)] f^b(r) \, dr,$$

and where $f^b(r) = \sum_{j=1}^{n} b_j \cdot f(r; a_j)$ for all $b \in P(\Omega)$. It is easily seen that if $s = 0$ then, for any $b \in P(\Omega)$, we have $V(b, s) = V(\pi, 1) > LV(b, s)$. The previously displayed equation may therefore be written in a manner suppressing the dependence on the indicator s as

$$V(b) = \max\left\{ V(\pi), E(b) + \delta \left[V(\pi) \int_{r < r^*} f^b(r) \, dr \right. \right.$$
$$\left. \left. + \int_{r \geq r^*} V(\beta(b, r)) f^b(r) \, dr \right] \right\}. \tag{10}$$

Given $b, b' \in P(\Omega)$, say that b *strongly (stochastically) dominates* b' if $b_j/b_k \geq b_j'/b_k'$ for $j > k$, that is, if b places relatively greater weight on higher types. It is not too difficult to see that strong stochastic dominance implies stochastic dominance; therefore, if b strongly dominates b' then, for any nonnegative numbers $x_1 < \cdots < x_n$, $\sum_{j=1}^{n} b_j \cdot x_j > \sum_{j=1}^{n} b_j' \cdot x_j$. For example, if b strongly dominates b' then $E(b) > E(b')$, since $\bar{r}(a_1) < \cdots < \bar{r}(a_n)$. Further, for all rewards $r \geq \hat{r}$, $f(r, a_j) > f(r, a_k)$ if $j > k$, so $f^b(r) > f^{b'}(r)$ for all $r \geq r^* \geq \hat{r}$. Finally, note that as long as the incumbent's rewards remain above r^*, the voter's current belief will strongly dominate the initial belief π, since after one such observation we have

$$\frac{b_j}{b_k} = \frac{\beta_j(\pi, r, a^*)}{\beta_k(\pi, r, a^*)} = \frac{\pi_j f(r, a_j)}{\pi_k f(r, a_k)} > \frac{\pi_j}{\pi_k}; \tag{11}$$

after two such observations we have

$$\frac{\beta_j(b, r, a^*)}{\beta_k(b, r, a^*)} = \frac{b_j f(r, a_j)}{b_k f(r, a_k)} > \frac{b_j}{b_k} > \frac{\pi_j}{\pi_k}; \tag{12}$$

and so forth. Therefore, if we can show that $V(b) > V(\pi)$ for all beliefs b that strongly dominate π, then the best response for the voter to a continual stream of rewards above r^* is to retain the incumbent, thereby proving the optimality of $\nu(\cdot)$.

So consider the difference $V(b) - V(\pi)$. By (10), we know that $V(\pi)$ can be written as

$$V(\pi) = E(\pi) + \delta \left[\int_D V(\pi) f^\pi(r) \, dr + \int_{D'} V(\beta(\pi, r)) f^\pi(r) \, dr \right], \tag{13}$$

where D, D' partition R, and where $D' \subset [r^*, \infty)$. Now since $V(\cdot)$ is the value of following an optimal strategy, we know that for any $b \in P(\Omega)$,

$$V(b) \geq E(b) + \delta \left[\int_D V(\pi) f^b(r) \, dr + \int_{D'} V(\beta(b, r)) f^b(r) \, dr \right], \tag{14}$$

where the sets D, D' are the same as those in (13). The RHS of (14) is the payoff associated with retaining the current incumbent, replacing him in the subsequent period if $r \in D$ and then proceeding according to the optimal strategy, and retaining him if $r \in D'$ and then proceeding according to the optimal strategy. Thus,

$$V(b) - V(\pi) \geq \{ E(b) - E(\pi) \}$$

$$+ \delta \left\{ V(\pi) \int_D [f^b(r) - f^\pi(r)] \, dr + \int_{D'} V(\beta(b, r)) f^b(r) \, dr \right.$$

$$\left. - \int_{D'} V(\beta(\pi, r)) f^\pi(r) \, dr \right\} \tag{15}$$

We can rewrite the term in large braces as

$$V(\pi) \int_D [f^b(r) - f^\pi(r)] \, dr + \int_{D'} V(\beta(\pi, r))[f^b(r) - f^\pi(r)] \, dr$$

$$+ \int_{D'} [V(\beta(b, r)) - V(\beta(\pi, r))] f^b(r) \, dr.$$

As noted earlier, if b dominates π then, for all $r \in D'$, $f^b(r) > f^\pi(r)$. Further, since by (10) $V(b') \geq V(\pi)$ for all $b' \in P(\Omega)$, the term just displayed is greater than or equal to

$$V(\pi) \int_D [f^b(r) - f^\pi(r)] \, dr + \int_{D'} V(\pi)[f^b(r) - f^\pi(r)] \, dr$$

$$+ \int_{D'} [V(\beta(b, r)) - V(\beta(\pi, r))] f^b(r) \, dr$$

$$= V(\pi) \left[\int_{D \cup D'} f^b(r) \, dr - \int_{D \cup D'} f^\pi(r) \, dr \right]$$

$$+ \int_{D'} [V(\beta(b,r)) - V(\beta(\pi,r))] f^b(r) \, dr$$

$$= \int_{D'} [V(\beta(b,r)) - V(\beta(\pi,r))] f^b(r) \, dr. \tag{16}$$

Therefore,

$$V(b) - V(\pi) \geq \{E(b) - E(\pi)\}$$

$$+ \delta \left\{ \int_{D'} [V(\beta(b,r)) - V(\beta(\pi,r))] f^b(r) \, dr \right\}, \tag{17}$$

where the first term in braces is strictly positive and the second is of undetermined sign.

Now if b dominates π then, as noted previously, $\beta(b,r)$ will dominate $\beta(\pi,r)$ for all $r \in D'$. Let $p = \beta(b,r)$ and $q = \beta(\pi,r)$ for some $r \in D'$, so p dominates q. Then, by definition of D',

$$V(q) = E(q) + \delta \left[\int_M V(\pi) f^q(r') \, dr' + \int_{M'} V(\beta(q,r') f^q(r') \, dr' \right], \tag{18}$$

where M' can depend on r and $M' \subset [r^*, \infty)$. Further,

$$V(p) \geq E(p) + \delta \left[\int_M V(\pi) f^p(r') \, dr' + \int_{M'} V(\beta(p,r') f^p(r') \, dr' \right], \tag{19}$$

where as before the RHS of (19) gives the payoffs for (potentially) departing from the stationary optimal strategy by retaining the current incumbent, and replacing him in the subsequent period if and only if $r \in M$. Now, using precisely the same arguments as before, we obtain

$$V(p) - V(q) \geq \{E(p) - E(q)\}$$

$$+ \delta \left\{ \int_{M'} [V(\beta(p,r')) - V(\beta(q,r'))] f^p(r') \, dr' \right\}. \tag{20}$$

Placing (20) into (17), we get

$$V(b) - V(\pi) \geq \{E(b) - E(\pi)\} + \delta \left\{ \int_{D'} [E(\beta(b,r)) - E(\beta(\pi,r))] f^b(r) \, dr \right\}$$

$$+ \delta^2 \left\{ \int_{D'} \left[\int_{M'} [V(\beta(\beta(b,r),r')) \right. \right.$$

$$\left. \left. - V(\beta(\beta(\pi,r),r'))] f^{\beta(b,r)}(r') \, dr' \right] f^b(r) \, dr \right\}, \tag{21}$$

where now the first and *second* terms in braces are strictly positive, while the third is of undetermined sign. But then for all $r \in D'$ and $r' \in M'$ we have $\beta(\beta(b, r), r')$ dominating $\beta(\beta(\pi, r), r')$, so we can apply this argument a third time, thereby generating three terms on the RHS that are strictly positive and a fourth of undetermined sign which is multiplied by δ^3. Continuing this logic, we see that $V(b) - V(\pi)$ will be greater than or equal to an infinite sum of strictly positive terms, plus a term on the order of $\delta^\infty \cdot K$, where K is bounded since $\delta < 1$. But then $\delta^\infty \cdot K = 0$, again since $\delta < 1$, thus proving $V(b) > V(\pi)$. $\square$

In the equilibria just described the voter has an incentive to play $\nu(\cdot)$, in part through the incumbent playing a "trigger" strategy and in part through the voter "learning" about the incumbent's type. The trigger-strategy aspect comes about by requiring the voter to replace an incumbent whenever a relatively low reward is witnessed: if the voter does not replace him, the incumbent reverts to $a = \underline{a}$ regardless of his type. These "punishments" are thus akin to those found in repeated Prisoner's Dilemma games of reverting to one-shot Nash equilibrium behavior upon observing a defection; the difference here is that only the currently employed candidate, and no other candidate, reverts to "myopic" play.

On the other hand, since we have assumed that candidates select actions based only on their own history of rewards, the same sort of trigger cannot be used to keep the voter retaining incumbents when relatively high rewards are witnessed, since a newly chosen candidate does not condition on the voter's responses to previous incumbents. What gives the voter the incentive to retain the incumbent upon observing such rewards is that the voter's belief shifts, placing relatively greater weight on higher types. That is, as long as the incumbent has continually generated rewards greater than r^*, the voter's belief about the incumbent will strongly stochastically dominate that of an untried candidate. This dominance implies that the voter receives a higher one-period payoff from the incumbent than from an untried candidate, and will continue to do so as long as the incumbent generates rewards greater than r^* (the incumbent is of course more *likely* to generate rewards greater than r^*). Therefore the voter wants to retain the incumbent, and thus does not need the behavior of subsequent incumbents to generate this incentive.

A number of issues are worthy of mention. The first is that, although the proof of the proposition assumed $r^* > \hat{r}$, this is not necessary. All that is actually required is for r^* to be such that, for all $r > r^*$, $f(r, a^*(\omega_k)) > f(r, a^*(\omega_j))$ for $k > j$ – that is, on the region $[r^*, \infty)$, the reward densities are "stacked" with densities from higher types strictly above those of lower types. Thus, for instance, as long as r^* is greater than the (unique) mode of $f(\cdot; a^*(\omega_n))$, the proof goes through without modification.

Second, we could have dispensed with the assumption of a bounded action space for the incumbent, in place of additional assumptions elsewhere. For instance, if we assume an upper bound on the candidates' discount factor of $\bar{\rho} < 1$, then for any $\omega \in \Omega$ the value function $V(\omega)$ will be bounded above by $u(\underline{a}, \omega)/(1 - \bar{\rho}) < \infty$. Therefore, we can let $A = [0, \infty)$, and as long as the Inada condition $u_1(a, \omega) \to -\infty$ as $a \to \infty$ continues to hold, we will effectively have an upper bound on the incumbent's actions.

Third, there is a continuum of equilibria of the form outlined in our proposition, parameterized by the critical value of rewards r^*. In terms of the players' preferences over these equilibria, it is easily shown that for all $\omega \in \Omega$ and for r^* high enough, $da^*(\omega)/dr^* < 0$, so lowering the cut-off increases the action choices by all types of candidates. This obviously increases the voter's immediate payoff; however, the long-term effects are not so transparent. It may well be that these new action choices are closer together than the old, implying the voter "learns" an incumbent's type more slowly, thereby lowering the voter's utility if she is sufficiently patient. Conversely, it is clear that candidates prefer lower values of r^* to higher, regardless of type while in office. Yet, if candidate i has not yet been employed, lowering the value of r^* pushes this higher payoff further into the future (in an expectational sense).

Fourth, we can address the issue of the "cost" borne by the voter to create the incentive for the candidate of type ω_j to take action $a^*(\omega_j)$ as long as previous rewards have been sufficiently high. Suppose the candidates' strategies were simply to play $a^*(\omega)$ regardless of history, that is, $\alpha(\omega) = a^*(\omega)$. Now, with the voter learning about the incumbent's type, the voter's best response would not be to maintain a time-invariant cut-off rule, but rather to make the retain/replace decision a function of the updated belief about the incumbent. For example, if $N = 2$ (so that there are exactly two types of candidates), Banks and Sundaram (1990) show that the best voter response to this candidate strategy is to retain or replace the incumbent depending on whether the incumbent generates a higher or lower expected one-period reward relative to an untried candidate; that is, the voter's optimal decision rule is myopic. Therefore, if enough high rewards have been observed from the current incumbent, then the voter would forgive an occasional low reward and continue to employ the incumbent – albeit lowering her belief that the incumbent is a hard-working type. On the other hand, if the voter adopted this "forgiving" rule in the current context, the candidates would obviously alter their action rule, possibly taking lower actions when confronted with a more lax standard. Hence in this equilibrium the voter will occasionally replace an incumbent even when the voter believes the incumbent is a relatively good type, in order to maintain incentives for candidates to take good actions.

Next, consider the probability of an incumbent's re-election and how this probability might change over time. Clearly, this probability is simply equal to $[1 - F(r^*, a^*(\omega)] \equiv \pi(\omega)$ for a type-ω candidate, where $\pi(\omega)$ is increasing in ω. Thus, from a candidate's perspective, the probability of his re-election is constant over time. From the voter's perspective, on the other hand, if the current belief about the incumbent is b^t then the probability of the incumbent being retained for the next period is $\sum_{j=1}^{n} b_j^t \cdot \pi(\omega_j)$. Now if the incumbent is in fact retained for period $t+1$, then the voter's belief will shift to $b^{t+1}(r)$, where the dependence of this belief on $r \in R$ is through Bayes's rule. And, by our previous discussion, we know that for all acceptable rewards (i.e., for all $r \in R$ such that the incumbent is retained), $b^{t+1}(r)$ strongly stochastically dominates b^t, implying in particular that

$$\sum_{j=1}^{n} b_j^{t+1}(r) \cdot \pi(\omega_j) > \sum_{j=1}^{n} b_j^t \cdot \pi(\omega_j).$$

Therefore, from the voter's perspective, the probability of retaining the incumbent is increasing with an incumbent's tenure, regardless of the actual history of rewards realized. Note that this increase occurs not because the incumbent works harder as his tenure increases, for in fact an incumbent's actions do not vary over time. Rather, it is due to the learning process of the voter, whose beliefs over time place greater weight on "better" (from the voter's perspective) types as long as the incumbent remains in office.

Finally, we note that the retrospective voting rule adopted by the voter is highly nonstationary in the voter's beliefs about the incumbent. That is, the voter's belief about the incumbent upon observing t rewards above r^* followed by a single reward below r^* could be the same as that from observing t' rewards above r^* and no rewards below r^*; yet, in the first instance the voter replaces the incumbent while in the second the incumbent is retained. Thus, it may be enlightening to characterize stationary simple equilibria where the voter's strategy and candidate i's strategy are functions only of the voter's current belief about i's type. Note that existence of such equilibria is not at issue, since the simple equilibrium in which all candidates adopt $a = q$ and the voter always replaces the incumbent trivially satisfies the stationarity requirement. Whether there exist more interesting stationary equilibria, and what the characteristics of such behavior might be, are as yet unanswered questions.

REFERENCES

Alesina, A. (1988), "Credibility and Policy Convergence in a Two-Party System with Rational Voters," *American Economic Review* 78: 796–806.
Alesina, A., and S. Spear (1988), "An Overlapping Generations Model of Electoral Competition," *Journal of Public Economics* 37: 359–79.

Austen-Smith, D., and J. Banks (1989), "Electoral Accountability and Incumbency," in P. Ordeshook (ed.), *Models of Strategic Choice in Politics*. Ann Arbor: University of Michigan Press.

Banks, J., and R. Sundaram (1990), "Incumbents, Challengers, and Bandits: Bayesian Learning in a Dynamic Choice Model," RCER Working Paper no. 235, University of Rochester, New York.

Barro, R. (1973), "The Control of Politicians: An Economic Model," *Public Choice* 14: 19-42.

Ferejohn, J. (1986), "Incumbent Performance and Electoral Control," *Public Choice* 50: 5-25.

Fiorina, M. (1981), *Retrospective Voting in American National Elections*. New Haven, CT: Yale University Press.

Kreps, D., and R. Wilson (1982), "Sequential Equilibria," *Econometrica* 50: 863-94.

Ledyard, J. (1989), "Information Aggregation in Two-Candidate Elections," in P. Ordeshook (ed.), *Models of Strategic Choice in Politics*. Ann Arbor: University of Michigan Press.

Maitra, A. (1968), "Discounted Dynamic Programming in Compact Metric Spaces," *Sankhyā Ser. A* 30: 211-16.

McKelvey, R., and R. Reizman (1992), "Seniority in Legislatures," *American Political Science Review* 86: 951-65.

Reed, R. (1991), "Retrospective and Prospective Voting in a Political Market with Finite-Lived Politicians," Working Paper, Department of Economics, Texas A&M University, College Station.

Rogoff, K. (1990), "Equilibrium Political Budget Cycles," *American Economic Review* 80: 21-37.

Rogoff, K., and A. Sibert (1988), "Elections and Macroeconomic Policy Cycles," *Review of Economic Studies* 55: 1-16.

CHAPTER 13

Campaign contributions and party-candidate competition in services and policies

David P. Baron and Jongryn Mo

1 Introduction

Political parties, their candidates, and their contributors are involved in a complex relationship in which policy positions are taken by parties, candidates campaign for votes and for campaign contributions, interest groups and individuals make campaign contributions, elections are held, and successful candidates take actions some of which may benefit their contributors. Electoral competition thus involves both parties and their candidates, and competition takes place both in policy positions and in services provided to constituents and interest groups. The model presented in this chapter represents electoral competition driven by bargaining between candidates and interest groups over the exchange of services for campaign contributions, where the bargaining power of the candidates is a function of the choices of policy positions by parties.

The model reflects the importance of services to contributors, and recognizes that it is candidates rather than parties that provide services. Furthermore, those services which are private can be provided by whichever candidate is the winner of the election, and hence interest groups can seek services from either candidate. The model also recognizes that the preferences of parties and candidates can differ, particularly because candidates and not parties are the providers of services. The theory presented characterizes the equilibrium relationship among (1) the strategies of parties as they compete through policy position taking and of candidates as they compete by pledging to provide services to interest groups, (2) the campaign contribution strategies of interest groups, and (3) the effect of

We would like to thank Keith Krehbiel and Thomas Romer for comments. The first author's research has been supported by National Science Foundation Grants No. SES-8808211 and SES-9109707.

those contributions on expectations about election outcomes. In the model, the sophisticated players are parties, candidates, and interest groups, and voters are assumed to be unsophisticated and to vote based on information provided through electoral campaigns financed by campaign contributions.

Parties are assumed to have preferences both for winning and for policy outcomes, and candidates have preferences for being in office but incur a cost of providing constituent services. Candidate preferences thus are not identical to those of their parties. Interest groups have preferences for the services provided by the successful candidate, and the benefits of services depend on the policy position of the candidate's party.

Parties move first by choosing policy positions (or platforms) and then, taking those positions as given, the parties' candidates choose the amount of services to offer to those who contribute to their campaigns. Candidates and interest groups then bargain over the contributions to be made, and both sides have a degree of bargaining power, depending on the policy positions taken by the candidate's party. The contributions received are expended in the campaign. In the model, voter behavior is represented by a reduced form that specifies election outcomes as a function of campaign expenditures. That is, voting strategies are not explicitly modeled.[1]

Interest groups make campaign contributions (1) to increase the likelihood that a candidate will be elected, and hence that more favorable policies will subsequently be implemented in the legislature; or (2) to obtain services such as intervention with the bureaucracy, favors, and private provisions in bills.[2] In the former case, what is exchanged is a collective good, since the election of a candidate and subsequent votes on legislation will benefit some interest groups and harm others. In the latter case, contributions are exchanged for private services that benefit the contributor often with little effect on other interest groups. In the model, the collective good is the policy chosen by the party, and that choice positions its candidate for raising campaign contributions from interest groups. Because party positions are chosen to position candidates, there is an endogenous relationship between campaign contributions and policy positions. This relationship is based on ex ante considerations and not on exchange of contributions for votes in the legislature. That is, this is not a model of bribes.[3]

---

[1] Hinich and Munger (1989) model the process by which campaign expenditures influence voters' voting decisions. Their model focuses on candidates' expenditure allocation problem and does not incorporate candidate competition over policy positions and constituency service offers.

[2] See Mayhew (1974) and Fiorina (1989).

[3] See Snyder (1991) for a model in which contributions are exchanged for the votes of legislators.

The private good is supplied by the candidates and represents services to contributors. A private good is such that (1) its provision to one contributor does not affect other contributors and (2) the services can be supplied by whichever candidate is elected. The services are costly to provide, however, so a candidate faces a supply decision. Because private services can be supplied by whichever candidate wins the election, when bargaining with one candidate an interest group has the option of breaking off that bargaining and commencing bargaining with the other candidate. The other candidate thus represents a pre-election outside option to a potential contributor.

If interest groups could obtain services only from one candidate, there would be no outside option. In that case, the model yields behavior analogous to that in the median-voter theorem. That is, the parties have incentives to choose party positions at the median because that best positions their candidates to generate contributions from interest groups. With services that can be provided by either candidate, the outside option can make the competition between candidates sufficiently intense that the parties choose positions away from the median so as to improve the bargaining positions of their candidates relative to interest groups.

In the market for campaign contributions, the rate of exchange is determined by the distribution of power on the demand and supply sides of the market, and that distribution depends on the opportunities available in the two sides. In an era in which election campaigns have become very expensive, candidates need contributions to fund their campaigns, and this gives contributors a degree of power in obtaining the services and the policy positions they prefer. There are, however, many potential contributors and relatively few candidates, and this gives candidates a degree of power on the supply side. This power may be enhanced by seniority and by leadership and committee positions in the legislature. Power thus is present on both sides of the exchange relationship, and the distribution of that power, and hence the equilibrium outcomes, will reflect the opportunities available to both sides.

Campaign contributions are made prior to an election, and services are provided and policies are implemented after the election. Since the exchange is unenforceable by any third-party mechanism such as the courts, the winner of an election has an opportunity to shirk on promises made. That shirking is restrained by an incumbent's interest in re-election as considered by Baron (1989b), but shirking remains a possibility. In the model considered here, parties and candidates are assumed to fulfill their promises as a consequence of their concern about re-election.[4] As an indication that re-election incentives may be sufficient to cause candidates

---

[4] This behavior can be supported as an equilibrium in a model with repeated play.

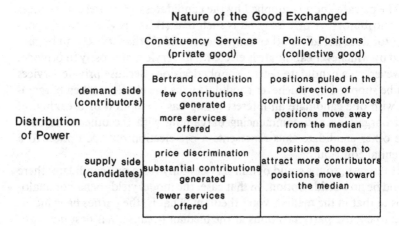

Figure 1. Typology of theories of campaign contributions.

to honor service pledges, the special counsel in the Senate Ethics Committee's investigation of the "Keating Five" quoted a memo written by Joy Jacobson, a fund-raiser, to Senator Alan Cranston: "Cases/legislation: Now that we [Democrats] are back in the majority, there are a number of individuals who have been very helpful to you who have cases or legislative matters pending within our office who will rightfully expect some kind of resolution. . . . Charlie Keating is continuing to have problems with the bank board and Ed Gray. Jim Grogan and the company's legal counsel, Bob Kieity, are coming to see you on Friday at 1 o'clock to get your advice on how to handle the current problem."[5]

2   Theories of campaign contributions

The market for campaign contributions can be categorized by the nature of the good exchanged and the distribution of the power in the market, as depicted in the typology in Figure 1. The columns correspond to the two aspects of party–candidate competition: private constituency services and collective party positions.

In the case of private constituency services that can be supplied by either candidate, if the market power is on the demand side then competition between the candidates would be expected to drive the contributions down. In the limit, contributions could be driven down to the level of the cost as in Bertrand competition.[6] In the model considered here, if the party posi-

[5] *The New York Times*, November 17, 1990.
[6] Morton and Cameron (1991) show another case of Bertrand competition in a model where candidates compete through providing private services, but the candidates have unconstrained capacity for providing the services.

tions are identical then candidates become perfect substitutes, and competition drives campaign contributions to zero. If those positions are different, however, the candidates are able to generate contributions.

If the power is on the supply side, however, the candidates would be expected to extract surplus from contributors in exchange for services. Snyder (1990a,b) assumes that candidates have power and hence can generate contributions from contributors. Baron (1989a) also assumes that there is power on the supply side but assumes that candidates do not know the value of the services to contributors. Candidates make take-it-or-leave-it offers to potential contributors, some of whom will choose to contribute and others will not. Baron (1989b) considers candidates who offer a schedule of service-contribution options and allow interest groups to select among those options based on their differing valuations of the services.

The collective good will be represented as a position in a unidimensional policy space. With this specification, if the power is on the demand side and the good is collective, contributions would be expected to pull party positions toward those desired by the contributors supporting that party's candidates. If, however, power is on the supply side, then parties would be expected to move toward the median to attract more contributors – those who would otherwise contribute to the candidate of the other party.

Among the models of campaign contributions in the collective-good case, Austen-Smith (1987), Brock and Magee (1978), Cameron and Enelow (1989), and Edelman (1989) assume win-seeking candidates or parties.[7] Edelman (1989) models the case in which the power is on the demand side – that is, there is only one PAC (political action committee) – and shows that the PAC's contributions induce both candidates to choose positions closer to its ideal point. In the other models (Austen-Smith 1987, Brock and Magee 1978, and Cameron and Enelow 1989), the power is with the candidates. These models have two interest groups, but interest groups' power is limited because when candidates choose locations they know that interest groups will contribute to whichever candidate is closer to their ideal point. Brock and Magee call this the "campaign contribution specialization theorem," and it creates an incentive for candidates to move toward the median. All three models show that, when everything is symmetric between candidates and between interest groups, candidates will choose identical locations. This convergence result is analogous to the median-voter theorem of Black (1958) and the strategic analogues of that theorem (Ledyard 1984; McKelvey and Ordeshook 1985).

In the model considered here, which side of the exchange has the greater power depends importantly on the policy positions chosen by the parties.

[7] See Morton and Cameron (1991) for a survey of this literature.

If both parties choose the same policy position, a contributor does not care which candidate is elected and hence will contribute to the candidate that makes the best offer of services. The candidates then are perfect substitutes, and interest groups can in effect play one group off against another. Competition in services then drives the contributions down. If the party positions differ then candidates are not perfect substitutes, and they are able to generate contributions.

3   Overview of the model

In the context of the typology in Figure 1, the model incorporates both collective and private goods and reflects power on both sides of the campaign contributions relation. The distribution of power is determined endogenously as a function of the strategies available to the interest groups and to the candidates as they bargain over contributions and constituency services. Interest groups receive benefits only from the services they receive, but the benefits from those services depend on the policy preferences of their members relative to the policy of the party of the candidate to whom they contribute. The positions chosen by the parties affect which interest groups will contribute to which candidate and how large those contributions will be. Potential contributors, of course, recognize that any promised services can only be delivered by the winning candidate, so their contributions will depend on their expectations about how likely the candidates are to win the election. Those expectations in turn must be consistent, in the sense of rational expectations, with the likely election outcome.

If parties move their policy positions closer to the position of the median interest group, their candidates become closer substitutes for all potential contributors. In the limit, contributions are driven to zero; that is, all the power is then on the demand side and contributions are zero as in Bertrand competition. Parties can raise campaign contributions by separating their positions and thereby differentiating their candidates. This improves the bargaining power of candidates relative to their potential contributors, since contributing to the candidate whose party has a more distant policy position is costly. Hence, contributions increase. If a party chooses too distant a position, however, the position may be less attractive to the potential contributors. The party's position is not, however, the only strategic instrument, since a candidate can choose the quantity of services to offer to contributors. The quantity of services to be provided is thus a substitute, albeit an imperfect one, for the policy position chosen by the party.

An equilibrium consists of: for each party, a policy position; for each candidate, the quantity of services to provide and a bargaining strategy taking policy positions as given; and, for interest groups, a bargaining strategy taking as given the policy positions and quantities of services offered. Equilibria do not exist for all configurations of the parameters of the model, but symmetric equilibria can be characterized in which the parties separate their policy positions so as to position their candidates to extract campaign contributions from interest groups. Each party thus responds to the policy preferences of the interest groups to increase the candidate's bargaining power relative to the interest groups. The theory thus establishes an endogenous relationship between contributions and policy positions, both of which are endogenous.

The ex ante policy positions of parties presumably have an (ex post) correlation with legislative outcomes. The literature on the relationship between campaign contributions and congressional voting, however, presents mixed results. Wilhite and Theilmann (1987) find that contributions have a significant influence on congressional voting, but Chappell (1982) and Wright (1990) find little direct influence of contributions. Contributors in our model are assumed to take candidates' positions as given and do not affect policy positions directly; that is, contributors do not buy votes ex post. Instead, anticipatory position taking by the parties causes contributors to exert an ex ante influence over parties' policy choice. That is, parties may choose policies closer to their contributors to be more attractive to them and to generate more contributions. This theory suggests that the influence of campaign contributions on congressional voting may operate indirectly through parties' general policy predispositions as reflected in ex ante electoral campaign positioning.

The equilibrium also identifies which interest groups support which candidates. In a symmetric equilibrium, all interest groups to the left of the median contribute to the candidate located on the left, and those to the right of the median contribute to the other candidate. This result is consistent with the empirical findings of Poole and Romer (1985) and Edelman (1989) that PACs contribute preferentially to ideologically close candidates – especially in open-seat elections that are more likely than elections with incumbents to display the characteristics of the model considered here.

The theory also has implications for lobbying. Constituency service can be interpreted as providing access to lobbyists. The theory then predicts that interest groups lobby those winners who received their contributions. Consequently, interest groups lobby those legislators who tend to be ideologically close in the policy dimension. The theory presented here does not incorporate any post-election exchange between the winning candidate and those interest groups that contributed to the loser, but Rothenberg (1990) finds that the particular interest group he studied concentrated its lobbying on marginal legislators, not their friends. Snyder (1991)

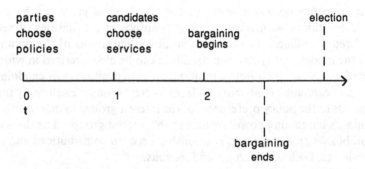

Figure 2. The sequence of moves.

provides a model that predicts that marginal legislators should be the targets of lobbying by an interest group. Rothenberg and Snyder's studies, however, do not analyze lobbying in the context of electoral competition. In the model here, it is the competition for contributors that causes parties to cater to interest groups with policy preferences similar to theirs. Ultimately, a theory is needed that incorporates both electoral competition and post-election activity.

4   The model

The model is intended to represent an open-seat election in which there is no incumbent who can deliver present services to contributors or has a name-recognition or other advantage over the challenger. The model incorporates two-party competition commencing with party conventions at which policy positions are chosen and ending after an election. The time line of the game is presented in Figure 2 and consists of the following sequence of moves.

At $t = 0$, parties choose policy positions. At $t = 1$, the campaign begins, and the candidates of the parties offer to provide constituent services to interest groups. Interest groups and candidates then bargain over the contributions to be made in exchange for the services. The election occurs when the bargaining is concluded, and then policies are implemented and constituent services are provided. The actors in the model are parties, their candidates, and interest groups.

Parties

At the beginning of the game, parties 1 and 2 choose positions α_1 and α_2, respectively, in a 1-dimensional policy space that without loss of generality will be assumed to be the unit interval [0, 1]. A policy position is to be interpreted as the policy the party will seek to implement if it wins the election. That policy position locates the party's candidate relative to the other candidate and relative to the interest groups. Parties in the model thus may be thought of as banners under which candidates raise contributions.

The parties have Euclidean policy preferences with ideal points, α_1^o and α_2^o, respectively. We assume that parties' ideal points are located in different halves of the policy space; namely, $\alpha_1^o \in [0, \frac{1}{2}]$ and $\alpha_2^o \in [\frac{1}{2}, 1]$. The parties choose policy positions in their respective regions; that is, $\alpha_1 \in [0, \frac{1}{2}]$ and $\alpha_2 \in [\frac{1}{2}, 1]$.

The election outcome is determined by voters who are assumed to base their voting strategies on the information that candidates provide in their campaigns. As mentioned previously, voting strategies are not modeled, and the electoral outcome is represented in a reduced form as a function of campaign expenditures, which are assumed to equal the campaign contributions. As indicated in what follows, in equilibrium the resulting contributions are a function of the services offered by candidates and of the positions chosen by parties. The parties form expectations about how likely they are to win the election, given the contributions they expect to be generated as a result of the positions they take. The function $f(\alpha_1, \alpha_2) \in [0, 1]$ represents these pre-campaign expectations of how likely party 1 is to win the election. The parties can infer the form of $f(\alpha_1, \alpha_2)$ because their choice of (α_1, α_2) conditions the actions at later stages of the game.

Parties have preferences over both holding office and the policy outcome to be implemented after the election. The utility y_1 of party 1 is specified as

$$y_1 = f(\alpha_1, \alpha_2)(v_1 - k(\alpha_1 - \alpha_1^o)^2) - (1 - f(\alpha_1, \alpha_2))k(\alpha_2 - \alpha_1^o)^2,$$

where the value of winning the election is denoted as $v_i \geq 0$ for party i and the value if the election is lost is normalized to zero. The parameter $k \geq 0$ is the weight the parties assign to policy preferences; for simplicity, it is assumed to be the same for both parties. When $k = 0$, the parties are interested only in winning the election.

The equilibrium to be characterized is a subgame-perfect Nash equilibrium, and hence a policy pair $(\bar{\alpha}_1, \bar{\alpha}_2)$ satisfies

$$\bar{\alpha}_1 \in \arg\max_{\alpha_1} f(\alpha_1, \bar{\alpha}_2)(v_1 - k(\alpha_1 - \alpha_1^o)^2) - (1 - f(\alpha_1, \bar{\alpha}_2))k(\bar{\alpha}_2 - \alpha_1^o)^2; \quad (1)$$

$$\bar{\alpha}_2 \in \arg\max_{\alpha_2}(1 - f(\bar{\alpha}_1, \alpha_2))(v_2 - k(\alpha_2 - \alpha_2^o)^2) - f(\bar{\alpha}_1, \alpha_2)k(\bar{\alpha}_1 - \alpha_2^o)^2. \quad (2)$$

Candidates and interest groups

Once the two parties have chosen their positions, their candidates compete for campaign contributions through the quantities q_1 and q_2, respectively, of services they provide to interest groups. The choice of services may be thought of as the choice of a campaign strategy.

An interest group a has a preferred policy position $\beta_a \in [0, 1]$, and interest group positions are distributed uniformly on the policy space. The assumption of a uniform distribution of interest groups is made so as not to bias the election outcome in favor of one of the candidates. All interest groups derive benefits from q_i units of constituency service, and thus benefits will be assumed to be normalized to q_i. Since contributions are made prior to the election which has an uncertain outcome, candidates' service offers are evaluated by interest groups according to their expectation about how likely the candidates are to win. Those expectations are assumed to be common to all interest groups, and $x = (x_1, x_2)$ denotes the probability beliefs x_i that candidate i will win the election. Interest groups are assumed to be risk-neutral, so the expected values of the two candidates' service offers are $x_1 q_1$ and $x_2 q_2$, respectively.

Once the candidates choose the quantity of services, they begin bargaining with interest groups over the contributions to be made in exchange for those services. The bargaining continues until a resolution is reached and, as will be demonstrated, is concluded immediately. The bargaining determines which interest groups contribute to which candidate, the number a_i of interest groups that contribute to candidate i, and the amount p_i that candidate i receives from each of its contributors.

Each interest group makes only one contribution, and in equilibrium, all interest groups contribute.[8] The total contributions for candidates 1 and 2 then are $C_1 = p_1 a_1$ and $C_2 = p_2 a_2$, respectively, and $a_1 + a_2 = 1$, where a_i is the "number" of interest groups that contribute to candidate i.

To represent the election outcome when both candidates are viable (i.e., $C_1 > 0$ and $C_2 > 0$), let $w(\cdot)$, the probability that candidate 1 wins, be represented by the reduced form[9]

$$w(\cdot) = \frac{C_1}{C_1 + C_2}. \tag{3}$$

The probability of winning is thus proportional to the candidate's share of campaign expenditures. This may be thought of as representing the effect of campaign expenditures, such as for political advertisements, to

---

[8] If they are allowed to make more than one contribution, they will still contribute only to one candidate.

[9] When $C_1 = 0$ and $C_2 = 0$, there are no campaign expenditures, in which case voters are assumed to vote randomly and so $w(\cdot) = \frac{1}{2}$. In cases where one of the candidates is not viable (i.e., that candidate receives negative contributions), his probability of winning is zero, since no money is spent on his behalf during the campaign.

influence uninformed voters.[10] Snyder (1990a,b) estimates this equation for open-seat House elections and for Senate elections for 1980–86, and finds that it fits the data well.

Candidates have preferences for being in office, represented by utilities u_i ($i = 1, 2$) and over the cost $n_i a_i q_i$ of providing the promised services to interest groups, where n_i is the marginal cost and $a_i q_i$ the total amount of service pledged to contributors.[11] The expected utility EU_i of candidate i is then

$$EU_i = w(\cdot)(u_i - n_i a_i q_i). \tag{4}$$

The expectations $x = (x_1, x_2)$ of interest groups at $t = 1$ are required to be rational in equilibrium or $x_1 = w$. The candidates are assumed not to have preferences for policies and may be thought of as having been selected because they are willing to serve interest groups in exchange for an opportunity to be in office.

An equilibrium at this stage of the game is thus a triple $(\bar{x}, \bar{q}_1, \bar{q}_2)$ such that[12]

$$\bar{q}_1 \in \arg\max_{q_1} w(q_1, \bar{q}_2; \alpha_1, \alpha_2)(u_1 - n_1 a_1 q_1), \tag{5}$$

$$\bar{q}_2 \in \arg\max_{q_2}(1 - w(\bar{q}_1, q_2; \alpha_1, \alpha_2))(u_2 - n_2 a_2 q_2), \quad \text{and} \tag{6}$$

$$\bar{x}_1 = w(\bar{q}_1, \bar{q}_2; \alpha_1, \alpha_2), \tag{7}$$

where $w(\bar{q}_1, \bar{q}_2; \alpha_1, \alpha_2)$ denotes the probability of the electoral outcome as a function of service choices, given policy positions (α_1, α_2). The expectations of interest groups about how likely a candidate is to win are formed simultaneously with the decisions of candidates about the amount of services to offer. If there exists a unique $\bar{x}_1$ for each policy pair then the equilibrium $\bar{x}_1$ is a function $\bar{x}_1(\alpha_1, \alpha_2)$ of the party positions. That function then is the expectations $f(\alpha_1, \alpha_2)$ used by the parties when choosing their positions in (1) and (2).

Bargaining over contributions

At the bargaining stage, $t \in [2, \infty)$, contributions $p_1(q_1, q_2, x, \alpha_1, \alpha_2)$ and $p_2(q_1, q_2, x, \alpha_1, \alpha_2)$ are determined as a function of party positions and candidate service offers. The net (expected) surplus an interest group derives from candidate i's offer q_i, when it contributes p_i, is then $x_i q_i - p_i$.

---

[10] Baron (1989a) considers a generalization of (3) that incorporates an incumbency advantage.

[11] Baron (1989a,b) considers models with these features.

[12] This formulation reflects the result, to be established subsequently, that the bargaining between interest groups and candidates is completed immediately.

Preferences in this bargaining game are defined over outcomes and the time at which these outcomes occur. Time preferences are represented by a discount factor $\delta_\tau \in (0, 1)$ that discounts interest groups' expected net surplus from services, and discounting from time t to time 2 involves the factor δ_τ^{t-2}.

The election is held as soon as the bargaining process is finished. This assumption is contrary to most election systems, but in addition to analytical convenience it may be thought of as corresponding to two features of electoral systems. First, in parliamentary systems, elections may be called before the mandated date, and in the context of this model the election may be viewed as called as soon as the bargaining has been concluded and the contributions received. Second, even in electoral systems (such as in the United States) where election dates are fixed, the beginning of a campaign, and particularly of fund-raising, is open.

The specification of interest-group preferences is intended to reflect both the benefits from services and the logic of the internal organization of interest groups. The potential beneficiaries of the services are assumed to care about the policy position of the candidate's party, and members of the interest group value the net benefits of the services less, the farther away is the party of the candidate with whom they are dealing. An alternative interpretation is that at the beginning of the campaign the interest group incurs internal organizational costs resulting from its alignment with the party of the candidate with whom it begins bargaining. Those alignment costs are greater the farther away is the party's position from its own. These alignment costs can also be thought of as the time it takes to "move" an interest group with given preferences to be willing to deal with a candidate whose party represents different policies.

An interest group's policy or alignment preferences are expressed as a function of the distance between its ideal point β_a and the position α_i of the party of the candidate to which the interest group contributes. This cost will be represented by a factor $e^{-c_p|\beta_a - \alpha_i|}$, where $c_p > 0$ is a parameter. With this specification, interest group preferences are single-peaked over candidate positions.

Once an interest group begins bargaining with a candidate, it may find the other candidate's offer to be more attractive. It then may realign itself with the other candidate and begin bargaining with that other candidate. Realignment, however, involves internal organization costs for the interest group. An agricultural association may lose members if its members expect to back a party that supports farm subsidies but then switches its support to a party that favors the elimination of subsidies and the opening of foreign markets. Similarly, the American Association of Retired Persons may experience membership problems if its members expect it to support a party that favors the control of pharmaceutical prices as a means of controlling Medicare costs but then switches its contributions to a party that favors an increase in co-payments. For simplicity, we represent this "switching" or realignment cost as $\delta_d^{c_d|\alpha_1 - \alpha_2|}$, where $\delta_d \in (0, 1)$ is the party distance discount factor and $c_d > 0$ is a cost parameter. That is, it is more costly to realign as the distance between the candidate positions increases. If the realignment costs are thought of as the time that it takes for an interest group to realign itself with the other party, then $\delta_d = \delta_r$.

Once the bargaining starts, candidates seek to obtain the highest contributions for the services they have offered. The campaign contribution p_i received by candidate i is discounted, and for simplicity, the same discount factor δ_r is used as for interest groups. One interpretation of discounting is that the effectiveness of campaign contributions in influencing the electoral outcome is greater when they are received earlier rather than later in the campaign. Candidates' utility functions in the bargaining with an interest group are then

$$u_i(p_i; t) = \delta_r^{t-2} p_i, \quad i = 1, 2.$$

The bargaining procedure is a modified version of Rubinstein's (1982) model of alternating offers and is based on a related model by Bester (1989). The realignment opportunity to break off negotiations with candidate i and begin bargaining with the other candidate generates an option value OV_i for the interest group bargaining with i which is determined in the equilibrium of the subgame commencing once the interest group has realigned to bargain with that candidate. For each candidate i, OV_i is taken to be independent of the history of the game. This assumption reflects a certain degree of anonymity, in that candidates are assumed to have no special relationship on which they can base their bargaining strategies. This means that candidates and interest groups have no information regarding any prior bargaining. Consequently, the candidate uses the same bargaining strategy with every interest group. The equilibrium contributions and outside option values thus are the same for each interest group.

When an interest group and candidate i begin bargaining at time t, one of the two, selected randomly, proposes a contribution p to be made in exchange for the services. With probability $(1 - \lambda) \in (0, 1)$, the first proposal is made by the candidate, and the bargaining game is denoted as Γ_{ic}. With probability λ, the interest group makes the first proposal, and the subsequent bargaining game, denoted as Γ_{ig}, is the same as Γ_{ic} with the exception of the order of moves. Due to the anonymity assumption, what transpired before time t has no bearing on the subsequent bargaining between the interest group and candidate i. The costs that the interest group incurred before beginning bargaining with candidate i - that

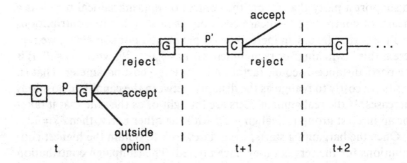

Figure 3. Extensive-form game (C – candidate; G – interest group).

is, those involving the initial alignment and any realignment – are sunk. Consequently, what induces the agreement after time t is the players' impatience.

Figure 3 provides the extensive-form representation of the subgame Γ_{ic}. When the candidate makes an offer p at $t > 2$, the interest group has one of three possible moves. First, it may break off bargaining with the candidate and realign itself with the other candidate. The associated payoffs in the subsequent subgame are $\delta_\tau^{t-2} OV_i$ for the interest group and zero for the candidate. Second, the interest group may accept the candidate's proposed contribution p, in which case the bargaining ends with payoffs $\delta_\tau^{t-2}(x_i q - p)$ and $\delta_\tau^{t-2} p$, respectively. Third, the interest group can make a counteroffer p' at $t+1$. If the candidate rejects this offer, then the outside option can be taken up only at $t+2$.[13] If the candidate accepts p' then the game ends at $t+1$ with payoffs $\delta_\tau^{t-1}(x_i q - p')$ and $\delta_\tau^{t-1} p'$, respectively. Alternatively, the candidate can make another offer at $t+2$, and the same pattern results. In this way, a candidate and an interest group alternate in making proposals, and the interest group can realign whenever the candidate has made an offer.

5   Equilibrium contributions

The equilibrium is characterized by working backward, starting with the bargaining stage at $t \in [2, \infty)$. At this stage, α_1, α_2, x, q_1, and q_2 are exogenous. The endogenous variables are the contributions (p_1, p_2) and which interest groups (a_1, a_2) contribute to which candidates.

[13]   That is, realignment can occur only after the candidate has made a proposal. If realignment could occur when the candidate rejects a proposal from the interest group, there may be multiple equilibria for certain values of the exogenous parameters. See Osborne and Rubinstein (1990).

5.1   Bargaining equilibrium

Consider the bargaining game with candidate i. Note that all interest groups bargaining with candidate i face the same situation regardless of their initial location β_a or how many times they have realigned between the candidates.[14] That is, the alignment and realignment costs incurred prior to the current bargaining with candidate i are effectively sunk and have no impact on the bargaining games Γ_{ic} and Γ_{ig}. Consequently, the policy preferences of interest groups do not affect the bargaining equilibrium, although the policy positions of the parties affect the amount of contributions through the outside option.

For a given outside option value OV_i, the bargaining strategies of the candidate and the interest group constitute a subgame-perfect equilibrium if the strategies restricted to every subgame of Γ_{ic} and Γ_{ig} form a Nash equilibrium. The contributions at which the agreement is reached will be denoted by p_{ic} and p_{ig}, respectively.

Proposition 1. *The equilibrium contributions of the bargaining games* Γ_{ic} *and* Γ_{ig}, *given* OV_i, *are unique and are given by* [15]

$$p_{ic} = \min\left\{ \frac{x_i q_i}{1+\delta_\tau}, x_i q_i - OV_i \right\} \quad and$$

$$p_{ig} = \min\left\{ \frac{\delta_\tau x_i q_i}{1+\delta_\tau}, \delta_\tau (x_i q_i - OV_i) \right\},$$

respectively.

Proof: The proof uses a technique developed by Shaked and Sutton (1984), and is presented in Baron and Mo (1991).

The outcome of the bargaining game is supported by the following strategies of a candidate and an interest group: Each player demands the equilibrium contributions in Proposition 1 when it makes a proposal; in the game Γ_{ic}, the interest group accepts any offer that does not exceed p_{ic}, and in the game Γ_{ig}, the candidate accepts any offer of at least p_{ig}. Consequently, agreement is reached immediately. The interest group never uses its outside option although, as indicated next, that option affects equilibrium contributions.

---

[14] A candidate, or his or her campaign staff, is assumed to be able to bargain simultaneously with an unlimited number of interest groups.

[15] For analytical convenience, contributions are allowed to be negative, which happens when $x_i q_i < OV_i$.

5.2   Contributions equilibrium

In an equilibrium, the contributions must be consistent with the bargaining equilibrium characterized by Proposition 1. Given p_{ic} and p_{ig}, the expected contribution p_i is $p_i = (1-\lambda)p_{ic} + \lambda p_{ig}$, which takes into account who makes the first proposal. The interest group can calculate the expected utility from breaking off negotiations with candidate i, which is the value of its outside option given by

$$OV_i = \rho(x_j q_j - p_j),\tag{8}$$

where

$$\rho \equiv \delta_d^{c_d|\alpha_i - \alpha_j|}\tag{9}$$

is the realignment cost and j denotes the other candidate. Note that OV_i depends on the positions of the parties.

The equilibrium contributions are attained if, for each candidate i, p_i is the expected contributions in the perfect equilibrium of the bargaining games Γ_{ic} and Γ_{ig} in which each interest group's outside option satisfies (8). Because of the anonymity assumption and the sunk cost of the policy position difference $|\alpha_i - \beta_a|$, the contributions are the same for all the interest groups that bargain with that candidate. Also, the interest groups benefit because $p_i < x_i q_i$.

Proposition 2. *Given α_1, α_2, q_1, q_2, and x, the equilibrium contributions $p = (p_1, p_2)$ are characterized by*

$$p_1 = \gamma \min\left\{\frac{x_1 q_1}{1 + \delta_\tau}, x_1 q_1 - \rho(x_2 q_2 - p_2)\right\} \quad and$$

$$p_2 = \gamma \min\left\{\frac{x_2 q_2}{1 + \delta_\tau}, x_2 q_2 - \rho(x_1 q_1 - p_1)\right\},$$

where $\gamma \equiv 1 - \lambda + \lambda\delta_\tau$ is the expected discount factor as a function of the probabilities that the candidate or the interest group makes the first offer.

Proof: Using the expressions for p_{ic} and p_{ig} from Proposition 1 and for OV_i from (8), solve for p_{ic} and p_{ig}, and substitute into the equation $p_i = (1 - \lambda)p_{ic} + \lambda p_{ig}$. □

Proposition 2 allows the three possible types of equilibrium contributions. A Type I equilibrium corresponds to the case where the outside option is not attractive to any interest group. A Type III equilibrium corresponds to the case where each interest group finds attractive the outside option corresponding to the other candidate. In a Type II equilibrium, the outside option is not attractive to the interest group bargaining with one candidate but is attractive to the interest group bargaining with the other candidate.

The equilibria will be presented here for the case in which the expected value of candidate 1's service offer is smaller than that of candidate 2, that is, $x_1 q_1 > x_2 q_2$.[16]

Type I: If $\delta_d^{Cd} \leq \rho < \rho^*$, then

$$p_1 = \frac{\gamma x_1 q_1}{1 + \delta_\tau} \quad \text{and} \tag{10}$$

$$p_2 = \frac{\gamma x_2 q_2}{1 + \delta_\tau}, \tag{11}$$

where

$$\rho^* \equiv \frac{x_2 q_2 \delta_\tau}{x_1 q_1 (1 + \delta_\tau - \gamma)}. \tag{12}$$

Type II: If $\max\{\delta_d^{Cd}, \rho^*\} \leq \rho \leq \rho^{**}$, then

$$p_1 = \frac{\gamma x_1 q_1}{1 + \delta_\tau} \quad \text{and} \tag{13}$$

$$p_2 = \gamma x_2 q_2 - \frac{\gamma(1 + \delta_\tau - \gamma)\rho x_1 q_1}{1 + \delta_\tau}, \tag{14}$$

where

$$\rho^{**} \equiv \frac{\sqrt{((1-\gamma)(1+\delta_\tau) x_2 q_2)^2 + 4\gamma\delta_\tau(1+\delta_\tau-\gamma)(x_1 q_1)^2} - (1-\gamma)(1+\delta_\tau) x_2 q_2}{2\gamma(1+\delta_\tau-\gamma) x_1 q_1}, \tag{15}$$

where $\rho^{**} > \rho^*$.[17]

Type III: If $\max\{\delta_d^{Cd}, \rho^{**}\} < \rho < 1$, then

$$p_1 = \frac{\gamma(1-\gamma\rho^2) x_1 q_1 - \gamma(1-\gamma)\rho x_2 q_2}{1 - (\gamma\rho)^2} \quad \text{and} \tag{16}$$

$$p_2 = \frac{\gamma(1-\gamma\rho^2) x_2 q_2 - \gamma(1-\gamma)\rho x_1 q_1}{1 + (\gamma\rho)^2}. \tag{17}$$

---

[16] The case of $x_1 q_1 < x_2 q_2$ can be described in a similar way. For example, in a Type II equilibrium, p_2 is a constant in ρ, whereas it is decreasing when $x_1 q_1 < x_2 q_2$. In addition, $x_1 q_1$ and $x_2 q_2$ are interchanged in the expressions for ρ^* and ρ^{**}.

[17] Since the policy space is the unit interval $[0,1]$, ρ has a minimum of δ_d^{Cd} when $\alpha_1 = 0$ and $\alpha_2 = 1$ and has a maximum of 1 when $\alpha_1 = \alpha_2$. It is straightforward to show that given (x_1, q_1, q_2), ρ^* is always smaller than ρ^{**}. To see this, note that

$$\rho^{**} - \rho^* > 0 \Leftrightarrow \sqrt{((1-\gamma)(1+\delta_\tau) x_2 q_2)^2 + 4\delta_\tau \gamma(1+\delta_\tau-\gamma)(x_1 q_1)^2} > ((1+\delta_\tau-\gamma) + 2\gamma\delta_\tau) x_2 q_2.$$

Squaring both sides of this inequality and subtracting establishes the result.

The type of bargaining equilibrium depends on the parameter ρ, which is a function of interest groups' realignment costs and the policies of the parties. When realignment costs are high or the party positions are not too close, the outside options are unattractive to all the interest groups and a Type I equilibrium results. When realignment costs are low or the party positions are close, every interest group may find the outside option attractive, and the equilibrium is of Type III. If the party positions and the realignment costs are such that one set of interest groups finds its outside option attractive and the other does not, the equilibrium is of Type II.

It is straightforward to show that, in all three equilibria, $\partial p_i/\partial q_i \geq 0$ and $\partial p_i/\partial q_j \leq 0$, so contributions are increasing in the services offered and decreasing in the opponent's service offer. This is summarized as follows.

Comment 1. The campaign contribution made by an interest group to a candidate is a (weakly) increasing function of her own service offer and a (weakly) decreasing function of her opponent's service offer.

Given q_1, q_2, and x, contributions are a (weakly) decreasing function of the closeness $\alpha_2 - \alpha_1$ of the policy positions of the candidates; that is, as ρ gets larger, both contributions in Type III are decreasing in ρ, one contribution is decreasing in ρ in Type II, and both are constant in ρ in Type I. Intuitively, when the policies of the parties' candidates are close to each other, interest groups have bargaining power relative to the candidates, and they thus make smaller contributions in equilibrium. When the candidate positions are separated, they have bargaining power relative to the interest group because realignment is more costly.

The result that the contributions in Type III are decreasing in ρ means that given the parties' positions (α_1 and α_2), the contributions are decreasing in δ_d and increasing in c_d, since $\rho = \delta_d^{c_d(\alpha_2 - \alpha_1)}$ and $\partial\rho/\partial\delta_d > 0$ and $\partial\rho/\partial c_d < 0$. This results because the bargaining power of the candidates relative to the interest groups is increasing in the realignment costs of interest groups.

The discount factor δ_r and the probability λ of the interest group making the first proposal also affect the contributions in a Type III equilibrium. Note that $\partial p_i/\partial\gamma > 0$.[18] Because $\gamma = 1 - \lambda + \lambda\delta_r$, $\partial\gamma/\partial\lambda < 0$, and

---

[18] Differentiating p_1 yields

$$\frac{\partial p_1}{\partial\gamma} = \frac{x_2 q_2((x_1 q_1/x_2 q_2)(\gamma^2\rho^2 - 2\gamma\rho^2 + 1) - ((\gamma^2\rho^2 + 1)\rho - 2\gamma\rho))}{(1 - (\gamma\rho)^2)^2}.$$

It is straightforward to show that $p_1 > 0$ and $p_2 > 0$ implies

$$\frac{(1-\gamma)\rho}{1-\gamma\rho^2} < \frac{x_1 q_1}{x_2 q_2} < \frac{1-\gamma\rho^2}{(1-\gamma)\rho},$$

and that $\partial p_1/\partial\gamma > 0$ in that case. Analogous reasoning establishes $\partial p_2/\partial\gamma > 0$.

$\partial \gamma / \partial \delta_\tau > 0$, the contributions in Type III are decreasing in λ and increasing in δ_τ. The result for λ is intuitive. The higher the probability (λ) of the interest group making the first proposal, the greater bargaining power the interest group has relative to the candidates. The result that δ_τ increases γ can be explained by the nature of a Type III bargaining equilibrium. When candidate i makes the first proposal and the bargaining equilibrium is of Type III, the candidate offers $x_i q_i - OV_i$ to make the interest group indifferent between taking the outside option and accepting her offer. Since OV_i is constant, the discount factor δ_τ does not affect the contribution to candidate i. When the interest group makes the proposal, the contributions are the amount that the interest group offers to candidate i, which equals $\delta_\tau(x_i q_i - OV_i)$. Therefore, the discount factor δ_τ increases the contributions to candidate i. Thus, whatever the probability λ of the interest group making the first proposal, an increase in δ_τ increases the contributions to the candidates. The following comment summarizes these results.

Comment 2. Given x, q_1, q_2, α_1, and α_2, the contributions in a Type III equilibrium are increasing in the discount factor δ_τ and decreasing in the probability λ of the interest group making the first proposal. As a function of ρ, in a Type III equilibrium the contributions increase with the distance between the parties' policy positions. In a Type I contributions equilibrium, the contributions are constant in ρ.

In the symmetric case in which $x_1 q_1 = x_2 q_2$, the following result obtains.

Comment 3. In a Type III equilibrium with $x_1 q_1 = x_2 q_2$, the contribution is a strictly decreasing function of ρ. The bargaining power of candidates relative to interest groups is thus greater as their positions are farther apart. As the policy positions converge, ρ approaches unity, and the contributions go to zero. This corresponds to the case in which the candidates have no bargaining power, and (as discussed in Section 2) the Bertrand outcome results.

When $x_1 q_1 = x_2 q_2$, note that $\rho^* = \rho^{**} = \delta_\tau / (1 + \delta_\tau - \gamma)$, so only Type I and Type III contributions equilibria exist and $p_1 = p_2$. For future reference, define

$$\rho^D \equiv \frac{\delta_\tau}{1 + \delta_\tau - \gamma}. \tag{18}$$

5.3   The indifferent interest group

Interest groups anticipate the bargaining stage and the equilibrium contributions, and decide with which candidate to begin bargaining. Since the bargaining will be concluded immediately, interest groups compare the two candidates in terms of the expected net surplus they will receive from the candidates' offers and the initial alignment costs $e^{-c_p|\alpha_i - \beta_a|}$. That is, an interest group with ideal point β_a will choose candidate 1 over candidate 2 if and only if $e^{-c_p|\alpha_1 - \beta_a|}(x_1 q_1 - p_1) - e^{-c_p|\alpha_2 - \beta_a|}(x_2 q_2 - p_2)$ is positive, that is,

$$-c_p(|\alpha_1 - \beta_a| - |\alpha_2 - \beta_a|) + \ln\left(\frac{x_1 q_1 - p_1}{x_2 q_2 - p_2}\right) \equiv CV(\beta_a) > 0.$$

The function $CV(\beta_a)$ depends in general on the location of an interest group's ideal point β_a, but when $\beta_a \le \alpha_1$,

$$CV(\beta_a) = c_p(\alpha_2 - \alpha_1) + \ln\left(\frac{x_1 q_1 - p_1}{x_2 q_2 - p_2}\right). \qquad (19)$$

That is, $CV(\beta_a)$ is independent of β_a, so all interest groups to the left of party 1's policy position α_1 contribute to the same candidate. Similarly, when $\beta \ge \alpha_2$,

$$CV(\beta_a) = -c_p(\alpha_2 - \alpha_1) + \ln\left(\frac{x_1 q_1 - p_1}{x_2 q_2 - p_2}\right), \qquad (20)$$

so those interest groups located to the right of party 2's policy position α_2 also contribute to the same candidate. When $\alpha_1 < \beta_a < \alpha_2$, however, the choice rule depends on β_a, since

$$CV(\beta_a) = c_p(\alpha_1 + \alpha_2 - 2\beta_a) + \ln\left(\frac{x_1 q_1 - p_1}{x_2 q_2 - p_2}\right). \qquad (21)$$

Since the interest groups located in either $[0, \alpha_1]$ or $[\alpha_2, 1]$ use the same choice rule – that is, the value of $CV(\beta_a)$ is the same in each interval – the signs of $CV(\alpha_1)$ and $CV(\alpha_2)$ are critical to determining the number a_1 and a_2 of contributors to candidate 1 and 2, respectively. Since $\alpha_2 \ge \alpha_1$ and $c_p > 0$, it is straightforward to show that $CV(\alpha_1) \ge CV(\alpha_2)$. Given this, there are three possible cases for the signs of $CV(\alpha_1)$ and $CV(\alpha_2)$:

(1) $CV(\alpha_1) > 0$ and $CV(\alpha_2) > 0$;
(2) $CV(\alpha_1) < 0$ and $CV(\alpha_2) < 0$; and
(3) $CV(\alpha_1) \ge 0$ and $CV(\alpha_2) \le 0$.

In the first case, where both $CV(\alpha_1)$ and $CV(\alpha_2)$ are positive, it follows that (21) is also positive, so all interest groups choose to contribute to candidate 1; that is, $a_1 = 1$ and $a_2 = 0$. For a similar reason, the second case implies that $a_1 = 0$ and $a_2 = 1$. Assume when $CV(\alpha_1) = 0$ that those in $[0, \alpha_1]$ contribute to candidate 1, and when $CV(\alpha_2) = 0$ that those in $[\alpha_2, 1]$ contribute to candidate 2. Then, when $CV(\alpha_1) \ge 0$ and $CV(\alpha_2) \le 0$, there exists $\beta_a = \bar{a} \in [\alpha_1, \alpha_2]$, where $CV(\bar{a}) = 0$ in (21); that is,

$$\tilde{a} = \frac{\alpha_1 + \alpha_2}{2} - \frac{1}{2c_p} \ln\left(\frac{x_2 q_2 - p_2}{x_1 q_1 - p_1}\right), \tag{22}$$

so that $a_1 = \tilde{a}$ and $a_2 = 1 - \tilde{a}$.[19]

To investigate how $\tilde{a}$ in (22) changes as a function of q_1, note that $\tilde{a}$ is a linear transformation of $\ln((x_1 q_1 - p_1)/(x_2 q_2 - p_2))$. The term within the larger parentheses is increasing and strictly concave in q_1 (see Baron and Mo 1991).

Comment 4. If candidate i increases the services she offers, the number of interest groups that contribute to her is increasing and strictly concave in q_i; that is, $\partial \tilde{a}/\partial q_1 > 0$ and $\partial \tilde{a}/\partial q_2 < 0$, and $\partial^2 \tilde{a}/\partial q_1^2 < 0$ and $\partial^2 \tilde{a}/\partial q_1^2 > 0$.

The total contributions received by the candidates are $C_1 = p_1 \tilde{a}$ and $C_2 = p_2(1 - \tilde{a})$. Therefore, the election outcome can be expressed as

$$w(q_1, q_2; \alpha_1, \alpha_2) = \frac{p_1 \tilde{a}}{p_1 \tilde{a} + p_2(1 - \tilde{a})}. \tag{23}$$

The general expression for the change in the probability $w(\cdot)$ of winning as a function of the services offered is, assuming differentiability,

$$\frac{\partial w}{\partial q_1} = \frac{\dfrac{\partial p_1}{\partial q_1}(1 - \tilde{a})\tilde{a}p_2 - (1 - \tilde{a})\tilde{a}p_1\dfrac{\partial p_2}{\partial q_1} + p_1 p_2\dfrac{\partial \tilde{a}}{\partial q_1}}{(p_1 \tilde{a} + p_2(1 - \tilde{a}))^2}. \tag{24}$$

Since $\partial p_1/\partial q_1 \geq 0$, $\partial p_2/\partial q_1 \leq 0$, and $\partial \tilde{a}/\partial q_1 > 0$ for all types of contributions equilibria, it follows that $\partial w/\partial q_1 > 0$. This result is summarized by the following comment.

Comment 5. The probability that candidate i wins is a strictly increasing function of i's own service offer.

Comment 5 follows because an increased service offer in turn increases both the contribution p_i and the number of interest groups that contribute to i. The provision of services is costly to the candidate, however, so unlimited services are not offered. The service equilibrium is characterized next.

6   Service equilibrium and rational expectations

When candidates choose the amount of services to promise and interest groups form expectations about who will win the election, only the

---

[19] To show this, note that $CV(\beta_a)$ in (21) is monotone decreasing in β_a in (α_1, α_2) and that $CV(\alpha_1) \geq 0$ and $CV(\alpha_2) \leq 0$, so there exists a β_a in which $CV(\beta_a)$ in (21) equals zero.

positions of the parties are exogenous. Candidates face the election outcome function $w(\cdot)$, which depends on the policy positions of the parties through the parameter ρ. Since there is no ex ante difference between the parties with respect to the electoral competition, only symmetric candidate–party equilibria will be characterized. Thus, assume that $v_1 = v_2 \equiv v$, $\alpha_1^o + \alpha_2^o = 1$, $u_1 = u_2 \equiv u$, and $n_1 = n_2 \equiv n$.

It can be shown (Baron and Mo 1991) that there exists no service equilibrium in which all interest groups contribute to one candidate, so $a_i \in (0, 1)$ for $i = 1, 2$. Thus, a service equilibrium, if it exists, is characterized by $a_1 = \bar{a}$; that is, the indifferent interest group is between the policy positions of the two parties. Letting $(\bar{x}, \bar{q}_1, \bar{q}_2)$ denote such a (local) service equilibrium for a given policy position pair (α_1, α_2), the necessary conditions for $(\bar{x}, \bar{q}_1, \bar{q}_2)$ from (5) and (6) are, assuming differentiability,

$$\frac{\partial w}{\partial q_1}(u - n\bar{a}q_1) - w(\cdot)n\left(\bar{a} + \frac{\partial \bar{a}}{\partial q_1}q_1\right) = 0; \tag{25}$$

$$\frac{\partial w}{\partial q_2}(u - n(1 - \bar{a})q_2) - (1 - w(\cdot))n\left(1 - \bar{a} - \frac{\partial \bar{a}}{\partial q_2}q_2\right) = 0; \tag{26}$$

$$\bar{x} = w(\cdot). \tag{27}$$

Let w denote the equilibrium expectations, that is, $w = \bar{x}$. Even if this local service equilibrium $(w, \bar{q}_1, \bar{q}_2)$ satisfies the second-order conditions[20] and is a unique solution to (25), (26), and (27), whether $q_i = \bar{q}_i$ is the globally optimal response to $\bar{q}_j$ $(j \neq i)$ is not clear. It is necessary to verify that $(w, \bar{q}_1, \bar{q}_2)$ is a global service equilibrium associated with (α_1, α_2). The difficulty in verifying this is that the types of contributions equilibria change as q_i varies, even though party positions are fixed. A detailed discussion of this issue is provided in Baron and Mo (1991, apx. E) and can be summarized as follows: A local service equilibrium is not a global service equilibrium if it is "close" to Type II competition – that is, if a slight change in q_1 or q_2 from its equilibrium level results in a Type II contributions equilibrium.

Since any global service equilibrium is a local service equilibrium, local service equilibria will be first characterized. Examples of global equilibria will be presented in Section 7. The following propositions establish the properties of some local service equilibria.

[20] Differentiating (25) with respect to q_1 yields an expression for a second-order condition:

$$\frac{\partial^2 w}{\partial q_1^2}(u - n\bar{a}q_1) - 2n\frac{\partial w}{\partial q_1}\left(\bar{a} + \frac{\partial \bar{a}}{\partial q_1}q_1\right) - wn\left(\frac{\partial \bar{a}}{\partial q_1} + \frac{\partial^2 \bar{a}}{\partial q_1^2}q_1\right).$$

Whether the second-order condition is satisfied cannot be directly determined by this expression, because $\partial^2 \bar{a}/\partial q_1^2 < 0$ and the sign of $\partial^2 w/\partial q_1^2$ is not known. Numerical examples show that second-order conditions are typically satisfied.

Proposition 3. *A Type I local service equilibrium is characterized by:*

$$\bar{q}_1 = \frac{2c_p\bar{a}(1-\bar{a})+1}{\bar{a}(6c_p\bar{a}(1-\bar{a})+2)}\frac{u}{n},$$ (28)

$$\bar{q}_2 = \frac{\bar{a}}{1-\bar{a}}\bar{q}_1,$$ (29)

$$w = \frac{\bar{a}(2c_p(1-\bar{a})+1)}{4c_p\bar{a}(1-\bar{a})+1}, \quad and$$ (30)

$$\bar{a} = \frac{\alpha_1+\alpha_2}{2} - \frac{1}{2c_p}\ln\left(\frac{2c_p\bar{a}+1}{2c_p(1-\bar{a})+1}\right).$$ (31)

Proof: Substituting the Type I equilibrium contributions into (25), (26), and (27) yields

$$\frac{w(1-w)(2c_p\bar{a}(1-\bar{a})+1)q_2}{(wq_1\bar{a}+(1-w)q_2(1-\bar{a}))^2}(u-nq_1\bar{a})-wn(2c_p\bar{a}+1)=0;$$ (32)

$$\frac{w(1-w)(2c_p\bar{a}(1-\bar{a})+1)q_1}{(wq_1\bar{a}+(1-w)q_2(1-\bar{a}))^2}(u-nq_2(1-\bar{a}))$$
$$-(1-w)n(2c_p(1-\bar{a})+1)=0;$$ (33)

$$q_1\bar{a} = q_2(1-\bar{a}).$$ (34)

Combining (32) and (33) and using (34) yields

$$q_1w(2c_p\bar{a}+1) = q_2(1-w)(2c_p(1-\bar{a})+1).$$ (35)

The indifferent interest group $\bar{a}$ is

$$\bar{a} = \frac{\alpha_1+\alpha_2}{2} - \frac{1}{2c_p}\ln\left(\frac{(1-w)q_2}{wq_1}\right)$$

$$= \frac{\alpha_1+\alpha_2}{2} - \frac{1}{2c_p}\ln\left(\frac{(1-w)\bar{a}}{w(1-\bar{a})}\right)$$

$$= \frac{\alpha_1+\alpha_2}{2} - \frac{1}{2c_p}\ln\left(\frac{2c_p\bar{a}+1}{2c_p(1-\bar{a})+1}\right).$$ (36)

The second step used (34) and the third step used

$$\frac{1-w}{w} = \frac{1-\bar{a}}{\bar{a}}\frac{2c_p\bar{a}+1}{2c_p(1-\bar{a})+1},$$ (37)

which can be derived from (34) and (35). Then, substituting (34) into (32) and solving for q_1 yields (28); substituting (34) into (33) yields a similar expression for q_2. Then, equating that expression with the expression for q_2 obtained by substituting (28) into (29) yields (30).   □

It is straightforward to verify that for all $\bar{a} \in [0,1]$, the equilibrium probability w of candidate 1 winning is in $[0,1]$. Furthermore, for all party policy positions, the indifferent interest group $\bar{a}$ is in $[0,1]$. Consequently, a Type I equilibrium is well behaved if it is a global equilibrium.

From (31), the indifferent interest group $\bar{a}$ is not a function of u and n. Therefore, the constituency services in (31) and (32) provided in equilibrium are increasing functions of the value of the office to the candidates and a decreasing function of the cost n of providing constituency service.[21] These results are summarized as follows.

Comment 6. For a Type I local service equilibrium, the equilibrium services are a strictly increasing function of u/n, whereas the probability of winning and the location of the indifferent interest group are independent of u/n.

When policy positions are symmetric (i.e., $\alpha_1 + \alpha_2 = 1$), a closed-form characterization of a local service equilibrium can be given.

Proposition 4. When (α_1, α_2) is such that $\alpha_1 + \alpha_2 = 1$ and $\rho < \rho^D$, a Type I symmetric local service equilibrium results with $w = \frac{1}{2}$ and

$$\bar{q}_1 = \bar{q}_2 = \frac{(2c_p + 4)u}{(3c_p + 4)n}. \tag{38}$$

Proof: The main part of the proof is to show that $\bar{a} = \frac{1}{2}$ is a unique solution to (31) when $\alpha_1 + \alpha_2 = 1$. It is easy to show that $\bar{a} = \frac{1}{2}$ is a solution. To show uniqueness, define

$$F(\bar{a}) = \bar{a} + \frac{1}{2c_p} \ln\left(\frac{2c_p\bar{a} + 1}{2c_p(1 - \bar{a}) + 1}\right) - \frac{1}{2}. \tag{39}$$

Then

$$\frac{\partial F}{\partial \bar{a}} = 1 + \frac{2(c_p + 1)}{(2c_p\bar{a} + 1)(2c_p(1 - \bar{a}) + 1)} > 0. \tag{40}$$

Therefore, there is only one $\bar{a}$ such that $F(\bar{a}) = 0$. Substituting $\bar{a} = \frac{1}{2}$ into (28) and (29) yields (38). Thus, $\bar{q}_1 = \bar{q}_2$ and $w = \frac{1}{2}$ result in a Type I contributions equilibrium when $\rho < \rho^D$. $\qquad \square$

In this equilibrium, the services provided are a decreasing function of the interest group's alignment cost parameter c_p, which pertains to the policy difference between the interest group's and the candidate's policy positions. As the cost to the interest groups of contributing to candidates farther from their ideal point increases, candidates offer more services.

---

[21] The effect of policy positions on the local service equilibrium is given in Proposition 6.

Since $C_1 = C_2 = \gamma \bar{q}_1 / 2(1 + \delta_r)$ in a Type I symmetric service equilibrium with symmetric policy positions, the result in (38) can be used to indicate the effect of the model parameters on the total contributions $C_1 + C_2$. Total contributions are increasing in u and decreasing in n. The more valuable the office, the more services candidates offer; as services become more costly, fewer services are offered. Since $\gamma = 1 - \lambda + \delta_r \lambda$, contributions are decreasing in λ, since a higher λ means that the interest groups are more likely to make the first proposal in the bargaining over contributions. Contributions are increasing (decreasing) in δ_r if λ is greater than (less than) 0.5, reflecting an advantage to the party that is less likely to make the first proposal. The total contributions inherit the properties of the equilibrium services, so contributions are a decreasing function of the alignment cost parameter c_p.

General results for Types II and III local service equilibria are not available in closed form, but symmetric local service equilibria can be characterized. In a symmetric local service equilibrium, candidates offer the same amount of services, have an equal chance of winning, and attract the support of half the interest groups.

Proposition 5. *A Type II symmetric local service equilibrium is characterized by*

$$\bar{q}_1 = \bar{q}_2 = \frac{u}{n} \frac{4(1 + \delta_r)(1 - \gamma) + 2c_p(1 + \delta_r)(1 + \delta_r - \gamma)}{4(1 + \delta_r)(1 - \gamma) + c_p(3 + \delta_r)(1 + \delta_r - \gamma)}. \tag{41}$$

This symmetric equilibrium exists only for $\rho = \rho^D$. A Type III symmetric local service equilibrium is characterized by

$$\bar{q}_1 = \bar{q}_2 = \frac{u}{n} \frac{2(c_p \rho^2 \gamma + c_p \rho \gamma - c_p \rho + 2\rho - c_p - 2)}{c_p \rho^2 \gamma + c_p \rho \gamma - c_p \rho + 4\rho - c_p - 4}. \tag{42}$$

Proof: Substituting the relevant types of contributions equilibria into (25), (26), and (27) and using $\bar{a} = \frac{1}{2}$, $w = \frac{1}{2}$, and $q_1 = q_2$ yields (41) and (42). □

The services in (42) for a Type III symmetric local service equilibria are a function of the policy distance ρ between the candidates. Differentiation shows that the services provided increase as the candidates' positions become closer (ρ becomes greater).[22] This results because the contributions made by an interest group are a decreasing function of ρ, and the

---

[22] Differentiating (42) yields

$$\frac{\partial \bar{q}_1}{\partial \rho} = \frac{4c_p(\gamma \rho^2 - 2\gamma \rho - \gamma + 2)}{(c_p \gamma \rho^2 + c_p \gamma \rho - c_p \rho + 4\rho - c_p - 4)^2}.$$

It is straightforward to show that the expression $\gamma \rho^2 - 2\gamma \rho + 2 - \gamma$ is positive.

candidates compensate by offering more services. Services and a more central policy position thus are complements. That is, as parties move their positions toward the median, the bargaining power of their candidates decreases, and the candidates compete more intensely by offering to provide more services. This is recorded in the next comment.

Comment 7. In a Type III symmetric local service equilibrium, as ρ increases the services offered increase, so closer policy positions result in more intense service competition.

For a Type I equilibrium, the expected utility of a candidate can be evaluated from (4), (28), (29), and (31), and a candidate's preference for the party's policy position can be determined.

Comment 8. In a Type I equilibrium, the expected utility of candidate 1 is

$$EU_1 = \left(\frac{\tilde{a}(2c_p(1-\tilde{a})+1)}{6c_p\tilde{a}(1-\tilde{a})+2} \right) u,$$

and the candidate prefers the party to choose a policy position that allows the candidate to obtain contributions from all interest groups.

This may be verified by observing that EU_1 is maximized at $\tilde{a} = 1$. A candidate thus prefers that his party choose a position that enables him to raise as much in campaign contributions as possible.

The following results establish properties of local service equilibria. In a Type I local service equilibrium, as either party moves its policy position to the right, the party on the left receives contributions from more interest groups and its probability of winning increases.

Proposition 6. *In a Type I local service equilibrium,*

$$\frac{\partial \tilde{a}}{\partial \alpha_1} = \frac{\partial \tilde{a}}{\partial \alpha_2} > 0 \quad and \quad \frac{\partial w}{\partial \alpha_1} = \frac{\partial w}{\partial \alpha_2} > 0.$$

Proof: Differentiating (38) yields, by the implicit function theorem,

$$\frac{\partial \tilde{a}}{\partial \alpha_1} = \frac{(2c_p\tilde{a}+1)(2c_p(1-\tilde{a})+1)}{4(c_p+1)+2(2c_p\tilde{a}+1)(2c_p(1-\tilde{a})+1)} > 0, \tag{43}$$

so if the candidate on the left moves toward the center, more interest groups will contribute to her. From (37), we know that

$$w = \frac{\tilde{a}(2c_p(1-\tilde{a})+1)}{1+4c_p\tilde{a}(1-\tilde{a})}.$$

It is straightforward to show that

$$\frac{\partial w}{\partial \bar{a}} = \frac{4c_p \bar{a}^2 - 4c_p \bar{a} + 1 + 2c_p}{(1 + 4c_p \bar{a}(1 - \bar{a}))^2} > 0. \tag{44}$$

Thus, $\partial w / \partial \alpha_1 = (\partial w / \partial \bar{a})(\partial \bar{a} / \partial \alpha_1) > 0$. The other results follow in a similar manner. $\square$

Comment 9.   In a symmetric Type I local service equilibrium, $\partial \bar{q}_1 / \partial \alpha_1 < 0$ and $\partial \bar{q}_1 / \partial \alpha_2 < 0$.

Note that $\partial \bar{q}_1 / \partial \alpha_1 = (\partial \bar{q}_1 / \partial \bar{a})(\partial \bar{a} / \partial \alpha_1)$. From (43), $\partial \bar{a} / \partial \alpha_1 > 0$, and differentiating (28) with respect to $\bar{a}$ yields

$$\frac{\partial \bar{q}_1}{\partial \bar{a}} = -\frac{6c_p^2 \bar{a}^2 (1 - \bar{a})^2 + 1 + c_p(6 - 7\bar{a})\bar{a}}{(\bar{a}(3c_p \bar{a}(1 - \bar{a}) + 1))^2} \frac{u}{n},$$

which is negative for $\bar{a} = \frac{1}{2}$. As party 1 moves toward the median, its candidate offers fewer services because with a higher probability of winning she prefers to offer fewer costly services. The same result obtains as candidate 2 moves farther from the median. Consequently, in a symmetric Type I local service equilibrium, candidate services and a party position closer to the median are substitutes. Note that $\partial \bar{q}_1 / \partial \bar{a} < 0$ for $\bar{a} < \frac{6}{7}$, so even in an asymmetric local service equilibrium, candidate 1 offers fewer services when her party moves toward the median.

The relationship of this model to the median-voter theorem can be indicated using the results in Proposition 6 and Comment 9. If realignment were impossible, a Type I bargaining equilibrium would exist for all party positions. For any symmetric locations for the parties, the probability that candidate 1 wins is $w = \frac{1}{2}$ and the equilibrium services are given in (38). The contributions are

$$p_1 = p_2 = \left(\frac{\gamma}{1 + \delta_\tau}\right)\left(\frac{c_p + 2}{3c_p + 4}\right)\frac{u}{n}. \tag{10a}$$

For symmetric but different policies, Proposition 6 indicates that party 1 has an incentive to move toward the median. A (marginal) movement toward the median causes candidate 1 to offer fewer services and candidate 2 to offer more services, as indicated by Comment 9. More interest groups, however, contribute to candidate 1, and her probability of winning increases. The parties thus have an incentive to move to the median, which is the unique equilibrium. The services offered are thus those in (38), and the contributions are those in (10a).

When interest groups are able to align, however, the contributions equilibrium as party positions move closer together becomes Type III;

that is, ρ becomes greater than ρ^D. Then, as they move closer, the candidates are more alike and the realignment costs are smaller. This reduces the bargaining power of the candidates, and their contributions decrease as indicated in Comment 3. The behavior in this case is considered next.

A limited characterization is available for a Type III local service equilibrium.[23] Extensive numerical analysis shows that in a Type III local service equilibrium, for certain parameter values, a party's probability of winning the election actually decreases if it chooses a position closer to the median. The parameter values that support this result belong to what will be called the "intense competition region." The question of which parameter values comprise this region will be discussed following an intuitive explanation of Proposition 6 and the following claim.

Claim. In the region that supports a Type III local service equilibrium, there is an intense competition region in which a party's probability of winning decreases if it chooses a policy position closer to the median, $\partial w/\partial\alpha_1 < 0$ and $\partial w/\partial\alpha_2 < 0$.

The basic intuition underlying this claim is that, because in the intensity parameter region the contributions by an interest group decrease as parties choose positions closer to the median, the parties thus have incentives to choose positions that differentiate their candidates. This gives their candidates more bargaining power relative to the interest groups, and contributions increase.

The following develops further the intuition underlying Proposition 6 and the claim. For given policy positions, draw $(x_1, w(\cdot))$ as illustrated in Figure 4. Note that a rational-expectations equilibrium occurs at the intersection of the 45-degree line and $w(\cdot)$. Denote the outcome function for symmetric locations as $w^S(\cdot)$ and the outcome function for asymmetric locations by $w^A(\cdot)$. Consider a particular asymmetric location pair in which party 1's position is slightly closer to the median than party 2's. For $w^A(\cdot) > w^S(\cdot)$, the situation is as in Proposition 6, and if the inequality is reversed then the situation is as in the claim with respect to the intense competition region.

Figures 5a and 5b, corresponding to Type I and Type III, show how $w(\cdot)$ changes as part 1 moves from the symmetric location toward the median, given a value of $x_1 = 0.5$.[24] The best response functions $q_1(q_2)$ and $q_2(q_1)$ are both upward-sloping in the $(q_1 q_2)$-plane, and candidate 1's best response function is steeper than candidate 2's. In Figure 5a for a Type I equilibrium, suppose that party 1 moves its policy position (mar-

---

[23] There is no result comparable to these propositions for Type II local service equilibria.
[24] The direction of change in $w(\cdot)$ is the same for other values of x_1.

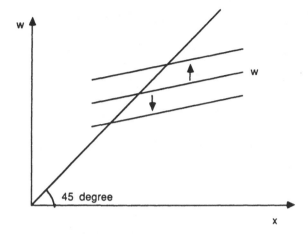

Figure 4. Illustration of rational expectations.

ginally) toward the median from its symmetric location. This creates an advantage for candidate 1, since contributions p_1 and p_2 are unaffected and the interest group that was indifferent between the two candidates now favors candidate 1. As Figure 5a illustrates, as a result of candidate 1's move, $q_1(q_2)$ shifts upward and $q_2(q_1)$ shifts downward. Candidate 1 can afford to offer fewer services for a given level of candidate 2's offer. The opposite is true for candidate 2. The result is that $q_2^A > q_1^A$ and $p_2^A > p_1^A$. This effect is called the *relaxation* effect, since candidate i need not compete as intensely. However, numerical analysis shows that this relaxation effect does not offset candidate 1's locational advantage. That is, in a Type I equilibrium candidate 2's total contributions $p_2^A(1 - \bar{a})$ are less than candidate 1's, $p_1^A \bar{a}$, even if $p_2^A > p_1^A$. Thus $w^A(\cdot) > w^S(\cdot)$, which confirms Proposition 6.

The same relaxation effect is present in a Type III service equilibrium, but there is an additional effect. In a Type III service equilibrium, when the parties' positions become closer, the candidates' bargaining powers weaken relative to interest groups because the outside options become more attractive when the parties' positions are closer – that is, ρ increases. As a result, both candidates have to offer more services. This will be called the *bargaining* effect of moving toward the median. Numerical analysis shows that the bargaining effect shifts $q_1(q_2)$ downward and $q_2(q_1)$ upward. The arrows in Figure 5b indicate this effect.[25] The net results are

---

[25] To isolate this bargaining effect, set the first term of (22), $(\alpha_1 + \alpha_2)/2$, equal to $\frac{1}{2}$, as in the original symmetric location. Note that the relaxation effect of a move toward the median works through the first term of (22).

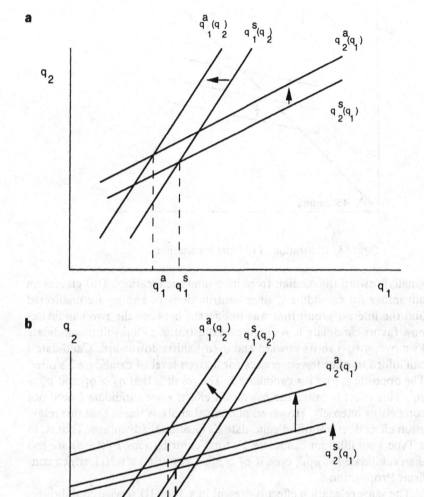

Figure 5. Candidates' best-response functions in services: (a) Type I service equilibrium; (b) Type III service equilibrium.

that $q_2(q_1)$ can move sharply to $q_2^A(q_1)$ and that $q_1(q_2)$ can move relatively little to $q_1^A(q_2)$. This creates a substantial difference between the candidates in equilibrium service offers and contributions. Candidate 2's contribution from an individual interest group is now much higher than candidate 1's, and for certain parameter values more than offsets candidate 1's advantage in the number $\bar{a}$ of interest groups that contribute to her. Thus $w^A(\cdot) < w^S(\cdot)$, which corresponds to the claim. Party 1 thus prefers to move its policy position away from rather than toward the median.

The condition under which the claim holds depends on whether the bargaining effect of moving toward the median is sufficiently great to offset the locational advantage. The bargaining effect is greater, the weaker is the bargaining power of the candidates relative to the interest groups. From Comment 2, the candidates' bargaining power is weaker if the time discount factor δ_r is lower, the probability λ of an interest group making the first proposal is higher, and the realignment costs are smaller – that is, δ_d is higher and c_d is lower. The intensity region thus consists of those values of the parameters that correspond to sufficiently weaker bargaining power of the candidates. That is, the claim holds if the realignment costs are sufficiently small and the probability of the interest group making the first proposal in the bargaining over contributions is sufficiently high. Numerical analysis shows that a given bargaining effect (i.e., the parameter values that affect the bargaining effect are fixed) offsets the locational advantage if the relaxation effect is great. The relaxation effect is greater, the greater is the competition to attract interest groups – that is, the policy costs of the interest groups are higher. Thus, the intensity parameter value region is also characterized by high c_p.[26]

7   Policy equilibria

To characterize policy equilibria, a unique global service equilibrium for each policy pair (α_1, α_2) is needed. The complete relationship between candidate positions and types of contributions equilibria is not known, but the relationship between symmetric locations and contributions equilibria can be characterized. Such a characterization is informative because a policy equilibrium would be expected to be symmetric in a situation where a party and its candidate have preferences and opportunities that are symmetric to the other party and its candidate.

As shown in Proposition 4, symmetric policy positions with $\rho < \rho^D$ result in a Type I symmetric local service equilibrium. Whether symmetric

---

[26] Numerical analysis shows that the candidates' value u of being in office and their marginal cost n of providing services do not affect the signs of the derivatives in the claim.

positions always result in a symmetric local service equilibrium is unclear. If symmetric policy positions do yield a symmetric local service equilibrium, as numerical examples indicate, Propositions 4 and 5 yield the following comment.

Comment 10.   Symmetric locations when $\rho > \rho^D$ (in (18)) result in a Type III symmetric local service equilibrium, whereas those with $\rho < \rho^D$ result in a Type I symmetric local service equilibrium. The symmetric location pair when $\rho = \rho^D$, given by

$$\alpha_1^D = \frac{1}{2}\left(1 - \frac{\ln \rho^D}{c_d \ln \delta_d}\right) \quad \text{and} \quad \alpha_2^D = \frac{1}{2}\left(1 + \frac{\ln \rho^D}{d_d \ln \delta_d}\right), \tag{45}$$

results in a Type II symmetric local service equilibrium. In symmetric equilibria, the contributions in Type I and Type III equilibria, respectively, are

$$p_1 = p_2 = \frac{\gamma}{2(1+\delta_r)}\bar{q}_I \quad \text{and} \quad p_1 = p_2 = \frac{\gamma(1-\rho)}{2(1-\gamma\rho)}\bar{q}_{III},$$

where $\bar{q}_I$ and $\bar{q}_{III}$ are the equilibrium services given in Propositions 4 and 5, respectively.

7.1   Parties that maximize the probability of winning

In this section, parties are assumed to care only about winning; that is, $k = 0$ in (1) and (2). First, consider the case of $\delta_d^{c_d} < \rho^D$.[27] At a symmetric policy pair with a Type I symmetric global service equilibrium, Proposition 6 indicates that there is an incentive for each party to move toward the median to increase its probability of winning. Then ρ necessarily increases above ρ^D, yielding a Type III local service equilibrium. The same incentive to move toward the median is present for a symmetric location pair with a Type III symmetric global service equilibrium if the parameter values are not in the intense competition region. Therefore, outside the intense competition region the parties' policies converge to the median. As the positions move toward the median, the contributions approach zero, in which case voters vote randomly when there are no contributions. Thus, there is an equilibrium in which both parties locate at the median.[28]

[27]   The policy cost $\delta_d^{c_d}$ corresponds to the extreme policy positions $\alpha_1 = 0$ and $\alpha_2 = 1$.

[28]   To show that there is an equilibrium at $\alpha_1 = \alpha_2 = \frac{1}{2}$, first note that the local symmetric service equilibrium is of Type III because $\rho = 1 > \rho^D$. From (42), the equilibrium service offer $\bar{q}$ is $\bar{q} = 2u/n$ when $\rho = 1$. So, $x_1 = \frac{1}{2}$ and $\bar{q}_1 = \bar{q}_2 = \bar{q}$ are a global service equilibrium if $q_1 = \bar{q}$ is a best response to $q_2 = \bar{q}$. Given $q_2 = \bar{q}$, $q_1 = \bar{q}$ yields to candidate 1 a utility $w(\cdot)(u - nq_1\bar{a}) = \frac{1}{2}(u - n\bar{q}/2)$, because $w(\cdot) = \frac{1}{2}$ (by assumption) and $\bar{a} = \frac{1}{2}$. Substituting

In the intense competition region, the claim indicates that there is an incentive to move away from the median. But then when $\delta_q^{c_d} < \rho^D$, moving away from the median leads to a Type I local service equilibrium, in which case there is an incentive to move toward the median. Thus, when the positions are close together, there is an incentive to move apart, and when the positions are far apart, there is an incentive to move closer. Therefore, when $\delta_q^{c_d} < \rho^D$, there is no symmetric policy equilibrium in the intensity region.

When $\delta_q^{c_d} > \rho^D$, every symmetric policy position pair results in a Type III symmetric local service equilibrium. Outside the intense competition region, there is an incentive to move toward the median, so both parties locating at the median is an equilibrium. In the intense competition region, there is an incentive to move away from the median, so the extreme positions $(0, 1)$ are the only possible policy equilibrium. The policy positions $(0, 1)$ are an equilibrium if a Type III symmetric local service equilibrium at that position is a global equilibrium; as indicated before, that condition is satisfied if the value $\delta_q^{c_d}$ of ρ at those positions is sufficiently greater than ρ^D.

The following proposition summarizes the preceding discussion.

Proposition 7. *Outside the intense competition region, there is an equilibrium in which both parties locate at the median if voters vote randomly when there are no contributions. In the intense competition region, the extreme positions $(\bar{\alpha}_1 = 0,\ \bar{\alpha}_2 = 1)$ can constitute a Nash policy equilibrium if $\delta_q^{c_d}$ is sufficiently greater than ρ^D.*

To develop the intuition of the second part of Proposition 7, suppose that the parties were to choose symmetric positions close to the median and that $x_1 = w = 0.5$ in a symmetric Type III contributions and service equilibrium. Figure 6 illustrates how candidates adjust their service offers in response to changes in parties' policies. The values of the parameters used in Figure 6 are $u = 1$, $n = 1.2$, $\delta_d = \delta_\tau = 0.05$, $\lambda = 0.5$, $c_p = 0.1054$, and $c_d = 0.51$. If party 1 moves its position (marginally) to the left, the candidates

---

$\bar{q} = 2u/n$, this equilibrium utility for candidate 1 equals zero. Service competition has thus competed away any gains to candidates. It is straightforward to show that if candidate 1 increases q_1 marginally from $\bar{q}$ then all interest groups align with candidate 1; that is, $a_1 = 1$, since q_{III}^a in Baron and Mo (1991, eq. (25)) is $\bar{q}$ in a symmetric service equilibrium with $\rho = 1$. Candidate 1's utility, however, becomes $w(\cdot)(u - nq_1 a_1) = -u$ because $w(\cdot) = 1$ with $a_1 = 1$ and $q_1 = \bar{q}$. Thus, candidate 1 is worse off by increasing her service. If candidate 1 decreases her service from $\bar{q}$ then no interest groups contribute to her and her probability of winning is zero, so her utility is zero, unchanged from the equilibrium utility. Therefore, $q_1 = \bar{q}$ is a best response to $q_2 = \bar{q}$, and a similar argument shows that $q_2 = \bar{q}$ is a best response to $q_1 = \bar{q}$.

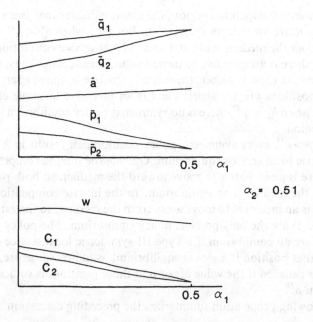

Figure 6. Movement away from the median, $k = 0$.

adjust their service levels and the contributions determined in the bargaining between candidates and interest groups change. As indicated in the previous section, in the intense competition region there are two effects. The bargaining effect leads both candidates to reduce their services, because services are costly to provide. The relaxation effect leads the candidate on the left to increase her services and the candidate on the right to decrease his services. The net effect on the services of the candidate on the left is unclear in general, but the candidate on the right reduces his services more because of the relaxation effect. Figure 6 illustrates that in this example q_1 decreases.

As is evident in (16) and (17), the contributions of each candidate change. However, the party positions are now farther apart, so ρ is lower, which (as indicated in Comment 2) causes both p_1 and p_2 to be higher than they would be with closer party positions. That is, policy positions that are farther apart increase the bargaining power of candidates relative to interest groups and cause contributions to increase. However, candidates reduce their services offered, which reduces the contributions. The net effect on contributions p_1 and p_2 is unclear in general, because of these two effects. Figure 6 illustrates that in the example the bargaining effect dominates – that is, the contributions to both candidates increase, although the services offered are lower. The contributions to candidate 1 increase more than those to candidate 2.

The change in party 1's position also affects which interest groups contribute to which candidates. The indifferent interest group is characterized in (22), and a movement to the left in α_1 has two effects. From the first term in (22) and holding beliefs and services fixed, the indifferent interest group shifts left. For fixed beliefs, the changes in the services offered affect the second term, so the indifferent interest group shifts to the right. The net effect is unclear in general and depends on the parameters of the model. In the example in Figure 6, the indifferent group shifts left.

Whether party 1 prefers to move its position to the left depends on the effect on the probability of winning. In the intensity region, however, it prefers to do so, as illustrated by the example in Figure 6. As party 1 moves to the left, its contributions increase by more than do the contributions to the candidate on the right.

To summarize the intuition, a movement away from the median increases the bargaining power of both candidates, which ceteris paribus increases contributions. Candidates, however, reduce their service offers, and although both offer fewer services, the candidate on the left reduces her services less than does the candidate on the right. This reduces the contribution by an interest group, but the contribution by an interest group on the left decreases by less than does the contribution by an interest group on the right. The net effect on the contributions p_1 and p_2 is unclear. The change in the position of party 1 and the resulting changes in the service offerings of the candidates also affect which interest groups give to which candidates. Holding service offerings fixed, the movement away from the median causes some interest groups now to contribute to the candidate of the party on the right. The candidate on the right, however, reduces his service offerings more than does the candidate on the left, and this – holding party positions fixed – causes some interest groups now to contribute to the party on the left. The net effect is unclear and depends on the parameters of the model. In the intensity region, however, the net effect of the change in policy position is to increase the relative contributions to the candidate on the left, so the probability of that candidate's winning increases. That party thus has an incentive to move away from the median. Recall that the candidates not only have preferences for winning but also have a disutility of providing services. Candidate 2 is willing to have a lower probability of winning because he can offer significantly fewer services.

To show that locating at the extremes can be a Nash policy equilibrium, it is necessary to show that a global service equilibrium exists for every unilateral deviation from those positions and that the properties of

w characterized by the claim holds globally. Under the same set of parameter values as in Figure 6, $\alpha_1 = 0$ and $\alpha_2 = 1$ are a Nash equilibrium. These parameter values yield $\rho^D = 0.0959$ and $\delta_d^{c_d} = 0.5$. To show $\bar{\alpha}_2 = 1$ is a best response to $\bar{\alpha}_1 = 0$, the response of w to changes in α_2 must be evaluated numerically. As α_2 decreases to $\frac{1}{2}$, party 1's equilibrium probability of winning, w, is strictly increasing to 0.7612; that is, the claim holds globally. A Type III global service equilibrium also exists for every unilateral deviation from (0, 1).

7.2   Parties with policy preferences

In the case where parties also have policy preferences ($k > 0$), interior policy equilibria can exist. The following proposition identifies which symmetric policy positions can be a policy equilibrium.

Proposition 8.   *When $k > 0$, for a symmetric policy pair $(\bar{\alpha}_1, \bar{\alpha}_2)$ with a Type I symmetric global service equilibrium to be a policy equilibrium, the policy positions must be between the median and the party ideal points. The same applies for a symmetric pair with a Type III symmetric global service equilibrium if the parameter values are outside the intense competition region. In the intense competition region, for a symmetric pair with a Type III symmetric global service equilibrium, a necessary condition is that the policy positions be farther from the median than are the respective party ideal points.*

Proof: An equilibrium location $(\bar{\alpha}_1, \bar{\alpha}_2)$ satisfies the following first-order conditions from (1) and (2), where w is substituted for $f(\cdot)$:

$$\frac{\partial w}{\partial \alpha_1}(v - k(\alpha_1 - \alpha_1^o)^2) - 2kw(\alpha_1 - \alpha_1^o) + k(\alpha_2 - \alpha_1^o)^2 \frac{\partial w}{\partial \alpha_1} = 0; \tag{46}$$

$$-\frac{\partial w}{\partial \alpha_2}(v - k(\alpha_2 - \alpha_2^o)^2) + 2wk(\alpha_2 - \alpha_2^o) - k(\alpha_1 - \alpha_2^o)^2 \frac{\partial w}{\partial \alpha_2} = 0. \tag{47}$$

Noting that $\partial w/\partial \alpha_1 > 0$ and $\partial w/\partial \alpha_2 > 0$ for a policy pair with a Type I global service equilibrium, and that $k(\alpha_2 - \alpha_1^o)^2 - k(\alpha_1 - \alpha_1^o)^2 + v > 0$ in (46) and $k(\alpha_2 - \alpha_2^o)^2 - k(\alpha_1 - \alpha_2^o)^2 - v < 0$ in (47), it is clear that only $\alpha_1 > \alpha_1^o$ and $\alpha_2 < \alpha_2^o$ can satisfy both first-order conditions. The result is analogous for a symmetric policy pair with a Type III symmetric global service equilibrium. $\square$

To interpret this result, consider first the case in which realignment is costly – that is, the policy distance cost c_d is large, so that ρ is smaller than ρ^D (unless the policy positions are very close). The contributions equilibrium then is of Type I, and the equilibrium policy positions are between the ideal points of the parties and the median. Thus, when the two parties' ideal points are apart, their election platforms are closer to the median. This results because as long as the contributions equilibrium is of Type I the contributions p_i remain constant as the party policy moves toward the median. That policy movement, however, allows the candidate to obtain contributions from more interest groups.

When the policy distance cost is small, so that $\rho > \rho^D$ and realignment is not costly, the contributions equilibrium is of Type III. If the parameter values are in the intense competition region, electoral incentives widen their policy differences; that is, the parties' policy positions differ by more than do their ideal points. This results because parties have incentives to improve their bargaining power relative to interest groups. Consequently, party positions can differ by more or less than the difference in their ideal points. Ouside the intense competition region, the results are the same as for a Type I equilibrium.

To characterize further the policy equilibrium, consider the case where the policy equilibrium has a Type I symmetric global service equilibrium.

Proposition 9. *When $k > 0$ and $\alpha_1^o + \alpha_2^o = 1$, a symmetric policy equilibrium with a Type I symmetric global service equilibrium satisfies*

$$\bar{\alpha}_1 = \frac{v + k(1 + 6\alpha_1^o + 2c_p\alpha_1^o)}{k(4(2 - \alpha_1^o) + 2c_p)}. \tag{48}$$

Proof: For a symmetric policy equilibrium (α_1, α_2), $\alpha_1 + \alpha_2 = 1$, $\bar{a} = \frac{1}{2}$, and $f = \frac{1}{2}$. Substituting these in (43) and (44) yields $\partial w / \partial \alpha_1 = 1/(6 + 2c_p)$. Substituting this expression into (46) and using $\alpha_2 = 1 - \alpha_1$ and $f = \frac{1}{2}$ yields (48). $\qquad\square$

The policy positions in (48) are a Nash equilibrium if every unilateral deviation from the equilibrium policy positions results in a Type I global service equilibrium. Conditions for this are provided in the appendix. Comparative statics properties are straightforward and are summarized in the following proposition.

Proposition 10. *The equilibrium policy position, $\bar{\alpha}_1$, in (48) is*

(a) *an increasing function of v,*
(b) *an increasing function of α_1^o, and*
(c) *a decreasing function of k.*

The effect of the parameter c_p is ambiguous.

Consequently, the policy position $\bar{\alpha}_1$ is positively responsive to the party's ideal point. The policy position is also increasing in the value v of winning, and as policy preferences become stronger (i.e., k larger), the policy moves toward the party's ideal point.

As an example, if $\alpha_1^o = 0$ and $\alpha_2^o = 1$ then

$$\bar{\alpha}_1 = \frac{1}{8+2c_p}\frac{v+k}{k} \quad \text{and} \quad \bar{\alpha}_2 = 1 - \frac{1}{8+2c_p}\frac{v+k}{k}. \tag{49}$$

For this to be an equilibrium, it must have a Type I global service equilibrium; that is, ρ must be sufficiently smaller than ρ^D:

$$\rho = \delta_d^{c_d|\bar{\alpha}_2 - \bar{\alpha}_1|} < \rho^D.$$

This requires that

$$\frac{v+k}{k} < (4+c_p)\left(1 - \frac{\ln \rho^D}{c_d \ln \delta_d}\right). \tag{50}$$

A necessary condition is that[29] $v/k < 3 + c_p$, and if c_d becomes large then this is a sufficient condition. Consequently, if the value v of office relative to the cost k of a policy deviation is not too large, the policy positions in (49) are an equilibrium.

8   Conclusions

Electoral competition is a complex process involving parties, their candidates, contributors, and voters. The strategic interactions among them involve the taking of policy positions, the promise of constituency services, and bargaining between political contributors and candidates. The model represents voters' strategies by a reduced form, whereas the strategies of parties, candidates, and contributors are explicitly modeled. Preferences are also complex and may involve more than just winning the election. In addition to preferences for services, the benefits to interest groups of those services can depend on the policy positions of the candidate's party. Candidates are assumed to have preferences for being in office, but incur a cost when they provide services. Parties are assumed to have preferences both for winning and for policy positions.

An equilibrium identifies the contributions made by the interest groups, which interest groups contribute to which candidates, the services provided by candidates, and the policy positions chosen by parties. Conditions are presented for there to be a symmetric equilibrium in which parties choose policy positions that are separated. The equilibrium reflects

---

[29] This condition is also necessary for the policy positions to be in the appropriate halves of the policy interval [0, 1].

the basic incentives present in electoral competition. Parties have incentives to choose policy positions toward the median in order to position their candidates to attract more contributors. Candidates have incentives to offer services to garner campaign contributions. Interest groups, however, can contribute to either candidate, so they have a degree of bargaining power. If parties choose positions close to the median of the policy space, interest groups can realign at low cost, which gives them bargaining power. There is thus an ex ante incentive for parties to choose policy positions that are separated so as to increase the costs of realignment. This in turn strengthens the bargaining power of the candidate relative to the interest groups and allows the candidate to generate more campaign contributions. Electoral competition thus can provide an incentive to move toward the median to attract more contributors, as well as an incentive to move away from the median so as to generate more contributions from interest groups. Equilibria, when they exist, reflect the relative strengths of these two competing incentives.

The equilibria also reflect the policy preferences of the parties and the value of winning. In a symmetric equilibrium in which the bargaining equilibrium between candidates and interest groups is of Type I, the parties choose a policy position between their ideal point and the median. This type of equilibrium occurs when parties have extreme ideal points or when the realignment cost parameter is high. When that is not the case and the bargaining equilibrium is of Type III, the parties choose equilibrium policy positions that are more extreme than their ideal points if the parameter values are in the intense competition region. If the parties care only about winning and the realignment cost is high, then the parties move toward the median. As they do, however, their bargaining power in the limit disappears as in Bertrand competition. The theory thus endogenously identifies the relative market power of candidates and interest groups and identifies how that distribution of power affects policy positions and campaign contributions. In the typology presented in Figure 1, the theory exhibits the behavior anticipated in each of the cells.

Appendix

Relative to benchmark positions, the Type I equilibrium policy positions as in (48) are located in the policy space as follows: $(0, \alpha_1^o, \bar{\alpha}_1, \alpha_1^D, \frac{1}{2}, \alpha_2^D, \bar{\alpha}_2, \alpha_2^o, 1)$. Conditions are provided next under which, with α_1 fixed at $\bar{\alpha}_1$, all positions of candidate 1 (i.e., $\alpha_2 \in [\frac{1}{2}, 1]$) result in a Type I global service equilibrium. At the equilibrium policy positions, $w = \frac{1}{2}$, $q_1 = q_2$, and $\rho < \rho^D = \rho^* = \rho^{**}$, so it must be determined how local service equilibria change as α_2 deviates from $\bar{\alpha}_2$.

Since the expressions for ρ^* and ρ^{**} change according to the sign of $w\bar{q}_1 - (1-w)\bar{q}_2$, that sign must be characterized in terms of α_2. For this purpose, define

$$G(\alpha_2) \equiv \frac{w\bar{q}_1}{(1-w)\bar{q}_2}.$$

When $\alpha_2 = \bar{\alpha}_2$, $G = 1$. Note that from (28) and (30), $\partial G/\partial \alpha_2 = (\partial G/\partial \bar{a}) \times (\partial \bar{a}/\partial \alpha_2)$. From Proposition 6, $\partial \bar{a}/\partial \alpha_2 > 0$. Substituting the expressions for $w/(1-w)$ from (30) and those for $\bar{q}_1/\bar{q}_2$ from (29), G can be expressed as $(1 - \bar{a} + 1/2c_p)/(\bar{a} + 1/2c_p)$, so

$$\frac{\partial G}{\partial \bar{a}} = -\frac{4c_p(c_p + 1)}{(2c_p\bar{a} + 1)^2} < 0.$$

Therefore, $G(\alpha_2)$ is a strictly decreasing function of α_2 with $G(\bar{\alpha}_2) = 1$. When α_2 increases from $\bar{\alpha}_2$, ρ decreases and G decreases below 1. When $G < 1$, $\rho^* = G\rho^D$ and

$$\rho^{**} = \frac{\sqrt{((1-\gamma)(1+\delta_\tau))^2 G^2 + 4\gamma\delta_\tau(1+\delta_\tau - \gamma)} - (1-\gamma)(1+\delta_\tau)G}{2\gamma(1+\delta_\tau - \gamma)}.$$

So, as G decreases, ρ^* decreases and ρ^{**} increases.[30] It can be shown that as α_2 increases, ρ decreases faster than ρ^*. Therefore $(\bar{\alpha}_1, \alpha_2)$, where $\alpha_2 \in (\bar{\alpha}_2, 1]$, results in a Type I global service equilibrium.[31] If α_2 decreases from $\bar{\alpha}_2$, G increases above 1. When $G > 1$, $\rho^* = \rho^D/G$ and

$$\rho^{**} = \frac{\sqrt{((1-\gamma)(1+\delta_\tau))^2 G^{-2} + 4\gamma\delta_\tau(1+\delta_\tau - \gamma)} - (1-\gamma)(1+\delta_\tau)G^{-1}}{2\gamma(1+\delta_\tau - \gamma)}.$$

So as α_2 decreases, G increases, ρ^* decreases, and ρ^{**} increases. Thus, there exists an α_2^* such that $\rho = \delta_d^{c_d|\alpha_2^* - \bar{\alpha}_1|} = \rho^D/G = \rho^*$. That is,

$$\alpha_2^* = \bar{\alpha}_1 + \frac{\ln(\rho^D/G)}{c_d \ln \delta_d}.$$

It is straightforward to show that a local service equilibrium at $(\bar{\alpha}_1, \alpha_2^*)$ is not a global equilibrium (see Baron and Mo 1991, apx. E). To ensure that there exists a global equilibrium for all α_2, a condition such that α_2^* is sufficiently smaller than $\frac{1}{2}$ is needed. This condition is not hard to satisfy

---

[30] To see this, differentiate to obtain

$$\frac{\partial \rho^{**}}{\partial G} = \frac{(1-\gamma)(1+\delta_\tau)}{(2\gamma(1+\delta_\tau - \gamma))^2} \frac{(1-\gamma)(1+\delta_\tau)G - \sqrt{((1-\gamma)(1+\delta_\tau))^2 G^2 + 4\gamma\delta_\tau(1+\delta_\tau - \gamma)}}{\sqrt{((1-\gamma)(1+\delta_\tau))^2 G^2 + 4\gamma\delta_\tau(1+\delta_\tau - \gamma)}} < 0.$$

[31] That these deviations result in a global service equilibrium can only be shown numerically. Intuitively, the equilibrium must be global because, as α_2 increases, ρ decreases.

because G does not depend on c_d and δ_d; α_2^* can be very small, even close to $\bar{\alpha}_1$ for very small δ_d or very large c_d. The comparable results for the policy equilibria of Type III service and contributions equilibria cannot be established analytically. Policy equilibria cannot be characterized in closed form, nor can existence conditions be explicitly provided. However, one condition under which Type III symmetric policy positions are a Nash equilibrium (i.e., the claim holds globally and every unilateral deviation from the equilibrium positions results in a global service equilibrium) can be illustrated. Relative to the benchmark positions, when the parameter values are in the intensity region, Type III equilibrium policy positions $(\bar{\alpha}_1, \bar{\alpha}_2)$ are located as follows: (1) when $\delta_d^{c_d} < \rho^D$, the locations are $(0, \alpha_1^D, \bar{\alpha}_1, \alpha_1^o, \frac{1}{2}, \alpha_2^o, \bar{\alpha}_2, \alpha_2^D, 1)$; (2) when $\delta_d^{c_d} > \rho^D$, the locations are $(0, \bar{\alpha}_1, \alpha_1^o, \frac{1}{2}, \alpha_2^o, \bar{\alpha}_2, 1)$. The first case is hard to analyze, but the second case is more tractable. An example has been presented in which $(0, 1)$ is a Nash equilibrium and every unilateral deviation in a policy results in a Type III global service equilibrium (see the discussion preceding Proposition 7). Since there are incentives in these Type III equilibria for the parties to locate farther from the median, and since it is the parties' policy preferences that sustain interior symmetric policy positions as equilibria, $(0, 1)$ can be a policy equilibrium if the parties' policy preferences are sufficiently weak – that is, if k is small.

REFERENCES

Austen-Smith, David (1987), "Interest Groups, Campaign Contributions, and Probabilistic Voting," *Public Choice* 54: 123-39.
Baron, David P. (1989a), "Service-Induced Campaign Contributions and the Electoral Equilibrium," *Quarterly Journal of Economics* 104: 45-72.
    (1989b), "Service-Induced Campaign Contributions, Incumbent Shirking, and Reelection Opportunities," in P. Ordeshook (ed.), *Models of Strategic Choice in Politics*. Ann Arbor: University of Michigan Press.
Baron, David P., and Jongryn Mo (1991), "Campaign Contributions and Party-Candidate Competition in Services and Policies," Research Paper no. 1151, Graduate School of Business, Stanford University.
Bester, Helmut (1989), "Noncooperative Bargaining and Spatial Competition," *Econometrica* 57: 97-113.
Black, Duncan (1958), *Theory of Committees and Elections*. Cambridge: Cambridge University Press.
Brock, William, and Stephen Magee (1978), "The Economics of Special Interest Politics: The Case of the Tariff," *American Economic Review* 68: 246-50.
Cameron, Charles M., and James M. Enelow (1989), "Asymmetric Policy Effects, Campaign Contributions, and the Spatial Theory of Elections," Working Paper, Department of Political Science, Columbia University, New York.
Chappell, Henry (1982), "Campaign Contributions and Congressional Voting: A Simultaneous Probit-Tobit Model," *Review of Economics and Statistics* 62: 77-83.

Edelman, Susan (1989), "Campaign Contributions and Political Action," Dissertation, Stanford University.

Fiorina, Morris P. (1989), *Congress: Keystone of the Washington Establishment,* 2nd ed. New Haven, CT: Yale University Press.

Hinich, Melvin, and Michael Munger (1989), "Political Investment, Voter Perceptions, and Candidate Strategy: An Equilibrium Spatial Anslysis," in P. Ordeshook (ed.), *Models of Strategic Choice in Politics.* Ann Arbor: University of Michigan Press.

Ledyard, John (1984), "The Pure Theory of Large Two Candidate Elections," *Public Choice* 44: 7–41.

Mayhew, David R. (1974), *Congress: The Electoral Connection.* New Haven, CT: Yale University Press.

McKelvey, Richard, and Peter Ordeshook (1985), "Elections with Limited Information: A Fulfilled Expectations Model Using Contemporaneous Poll and Endogenous Data as Information Sources," *Journal of Economic Theory* 36: 55–85.

Morton, Rebecca, and Charles Cameron (1991), "Elections and the Theory of Campaign Contributions: A Survey and Critical Analysis," *Economics and Politics* 4: 79–108.

Osborne, Martin J., and Ariel Rubinstein (1990), *Bargaining and Markets.* San Diego: Academic Press.

Poole, Keith T., and Thomas Romer (1985), "Patterns of Political Action Committee Contributions to the 1980 Campaigns for the United States House of Representatives," *Public Choice* 47: 63–111.

Rothenberg, Lawrence (1990), "Interest Group Influence and Public Policy," Mimeo, University of Rochester, New York.

Rubinstein, A. (1982), "Perfect Equilibrium in a Bargaining Model," *Econometrica* 50: 97–109.

Shaked, A., and J. Sutton (1984), "Involuntary Unemployment as a Perfect Equilibrium in a Bargaining Model," *Econometrica* 52: 1351–64.

Snyder, James M. (1990a), "Campaign Contributions as Investments: The U.S. House of Representatives 1980–1986," *Journal of Political Economy* 98: 1195–1227.

(1990b), "The Market for Campaign Contributions: Evidence for the U.S. Senate 1980–1986," Working Paper, Department of Economics, University of Chicago.

(1991), "On Buying Legislatures," *Economics and Politics* 3: 93–109.

Wilhite, Allen, and John Theilmann (1987), "Labor PAC Contributions and Labor Legislation: A Simultaneous Logit Approach," *Public Choice* 53: 267–76.

Wright, John (1990), "Contributions, Lobbying, and Committee Voting in the U.S. House of Representatives," *American Political Science Review* 84: 417–38.

CHAPTER 14

Polarization, incumbency, and the personal vote

John Londregan and Thomas Romer

1   Introduction

Many observers have noted the rising importance since the late 1950s of constituent services or the "personal vote" for U.S. congressional politics. For example, Cain, Ferejohn, and Fiorina (1987) find that constituency attentiveness became a more important source of positive evaluations of congressmen between 1958 and 1978. In addition, in 1978 constituents were twice as likely to recall a legislator's work on local problems and projects as they were to recall his or her overall legislative record. In 1958 the two probabilities were more nearly even. Paralleling these observations are those of Alford and Brady (1988) and Gelman and King (1990), who have charted the importance of the incumbency advantage. They show that this advantage increased considerably from the 1950s to the 1980s.

Poole and Rosenthal (1984) discuss the history of polarization in Senate roll-call voting since the mid-1950s. They note an increase in spatial separation between the parties. In Poole and Rosenthal (1991), using a different scaling technique on House roll calls, they again note an increase in distance between the party centroids starting in the 1960s.[1]

We address these observations by developing a model that is a variant of the oft-used probabilistic model of spatial voting. Our model has some

This chapter is a revised version of a paper presented at the Political Economy Conference, Washington University, St. Louis, Mo., May 23-25, 1991. We thank Barry Nalebuff, Mary Olson, and Howard Rosenthal for helpful comments, and David Brady for providing the election data. A preliminary version of some of this material was presented at the Public Choice Society meetings, Tucson, Ariz., March 16-17, 1990. The Center for the Study of Public Policy at Carnegie Mellon University provided research support.

[1]   Although on the increase, the polarization between the parties by the early 1980s is still small compared to that of a century earlier (Poole and Rosenthal 1991, fig. 9). Poole and Rosenthal (1984, fig. 5) also find that the gap between Republican and Democratic senators from the same state declined from 1968 to 1980.

elements in common with those of Wittman (1977, 1983) and others, in that candidates represent parties with divergent policy preferences. At the same time, we assume that voters' evaluation of candidates depends not only on the candidates' location on a policy dimension, but also on a nonpolicy dimension. In this respect, our approach resembles (but is not equivalent to) those of Enelow and Hinich (1982) and Cukierman (1991). We interpret the nonpolicy dimension as measuring a personal characteristic of candidates, such as "ability to deliver the goods" or constituent services. We assume that all voters agree that, independent of policy position, more of this ability is better than less. So while there is disagreement among voters on policy issues, there is consensus on the service dimension. In this regard, our formulation also recalls Stokes's (1963) "position" and "valence" dimensions.

Uncertainty plays an important role in our analysis. At the time that candidates for an open seat are nominated, parties have only a noisy signal about candidates' service provision abilities. The campaign provides voters information about the ability variable. (For example, think of the campaign as telling voters about which candidate "really cares" or which candidate has a more effective organization.)

The ex ante uncertainty about what voters will learn during the campaign about candidates' abilities leaves the parties uncertain about electoral response to their candidates at the time the policy platforms are selected. Unlike many models of probabilistic voting, our framework explicitly links the uncertainty faced by parties to the voters' optimizing behavior.[2]

As with the standard probabilistic voting models in which the two parties have policy preferences, our model predicts that candidate locations will diverge in a 1-dimensional (left–right) policy space. But this polarization is related to parties' uncertainty about how voters will evaluate candidates' abilities to deliver constituent services, rather than to the parties' uncertainty about turnout or the location of the pivotal voter's ideal point.

Moreover, for a given distribution of voter ideal points on the policy dimension, the more weight voters place on the consensus "service" dimension, the greater the degree of polarization. To be more precise, we find that the set of policy platform pairs that could be Nash equilibria moves farther from the pivotal voter's ideal point, the greater is the relative importance of the consensus dimension. In a sense, then, increasing weight on the service variable leads to increasing the spread between candidates on policy issues.

[2] Although – unlike Ledyard (1984), who does make this link in a model with purely policy-oriented voting and office-motivated candidates – we do not address turnout issues.

We also investigate the case when one of the candidates is an incumbent whose ability and platform position are known and fixed. Again, we find that increasing weight on the service dimension favors the incumbent's party, in the sense of according a higher ex ante expected utility, and it can lead to increasing the gap between challenger and incumbent positions on the policy dimension.

In the next section we present our analytical framework. We then go on to a preliminary empirical analysis, using data from the 1978 National Election Study survey.

2 Two-party competition with service

We assume that there is a continuum of voters indexed by $\beta \in [\beta_0, \beta^0]$, where $\beta_0 < 0$ and $\beta^0 > 1$. Let $F(x)$ be the cumulative density function of voters' types. We normalize this density so that $F(\beta^0) = 1$, and assume that all voters cast ballots. Let β^μ be the median β, with $\beta^\mu \in (0, 1)$. There are two political parties, each of which selects a platform $\pi \in \mathbb{R}$ and a candidate to represent that platform. A candidate is indexed by $\alpha \in \mathbb{R}$. We think of π as representing candidate location on a policy dimension, and of α as a "quality" or "ability" index.[3]

Payoffs to the voters depend on both the post-election policy outcome and on the quality of constituent services provided by the winning candidate. Quality of post-election services is a function of the candidate's ability α. A voter of type β values an officeholder of type (π, α) according to

$$V(\pi, \alpha; \beta, \gamma) = -d(\beta, \pi) + \gamma g(\alpha), \tag{1}$$

where $d(a, b)$ is an increasing, continuously differentiable, convex function of the distance between positions a and b, with $d(a, a) = 0$ and $d(0, 1) = 1$. Let $\partial d(a, b)/\partial a = d_1(a, b)$ and $\partial d(a, b)/\partial b = d_2(a, b)$. Note that $d_2(a, b) > 0$ for $b > a$ and $d_2(a, b) < 0$ for $b < a$. By continuity, $d_2(a, a) = 0$.

The parameter γ calibrates the intensity with which a voter cares about the provision of constituent services, where the level of services $g(\alpha)$ is an increasing function of a candidate's ability level α. In what follows, we assume that all voters have the same γ parameter (with $\gamma > 0$) and face the same $g(\alpha)$, while their β values are heterogeneous.[4]

---

[3] Alternatively, we could think of each candidate being indexed by the vector $(\pi, \alpha) \in \mathbb{R}^2$.

[4] This characterization of voter preferences is quite similar to that used in Enelow and Hinich (1982). They examine a model in which neither candidates nor parties have policy preferences, and thus in equilibrium converge on the policy dimension (though usually not to the median of voters' spatial ideal points). Cukierman (1991) also adopts a similar specification of voter preferences. Candidates differ in ability but have no policy preferences. In

Candidates for election represent platforms selected by two political parties, the Left Party (henceforth L) and the Right Party (R). Payoffs to the parties depend only on the policy actually implemented after the election. For party j ($j = L, R$) the payoff is given by $-d(\theta^j, \pi)$, where θ^j is the ideal point of party j.[5] These ideal points[6] are $\theta^L = 0$ and $\theta^R = 1$.

Each candidate, if successful, is assumed to implement the party platform after the election. We thus do not model candidates' preferences directly. The candidates play the role of passive instruments in this analysis.

2.1   Open-seat contests

We begin with an election in which there is no incumbent running. At the beginning of the game (i.e., prior to the election campaign), each party observes a signal of a candidate's ability. (This may come from the candidate's record of prior public service, business background, party activism, etc.) Each party then selects one candidate to nominate. Label π_j the policy position of the candidate chosen by party $j \in \{L, R\}$.

The election campaign provides information to voters about the candidates' abilities. Such signals may come from the effectiveness of the campaign itself, the apparent credibility of the candidate, and so forth. To simplify the analysis, we will suppose that by the end of the campaign and immediately before the election, voters are able to infer perfectly the ability levels of the candidates. Moreover, all voters make the same assessments. So the abilities of the two candidates, as perceived by voters at the time of the election, are given by $\{\alpha_L, \alpha_R\}$, which has joint density $\phi(\alpha_L, \alpha_R)$ and cumulative density $\Phi(\alpha_L, \alpha_R)$. We assume that $\Phi_1(\alpha_L, \alpha_R) > 0$ and $\Phi_2(\alpha_L, \alpha_R) > 0$ everywhere on the support of Φ.

Each voter then casts one vote for her most preferred candidate (abstention is ruled out). The candidate preferred by the majority is elected. Notice that the voters possess more information about the candidates when they cast their ballots than the parties have at the time platforms are selected. In choosing platforms, however, parties take into account the

---

his model, voters gain information about candidate ability during the campaign by means of polls. Cukierman does not analyze the effects on equilibrium candidate positions that result from changes in the weight voters place on the nonpolicy dimension.

[5] As we point out in note 9, adding a term to capture a party's utility for being in office would not affect our results.

[6] Placement of the parties' most-preferred policies at 0 and 1 is somewhat arbitrary. What is essential to the rest of the analysis is that θ^L and θ^R are both interior to the support of $F(\cdot)$ – so that there are some voters who are more extreme than each party – and that the party ideal points are on opposite sides of the median voter's most preferred policy: $\theta^L < \beta^\mu < \theta^R$.

fact that voters will cast their ballots on the basis of updated information about candidates' abilities.[7]

Given issue positions π_L and π_R and a realization of (α_L, α_R), a voter with ideal point β will vote for party L if

$$\gamma[g(\alpha_R) - g(\alpha_L)] < d(\beta, \pi_R) - d(\beta, \pi_L). \tag{2}$$

The RHS of (2) is monotone in β. Thus, for $\pi_L < \pi_R$, if voter β' votes for party L's candidate then so will voters with $\beta < \beta'$.[8] With this in mind, we can express the ex ante probability that party L's candidate wins the election in terms of the probability that the voter with median ideal point on the issue dimension β^μ casts her vote for the L candidate.

Let

$$q(\pi_L, \pi_R; \beta^\mu, \gamma) \equiv \Pr\{V(\pi_L, \alpha_L; \beta^\mu, \gamma) > V(\pi_R, \alpha_R; \beta^\mu, \gamma) \,|\, (\pi_L, \pi_R)\}$$

$$= \Pr\{g(\alpha_R) - g(\alpha_L) < [d(\beta^\mu, \pi_R) - d(\beta^\mu, \pi_L)]/\gamma\}.$$

Define the random variable $\delta \equiv g(\alpha_R) - g(\alpha_L)$. We can think of δ as the effective ability gap between the two candidates. For invertible $g(\cdot)$, the density of δ, $h(\delta)$, is given by

$$h(\delta) = \int_{-\infty}^{\infty} \phi[w, g^{-1}(g(w) + \delta)] \,|g^{-1\prime}[g(w) + \delta]| \, dw.$$

Denote the cumulative density of δ by $H(\delta)$.

For each pair of policy platforms (π_L, π_R) and for each set of voter preferences (β^μ, γ), there is a value δ^* of the ability gap that leaves the median voter just indifferent between the two candidates. The function $\delta^*(\pi_L, \pi_R; \beta^\mu, \gamma)$ is then defined implicitly by

$$\delta^*(\pi_L, \pi_R; \beta^\mu, \gamma) = [d(\beta^\mu, \pi_R) - d(\beta^\mu, \pi_L)]/\gamma. \tag{3}$$

We can express the ex ante probability of a party L victory – that is, the pre-campaign probability that voter β^μ casts her ballot for party L's candidate – as

$$q(\pi_L, \pi_R; \beta^\mu, \gamma) = H(\delta^*(\pi_L, \pi_R; \beta^\mu, \gamma)) = \int_{-\infty}^{\delta^*(\pi_L, \pi_R; \beta^\mu, \gamma)} h(\delta) \, d\delta. \tag{4}$$

Hence

$$q_{\pi_L}(\pi_L, \pi_R; \beta^\mu, \gamma) = H'(\delta^*(\pi_L, \pi_R; \beta^\mu, \gamma)) \delta^*_{\pi_L}(\pi_L, \pi_R; \beta^\mu, \gamma),$$

where $q_{\pi_L} \equiv \partial q(\cdot)/\partial \pi_L$ and $\delta^*_{\pi_L}(\cdot) \equiv \partial \delta^*(\cdot)/\partial \pi_L$.

---

[7] We assume that neither voters nor parties take into account the prospect that the winner of the open-seat election may run as an incumbent in a later election.

[8] Similarly, if $\pi_L > \pi_R$, then if voter β'' votes for party L's candidate, so will voters with $\beta > \beta''$. As we show in what follows, choosing $\pi_L > \pi_R$ is a dominated strategy for party L.

From (3), we have

$$\delta^*_{\pi_L}(\pi_L, \pi_R; \beta^\mu, \gamma) = -d_2(\beta^\mu, \pi_L)/\gamma.$$

Thus,

$$q_{\pi_L}(\pi_L, \pi_R; \beta^\mu, \gamma) = -H'(\delta^*(\pi_L, \pi_R; \beta^\mu, \gamma))d_2(\beta^\mu, \pi_L)/\gamma. \qquad (5)$$

If $\pi_L < \beta^\mu$ then $q_{\pi_L}(\pi_L, \pi_R; \beta^\mu, \gamma) > 0$, so that, as the left-wing candidate's platform approaches the median ideal point from the left, the probability of a party L victory increases. Likewise, this probability increases as the policy advocated by the right-wing candidate moves away and to the right of β^μ; that is, $q_{\pi_R}(\pi_L, \pi_R; \beta^\mu, \gamma) > 0$ if $\pi_R > \beta^\mu$.

We denote by $U(\pi_L, \pi_R; \theta^j, \beta^\mu, \gamma)$ the expected utility of party j after the two parties have nominated their candidates, but before the campaign begins: [9]

$$U(\pi_L, \pi_R; \theta^j, \beta^\mu, \gamma) = -q(\pi_L, \pi_R; \beta^\mu, \gamma)d(\theta^j, \pi_L)$$
$$-[1 - q(\pi_L, \pi_R; \beta^\mu, \gamma)]d(\theta^j, \pi_R). \qquad (6)$$

Let $U_{\pi_L} \equiv \partial U(\cdot)/\partial \pi_L$. Then

$$U_{\pi_L}(\pi_L, \pi_R; 0, \beta^\mu, \gamma) = -d_2(0, \pi_L)q(\pi_L, \pi_R; \beta^\mu, \gamma)$$
$$+[d(0, \pi_R) - d(0, \pi_L)]q_{\pi_L}(\pi_L, \pi_R; \beta^\mu, \gamma).$$

Note first that $\pi_L > \pi_R$ is a dominated strategy for party L for any $\pi_R \geq 0$. (If $\pi_L > \pi_R \geq 0$, then party L is better off having party R in office.) For $\pi_R \geq \pi_L > \beta^\mu$, $U_{\pi_L}(\pi_L, \pi_R; 0, \beta^\mu, \gamma) < 0$, since $q_{\pi_L}(\pi_L, \pi_R; \beta^\mu, \gamma) < 0$. Moreover, $q_{\pi_L}(\beta^\mu, \pi_R; \beta^\mu, \gamma) = 0$ because $d_2(\beta^\mu, \beta^\mu) = 0$, so that $U_{\pi_L}(\beta^\mu, \pi_R; 0, \beta^\mu, \gamma) < 0$ for all π_R. Therefore, $\pi_L \in [0, \beta^\mu)$ for all π_R, γ. Similarly, we can show that $\pi_R \in (\beta^\mu, 1]$ for all π_L, γ. (In fact, except in special cases, we will have $\pi_L \in (0, \beta^\mu)$ and $\pi_R \in (\beta^\mu, 1).$[10]) This establishes the following proposition.

[9] If, in addition to policy, each party cares about holding office, then the RHS of (6) should account for this as well. A standard way to do this is by letting $W > 0$ represent the utility of holding office, and adding a term qW to the expected utility for party L and a term $(1 - q)W$ to the expected utility for party R. None of our qualitative results changes with this modification, though we would have an extra parameter to carry around. Although party platforms would still be separated in equilibrium, with $W > 0$ each party would locate closer to β^μ than with $W = 0$.

[10] $U_{\pi_L}(0, \pi_R; 0, \beta^\mu, \gamma) = d(0, \pi_R)q_{\pi_L}(0, \pi_R; \beta^\mu, \gamma)$, which is positive, except possibly when π_R is such that $q(0, \pi_R; \beta^\mu, \gamma) = 1$. In other words, a necessary condition for $\pi_L = 0$ to be a best response is that $q(0, \pi_R; \beta^\mu, \gamma) = 1$. So, unless party L is guaranteed to win the election when its candidate locates at $\pi_L = 0$ (and even then, this need not be an equilibrium), we will not see it advocating its policy ideal point. A similar result holds for party R.

Proposition 1. *In an open-seat contest, no pure strategy equilibrium candidate locations in the policy dimension exist such that* $\pi_R \in [0, \beta^{\mu}]$ *or* $\pi_L \in [\beta^{\mu}, 1]$; *thus, no equilibrium exists in which the parties nominate candidates who advocate the same policy platform.*

As in other probabilistic voting models of electoral competition with candidates having policy preferences (e.g. Wittman 1977, 1983), the parties will not choose candidates whose policies converge.[11]

Although it is easy to show that the parties will not converge in equilibrium, placing a lower bound on the policy wedge between them takes more work. Divergence in party platforms in our model depends on both the divergence of party policy preferences and the willingness of voters to sacrifice proximity on the spatial ("issue") dimension for greater service provision ability.[12]

For relatively simple structures (such as that used in the example below: α_L and α_R i.i.d. and uniform; linear $g(\cdot)$; quadratic $d(\cdot)$), the gap between the candidate platforms in equilibrium can be shown to be increasing in γ, as long as it is not optimal for at least one candidate to locate at his party's ideal point.

More generally, we can show that the intensity of voter preferences in the nonpolicy dimension (as calibrated by γ) polarizes the party issue platforms. In equilibrium, the distance between the platforms on the policy dimension is bounded below by an increasing function of the degree to which the voters care about the nonpolicy dimension.

More concretely, in the appendix we establish the next proposition.

Proposition 2. *In equilibrium, π_L and π_R will lie outside an interval $[\bar{\pi}_L(\gamma), \bar{\pi}_R(\gamma)]$ that contains β^{μ}, with $\pi_L \leq \bar{\pi}_L(\gamma)$ and $\pi_R \geq \bar{\pi}_R(\gamma)$. Moreover, $\bar{\pi}'_L(\gamma) < 0$ for $\bar{\pi}_L(\gamma) > 0$ and $\bar{\pi}'_R(\gamma) > 0$ for $\bar{\pi}_R(\gamma) < 1$.*

This proposition implies that, if voters become more service-motivated (as measured by an increase in γ), the interval on the policy dimension in which candidates will *not* locate becomes larger. In this sense, then, an increase in the weight voters place on the candidates' personal attributes

---

[11] In our model, unlike most standard probabilistic voting models, the probabilities of electoral victory are endogenous. For conditions guaranteeing existence of equilibrium, see the appendix.

[12] Although we focus on the effects of changes in γ, these shifts need not occur because of a change in voter preferences. Shifts in $g(\cdot)$ would have qualitatively similar effects, by changing the weight accorded the ability dimension. Changes in $g(\cdot)$ might come about because of improvements in the technology of providing constituent services (computers, communications, advertising, office management, etc.).

(as opposed to policy positions) leads to an increase in the polarization between the parties, as measured by the distance between their candidates' policy positions.

2.2   An example

The following example illustrates the impact of the salience of personal services on the divergence of candidates in policy space. Suppose that a voter's utility function is given by $V(\pi, \alpha; \beta, \gamma) = -(\beta - \pi)^2 + \gamma\alpha$. Let $\beta^\mu = 1/2$, so that the utility function of the median voter is given by

$$V(\pi, \alpha; 1/2, \gamma) = -(1/2 - \pi)^2 + \gamma\alpha.$$

The median voter prefers the party L candidate (who therefore wins the election) whenever

$$-(1/2 - \pi_R)^2 + \gamma\alpha_R < -(1/2 - \pi_L)^2 + \gamma\alpha_L,$$

that is, whenever

$$\delta = \alpha_R - \alpha_L < \delta^*(\pi_L, \pi_R; 1/2, \gamma) = [(1/2 - \pi_R)^2 - (1/2 - \pi_L)^2]/\gamma.$$

Assume that α_L and α_R are independently distributed, each with uniform density on the interval $[-1/8, 1/8]$. The ex ante probability that party L wins the election is given by

$$q(\pi_L, \pi_R; 1/2, \gamma) = H(\delta^*(\pi_L, \pi_R; 1/2, \gamma))$$

$$= \begin{cases} 0 & \text{if } \Delta(\pi_L, \pi_R) < -\gamma/4, \\ 8(1/4 + \Delta/\gamma)^2 & \text{if } -\gamma/4 \leq \Delta(\pi_L, \pi_R) < 0, \\ 1 - 8(1/4 - \Delta/\gamma)^2 & \text{if } 0 \leq \Delta(\pi_L, \pi_R) < \gamma/4, \\ 1 & \text{if } \Delta(\pi_L, \pi_R) \geq \gamma/4, \end{cases} \quad (7)$$

where $\Delta(\pi_L, \pi_R) = (1/2 - \pi_R)^2 - (1/2 - \pi_L)^2$.

Let the post-election utility function for party L from the election of a candidate with platform π be $u^L(\pi) = -\pi^2$, and suppose that the utility function for party R is given by $u^R(\pi) = -(1 - \pi)^2$. The ex ante expected payoff to party L is

$$U(\pi_L, \pi_R; 0, 1/2, \gamma) = -\pi_L^2 q(\pi_L, \pi_R; 1/2, \gamma) - \pi_R^2[1 - q(\pi_L, \pi_R; 1/2, \gamma)],$$

and to party R it is

$$U(\pi_L, \pi_R; 1, 1/2, \gamma) = -(1 - \pi_L)^2 q(\pi_L, \pi_R; 1/2, \gamma)$$
$$- (1 - \pi_R)^2[1 - q(\pi_L, \pi_R; 1/2, \gamma)].$$

The following table lists pure strategy Nash equilibrium platforms for various values of γ.

γ	π_L	π_R	$|\pi_L - \pi_R|$
0.5	0.38965	0.61035	0.22070
1.0	0.35173	0.64827	0.29654
2.0	0.3048	0.6952	0.3904
4.0	0.25	0.75	0.5
32.4	0.08503	0.91497	0.82994

The policy gap separating the candidates increases as the weight voters place on personal services increases.

From note 10, we have that $\pi_L = 0$ only if $q(0, \pi_R; 1/2, \gamma) = 1$. From (7), this requires that $(1/2 - \pi_R)^2 - 1/4 \geq \gamma/4$, which is inconsistent with any equilibrium π_R for $\gamma > 0$. Similarly, we can rule out $\pi_R = 1$ for $\gamma > 0$. So, while the salience of personal services causes policy polarization, in equilibrium neither party will locate at its policy ideal point.

2.3   Elections with an incumbent

We next consider the nature of a contest when there is an incumbent candidate. To keep things simple, we assume that the sequence of events when there is an open seat is as follows: First, the party of the incumbent candidate announces whether that candidate will be renominated. Next, if the party decides to renominate the incumbent, the out-of-power party then chooses a candidate to contest the seat. Otherwise, both parties then simultaneously nominate candidates, and the race is effectively a race for an open seat. (The incumbent may not seek office as a third-party candidate.)

We will focus on the case when a party renominates the incumbent. We will assume that the incumbent's ability parameter is fully known to both parties and to the voters, as is his position on the policy dimension. Without loss of generality, consider the case in which party R has chosen to renominate its incumbent, whose attributes are (π_R, α_R). Party L selects its platform π_L knowing (π_R, α_R) but knowing only the distribution of its own candidate's ability. We denote the cumulative density of this distribution by $\Phi^L(\alpha_L)$.

As with an open-seat race, during the campaign voters will observe not only the policy location of the party L candidate but also his ability level α_L. The realization of α_L that leaves the median voter indifferent between the challenger and the incumbent is given implicitly by:

$$g(\alpha_L) = [d(\beta^\mu, \pi_L) - d(\beta^\mu, \pi_R)]/\gamma + g(\alpha_R) \equiv K(\pi_L, \pi_R, \alpha_R; \beta^\mu, \gamma). \tag{8}$$

This implies that, if $g(\cdot)$ is invertible, we can rewrite the probability that voter β^μ casts her ballot for the party L candidate as:

$$r(\pi_L, \pi_R, \alpha_R; \beta^\mu, \gamma) = 1 - \Phi^L[g^{-1}(K(\pi_L, \pi_R, \alpha_R; \beta^\mu, \gamma))]. \tag{9}$$

Differentiation of (9) yields

$$r_{\pi_L}(\pi_L, \pi_R, \alpha_R; \beta^\mu, \gamma) = -\Phi^{L'}(\cdot)g^{-1'}(\cdot)d_2(\beta^\mu, \pi_L)/\gamma, \tag{10}$$

so $r_{\pi_L}(\pi_L, \pi_R, \alpha_R; \beta^\mu, \gamma) > 0$ if $\pi_L < \beta^\mu$. As with open-seat races, convergence toward the median ideal point increases the out-party's election probability.[13]

An increase in γ, ceteris paribus, reduces the electoral advantage of locating closer to β^μ than the opponent. Thus, an increase in the weight placed on personal services works to the advantage of a challenger who has staked out a position farther from the median than the incumbent:

$$\text{sign } r_\gamma = \text{sign}[d(\beta^\mu, \pi_L) - d(\beta^\mu, \pi_R)].$$

The effect of an increase in γ on the equilibrium policy distance between challenger and incumbent is therefore ambiguous. We have

$$\text{sign } d\pi_L/d\gamma = \text{sign}\{[d(0, \pi_R) - d(0, \pi_L)]r_{\pi_L\gamma} - d_2(0, \pi_L)r_\gamma\}.$$

The sign of $r_{\pi_L\gamma}$ depends on r_γ as well as on $\Phi^{L''}(\cdot)$ and $g^{-1''}(\cdot)$, so in general we cannot say what the net effect will be.

Incumbent ability also affects challenger platform and election probability. First, note that

$$r_{\alpha_R}(\pi_L, \pi_R, \alpha_R; \beta^\mu, \gamma) = -\Phi^{L'}(\cdot)g^{-1'}(\cdot)g'(\alpha_R) < 0.$$

For any challenger chosen by the out-party, the incumbent is more likely to prevail the higher is α_R. We would expect that, with a party R incumbent, $\alpha_R > E(\alpha_L)$. In an otherwise symmetric race, therefore, our model implies an electoral advantage to incumbents. The equilibrium effect of higher α_R on the probability that a challenger from party L wins depends, however, on the effect of a change in α_R on L's best policy response. As with the effects of γ, the net effect of a change in α_R is ambiguous. Both $d\pi_L/d\alpha_R$ and $dr/d\alpha_R$ depend on the curvature of $r(\cdot)$. Nonetheless, controlling for the response of the challenger's platform, it is unambiguously the case that higher-ability incumbents have a higher probability of winning re-election.

We can obtain stronger implications from the added structure afforded by simple specifications, such as the one we used in the example for open-seat contests (uniform distribution of α_L, quadratic $d(\cdot)$, and linear $g(\cdot)$). In that setting, for values of π_R not very close to 1, we find that $d\pi_L/d\gamma < 0$. In these cases, as the weight on personal services increases, so does the

---

[13] For conditions guaranteeing uniqueness of the out-of-power party's best response, see the appendix.

policy distance between an arbitrarily positioned incumbent (with $\beta^\mu <$ $\pi_R < 1$) and the optimal policy location of his challenger. So, in this environment, increasing "personal vote" is associated with more polarized policy positions.

Furthermore, in such a setting, the equilibrium probability of the incumbent being re-elected increases (r decreases) as γ increases, for values of π_R not very close to β^μ – at least until γ becomes very large, when the re-election probability becomes virtually independent of π_R. So the incumbency advantage is also increasing with the weight that voters attach to constituent service.

These points are illustrated in Figure 1, using the example from the discussion of open-seat races. We have let $\alpha_L \sim U[-1/8, 1/8]$ and set $\alpha_R =$ $E(\alpha_L) + 0.05 = 0.05$. The top panel illustrates best-response challenger platforms (π_L) for various values of γ, while the bottom panel shows how the equilibrium probability of challenger victory (r) varies.

3   Some shreds of evidence

The main result in our discussion of electoral equilibrium in open-seat races, summarized as Proposition 2, is that the ideological "no-man's land" – within which neither party will nominate candidates – expands as voters place more weight on the provision of personal services. This strongly suggests that the actual gap between candidates will expand, on average, with the degree of constituent service motivation, as in the context of our example. We state this hypothesis as follows:[14]

H1.   Other things being equal, in constituencies that place greater weight on personal services, candidates for an open congressional seat will be more ideologically polarized.

Our analysis also suggests that service-motivated constituents are more loyal to their incumbent representatives; that is:

H2.   The incumbency advantage is higher in districts whose constituents place greater weight on the service dimension.

The winners of open-seat races will, on average, be of higher quality than the average open-seat contender. (In the equilibrium of our model,

---

[14] This hypothesis requires a theoretical and a practical caveat. On a note of theoretical caution: It is possible to construct examples satisfying the conditions requisite for Proposition 2 that nevertheless yield reduced polarization as service motivation increases. These equilibria are still sufficiently polarized to remain outside the expanding ideological "no-man's land" identified in Proposition 2. On the practical side, H1, like our other hypotheses, concerns preferences rather than behavior, requiring us to rely on voters' self-reported electoral motives.

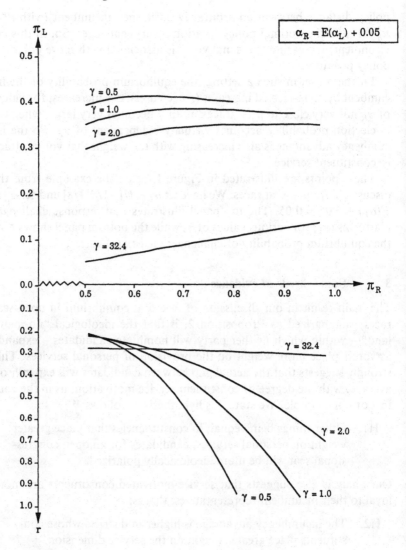

Figure 1.

an average winning candidate for an open seat has competence above α^0, the average realization for challengers.) In our analysis of incumbent races, we showed that ceteris paribus the incumbent has a higher chance of re-election the higher her level of competence. Of course, the out-of-power party will strive to see that *ceteris* are not *paribus,* adjusting the challenger's platform in response to the higher ability of the proven incumbent. However, although we cannot rule this out on a priori theoretical grounds, it would take a lot of adjustment indeed to more than offset the average advantage to incumbents, whose previous election victories have shown them to be above-average candidates.

The first two hypotheses, which are suggested by our theory, in turn point to a third, which follows by a sort of "chain rule":

H3. Other things being equal, there will be a positive relationship between incumbency advantage and the degree of polarization between the candidates.

There are two mechanisms by which this association could arise. The first is that both the gap in candidate positions and the incumbency advantage are hypothesized to increase with higher levels of service motivation. Then districts with high levels of service motivation will tend to have entrenched incumbents and polarized politics, whereas low levels of service motivation will tend to simultaneously produce vulnerable incumbents and moderate ideology. This would generate the hypothesized positive association between incumbency advantage and polarization.

A second process could also lead to this outcome. In the theoretical model, candidates' policy locations (though not their competence) were assumed to be known in advance by the parties. However, if the parties had only unbiased estimates of candidate policy positions (π in our model), then the actual locations would be distributed around the equilibrium platforms. Candidates who happened to be more polarized than average would, on average, tend to lose open-seat contests. For a given distribution of voter policy preferences within a district, more polarized incumbents will, on average, be those whose high service ability enabled them to prevail despite their positional handicap. This will happen more frequently in districts that place greater weight on service provision, and hence, according to H2, afford incumbents larger margins. This means that polarized candidates are more likely to survive in districts with high incumbency advantage.

To gauge these hypotheses, we use data from the 1978 National Election Survey (NES). In that year, respondents were asked detailed questions about the criteria they used to evaluate their candidates for the House of Representatives in 108 congressional districts. One series of questions asked a respondent to rank the relative importance (from the respondent's viewpoint) of each of the following activities of a legislator:

(A) helping people in the district who have personal problems with the government;

(B) making sure the district gets its fair share of government money and projects;

(C) keeping track of the way government agencies are carrying out laws passed by Congress;

(D) keeping in touch with the people about what government is doing; and

(E) working in Congress on bills concerning national issues.

Activities (A) and (B) are generally interpreted as constituent service by such writers as Cain et al. (1987) and Johannes (1984). More narrowly, one can think of activity (A) as "personal services" and (B) as "pork-barrel" services.

NES respondents could rate each activity as "most important," "second most important,"..., "least important." Respondents were also given the option of asserting that all five activities were equally important, or that none of the five was particularly important. To create a "salience of personal services" variable, we assigned a score of 5 to respondents who ranked (A) as the most important activity, a 4 to those who ranked it second, and so forth. If personal services were ranked least important, the response was coded as a 1. If a respondent claimed that all five activities were equally important, we assigned a score of 3, whereas if none of the activities was considered important, the response received a score of 1.[15] Our variable SPS (salience of personal service) is the average scored response in each district, and serves as a measure of γ, the weight placed on personal services.[16]

Measuring political polarization in congressional races is a challenge. Although interest-group ratings and scalings are available for the winners of these races, losers often disappear from congressional politics without ever making it into Congress, and hence without generating roll-call voting records. However, respondents to the 1978 NES were asked to locate both House candidates for office (plus retiring incumbents) on a seven-point liberal–conservative ideological scale, with 1 being most liberal, 4 corresponding to moderate ideology, and 7 indicating most conservative. The NES sample covered 108 House districts, of which 86 had elections that were contested by both parties in 1978. In five of these districts either the Republican candidate or the Democratic candidate was not located on

[15] We made no attempt to assign scores when the respondent did not answer this set of questions. Of the 2,304 interviews conducted for the 1978 NES, 25 contained logically inconsistent responses to the activities; for example, one respondent rated three services as "most important." Rather than attempt to impute responses for these cases, we simply discarded them, leaving us with 2,279 potentially usable interviews.

[16] We also constructed an alternative measure, in exactly the same way, using activity (B) as the measure of the salience of personal services. Our empirical results were not affected by whether we used the measure in the text or this alternative "porkability" measure. Other alternatives, such as scaled ranking of (A) divided by scaled ranking of (E), yielded similar results.

the seven-point scale by *any* respondent. This left us with usable data for 81 districts.

As a check of the accuracy of respondents' subjective evaluations of candidates' ideological locations, we calculated the correlation between respondents' assessments of the location of the district's incumbent (whether running for re-election or not) and the incumbent's 1978 ADA rating. If constituent evaluations were in perfect accord with ADA ratings then we would observe a correlation of −1, as the ADA ratings assign high numbers to liberals and low numbers to conservatives, while the seven-point scale of the NES assigns low numbers to liberals and high numbers to conservatives.

A total of 810 respondents evaluated the incumbent's location. The observed correlation between constituent evaluations and ADA ratings was −0.659, with an associated standard error of 0.059. This is significantly negative at all standard levels of significance, indicating that House members with high ADA scores tend to be viewed by respondents as more liberal than those with low ADA ratings. However, the measured correlation is also significantly different from −1. Respondents do not simply replicate ADA ratings, but have their own ideas about the precise definitions of the words "liberal" and "conservative."

For each of the 81 districts, we computed the location of each of the two parties' candidates, using the mean of the NES responses in the district.[17] We define the distance between candidates as:

$$\text{GAP} = |\text{Mean Democratic candidate location}$$
$$- \text{Mean Republican candidate location}|.$$

3.1   GAP and salience of personal sevices in open-seat races

Only 11 of our 81 districts had open-seat races. We therefore looked at only the simplest empirical test of H1. The correlation between SPS and GAP for these districts was 0.239, with a standard error of 0.217. This correlation is of the predicted sign, but falls well short of significance. This is not surprising in light of the small sample size. Given the small number of open-seat races for the House of Representatives, a conclusive test of this hypothesis would require that questions about ideology and the salience of personal services be asked in several waves of future surveys, in order to accumulate a large enough sample to obtain precise parameter estimates.

---

[17] Our scaling of the Democratic candidates was based on 621 responses with an average of 7.67 responses per district; Republican candidate locations were based on 532 responses with an average of 6.57 per district.

3.2   Incumbency advantage

The other two hypotheses pertain to the strength of the incumbency advantage. Measurement of the advantage of incumbency is complicated by the partisan nature of some congressional districts. During every legislative reapportionment, major parties exert tremendous effort to gerrymander House districts, concentrating hostile majorities in single districts and creating small but safe margins in others. The offshoot is that part of an incumbent's winning margin will typically be attributable to the incumbent's partisan affiliation, and would have accrued to *any* member of the incumbent's party; some other component correponds to personal loyalty to the incumbent. It is this second component that we seek to measure and relate to the salience of personal services and the degree of partisan polarization.

To separate the two sources of incumbency advantage we attempt to control for the "normal" vote in the district, and attribute what remains of the incumbency advantage to personal loyalty to the incumbent candidate. We follow Gelman and King (1990) and use as our basic specification[18]

$$E(V_t) = b_0 + b_1 V_{t-1} + b_2 I_t, \tag{11}$$

where V_t is the Democratic share of the two-party vote in election year t (so that $t-1$ occurs two years earlier) and I_t is a measure of incumbency status in election t: I_t equals 1 if a Democratic incumbent is running for re-election, it is -1 if a Republican incumbent is running, and it is 0 for an open-seat race.

Using the 81 contested congressional districts for which we have NES data, we estimated (11) by OLS using V^{1978}, the Democratic share of the two-party vote in 1978, as the dependent variable. The results, reported in column 1 of Table 1, indicate a 10-point advantage to 1978 incumbents. This estimate is close to that found by Gelman and King (1990) for their complete sample of contested 1978 elections (see their fig. 2).

By H2, the incumbency advantage IAD, as measured by the extra vote margin accruing to incumbents not encompassed by the partisan leanings of the district, depends on the salience of personal services SPS. The simplest way to capture this is to let

$$IAD = a_0 + a_1 SPS. \tag{12}$$

Our specification becomes:

[18] Gelman and King (1990) suggest the specification $V_t = b_0 + b_1 V_{t-1} + b_2 I_t + b_3 P_{t-1}$, where P_{t-1} equals 1 if the district was won by a Democrat at $t-1$ and -1 if a Republican won at $t-1$. We found that inclusion of such a variable contributed nothing to the specification (except collinearity with I_t).

Table 1. *Dependent variable: Democratic
share of 1978 two-party vote* $(N = 81)$

	(1)	(2)	(3)
Constant	30.409	30.383	29.705
	(3.915)	(3.960)	(3.795)
V^{1976}	0.396	0.396	0.406
	(0.068)	(0.069)	(0.066)
I	10.316	9.836	6.513
	(1.606)	(7.424)	(2.157)
$I \cdot$ SPS		0.184	
		(2.784)	
$I \cdot$ GAP			3.330
			(1.311)
$\bar{R}^2$	0.763	0.760	0.779

Note: estimated standard errors are shown in parentheses.

$$E(V^{1978}) = b_0 + b_1 V^{1976} + b_2 I \cdot \text{IAD}.$$

Substituting from (12), we obtain:

$$E(V^{1978}) = b_0 + b_1 V^{1976} + b_2' I + b_3 I \cdot \text{SPS}, \tag{13}$$

where $b_2' = a_0 b_2$ and $b_3 = a_1 b_2$.

Hypothesis H2 suggests that $b_2' > 0$ and $b_3 > 0$. Results of our regression are reported in column 2 of Table 1. The estimates of b_2' and b_3 are not statistically significant, while the associated standard errors are very large. The reason is not difficult to ascertain. The correlation between the incumbency variable I and the interaction term $I \cdot$ SPS is 0.988. This high degree of collinearity greatly inflates our estimated standard errors. The collinearity is due to the high degree of "bunching" in the respondents' rating of personal services. The mean value of SPS is 2.597, and the standard deviation is 0.407. Of the 81 districts in our sample, 64 have SPS values between 2 and 3. Thus, the interaction term used to assess the effect of SPS in the incumbency advantage, $I \cdot$ SPS, behaves very much like $I \cdot 2.597$, resulting in severe collinearity. As with the hypothesis that the salience of personal services and polarization are positively correlated, the hypothesis that the incumbency advantage and personal services are positively correlated requires considerably more data to evaluate.[19]

---

[19] Nonlinear specifications of IAD, while helping to reduce collinearity, did not significantly change our results. For instance, we hypothesized that the salience of personal

Hypothesis H3, that the incumbency advantage and the GAP between candidates are positively related, can be tested in a similar manner. We now take

$$IAD = c_0 + c_1 GAP \tag{14}$$

and use (14) to estimate

$$
\begin{aligned}
E(V^{1978}) &= b_0 + b_1 V^{1976} + b_2 I \cdot IAD \\
&= b_0 + b_1 V^{1976} + b_2'' I + b_3' I \cdot GAP, \tag{15}
\end{aligned}
$$

where $b_2'' = c_0 b_2$ and $b_3' = c_1 b_2$.

Hypothesis H3 implies that $b_2'' > 0$ and $b_3' > 0$. Results of our regression are reported in column 3 of Table 1. The estimates lend support to the hypothesis that high values of incumbency advantage and candidate polarization are positively associated. Our regression results indicate that, for each additional point on the NES seven-point ideological scale that separates candidates,[20] the incumbency advantage rises by about three points.

Obviously, these empirical exercises are meant only to be suggestive. More careful analysis awaits a richer data set, particularly with regard to measures of the salience of personal services over a time series, as well as better measures of candidate locations in congressional races.

4   Conclusion

Our model encompasses constituent evaluation of congressional candidates on two dimensions: the conventional left–right ideological dimension, along which voters' preferred outcomes are heterogeneous, and a second dimension – candidate ability to provide ombudsman services for constituents. Voters in our model are unanimous in preferring a candidate with high service provision ability to one with limited ability at providing services, if both have identical ideological positions. Voters are willing to trade off greater distance in ideological space for increased service provision ability. The probability of a candidate winning the election is determined endogenously as a function of voters' assessments of candidate policy positions and abilities to deliver personal services.

services affects elections only where it is sufficiently great. Thus, we set SPS* = SPS if SPS ≥ 2.5 and SPS* = 0 otherwise. We then found:

$$V^{1978} = 30.149 + 0.399 V^{1976} + 9.439 I + 0.461 I \cdot SPS^*, \quad \bar{R}^2 = 0.761.$$
$$\quad\;\; (3.958) \;\; (0.069) \qquad (2.229) \quad\;\; (0.810)$$

(Estimated standard errors in parentheses.)

[20] The mean gap between candidates in our sample is 1.09.

The combination of voters' willingness to sacrifice ideological purity for the ability to provide services, combined with parties' uncertainty about candidates' abilities at the time they are nominated, produces ideological separation. This separation occurs in both open-seat races and those in which an incumbent is running. As constituencies place greater weight on the nonpolicy dimension, the lower bound on the distance by which candidates in open-seat races will be separated on the policy dimension increases. In races involving an incumbent, greater weight on ability raises the re-election probability of the average incumbent, holding fixed the challenger's issue position, while it also favors polarized challengers.

The model suggests three empirically testable hypotheses. The first, which follows most directly from the model, is that the degree of ideological polarization between contending candidates for an open congressional seat increases with the salience to voters of service provision ability. A test of this hypothesis, based on data from the 1978 National Election Survey, is hampered by the small number of open-seat races in the sample; although the salience of service provision is positively correlated with polarization in the NES data, this correlation is not statistically significant. A second hypothesis suggested by our model is that the incumbency advantage will be higher in districts with high salience of service ability. Our test of this hypothesis is inconclusive, thwarted by high collinearity in the 1978 NES data. A third hypothesis, which receives support in our data, is that the incumbency advantage will be more pronounced in ideologically polarized districts.

Appendix

A.1   *Existence of equilibrium in an open-seat contest*

Continuity of each of the payoff functions in (π_L, π_R), and quasiconcavity of L's payoff in π_L and of R's payoff in π_R, are sufficient for existence of a pure strategy Nash equilibrium (Dasgupta and Maskin 1986, p. 4). Ruling out dominated strategies, sufficient conditions for existence of a pure strategy equilibrium are that

(i) q is continuous,
(ii) d is continuous,
(iii) $q_{\pi_L \pi_L}(\pi_L, \pi_R; \beta^\mu, \gamma) \leq 0$,
(iv) $d_{22}(0, \pi_L) \geq 0$,
(v) $q_{\pi_R \pi_R}(\pi_L, \pi_R; \beta^\mu, \gamma) \geq 0$,
(vi) $d_{22}(1, \pi_R) \geq 0$.

Conditions (i) and (ii) insure that $U(\pi_L, \pi_R; 0, \beta^\mu, \gamma)$ is continuous in (π_L, π_R); conditions (iii) and (iv) are sufficient to give us

$$U_{\pi_L \pi_L}(\pi_L, \pi_R; 0, \beta^\mu, \gamma) < 0,$$

while conditions (v) and (vi) guarantee that

$$U_{\pi_R \pi_R}(\pi_L, \pi_R; 1, \beta^\mu, \gamma) < 0.$$

A.2   *Uniqueness of equilibrium in incumbent contests*

Uniqueness of the out-of-power party's best response can be guaranteed by condition (iv) from the discussion of an open-seat race, plus the additional restriction that

(vii) $r_{\pi_L \pi_L}(\pi_L, \pi_R, \alpha_R; \beta^\mu, \gamma) \le 0.$

Note that for the case of a party L incumbent facing a party R challenger, we would need condition (vi) as well as

(viii) $r_{\pi_R \pi_R}(\pi_L, \pi_R, \alpha_R; \beta^\mu, \gamma) \ge 0.$

A.3   *Proof of Proposition 2*

Let $\bar{h} \equiv \max_\tau H'(\tau)$ and define the function $\psi(\pi_L, \gamma; \beta^\mu)$ such that:[21]

$$\psi(\pi_L, \gamma; \beta^\mu) = -\bar{h}d_2(\beta^\mu, \pi_L)/\gamma - q(\pi_L, \beta^\mu; \beta^\mu, \gamma)d_2(0, \pi_L).$$

Lemma 1.   *For all $\pi_L \in [0, \beta^\mu]$, and given any $\pi_R \in [\beta^\mu, 1]$, $\psi(\pi_L, \gamma; \beta^\mu) \ge U_{\pi_L}(\pi_L, \pi_R; 0, \beta^\mu, \gamma).$*

Remark.   This lemma states that the ψ function serves as an upper bound on the first partial derivative of party L's utility function with respect to the policy advocated by its candidate. This bound is independent of π_R. We require only that neither party use a dominated strategy.

Proof of Lemma 1:

$$U_{\pi_L}(\pi_L, \pi_R; 0, \beta^\mu, \gamma)$$
$$= q_{\pi_L}(\pi_L, \pi_R; \beta^\mu, \gamma)[d(0, \pi_R) - d(0, \pi_L)] - q(\pi_L, \pi_R; \beta^\mu, \gamma)d_2(0, \pi_L)$$
$$= -H'(\delta^*(\pi_L, \pi_R; \beta^\mu, \gamma))d_2(\beta^\mu, \pi_L)[d(0, \pi_R) - d(0, \pi_L)]/\gamma$$
$$\quad - q(\pi_L, \pi_R; \beta^\mu, \gamma)d_2(0, \pi_L)$$
$$\le -\bar{h}d_2(\beta^\mu, \pi_L)/\gamma - q(\pi_L, \pi_R; \beta^\mu, \gamma)d_2(0, \pi_L) \tag{A1}$$

---

[21] If, as in note 9, we include an additive term $q(\cdot)W$ in party L's expected payoff function to capture the expected utility of being in office, then we would define $\psi(\pi_L, \gamma; \beta^\mu)$ as

$$\psi(\pi_L, \gamma; \beta^\mu) = -\bar{h}(1 + W)d_2(\beta^\mu, \pi_L)/\gamma - q(\pi_L, \beta^\mu; \beta^\mu, \gamma)d_2(0, \pi_L).$$

The lemmas then hold with this definition of ψ.

$$\leq -\bar{h}d_2(\beta^\mu, \pi_L)/\gamma - q(\pi_L, \beta^\mu; \beta^\mu, \gamma)d_2(0, \pi_L) \qquad (A2)$$
$$= \psi(\pi_L, \gamma; \beta^\mu).$$

Step (A1) uses $d_2(\beta^\mu, \pi_L) \leq 0$ and $[d(0, \pi_R) - d(0, \pi_L)] \leq 1$ for $\pi_L \in [0, \beta^\mu]$, $\pi_R \in [\beta^\mu, 1]$. Step (A2) uses $q(\pi_L, \pi_R; \beta^\mu, \gamma) \geq q(\pi_L, \beta^\mu; \beta^\mu, \gamma)$ together with $d_2(0, \pi_L) > 0$. $\qquad\square$

Lemma 2. $\psi(\beta^\mu, \gamma; \beta^\mu) < 0.$

Proof:

$$\psi(\beta^\mu, \gamma; \beta^\mu) = -\bar{h}d_2(\beta^\mu, \beta^\mu)/\gamma - q(\beta^\mu, \beta^\mu; \beta^\mu, \gamma)d_2(0, \beta^\mu)$$
$$= -H(0)d_2(0, \beta^\mu) < 0. \qquad\square$$

Lemma 3. *There exist $\hat{\pi}_L \in (0, \beta^\mu)$ such that $\psi(\hat{\pi}_L, \gamma; \beta^\mu) = 0$.*

Proof:

$$\psi(0, \gamma; \beta^\mu) = -\bar{h}d_2(\beta^\mu, 0)/\gamma - q(0, \beta^\mu; \beta^\mu, \gamma)d_2(0, 0)$$
$$= -\bar{h}d_2(\beta^\mu, 0)/\gamma > 0.$$

From Lemma 2, $\psi(\beta^\mu, \gamma; \beta^\mu) < 0$. Continuity of $\psi(\pi_L, \gamma; \beta^\mu)$, which follows from continuity of $d_2(\cdot)$ and $q(\cdot)$, implies the existence of $\hat{\pi}_L \in (0, \beta^\mu)$ such that $\psi(\hat{\pi}_L, \gamma; \beta^\mu) = 0$. $\qquad\square$

Next, we define $\tilde{\pi}_L(\gamma)$ as follows:

$$\tilde{\pi}_L(\gamma) = \max\{\pi_L \in [0, \beta^\mu] \mid \psi(\pi_L, \gamma; \beta^\mu) = 0\}.$$

Corollary to Lemma 3. $\tilde{\pi}_L(\gamma) \in (0, \beta^\mu).$

Next, let π_L^e and π_R^e be equilibrium platforms.

Lemma 4. $\pi_L^e \leq \tilde{\pi}_L(\gamma).$

Remark. Lemma 4 says that the $\tilde{\pi}_L(\gamma)$ function serves as an upper bound on the policy advocated by party L in any equilibrium.

Proof: We know that if the parties use undominated strategies, then $\pi_R^e \in (\beta^\mu, 1]$ while $\pi_L^e \in [0, \beta^\mu)$. Suppose that, in contradiction to the lemma, $\pi_L^e \in (\pi_L^*(\gamma), \beta^\mu]$. By Lemmas 1–3,

$$U_{\pi_L}(\pi_L^e, \pi_R^e; 0, \gamma, \beta^\mu) \leq \psi(\pi_L^e, \gamma; \beta^\mu) < 0 \quad \text{for } \pi_L^e \in (\pi_L^*(\gamma), \beta^\mu],$$

in contradiction to the equilibrium condition $U_{\pi_L}(\pi_L^e, \pi_R^e; \theta^L, \gamma) = 0$. $\qquad\square$

Lemma 5. $\bar{\pi}'_L(\gamma) < 0$.

Proof: By the definition of $\bar{\pi}_L(\gamma)$, $\psi(\bar{\pi}_L(\gamma), \gamma; \beta^\mu) = 0$. By implicit differentiation,

$$\bar{\pi}'_L(\gamma) = -\psi_\gamma(\bar{\pi}_L(\gamma), \gamma; \beta^\mu)/\psi_\pi(\bar{\pi}_L(\gamma), \gamma; \beta^\mu);$$

$$\psi_\gamma(\bar{\pi}_L(\gamma), \gamma; \beta^\mu)$$
$$= \gamma^{-2}\{\bar{h}d_2(\beta^\mu, \bar{\pi}_L(\gamma))$$
$$- H'[\delta^*(\bar{\pi}_L(\gamma), \beta^\mu; \beta^\mu, \gamma)]d(\beta^\mu, \bar{\pi}_L(\gamma))d_2(0, \bar{\pi}_L(\gamma))\}$$
$$< 0 \quad \text{since } \bar{\pi}_L(\gamma) \in (0, \beta^\mu).$$

So $\text{sign}[\bar{\pi}'_L(\gamma)] = \text{sign}[\psi_\pi(\bar{\pi}_L(\gamma), \gamma; \beta^\mu)]$. But since $\psi(\beta^\mu, \gamma; \beta^\mu) < 0$, we must have $\psi_\pi(\bar{\pi}_L(\gamma), \gamma; \beta^\mu) < 0$, or else $\bar{\pi}_L(\gamma)$ would not be maximal.   □

Results analogous to Lemmas 1–5 can be derived for party R along exactly symmetric lines.

Proof of Proposition 2: The proof follows immediately from the corollary to Lemma 3, Lemmas 4 and 5, and the analogous results for party R.   □

REFERENCES

Alford, J. R., and D. W. Brady (1988), "Personal and Partisan Advantage in U.S. House Elections, 1846–1986," Unpublished Manuscript, Department of Political Science, Rice University, Houston.

Cain, B., J. Ferejohn, and M. Fiorina (1987), *The Personal Vote: Personal Service and Electoral Independence.* Cambridge, MA: Harvard University Press.

Cukierman, A. (1991), "Asymmetric Information and the Electoral Momentum of Public Opinion Polls," *Public Choice* 70: 181–213.

Dasgupta, P., and E. Maskin (1986), "The Existence of Equilibria in Discontinuous Economic Games, I: Theory," *Review of Economic Studies* 53: 1–26.

Enelow, J., and M. Hinich (1982), "Nonspatial Candidate Characteristics and Electoral Competition," *Journal of Politics* 44: 115–30.

Gelman, A., and G. King (1990), "Estimating Incumbency Advantage without Bias," *American Journal of Political Science* 34: 1142–64.

Johannes, J. (1984), *To Serve the People: Congress and Constituency Service,* Lincoln: University of Nebraska Press.

Ledyard, J. (1984), "The Pure Theory of Large Two-Candidate Elections," *Public Choice* 44: 7–42.

Poole, K., and H. Rosenthal (1984), "The Polarization of American Politics," *Journal of Politics* 46: 1061–79.

(1991), "Patterns of Congressional Voting," *American Journal of Political Science* 35: 228–78.

Stokes, D. (1963), "Spatial Models of Party Competition," *American Political Science Review* 57: 368-77.

Wittman, D. (1977), "Candidates with Policy Preferences: A Dynamic Model," *Journal of Economic Theory* 14: 180-9.

  (1983), "Candidate Motivation: A Synthesis of Alternative Theories," *American Political Science Review* 52: 142-57.

CHAPTER 15

Credibility and the responsiveness of direct legislation

Arthur Lupia

1   Introduction

Scholars and pundits alike have documented the ignorance of the common voter. They often point to the unsavory folks who run large-scale campaigns, assert that voters can be manipulated, and conclude that popular elections do not provide accurate representations of voter preferences. In this chapter, I identify conditions under which this type of conclusion is true (false) for a substantively interesting and widely used class of electoral rules.

Direct legislation (the initiative and referendum) allows voters to choose among specific policy alternatives. In the most basic and commonly used form of direct legislation, voters are asked to vote for either the *Status Quo* or a single "alternative to the Status Quo." Although majority rule is often used to determine which alternative will prevail, the extent to which direct legislation produces "majority preferred outcomes" is the subject of considerable debate.[1] For instance, a relatively uninformed voter may not be able to determine which alternative is better for her and, as a consequence, may not cast the same vote she would have cast if she had possessed better or complete information. If many voters are relatively uninformed, then the alternative that is the electoral winner may not be the same as the alternative that a majority of voters in the same electorate would have chosen if they had better or complete information.

Prepared for International Symposia on Economic Theory and Econometrics, volume 8. I thank Gary Cox, Elisabeth Gerber, Susanne Lohmann, Mat McCubbins, Richard Mc-Kelvey, Roger Myerson, Peter Ordeshook, and Barry Weingast for helpful comments and advice.
[1] Magleby (1984) and Cronin (1989) provide detailed accounts of the history and use of direct legislation.

In the presence of complex alternatives, one option for voters is to rely on information provided by others.[2] If the provision of information is costly, we might expect only those groups interested in affecting the outcome of the election to provide information. Whether or not these groups provide truthful information depends on their incentives. For instance, groups who care about the outcome of a particular direct legislation election, and who do not have a reputation for providing truthful information that they want to protect, may be more likely – than groups who have something to lose from lying – to attempt to influence an electoral outcome by misleading voters. If voters do not acquire costly political information, if it is difficult for them to verify the claims made by others, and if a voter is uncertain about the preferences of an information provider, then the voter's beliefs about an information provider's credibility may be an important determinant of how the policy alternatives chosen by direct legislation are related to the preferences of individual voters.

In this chapter, I develop a model of direct legislation that shows how certain regular characteristics of political communication affect voter inferences, voter behavior, and electoral outcomes. I identify these effects by examining the model under different assumptions about the credibility of an information-providing monopoly agenda setter. The agenda setter can propose a single alternative to the Status Quo and provide information to incompletely informed voters about the alternative she has proposed. (In direct legislation elections, it is frequently the case that a single group both places a policy alternative on a ballot and provides information to voters about the alternative.)

I first examine the model under the assumption that all voters can costlessly verify the truthfulness of the information that the agenda setter provides. I then examine the model under the assumption that voters do not verify the truthfulness of the information provided by the agenda setter at the time they choose their strategies. In a third version of the model, I not only assume that voters are unable to verify the truthfulness of the agenda setter's message, I also assume that the agenda setter faces a penalty for providing untruthful information. The motivation for this penalty comes from the observation that political information providers tend to operate in the presence of disclosure laws, truth-in-advertising laws, or situations under which there exist long-term benefits from culti-

---

[2] Campbell et al. (1960), Fiorina (1981), and Popkin (1991) are among those who have provided influential arguments about the ways in which voters in candidate-based elections adapt to their information problems. Also see Spence (1973) and Crawford and Sobel (1982) for seminal signaling models that are directly relevant to our understanding of the role of communication in collective choice settings.

vating a reputation for providing truthful information. For each version of the model, I derive an equilibrium and show how the agenda setter's credibility affects voter behavior, the content of the alternative to the Status Quo, and whether the alternative or the Status Quo wins the election. I also show the conditions under which voters can be misled by the information they receive and the conditions under which this information allows voters to cast the same vote they would have cast if they had better or complete information. Knowing each of these relationships allows us to be more precise about the responsiveness of direct legislation outcomes to (complete-information) voter preferences.

The sequence of the chapter is as follows. In Section 2, the foundations of the model are presented. In Section 3, I derive electoral equilibria that allow me to demonstrate how different forms of credible and noncredible communication affect inferences, behavior, and electoral outcomes. Section 4 summarizes the findings and an appendix includes a series of proofs and formal statements of equilibria. Notice that this model differs from previous work on signaling and credibility in that neither complete information, historical information about the agenda setter's actions (Sobel 1985), certifiably truthful statements (Okuno-Fujiwara, Postlewaite, and Suzumura 1990), nor competition among interested information providers (Milgrom and Roberts 1986) are among the conditions necessary for a decison maker to make a more accurate inference about competing alternatives after receiving information from a potentially noncredible source.

2   Description of the model

I model *direct legislation* as a one-period, multistage game of incomplete information. The object of the game is to choose one policy from a finite continuum of possible policy alternatives. A monopoly agenda setter first decides whether or not to pay an exogenously determined cost of entry that allows her to challenge a common-knowledge Status Quo. If the agenda setter pays this cost, she can propose a single *Alternative,* provide an electorate of incompletely informed voters with information about the Alternative, and force an election where each voter must cast a vote for either the Alternative or the Status Quo. If the agenda setter does not pay this cost, the game ends and the Status Quo is the outcome. All players have policy preferences and are restricted to the use of pure strategies. Majority rule determines the outcome of the election.

Consider the policy space [0, 1]. There exists an exogenously determined and common-knowledge Status Quo, $SQ \in [0, 1]$. The game is played by $n+1$ players; n of the players ($N = \{1, ..., n\}$) are called *voters,* and one player is called the *setter.*

A player's policy preferences can be identified by the location of her ideal point. The setter's ideal point, $X \in [0,1]$, is drawn from the common-knowledge, cumulative distribution function $F(X)$, which has density f. Each voter's type, $T_i \in [0,1]$, is drawn from the common-knowledge cumulative distribution function $G(T)$, which has density g. The distribution $F(X)$ represents the prior beliefs that voters have about the setter's preferences. For simplicity, I discuss the case where it is common knowledge that the distribution $G(T)$ is the actual draw of voter ideal points.[3]

After player types are determined, the setter chooses a strategy. The setter's strategy, $s(X, K)$, has three components. The first strategic decision is whether to challenge SQ by forcing an election. The decision to challenge SQ is nontrivial because the setter will face a common-knowledge *cost of entry*, $K \in \mathbb{R}^+$, if she decides to challenge SQ. This aspect of the setter's decision is denoted $s_{chal}(X, K)$, which equals 1 if the setter decides to challenge SQ and 0 otherwise. If the setter decides not to challenge SQ, the game ends and SQ is the outcome. Otherwise, the setter enters and chooses the second component of her strategy – a location for (the content of) the Alternative – $s_{loc}(X) \in [0,1]$.[4]

The third component of the setter's strategy, $s_{mes}(X) \in \{-1, 1\}$, is a decision about the content of a message that the setter can send to voters: $s_{mes}(X) = -1$ when the setter sends the message "$s_{loc}(X)$ is to the left of SQ"; $s_{mes}(X) = 1$ when the setter sends the message "$s_{loc}(X)$ is to the right of SQ."[5] The setter's strategy set is $S_{set} = \{s: [0,1] \times \mathbb{R}^+ \rightarrow \{0,1\} \times [0,1] \times \{-1,1\}\}$, where the particular strategy chosen by the setter takes the form $s(X, K) = (s_{chal}(X, K), s_{loc}(X), s_{mes}(X))$. For notational simplicity, I henceforth denote $s(X, K)$ as s, $s_{chal}(X, K)$ as s_{chal}, and so on. It follows that when an election is held it is of the form SQ versus s_{loc}.

After the setter moves, the voters choose a strategy. A voter can condition her strategy on the setter's expenditure (K) and/or on the content of the message provided by the setter (s_{mes}). All actions taken by and all information obtained by voters are assumed to be costless to them. A voter's strategy is a binary decision, where $v_i(T_i, K, s_{mes}) = -1$ represents a vote for SQ and $v_i(T_i, K, s_{mes}) = 1$ represents a vote for s_{loc}. The voter's strategy set is defined as

[3] Alternatively, I could have assumed that either $G(T)$ is the distribution from which voter ideal points are drawn or, for each $i \in N$, $G(T_i)$ is the common-knowledge distribution from which voter i's ideal point is drawn. The assumption used in the exposition is relatively restrictive, but it allows me to simplify the notation and exposition. The results of this chapter are robust to each of the assumptions.

[4] For notational convenience, I denote $s_{loc}(X) = SQ$ when $s_{chal}(X, K) = 0$ (i.e., the setter chooses to accept SQ).

[5] Since $F(X)$ and $[0,1]$ are continuous, $SQ = s_{loc}$ occurs with near zero probability. If this event does occur, it follows trivially that SQ is the direct legislation outcome.

$$S_i := \{v_i : [0,1] \times \mathbb{R}^+ \times \{-1,1\} \to \{-1,1\}\}.$$

I describe the case where the electoral winner is determined by simple majority rule.[6] The outcome function is, for any $s \in \{1\} \times [0,1] \times \{-1,1\}$ and $v_i \in \{-1,1\}$,

$$o(s, v_1, \ldots, v_n) = \begin{cases} s_{\text{loc}} & \text{if } \sum_{i=1}^n v_i > 0, \\ SQ & \text{if } \sum_{i=1}^n v_i \le 0. \end{cases}$$

The outcome determines the payoffs to all players.[7]

For expositional and notational simplicity, I describe the case where the setter and the voters have symmetric and single-peaked utility functions. I also assume that the shape of player utility functions are common knowledge, though the location of any particular player's ideal point may not be. For outcome $x \in [0,1]$, I define *voter i's utility function* to be $T_i \in [0,1]$: $U_i(x, T_i) = -|x - T_i|$, and the setter *policy* utility function to be $U_{\text{set}}(x, X) = -|x - X|$. Since the setter's incentives are also affected by the cost of entry, I define the setter's utility function as the setter's policy utility minus the cost of contesting the election: $U_{\text{set}}(x, X) - [K \times s_{\text{chal}}]$.

This chapter's equilibrium concept is constructed by starting with the Bayes–Nash concept and incorporating the assumptions of this model.[8] I first incorporate the assumption that voters always vote as if they are the pivotal voter. This strategy is weakly dominant with respect to the strategies of other voters. The incorporation of this assumption transforms the equilibrium concept into a variant of the sequential equilibrium concept of Kreps and Wilson (1982). I next incorporate the assumption that $G(T)$ is the actual distribution of voter ideal points; this is not necessary for my results to hold, but does considerably simplify the description of the setter's objective function. The third assumption, which is essentially the same made by Kreps and Wilson, is that voter beliefs are consistent.

Let $C(SQ, K, s_{\text{mes}})$ be the set of voter types for whom the observation that the setter pays K and sends a message with content s_{mes} reveals that the certain utility from SQ is greater than or equal to the expected utility from s_{loc}. For all $(K, j) \in \mathbb{R}^+ \times \{-1,1\}$, let $A(K, j) \subseteq F(X)$ be the set of all setter types who could find it profitable to pay K and send message j. The equilibrium concept used in this chapter is defined as a set of strategies

---

[6] Supermajorities follow straightforwardly by changing the values of v_i.

[7] I have assumed that the SQ wins ties. This assumption is consistent with the tie-breaking rule used in many of direct legislation environments. Changing this assumption does not alter the power of the results that follow, but it does influence boundary conditions in straightforward ways.

[8] A closely related derivation is in Lupia (1992). The actual derivation is available upon request.

$s \in S_{\text{set}}$, $v_i \in S_i$ and voter beliefs $f(X \mid K, s_{\text{mes}})$ such that, for each $K \in \mathbb{R}^+$ and $s_{\text{mes}} \in \{-1, 1\}$, we have the following.

(1) *Setter:* for all X, $s = (s_{\text{chal}}, s_{\text{loc}}, s_{\text{mes}})$ satisfies:

$$\max_{s \in [0,1] \times [0,1] \times \{-1,1\}};$$

$$\Phi_{\text{set}}(s \mid K, G(T), X)$$

$$= \begin{cases} U_{\text{set}}(SQ, X) - (K \times s_{\text{chal}}) & \text{if } \int_{C(SQ, K, j)} dG(T) \geq \frac{1}{2}, \\ U_{\text{set}}(s_{\text{loc}}, X) - (K \times s_{\text{chal}}) & \text{if } \int_{C(SQ, K, j)} dG(T) < \frac{1}{2}. \end{cases}$$

(2) *Voters:* for all T_i ($i \in N$), $K \in \mathbb{R}^+$, and for all $j \in \{-1, 1\}$, $v_i(T_i, K, j)$ satisfies:

$$v_i = \begin{cases} 1 & \text{if } \int_0^1 U_i(s_{\text{loc}}, T_i) \, dF(X \mid K, j) > U_i(SQ, T_i), \\ -1 & \text{otherwise.} \end{cases}$$

(3) *Beliefs:* for all $(K, j) \in \mathbb{R}^+ \times \{-1, 1\}$:

$$f(X \mid K, j) = \begin{cases} f(x)/\text{pr}(K, j) & \text{if } x \in A(K, j), \\ 0 & \text{otherwise,} \end{cases}$$

where $\text{pr}(K, j) = \int_{A(K, j)} F(x) \, dx$.

3   Identifying the power of information

I now use the model to show how voter inferences are affected by costly setter effort and the content of the setter's message. In Section 3.1, I show how voters can use the observation of costly setter effort (the costs associated with the setter's decision to challenge SQ) to make more accurate inferences about the magnitude of the difference between s_{loc} and SQ. I then examine the effect of the content of the setter's message on voter inferences. I claim that the inference a voter makes after receiving a message from the setter depends on how much the voter believes that the information provider knows (i.e., does the information provider have the information necessary to make a statement like "s_{loc} is better for a voter like you than SQ") and on whether or not the voters believe that the information provider would tell the truth if she knew it (i.e., is the information provider credible). In this model, I assume that it is common knowledge that the setter knows the actual location of s_{loc}; I examine behavior and electoral outcomes for three different versions of the model where, in each version, I make a different assumption about the setter's credibility. In each case, I assume that all players know which circumstance prevails.

In the first version (Section 3.2), the setter is *perfectly credible* (because she is restricted from sending untruthful messages). In the second version

(Section 3.3), the setter is *noncredible* in that no voter is able to verify the truthfulness of the setter's message until after the election. I then examine a third version (Section 3.4) of the model where the setter is noncredible and there exists a positive penalty for lying. The penalty for lying is introduced in order to identify how the knowledge that the setter has something to lose from lying affects a voter's interpretation of a potentially untruthful message.

The equilibria of each version show how voters and the setter adapt their strategies to voter information problems. The comparison of the perfectly credible and the noncredible equilibria allows me to identify the effect of credibility on the relationship between player preferences and direct legislation electoral outcomes. The comparison of the noncredible equilibria with and without a penalty for lying allows me to demonstrate the conditions under which information providers who care about their reputations, or institutional characteristics that have been designed to penalize liars, can affect the relationship between individual preferences and electoral outcomes. In short, I identify how certain regular characteristics of political communication affect the likelihood that the direct legislation electoral outcome chosen by an incompletely informed electorate is the same as the outcome that the same electorate, if better or completely informed, would have chosen.

3.1   *Costly setter effort and voter updating*

The setter must decide whether or not to spend K (> 0 and common knowledge) in order to challenge SQ. Challenging SQ allows the setter to propose an alternative s_{loc} that the voters do not observe, and choose the content of a message s_{mes} that will be sent to voters.[9] Lemma 1 and Lemma 2 characterize the setter's entry and location strategies, respectively. Lemma 1 is a straightforward incentive-compatibility condition that defines the conditions under which the setter will find it profitable to challenge SQ. Lemma 2 states that if voters are uncertain about the location of s_{loc} when it is time for them to vote, then a dominant strategy for the setter is to choose her ideal point. (The proofs of Lemma 2 and Lemma 6 are in Appendix A. The proofs of all other lemmas are straightforward and are available upon request.)

Lemma 1.   *The setter contests an election if and only if the expected benefit from contesting the election is greater than the cost.*

---

[9] The findings described in this section are originally derived in Lupia (1992), do not depend on the setter's credibility, and are shown in Appendix A to hold for all three versions of the model presented in this chapter.

Lemma 2. *A weakly dominant location strategy for the setter is* $s_{loc} = X$.

Lemma 2 is interesting as it tells us that voter uncertainty about the location of s_{loc} is sufficient for a monopoly agenda setter to ignore voter preferences when she chooses the location of s_{loc} (i.e., the content of the Alternative is not responsive to voter preferences).[10] For notational convenience in describing equilibria, I will henceforth refer to voter beliefs about the location of s_{loc} on $[0, 1]$ as $F(X)$. In the absence of any additional information, voters would have to make a choice between s_{loc} and SQ based on their complete information about SQ and their beliefs about s_{loc}. However, we assume that voters can observe the setter's expenditure K when she decides to challenge SQ. The fact that the setter decides to pay K in order to challenge SQ sends a signal to the voters. From Lemma 1, it follows that voters can infer that the setter believes she can recover (at least) the cost of contesting the election. For $K > 0$, the fact that the setter contests the election, along with the voter's knowledge of the shape of the setter's utility function, implies that s_{loc} is not within a well-specified neighborhood of SQ, since electoral outcomes near SQ will not provide enough extra utility for a setter to make contesting the election a profitable endeavor.

Let $\epsilon(K)$ (henceforth referred to as ϵ) be a distance on the continuum that is an increasing function of K.[11] The distance ϵ determines the range of alternatives within which it will never be profitable for the setter to contest an election. Since K and the shape of the setter's utility function are known, the correspondence between K and ϵ is common knowledge, as is the distance from SQ within which it is impossible for the setter to recover the cost of contesting the election. Lemma 3 shows that for setters whose ideal points are located within the "range of unprofitable alternatives," $[SQ - \epsilon, SQ + \epsilon]$, there exist no policies which, given the cost K of contesting the election, will provide the setter with a higher level of utility than costlessly accepting SQ.

Lemma 3. *If the setter's ideal point is located in the range of unprofitable alternatives, the setter should not challenge SQ.*

---

[10] A comparison of this finding to the agenda setter's equilibrium location strategy in a complete-information monopoly agenda setter model (Romer and Rosenthal 1978) shows the effect of voter uncertainty on the location of the alternative to SQ. In Romer and Rosenthal, the presence of completely informed voters forces the setter to propose an alternative that a majority of voters prefer to SQ in order to obtain a new outcome. Similar results are achieved when voters have incomplete information about SQ (Banks 1990) or the setter has incomplete information about voters (Denzau and Mackay 1983).

[11] Both $d\epsilon/dK$ and $d^2\epsilon/dK^2$ are positive.

When $K > 0$ and the setter challenges SQ, voters know that $X \notin [SQ - \epsilon, SQ + \epsilon]$. Independent of the message that the setter sends, the voters' updated beliefs should have no support over this range. When the setter enters, voters use Bayes's rule to update their beliefs about the location of s_{loc}. Updated voter beliefs $F(X \mid K, s_{\text{mes}})$ are related to voter prior beliefs $F(X)$ in the following way:

$$f(X \mid K, s_{\text{mes}})$$

$$= \begin{cases} 0 & \text{in } [SQ - \epsilon, SQ + \epsilon], \\ f(X) \times 1/(1 - F(SQ + \epsilon) + F(SQ - \epsilon)) & \text{in } [0, SQ - \epsilon), (SQ + \epsilon, 1]. \end{cases}$$

In addition to the updating process just described, the size and location of the range of unprofitable alternatives will determine the number of voters that are members of one of two partitions of the electorate. The members of the first partition are called *centrist voters* $\{i \mid T_i \in [SQ - \epsilon/2, SQ + \epsilon/2]\}$ and the members of the second partition are called *noncentrist voters* $\{i \mid T_i \notin [SQ - \epsilon/2, SQ + \epsilon/2]\}$. Lemma 4 tells us that centrist voters know that if the setter paid K to contest SQ, then s_{loc} will definitely provide a lower level of utility than SQ.

Lemma 4. *"Vote for the SQ" is an undominated strategy for all centrist voters.*

Observing costly setter effort has a stronger effect on centrist voters than it does on noncentrist voters. Centrist voters *always* vote for SQ and cast the same vote they would have cast if they were completely informed about s_{loc}. In contrast, noncentrist voters merely increase the likelihood that they cast the same vote they would have cast if they were completely informed about s_{loc} (i.e., were a noncentrist voter given a single opportunity to guess either the exact location of s_{loc} or a range within which s_{loc} is located, before and after observing costly setter entry, it is at least as likely that she will guess correctly after the observation). It is generally true that all voters are able to use their observation of costly setter effort to make more accurate inferences about the location of s_{loc}. Therefore, voters are generally more likely to cast the same vote they would have cast if they were completely informed.

3.2 *Verifiable messages*

I now use the model to identify what a voter can learn when a perfectly credible setter provides information about s_{loc}. The content of the perfectly credible message $s_{mes} = -1$ is that s_{loc} is to the left of SQ and the content of $s_{mes} = 1$ is that s_{loc} is to the right of SQ.[12]

The inference that voters can make from the content of a perfectly credible message is straightforward. For example, if a voter is told by a perfectly credible information provider that s_{loc} is to the left of SQ, she can eliminate from her voting calculus any beliefs about s_{loc} which place it to the right of SQ. The voter is not necessarily learning the exact location of s_{loc}, but she is able to make a definite directional inference about s_{loc} and SQ. If a voter is uncertain about this directional relationship before receiving the message, then receiving the message allows her to make a more accurate inference about the location of s_{loc}. When voters observe that a perfectly credible setter has paid K to challenge SQ and send message $s_{mes} \in \{-1, 1\}$, their updated beliefs $F(X|K, \{-1, 1\})$ about the location of s_{loc} are related to their prior beliefs $F(X)$ in the following way.

(a)   For $s_{mes} = -1$:

$$f(X|K, -1) = f(X) \times \frac{1}{F(SQ-\epsilon)} \in [0, SQ-\epsilon);$$

$$f(X|K, -1) = 0 \in (SQ-\epsilon, 1].$$

(b)   For $s_{mes} = 1$:

$$f(X|K, 1) = 0 \in [0, SQ+\epsilon);$$

$$f(X|K, 1) = f(X) \times \frac{1}{1-F(SQ+\epsilon)} \in (SQ+\epsilon, 1].$$

As was the case with costly setter effort, a perfectly credible message divides the electorate into two partitions. Let those voters whose ideal points are located in the range where $f(X|K, 1) = 0$ or $f(X|K, -1) = 0$ be called *opposite* voters ($\{i \mid T_i \in [0, SQ)$ if $s_{mes} = -1\}$, $\{i \mid T_i \in (SQ, 1]$ if $s_{mes} = 1\}$). Let all other voters be known as *nonopposite* voters.

Observing the content of a perfectly credible message has the same effect on opposite voters that observing costly setter effort had on centrist voters. An opposite voter knows that her ideal point is not on the same side of SQ as s_{loc}, (from Lemma 4) always votes for SQ, and always casts the same vote she would have cast if she were completely informed. A nonopposite voter who receives a perfectly credible message is generally more likely to cast the same vote she would have cast were she completely informed, since the perfectly credible message allows her to make a correct directional inference about s_{loc} and SQ.

---

[12] The concept of a perfectly credible message has also been used in models of voting behavior in multicandidate elections by McKelvey and Ordeshook (1985) and Calvert (1985).

In the "perfectly credible" equilibrium (see Appendix B for the formal statement of this and other equilibria), a perfectly credible setter challenges SQ, chooses $s_{loc} = X$, and sends a truthful message if and only if her ideal point is not located within the range of unprofitable alternatives and updated voter beliefs will lead a majority of voters to vote for s_{loc}. From the common knowledge and the fact that the setter knows the actual distribution of voter types, she can accurately predict what the electorate will do.[13] Otherwise, she does not challenge SQ. Because all voters can make correct directional inferences about s_{loc} and SQ, a perfectly credible setter will only challenge SQ when her ideal point is on the same side of SQ as the median voter's ideal point. In other words, a perfectly credible setter whose ideal point is on the *opposite* side of SQ as the ideal points of a majority of voters is unable to obtain an electoral outcome that she prefers to SQ.

Centrist and opposite voters vote for SQ. Nonopposite and noncentrist voters maximize expected utility, where the expectation is conditioned on their beliefs about s_{loc}, which are themselves conditioned on the value of K and s_{mes}. Since the presence of a perfectly credible message allows all voters to make more accurate inferences about the location of s_{loc}, its presence generally increases the likelihood that an incompletely informed electorate chooses the same outcome it would have chosen if it were completely informed. Independent of its true location, s_{loc} is the electoral outcome if and only if the number of noncentrist voters for whom the updated expected utility from s_{loc} is greater than the utility from SQ is a majority of all voters.

The discussion so far suggests that the voters' access to simple and publicly available sources of information, like the cost of contesting an election or perfectly credible messages, can help incompletely informed voters make (ex post) better decisions. If obtaining these forms of information requires less effort than obtaining information about the true location of an alternative, then voters can cast an "informed" vote while possessing very little information. Thus, we can say that the existence of these types of information makes direct legislation outcomes more responsive to complete-information voter preferences.

3.3   Nonverifiable messages

In many collective choice situations, those who have the resources to provide information sometimes have an incentive to mislead those who receive it. To examine what a voter can learn from a potential liar and how

---

[13] Under the two less restrictive assumptions about setter beliefs mentioned in note 3, the setter could condition her strategy on her *beliefs* about likely voter preference profiles.

this interaction affects beliefs, strategies, and electoral outcomes, I re-examine the previous model under the assumptions that the setter is not restricted to the provision of truthful information, the truthfulness of a message cannot be verified, and the cost of sending truthful messages equals the cost of sending untruthful messages.

Lemma 5 shows that an undominated partial strategy for a noncredible setter is to send the message that she believes is most likely to lead to s_{loc} as the electoral outcome. This implies that the content of a noncredible setter's message does not necessarily depend on the true relationship between s_{loc} and SQ. (In contrast, the perfectly credible setter is prevented from sending a message if it is untrue.) This lemma, while not surprising, helps us understand how an interaction between an incompletely informed voter and a potentially noncredible information provider (who does not face a penalty for lying) affects direct legislation strategies and outcomes.

Lemma 5. *A weakly dominant partial strategy for a noncredible setter is to send the message that is most likely to lead to s_{loc} as the electoral outcome.*

There are two ways that a voter can react to the content of a nonverifiable message. A voter can either ignore the content of a nonverifiable message, because she believes that it may be an attempt to mislead her, or she can use other information about the setter to assess the probability that the message is truthful. When a voter is uncertain about the setter's preferences, the act of conditioning her strategy on the content of a nonverifiable message is often risky. In order to show how voters condition their strategies on the content of a nonverifiable message in the absence of a penalty for lying, I compare voter inferences under two methods of updating prior beliefs that uncertain voters could use in equilibrium, and discuss how a voter's preferences for risk influence which updating method we should expect a voter to use.

Consider, for a moment, the case where it is common knowledge that a noncredible setter has the same ideal point as a majority of voters. In equilibrium, the setter always sends a truthful signal (Lemma 5), because she wants a majority of voters to make the same choice she would make if she could vote and voters (using Bayes's rule) always condition their strategy on the message as though the content were true. Now consider a case where it is common knowledge that the noncredible setter and a majority of voters have different preferences over outcomes. In the absence of any penalty for lying, voters may not want to condition their beliefs or their strategies on the content of a nonverifiable message, as there is no reason to believe that the content of the message depends on the actual directional relationship between s_{loc} and SQ.

When the probability that the setter and a majority of voters have the same preferences over outcomes is relatively high, voters can maximize their expected utility by using their prior beliefs about the setter's preferences to make an inference about the probability that the nonverifiable message is truthful. In these cases, voters use their beliefs about the location of the setter's ideal point to make an inference that "the probability that the setter has the same preferences over outcomes as a majority of voters when she signals $s_{mes} = 1$ (resp. -1)" divided by 1 minus "the probability that the setter has the same preferences over outcomes as a majority of voters when she signals $s_{mes} = -1$ (resp. 1)" is equal to the minimum probability that the content of the message $s_{mes} = 1$ (resp. -1) is true. With 1 minus the probability of the event just described, voters cannot make a more accurate inference about the truthfulness of the message.

Let T_{DV} be the ideal point of the decisive voter, let $same_{-1}$ be the probability that $s_{loc} = X$ is closer to T_{DV} than SQ when $s_{mes} = -1$, and let $same_1$ be the probability that $s_{loc} = X$ is closer to T_{DV} than SQ when $s_{mes} = 1$, where $same_{-1} = \text{prob}(-|X - T_{DV}| < -|X - SQ| \text{ and } X < SQ)$ and $same_1$ is defined in a similar manner. When voters observe that the setter sends nonverifiable message $s_{mes} = -1$ and use information about setter preferences, their updated beliefs $F(X|0, -1)$ about the location of s_{loc} are related to their prior beliefs $F(X)$ in the following way (for $same_1 < 1$ and $K = 0$):

$$f(X|0, -1) = \left(\frac{same_{-1}}{1 - same_1} \times \frac{f(X)}{F(SQ)} \right) + \left(\frac{1 - same_{-1}}{1 - same_1} \times f(X) \right) \in [0, SQ);$$

$$f(X|0, -1) = \left(\frac{1 - same_{-1}}{1 - same_1} \times f(X) \right) \in (SQ, 1].$$

Similarly, for nonverifiable message $s_{mes} = 1$, voters update their beliefs in the following way (for $same_{-1} < 1$):

$$f(X|0, 1) = \left(\frac{1 - same_1}{1 - same_{-1}} \times f(X) \right) \in [0, SQ);$$

$$f(X|0, 1) = \left(\frac{same_1}{1 - same_{-1}} \times \frac{f(X)}{1 - F(SQ)} \right) + \left(\frac{1 - same_1}{1 - same_{-1}} \times f(X) \right) \in (SQ, 1].$$

When $same_1$ (resp. $same_{-1}$) equals 1, and voters update in the manner just described, $s_{mes} = -1$ (resp. $s_{mes} = 1$) should never be seen in equilibrium and voters update as though the message were perfectly credible (Section 3.2).

The type of inference described here is similar to the relationship between player preferences and communication identified in Crawford and Sobel (1982). That is, as the preferences of the setter and a majority of voters become more alike (in probability), so does one of the *same* terms, so does the probability that the message is truthful, and – everything else held constant – so does the probability that a voter makes more accurate inferences about the location of s_{loc}. (Notice that voter beliefs about the proximity of setter and voter preferences are derived exclusively from the common knowledge.)

While the method of updating just described has intuitive appeal, it cannot always be used. For instance, consider the case where $s_{mes} = -1$ and our updating method leads a majority of voters to believe that s_{loc} offers higher expected utility than SQ. In the absence of a penalty for lying, all setter types will want to send this message (Lemma 5). A voter who adopts the previous updating method can infer (from the common knowledge) the probability with which she will be led to choose the alternative that she would not have chosen if she were either completely informed or had not conditioned her strategy on the content of the message. If the expected loss from being misled (the probability that the setter's untruthful message affects the electoral outcome given that voters update in the manner just described, multiplied by the expected loss in a voter's utility from the outcome s_{loc} when the voter is misled) is greater than the expected gain from the use of prior beliefs about setter preferences to update beliefs, then the voter is better off using a second updating method – ignoring the content of the message when she chooses her strategy. When voters use this updating method, the equilibrium response of the setter is to babble; it does not matter which message she sends. Since the expected return of each updating scheme for each voter is always based exclusively on common knowledge, I assume that the updating scheme used by each type of voter is common knowledge. In the case where voters do not use beliefs about setter preferences to make an inference about the truthfulness of a nonverifiable message, $F(X) = F(X\,|\,0, -1) = F(X\,|\,0, 1)$.

In addition to making inferences about the truthfulness of a message from information about the setter's ideal point, a voter can also make more accurate inferences about the location of s_{loc} from her observation of costly setter effort. For cases where voters maximize expected utility by ignoring the content of the message, voter updating can be described as in Section 3.1. For cases where voters use their priors about setter preferences, a voter can make more accurate inferences about the location of s_{loc} than from using either piece of information exclusively. For instance, $F(X\,|\,K, -1)$ is related to $F(X)$ in the following way: for $s_{mes} = -1$,

$$f(X\,|\,K, -1) = \left(\frac{same_{-1}}{1 - same_1} \times \frac{f(X)}{F(SQ + \epsilon)} \right)$$

$$+ \left(\frac{1 - same_{-1}}{1 - same_1} \times \frac{f(X)}{1 - F(SQ + \epsilon) + F(SQ - \epsilon)} \right) \in [0, SQ - \epsilon);$$

$$f(X \mid K, -1) = 0 \in [SQ - \epsilon, SQ + \epsilon];$$

$$f(X \mid K, -1) = \frac{1 - same_{-1}}{1 - same_1} \times \frac{f(X)}{1 - F(SQ + \epsilon) + F(SQ - \epsilon)} \in (SQ + \epsilon, 1].$$

In the noncredible equilibrium, the setter challenges SQ, chooses $s_{loc} = X$, and sends a message if and only if her ideal point is outside the range of unprofitable alternatives and the setter expects that updated voter inferences will result in s_{loc} as the electoral outcome. Otherwise, the setter does not challenge SQ. Voters use any observable costly effort by the setter to make an inference about the distance between SQ and s_{loc}. Voters may also choose to update their beliefs about the location of s_{loc} by using their beliefs about the setter's ideal point to make an inference about the truthfulness of the message, if they expect this information to increase their ex post utility.

Centrist voters vote for SQ and always cast the same vote that they would have if they had complete information. Noncentrist voters maximize expected utility, where the expectation is conditioned on their updated beliefs. Voters who observe costly setter effort and receive a message are able to make more accurate inferences about the location of s_{loc} than they would have in the absence of these signals. Again, s_{loc} is the electoral outcome if and only if the number of noncentrist voters for whom the updated expected utility from s_{loc} is greater than the utility from SQ is a majority of all voters. For small K, voters are generally not able to make inferences as accurate as would have been the case if the setter were perfectly credible. As a result, noncredible setters can select s_{loc} to be on the opposite side of SQ as the median voter's ideal point.

A comparison of the perfectly credible and the noncredible equilibria suggests that a perfectly credible setter must be more responsive to voter preferences than a noncredible setter. Although Lemma 2 shows that voters in neither circumstance have enough information to compel the setter to choose some point other than her own ideal point as the location of s_{loc}, only the perfectly credible setter – whose ideal point is on the opposite side of SQ as the median voter's ideal point – is effectively prevented from challenging SQ by the knowledge that voters will receive a credible message about the directional relationship between SQ and s_{loc} and will vote against any policy that the setter prefers to SQ. This difference suggests that providing a noncredible setter with incentives to act like a perfectly credible setter can protect a majority of voters by decreasing the likelihood of electoral outcomes that are on the opposite side of SQ as the median voter's ideal point. In the next section, such incentives are shown to be one effect of the implementation of a penalty for lying on the responsiveness of direct legislation.

3.4   The effect of a penalty for lying

I now introduce a penalty for lying and re-examine the noncredible setter model. The penalty for lying can be thought of as the expected future cost of sending an untruthful message, or as a simple fine. In this model, the "future" is the payoff stage of the game and serves as a metaphor for the fact that signaling strategies chosen now can affect one's future opportunities. Although I have not developed a model of multiperiod interaction in this chapter, the penalty for lying does allow present actions to have common-knowledge consequences. (In order to clearly identify the effect of the penalty for lying, I examine the case where voters do not use their beliefs about the setter's ideal point to compute the probability that a nonverifiable message is true. The exposition and results of this section are robust with respect to both types of updating discussed in the preceding section, but are easier to present under the current assumption.)

I now assume that there is a common-knowledge cost to the setter, $Z > 0$, for sending an untruthful message. Even though the magnitude of Z is common knowledge, voters do not know whether or not the setter has paid Z at the time that they vote. Z can be thought of as a common-knowledge fine or a common belief that the expected penalty for lying (perhaps, the amount of a common-knowledge penalty multiplied by the common expectation of the probability of being "caught lying") is Z. It follows that the cost to the setter of not challenging SQ is zero, the cost of challenging SQ and sending a truthful message is K, and the cost of challenging SQ and sending an untruthful message is $K + Z$. For simplicity, I assume that $K + Z$ is less than the initial endowment of every setter type.[14]

Let $\zeta(Z)$ (henceforth referred to as ζ) be a distance on $[0, 1]$ which is an increasing function of Z.[15] Hence $\epsilon + \zeta$ determines a range of locations of s_{loc} within which it would never be profitable for the setter to send an untruthful message. Since Z and the shape of the setter's utility function are known, the correspondence between Z and ζ is common knowledge. For $s_{loc} \in [0, SQ)$ the range$_{pen}$ of unprofitable alternatives is $[SQ - \epsilon, SQ + \epsilon + \zeta]$, and for $s_{loc} \in (SQ, 1]$ the range$_{pen}$ of unprofitable alternatives is $[SQ - \epsilon - \zeta, SQ + \epsilon]$ (where the subscript "pen" denotes consideration of the penalty for lying). Since the exact boundaries of this range become common knowledge when the voters observe the content of the message, range$_{pen}$ is common knowledge at the time that voters choose their strategies. It follows from Lemma 3 that sending an untruthful message is a

---

[14] We can adapt the definition of the setter's utility and objective function to the presence of a penalty for lying by subtracting a constant Z when the message is untruthful.

[15] Note that $\zeta(0) = 0$.

dominated strategy for setters when s_{loc} is located within the range$_{pen}$ of unprofitable alternatives.

The size and location of the range$_{pen}$ of unprofitable alternatives determine the number of voters that are members of one of two partitions of the electorate: centrist$_{pen}$ voters and noncentrist$_{pen}$ voters. If $s_{mes} = 1$, then centrist$_{pen}$ voters are $\{i \mid T_i \in [SQ - \epsilon/2, SQ + (\epsilon + \zeta)/2]\}$; if $s_{mes} = -1$, then centrist$_{pen}$ voters are $\{i \mid T_i \in [SQ - (\epsilon + \zeta)/2, SQ + \epsilon/2]\}$. All voters not in the set of centrist$_{pen}$ voters comprise the set of noncentrist$_{pen}$ voters. The previous results for centrist voters apply to centrist$_{pen}$ voters.

When there exists a positive penalty for lying, voters can, in equilibrium, condition their strategies on the content of the setter's message. The voter does not necessarily believe that the content is true, but she can use the content to form more accurate beliefs about the true location of s_{loc}. For any particular s_{loc}, only one of the nonzero messages can be untruthful. For instance, if the content of the setter's message is "s_{loc} is to the left of SQ," then a voter can infer that either "the setter has paid K to tell me the truth" or "the setter finds it worthwhile to pay $K + Z$ to tell me that s_{loc} is to the left of SQ when it is, in fact, to the right." If, instead, the content of the setter's message is "s_{loc} is to the right of SQ," one inference a voter can make is that "the setter finds it worthwhile to pay $K + Z$ to tell me that s_{loc} is to the right of SQ, when it is, in fact, to the left." The penalty for lying makes the set of possible locations of s_{loc} for which it would be profitable for a setter to send the "left" message different than the set of possible locations of s_{loc} for which it would be profitable for a setter to send the "right" message. The fact that these sets are different allows voters to make different inferences about the location of s_{loc} based on which value of s_{mes} they observe. That is, the existence of a nonzero penalty for lying allows an incompletely informed voter to condition her strategy on the content of a message sent by a noncredible setter.

This type of inference leads to revised beliefs about the location of s_{loc} that are related to prior beliefs $F(X)$ in the following way.

(a) If $s_{mes} = 1$:

$$f(X \mid K, Z, 1) = 0 \in (SQ - \epsilon, SQ + \epsilon + \zeta);$$

$$f(X \mid K, Z, 1) = f \times \frac{1}{1 - F(SQ + \epsilon + \zeta) + F(SQ - \epsilon)}$$

$$\in [0, SQ - \epsilon] \cup [SQ + \epsilon + \zeta, 1].$$

(b) If $s_{mes} = -1$:

$$f(X \mid K, Z, -1) = 0 \in (SQ - \epsilon - \zeta, SQ + \epsilon);$$

$$f(X \mid K, Z, -1) = f \times \frac{1}{1 - F(SQ + \epsilon) + F(SQ - \epsilon - \zeta)}$$

$$\in [0, SQ - \epsilon - \zeta) \cup (SQ + \epsilon, 1].$$

All other factors held constant, *the penalty for lying may decrease the likelihood that an untruthful message will be sent,* and allows all voters to make more accurate inferences about the location of s_{loc}. The likelihood that an untruthful message is sent decreases when there exist actualizations of s_{loc} for which a setter, who would have sent an untruthful message in the absence of a penalty for lying, will no longer find it profitable to challenge SQ (send a message)

$$[X \in [0, 1]: U_{\text{set}}(s_{\text{loc}}, X) - K > U(SQ, X) > U_{\text{set}}(s_{\text{loc}}, X) - K - Z].$$

The penalty for lying allows voters to make more accurate inferences about the location of s_{loc} than would be the case if there were no penalty. This follows because the range$_{\text{pen}}$ of unprofitable alternatives is wider than the range of unprofitable alternatives, and each range includes only points on $[0, 1]$ that result in ex post false responses to the question "Is this point the location of s_{loc}?"

The existence of a penalty for lying can, under certain circumstances, induce noncredible setters to send only truthful messages. For instance, Z may be large enough so that it is common knowledge that the setter would only find it worthwhile to send a truthful message. That is, for almost any set of parameters, we can make the penalty for lying sufficiently large so as to ensure that no untruthful messages would be sent. An arbitrarily large value of Z is not the only way to ensure that noncredible setters send only credible messages in equilibrium. If a majority of voters would vote for s_{loc} after observing any message but would vote for SQ otherwise, then any setter type for whom it would be profitable to challenge SQ should send the least expensive message. In this case, the least expensive message is the truthful message. This case is the intuition that produces a set of sufficient conditions (Lemma 6) under which noncredible setters send only truthful messages.

Lemma 6. *If sending a message is costly, if there exists a positive penalty for sending an untruthful message, and if it is common knowledge that either message will cause the expected utility from s_{loc} to be greater than the utility from SQ for a majority of voters, then all messages sent are truthful and voters treat any message as though it is perfectly credible.*

When it is common knowledge that Z is large enough to prevent untruthful messages, or if the conditions listed in Lemma 6 hold, it is then common knowledge that a noncredible setter will send a truthful message. In either case, our description of voter inferences, equilibrium player strategies, and electoral outcomes will be the same whether we used this section's equilibrium or borrowed the descriptions from the version of the model where the setter was perfectly credible (Section 3.2).

In the "noncredible setter with penalty" equilibrium, the setter challenges SQ, chooses $s_{loc} = X$, and sends a message if and only if she expects that s_{loc} will be the electoral outcome and the benefit from affecting the outcome is greater than the cost of challenging SQ. It is common knowledge that the message is truthful if either the conditions of Lemma 6 hold or K is sufficiently large.

Centrist$_{pen}$ voters vote for SQ and always cast the same vote that they would have if they had complete information. Noncentrist$_{pen}$ voters maximize expected utility, where the expectation is conditioned on their beliefs about s_{loc}, which in turn is conditioned on K and Z. If it is common knowledge that any message the setter sends will result in s_{loc} as the outcome, voters also believe s_{mes} and make a directional inference about the relationship between s_{loc} and SQ. Regardless of its true location, s_{loc} is the electoral outcome if and only if the number of noncentrist$_{pen}$ voters for whom the updated expected utility from s_{loc} is greater than the utility from SQ is a majority of all voters.

A comparison of the last two equilibria shows the effect of a penalty for lying. When s_{loc} is located in the range$_{pen}$ of unprofitable alternatives, setters do not send a message in the presence of a penalty for lying. Thus, the penalty for lying can reduce the likelihood that a message is untruthful. Also, noncentrist$_{pen}$ voters condition their strategies on more accurate beliefs than they would if no penalty existed, since the range$_{pen}$ of unprofitable alternatives is wider than the range of unprofitable alternatives. It follows that the introduction of a penalty for lying leads to an increase in the likelihood that the complete-information electoral outcome is the same as the outcome that the incompletely informed voters choose, as well as an increase in the responsiveness of direct legislation outcomes to complete-information voter preferences.

4   Conclusion

I have developed a model that allows me to demonstrate how credible and noncredible signals affect the likelihood that (1) an incompletely informed voter casts the same vote she would have cast if she had complete information, and (2) the outcome that an incompletely informed electorate chooses is the same as the outcome that the same electorate, if completely informed, would have chosen. The intuition that generates these results is that voters can make more accurate inferences by conditioning their voting behavior on the content of a message if either the setter is perfectly credible, or the setter is known to have the same preferences over outcomes as a majority of voters, or there exists a penalty for lying. If there exists no penalty and the information provider is not credible, voters can still make better inferences about which of the potential electoral outcomes would lead to a preferred state of the world by their ability to observe how much effort the setter put into attempting to change the electoral outcome and by their beliefs about setter preferences. I also showed that the agenda setter's decision to challenge SQ was affected by her expectation of the types of information voters would receive – an agenda setter with different preferences over outcomes than a majority of voters was less likely to enter as the accuracy of voter inferences about the electoral alternatives increased.

My findings have at least two implications for collective choice institutions that include badly informed decision makers. First, many people who are asked to make decisions have neither the time nor the resources either to gather information about complex issues or to verify the validity of arguments made for or against certain potential outcomes. Oftentimes, the only information available to decision makers comes from sources whose preferences or incentives are unknown. My analysis shows that these conditions are not sufficient for us to conclude that decision makers cannot make the same choice that they would if they were fully informed.

Second, a positive penalty for lying was shown to enable an incompletely informed decision maker to use the content of a noncredible message to make more accurate inferences about the relationship between her actions and subsequent outcomes. This implies that institutional designers may want to consider introducing this type of penalty if they desire outcomes that are more likely to correspond to the outcomes that would be chosen by completely informed decision makers. Introducing, enforcing, and publicizing the existence of penalties for lying should provide incompletely informed decision makers with the ability to ask "What does this information provider have to lose by misleading me?" – a question that this research shows will produce more accurate inferences by decision makers. Of course, there are problems associated with the definition of "truth," but as long as there exists a set of possible messages that are clearly false then common-knowledge penalties for lying might be an efficient way of increasing the likelihood that actual collective choice outcomes are the same as those that a completely informed electorate would choose.

Uncertainty is a common feature of collective choice. In order to make the claim that a particular direct legislation electoral outcome represents some aspect of public opinion on a particular policy issue, we must understand how the institution converts individual preferences into electoral outcomes. In an attempt to better understand this process, and to broaden the applicability of the intuition provided by the model, my own ongoing research focuses on the effect of different types of electoral competition on voter inferences and the responsiveness of direct legislation. The presence of incompletely informed voters generates the potential effectiveness of information cues. If political elites expect cues to have an effect on voting behavior, we should not be surprised when they incorporate the provision of information cues into their electoral strategies. I expect that competition among potential agenda controllers and competition among information providers will affect the type and content of information available to voters. Identifying the conditions under which competition affects information, and the conditions under which information affects voting behavior, should provide a dynamic and relatively comprehensive description of the relationship between individual policy preferences and electoral outcomes in a substantively interesting class of collective choice rules.

Appendix A: Selected proofs

A.1   *Proof of Lemma 2 for a noncredible setter*

The setter's choice of strategy relays information to the voters. Voters condition their choice on the communication $s_{mes} \in \{-1, 1\}$, $s_{mes} = (s_{chal}, s_{loc}, s_{mes})$. I now establish the dominance of the strategy when the setter is noncredible. The proof of this lemma for the case of a perfectly credible setter follows straightforwardly from Lupia (1992).

To show that $s_{loc} = X$ is a weakly dominant strategy for the noncredible setters, it must be true that this strategy is dominant independent of the setter's choice of message content. Consider the following two mutually exclusive and collectively exhaustive cases.

Case 1: The setter sends a truthful message.   Let $s'_{loc} \neq X$ and $s_{loc} = X$, where $s' = (1, s'_{loc}, s'_{mes})$ and $s = (1, X, s_{mes})$. In the case where the setter sends a truthful message, there are two possible subcases: $s_{mes} = s'_{mes}$ and $s_{mes} \neq s'_{mes}$.

(a)   If $s'_{loc} \neq X$ and $s_{mes} = s'_{mes}$ then $U_{set}(X, X) > U_{set}(s'_{loc}, X)$, which implies

$$\Phi_{set}(s \mid K, Z, X) \geq \Phi_{set}(s' \mid K, Z, X).$$

(That is, since $s_{mes} = s'_{mes}$, voters cannot differentiate amongst the setter types that would send each message.) Thus, $s_{loc} = X$ is a weakly dominant setter location strategy for this subcase.

(b) If $s'_{loc} \neq X$ and $s_{mes} \neq s'_{mes}$, then $s'_{loc} \neq SQ$ (unless $s_{loc} = SQ$, in which case the outcome is trivially SQ). Let

$$s''_{loc} = \frac{s_{chal} + SQ}{2}.$$

In the truthful-message case, $s_{mes} \neq s'_{mes}$ implies that X and s_{loc} are on opposite sides of SQ. Thus, any s''_{loc} that is closer to SQ gives higher utility to the setter: $U_{set}(s''_{loc}, X) > U_{set}(s'_{loc}, X)$. So, changing from s'_{loc} to s''_{loc} gives the setter a higher level of utility. If $\int_{C(SQ, K, z, s_{mes})} dG(T) \geq \frac{1}{2}$, the setter receives $U_{set}(SQ, X) - K$ independent of her choice of s_{loc}; if $\int_{C(SQ, K, z, s_{mes})} dG(T) < \frac{1}{2}$, the setter receives $U_{set}(s''_{loc}, X) - K$. But

$$U_{set}(s''_{loc}, X) - K < U_{set}(s'_{loc}, X) < U_{set}(SQ, X)$$

by assumption. Only s''_{loc} closer to X than SQ would give the setter higher utility if $\int_{C(SQ, K, z, s_{mes})} dG(T) < \frac{1}{2}$, but – from subcase (a) – $s_{loc} = X$ is a weakly dominant setter location strategy. Thus, $s_{loc} = X$ is a weakly dominant setter location strategy for this subcase also.

Case 2: The setter sends an untruthful message. Let $s'_{loc} \neq X$ and $s_{loc} = X$, where $s' = (1, s'_{loc}, s'_{mes})$ and $s = (1, X, s_{mes})$. We consider two collectively exhaustive subcases, one where s_{loc} and s'_{loc} are on the same side of SQ and the other where s_{loc} and s'_{loc} are on opposite sides of SQ.[16]

(a) Let $s'_{loc} \neq X$ and $s_{loc} = X$, and let s'_{loc} and X be on the same side of SQ. In this case the untruthful messages are the same for both strategies, $s_{mes} = s'_{mes}$, as is the cost of sending a message, and voters cannot distinguish among (or reward) setter types who send the same message. Therefore, for any s_{loc},

$$\Phi_{set}(s \mid K, Z, X) \geq \Phi_{set}(s' \mid K, Z, X).$$

(b) Let $s'_{loc} \neq X$ and $s_{loc} = X$, and let s'_{loc} and X be on opposite sides of SQ. In this case, corresponding untruthful messages are unequal, $s_{mes} \neq s'_{mes}$. For any $X \in [0, 1]$ it must be the case that either $o(s', v_N(T_N, s'_{mes})) = o(s, v_N(T_N, s_{mes}))$ or $o(s', v_N(T_N, s'_{mes})) \neq$

---

[16] The case where $s'_{loc} = SQ$ is shown as part of the "opposite" case. In the case where $s_{loc} = SQ$, the outcome is SQ.

$o(s, v_N(T_N, s_{mes}))$. If the equality holds (choice of untruthful message does not affect outcome), then it follows straightforwardly that

$$\Phi_{set}(s \mid K, Z, X) \geq \Phi_{set}(s' \mid K, Z, X)$$

and $X = s_{loc}$ is a weakly dominant partial strategy.

Now consider the two circumstances under which the inequality holds. If $\int_{C(SQ, K, Z, s'_{mes})} dG(T) < \frac{1}{2}$ (the setter chooses an alternative that is on the opposite side of SQ from her ideal point, sends an "untruthful message," and knows that she will win the election if she sends that message). Then the setter receives $U_{set}(s'_{loc}, X) - K$, but in this case an undominated strategy for the setter is to choose $s_{loc} = X$ (and the untruthful message changes to a truthful message). If $\int_{C(SQ, K, Z, s'_{mes})} dG(T) \geq \frac{1}{2}$ (the setter chooses an alternative that is on the opposite side of SQ from her ideal point, sends an "untruthful message," and knows that she will lose the election if she sends that message), then the same outcome is true for all s'_{loc} on the opposite side of SQ, which implies that such a choice of s_{loc} is at least weakly dominated by the choice of s'_{loc} on the same side of SQ as X (in which case $s_{loc} = X$ is undominated).

Since $s_{loc} = X$ is weakly dominant for all cases, it is weakly dominant for all noncredible setters in this model.   □

A.2   Proof of Lemma 6

From the assumption that SQ, F, $G(T)$, ϵ, ζ, and the shape of voter utility functions are common knowledge, it follows that one and only one of the following statements can be true:

1. Neither of the messages a setter can send will lead to s_{loc} as the electoral outcome.
2. Only one of the messages a setter can send will lead to s_{loc} as the electoral outcome.
3. Both of the messages a setter can send will lead to s_{loc} as the electoral outcome.

If it is common knowledge that case 1 is the true state of the world then, from Lemma 1, no setter will challenge SQ. If it is common knowledge that case 2 is the true state of the world, then only some setter types can be expected to provide truthful information (Lemma 5), and voters cannot be certain the message contains truthful information. If it is common knowledge that case 3 is the true state of the world then all setters who send messages send truthful messages. Consider the case $SQ > s_{loc}$ (the case $s_{loc} > SQ$ is equivalent). Let $v_N = v_1, ..., v_n$. If $o((1, s_{loc}, 1), v_N) = s_{loc}$ and $o((1, s_{loc}, -1), v_N) = s_{loc}$ then, for all $X \in [0, 1]$,

$$\phi_{set}(1, s_{loc}, -1 \mid K, G, X) = U_{set}(s_{loc}, X) - K;$$

$$\phi_{set}(1, s_{loc}, 1 \mid K, G, X) = U_{set}(s_{loc}, X) - (K + Z).$$

Since $Z > 0$, $\phi_{set}(1, s_{loc}, -1 \mid K, G, X)$ dominates $\phi_{set}(1, s_{loc}, 1 \mid K, G, X)$.

□

Appendix B: Formal statement of equilibria

B.1   *Verifiable-message equilibrium*

(a)   For all $X \in [SQ - \epsilon, SQ + \epsilon]$, $s_{chal} = 0$.

(b)   For all $X \in [0, SQ - \epsilon] \cup (SQ + \epsilon, 1]$:

$$s_{chal} = \begin{cases} 1 & \text{if } s_{loc} < SQ \text{ and } C(SQ, K, -1) < N/2, \\ 1 & \text{if } s_{loc} > SQ \text{ and } C(SQ, K, 1) < N/2, \\ 0 & \text{otherwise.} \end{cases}$$

(c)   For all $X \in [0, 1]$, $s_{loc} = X$.

(d)   For all $T_i \in [0, SQ - \epsilon)$:

$$v_i(T_i, K, s_{mes}) = \begin{cases} 1 & \text{if } s_{mes} = -1 \text{ and} \\ & \int_0^1 [U_i(X, T_i) f(X \mid K, -1)] > U_i(SQ, T_i) \\ & \text{and } s_{chal} = 1, \\ -1 & \text{otherwise.} \end{cases}$$

(e)   For all $T_i \in (SQ + \epsilon, 1]$:

$$v_i(T_i, K, s_{mes}) = \begin{cases} 1 & \text{if } s_{mes} = 1 \text{ and} \\ & \int_0^1 [U_i(X, T_i) f(X \mid K, 1)] > U_i(SQ, T_i) \\ & \text{and } s_{chal} = 1, \\ -1 & \text{otherwise.} \end{cases}$$

Beliefs can be characterized by $f(X \mid K, -1)$ or $f(X \mid X \mid K, 1)$.

B.2   *Nonverifiable-message equilibrium*

(a)   For all $X \in [SQ - \epsilon, SQ + \epsilon]$, $s_{chal} = 0$.

(b)   For all $X \in [0, 1]$, $s_{loc} = X$.

(c)   If $o(1, v_N) = s_{loc}$ and $o(-1, v_N) = s_{loc}$, then

$s_{\text{loc}} < SQ \rightarrow s_{\text{mes}} = -1$ and $s_{\text{loc}} > SQ \rightarrow s_{\text{mes}} = 1$.

Otherwise,

$$
s_{\text{mes}} = \begin{cases} -1 & \text{if } \int_{C(SQ,K,Z,-1)} dG(T) < \frac{1}{2} \text{ and} \\ & s_{\text{loc}} \notin [SQ+\epsilon, SQ+\epsilon+\zeta]; \\ 1 & \text{if } \int_{C(SQ,K,Z,1)} dG(T) < \frac{1}{2} \text{ and} \\ & s_{\text{loc}} \notin [SQ-\epsilon-\zeta, SQ-\epsilon]; \\ s_{\text{chal}} = 0 & \text{otherwise.} \end{cases}
$$

(d)   If $s_{\text{mes}} = -1$ then:

$\forall T_i \in [SQ - \epsilon/2, SQ + (\epsilon + \zeta)/2], \quad v_i(T_i, K, Z, -1) = -1;$

$\forall T_i \in [0, SQ - \epsilon/2) \cup (SQ + (\epsilon + \zeta)/2, 1],$

$$
v_i(T_i, K, Z, -1) = \begin{cases} 1 & \text{if } \int_0^1 [U_i(X, T_i) f(X \mid K, Z, -1)] \\ & \qquad\qquad\qquad\qquad > U_i(SQ, T_i), \\ -1 & \text{otherwise.} \end{cases}
$$

(e)   If $s_{\text{mes}} = 1$ then:

$\forall T_i \in [SQ - (\epsilon + \zeta)/2, SQ + \epsilon/2], \quad v_i(T_i, K, Z, 1) = -1;$

$\forall T_i \in [0, SQ - (\epsilon + \zeta)/2) \cup (SQ + \epsilon/2, 1],$

$$
v_i(T_i, K, Z, 1) = \begin{cases} 1 & \text{if } \int_0^1 [U_i(X, T_i) f(X \mid K, Z, 1)] \\ & \qquad\qquad\qquad\qquad > U_i(SQ, T_i), \\ -1 & \text{otherwise.} \end{cases}
$$

Beliefs can be characterized by $f(X \mid K, Z, -1)$, $f(X \mid K, Z, 1)$, $f'(X \mid K, Z, -1)$, or $f'(X \mid K, Z, 1)$.

REFERENCES

Banks, Jeffrey S. (1990), "Monopoly Agenda Control and Asymmetric Information," *Quarterly Journal of Economics* 105: 445-64.

Calvert, Randall (1985), "The Value of Biased Information: A Rational Choice Model of Political Advice," *Journal of Politics* 47: 530-55.

Campbell, Angus, Philip E. Converse, Warren E. Miller, and Donald E. Stokes (1960), *The American Voter.* New York: Wiley.

Crawford, Vincent, and Joel Sobel (1982), "Strategic Information Transmission," *Econometrica* 50: 1431-51.

Cronin, Thomas E. (1989), *Direct Democracy: The Politics of Referendum, Initiative and Recall.* Cambridge, MA: Harvard University Press.

Denzau, Arthur, and Robert Mackay (1983), "Gatekeeping and Monopoly Power of Committees: An Analysis of Sincere and Sophisticated Behavior," *American Journal of Political Science* 27: 740-61.

Fiorina, Morris P. (1981), *Retrospective Voting in American National Elections.* New Haven, CT: Yale University Press.

Kreps, David M., and Robert Wilson (1982), "Sequential Equilibria," *Econometrica* 50: 863–94.

Lupia, Arthur (1992), "Busy Voters, Agenda Control and the Power of Information," *American Political Science Review* 86: 390–403.

Magleby, David B. (1984), *Direct Legislation: Voting on Ballot Propositions in the United States.* Baltimore: Johns Hopkins.

McKelvey, Richard D., and Peter C. Ordeshook (1985), "Elections with Limited Information: A Fulfilled Expectations Model Using Contemporaneous Poll and Endorsement Data as Information Sources," *Journal of Economic Theory* 36: 55–85.

Milgrom, Paul, and John Roberts (1986), "Relying on the Information of Interested Parties," *RAND Journal of Economics* 17: 18–32.

Okuno-Fujiwara, Masahiro, Andrew Postlewaite, and Kotaro Suzumura (1990), "Strategic Information Revelation," *Review of Economic Studies* 57: 25–48.

Popkin, Samuel L. (1991), *The Reasoning Voter: Communication and Persuasion in Presidential Campaigns.* Chicago: University of Chicago Press.

Romer, Thomas, and Howard Rosenthal (1978), "Political Resource Allocation, Controlled Agendas, and the Status Quo," *Public Choice* 33: 27–44.

Sobel, Joel (1985), "A Theory of Credibility," *Review of Economic Studies* 52: 557–73.

Spence, Michael (1973), "Job Market Signaling," *Quarterly Journal of Economics* 87: 355–74.

PART V

Information acquisition by government

CHAPTER 16

Information acquisition and orthogonal argument

David Austen-Smith

1   Introduction

Political rhetoric is effective in influencing political decision making to the extent that it alters individuals' beliefs about how actions are related to consequences. Although this is, I would argue, as true of moral debate as it is of purely technical argument, this chapter is concerned primarily with the latter. In particular, the focus is on a single decision maker who must choose an alternative from some feasible set; the consequences of her choice, however, are known only with uncertainty, and she can receive information about how actions and consequences are related only through the (cheap-talk) advice of one or two "experts." Strategic issues arise because experts too have preferences over outcomes.

The seminal papers on strategic information transmission of the sort considered here are Crawford and Sobel (1982) and Farrell (1985). In explicitly political settings, Austen-Smith (1990a,b, 1993), Matthews (1989), and – when discussing committee decision making under open rule – Gilligan and Krehbiel (1987, 1989, 1990) have all considered costless signaling models of rhetoric as strategic information sharing. Although these models vary in the assumptions made about the institutional setting, the extent to which experts are fully or partially informed, the number of experts and decision makers, and so forth, they all have two assumptions in common. First, the action set for any decision maker is the real line; and second, the extent to which experts are informed relative to decision makers is given exogenously.[1] Consequently, the models do not address questions

This is an extensively revised version of a paper originally prepared for presentation at the Conference in Political Economy, Washington University, St. Louis, Mo., May 23–25, 1991. I am grateful to the anonymous referees for useful comments, and to the National Science Foundation for financial support.
[1] One exception is Gilligan and Krehbiel (1987), who consider the incentives for committees (experts) to become informed. In their models, a potential expert can choose to become fully informed at some cost, or acquire no information at all.

407

about rhetoric designed to influence decisions over a fixed agenda, or about how much information to acquire on particular issues of a multidimensional policy decision.

Casual empiricism and more careful empirical work suggest that when policy decisions are multidimensional, prima facie antagonists on some decision tend to argue their respective cases on orthogonal issues. For example (casual empiricism), a reading of the House debates on the 1977 Clean Air Act (*Congressional Record* 1977) reveals that while proponents of tightening regulation on emissions and so forth presented a host of information on the health and environmental consequences of the bill, they almost wholly ignored the focus of their opponents, who in turn argued against further regulation almost exclusively on economic grounds (especially rising unemployment in the auto industry). Similarly (careful empiricism), in his study of the rhetoric of the ratification campaigns in the late eighteenth century, Riker (1991) was struck by two regularities that he termed the dominance and the dispersion principles, jointly summarized in the statement: "When one side has an advantage on an issue, the other side ignores it: but when neither side has an an advantage, both seek new and advantageous issues" (1991, p. 38). In effect, the principles amount to a claim that two sides of a debate will generally argue on orthogonal issues. However, not all debates follow this pattern. Richard Smith (1989) discusses the interaction between the two major teachers' unions who opposed each other on whether Education should become an agency in its own right or be left under the HEW umbrella. In this case, the "pro" and "anti" camps debated on essentially the same issue: will Education get a larger budget as a separate agency, or is it better off being "carried" by the two huge budgets commanded by Health and Welfare? Neither side, of course, could provide a definitive answer, but both sides marshaled an array of economic estimates and distributive arguments to support their claims.

Given such examples, then, natural questions to ask are: Under what circumstances can we expect to observe two sides of an issue debating on the same ground or on orthogonal grounds; and can we say anything about the influence of one type of argument (e.g., specialist, single-issue, or generalist) relative to another? Related questions concern the choice of how much information to acquire before engaging in trying to influence some decision maker(s). In some instances, proponents of a bill choose *not* to obtain information on some issue, despite it being both relevant and (to them) readily available (e.g. Mansbridge 1986). A rationale behind such actions appears to be that the risk of discovering information unfavorable to the group's cause is too high and, furthermore, it would likely become common knowledge that the group had the information whether or not they used it – in which case, not to use it would be seen as a signal that it was indeed unfavorable. What follows is an attempt to shed some light on these questions.

The plan of the chapter is as follows. Section 2 describes the model; Section 3 examines the strategic incentives when the agenda is a predetermined pair of alternatives in a 2-dimensional Euclidean space; and Section 4 does the same assuming the decision maker is free to pick any point in the space. Section 5 draws the threads together and concludes. It must be emphasized at the outset that this chapter is distinctly exploratory: none of the results can claim any generality, and most of the discussion is conducted through a sequence of more-or-less complex examples.

2   The model

2.0   *Overview*

The model involves a decision maker and two possible advisors. The decision maker has to select some action, or policy; in one case, the possible decision is binary (e.g., vote for A or vote for B), and in the other there are essentially no effective constraints on what to choose (e.g., pick any tax rate between 0 and 100 percent). So, for example, when the decision is binary, the decision maker might be a pivotal voter with the advisors being advocates for the alternatives; and when there are no constraints, the decision maker might represent a pivotal legislator in the House with the advisors being (unitary-actor) committees making proposals under open rule.

Actions map into consequences only with uncertainty: legislation is a means to an end, not an end in itself, and the outcome associated with any legislative decision depends not only on the decision itself but also on the realization of some stochastic parameters. For instance, total milk production depends partly on the level of price support (which can be legislated unequivocally) and partly on how nature "chooses" the health of the dairy herds (which is stochastic). In view of this, the decision maker chooses actions under uncertainty. An *expert* in this chapter is understood to be an individual possessing relatively more information about the likely consequences of any action than the decision maker. In particular, the possible advisors are assumed to be able to observe something about the distribution of the random component to consequences and, therefore, be able in principle to influence the decision maker's choice by volunteering policy-relevant information. However, since all individuals' preferences over consequences are presumed to be common knowledge and since giving advice is costless, the extent and character of such influence depends on the strategic interaction between advisors and decision maker and on the extent to which advisors possess information that the decision maker does not. And with respect to this last point, advisors are assumed free to acquire more or less information up to some exogenously given limit, beyond which the cost of information becomes prohibitive. In general, information acquisition is costly with more information requiring higher expenditures, so the assumption made here requires justification. This is offered during the formal development of the model, to which I now turn.

2.1   Players, preferences, and technology

There are three individuals, indexed $i \in \{R, 1, 2\}$. Each individual i has preferences on the outcome space, $X = \mathbb{R}^2$, given by

$$U^i(y) = -(x^i - y)W^i(x^i - y)' \quad \forall y \in X, \tag{1}$$

where $x^i \in X$ is i's ideal point and

$$W^i \equiv \begin{bmatrix} a^i & c^i \\ c^i & b^i \end{bmatrix}$$

is a positive-definite matrix of scalars. To save on notation, normalize X by setting $x^R \equiv 0$.

Individual R (the receiver, or decision maker) must choose a policy from some set $P \subseteq \mathbb{R}^2$. Policies map into outcomes according to the technology

$$y(p; \omega) = p - \omega \quad \forall p \in P, \tag{2}$$

where ω is the realization of a 2-dimensional random variable $\Omega = (\Omega_1, \Omega_2)$ distributed on $\{0, 1\}^2$. Thus the outcome from any particular policy choice is known only with uncertainty.

Substituting for y into U^i and taking expectations yields i's induced preferences over P:

$$u^i(p) \equiv EU^i(p - \Omega) = -(x^i + E\Omega - p)W^i(x^i + E\Omega - p)' - V^i, \tag{3}$$

where $V^i \equiv (a^i, b^i, 2c^i) \cdot (\text{var}[\Omega_1], \text{var}[\Omega_2], \text{cov}[\Omega_1, \Omega_2])'$.

2.2   Information

Players' preferences $U^i(\cdot)$ are common knowledge, as is the technology $y(\cdot, \cdot)$. Assume that Ω_l has a Bernoulli distribution with unknown parameter $q_l \in (0, 1)$, $l = 1, 2$, and that $\text{cov}[\Omega_1, \Omega_2] \equiv 0$. All players share a common prior on q_l given by a beta distribution with parameters $\alpha_l, \beta_l > 0$.

Although certainly not pathological, the nature of uncertainty here is somewhat special; each component of a 2-dimensional policy decision is subject to a stochastic binary shock (high or low), and these shocks are independent across dimensions. More general settings include richer descriptions of uncertainty; for example, Ω might be distributed on a connected subset of $\mathbb{R}^2$, or its distribution might be correlated in some way with the policy choice itself. The justification for the specification used here is simply that it generates a tractable model yielding some intuition about the more general environments.

Players 1 and 2 are the potential advisors, or experts. They have no decision-making rights but are able to acquire firsthand information on the likely value of Ω_l. Specifically, for $i, l \in \{1, 2\}$, i may freely choose to observe a sample of $n_l^i \in N_l^i \subseteq \{0, 1, 2, 3, \ldots\}$ random draws from the distribution of Ω_l. Assume that $|N_l^i| < \infty$ is exogenously fixed.

The implicit information acquisition cost function used here is extreme: a potential advisor can obtain any amount of information at no cost up to some maximum (finite) level, beyond which the cost becomes prohibitive. The rationale for this assumption derives from the concern to treat advisors' specialization choices as endogenous. In particular, the observations in Section 1 suggest that advisors' selection of the issue on which to focus depends at least in part upon the decision maker's inferences from anything the advisor might say. By letting information acquisition costs be zero up to some point, therefore, the influence of these sorts of endogenous strategic considerations on data acquisition is unequivocal. With explicit and positive costs, additional budget-based incentives would obscure the link between strategic information signaling per se and information acquisition. Moreover, if both advisors faced identical cost acquisition schedules, then the assumption here is simply a normalization with differences in $|N_l^i|$ reflecting budget asymmetries.

For $i = 1, 2$, assume $n^i \in N^i = N_1^i \times N_2^i$ is common knowledge but that realizations of i's sample are private information to i. So when an advisor seeks to influence the decision maker's choice, the decision maker knows just how expert is the advisor. (An alternative interpretation here is that an interest group i, say, with preferences U^i, chooses what type of lobbyist or expert to hire to argue its case. By assuming that, once hired, such a lobbyist has no goal save to promote the group, "choosing a level of expertise" and "choosing an expert" become analytically equivalent.) The decision maker ($i = R$) can receive further information on the distribution of Ω only through the advice of 1 and 2; that is, assume $N_l^R = \{0\}$ for all l. So if $n_l^i \neq 0$ for some $i \in \{1, 2\}$, i is better informed than R with respect to the likely consequences of a policy p for issue l. However, $n_l^i < \infty$ implies that i is not fully informed.

For a given sample of n_j^i observations from the distribution of Ω_l, let $t_j^i \in T(n_j^i) = \{0, 1, \ldots, n_j^i\}$ denote the number of observations in the sample with value 1. Once chosen, n^i is common knowledge; consequently, i's *type* is completely described by $t^i \in T(n^i) = T(n_1^i) \times T(n_2^i)$ and t^i is private information to i. Evidently, $T(0) = \emptyset$. In this model, then, i's type summarizes the information that i possesses about how policies are likely to map into consequences. Furthermore, the larger is n^i the greater the informative content of any given value of $t^i \in T(n^i)$ – that is, the more expert is advisor i about the issues.

2.3   Decision sequence and strategies

There are three decision stages. First, each $i \in \{1, 2\}$ simultaneously selects $n^i \in N^i$, and nature determines t^i; second, each $i \in \{1, 2\}$ simultaneously makes a cheap-talk speech (sends a message) to R; and third, having heard the messages, R selects a policy from P. Finally, nature draws ω and all players receive their payoffs.

A strategy for $i \in \{1, 2\}$ has two parts: an information acquisition strategy and a talking strategy. An *information acquisition strategy* for i is a choice of $n^i \in N^i$; given n^i, a *talking strategy* for i is a map

$$\mu_i : T(n^i) \to M,$$

where M is an arbitrary uncountable message space. Given that sending messages is costless (cheap talk), excluding mixed strategies here is with little loss of generality (see Austen-Smith 1992 for a more formal justification). If $\mu_i(t) = \mu_i(t')$ for all $t, t' \in T(n^i)$, then μ_i is a pooling strategy; if $\mu_i(t) \neq \mu_i(t')$ for all $t, t' \in T(n^i)$, then μ_i is a separating strategy.

A *decision strategy* for R is a map

$$\delta : M \times M \to P.$$

By (3), the circumstances under which R might use a mixed strategy in equilibrium are nongeneric, and so ignored.

2.4   Equilibrium

The solution concept used here is sequential equilibrium with undominated strategies: at each decision stage, players' strategies must be mutually (undominated) best responses relative to the beliefs held at that stage, and beliefs must be consistent with Bayes's rule where this is defined. Because talk is costless and all players are risk-averse, there is always an equilibrium in which $i \in \{1, 2\}$ selects $n^i = (|N_1^i|, |N_2^i|)$ and adopts a pooling strategy, and in which R selects the policy $p \in P$ that maximizes her expected payoff with respect to the prior beliefs on Ω. Under some circumstances, such equilibria are essentially the only equilibria. This is not always so, however, in which case I shall focus on the most informative available equilibria.[2] In particular, I am interested in influential equilibria. Fix an equilibrium set of strategies, (n^*, μ^*, δ^*).[3] Then i's talking strategy μ_i^* is *influential* if and only if R's strategy δ^* is not constant for all messages sent under μ_j^*, $j \neq i$. An equilibrium in which μ_i^* is influential for at least some $i \in \{1, 2\}$ is said to be an *influential equilibrium*.

3   Constrained agenda: $P = \{A, B\}$

In this section, R is assumed to be constrained to choose between two distinct alternatives, A and B. For example, R may be the pivotal voter in some majoritarian decision process. So $p = (p_1, p_2) \in P = \{A, B\} \subseteq \mathbb{R}^2$. Manipulating expression (3) gives

$$u^i(A) \gtreqless u^i(B) \quad \text{as} \quad Z^i \gtreqless \hat{\Omega}(\cdot)L^i, \tag{4}$$

where $\hat{\Omega}(\cdot)L^i \equiv [\hat{\Omega}_1(\cdot)L_1^i + \hat{\Omega}_2(\cdot)L_2^i]$, $\hat{\Omega}_l(\cdot) \equiv E[\Omega_l | \cdot]$, and

$$Z^i \equiv a^i d_1 \Delta_1 + b^i d_2 \Delta_2 - [x_1^i L_1^i + x_2^i L_2^i];$$

$$L_1^i \equiv a^i \Delta_1 + c^i \Delta_2; \qquad L_2^i \equiv b^i \Delta_2 + c^i \Delta_1;$$

$$d_l \equiv (A_l + B_l)/2; \qquad \Delta_l \equiv B_l - A_l.$$

Thus there exists a line in $\mathbb{R}^2$ such that for $E\Omega$ lying on one side of the line, i strictly prefers B to A; and conversely for $E\Omega$ lying on the other side of the line. Figure 1 illustrates the decision rule.

For any $i \in \{1, 2\}$, let $T_A(n^i)$ describe any information, given n^i, that induces i to weakly prefer alternative A to B:

$$T_A(n^i) = \{t \in T(n^i) \mid Z^i \geq \hat{\Omega}(t)L^i\}.$$

Let $T_B(n^i) = T(n^i) \setminus T_A(n^i)$. Then the following simple result characterizes informative and influential equilibria.

Proposition 1.   *In any influential equilibrium* (n^*, μ^*, δ^*):

(1.1) $\forall i \neq R$, $\mu_i^*(t) \in M_A \subset M$ $\forall t \in T_A(n^{i*})$ *and*
$\mu_i^*(t') \in M \setminus M_A$ $\forall t' \in T_B(n^{i*})$;

---

[2] An equilibrium is *informative* if there exist equilibrium messages from $i \in \{1, 2\}$ such that R's posterior on the expected value of Ω, conditional on hearing these messages, is distinct from R's prior.

[3] Throughout, $n = (n^1, n^2)$ and $\mu = (\mu^1, \mu^2)$. When there is only one sender, say i, it is understood that $n \equiv n^i$ and $\mu \equiv \mu^i$. Also, E_μ is the expectation operator conditional on strategies μ, etc.

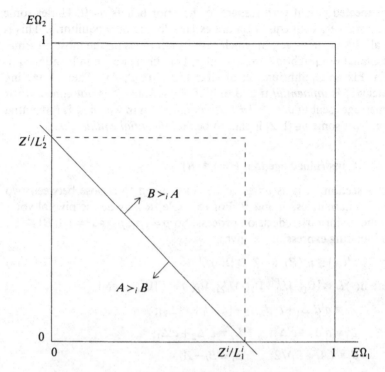

Figure 1. Agent i's induced preferences over $\{A, B\}$, with $x >_i y \equiv u^i(x) > u^i(y)$.

(1.2) $\forall (m, m') \in M \times M, \delta^*(m, m') = A\ [B]\ as$
$Z^R > [<]\ E_{\mu^*}[\Omega \mid m, m']L^R.$

(The proof of Proposition 1 and all subsequent formal claims are confined to the appendix.) Essentially, therefore, at most two messages are sent in equilibrium by any advisor i; "choose A" if $t^i \in T_A(n^i)$ and "choose B" otherwise (let these messages be m_A and m_B, respectively). In particular, even if $n_l^i > 0$ for some i and all l, i cannot credibly provide any less aggregated information about his type than that captured in the speech "choose p."

The messages (or speeches) given by the advisors accurately reflect the interests of the speaker, but not necessarily the interests of the decision maker R. For instance, suppose $x^1 \neq x^R$. Then for some n^1, there will typically exist $t \in T_A(n^1)$ such that the decision maker, were she to know t surely, would choose B. Nevertheless, if condition (1.2) holds, R rationally chooses A on hearing the advice from $i = 1$, "choose A," even though there is a chance that her full-information decision is B. In other words, in any influential equilibrium advisors tell the truth but are incapable of credibly telling "the whole truth," even when they so wish.

It follows from Proposition 1 that a necessary condition for an influential equilibrium to exist is that, for some $i \in \{1, 2\}$, $T_A(n^i) \neq \{\emptyset, T(n^i)\}$ – that is, that i have state-dependent induced preferences over $\{A, B\}$. It is apparent from (4) and Figure 1 that an agent can have state-independent preferences on each dimension l separately yet have state-dependent preferences on the two dimensions considered jointly; for example, in Figure 1 let the prior $E\Omega_l > Z^i/L_l^i$ for $l = 1, 2$. Consequently, an advisor may be unable to send informative messages if constrained to acquire data on at most one issue l, yet be capable of sending informative messages if allowed to acquire data on both issues together. Somewhat less apparent is the possibility that, while i may have state-dependent preferences on each issue separately and on both issues jointly, i may have an influential message strategy only if i acquires information on a single issue. This claim is established by Example 1.

Example 1. For $l \in \{1, 2\}$, let $N_l^2 = \{0\}$, $N_l^1 = \{0, 1\}$, and $\alpha_l = \beta_l = 1$. Choose W^1, W^R, x^1, and P so that Figure 2 describes the situation.[4] It is straightforward to check that 1 has state-dependent preferences on each issue l taken separately, and on the two issues considered jointly. Ex ante ($n^1 = (0, 0)$), R strictly prefers A to B. Suppose $n^1 = (1, 1)$. Then $T_A(n^1) = \{(0, 0)\}$, so

$$\mu_1^*((0, 0)) = m_A \quad \text{and} \quad \mu_1^*(t) = m_B \quad \text{for all } t \in T_B(n^1).$$

Clearly, $\delta^*(m_A) = A$. Suppose 1 says "choose B." Then Bayes's rule yields (DeGroot 1970, p. 160)

$$\begin{aligned} E_\mu[\Omega_1 \mid m_B] &= \Pr[t_2^1 = 1]\hat{\Omega}_1(t_2^1 = 1, t^1 \notin T_A(n^1)) \\ &\quad + \Pr[t_2^1 = 0]\hat{\Omega}_1(t_2^1 = 0, t^1 \notin T_A(n^1)) \\ &= (1/2)[(1/2)(2/3) + (1/2)(1/3)] + (1/2)(2/3) \\ &= 7/12. \end{aligned}$$

Similarly, compute $E_\mu[\Omega_2 \mid m_B] = 7/12$. Hence, $Z^R > \hat{\Omega}(m_B)L^R$ implying $\delta^*(m_B) = A$, in which case μ_1^* is informative but not influential. Now suppose $n^1 = (0, 1)$. Then $T_A(n^1) \equiv T_A(n_2^1) = \{0\}$, $\mu_1^*(0) = m_A$, and $\mu_1^*(1) = m_B$.

---

[4] Such a situation surely exists. For example, let $A = (0, 1)$, $B = (1, 0)$, and set $x_1^i = x_2^i = \bar{x}^i$. Substituting into (4), the decision criterion for i can be written

$$u^i(A) \gtreqless u^i(B) \quad \text{as} \quad (b^i - a^i)(1 - 2\bar{x}^i)/2 \gtreqless (c^i - a^i)\hat{\Omega}_1(\cdot) + (b^i - c^i)\hat{\Omega}_2(\cdot).$$

Suitably choosing $\{a^i, b^i, c^i, \bar{x}^i\}$ then supports the situation depicted in Figure 2.

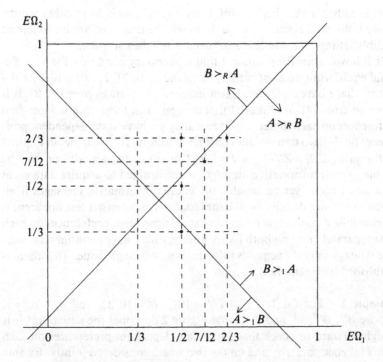

Figure 2. Induced preferences of $i \in \{1, R\}$ in Example 1,
with $x >_i y \equiv u^i(x) > u^i(y)$.

Hence $E_\mu[\Omega_1 | m] = 1/2$ for all m, and $E_\mu[\Omega_2 | m_p] = 2/3$ [1/3] if $p = B$ [A]. Therefore, $\delta^*(m_A) = A$, $\delta^*(m_B) = B$, and μ_1^* is both informative and influential. Finally, it is easy to check from Figure 2 that there can be no informative messages sent if $n^1 = (1, 0)$ (1 and R have diametrically opposed preferences here). Consequently, the only possible influential equilibrium in the current situation is for 1 to acquire information only on issue 2 and to adopt the separating talking strategy described previously. Furthermore, there exist parameter specifications for which $n^{1*} = (0, 1)$ is an equilibrium strategy – for example, when $A = (1, 0)$, $B = (0, 1)$, $b^1 > c^1 > a^1 > 0$, $c^1 \approx a^1$, and $x^1 \approx 0$).

It is tempting to interpret Example 1 as illustrating a principle that specialists can be more influential than generalists. However, advisor 1 is no more a specialist on issue 2 when $n^1 = (0, 1)$ than when $n^1 = (1, 1)$. Rather, it is R's knowledge that 1 possesses information on both issues when $n^1 = (1, 1)$, coupled with 1 being unable credibly to convey anything but aggregate information to R, that leads to the "generalist" being informative

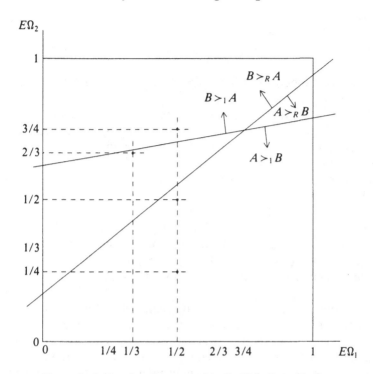

Figure 3. Induced preferences of $i \in \{1, R\}$ in Example 2, with $x >_i y \equiv u^i(x) > u^i(y)$.

but uninfluential. Having said this, despite the coarse structure of equilibrium message strategies, there are circumstances under which specialists (relatively high n_l^j on l alone) can be influential when generalists (relatively low n_l^j on each l) cannot. Example 2 illustrates the possibility.

Example 2. Let $N^1 = \{(n_1^1, n_2^1) \mid n_1^1 + n_2^1 \leq 2\}$, $\alpha_l = \beta_l = 1$, and $N_l^2 = \{0\}$ for each l. Pick parameters so that the situation is as described in Figure 3. Clearly, if $n^1 = (1, 1)$ then 1 has state-independent preferences on each issue separately and on both issues jointly. Hence there can be no informative talking strategy. However, if $n^1 = (0, 2)$, the advisor does have state-dependent preferences relative to n^1, and $\mu_1^*(t_2^1 = 2) = m_B$, $\mu_1^*(t_2^1 < 2) = m_A$ is an influential talking strategy.

The relationship between the level of expertise of some $i \in \{1, 2\}$ (as measured by n_l^j) and the existence of an influential equilibrium is not monotonic. In particular, it is possible for there to exist an influential equilibrium with low and high values of n_l^j but not for intermediate values, and it is possible for there to exist an influential equilibrium with intermediate values of n_i^j but not for low (positive) or for high values. These assertions are demonstrated in Example 3, in which only issue 1 is decision-relevant.

Example 3. Suppose $A_2 = B_2 = 0$; $N_l^2 = \{0\}$, $l = 1, 2$; and $N_2^1 = \{0\}$. Assume $a^i = b^i = 1$ and $c^i = 0$, $i = 1, R$.

(i) Let $N_1^1 = \{0, 1, 2, 3, 4\}$; $d_1 \in (7/12, 13/22)$; $d_1 - x_1^1 \in (1/3, 2/5)$; and $\alpha_1 = \beta_1 = 1$. Then ex ante $(n_1^1 = 0)$, $d_1 > E\Omega_1 = 1/2 > d_1 - x_1^1$ and so (4) implies that, in the absence of any further information, R would choose B while $i = 1$ prefers A. By Bayes's rule, $E[\Omega_1 | s, n^1 \equiv n_1^1] = (1+s)/(2+n^1)$. Hence, as is easy to check, $T_A(n^1) \neq \{\emptyset, T(n^1)\}$ for all $n_1^1 \in \{1, ..., 4\}$. However, by Proposition 1.2, there can exist an influential equilibrium talking strategy only for $n_1^1 \in \{1, 4\}$.

(ii) Let $N_1^1 = \{0, 1, 2, 3\}$; $d_1 = 11/20$; $d_1 - x_1^1 = 3/10$; and $\alpha_1 = \beta_1 = 1$. Then ex ante $(n_1^1 = 0)$, $d_1 > E\Omega_1 = 1/2 > d_1 - x_1^1$. Proceeding as for (i), compute that $T_A(n^1) \neq \{\emptyset, T(n^1)\}$ only for $n_1^1 \in \{2, 3\}$. However, there can exist an influential equilibrium talking strategy only if $n_1^1 = 2$.

Now suppose both senders $i = 1, 2$ have nonempty information acquisition sets. In this case, R typically receives more information than with only one sender. However, the existence of a competing source of advice can influence any given sender's data acquisition decision. In particular, although some sender, say 1, has an influential talking strategy available conditional on acquiring information on both issues, 1 may choose not to get much information if 2 has a similar talking strategy. In other words, given that both senders offer R advice, 1 is relatively more influential than 2 when he acquires information on only one issue than when he acquires information on both issues. Consider Example 4.

Example 4. For $i, l \in \{1, 2\}$, let $N_l^i = \{0, 1\}$ and $\alpha_l = \beta_l = 1$. Choose preferences and P so that Figure 4 describes the situation. In the absence of any further information, R strictly prefers A to B.

It is easy to see that both advisors have state-dependent preferences on both issues taken together; that $i = 1$ has state-dependent preferences on both issues taken separately; and that $i = 2$ has state-dependent preferences on issue 1 taken separately, but not on issue 2 (relative to the information acquisition sets N^i). Furthermore, if $i \in \{1, 2\}$ is the only sender, then, by the same reasoning as in Example 1, i has an influential talking strategy given $t^i \in T((1, 1))$. Specifically,

$$E_{\mu_1}[\Omega_l | m_B] = 7/12 \quad \text{and} \quad E_{\mu_1}[\Omega_l | m_A] = 1/3, \quad l = 1, 2;$$

$$E_{\mu_2}[\Omega_l | m_A] = 5/12 \quad \text{and} \quad E_{\mu_2}[\Omega_l | m_B] = 2/3, \quad l = 1, 2.$$

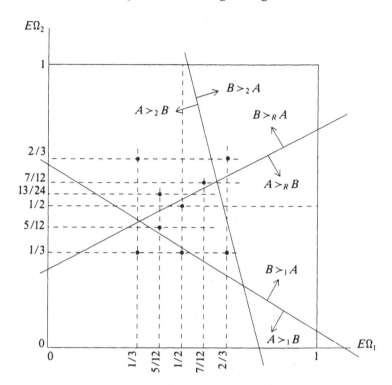

Figure 4. Induced preferences of $i \in \{1, 2, R\}$ in Example 4,
with $x >_i y \equiv u^i(x) > u^i(y)$.

Consequently, conditional on only one sender giving advice and that
sender having information on both issues, R will (in equilibrium) take
the advice offered. And selecting $n^i = (1, 1)$ is the unique equilibrium decision for i under these circumstances. Now suppose there are two senders
and $n^i = (1, 1)$ for all $i \in \{1, 2\}$, and let the first component of any pair
$(m, m') \in M \times M$ be advisor 1's message. Then it is straightforward to
check that

$$\delta^*(m_p, m_p) = p \ \forall p \in \{A, B\} \quad \text{and} \quad \delta^*(m_p, m_{p'}) = A \ \forall p \neq p'.$$

Hence, whenever 1 and 2 give conflicting advice, R's best response is to
choose A (because her posterior on Ω coincides with the prior); otherwise, R accepts the sender's recommendation. But $n^1 = (1, 1)$ is not a best-
response data acquisition decision. To see this, let $n^1 = (0, 1)$ so $T_A(n^1) \equiv$
$T_A(n_2^1) = \{0\}$. Then, given $n^2 = (1, 1)$, Bayes's rule yields

$$E_\mu[\Omega_1 \mid m_A, m_B] = 2/3 \quad \text{and} \quad E_\mu[\Omega_2 \mid m_A, m_B] = 1/2,$$

which together imply $\delta^*(m_A, m_B) = A$. Similarly,

$E_\mu[\Omega_1 | m_B, m_A] = 5/12$ and

$E_\mu[\Omega_2 | m_B, m_A] = (1/2)[(2/3)(3/4) + (1/3)(1/4)] + (1/2)(1/2) = 13/24$,

which together imply $\delta^*(m_B, m_A) = B$. Finally, it is evident that

$$\delta^*(m_p, m_p) = p \quad \forall p \in P.$$

Therefore, while 2's messages are informative (and influential in the absence of 1's advice), 1 is relatively more influential than 2: R invariably accepts 1's advice. If $n^1 = (1, 0)$ and $n^2 = (1, 1)$ then it can be checked that 2 is relatively more influential than 1; whenever the senders offer conflicting advice, R accepts 2's recommendation. And, as in Example 1, there exist parameter specifications for which $n^{1*} = (0, 1)$ is a best response to $n^2 = (1, 1)$. Indeed, in such cases it can be checked that n^{1*} is the unique best response to any $n^2 \in N^2 \setminus \{(0, 0)\}$, and that $n^{2*} = (1, 1)$ is 2's unique best response to n^{1*}.

In sum, for some parameterizations, the unique influential equilibrium here involves 1 specializing on issue 2 alone and 2 acquiring information on both issues. And when 1 and 2 offer conflicting advice, R accepts 1's recommendation.

It is worth noting here that the equilibrium of Example 4 does not depend on R's prior belief leading her to vote for A, or on 1 having state-dependent preferences on issue 1 (relative to N^1). However, the equilibrium does depend on 2 having state-independent preferences on issue 2. Were this not so, 2's best response to $n^{1*} = (0, 1)$ would then be $n^2 = (0, 1)$; in this case, the situation is strategically equivalent to that when $n^i = (1, 1)$ for both i.

4   Unconstrained agenda: $P = \mathbb{R}^l$

In contrast to the previous section, the decision maker here is presumed free to choose any point in the issue space. Not surprisingly, it turns out that the senders' message strategies can be more complex than when R must make a binary choice. This follows from R's best-response decision strategy; it is immediate from (3) and sequential rationality that δ^* is given by the following.

Lemma 1.   *For all* $(m_1, m_2) \in M \times M$, $\delta^*(m_1, m_2) = E_\mu[\Omega | m_1, m_2]$.

For $l \in \{1, 2\}$, let $H_l(n) = 1/(\alpha_l + \beta_l + n_l^1 + n_l^2)$. Then we have the following proposition.

Proposition 2. *Fix $n = (n^1, n^2)$. Then there exists an equilibrium in which μ_i^* is a separating talking strategy for all $i \in \{1, 2\}$ if and only if, for all $\gamma_j^i \in \{-1, 0, 1\}$ such that $n_j^i = 0$ implies $\gamma_j^i = 0$,*

$$(2.1) \quad 2x_1^i[\gamma_1^i a^i/H_1(n) + \gamma_2^i c^i/H_2(n)] + 2x_2^i[\gamma_2^i b^2/H_2(n) + \gamma_1^i c^i/H_1(n)]$$
$$\leq a^i[\gamma_1^i/H_1(n)]^2 + b^i[\gamma_2^i/H_2(n)]^2 + 2\gamma_1^i \gamma_2^i c^i/H_1(n)H_2(n).$$

By setting $n_j^i = 0$ appropriately, (2.1) characterizes the circumstances under which a sender has a separating talking strategy (in equilibrium) on one issue alone, on both issues, and when only one or both senders give advice. Note that Proposition 2 implies a sender is capable of sending finer information in equilibrium than is possible when the receiver must choose from a constrained alternative set $\{A, B\}$, where the sender can only transmit coarse information ("choose A" or "choose B") irrespective of whether he has information on both issues.

Given the number of parameters relevant for any sender's decision, it is not surprising that there are circumstances in which a sender might be able to separate on both issues considered jointly but not on either issue taken separately, and conversely. Of more interest is that Proposition 2 reveals an externality in data acquisition; specifically, neither sender may be able to adopt a separating strategy in equilibrium when both are giving advice to R, even though each sender on his own does have a credible talking strategy. For example, suppose that $n_2^i = 0$ (so $\gamma_2^i = 0$), $i = 1, 2$, and $n_1^1 = k \cdot n_1^2 = k \geq 1$. Then, for x^i sufficiently close to (but distinct from) x^R, both advisors can use a separating talking strategy in equilibrium to give advice focused on issue 1 when $k = 1$; however, for k large enough, neither advisor will be able to transmit any credible information to R.

To see why the externality arises, recall that when only one sender (say $i = 1$) is giving advice, 1's separating talking strategy is credible if no type can gain by sending another type's message; this is a function of R's decision strategy, which in turn depends only on $T(n^1)$. However, when $i = 2$ also gives advice to R using a separating strategy, R's response to 1's message will be conditioned on 2's strategy; in particular, R's decision for any given message from 1 will vary with 2's message (Lemma 1). But now, because any message from 1 can elicit multiple decisions from R and because every type t^1 has a better (interim) estimate of 2's type than R, some types $t^1 \in T(n^1)$ may find it profitable to deviate from the initial separating strategy. In effect, it is R's inability to commit credibly to treating each advisor's message independently of the other that generates the externality.

Despite the externality, it is important to recognize that an informative but not separating talking strategy (for some sender i) with high n^i may in fact convey more information to R than a separating talking strategy with low n^i. The reason for this is simply that $|T(n^i)|$ is increasing in n^i, so that a type $t \in T(n)$ has more information than the type $t \in T(n')$ for $n' < n$.

The preceding discussion suggests that, when there are two effective senders, one might strategically choose a sample size to block the effective transmission of information by the other. Ideally, one wants a characterization result here on the senders' best response correspondences for data acquisition, but as yet I have been unable to provide such a result. However, assuming that for all acquisition decisions $n = (n^1, n^2)$, $i = 1, 2$ use the most informative available equilibrium talking strategies, Example 5 illustrates the suggestion. In the example, the data acquisition sets are symmetric and there are two possible influential equilibria, each involving one sender credibly revealing all of his data and the other offering no information to R.

Example 5.   Suppose $P = \{p \in \mathbb{R}^2 \mid p_2 = 0\}$; $N_2^i = \{0, 1, 2\}$, $i = 1, 2$. Assume that $a^i = b^i = 1$ and $c^i = 0$ for all $i \in \{R, 1, 2\}$. Let $x_1^1 \in (1/10, 1/8)$, $|x_1^2| \in (1/12, 1/10)$, and $\alpha_l = \beta_l = 1$, $l = 1, 2$. Write $n = (n_1^1, n_1^2)$. Then the most informative equilibrium talking strategies are (see the appendix):

$$n = (1, 1) \Rightarrow \mu_i^* \text{ is separating, } i = 1, 2;$$
$$n = (1, 2) \Rightarrow \mu_1^* \text{ is pooling and } \mu_2^* \text{ is separating;}$$
$$n = (2, 1) \Rightarrow i = 1 \text{ uses the strategy } \mu_1^0 \text{ (defined hereunder) and}$$
$$\mu_2^* \text{ is separating;}$$
$$n = (2, 2) \Rightarrow \mu_i^* \text{ is separating and } \mu_j^* \text{ is pooling, } i \neq j.$$

Here: $\mu_1^0(0) = m$ and, for all $t > 0$, $\mu_1^0(t) = m' \neq m$. From R's perspective, the best situation available is $n = (2, 1)$, since this generates the most information on Ω_1. However, as shown in the appendix, whichever of the two available informative equilibria is played, the unique best response pair n^* is $(2, 2)$. Thus both advisors acquire as much information as possible, but at most one of them gives credible advice to R. Further, although R is indifferent about which sender gives influential advice, each advisor strictly prefers (ex ante) the equilibrium in which he separates.

An important topic in the 2-dimensional case concerns any potential advisor's decision to specialize on only one dimension or to acquire (and possibly send) information on both dimensions. The remainder of this section, then, discusses several of the issues involved, beginning with the role of nonseparable preferences in governing the ability of a single advisor to transmit information on only one issue.

Although the distributions of the random variables Ω_1 and Ω_2 are assumed to be independent, nonseparability in any advisor i's preferences can lead R to make inferences about what i knows concerning issue 2,

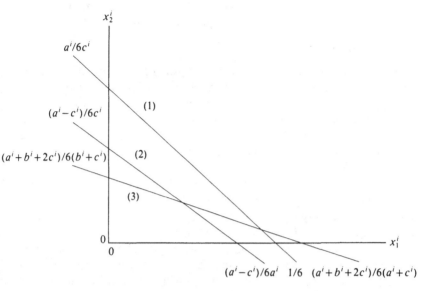

Figure 5. Equilibrium talking strategies for Example 6. For (x_1^i, x_2^i) lying below line (1), μ_i separating on $T((1, 0))$ is equilibrium behavior; for (x_1^i, x_2^i) lying below line (2), μ_i^1 is equilibrium behavior with $n^1 = (1, 1)$; and for (x_1^i, x_2^i) lying below line (3), μ_i separating on $T((1, 1))$ is equilibrium behavior.

say, on the basis of a speech by i concerned exclusively with issue 1. Consequently, 1 may choose to get information on only one issue l, rather than acquire information on both issues and give advice only on l. To see this, consider Example 6.

Example 6. Suppose $N^j = \{(0, 0)\}$ and $N^i = \{(1, 0), (1, 1)\}$. For all $l = 1, 2$, let $\alpha_l = \beta_l = 1$ and $x_l^j \geq 0$. Suppose $a^i > b^i = c^i > 0$. Assume $n^i = (1, 1)$, and consider the talking strategy

$$\mu_i^1(t = (1, 0)) = \mu_i^1(t = (1, 1)) = m;$$
$$\mu_i^1(t = (0, 0)) = \mu_i^1(t = (0, 1)) = m' \neq m.$$

So μ_i^1 is a strategy by which advisor i separates with respect to his information on issue 1, but reveals no information on issue 2. In the appendix it is shown that μ_i^1 constitutes an equilibrium strategy if and only if

$$x_1^i \leq 1/6 - c^i[x_2^i + (1/6)]/a^i.$$

Moreover, there exist W^i such that μ_i^1 is the most informative available equilibrium talking strategy relative to $n^i = (1, 1)$; see Figure 5. On the other hand, when $n^i = (1, 0)$, Proposition 2 implies for this example that i has a separating talking strategy in equilibrium if and only if

$$x_1^i \le 1/6 - c^i x_2^i / a^i.$$

Thus the mere fact that R knows that advisor i has information on the second issue compromises i's ability to reveal his information on issue 1 alone, given that i has nonseparable preferences – that is, given $c^i \ne 0$. In view of this, i's ex ante best choice of $n^i \in N^i$ depends on the equilibrium that will be played conditional on his decision. Assume, as usual, that the most informative available equilibrium will be played in all circumstances. There are basically two cases, depending on i's preferences.

First: x^i and W^i are such that either the fully separating strategy – that is, separate on $T((1, 1))$ – is available relative to $n^i = (1, 1)$; or μ_i^1 is available but not the fully separating strategy; or there is no informative talking strategy available in equilibrium. Then $n^{i*} = (1, 1)$.

Second: x^i and W^i are such that μ_i^1 is not an available equilibrium strategy relative to $n^i = (1, 1)$, but the separating strategy on $T((1, 0))$ exists – that is, by acquiring information only on issue 1, advisor i can credibly reveal his type to R. The first question here then concerns what is the most informative equilibrium relative to $n^i = (1, 1)$, given that μ_i^1 is not available. There are essentially two possible informative strategies:

$$\mu_i'(t = (0, 0)) = m; \quad \mu_i'(t \ne (0, 0)) = m' \ne m;$$

$$\mu_i''(t = (0, 1)) = m; \quad \mu_i''(t \ne (0, 1)) = m' \ne m.$$

In the appendix it is shown that, if μ_i' can be part of an equilibrium relative to $n^i = (1, 1)$, then there also exists an equilibrium in which i uses the fully separating talking strategy; and that, generically, μ_i'' cannot be an equilibrium strategy here. In other words, for x^i and W^i of this second case, the only equilibrium talking strategy relative to $n^i = (1, 1)$ is wholly uninformative. Therefore, i's ex ante information acquisition decision depends on whether he prefers $n^i = (1, 0)$ and being able to transmit his information credibly to R, or $n^i = (1, 1)$ and being better informed but unable to transmit any of his information credibly. It turns out (see the appendix) that $n^{i*} = (1, 0)$: i prefers not to acquire as much information as possible.

Proposition 2 implies that it is possible for a given advisor, say i, to be able to adopt a separating strategy (in equilibrium) on issue $l = 1, 2$ taken separately, given that he has information on at most issue l, yet not be able to adopt a separating strategy on both issues taken jointly. And the logic of Example 6 suggests that, under such circumstances, if i acquires information on both issues then he will be unable to transmit *any* information credibly to R. Consequently, i must choose between (1) acquiring information on both issues and being unable to reveal it, and (2) acquiring information on issue $l \in \{1, 2\}$ only and being able to use a separating talking strategy in equilibrium. Suppose (1) is unavailable or that (2) dominates (1) ex ante; so the effective choice concerns the issue on which to specialize (given that the most informative equilibrium is played in each case).

Example 7. Suppose $N^2 = \{(0, 0)\}$ and $N^1 = \{(v, 0), (0, v)\}$, where $v > 0$ and x^1 and W^1 are such that $i = 1$ can separate on both issues taken separately but not jointly. Then

$$n^{1*} = (v, 0) \ [(0, v)] \text{ as } a^1/b^1 > [<] \ (\hat{v}_2(0) - \hat{v}_2(v))/(\hat{v}_1(0) - \hat{v}_1(v)), \tag{5}$$

where

$$\hat{v}_l(n_l^1) \equiv \sum_{T(n_l^1)} \Pr[t_l^1](\text{var}[\Omega_l \,|\, E[q_l \,|\, t_l^1]] + \text{var}[q_l \,|\, t_l^1]).$$

Expression (5) follows because, under separating talking strategies, Lemma 1 implies that the only ex ante difference between specializing on issue 1 and on issue 2 lies in the relative differences between the variance terms. If $\alpha_l = \alpha$ and $\beta_l = \beta$ for all l, then the RHS of (5) equals 1 and the expression says $i = 1$ will acquire information on the issue most salient to him. On the other hand, if the prior on one issue is sufficiently skewed relative to that on the other, (5) says that 1 will acquire information on the issue about which there is a priori more uncertainty. For instance, suppose $a^1 > b^1$ so that issue 1 is relatively salient for $i = 1$. Then 1 will acquire information on issue 2 if the prior on q_1 is sufficiently skewed relative to that on q_2; for in this case, the numerator of the RHS of (5) will be large relative to the denominator.

When there are two advisors, the interesting question concerns the circumstances under which they will acquire and transmit information on both issues, or on a given issue, or on orthogonal issues. Although I do not as yet have a general answer to this question, some insight is available from the final example.

Example 8. For each $i \in \{1, 2\}$, suppose $N^i = \{(n_1^i, n_2^i) \,|\, n_1^i + n_2^i \leq 2\}$. Suppose $\alpha_l = \beta_l = 1$, $l = 1, 2$, and let x^i, W^i be such that, for all $n^i \in N^i$, i can use a (fully) separating talking strategy in equilibrium. Then, assuming the most informative available equilibrium is played conditional upon $n^* = (n^{1*}, n^{2*})$, there exist $\zeta_1 > 1 > \zeta_2 > \zeta_3 > 0$ such that:

$$[\varsigma_2 > a^1/b^1 > \varsigma_3] \& [\varsigma_2 > b^2/a^2 > \varsigma_3] \Rightarrow n^* = ((1,1),(1,1));$$
$$[\varsigma_1 > a^1/b^1 > \varsigma_2] \& [\varsigma_1 > b^2/a^2 > \varsigma_2]$$
$$\Rightarrow n^* \in \{((2,0),(0,2)),((1,1),(1,1))\};$$
$$[a^1/b^1 > \varsigma_1] \& [b^2/a^2 > \varsigma_1] \Rightarrow n^* = ((2,0),(0,2)).$$

(See the appendix.) As the salience of one issue increases relative to the other, the incentive to acquire information on only the most salient issue likewise increases; for sufficiently disparate views on salience, the senders will acquire information and offer advice to R on orthogonal issues.

It is worth noting here that the incentives for specialization facing the senders do not involve the relative salience of the issues for the receiver R; this stands in contrast to the situation with a constrained agenda. The reason for the disparity is implicit in Lemma 1: with an unconstrained agenda, R will choose a policy in $\mathbb{R}^2$ that corresponds to her induced ideal point, irrespective of the importance for her of one issue relative to the other.

5   Discussion

Although the preceding analysis falls short of providing a class of characterization results identifying the circumstances under which, for example, individuals or groups will attempt to influence policy by focusing on one set of issues rather than another, it does offer some clues about the strategic interactions involved. There are four main observations to be made.

1. Least surprisingly, the structure of messages sent in equilibrium is coarser when the agenda is finite and predetermined than when the decision maker is free to pick any alternative in the space (compare Proposition 1 with Proposition 2). This is to be expected because, although (ceteris paribus) more information is preferable to less by risk aversion, the only decision-relevant fact for any agent confronting a binary agenda $\{A, B\}$ is whether the expected state of the world is such that A is better than B. Given an expert's preferences over consequences and the common prior on the state of the world, a choice of sample size by the expert induces a binary partition on the type set such that all types in one element of the partition prefer A and all types in the other prefer B. Consequently, in equilibrium an expert can only report whether he prefers A or B. Whether his message is persuasive then depends on the decision maker's updated beliefs conditioned on common-knowledge data about the expert's preferences and the extent of his information: so, unless the binary partition induced by the expert's choice of sample size coincides with that of the decision maker, the expert's advice can be informative but not influential. On the other hand, when the decision maker is free to choose any point

in a Euclidean space, all informative messages are influential (Lemma 1). And in this case, therefore, equilibrium messages can be relatively fine, with senders offering more-or-less detailed information about what they have learned.

The fixed binary agenda and the completely free choice set of this chapter define the polar extremes. It seems evident that as the number of alternatives in an agenda increases, the richness of the possible (equilibrium) advice that experts can give will likewise increase. In turn, this suggests that debate about how to choose from a given agenda is likely to be less informative than debate about what to put on the agenda.

2. The second observation concerns a potential expert's decision to specialize on a single issue, despite having the opportunity to acquire data freely on both issues jointly.[5] Specialization takes two forms here, depending on the structure of the data acquisition sets with which the potential experts are endowed: (i) an expert has the option of acquiring a given amount of information on both issues jointly or separately (e.g., $N^i = \{(\nu, 0), (0, \nu), (\nu, \nu)\}$); and (ii) he can allocate a given level of resources freely between data gathering on either or both of the two issues (e.g., $N^i = \{(n_1^i, n_2^i) \mid n_1^i + n_2^i \le \nu\}$). In all cases, however, the decision to specialize depends on a trade-off between being relatively well informed and being influential. In Examples 1 and 2 with the binary agenda, and in Examples 6 and 7 with the unconstrained agenda, the sender is influential only if he specializes on a single issue (although, in Example 1, he can be informative if he acquires data on both issues). Further, what blocks the sender from being influential in Examples 1 and 6 if he does not specialize is the decision maker's knowledge that the sender possesses information on both issues coupled with the fact that, in each instance, the sender has no message strategy capable of disaggregating his (general) data credibly. In contrast, the sender in Example 2, if he does not specialize, is simply insufficiently expert on either issue to be capable of affecting the decision.

3. Closely related to the preceding discussion is the intuitive observation that the mere existence of more than one sender can significantly influence senders' data acquisition decisions. This is illustrated through Example 4 (binary agenda) and Examples 5 and 8 (unconstrained agenda).[6]

In Example 4, both senders are influential if giving advice alone and if they have data on both issues. However, when both senders are giving advice and have data on both issues, one sender can become relatively

<hr />

[5] Recall the alternative interpretation suggested previously for the data acquisition decision. Rather than think of a given agent choosing how much information to acquire, the decision can be considered in terms of an interest group selecting a particular type of lobbyist or technical expert to make their case before the decision maker. Thus the results on specialization decisions can be thought of as results on analyzing choice of lobbyist.

[6] See also Demange (1990).

more influential than the other by specializing in the sense of (i) in observation 2 – that is, simply by not getting data on one issue rather than by getting more data on a given issue. In Example 8, the incentive to specialize increases with the relative salience of the issues for the two senders. It is worth noting that, in the binary-agenda examples, it is primarily the salience of the issues to the decision maker that tips the trade-off one way rather than another; for an unconstrained agenda, it is exclusively the salience of the issues to the sender that matters (compare Examples 1 and 4 with Examples 7 and 8).

Although Examples 4 and 8 refer to 2-dimensional policies, Example 5 illustrates the mutual externalities generated by both senders offering advice when only one dimension is subject to asymmetric information. In Example 5, it is because the decision maker's policy choice is derived by aggregating the advice of both experts that at least one expert is rendered incapable of credibly transmitting all of his data. In effect, because the induced preferences of the senders are correlated, the existence of more than one sender leads to an additional trade-off – between the desire to share information to obtain a better estimate of what policy is best in one's interests, and a desire to reveal information strategically to manipulate the policy decision.

4. Finally, it turns out that having more information in the settings discussed here is not always better, irrespective of any incentive to specialize. This is demonstrated in Example 3 for the binary agenda, and similar examples can readily be constructed for unconstrained agendas. As in the case of specialization, however, the fundamental trade-off is between being better informed and being influential. What is surprising about Example 3 is that the relationship between influence and level of expertise is not necessarily monotonic. Under some circumstances, it is better to be relatively well informed but not as informed as one (freely) could be (Example 3(ii)); in other circumstances, it is possible to be influential at low and at high levels of expertise, but not at intermediate levels (Example 3(i)).

Appendix

The following implications of Bayes's rule are used repeatedly in the appendix. Suppose there are t observations with value 1 in a random sample of n draws from a Bernoulli distribution with unknown mean q, and suppose the prior on the mean is a beta distribution with parameters $\alpha, \beta > 0$. Then (DeGroot 1970, p. 160)

$$E[\Omega \mid n, t] \equiv \hat{q}(n, t) = (\alpha + t)/(\alpha + \beta + n);$$

$$\text{var}[\Omega \,|\, n, t] = \text{var}[\Omega \,|\, \hat{q}(n, t)] + \text{var}[q \,|\, n, t]$$
$$= \hat{q}(n, t)[1 - \hat{q}(n, t)]$$
$$+ (\alpha + t)(\beta + n - t)/(\alpha + \beta + n)^2(\alpha + \beta + n + 1).$$

Proof of Proposition 1: (1.1) For all $m \in M \times M$, $\delta^*(m) \in \{A, B\}$. Fix, say, $\mu_j^*(t^j)$; then either $i \neq j$ has an influential talking strategy or not. In the latter case, j must be influential, by the supposition that (n^*, μ^*, δ^*) is an influential equilibrium; hence, μ_i^* is vacuously a best response. In the former instance, since $\delta^*(m) \in \{A, B\}$, i can send a message inducing A or B, and must be indifferent over any message inducing a given action. So by weak dominance, $t^i \in T_A(n^{i*})$ implies i chooses $\mu_i^*(t^i)$ to induce A; and similarly for $t^i \in T_B(n^{i*})$.

(1.2) This is immediate from sequential rationality, (4), and the requirement that beliefs be consistent with Bayes's rule where defined. □

Proof of Proposition 2: Fix $n = (n^1, n^2)$ and suppose μ_2^* is a separating talking strategy. If μ_1^* is also a separating talking strategy, then Lemma 1 and Bayes's rule imply that, for all $t^1 \in T(n^1)$,

$$E[u^1(p) \,|\, \mu_1^*(t^1), \mu_2^*, \delta^*; t^1] = -x^1 W^1 x^{1\prime} - \hat{V}^1(t^1),$$

where

$$\hat{V}^1(t^1) \equiv \sum_{T(n^2)} \Pr[t^2 \,|\, t^1] \, \text{var}[\Omega \,|\, n, t^1, t^2].$$

Suppose type $t^1 \in T(n^1)$ deviates from μ_1^* and sends the message that type $s \neq t^1$ is supposed to send under μ_1^*. Assume first that $s_l > t_l^1$ and that $n_l^1 > 0$, $l = 1, 2$. Then

$$E[u^1(p) \,|\, \mu_1^*(s), \mu_2^*, \delta^*; t^1]$$
$$= -\sum_{T(n^2)} \Pr[t^2 \,|\, t^1][z(s, t^1, t^2) W^1 z(s, t^1, t^2)'] - \hat{V}^1(t^1),$$

where $z(s, t^1, t^2) \equiv (x^1 + E[\Omega \,|\, t^1, t^2] - \delta^*(\mu_1^*(s), \mu_2^*(t^2)))$. Substituting for $E[\Omega \,|\, \cdot]$ from above and using Lemma 1 yields

$$z(s, t^1, t^2) = (x_1^1 + (t_1^1 - s_1)/H_1(n), x_2^1 + (t_2^1 - s_2)/H_2(n)),$$

which is independent of t^2. Therefore, substituting and collecting terms yields

$$E[u^1(p) \,|\, \mu_1^*(t^1), \mu_2^*, \delta^*; t^1] \geq E[u^1(p) \,|\, \mu_1^*(s), \mu_2^*, \delta^*; t^1] \quad \text{for all } s \neq t^1$$

if and only if (2.1) holds with $\gamma_l^1 = 1$, $l = 1, 2$. Similarly, when $s_l \leq t_l^1$, (2.1) must hold with $\gamma_l^1 = -1$. Finally, if $n_l^1 = 0$, it is common knowledge that $i = 1$ has no more information on issue l than R and so all deviations s_l are ignored - hence, set $\gamma_l^1 = 0$ to obtain the relevant expression. □

Proof of claims in Example 5:   By construction, all agents' preferences over consequences are strictly Euclidean, and so separable. Further, $p_2 = 0$ for all $p \in P$, so only issue 1 is germane to R's decision. We can therefore considerably simplify notation by observing that (3) implies, for all $p, p' \in P$,

$$u^i(p) > u^i(p') \quad \text{if and only if} \quad (x_1^i + E[\Omega_1 | \cdot] - p_1')^2 > (x_1^i + E[\Omega_1 | \cdot] - p_1)^2.$$

Without ambiguity, the issue subscript $l = 1$ can be taken as understood for the remainder of the argument. Now check that the most informative equilibrium for each n is that specified in the text.

$n = (1, 1)$: By Proposition 2, both senders separating is the most informative equilibrium here (with δ^*).

$n = (1, 2)$: Proposition 2 implies that not both senders can separate. And clearly, $i = 2$ pooling and $i = 1$ separating is less informative than the converse, since $n = (1, 2)$. Therefore, because $T(n^1) = \{0, 1\}$, the most informative equilibrium is $i = 1$ pooling and $i = 2$ separating.

$n = (2, 1)$: By Proposition 2, not both senders can separate. Because $n = (2, 1)$, the postulated strategies are certainly a most informative pair; so it is enough to check that there is no other most informative pair of strategies that can constitute equilibrium behavior, and that (μ_1°, μ_2^*) is indeed an equilibrium pair of talking strategies. Consider these issues in turn.

Given $n^2 = 1$, $i = 2$ either pools or separates. Given that $i = 2$ separates, the only other possibilities for $i = 1$'s talking strategy (modulo message-labeling conventions) are: (a) $\mu_1(0) = \mu_1(2) \neq \mu_1(1)$; and (b) $\mu_1(0) = \mu_1(1) = \underline{m} \neq \mu_1(2) = \bar{m}$. But from our decision criterion and $x^1 > 0$, higher types strictly prefer higher decisions; hence equilibrium talking strategies are necessarily monotonic, so (a) cannot occur. Consider (b). By Bayes's rule and Lemma 1,

$$\delta^*(\bar{m}) = (\alpha + 2)/H(2);$$

$$\delta^*(\underline{m}) = \sum_0^1 \binom{2}{s} \alpha^s \beta^{2-s}(\alpha + s) \bigg/ H(2) \sum_0^1 \binom{2}{s} \alpha^s \beta^{2-s}.$$

Hence,

$$E[u^1(\delta^*(\underline{m})) | t^1 = 1] = -(x^1 + (\alpha + 1)/H(2) - \delta^*(\underline{m}))^2 - \text{var}[\Omega | 2, 1];$$

$$E[u^1(\delta^*(\bar{m})) | t^1 = 1] = -(x^1 + (\alpha + 1)/H(2) - \delta^*(\bar{m}))^2 - \text{var}[\Omega | 2, 1].$$

Therefore

$$E[u^1(\delta^*(\underline{m})) | t^1 = 1] \geq E[u^1(\delta^*(\bar{m})) | t^1 = 1]$$
$$\text{if and only if} \quad x^1 \leq \alpha/(\beta + 2\alpha)H(2).$$

By assumption, $\alpha = \beta = 1$ and $x^1 > 1/10$. Hence μ_1 cannot be an equilibrium talking strategy; so (b) cannot occur.

Now check that (μ_1°, μ_2^*) is an equilibrium pair of strategies. Fix μ_2^* to be separating,

$$\mu_2^*(0) = m, \quad \mu_2^*(1) = m', \quad m \neq m'.$$

Let $i = 1$ use μ_1°. Then Bayes's rule, $\alpha = \beta = 1$, and Lemma 1 imply:

$$\delta^*(m, m) = 1/5; \quad \delta^*(m, m') = 2/5; \quad \delta^*(m', m) = 9/25; \quad \delta^*(m', m') = 7/10.$$

For example,

$$\delta^*(m', m') = \sum_1^2 \binom{2}{s}(\alpha+1)^s \beta^{2-s}(\alpha+1+s) \bigg/ H(3) \sum_1^2 \binom{2}{s}(\alpha+1)^s \beta^{2-s}.$$

Hence,

$$E[u^1(p) \mid \mu_1^\circ(0), \mu_2^*, \delta^*, t^1 = 0] = -(x^1)^2 - \hat{V}^1(0);$$

$$E[u^1(p) \mid \mu_1^\circ(t^1 > 0), \mu_2^*, \delta^*, t^1 = 0]$$

$$= -\sum_{T(n^2)} \Pr[t^2 \mid t^1 = 0] E[u^1(\delta^*(m', \mu_2^*(t^2)))]$$

$$= -(3/4)(x^1 + 1/5 - 9/25)^2 - (1/4)(x^1 + 2/5 - 7/10)^2 - \hat{V}^1(0).$$

Therefore,

$$E[u^1(p) \mid \mu_1^\circ(0), \mu_2^*, \delta^*, t^1 = 0] \geq E[u^1(p) \mid \mu_1^\circ(t^1 > 0), \mu_2^*, \delta^*, t^1 = 0]$$
$$\text{if and only if } x^1 \leq 289/2300.$$

Since $x^1 < 1/8$, μ_1° is a best response to (μ_2^*, δ^*). It remains to check that μ_2^* is a best response to μ_1°. Given (μ_1°, μ_2^*), δ^* is as described before. So,

$$E[u^2(p) \mid \mu_1^\circ, \mu_2^*(0), \delta^*, t^2 = 0]$$
$$= -(4/9)(x^2)^2 - (4/9)(x^2 + 2/5 - 9/25)^2$$
$$\quad - (4/9)(x^2 + 3/5 - 9/25)^2 - \hat{V}^2(0);$$

$$E[u^2(p) \mid \mu_1^\circ, \mu_2^*(1), \delta^*, t^2 = 0]$$
$$= -(4/9)(x^2 + 1/5 - 2/5)^2 - (4/9)(x^2 + 2/5 - 7/10)^2$$
$$\quad - (4/9)(x^2 + 3/5 - 7/10)^2 - \hat{V}^2(0).$$

Hence

$$E[u^2(p) \mid \mu_1^\circ, \mu_2^*(0), \delta^*, t^2 = 0] \geq E[u^2(p) \mid \mu_1^\circ, \mu_2^*(1), \delta^*, t^2 = 0]$$
$$\text{if and only if } x^2 \leq 233/2180.$$

Similar computations yield

$$E[u^2(p) \mid \mu_1^\circ, \mu_2^*(1), \delta^*, t^2 = 1] \geq E[u^2(p) \mid \mu_1^\circ, \mu_2^*(0), \delta^*, t^2 = 1]$$
$$\text{if and only if } x^2 \geq -603/146.$$

Therefore, since $|x^2| \in (1/12, 1/10)$ by assumption, μ_2^* is a best response to (μ_1^o, δ^*) as required.

$n = (2, 2)$: Again, Proposition 2 implies that not both senders can separate, and that there exists an equilibrium in which one sender separates and the other pools. To show that these are the most informative equilibria available, we must check (i) that one sender separating and the other adopting the semiseparating strategy μ_i^o is not an equilibrium, and (ii) that both senders using a semiseparating strategy is not an equilibrium. However, if (ii) is true then, a fortiori, (i) is true. So suppose $x^2 < 0$, and assume $i = 1$ uses the talking strategy μ_1^o and $i = 2$ uses the equivalent strategy,

$$\mu_2^o(t^2 = 2) = m', \quad \mu_2^o(t^2 < 2) = m'' \neq m'.$$

(Given $x^2 < 0$, similar reasoning as before shows that $i = 2$ could not use a semiseparating strategy in equilibrium in which the low types pool and the high type separates.) Bayes's rule, Lemma 1, and $\alpha = \beta = 1$ yield

$$\delta^*(m, m') = 1/2; \quad \delta^*(m, m'') = 7/30;$$
$$\delta^*(m', m') = 23/30; \quad \delta^*(m', m'') = 1/2.$$

Hence,

$$E[u^1(p) \mid \mu_1^o(0), \mu_2^o, \delta^*, t^1 = 0]$$
$$= -(1/16)(x^1)^2 - (9/16)(x^1 + 1/6 - 7/30)^2$$
$$\quad - (6/16)(x^1 + 2/6 - 7/30)^2 - \hat{V}^1(0);$$

$$E[u^1(p) \mid \mu_1^o(t^1 > 0), \mu_2^o, \delta^*, t^1 = 0]$$
$$= -(1/16)(x^1 + 1/2 - 23/30)^2 - (9/16)(x^1 + 1/6 - 1/2)^2$$
$$\quad - (6/16)(x^1 + 2/6 - 1/2)^2 - \hat{V}^1(0).$$

Thus

$$E[u^1(p) \mid \mu_1^o(0), \mu_2^o, \delta^*, t^1 = 0] \geq E[u^1(p) \mid \mu_1^o(t^1 > 0), \mu_2^o, \delta^*, t^1 = 0]$$
$$\text{if and only if } x^1 \leq 503/4200.$$

But $x^1 > 1/10$. Therefore, μ_1^o is not a best response to (μ_2^o, δ^*). Mutatis mutandis, a similar argument applies if $x^2 > 0$ and $\mu_2^o = \mu_1^o$; we omit the details.

Given the equilibrium talking strategies for each $n \in N^1 \times N^2$, it remains to show that $n^* = (2, 2)$. First note that if μ_i is pooling in equilibrium, then surely $n^{i*} = 2$, by u^i quadratic. Similarly, it is straightforward to check that if $n^2 = 1$ (so μ_2^* is separating) then $i = 1$ strictly prefers $n^1 = 2$ (with μ_1^o) to $n^1 = 1$ (with μ_1^* separating). Therefore, given the specified equilibrium pairs of talking strategies, $n^{1*} = 2$ is a best response to all $n^2 \in N^2$. It remains to check that $n^{2*} = 2$ is a best response to $n^{1*} = 2$. Using the interim expected payoffs from the specified equilibrium talking strategies and δ^*,

$E[u^2 \mid n = (2,2), i = 1 \text{ pools}, i = 2 \text{ separates}, \delta^*]$

$\qquad = -(x^2)^2 - \hat{v}^2(n, (\text{pools, separates}));$

$E[u^2 \mid n = (2,2), i = 1 \text{ separates}, i = 2 \text{ pools}, \delta^*]$

$$\qquad = -\sum_{T(2)} \Pr[t^2 \mid \emptyset]\left(\sum_{T(2)} \Pr[t^1 \mid t^2] E[u^2(p) \mid \mu_1^*(t^1), \delta^*, t^2] \right)$$

$$\qquad = -(x^2)^2 - 15/1152 - \hat{v}^2(n, (\text{separates, pools})).$$

By Bayes's rule,

$$\hat{v}^2(n, (\text{pools, separates})) = 21/80 \quad \text{and} \quad \hat{v}^2(n, (\text{separates, pools})) = 16/63.$$

Hence,

$\qquad E[u^2 \mid n = (2,2), \text{pools, separates}, \delta^*]$

$\qquad\qquad > E[u^2 \mid n = (2,2), \text{separates, pools}, \delta^*].$

Similarly,

$\qquad E[u^2 \mid n = (2,1), \mu_1^\circ, i = 2 \text{ separates}, \delta^*]$

$\qquad\qquad = -(1/2)[(4/9)(x^2)^2 + (4/9)(x^2 + 2/5 - 11/25)^2$

$\qquad\qquad\quad + (1/9)(x^2 + 3/5 - 11/25)^2]$

$\qquad\qquad\quad - (1/2)[(1/9)(x^2)^2 + (4/9)(x^2 + 3/5 - 7/10)^2$

$\qquad\qquad\quad + (4/9)(x^2 + 4/5 - 7/10)^2] - \hat{v}^2((2,1), (\mu_1^\circ, \text{separates})),$

where, recalling that $\mu_1^\circ(t^1 = 0) = m$, $\mu_1^\circ(t^1 > 0) = m' \neq m$, $\mu_2^*(t^2 = 0) = m$, and $\mu_2^*(t^2 = 1) = m' \neq m$, we have used Bayes's rule to compute $\delta^*(m', m) = 11/25$ and $\delta^*(m', m') = 7/10$, and so on. Doing the algebra,

$\qquad E[u^2 \mid n = (2,1), \mu_1^\circ, i = 2 \text{ separates}, \delta^*] \gtrless \min E[u^2 \mid n = (2,2), \cdot]$

$\qquad\qquad \text{if and only if} \quad 15/1152 + \hat{v}^2((2,2), (\text{separates, pools}))$

$$\qquad\qquad\qquad\qquad \gtrless 14/125 + \hat{v}^2((2,1), (\mu_1^\circ, \mu_2^*)).$$

By Bayes's rule,

$\qquad \hat{v}^2((2,1), (\mu_1^\circ, \mu_2^*)) > \hat{v}^2((2,2), (\text{separates, separates}))$

$\qquad\qquad\qquad\qquad = \hat{v}^2((2,2), (\text{separates, pools})).$

Therefore,

$\qquad E[u^2 \mid n = (2,1), \mu_1^\circ, i = 2 \text{ separates}, \delta^*] < \min E[u^2 \mid n = (2,2), \cdot],$

and so $n^{2*} = 2$ is a best response to $n^{1*} = 2$. $\square$

Proof of claims in Example 6: Given $n^i = (1,1)$ and μ_i^l as specified in the text, Bayes's rule, $\alpha_l = \beta_l = 1$ for all l, and Lemma 1 imply

$$\delta^*(m) = (2/3, 1/2) \quad \text{and} \quad \delta^*(m') = (1/3, 1/2).$$

Consequently, for all $t^i \in T((1, 1))$,

$$E[u^i(p)|\mu_i^1(t^i), \delta^*, t^i]$$
$$= -a^1(x_1^i)^2 - 2c^i x_1^i(x_2^i + \eta(t_2^i)) - b^i(x_2^i + \eta(t_2^i))^2 - V^i(\cdot),$$

where $\eta(t_2^i) = (1 + t_2^i)/3 - 1/2$. Suppose $t^i = (t_1^i, t_2^i)$ deviates from $\mu_i^1(t^i)$ and sends $\mu_i^1(s)$, $s = ((1 - t_1^i), t_2^i)$. Then

$$E[u^i(p)|\mu_i^1(s), \delta^*, t^i] = -a^i(x_1^i + (1 + t_1^i)/3 - (2 - t_1^i)/3)^2$$
$$- 2c^i x_1^i(x_2^i + \eta(t_2^i)) - b^i(x_2^i + \eta(t_2^i))^2 - V^i(\cdot).$$

Hence, for all $t^i \in T((1, 1))$,

$$E[u^i(p)|\mu_i^1(t^i), \delta^*, t^i] \geq E[u^i(p)|\mu_i^1(s), \delta^*, t^i]$$
$$\text{if and only if } x_1^i \leq 1/6 - c^i[x_2^i + \eta(t_2^i)]/a^i.$$

So, because $x_l^i \geq 0$ by assumption, (μ_i^1, δ^*) is an equilibrium pair of strategies if and only if $x_1^i \leq 1/6 - c^i[x_2^i + (1/6)]/a^i$, as required.

Suppose μ_i^1 is not available as an equilibrium strategy relative to $n^i = (1, 1)$, but that i can separate in equilibrium if $n^i = (1, 0)$. Given μ_i^1 is unavailable, one possible equilibrium informative strategy on $T((1, 1))$ is μ_i' as described in the text: with this strategy, $t^i = (0, 0)$ distinguishes himself while $t^i \neq (0, 0)$ pool. Given μ_i', derive δ^* as

$$\delta^*(m) = (1/3, 1/3) \quad \text{and} \quad \delta^*(m') = (5/9, 5/9).$$

Computing interim expected payoffs for each type $t^i \in T((1, 1))$ in the same way as in preceding arguments, it turns out that (μ_i', δ^*) is an equilibrium pair of strategies if and only if

$$(1/9)[a^i + b^i + 2c^i] \geq x_1^i(a^i + c^i) + x_2^i(b^i + c^i) \geq (1/9)[a^i - 2b^i - c^i].$$

But since $x_l^i \geq 0$ for all l, and since a^i, b^i, c^i are strictly positive, Proposition 2 implies that there exists a separating talking strategy in equilibrium if

$$(1/9)[a^i + b^i + 2c^i] \geq (2/3)[x_1^i(a^i + c^i) + x_2^i(b^i + c^i)].$$

Therefore, whenever μ_i' is part of an equilibrium, there exists another equilibrium in which i separates fully on $T((1, 1))$; that is, μ_i' cannot be part of the most informative available equilibrium when μ_i^1 is unavailable. Similarly, if the other possible informative strategy μ_i'' – in which $t^i = (0, 1)$ separates and $t^i \neq (0, 1)$ pool – is used, then

$$\delta^*(m) = (1/3, 2/3) \quad \text{and} \quad \delta^*(m') = (5/9, 4/9).$$

In this case, proceeding as above, μ_i'' can be a best response to δ^* if and only if

$(1/9)[a^i + b^i - 2c^i] \geq x_1^i(a^i - c^i) + x_2^i(c^i - b^i) \geq (1/9)[a^i - 2b^i + c^i]$.

But $a^i > b^i = c^i > 0$ by assumption, and so this constraint set is empty unless $x_1^i = 1/9$. Hence, generically μ_i'' cannot be part of an equilibrium. And since $x_l^i \geq 0$ for all l, there surely can be no equilibrium in which $t^i = (1, 1)$ separates and $t^i \neq (1, 1)$ pool.

Finally, we have to check that $n^{1*} = (1, 0)$. Given that i can reveal no information credibly if $n^i = (1, 1)$, $\delta^*(m) = (1/2, 1/2)$ for all $m \in M$ and, after doing the algebra:

$$E[u^i \mid n^i = (1, 1), \delta^*] = -a^i[((x_1^i)^2 + 1/36) + \hat{v}_1^i(1)]$$
$$- 2c^i x_1^i x_2^i - b^i[((x_2^i)^2 + 1/36) - \hat{v}_2^i(1)].$$

Similarly, since i reveals all of his information if $n^i = (1, 0)$,

$$E[u^i \mid n^i = (1, 0), \mu^*, \delta^*] = -a^i[(x_1^i)^2 + \hat{v}_1^i(1)] - 2c^i x_1^i x_2^i - b^i[(x_2^i)^2 + \hat{v}_2^i(0)].$$

Bayes's rule implies $\hat{v}_l^j(1) = 5/18$ and $\hat{v}_l^j(0) = 1/3$. Hence

$$E[u^i \mid n^i = (1, 0), \mu^*, \cdot] > E[u^i \mid n^i = (1, 1), \cdot] \quad \text{if } a^i/b^i > 1.$$

Therefore, $n^{i*} = (1, 0)$, as claimed. $\qquad\qquad\square$

Proof of claims in Example 8: Suppose preferences are such that the most informative available equilibrium for all $n \in N^1 \times N^2$ involves both senders separating. For all n, let μ^* denote these talking strategies. Fix (n^j, μ^*) and consider i's decision on $n^i \in N^i$, $i \neq j$. Given μ^* and δ^* (Lemma 1), the difference in i's ex ante expected payoffs between choosing n^i and $n^{i'}$ depends exclusively on the respective weighted variance terms. Specifically, for all $n^i, n^{i'} \in N^i$:

$$E[u^i \mid n^i, n^j, \mu^*, \delta^*] = -a^i(x_1^i)^2 - 2c^i x_1^i x_2^i - b^i(x_2^i)^2$$
$$- a^i \hat{v}_1^i(n, \mu^*) - b^i \hat{v}_2^i(n, \mu^*),$$

where

$$\hat{v}_l^j(n, \mu^*) \equiv \sum_{t \in T(n_l^i + n_l^j)} \Pr[t]\, \mathrm{var}[\Omega_l \mid n, t].$$

Because $\hat{v}_l^j$ is strictly decreasing in n^i, no $n^i \in N^i$ such that $n_1^i + n_2^i < 2$ can be a best response to (n^j, μ^*, δ^*). Assuming $n^i > n^{i'}$ and writing $n' = (n^{i'}, n^j), \ldots,$

$$E[u^i \mid n^i, n^j, \mu^*, \delta^*] \geq E[u^i \mid n^{i'}, n^j, \mu^*, \delta^*] \quad \text{if and only if}$$
$$a^i/b^i \geq [\hat{v}_2^j(n, \mu^*) - \hat{v}_2^j(n', \mu^*)]/[\hat{v}_1^j(n', \mu^*) - \hat{v}_1^j(n, \mu^*)].$$

In view of the definition of $\hat{v}_l^j(n, \mu^*)$, it is convenient to write $\hat{v}_l^j(n, \mu^*) \equiv \hat{v}_l^j(n_l^i + n_l^j)$. Then, using Bayes's rule and $\alpha_l = \beta_l = 1$, compute for all i, l:

$$\hat{v}_l^j(0) = 1/3; \quad \hat{v}_l^j(1) = 5/18; \quad \hat{v}_l^j(2) = 21/80;$$

$$\hat{v}_i^j(3) = 77/300; \quad \hat{v}_i^j(4) = 16/63.$$

Substituting as appropriate into the previous inequality yields the claims.

□

REFERENCES

Austen-Smith, D. (1990a), "Information Transmission in Debate," *American Journal of Political Science* 34: 124–52.

(1990b), "Credible Debate Equilibria," *Social Choice and Welfare* 7: 75–93.

(1993), "Interested Experts and Policy Advice: Multiple Referrals under Open Rule," *Games and Economic Behavior* 5: 3–43.

Congressional Record, May 1977.

Crawford, V., and J. Sobel (1982), "Strategic Information Transmission," *Econometrica* 50: 1431–51.

DeGroot, M. (1970), *Optimal Statistical Decisions.* New York: McGraw-Hill.

Demange, G. (1990), "Are Two Heads Better than One?" Mimeo, Laboratoire d'Econometrie de l'Ecole Polytechnique, Paris.

Farrell, J. (1985), "Credible Neologisms in Games of Communication," Working Paper no. 386, Department of Economics, Massachusetts Institute of Technology, Cambridge.

Gilligan, T., and K. Krehbiel (1987), "Collective Decision Making and Standing Committees: An Informational Rationale for Restrictive Amendment Procedures," *Journal of Law, Economics and Organization* 3: 145–93.

(1989), "Asymmetric Information and Legislative Rules with a Heterogeneous Committee," *American Journal of Political Science* 33: 459–90.

(1990), "Organization of Informative Committees by a Rational Legislature," *American Journal of Political Science* 34: 531–64.

Mansbridge, J. (1986), *Why We Lost the ERA.* Chicago: University of Chicago Press.

Matthews, S. (1989), "Veto Threats: Rhetoric in a Bargaining Game," *Quarterly Journal of Economics* 104: 347–69.

Riker, W. H. (1991), "Rhetorical Interaction in the Ratification Campaigns," Working Paper, Department of Political Science, University of Rochester.

Smith, R. (1989), "Interpretation, Pressure, and the Stability of Interest Group Influence in the U.S. Congress," Paper presented at the 1989 APSA meetings, Atlanta, GA.

CHAPTER 17

A welfare analysis of political action

Susanne Lohmann

1   Introduction

A common theme in political science is that an office-motivated leader will be responsive to shifts in voter preferences. A leader who is out of touch with the voters will be replaced by a challenger whose policy positions are more popular.

Policy shifts and changes in leadership personnel are often preceded by political action: people sign petitions, take part in demonstrations, or participate in violent riots. Social scientists commonly question whether these forms of political participation are an effective or desirable means by which the members of a society express their policy preferences.[1]

In earlier work, I show that political action may be an effective means by which the populace can influence political outcomes (Lohmann 1992a, b,c, 1993). Some information pertinent to political decisions may be dispersed among the members of a society. In this situation, rational and self-interested individuals may have incentives to take costly political action in order to signal their private information to political decision makers. Voters or political leaders may rationally take a cue from a simple aggregate statistic: the publicly observed number of political actions. By contributing information prior to political decisions, political action has the potential to increase the likelihood that political outcomes will be in line with the policy preferences of the people. This benefit comes at a deadweight cost privately incurred by the activists.

This work is based on Chapter Four of my doctoral dissertation at Carnegie-Mellon University. I am deeply indebted to Howard Rosenthal for numerous insightful comments and corrections. I would also like to thank Arthur Lupia, Gary Miller, and other participants of the Conference on Political Economy: Institutions, Information, Competition and Representation at Washington University in St. Louis in May 1991 for their comments. Fellowship support from the John M. Olin Foundation and the Alfred P. Sloan Foundation is gratefully acknowledged.
[1]   See Lohmann (1992a,b,c, 1993) for a literature review.

This chapter examines whether political action is a socially desirable means of disciplining political decision making.[2] The welfare analysis identifies a number of sources that render the equilibrium supply of political action socially suboptimal. Perhaps surprisingly, costly political action may be under- *and* oversupplied in equilibrium.

Section 2 develops a welfare analysis of the equilibria that arise when members of a homogeneous society can take costly political action prior to a vote.[3] In a sense, the individuals have the option to contribute to a public good (information) at a private cost. The welfare analysis establishes that the existence of this cost may lead to a socially suboptimal supply of political action in equilibrium.

The information transmission that precedes the vote is decentralized. The multiple senders and receivers of costly political action messages are drawn from the electorate. If the individuals' private information is not fully revealed prior to the vote, their residual private information affects their votes. As a consequence, some information is aggregated through the voting mechanism. The welfare analysis focuses on the marginal informational contribution of the political action mechanism.

Section 3 presents a welfare analysis of the equilibria that arise when members of a heterogeneous society can take political action to influence the policy decision made by a political leader. Because information flows to one receiver only, the signaling and updating strategies are simpler in this setting. On the other hand, I now assume that individuals have heterogeneous preferences over policy outcomes. As a consequence, some individuals may have disincentives to truthfully reveal their private information, which complicates the leader's signal-extraction problem. The welfare analysis examines how conflicts of interest among the members of a society may drive a wedge between the equilibrium and the socially optimal supply of political action.

Section 4 summarizes the results and contains some conclusions on the social role of political action.

2   Pre-election political action

2.1   *The model*

I first present a formal signaling model of political action in which the members of a homogeneous society can take costly political action prior to a vote.[4]

---

[2] In a related paper, Ball (1991) develops a welfare analysis of lobbying.

[3] See also Lupia (1992) and Lupia's Chapter 15 in this volume.

[4] The model is a special case of Lohmann (1992b).

The society consists of n identical individuals, indexed by $i = 1, ..., n$. The size n of the population is assumed to be large but finite and odd. Individual i's loss function is given by

$$L_i = x^2 + d_i c,$$ (1)

where x is the policy outcome, c is the cost incurred by individual i when taking political action, and d_i is an index variable which takes on the value 1 if individual i takes political action, and value 0 otherwise. The policy outcome x is determined by the policy p and the state of the world s:

$$x = p - s.$$ (2)

The state of the world s is drawn from a uniform distribution $\beta(s)$ over the unit interval. The common prior on the density of the states of the world is given by $\beta(s)$. The policy p is chosen from the set $\{Q, A\}$, where the status quo Q and the policy alternative A are two exogenously fixed and distinct points on the unit interval, $0 \le Q < A \le 1$. The population is better off under the status quo for states of the world that satisfy $s \in [0, (Q+A)/2)$, but under the policy alternative for other states $s \in ((Q+A)/2, 1]$.

The time sequence of events in the homogeneous model is given in Figure 1. Nature draws the state of the world s. Then, each individual observes an independent realization of a binary signal σ. The probability that an individual observes the realization $\sigma = 1$ is equal to s, while the probability of the realization $\sigma = 0$ is given by $(1-s)$. Thus, the signal σ is informative about the state of the world. Since the individual experiences are made privately, each individual is very imperfectly informed about the state of the world s. In the aggregate, the population observes n independent draws of the signal σ and is thus very well informed. However, no single individual is informed about the aggregate number of individuals of type $\sigma = 1$ or $\sigma = 0$.

Given her private information at the political action stage, σ, each individual chooses whether to take political action or to abstain. Formally, her political action strategy is given by the probability $\pi(\sigma)$. An individual who takes political action ($\pi = 1$) privately incurs the cost c; an individual who abstains ($\pi = 0$) does not.

It is commonly understood that an individual who takes political action wishes to indicate that she is of type $\sigma = 1$, or (equivalently) that she is in favor of the policy alternative. That is, individuals can choose whether to send the costly message "I am type $\sigma = 1$" or to abstain from sending this message. The analysis of the case in which the message implicit in a

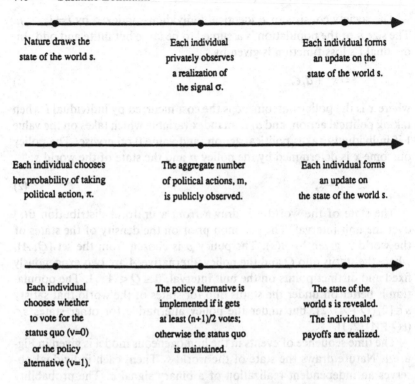

Nature draws the
state of the world s.

Each individual
privately observes
a realization of
the signal σ.

Each individual forms
an update on the
state of the world s.

Each individual chooses
her probability of taking
political action, π.

The aggregate number
of political actions, m,
is publicly observed.

Each individual forms
an update on
the state of the world s.

Each individual
chooses whether
to vote for the
status quo (v=0)
or the policy
alternative (v=1).

The policy alternative is
implemented if it gets
at least (n+1)/2 votes;
otherwise the status quo
is maintained.

The state of the
world s is revealed.
The individuals'
payoffs are realized.

Figure 1. Time sequence of events in the homogeneous model.

political action is "I am type $\sigma = 0$" or (equivalently) "I am in favor of the status quo" is symmetric.[5]

At the voting stage, m individuals are publicly observed to take political action. At this time, each individual's information set contains the publicly observed number of political actions, m, and the individual's private information, σ and π. (In addition to her private information about her type σ, an individual who chose to follow a mixed strategy of taking political action knows whether the realization of this probability π was zero or unity.) Based on this information, each individual forms an update on the state of the world s.

Next, a majority-rule referendum takes place. Formally, the individuals' voting strategies are given by $v(m, \sigma, \pi)$. Each individual chooses whether to vote for the policy alternative A ($v = 1$) or the status quo Q ($v = 0$). (The individuals' voting strategies are generally pure in this model.)

---

[5] Lohmann (1992a) develops a model in which individuals can choose to send one (or both) of the messages "I am type $\sigma = 1$" and "I am type $\sigma = 0$," or abstain from sending a message.

The policy alternative is implemented if at least $(n+1)/2$ voters cast their votes in its favor; otherwise the status quo is maintained.[6] Finally, individual losses are realized as a function of the policy passed in the referendum and the state of the world.

The structure of the game is common knowledge. The equilibrium concept is a refinement of sequential equilibrium (Kreps and Wilson 1982) with symmetric, weakly undominated strategies.[7] The equilibrium is defined as follows.

Definition. An equilibrium of the game is given by the individuals' political action strategies, $\{\pi(\sigma)\}$; their beliefs at the political action stage, $\{\beta(s\,|\,\sigma)\}$; their voting strategies, $\{\nu(\sigma, \pi, m)\}$; and their beliefs at the voting stage, $\beta(s\,|\,\sigma, \pi, m)$. The strategies and beliefs are consistent with each other and fulfill the following conditions.[8]

(A1) Individual i's political action strategy $\pi(\sigma)$ minimizes her expected loss at the political action stage,

$$E(L_i\,|\,\sigma) = \int \sum_{m=0}^{n} \sum_{k=0}^{n} \left\{ \text{prob}\left[\sum_{j=1}^{n} \nu_j < \frac{n+1}{2} \Big| m \right] (Q-s)^2 \right.$$
$$\left. + \text{prob}\left[\sum_{j=1}^{n} \nu_j \geq \frac{n+1}{2} \Big| m \right] (A-s)^2 \right\}$$
$$\cdot b(m; k, \pi) b(k; n, s) \beta(s\,|\,\sigma)\,ds + \pi_i c, \tag{3}$$

where $E(\cdot)$ is an expectations operator, and $b(b_1; b_2, b_3)$ is the binomial probability that b_2 Bernoulli trials will result in b_1 successes if the probability of a success is given by b_3.

(A2) Individual i uses Bayes's rule to update that $\beta(s\,|\,\sigma)$ is the posterior density of the state of the world s conditional on the private information σ.

(A3) Individual i's voting strategy $\nu(\sigma, \pi, m)$ minimizes her expected loss at the policy decision stage,

$$E(L_i\,|\,\sigma, \pi, m) = \int \left\{ \text{prob}\left[\sum_{j=1}^{n} \nu_j < \frac{n+1}{2} \Big| m \right] (Q-s)^2 \right.$$
$$\left. + \text{prob}\left[\sum_{j=1}^{n} \nu_j \geq \frac{n+1}{2} \Big| m \right] (A-s)^2 \right\}$$
$$\cdot \beta(s\,|\,\sigma, \pi, m)\,ds + d_i c. \tag{4}$$

---

[6] The analysis of a majority-rule election in which voters choose between an incumbent and a challenger with distinct policy preferences is formally equivalent.

[7] The equilibrium concept is extensively discussed in Lohmann (1992b).

[8] The separability of the individuals' best responses at the political action and voting stages underlying the equilibrium conditions is established in Lohmann (1992b).

(A4)   Individual i uses Bayes's rule to update that $\beta(s\,|\,\sigma, \pi, m)$ is the posterior density of the state of the world s conditional on the public information m and the private information σ and π.

(A5)   For the zero political action equilibrium, the individuals' out-of-equilibrium updating rule is assumed to be given by

$$\beta(s\,|\,\sigma, \pi, m) = \beta(\sigma) \quad \text{for all } m > 0.$$

2.2   The normative benchmark

This section develops a normative benchmark for the welfare analysis. The socially optimal supply of political action might be thought of as solving a standard two-stage statistical decision problem (DeGroot 1970). A random variable is correlated with the state of the world. At the first stage, the statistician chooses how many realizations of a random variable are to be observed at a fixed cost per observation. At the second stage, the statistician chooses a decision from a decision set. The loss generated by the decision increases in the quadratic difference between the decision and the state of the world. The higher is the number of observations made in the first stage, the better informed is the statistician about the state of the world, and, in expectation, the lower is the quadratic distance between the decision and the state of the world; but the higher is the total cost of sampling. For zero (low, prohibitive) sampling costs, the statistician chooses to sample all (some, none) of the realizations of the random variable.

The statistical decision problem in this chapter is more complicated, but the underlying intuition is similar. The members of the society ultimately care about policy outcomes. Since the policy and the state of the world jointly determine the policy outcome, the individuals' preferences over policies depend on the state of the world. If no information is publicly revealed prior to the vote, the individuals' voting decisions are a function of their private information only. The voting mechanism then allows for some aggregation of information. In many states of the world, a majority of the imperfectly informed voters choose the policy that would also be implemented if the voters were fully informed. However, in some states of the world, a majority of voters may cast their votes in favor of one policy although they would be better off under the alternative policy. If the information dispersed in the population were partially or fully revealed prior to the vote, the individuals might be less likely to cast "mistaken" votes. However, information revelation through political action comes at a cost privately incurred by the activists. This setting gives rise to a trade-off between the aggregate expected benefits generated by a reduction in the likelihood of a mistaken voting outcome, on the one hand, and the aggregate costs of political action, on the other.

Let the social loss be measured by the sum of equiweighted individual losses,

$$L^W = \sum_{i=1}^{n} L_i = nx^2 + \sum_{i=1}^{n} d_i c. \tag{5}$$

(The superscript W stands for welfare.) The specification of the social loss function is motivated as follows. An outcome that minimizes the sum of individual losses is Pareto efficient if utility is transferable between individuals.

As a normative benchmark, I take the supply of political action that is prescribed by a benevolent dictator to minimize the ex ante expected social loss. The first-best supply of political action would be obtained if incentive-compatibility constraints were not binding and the individuals could coordinate their beliefs on a particular equilibrium.

At the beginning of the game, the dictator publicly announces a mapping $\pi^W(\sigma)$. This mapping specifies the probability of taking political action for each individual as a function of that individual's private information at the political action stage. To ensure that the socially optimal and equilibrium supplies of taking political action are comparable, the dictator is constrained to choose symmetric probabilities of taking political action; that is, identical types are constrained to take political action with identical probabilities.

Each individual takes political action with the probability prescribed for her private information σ. After m political actions are publicly observed, each individual forms a Bayesian update on the state of the world s. This update is based on the publicly available information m as well as her residual private information, σ and π. The individual (correctly) presumes that all individuals have followed the dictator's prescription, $\pi^W(\sigma)$.

To focus on the optimality properties of the political action mechanism (as opposed to those of the voting mechanism), I restrict attention to the setting in which the benevolent dictator plays a role at the political action stage only. Based on the dictator's announcement and the subsequently observed number of political actions, a voting-stage equilibrium will be realized. The voting mechanism allows for some information aggregation. The welfare analysis separates the marginal informational contribution of pre-election communication from the contribution of the voting mechanism.

To simplify the presentation of the welfare analysis, I initially restrict attention to the case in which the socially optimal "message space" involves individuals of type $\sigma = 1$ taking political action, while individuals of type $\sigma = 0$ abstain. (Later on, I will allow the benevolent dictator to choose the message space; that is, he can then determine whether political action is to be taken by individuals of type $\sigma = 1$ or $\sigma = 0$.) Given this restriction, the social optimum is defined as follows.

Definition. The social optimum is given by the socially optimal probability π^W of taking political action for individuals of type $\sigma = 1$; the individuals' voting strategies, $\{v(\sigma, \pi, m)\}$; and their beliefs at the voting stage, $\{\beta(s \mid \sigma, \pi, m)\}$. All of these are consistent with each other and satisfy conditions (A3) and (A4), as well as the following condition.

(B1)   The socially optimal probability of taking political action for individuals of type $\sigma = 1$, π^W, minimizes the ex ante expected social loss,

$$E(L^W) = n \int \sum_{m=0}^{n} \sum_{k=0}^{n} \left\{ \text{prob}\left[\sum_{i=1}^{n} v_i < \frac{n+1}{2} \,\middle|\, m \right] (Q-s)^2 \right.$$

$$+ \text{prob}\left[\sum_{i=1}^{n} v_i \geq \frac{n+1}{2} \,\middle|\, m \right] (A-s)^2 \Big\}$$

$$\cdot b(m; k, \pi^W) b(k; n, s) \beta(s) \, ds$$

$$+ c\pi^W \int \sum_{k=0}^{n} k b(k; n, s) \beta(s) \, ds. \tag{6}$$

In the following analysis, three cases are distinguished: zero, strictly positive but not prohibitive, and prohibitive costs of taking political action. Costs are defined as "strictly positive but not prohibitive" if they are strictly positive and are associated with at least one equilibrium characterized by strictly positive political action turnout; costs are referred to as "prohibitive" if they are associated with a unique zero political action equilibrium.

Zero cost
The individuals' posterior beliefs at the political action stage are given by

$$\beta(s \mid \sigma) = \begin{cases} 2s & \text{if } \sigma = 1, \\ 2(1-s) & \text{if } \sigma = 0. \end{cases} \tag{7}$$

Individuals of type $\sigma = 1$ expect to be better off if the policy alternative were implemented, while individuals of type $\sigma = 0$ prefer the status quo to be maintained:

$$E(s \mid \sigma = 1) = 2/3 > 1/3 = E(s \mid \sigma = 0). \tag{8}$$

Given that political action can be taken at zero cost, individuals of type $\sigma = 1$ take action in favor of the policy alternative; all others abstain. The equilibrium is fully revealing.

The observed number of political actions m is exactly equal to the number of individuals of type $\sigma = 1$. Given the correlation between the individuals' private information σ and the state of the world s, the probability that m individuals in a population of size n are of type $\sigma = 1$ if the state of the world is given by s is equal to the binomial probability that n Bernoulli trials result in m successes if the probability of a success is given by s and $b(m; n, s)$. Thus, the voters' posterior beliefs about the state of the world are based on the number m:

$$\beta(s \mid m) = \frac{b(m; n, s)\beta(s)}{\int b(m; n, s)\beta(s)\, ds}. \tag{9}$$

The higher is the number of political actions m, the higher is the posterior expectation of the state of the world $E(s \mid m)$. If the number m exceeds a critical level $\tilde{m}$, all voters update that they would be better off under the policy alternative and unanimously vote in its favor; otherwise, all individuals cast their votes in favor of the status quo. The threshold $\tilde{m}$ is given by the natural number that solves

$$E(s \mid m = \tilde{m}) \geq (Q + A)/2; \tag{10}$$

$$E(s \mid m = \tilde{m} - 1) < (Q + A)/2. \tag{11}$$

This fully revealing equilibrium co-exists with another informative equilibrium in which all individuals of type $\sigma = 0$ take political action while all individuals of type $\sigma = 1$ abstain. Moreover, there exists a multiplicity of uninformative equilibria. First, if individuals believe that they are in a zero political action equilibrium, their beliefs are fulfilled in equilibrium. Second, uninformative babbling equilibria are characterized by the feature that all individuals take political action with identical, strictly positive probabilities.

The supply of political action in the two fully revealing equilibria is socially optimal. Given that the transmission of information is costless, the benevolent dictator chooses to have all information revealed in order to minimize the likelihood of a mistaken voting outcome. In contrast, informative political action is undersupplied in the nonrevealing equilibria. In this case, the individuals are trapped into Pareto-dominated equilibria by their exogenously given beliefs.

Strictly positive but not prohibitive costs
For a nonempty set of strictly positive but not prohibitive costs of taking political action, a partially revealing equilibrium emerges. The model is

solved by backward induction. I first analyze the voting stage and then the political action stage.

At the voting stage, m political actions are publicly observed. There exist three types of individuals with different information sets. The posterior density of an individual of type $\sigma = 0$ is given by

$$\beta(s\,|\,\sigma = 0, m) = \frac{b(m; k, \pi)b(k; n-1, s)\beta(s\,|\,\sigma = 0)}{\int b(m; k, \pi)b(k; n-1, s)\beta(s\,|\,\sigma = 0)\,ds}. \tag{12}$$

The posterior density of an individual of type $\sigma = 1$ whose political action probability was realized as unity ($\pi = 1$) is given by

$$\beta(s\,|\,\sigma = 1, \pi = 1, m) = \frac{b(m-1; k, \pi)b(k; n-1, s)\beta(s\,|\,\sigma = 1)}{\int b(m-1; k, \pi)b(k; n-1, s)\beta(s\,|\,\sigma = 1)\,ds}. \tag{13}$$

The posterior density of an individual of type $\sigma = 1$ whose political action probability was realized as zero ($\pi = 0$) is given by

$$\beta(s\,|\,\sigma = 1, \pi = 0, m) = \frac{b(m; k, \pi)b(k; n-1, s)\beta(s\,|\,\sigma = 1)}{\int b(m; k, \pi)b(k; n-1, s)\beta(s\,|\,\sigma = 1)\,ds}. \tag{14}$$

As before, each individual follows a cutpoint voting rule. The type-specific voting cutpoints, $\tilde{m}_0$, $\tilde{m}_{11}$, and $\tilde{m}_{10}$, are given by the natural numbers that solve

$$E(s\,|\,\sigma = 0, m = \tilde{m}_0) \geq (Q+A)/2, \tag{15}$$

$$E(s\,|\,\sigma = 0, m = \tilde{m}_0 - 1) < (Q+A)/2, \tag{16}$$

$$E(s\,|\,\sigma = 1, \pi = 1, m = \tilde{m}_{11}) \geq (Q+A)/2, \tag{17}$$

$$E(s\,|\,\sigma = 1, \pi = 1, m = \tilde{m}_{11} - 1) < (Q+A)/2, \tag{18}$$

$$E(s\,|\,\sigma = 1, \pi = 0, m = \tilde{m}_{10}) \geq (Q+A)/2, \tag{19}$$

$$E(s\,|\,\sigma = 1, \pi = 0, m = \tilde{m}_{10} - 1) < (Q+A)/2. \tag{20}$$

Equations (12)–(20) imply that

$$\tilde{m}_0 \geq \tilde{m}_{11} \geq \tilde{m}_{10}. \tag{21}$$

The policy alternative receives a majority of the vote if the realized number of political actions lies above the voting cutpoint of $(n+1)/2$ or more individuals. The ex ante probability that this happens as a function of the number of political actions is given by

$$\text{prob}\left[\sum_{i=1}^{n} v_i \geq \frac{n+1}{2}\,\bigg|\,m\right]$$

$$= \begin{cases} 1 & \text{if } m \geq \tilde{m}_0, \\ \int \sum_{k=(n+1)/2}^{n} b(k; n, s)\beta(s)\,ds & \text{if } m = \tilde{m}_{11}, \\ \int \sum_{k=(n+1)/2+\tilde{m}_{10}}^{n} b(k; n, s)\beta(s)\,ds & \text{if } m = \tilde{m}_{10}, \\ 0 & \text{if } m < \tilde{m}_{10}. \end{cases} \tag{22}$$

I now turn to the analysis of the political action stage. An individual of type $\sigma = 1$ strictly prefers the policy alternative to receive a majority of the vote. Her political action decision is based on the expected private benefits and costs generated by her action. She compares the cost of taking political action with the expected probability that her action will be pivotal for triggering a policy shift, multiplied by the benefits expected from a policy shift. In equilibrium, the individual is indifferent between having her political action probability realize as unity ($\pi = 1$) or zero ($\pi = 0$) if the following indifference condition holds:

$$\int \left\{ b(\tilde{m}_0; k, \pi) + \sum_{k=(n+1)/2}^{n} b(\tilde{m}_{11}; k, \pi) + \sum_{k=(n+1)/2+\tilde{m}_{10}}^{n} b(\tilde{m}_{10}; k, \pi) \right\}$$
$$\cdot [(Q-s)^2 - (A-s)^2] b(k; n, s) \beta(s \mid \sigma = 1)\, ds = c. \quad (23)$$

The symmetry restriction (identical types follow identical strategies) implies that the indifference condition must hold for all individuals of type $\sigma = 1$. The type $\sigma = 1$ equilibrium probability π of taking political action solves this condition and lies strictly between zero and unity. As before, individuals of type $\sigma = 0$ abstain from taking political action, as they do not wish to improve the chances that the policy alternative receives a majority of the vote.

Due to the random realization of the individuals' mixed strategies of taking political action, the equilibrium is partially revealing. In equilibrium, the public knows that an individual who took political action is of type $\sigma = 1$. But voters cannot distinguish between a type $\sigma = 1$ individual who abstained from political action because her probability of taking action realized as zero and a type $\sigma = 0$ individual who has a dominant strategy of abstaining.

This partially revealing equilibrium co-exists with an equilibrium in which political action is taken by individuals of type $\sigma = 0$ while individuals of type $\sigma = 1$ abstain. Moreover, the individuals may be trapped into a zero political action equilibrum due to their beliefs.

In the welfare analysis, I first focus on the case where the socially optimal supply of political action for individuals of type $\sigma = 1$ is characterized by an interior solution for π^W. The benevolent dictator compares the ex ante expected aggregate benefits and costs that are derived from a marginal increase in the type $\sigma = 1$ probability of taking political action. In forming an expectation of the probability that an individual action will be pivotal, the benevolent dictator rationally anticipates the play of the game at the voting stage. The dictator's indifference condition is given by

$$\int \left\{ b(\tilde{m}_0; k, \pi^W) + \sum_{k=(n+1)/2}^{n} b(\tilde{m}_{11}; k, \pi^W) + \sum_{k=(n+1)/2+\tilde{m}_{10}}^{n} b(\tilde{m}_{10}; k, \pi^W) \right\}$$
$$\cdot [(Q-s)^2 - (A-s)^2] b(k; n, s) \beta(s)\, ds =$$

$$= \left[c \int \sum_{k=0}^{n} b(k; n, s)\beta(s) \, ds \right] \Big/ n. \tag{24}$$

The socially optimal political action probability π^W for individuals of type $\sigma = 1$, together with the equilibrium cutpoints $\tilde{m}_0$, $\tilde{m}_{11}$, and $\tilde{m}_{10}$, implicitly solves the system of equations (7), (12)–(20), and (24). If there exists more than one solution to the system of equations that defines the social optimum, then the benevolent dictator selects the one that minimizes the ex ante expected social loss. The dictator also compares the interior solution to corner solutions that prescribe political action probabilities of zero or unity for individuals of type $\sigma = 1$. Finally, the dictator chooses the message space that is associated with a lower ex ante expected social loss; that is, he determines whether political action is to be taken by individuals of type $\sigma = 1$ or $\sigma = 0$.

In order to specify some sources that render the equilibrium supply of political action socially suboptimal, it is useful to compare the equilibrium minimization problem solved by the individuals and the social minimization problem faced by the benevolent dictator.

First, compared to the equilibrium indifference condition of an individual of type $\sigma = 1$, the right-hand side of the dictator's indifference condition contains an additional term (see equations (23) and (24)). All else being equal, the probability that an individual action will be pivotal for the voting outcome is higher in equilibrium than in the social optimum. In equilibrium, the individuals do not take into account the informational externalities exerted by their actions; they only care about the private benefits and costs of taking political action. In contrast, the benevolent dictator's political action prescription optimally trades off the *aggregate* expected benefits and costs generated by an individual action.

Second, the benevolent dictator uses the prior density $\beta(s)$ to form an expectation of the probability that an individual action will be pivotal and of the resulting expected benefits. In contrast, the individuals' calculus is based on the posterior density $\beta(s \mid \sigma)$. From the point of view of the benevolent dictator, individuals tend to overestimate the number of "like-minded" individuals at the political action stage. An activist expects the protest movement to be larger and more likely to succeed than does the benevolent dictator.

Third, the individual political action probabilities, beliefs, and voting cutpoints are endogenous with regard to the dictator's announcement. In contrast, each individual's equilibrium behavior takes other individuals' political action and voting behavior as exogenously given. If there exist multiple solutions to the system of equations that defines the equilibrium, the individuals may be trapped into a Pareto-dominated solution owing to their exogenously given beliefs.

In some partially informative equilibria, political action is taken by individuals of type $\sigma = 1$; in others, by individuals of type $\sigma = 0$. The welfare analysis suggests that it is misleading to classify these equilibria as "essentially equivalent" (Palfrey and Rosenthal 1991). In general, one of these equilibria is more efficient in the following sense: it is associated with a higher likelihood that the socially preferred political decision will be made or with a lower aggregate deadweight cost of political action.

The political action mechanism aggregates some of the individuals' private information prior to the vote at a cost privately incurred by the activists. This mechanism co-exists with the voting mechanism that costlessly aggregates some of the dispersed information via the vote. Given that some information is aggregated by the vote, the marginal contribution of the political action mechanism may consist of adding noise. In some cases, the voting mechanism is ex ante more likely to implement the full-information voting outcome in the absence of pre-election political action.

This insight can be illustrated as follows. The optimal policy decision rule for the society is to shift policy if the number of individuals of type $\sigma = 1$ is greater than k^* and maintain the status quo otherwise, where k^* is the natural number that solves

$$\frac{\int sb(k^*; n, s)\beta(s)\,ds}{\int b(k^*; n, s)\beta(s)\,ds} \geq \frac{Q+A}{2}; \tag{25}$$

$$\frac{\int sb(k^*-1; n, s)\beta(s)\,ds}{\int b(k^*-1; n, s)\beta(s)\,ds} < \frac{Q+A}{2}. \tag{26}$$

Given the dispersed private information, this decision rule is implemented by the following $(k^*/n) \cdot 100\%$ voting rule: if k^* or more individuals vote in favor of the policy alternative, then the status quo is overturned; otherwise, the status quo is maintained. This rule costlessly implements the full-information outcome even though each individual voter is very imperfectly informed.

In contrast, an equilibrium characterized by a strictly positive political action turnout is associated with the "noise" of the random realizations of the individuals' mixed strategies of taking political action. The realized number of political actions may be a misleading indicator of the state of the world, so that some individuals may cast mistaken votes. It follows that the probability that the socially preferred policy is implemented is strictly smaller than unity. In addition, the deadweight costs of information aggregation are strictly positive.

It is interesting to note that a homogeneous group of individuals might choose *not* to make decisions by consensus, as suggested by the Condorcet jury theorem (Condorcet 1785; Grofman, Owen, and Feld 1983). An appropriately chosen voting rule can ensure that the private information dispersed in the population is costlessly utilized in the individuals' collective decision. Moreover, in the presence of the optimal voting rule, the members of the society would choose to disallow communication prior to a vote.[9]

Prohibitive costs

For prohibitive cost parameters, the zero political action equilibrium is unique. No information is revealed prior to the referendum, and no individual incurs the cost of taking political action. Each individual bases her vote on her private information only. As a result, each individual of type $\sigma = 1$ casts her vote in favor of the policy alternative, and each individual of type $\sigma = 0$ votes for the status quo. The political alternative is implemented if and only if the individuals of type $\sigma = 1$ form a majority.

For the range of costs that are prohibitive from both the individual and the social point of view, the equilibrium supply of political action (zero) is socially optimal. For cost parameters that are prohibitive from an individual but not from a social point of view, or vice versa, the supply of political action is socially suboptimal.

It is interesting to note that if the status quo is ex ante preferred by the population, that is, if

$$E(s) < (Q + A)/2, \tag{27}$$

then the ex ante probability that a fully informed population would vote in favor of the policy alternative is strictly greater than the ex ante probability that $(n + 1)/2$ or more partially informed individuals will vote in favor of the policy alternative:

$$\int \sum_{k=k^*}^{n} b(k; n, s)\beta(s)\,ds > \int \sum_{k=(n+1)/2}^{n} b(k; n, s)\beta(s)\,ds. \tag{28}$$

In this case, uninformed decision making by simple majority rule is associated with a bias toward the status quo.

3   Informative versus manipulative political action

3.1   The model

I now review a model in which the members of a heterogeneous society can take political action to influence the policy decision made by a political leader (Lohmann 1993). Individual i's loss function is now modified to

[9] The argument must be modified if voting is costly. In this case, the socially optimal supply of political action and the socially optimal voting rule would be jointly chosen to minimize the expected social loss.

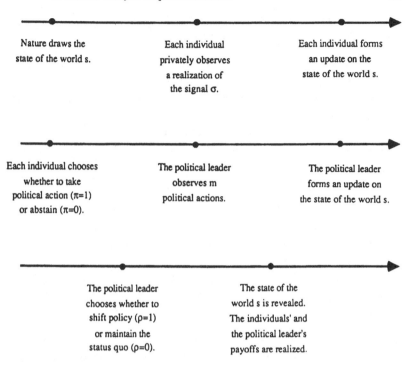

Figure 2. Time sequence of events in the heterogeneous model.

$$\Lambda_i = (x - x_i)^2 + d_i c, \tag{29}$$

where x_i is individual i's bliss point for policy outcomes. For simplicity, the bliss points are assumed to be uniformly distributed between $-\bar{x}$ and $\bar{x}$, $\bar{x} > 0$. The distribution of bliss points is common knowledge, but each individual is privately informed about her own bliss point. The parameter $\bar{x}$ measures the heterogeneity of the population.

The political leader is motivated to minimize the loss function of the median individual, whose bliss point is equal to zero:

$$\Lambda_0 = x^2. \tag{30}$$

This specification reflects the leader's desire to set the policy that benefits a majority. The costs of political action incurred by the activists are sunk costs at the policy-decision stage, so the cost term can be omitted.

The time sequence of events in the heterogeneous model is given in Figure 2. The game is similar to the one presented in Section 2, except that the individuals are differentiated with respect to their bliss points and information sets. Formally, the individuals' political action strategies are given by $\pi(i, \sigma)$. Given her private information at the political action stage, x_i and σ, each individual chooses whether to take political action ($\pi = 1$) or abstain ($\pi = 0$). (Except in mixed-strategy babbling equilibria, the individuals' strategies are generally pure in this model.) As before, I focus on the analysis of the case in which an individual who takes political action wishes to indicate that she is of type $\sigma = 1$, or (equivalently) that she is in favor of a policy shift.

At the policy-decision stage, the political leader observes m individuals engaged in political action. The leader has no private information. His information set at the policy decision stage contains the publicly observed number of political actions m. Formally, the leader's policy decision strategy is given by $\rho(m)$. Based on the public information m, the leader chooses whether to shift policy ($\rho = 1$) or maintain the status quo ($\rho = 0$). (The leader's strategy is generally pure in this model.)

After the leader's policy decision is made, the individuals' and the political leader's losses are realized as a function of the state of the world and the leader's policy decision. The structure of the game is common knowledge. The equilibrium concept employed is a refinement of sequential equilibrium.[10] The equilibrium is defined as follows.

Definition. An equilibrium of the game is given by the individuals' political action strategies, $\{\pi(i, \sigma)\}$; their beliefs at the political action stage, $\{\beta(s \mid \sigma)\}$; the political leader's decision rule, $\rho(m)$; and his beliefs at the policy decision stage, $\beta(s \mid m)$. The strategies and beliefs are consistent with each other and fulfill the following conditions.

(C1) Individual i's political action strategy $\pi(i, \sigma)$ minimizes her expected loss at the political action stage,

$$E(\Lambda_i \mid \sigma) = \int \sum_{m = \underline{m}}^{\bar{m}} \{ \text{prob}[\rho(m) = 0](Q - s - x_i)^2 + \text{prob}[\rho(m) = 1](A - s - x_i)^2 \}$$
$$\cdot b(m - \underline{m}; \bar{m} - \underline{m}, s)\beta(s \mid \sigma) \, ds + \pi_i c, \tag{31}$$

where $\underline{m}$ and $\bar{m}$ are the minimum and maximum number of political actions that can possibly be observed in equilibrium, respectively.

(C2) Individual i uses Bayes's rule to update that $\beta(s \mid \sigma)$ is the posterior density of the state of the world s conditional on the private information σ.

(C3) The political leader's policy decision rule $\rho(m)$ minimizes his expected loss at the policy decision stage,

[10] The equilibrium concept is extensively discussed in Lohmann (1993).

$$E(\Lambda_0 \mid m) = \int \{\text{prob}[\rho(m) = 0](Q - s)^2$$
$$+ \text{prob}[\rho(m) = 1](A - s)^2\}\beta(s \mid m)\,ds. \tag{32}$$

(C4) The political leader uses Bayes's rule to update that $\beta(s \mid m)$ is the posterior density of the state of the world s conditional on the public information m.

(C5) The political leader's out-of-equilibrium updating rule is assumed to be given by $\beta(s \mid m) = \beta(s \mid \underline{m})$ for all $m < \underline{m}$ and by $\beta(s \mid m) = \beta(s \mid \bar{m})$ for all $m > \bar{m}$.

3.2   The normative benchmark

As before, the socially optimal supply of political action is chosen by a benevolent dictator who minimizes the ex ante expected social loss. The social loss function for a heterogeneous society differs from the loss function for the homogeneous case by a constant:

$$\Lambda^W = \sum_{i=1}^{n} \Lambda_i = \sum_{i=1}^{n} x_i^2 + nx^2 + \sum_{i=1}^{n} d_i c. \tag{33}$$

The revelation of information prior to the policy decision affects the likelihood that the status quo Q or the policy alternative A is implemented. Given the heterogeneity of the individuals' preferences over policy outcomes, some individuals might benefit from more informed political decision making, while others lose. The benevolent dictator does not care about the distributional effects of information revelation, since the effects for the individuals on each side of the median (and mean) individual exactly cancel out. In contrast, the individuals care about the distributional effects. In equilibrium, some individuals may have incentives to contribute or misrepresent their private information in order to influence the decision to their advantage. Incentive-compatibility conditions that arise owing to the heterogeneity of the population may render the equilibrium supply of political action socially suboptimal.

The benevolent dictator announces a mapping of the cross-product of the individuals' bliss points x_i and their private information σ into a probability of taking political action, $\pi^W(i, \sigma)$. The individuals follow the dictator's prescription. Based on the observed number of political actions m, the political leader then forms an update on the state of the world. The leader (correctly) presumes that the individuals followed the dictator's political action prescription, $\pi^W(i, \sigma)$.

In Lohmann (1993), I show that all informative equilibria in the heterogeneous case are characterized by pure strategies. To ensure that the equilibrium and the socially optimal supplies of political action are comparable, the dictator is constrained to choose probabilities of political action that are equal to zero or unity. The dictator's choice of a mapping, $\pi^W(i, \sigma)$, then reflects his choice of the number of individuals who are to take political action conditional on privately observing that they are of type σ.

Ex ante, all individuals have the same probability of observing the realizations $\sigma = 1$ or $\sigma = 0$. The dictator cares about the number but not the specific identities of the individuals who take political action. The socially optimal number of individuals who take political action conditional on their private information is defined as N^W.

As in the welfare analysis of the homogeneous case, I restrict attention to the case in which the socially optimal message space involves individuals of type $\sigma = 1$ taking political action while individuals of type $\sigma = 0$ abstain. Given this restriction, the social optimum is defined as follows.

Definition. The social optimum is given by the socially optimal number of individuals N^W who are to take political action conditional on being type $\sigma = 1$; the political leader's decision rule, $\rho(m)$; and his beliefs at the policy decision stage, $\{\beta(s \mid m)\}$. All of these are consistent with each other and satisfy conditions (C3), (C4), and (D1):

(D1)   The number N^W minimizes the ex ante expected social loss,

$$
\begin{aligned}
E(\Lambda^W) = n \int \sum_{m=0}^{N^W} \{ \mathrm{prob}[\rho(m) = 0](Q - s)^2 \\
+ \mathrm{prob}[\rho(m) = 1](A - s)^2 \} \cdot b(m; N^W, s)\beta(s)\, ds \\
+ c \int \sum_{m=0}^{N^W} mb(m; N^W, s)\beta(s)\, ds.
\end{aligned}
\tag{34}
$$

In Section 2, I identified a number of sources that may render the equilibrium supply of political action socially suboptimal. In the following welfare analysis, I focus on the additional sources of suboptimality that arise from the conflicts of interest among the members of the society. I first discuss the zero-cost case and then the case of strictly positive costs.

Zero cost
At the political action stage, an individual of type $\sigma = 1$ will tend to favor the policy alternative A, while an individual of type $\sigma = 0$ will tend to prefer the status quo Q. However, the individual's preferences over policies also depend on her preferences over policy outcomes, as summarized by her bliss point x_i. An individual of type $\sigma = 1$ whose bliss point is exactly equal to

$$\tilde{s}_1 = (Q+A)/2 - E(s \mid \sigma = 1) = (Q+A)/2 - 2/3 \tag{35}$$

is indifferent between the status quo and the policy alternative. This individual does not care whether her action is decisive for the policy decision. In the absence of a strictly positive cost of taking political action, the individual is indifferent toward taking political action. The bliss point $\tilde{s}_1$ will be referred to as the political action cutpoint of the individuals of type $\sigma = 1$.

Similarly, an individual of type $\sigma = 0$ whose bliss point is exactly equal to

$$\tilde{s}_0 = (Q+A)/2 - E(s \mid \sigma = 0) = (Q+A)/2 - 1/3 \tag{36}$$

is indifferent between the status quo and the policy alternative, and thus indifferent toward taking action. The bliss point $\tilde{s}_0$ will be referred to as the political action cutpoint of the individuals of type $\sigma = 0$.

All individuals whose bliss points lie above their type-specific cutpoints strictly prefer to take political action; all others strictly prefer to abstain. Individuals whose bliss points lie in the interval $[\tilde{s}_1, \tilde{s}_0)$ take political action if and only if they are of type $\sigma = 1$. The actions or abstentions of all other individuals are uninformative. It follows that the equilibrium is informative if and only if the number of individuals whose bliss points lie in this separating interval is strictly positive.

If the population is relatively homogeneous, the support of the bliss point distribution $[-\bar{x}, \bar{x}]$ lies within the separating interval $[\tilde{s}_1, \tilde{s}_0)$ (see Figure 3). In this case, the equilibrium is fully revealing. All individuals of type $\sigma = 1$ take political action, while all others abstain. The political leader forms a perfect inference on the number of individuals m of type $\sigma = 1$. His posterior beliefs are given in equation (9). If the number of political actions exceeds the critical threshold $\tilde{m}$, the leader expects the state of the world s to be greater than $(Q+A)/2$ and shifts policy; otherwise the status quo is maintained (see equations (10) and (11)).

If the population is relatively heterogeneous, the separating interval $[\tilde{s}_1, \tilde{s}_0)$ lies strictly within the support of the bliss point distribution $[-\bar{x}, \bar{x}]$ (see Figure 3). In this case, the equilibrium is partially revealing. Moderates, whose bliss points lie in the interval $[\tilde{s}_1, \tilde{s}_0)$, take political action if and only if they are type $\sigma = 1$. Anti-status quo extremists, whose bliss points lie above $\tilde{s}_0$, take political action regardless of their private information in an attempt to manipulate the leader's decision. The bliss points of pro–status quo extremists lie below $\tilde{s}_1$. They abstain from taking political action regardless of their private information because they do not wish to increase the likelihood that the leader will shift policy.

The distribution of the individual bliss points is commonly known. The political leader discounts the observed number of political actions

Homogeneous society.

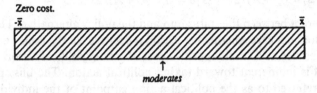

Heterogeneous Society.

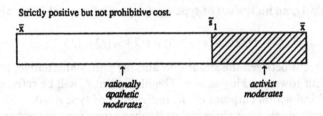

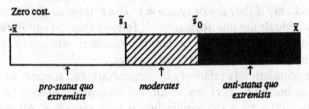

Figure 3. Pattern of participation in the heterogeneous model, where $-\bar{x}, \bar{x}$ denote the lower and upper support of the bliss point distribution (resp.); $\tilde{s}_0, \tilde{s}_1$ denote the bliss point of an individual who observed signal $\sigma = 0$ or $\sigma = 1$ (resp.), and is indifferent between taking political action and abstaining.

by $\underline{m}$, the number of anti-status quo extremists who engage in manipulative political action. Similarly, the leader knows that the abstentions of the $n - \bar{m}$ pro-status quo extremists are uninformative. Thus, he perfectly infers how many of the $\bar{m} - \underline{m}$ activist moderates with bliss points in the interval $[\tilde{s}_1, \tilde{s}_0)$ are of type $\sigma = 1$. The posterior probability that there are $m - \underline{m}$ individuals of type $\sigma = 1$ whose bliss points lie in the interval $[\tilde{s}_1, \tilde{s}_0)$ is equal to the binomial probability that $\bar{m} - \underline{m}$ Bernoulli trials result in $m - \underline{m}$ successes if the probability of a success is given by s. The leader's posterior beliefs on the state of the world s are given by

$$\beta(s \mid m) = \frac{b[m - \underline{m}; \bar{m} - \underline{m}, s]\beta(s)}{\int b[m - \underline{m}; \bar{m} - \underline{m}, s]\beta(s)\, ds}. \tag{37}$$

The higher the number of individuals of type $\sigma = 1$ whose bliss points lie in the interval $[\tilde{s}_1, \tilde{s}_0)$, the higher is the political leader's expectation of the state of the world s. As before, if the observed number of political actions m exceeds the critical level $\bar{m}$, the leader prefers to shift policy; otherwise, he maintains the status quo (see equations (10) and (11)). The critical threshold $\bar{m}$ reflects the leader's awareness of the individuals' incentives to inform or manipulate his decision.

I now turn to the welfare analysis. If the cost of taking political action is zero, then the information dispersed in the population can be aggregated at no cost. The dictator prescribes that all individuals of type $\sigma = 1$ take political action with probability 1, while all others abstain. This social optimum coincides with the political action equilibrium if the population is sufficiently homogeneous.

If the population is too heterogeneous, then political action is undersupplied by pro-status quo extremists, oversupplied by anti-status quo extremists, and optimally supplied by moderates.[11] Thus, in the presence of severe conflicts of interest among the members of the society, the equilibrium supply of political action may be socially suboptimal even when the cost of taking political action is zero.

In equilibrium, some information that is pertinent to the policy decision is trapped in extremist pockets of the society. In the aggregate, the population observes n independent draws of the signal σ; but only the $\bar{m} - \underline{m}$ draws made by the individuals whose bliss points lie in the separating interval $[\tilde{s}_1, \tilde{s}_0)$ are revealed. The likelihood that the political leader makes a mistaken decision is strictly higher in the partially revealing equilibrium than in the fully revealing one.

---

[11] Political action is oversupplied by anti- and pro-status quo extremists in an extension of the model that allows for counteracting political action on both sides of the issue (Lohmann 1992a).

Strictly positive costs

If the cost of taking political action is strictly positive but not prohibitive, a partially revealing equilibrium arises that is similar to the one in the zero-cost case. However, an individual who takes political action now derives some disutility from doing so, due to the cost of taking political action. She has an incentive to engage in costly political action only if the private cost of taking political action is dominated by private benefits expected from a policy shift, multiplied by the expected probability that her action will be decisive in triggering a policy shift. Compared to the partially revealing zero-cost case, the political action cutpoints $\bar{s}_1$ and $\bar{s}_0$ shift (see Figure 3). The cutpoints implicitly solve the following indifference conditions:

$$\int b(\bar{m}-\underline{m}; \bar{m}-\underline{m}, s)[(Q-s-\bar{s}_1)^2 - (A-s-\bar{s}_1)^2]\beta(s\,|\,\sigma=1)\,ds = c; \quad (38)$$

$$\int b(\bar{m}-\underline{m}; \bar{m}-\underline{m}, s)[(Q-s-\bar{s}_0)^2 - (A-s-\bar{s}_0)^2]\beta(s\,|\,\sigma=0)\,ds = c. \quad (39)$$

As in the zero-cost case, activist moderates take informative political action. However, some moderates now abstain from political action even if they expect to be better off if the political leader shifted policy. These rationally apathetic moderates are close to indifferent between the status quo and the policy alternative, and do not have an incentive to pay the private cost of taking political action. They free-ride on the informational efforts of the activist moderates. Thus, even if the population is fairly homogeneous, some information will be trapped in rationally apathetic pockets of society (see Figure 3). As in the zero-cost case, if the population is very heterogeneous, the private information held by anti-status quo extremists is not revealed due to the distributional effects of information revelation (see Figure 3).

An interior solution for the optimal number N^W of individuals who are to take political action conditional on being type $\sigma = 1$ is defined by

$$\int b(\bar{m}; N^W, s)[(Q-s)^2 - (A-s)^2]\beta(s)\,ds \geq c/n; \quad (40)$$

$$\int b(\bar{m}; N^W-1, s)[(Q-s)^2 - (A-s)^2]\beta(s)\,ds < c/n. \quad (41)$$

If there exist multiple interior solutions, the dictator chooses the one that minimizes the ex ante expected loss.

A comparison of the indifference conditions (38)–(41) indicates that the socially optimal number N^W is generally different from the number of individuals $\bar{m}-\underline{m}$ whose bliss points lie in the separating interval $[\bar{s}_1, \bar{s}_0]$.

That is, the number of individuals who take political action conditional on being type $\sigma = 1$ is socially suboptimal in equilibrium, owing to binding incentive-compatibility conditions that arise from the cost of taking political action and the heterogeneity of the population.

In addition, m political actions are oversupplied in equilibrium. In their futile attempt to manipulate the political leader's decision, anti–status quo extremists are trapped into taking costly but uninformative political action. They know that the political leader discounts the size of the protest movement for their actions. Given the leader's updating rule, they are "forced" to take political action to prevent an unacceptable reduction in the probability that the leader will shift policy. Political action is oversupplied by these extremists because the political leader cannot observe the extremists' identities but is aware of their incentives to manipulate his decision.

The analysis of the prohibitive cost case compares to the corresponding analysis in Section 2.

4 Discussion

In earlier work, I establish that political action has the potential to make political outcomes more representative (Lohmann 1992a,b,c, 1993). The welfare analysis developed in this chapter identifies a number of sources that render the equilibrium supply of political action socially suboptimal.

First, people may be trapped into inefficient equilibria by their exogenously given beliefs. An informative equilibrium generally co-exists with an uninformative zero political action equilibrium and, in the zero-cost case, with a continuum of uninformative babbling equilibria. An informative equilibrium dominates the zero political action equilibrium if it is associated with a relatively high likelihood that the socially preferred political decision will be made and with a relatively low aggregate deadweight cost of political action.

Second, strictly positive but not prohibitive costs of taking political action drive a wedge between the equilibrium and the socially optimal supply of political action. In equilibrium, individuals do not take into account the informational externalities exerted by their actions. Moreover, they base their political action decisions on their private information, and consequently tend to overestimate the number of like-minded individuals.

Third, severe conflicts of interest among the members of the society lead to a socially suboptimal supply of political action in equilibrium. Even if the cost of taking political action is zero, extremists have disincentives to truthfully reveal their private information owing to the distributional consequences of information revelation. If the cost of taking political action is strictly positive, some extremists are trapped into over-supplying uninformative political action at a deadweight cost.

Moreover, political action may ex ante be oversupplied in the sense that an equilibrium with a strictly positive political action turnout is dominated by the zero political action equilibrium. For example, if the political action mechanism co-exists with a voting mechanism that costlessly aggregates some of the dispersed information, the marginal contribution of the political action mechanism may consist of adding noise. In this case, the voting mechanism is ex ante more likely to implement the full-information voting outcome in the absence of pre-election political action.

In other cases, political action reduces the ex ante likelihood of mistaken political decisions, but the number of political actions may ex post be a misleading indicator of the state of the world. In the homogeneous model, activists follow mixed strategies of taking political action when faced with a strictly positive but not prohibitive cost. Due to the random realization of their political action probabilities, political action may ex post be over- or undersupplied. As a consequence, voters may cast mistaken votes. In the heterogeneous model, activists follow pure strategies of taking political action. However, the private experiences made by individuals who take political action conditional on being of type $\sigma = 1$ may not be representative; a mistaken policy decision may result.

Social scientists who ignore the distinction between the ex ante likelihood of mistaken political decisions and ex post realizations may come to misleading conclusions about the link between public protest activities and the representativeness of political outcomes. If political action is ex post oversupplied, activists might be thought of as emotionally overreacting to some unusual, privately observed events, and voters as irrationally overresponding to political action – although these observations are consistent with rational, utility-maximizing behavior. If political action is ex post undersupplied, a scholar might erroneously interpret observations of this kind as empirical evidence in favor of Olson's (1965) free-rider hypothesis.

The institutions of representative democracy are based on the idea that ongoing and extensive mass participation is impractical and undesirable (Schumpeter 1942). Indirectly elected politicians, a professional civil service, a depoliticized central bank, and an independent system of courts isolate political decision makers from popular pressures. However, the isolation is not complete. The political commitment to particular policies, leadership personnel, and institutional arrangements may fail. Empirically, major changes of this kind are often preceded by political action.

By informing political decision making, extra-institutional activities have the potential to enhance the performance of formal institutions.

However, political action may be under- or oversupplied in equilibrium. This welfare analysis might serve to motivate the emergence of institutional arrangements that influence individual incentives to participate in representative democracies and thus affect the likelihood that political outcomes are representative.

REFERENCES

Ball, Richard (1991), "Political Lobbying as Welfare Improving Signaling," Mimeo, Department of Agricultural and Resource Economics, University of California at Berkeley.

Condorcet, Marie J. A. N. C., Marquis de (1785), *Essai sur l'application de l'analyse à la probabilité des decisions rendues à la pluralité des voix*. Paris: Impr. royale.

DeGroot, Morris H. (1970), *Optimal Statistical Decisions*. New York: McGraw-Hill.

Feller, William (1968), *An Introduction to Probability Theory and Its Applications,* v. 1, 3rd ed. New York: Wiley.

Grofman, Bernard, Guillermo Owen, and Scott L. Feld (1983), "Thirteen Theorems in Search of the Truth," *Theory and Decision* 15: 261–78.

Kreps, David M., and Robert Wilson (1982), "Sequential Equilibria," *Econometrica* 50: 863–93.

Lohmann, Susanne (1992a), "Competitive Political Action," Graduate School of Business Research Paper no. 1202a, Stanford University.

  (1992b), "Information Aggregation through Costly Political Action," Graduate School of Business Research Paper no. 1130b, Stanford University.

  (1992c), "Rationality, Revolution and Revolt: The Dynamics of Informational Cascades," Graduate School of Business Research Paper no. 1213, Stanford University.

  (1993), "A Signaling Model of Informative and Manipulative Political Action," *American Political Science Review* 87: 319–33.

Lupia, Arthur (1992), "Busy Voters, Agenda Control, and the Power of Information," *American Political Science Review* 86: 390–403.

Olson, Mancur (1965), *The Logic of Collective Action*. Cambridge, MA: Harvard University Press.

Palfrey, Thomas R., and Howard Rosenthal (1991), "Testing for Effects of Cheap Talk in a Public Goods Game with Private Information," *Games and Economic Behavior* 3: 183–220.

Schumpeter, Joseph A. (1942), *Capitalism, Socialism and Democracy*. New York: Harper.

Government behavior

CHAPTER 18

Monetary policy and credibility under exact monetary aggregation

William A. Barnett

1   Introduction

1.1   *Objectives*

The purpose of this chapter is to raise a difficult question without providing a definitive answer. In particular, this chapter observes that the literature on the time inconsistency of replanned discretionary policy overlooks a complicating factor, which might substantially increase the central bank's credibility problems. This complication has implications for time inconsistency and its proposed solutions, such as reputational equilibrium. The extent of the game-theoretic complications produced by this theoretical problem are not clear from the current stage of this research, and hence the purpose of this chapter is to identify the problem and measure its empirical magnitude without fully solving the resulting game.

However, in this regard it is worth observing that in recent years the time-inconsistency issue has become the central issue in the ongoing debate on rules versus discretion (see, e.g., Mankiw 1990). In addition, the time-inconsistency issue has become the basis for the growing research on the connection between monetary economics, political economy, and social choice theory; see, for example, Alesina (1988), Alesina and Tabellini (1988), and Persson and Tabellini (1990).

In the existing literature on time inconsistency, the consumer typically is modeled as a Nash follower who conditions upon her expectations of the government's selection of the nominal stock of money. The government, on the other hand, is modeled as a Stackelberg leader who sets the nominal monetary stock path as a control variable path. In both cases,

Presented at the Seventh International Symposium in Economic Theory and Econometrics on Political Economy: Institutions, Information, Competition and Representation, Washington University in St. Louis, May 22–25, 1991.

the nominal stock of money is the same variable for all economic agents in any period. The difference is in the way in which that variable is treated by each agent. The consumer treats the variable as if it is beyond her control and must be estimated, while the government controls the variable.

As we shall show, this assumed agreement between all economic agents on the identity of the relevant monetary variable is inconsistent with the structure of those models. This internal inconsistency becomes evident as soon as the models are extended from the case of a single monetary asset to the case of a monetary aggregate over multiple monetary assets.

Since outside money enters the government's decision through the government's budget constraint, money growth produces "seigniorage." But the consumer uses monetary assets for their services, as in transactions. There is no reason to believe that those two motives produce the same aggregated monetary asset. For example, if changes in the monetary base produce seigniorage, then the monetary base is the monetary aggregate that will enter the government's budget constraint. But there is no reason to believe that the monetary base measures the monetary services received by the consumer, and hence the monetary base cannot be entered into her utility function. Yet in the existing research on the time inconsistency of discretionary monetary policy, the same monetary variable is usually entered both into the consumer's utility function and into the government's budget constraint.

Barnett and Yue (1991) formulated the consumer's decision to identify the monetary service flow received by the consumer when more than one monetary asset exists. In the current chapter, we find that the resulting monetary aggregate does not appear in the government's budget constraint. In addition, the monetary aggregate over imperfectly substitutable components cannot be a simple-sum aggregate, despite the fact that central banks routinely use simple-sum aggregates as intermediate targets. However, a simple-sum monetary aggregate over outside money may enter into the government's budget constraint. Hence the monetary control variable in the Stackelberg leader's decision cannot correspond with the monetary variable upon which the consumer conditions in solving her decision problem. The resulting slackness in monetary policy poses unsolved problems for discretionary policy and potentially increases the central bank's difficulty in establishing a reputational equilibrium.

1.2   *Approach*

The approach used to identify the relevant monetary variable to the consumer is that of exact aggregation. Some relevant references in that area include Barnett (1980, 1982, 1983, 1987), Barnett, Fisher, and Serletis

(1992), Belongia and Chalfant (1989), and Belongia and Chrystal (1991). However, the approach to the derivation and specification of aggregator functions in most of that research implicitly assumes either perfect certainty or risk neutrality, as is the case in virtually all of the literature on economic aggregation and index number theory. The needed theorems on duality, two-stage budgeting, and nonparametric approximation to aggregator functions do not yet exist for the case of risk aversion. Nevertheless, although nonparametric statistical index numbers with known properties are not yet available under risk aversion, Poterba and Rotemberg (1987) have demonstrated that parametric econometric estimation of theoretical economic monetary aggregator functions is presently possible under risk aversion. Their approach has been applied and further developed by Barnett and Yue (1991); we use that approach here.

1.3   The Calvo model

As a means of providing a context within which this issue can be presented, it is useful to review the Calvo (1978) model, which is a model commonly used in discussing the time inconsistency of continuously replanned discretionary monetary policy. The Calvo model presents monetary policy as a team dynamic game. It is a team game because both economic agents have the same objective function, which is an intertemporal utility function of the form

$$u = \sum_{t=1}^{\infty} \beta^t u(x_t, M_{t+1}/p_t) \tag{1.1}$$

for $0 < \beta < 1$, where M_{t+1} is nominal monetary balances in period $t+1$, x_t is consumption of goods in period t, and p_t is the price of goods in period t. The consumer maximizes intertemporal utility subject to the sequence of budget constraints

$$x_t + \tau_t + M_{t+1}/p_t = y(\tau_t) + M_t/p_t \quad (t = 1, \dots, \infty), \tag{1.2}$$

where τ_t is taxes paid during period t and $y(\tau_t)$ is income received by the consumer during period t. Multiplying through by p_t, we can rewrite (1.2) as

$$x_t p_t + \tau_t p_t = y(\tau_t) + M_t - M_{t+1} \quad (t = 1, \dots, \infty). \tag{1.3}$$

Since income depends upon the tax, the tax is distortionary.

The consumer solves her dynamic programming problem for (x_t, p_t) conditionally upon the government's choice of taxes and nominal money supply. Since the government chooses nominal money balances, the consumer's choice of p_t amounts to a choice of real money balances, conditional upon the government's choice of M_t.

The solution feedback rule to this dynamic programming problem in each period is of the form

$$(x_t, p_t) = h(g_t, \tau_t; M_t, M_{t+1}, M_{t+2}, M_{t+3}, \ldots). \tag{1.4}$$

The dependency upon future values of the money supply is unusual in dynamic programming feedback rules, since feedback rules usually provide the relationship between the current control and current state variables along the solution path. But in equation (1.4), the consumer's current choice of controls depends upon all future expected values - as well as the current value - of the money supply.

The reason is that the consumer's decision contains no law of motion dictating the endogenous evolution of the money supply conditional upon her choice of control variables. Instead, equation (1.3) constrains the consumer's choice of her control variables conditionally upon the government's exogenous choice of the consumer's state variables. Furthermore, the money supply appears in the intertemporal utility function for all future periods. Without the ability to absorb the law of motion of M_t into the feedback rule function h, we must insert the entire future path of M_t into h, because the entire future path of the money supply - without an endogenous law of motion within the consumer's decision - is acting as a sequence of shift variables within the future tastes of the consumer.

Hence the feedback rule feeds back not only current values of the money supply but also future ones in determining the consumer's optimal choice of her control variables (x_t, p_t) during each period. Since the consumer conditions upon the values of the government's selection of its controls, rather than upon the structure of the government's decision problem, the consumer behaves as a Nash-Cournot follower.

The government treats its committed level of government spending g_t as exogenous (perhaps fixed by Congress). The government then chooses (M_t, τ_t) to maximize utility, (1.1), subject to the economy's resource constraint

$$x_t + g_t = y(\tau_t) \quad (t = 1, \ldots, \infty) \tag{1.5}$$

and the government's budget constraint

$$g_t = \tau_t + (M_{t+1} - M_t)/p_t \quad (t = 1, \ldots, \infty). \tag{1.6}$$

However, in solving its problem the government does not merely condition upon expected values of the consumer's control variables, but instead conditions upon knowledge of the consumer's feedback rule (1.4), which tells the government the way in which the consumer will respond to any potential choice by the government of its control variables. Hence the government acts as a Stackelberg leader. Once the government has chosen its control variables, the consumer will select her control variables, and that choice by the consumer will be exactly as had been expected by the government. Unlike the Nash game solution, which iterates back and forth between the expectations of each economic agent until convergence of the expectations of all agents (each of whom is a follower), Calvo's team dynamic game converges immediately to the point selected by the government.

1.4   Time inconsistency

The time-inconsistency problem in this model is produced by the non-recursive form of the government's decision. Consider, for example, that the government is solving for its planned setting of its control variables (M_s, τ_s) for future period $s > 1$, where $t = 1$ is the current time period. Then the government maximizes

$$u = \sum_{t=s}^{\infty} \beta^t u(x_t, M_{t+1}/p_t) \tag{1.7}$$

subject to

$$x_t + g_t = y(\tau_t) \quad (t = s, ..., \infty); \tag{1.8}$$

$$g_t = \tau_t + (M_{t+1} - M_t)/p_t \quad (t = s, ..., \infty); \tag{1.9}$$

$$(x_t, p_t) = h(g_t, \tau_t; M_t, M_{t+1}, M_{t+2}, M_{t+3}, ...) \quad (t = 1, ..., \infty). \tag{1.10}$$

Observe that the last constraint applies for $t = 1, ..., \infty$, not just for $t = s, ..., \infty$. But periods $1, 2, ..., s-1$ precede the period for which the government is planning.

This backward feedback violates the forward-looking recursiveness property that is required if the problem is to be a dynamic programming problem for which Bellman's principle would be relevant. In planning for future period s, the government must consider the effect of its decision on the consumer's behavior during the periods $1, 2, ..., s-1$, since the consumer's decision during periods $1, 2, ..., s-1$ depends upon her expectations of the government's decision in period s.

The importance of this observation results from the fact that continuous replanning, which characterizes discretionary policy, is typically formulated as being a Bellman solution that considers effects only on the present and future. But since the Bellman method is irrelevant to solving the government's optimization problem for future periods $s > 1$, the government must directly solve its full constrained optimization decision simultaneously for all periods $t = 1, ..., \infty$. The government, in order to follow the resulting optimal path, must commit to that path and follow it without future replanning. The replanned Bellman path, not solving the government's nonrecursive decision problem, cannot track the true solution path to the government's intertemporal optimization; see, for example, Kydland and Prescott (1977).

The time-inconsistency problem is that the true intertemporal solution to the government's decision problem is not the same as the continuously replanned "discretionary" solution. On the face of it, this issue does not seem particularly interesting, since it is merely the observation that Bellman's recursive solution method should not be used when the decision is not in the Bellman form. Following this trivial observation, we might argue that under these circumstances the government simply should correctly solve its decision of maximizing (1.7) subject to (1.8), (1.9), and (1.10), and should not use Bellman's method or any other irrelevant or inapplicable solution method. But the paradox is that the government has an incentive nevertheless to use Bellman's forward-looking solution method, ignoring the backward feedback, on the grounds that what is past is past. In Hurwicz's (1972) terminology, the consumer views the government's commitment to the true intertemporally optimal solution to be incentive incompatible. As observed by Kydland and Prescott (1977), the consumer may then assume that the government will replan, and a Prisoner's Dilemma problem arises.

To see this, consider the feedback rule for the price level

$$p_t = h(g_t, \tau_t; M_t, M_{t+1}, M_{t+2}, M_{t+3}, \ldots) \quad (t = 1, \ldots, \infty). \quad (1.11)$$

The price level depends upon the consumer's expectations of future monetary growth. Suppose the government optimally solves its decision and claims to be following the optimal path for money growth. If that growth rate is moderate, then the inflation rate produced by (1.11) may be low. With low inflation, the consumer may decide to hold substantial real balances of money. This will all work out to produce the optimal intertemporal solution, if the government does indeed stick to its optimal path for money growth. But once time has passed – and the government has observed that the consumer is holding substantial real balances of money – the government will observe that the tax base (i.e. real balances) for the seigniorage tax is large, and hence may decide to inflate more rapidly in order to increase its current seigniorage tax. In fact, replanning according to Bellman's recursive method and ignoring the backward feedback on expectations would indeed exploit that opportunity to fool the consumer.

But the consumer may recognize this temptation to the government and so base her expectations of money growth on the assumption that the government will succumb to the temptation to discretionary replanning, despite its stated commitment to its optimal solution rule. If the consumer forms expectations in this manner, then the optimal solution to the game becomes impossible to attain. Hence we see that the optimal solution can be attained only if government's commitment to the optimal Stackelberg solution is completely credible and is believed by the consumer.

However, we shall demonstrate in what follows that the monetary variable that is relevant to the consumer's decision is not the one that enters the government's budget constraint, and is not the one that is being controlled by central banks at the present time. Furthermore, we shall observe that a broad set of values of the monetary service flow is consistent with any one fixed value of the monetary variable targeted by central banks. The result is a slackness in monetary policy. This observation raises serious questions about the ability of the central bank to establish credibility of its commitment to the optimal money growth path.

2   Microfoundations for consumer demand for money

2.1   *Introduction*

In this section we replace Calvo's utility function with Barnett and Yue's (1991) model of consumer behavior, which generalizes Calvo's in two directions. The central generalization is the introduction of multiple monetary assets into the utility function under conditions sufficient for exact aggregation over monetary assets (the Calvo model contains only one monetary asset). Barnett and Yue also introduce uncertainty into the model, so that the consumer maximizes expected utility rather than just utility. We believe that full analysis of the effects of exact monetary aggregation in the dynamic game may require the simultaneous extension from risk neutrality to risk aversion. Hence we use both of Barnett and Yue's generalizations at once.

Although we continue to use the analogy with the Calvo model to discuss the time-inconsistency issue, we specify our empirical model for estimation in a more general form, in which there may be manufacturing firms and financial intermediaries as well as consumers and government.

2.2   *Shocks*

We assume that all stochastic shocks are Markovian. Hence, at each time period, economic agents make decisions regarding current and subsequent actions given the current state of the economy and relevant information about the future. The past contains no information about the future.

Uncertainty in the economy is produced by a random vector of shocks, λ_t. We assume that the vector of random shocks λ_t follows a stationary Markov process with the bounded ergodic realization set Λ defined by

$$\Lambda = \{\lambda_t \in \mathbb{R}^K : P[\sup\|\lambda_t\| \le D] \ge \beta\},$$

where D is a finite number, P is a probability measure, $\mathbb{R}^K$ is K-dimensional Euclidean space, $\|\cdot\|$ is the Euclidean norm, and β is a positive number less than 1. Since λ_t follows a Markov process, the distribution of λ_t depends only upon the value of λ_{t-1}. The dynamic properties of the random shocks are described by the transition function $F(\lambda_{t+1}|\lambda_t)$, which is the conditional distribution of the random shocks. Since the shocks are stationary, the conditional distribution F is invariant to time t. We assume that $F(\lambda_{t+1}|\lambda_t)$ is continuous in both of its arguments. The Markov stochastic shocks are assumed to be to the technology of firms, not to tastes. As a result, the shocks will not explicitly appear again in the following discussion, which will relate solely to consumer demand. However, these assumptions have implications for the equilibrium stochastic behavior of the prices and interest rates that will be given to the consumer.

Although this convention simplifies exposition, the results would be unchanged if the stochastic shocks were to future tastes rather than to technology. This latter alternative assumption will be implicit when we discuss the effects of our extension on the Calvo model, which contains no firms.

2.3   Consumer demand for monetary assets

In this section we formulate a representative consumer's stochastic decision problem over consumer goods and monetary assets.[1] The formulation is based upon Barnett and Yue (1991), but is adapted to merge with the Calvo model's government sector. The consumer's decisions are made in discrete time over a finite planning horizon for the time intervals $t, t+1, \ldots, s, \ldots, t+T$, where t is the current time period and $t+T$ is the terminal planning period. Hence the time interval s satisfies $s \in \{t, t+1, \ldots, t+T\}$. The variables used in defining the consumer's decision are as follows:

$\mathbf{x}_s$ = n-dimensional vector of planned real consumption of goods and services during period s;

$\mathbf{p}_s$ = n-dimensional vector of goods and services' expected prices and of durable goods' expected rental prices during period s;

---

[1] In later research we plan to delete the representative consumer assumption and aggregate over consumers by weaker means. See Barnett (1981, apx. B1.2), Barnett (1987, sect. 9), and Barnett and Serletis (1990).

$\mathbf{a}_s = k$-dimensional vector of planned real balances of monetary assets during period s;

$\mathbf{\rho}_s = k$-dimensional vector of expected nominal holding-period yields of monetary assets;

$A_s =$ planned holdings of the benchmark (pure savings) assets during period s;

$R_s =$ expected one-period holding yield on the benchmark asset during period s;

$L_s =$ planned labor supply during period s;

$w_s =$ expected wage rate during period s;

$\mathbf{I}_s(\tau_s) =$ sum of all other sources of after-tax income during period s;

$\tau_s =$ income tax paid by the consumer during period s;

$p_s^* = p_s^*(\mathbf{p}_s) =$ true cost-of-living index.

Define Y to be a compact subset of the $(n+k+2)$-dimensional non-negative orthant. Barnett and Yue define the consumer's consumption possibility sets $S(s)$, for $s \in \{t, ..., t+T\}$, as follows:

$$S(s) = \left\{ (\mathbf{a}_s, L_s, \mathbf{x}_s, A_s) \in Y : \sum_{i=1}^{n} p_{is} x_{is} = w_s L_s \right.$$
$$+ \sum_{i=1}^{k} [(1 + \rho_{i,s-1}) p_{s-1}^* a_{i,s-1} - p_s^* a_{is}]$$
$$\left. + (1 + R_{s-1}) p_{s-1}^* A_{s-1} - p_s^* A_s + \mathbf{I}_s(\tau_s) \right\}. \quad (2.1)$$

Under the assumption of rational expectations, $F(\lambda_{t+1} | \lambda_t)$ is known to the consumer. Since current-period interest rates are not paid until the end of the period, they may be contemporaneously unknown to the consumer. Nevertheless, observe that during period t the only interest rates that enter into $S(t)$ are interest rates paid during period $t-1$, which are known at the start of period t. Similarly $\mathbf{p}_t$ and p_t^* are determined and known to the consumer at the start of period t. Hence $(\mathbf{a}_t, L_t, \mathbf{x}_t, A_t)$ can be chosen deterministically in a manner that assures that $(\mathbf{a}_t, L_t, \mathbf{x}_t, A_t) \in S(t)$ with certainty. However, this is not possible for $s > t$, since at the beginning of time period t, when the intertemporal decision is solved, the constraint sets $S(s)$ for $s > t$ are random sets. For example, during period $s = t+1$, $(\rho_t, R_t, w_{t+1}, \mathbf{p}_{t+1}, p_{t+1}^*)$ are random in the definition of the feasible set $S(t+1)$. Hence for $s > t$, the values of $(\mathbf{a}_s, L_s, \mathbf{x}_s, A_s)$ must be selected as random points to assure that the constraints will all be satisfied with probability 1. Note that during periods $s > t+1$, $(\rho_{s-1}, R_{s-1}, w_s, \mathbf{p}_s, p_s^*, p_{s-1}^*, \mathbf{a}_{s-1}, A_{s-1})$ are all random in $S(s)$.

In brief, for $s \in \{t+1, ..., t+T\}$ the consumer's choices at time t of planned $(\mathbf{a}_s, L_s, \mathbf{x}_s, A_s)$ produce stochastic processes, since only stochastic processes for $(\mathbf{a}_s, L_s, \mathbf{x}_s, A_s)$ can satisfy the budget constraint equality in the definition of $S(s)$. This follows from the fact that only information available at t is used in solving the decision. In addition, stochastic plans regarding future purchases are possible, since planned future purchases are assumed not to result in binding futures contracts. However, the choice of $(\mathbf{a}_t, L_t, \mathbf{x}_t, A_t)$ from $S(t)$ in the current period will be deterministic, since $S(t)$ is a deterministic set and since current-period purchases are assumed to be binding. Observe that for $s \in \{t+2, \ldots, t+T\}$ the randomness in the feasible set $S(s)$ is produced not only from uncertainty regarding future interest rates and prices, but also from the randomness in the lagged choice variables $(\mathbf{a}_{s-1}, A_{s-1})$, which are not known with certainty at time t.

The benchmark asset A_s is defined to provide no services other than its yield R_s, and hence is a vehicle for pure savings. As a result, the benchmark asset does not enter the consumer's intertemporal utility function except in the last instant of the planning horizon. The asset is held only as a means of accumulating wealth to endow the next planning horizons. The consumer's intertemporal utility function is

$$U = U(\mathbf{a}_t, \ldots, \mathbf{a}_s, \ldots, \mathbf{a}_{t+T}; L_t, \ldots, L_s, \ldots, L_{t+T}; \mathbf{x}_t, \ldots, \mathbf{x}_s, \ldots, \mathbf{x}_{t+T}; A_{t+T}),$$

where U is assumed to be intertemporally additively (strongly) separable, such that

$$
\begin{aligned}
U = {} & u(\mathbf{a}_t, L_t, \mathbf{x}_t) + \left(\frac{1}{1+\xi}\right) u(\mathbf{a}_{t+1}, L_{t+1}, \mathbf{x}_{t+1}) + \cdots \\
& + \left(\frac{1}{1+\xi}\right)^{T-1} u(\mathbf{a}_{t+T-1}, L_{t+T-1}, \mathbf{x}_{t+T-1}) \\
& + \left(\frac{1}{1+\xi}\right)^{T} u(\mathbf{a}_{t+T}, L_{t+T}, \mathbf{x}_{t+T}, A_{t+T}) \\
= {} & \sum_{s=t}^{t+T-1} \left(\frac{1}{1+\xi}\right)^{s-t} u(\mathbf{a}_s, L_s, \mathbf{x}_s) \\
& + \left(\frac{1}{1+\xi}\right)^{T} u_T(\mathbf{a}_{t+T}, L_{t+T}, \mathbf{x}_{t+T}, A_{t+T}),
\end{aligned}
\tag{2.2}
$$

and the consumer's subjective rate of time preference, ξ, is assumed to be constant.[2] The single-period utility functions u and u_T are assumed to be increasing and strictly quasiconcave.

---

[2] Although money may not exist in the elementary utility function, there exists a derived utility function that contains money so long as money has positive value in equilibrium. See, e.g., Arrow and Hahn (1971), Phlips and Spinnewyn (1982), and Feenstra (1986). We implicitly are using that derived utility function.

Given the price, wage, and interest-rate processes, the consumer selects the deterministic point $(\mathbf{a}_t, L_t, \mathbf{x}_t, A_t)$ and the stochastic process $(\mathbf{a}_s, L_s, \mathbf{x}_s, A_s)$, $s = t+1, \ldots, t+T$, to maximize the expected value of U over the planning horizon, subject to the sequence of choice set constraints. Formally, the consumer's decision problem is the following.

Problem 1. Choose the deterministic point $(\mathbf{a}_t, L_t, \mathbf{x}_t, A_t)$ and the stochastic process $(\mathbf{a}_s, L_s, \mathbf{x}_s, A_s)$, $s = t+1, \ldots, t+T$, to maximize

$$
u(\mathbf{a}_t, L_t, \mathbf{x}_t) + E_t \left[\sum_{s=t+1}^{t+T-1} \left(\frac{1}{1+\xi} \right)^{s-t} u(\mathbf{a}_s, L_s, \mathbf{x}_s) \right.
$$
$$
\left. + \left(\frac{1}{1+\xi} \right)^T u_T(\mathbf{a}_{t+T}, L_{t+T}, \mathbf{x}_{t+T}, A_{t+T}) \right], \quad (2.3)
$$

subject to $(\mathbf{a}_s, L_s, \mathbf{x}_s, A_s) \in S(F, s)$ for $s = t, \ldots, t+T$.

By equation (2.1) we have that $S(s)$ is the deterministic current-period choice set, while $S(s)$ for $s \in \{t+1, \ldots, t+T\}$ are random expected future choice sets. We use E_t to designate the expectations operator, conditional upon the information that exists at time t.

In the infinite–planning horizon case, the decision problem is as follows.

Problem 2. Choose the deterministic point $(\mathbf{a}_t, L_t, \mathbf{x}_t, A_t)$ and the stochastic process $(\mathbf{a}_s, L_s, \mathbf{x}_s, A_s)$, $s = t+1, \ldots, \infty$, to maximize

$$
u(\mathbf{a}_t, L_t, \mathbf{x}_t) + E_t \left[\sum_{s=t+1}^{\infty} \left(\frac{1}{1+\xi} \right)^{s-t} u(\mathbf{a}_s, L_s, \mathbf{x}_s) \right], \quad (2.4)
$$

subject to $(\mathbf{a}_s, L_s, \mathbf{x}_s, A_s) \in S(s)$ for $s \geq t$, and also subject to

$$
\lim_{s \to \infty} E_t \left(\frac{1}{1+\xi} \right)^{s-t} A_s = 0.
$$

The latter constraint rules out perpetual borrowing at the benchmark rate of return R_t.[3] By equation (2.1) we have that $S(t)$ is the deterministic current-period choice set, while $S(s)$ for $s \geq t+1$ are random expected future choice sets.

A nonzero probability must exist that the holding-period return R_s on the benchmark asset will exceed that of any other asset during period s, since no other motivation for holding the benchmark asset exists within Problem 2 at any s. In fact, since the variance of the distribution of R_s

---

[3] This constraint is common in infinite-horizon stochastic control problems. See, e.g., Sargent (1987, pp. 31, 33).

is likely to be high relative to that of r_{is} for any i, we should expect the mean of R_s to exceed that of any element of r_s.

2.4   Existence of a monetary aggregate for the consumer

In order to assure the existence of a monetary aggregate for the consumer, Barnett and Yue partition the vector of monetary asset quantities a_s so that $a_s = (m_s, \bar{m}_s)$. We correspondingly partition the vector of interest rates of those assets, ρ_s, so that $\rho_s = (r_s, \bar{r}_s)$. We then assume that the utility function u is blockwise weakly separable in m_s. Hence there exists a monetary aggregator ("category utility") function M and a utility function u^* such that

$$u(a_s, L_s, x_s) = u^*(M(m_s), \bar{m}_s, L_s, x_s). \qquad (2.5)$$

We assume that the terminal-period utility function in the finite–planning horizon case is correspondingly weakly separable, such that

$$u_T(a_s, L_s, x_s, A_s) = u_T^*(M(m_s), \bar{m}_s, L_s, x_s, A_s).$$

Then it follows that the exact monetary aggregate, measuring the welfare acquired from consuming the services of m_s, is

$$M_s = M(m_s). \qquad (2.6)$$

Note that we assume only that there exists a partition $a_s = (m_s, \bar{m}_s)$ such that (2.5) holds. Testing for which partition satisfies the weak separability assumption (2.5) is an empirical matter. Considering the number of combinations of possible weakly separable blockings, the assumption that there exists one that would pass the empirical test is reasonable. We define the dimension of m_s to be k_1 and the dimension of $\bar{m}_s$ to be k_2, so that $k = k_1 + k_2$.

It is clear that equation (2.6) does define the exact monetary aggregate in the welfare sense, since M_s measures the consumer's subjective evaluation of the services that she receives from holding m_s. However, it also can be shown that equation (2.6) defines the exact monetary aggregate in the aggregation-theoretic sense. In particular, the stochastic process M_s, $s \geq t$, contains all of the information about m_s that is needed by the consumer in order optimally to solve the rest of her decision problem. This conclusion is proven as a theorem in Barnett and Yue (1991). This fundamental aggregation theorem applies not only when M_s is produced by voluntary behavior but also when the M_s process is exogenously imposed upon the consumer, as through a perfectly inelastic supply function for M_s imposed by central bank policy. Hence we find that M_s is the monetary aggregate that is relevant to the consumer's problem in the Calvo model.

Alternatively, information about the simple-sum aggregate over the components of $\mathbf{m}_s$ is of no use in solving the consumer's decision problem unless that monetary aggregator function M happens to be a simple sum. In other words, the simple-sum aggregate contains useful information about behavior only if the components of $\mathbf{m}_s$ are perfect substitutes in identical ratios (linear aggregation with *equal* coefficients).

3   Time inconsistency

Having determined the economic monetary aggregate that is relevant to the consumer, we now seek to close the model by introducing government as in the Calvo model. In the Calvo model the consumer selects the path for the price level along with the path for consumption of goods, conditional upon the government's choice of the paths for nominal monetary balances and taxes. In our extended model, the analogous decision for the consumer would be to choose the process for the true cost-of-living index p_s^* along with $(\bar{\mathbf{m}}_s, L_s, \mathbf{x}_s, A_s)$ for $s \geq t$, conditional upon the government's choice of the path for the exact nominal monetary aggregate $p_s^* M_s = p_s^* M(\mathbf{m}_s)$ and for taxes τ_s.

But, in fact, the exact nominal monetary aggregate does not appear in the government's budget constraint, and no central bank targets that exact aggregate. Instead, central banks target the nominal simple-sum aggregate, $\sum_{i=1}^{k_1} m_{is} p_s^*$. This phenomenon is very puzzling because the simple-sum aggregate does not appear in the consumer's decision, and would not appear in the government's budget constraint, unless all of the components of that aggregate were outside money. Since we are assuming that monetary assets can yield interest, we should not expect all of the components of the simple-sum aggregate to be outside money.

Nevertheless, in an attempt to parallel central bank policy, let us assume initially that every component of the simple-sum monetary aggregate is outside money. Then the government's budget constraint would become

$$g_t = \tau_t + \left(p_{t+1}^* \sum_{i=1}^{k_1} m_{it+1} - p_t^* \sum_{i=1}^{k_1} m_{it} \right) \Big/ p_t^*.$$

Under these circumstances, the Calvo model would produce the conclusion that the government will select the path for the simple-sum aggregate along with the path for taxes. But a wedge then appears between what the government actually is controlling and what the consumer thinks the government is controlling. The consumer thinks that the government is controlling $p_s^* M_s = p_s^* M(\mathbf{m}_s)$, while in fact the government is controlling $\sum_{i=1}^{k_1} m_{is} p_s^*$. This confusion could only aggravate the central bank's time-inconsistency problem.

Alternatively, it is possible that the central bank uses the monetary base as an instrument of policy (i.e., as a control variable), and that the monetary base appears in the government's budget constraint as the relevant measure of the seigniorage tax base. That instrument then could be used to target the simple-sum monetary aggregate, $\sum_{i=1}^{k_1} m_{is} p_s^*$, as an intermediate target of policy. Under that strategy, the base would be the instrument, the simple-sum aggregate would be the intermediate target, and the consumer's consumption path could be the final target. In this case, there need be no assumption that all components of the simple-sum aggregate be outside money. Finally, it is possible that the consumer is aware of this policy, and solves her decision conditionally upon the expected level of that simple-sum aggregate as a constraint.[4]

If, for example, there were perfect foresight, the consumer would determine the composition of her monetary asset portfolio by maximizing $M(\mathbf{m}_s)$ subject to the government's fixed level for the nominal simple-sum monetary aggregate $\sum_{i=1}^{k_1} m_{is} p_s^*$. The consumer then would determine the resulting level of the exact aggregate $M_s = M(\mathbf{m}_s)$ at the solution value for $\mathbf{m}_s$. Observe that fixing the level of the simple-sum aggregate does not fix the level of the exact aggregate but does constrain its feasible range, in much the same way that a budget constraint defines the feasible set for a consumer but does not fix the consumer's solution point. This remaining slackness in monetary policy need not necessarily aggravate the time-inconsistency problem, but in practice it seems clear from our discussion that the complex relationship that exists between the three monetary aggregates in the economy – the simple-sum aggregate, the monetary base, and the consumer's exact aggregate – will greatly complicate the solution of the team dynamic game. Establishing credibility of the central bank's commitment to the optimal policy seems difficult under these circumstances.[5] Even if the central bank never does replan, the appearance of replanning is likely to arise periodically.

In fact, the reason that the simple-sum aggregate is intermediating between the base and the consumer's exact aggregate is unclear, to say the least. Furthermore, any attempt to estimate the demand function for the exact aggregate under these circumstances would produce a Lucas critique issue, since the simple-sum constraint on the consumer's decision

[4] However, as has been observed by Poterba and Rotemberg (1990), there is a limit to the degree of understanding of monetary policy that reasonably can be imputed to the public. For example, the public has little understanding of the relationship between the monetary base and seigniorage. Yet the actual importance of seigniorage and hence of the base, even during periods of moderate inflation, has been demonstrated by Mankiw (1987).

[5] On the subject of credibility and reputational equilibrium, see Kreps and Wilson (1982), Barro and Gordon (1983), Backus and Driffill (1985), Barro (1986), Cukierman (1986), and Grossman and van Huyck (1986).

produces a direct connection between demand and supply not operating through interest rates. The distribution of the stochastic process of the simple-sum aggregate is embedded directly within the demand function for the consumer's exact aggregate. Hence the parameters of the demand function for the exact aggregate would not be invariant to policy.

The importance of this issue depends upon the magnitude of the divergence between the exact theoretical monetary aggregate and the simple-sum aggregate. To explore the magnitude of that divergence, Barnett and Yue produced both aggregates. They produce the exact aggregate in two manners: by using the Divisia index under the assumption of risk neutrality, and by using generalized method-of-moments estimation to estimate the parameters of the Euler equations under risk aversion. They displayed the resulting three data series. In the discussion that follows, we call $M(\mathbf{m}_s)$ the *Theoretical monetary aggregate*.

In order to acquire the existence of a monetary aggregate, we accept the admissibility (weak separability) assumption in equation (2.5). Hence there exists some partition of the vector of monetary asset quantities $\mathbf{a}_s = (\mathbf{m}_s, \bar{\mathbf{m}}_s)$ such that $u(\mathbf{a}_s, L_s, \mathbf{x}_s) = u^*(M(\mathbf{m}_s), \bar{\mathbf{m}}_s, L_s, \mathbf{x}_s)$. The consumer's exact monetary aggregate, $M_s = M(\mathbf{m}_s)$, exists where the dimension of $\mathbf{m}_s$ is k_1. In later research, we plan to separate the demand for money by consumers from that by firms.

In order to simplify the illustration, we accept a common clustering of components without weak separability testing. We shall first set $\mathbf{m}_s$ equal to those components of M1 found by Belongia and Chalfant (1989) to be weakly separable. We then repeat our analysis with $\mathbf{m}_s$ set equal to the components of M2, but with those components clustered into three groups with prior aggregation within groups, so that $\mathbf{m}_s$ contains three aggregated elements. Hence we implicitly assume that $\mathbf{a}_s$ is partitioned in accordance with a recursively nested two-level separable blocking such that the components of our M1 aggregate are separable within the components of our M2 aggregate, which in turn are separable within $\mathbf{a}_s$. Considering the little that is known about testing for separability in the risk-averse case, the clustering that we have chosen without explicit separability testing is hardly the last word on that subject.

Barnett and Yue selected a specification for the function u satisfying the existence condition (2.5), and estimated the parameters by GMM (generalized method of moments). In that estimation, the data used is the monthly monetary component data available in Fayyad (1986) for January 1969 to March 1985. We begin by defining $\mathbf{m}_s$ to contain two components: currency and demand deposits, which Belongia and Chalfant (1989) found to be blockwise weakly separable (at least under risk neutrality) from other goods and assets. In the utility function $u^*(M(\mathbf{m}_s), \bar{\mathbf{m}}_s, L_s, \mathbf{x}_s)$, we assume a further higher level of nested blockwise strong separability such that

$$u(\mathbf{m}_s, \bar{\mathbf{m}}_s, L_s, \mathbf{x}_s) = V(M(\mathbf{m}_s), X_s) + H(\bar{\mathbf{m}}_s, L_s), \tag{3.1}$$

where $X_s = X(\mathbf{x}_s)$ is the exact quantity aggregate over consumer goods.[6] The utility function that Barnett and Yue specified and estimated is the category utility function $V(M(\mathbf{m}_s), X_s)$.[7]

Because the variables in $V(M(\mathbf{m}_s), X_s)$ are disjoint from those in $H(\bar{\mathbf{m}}_s, L_s)$, we can restrict the original decision to be defined in terms of the utility function $V(M(\mathbf{m}_s), X_s)$ in the following manner, without altering the solution for the variables $(\mathbf{m}_s, X_s)$: Redefine the utility function in Problem 2 to be

$$V(M(\mathbf{m}_t), X_t) + E_t \left[\sum_{s=t+1}^{\infty} \left(\frac{1}{1+\xi} \right)^{s-t} V(M(\mathbf{m}_s), X_s) \right]. \tag{3.2}$$

The utility function in Problem 1 can be restricted in an analogous manner. The budget constraint in either case is constructed as follows. All terms containing the variables $(\bar{\mathbf{m}}_s, \bar{\mathbf{m}}_{s-1}, L_s)$ are absorbed into the "other income" variable, $\mathbf{I}_s(\tau_t)$, with $(\bar{\mathbf{m}}_s, \bar{\mathbf{m}}_{s-1}, L_s)$ replaced by their stochastic processes solving the complete unrestricted decision (Problem 1 or 2).

The budget constraint then becomes:

$$\Phi(s) = \left\{ (\mathbf{m}_s, X_s, A_s) \in H : p_s^* X_s = \sum_{i=1}^{k_1} [(1+r_{i,s-1}) p_{s-1}^* m_{i,s-1} - p_s^* m_{is}] \right.$$
$$+ (1+R_{s-1}) p_{s-1}^* A_{s-1} - p_s^* A_s$$
$$\left. + \mathbf{I}_s(\tau_t) \right\}, \tag{3.3}$$

where H is a compact subset of the $(n+k)$-dimensional nonnegative orthant. Decision problems 1 and 2 are then amended as follows.

Problem 1a. Choose the deterministic point $(\mathbf{m}_t, X_t, A_t)$ and the stochastic process $(\mathbf{m}_s, X_s, A_s)$, $s = t+1, \dots, t+T$, to maximize

$$V(M(\mathbf{m}_t), X_t) + E_t \left[\sum_{s=t+1}^{t+T-1} \left(\frac{1}{1+\xi} \right)^{s-t} V(M(\mathbf{m}_s), X_s) \right]$$

---

[6] Formally, we assume that $\mathbf{x}_s$ is a weakly separable block within u with linearly homogeneous category utility function $X(\mathbf{x}_s)$. The true cost-of-living index $p_s^* = p^*(\mathbf{p}_s)$ hence is the unit cost function dual to the quantity aggregator function X_s. We are able to appeal to perfect-certainty aggregation theory in this case, since current-period prices, unlike current-period interest rates, are known in the current period. Hence two-stage budgeting over consumer goods is possible, and thereby perfect-certainty aggregation and index number theory are applicable to consumer goods.

[7] The strong separability assumption is largely for expository convenience. Weak separability of the form $u(\mathbf{m}_{1s}, \mathbf{m}_{2s}, L_s, \mathbf{x}_s) = U[V(M(\mathbf{m}_{1s}), X_s), \mathbf{m}_{2s}, L_s]$ would be sufficient to assure the existence of the function $V(M(\mathbf{m}_{1s}), X_s)$ that we use in what follows.

$$+ \left(\frac{1}{1+\xi}\right)^T V_T(M(\mathbf{m}_{t+T}), X_{t+T}, A_{t+T})\Bigg],$$

subject to $(\mathbf{m}_s, X_s, A_s) \in \Phi(F, s)$ for $s = t, \ldots, t+T$.

Problem 2a. Choose the deterministic point $(\mathbf{m}_t, X_t, A_t)$ and the stochastic process $(\mathbf{m}_s, X_s, A_s)$, $s = t+1, \ldots, \infty$, to maximize

$$V(M(\mathbf{m}_t), X_t) + E_t\left[\sum_{s=t+1}^{\infty} \left(\frac{1}{1+\xi}\right)^{s-t} V(M(\mathbf{m}_s), X_s)\right],$$

subject to $(\mathbf{m}_s, X_s, A_s) \in \Phi(F, s)$ for $s \geq t$, and also subject to

$$\lim_{s \to \infty} E_t\left(\frac{1}{1+\xi}\right)^{s-t} A_s = 0.$$

In short, with M1 components we estimate a three-goods model, including two monetary components and the aggregate quantity of consumer goods X_s. With M2 components we estimate a four-goods model, including three aggregated monetary components and the aggregate quantity of consumer goods X_s. Barnett and Yue used the same aggregator function specifications (nested CES, with constant proportional risk aversion) used by Poterba and Rotemberg (1987), although we believe that at a later stage of this research the aggregator functions should be replaced by those of the highly flexible seminonparametric AIM (asymptotically ideal model) specification; see, for example, Barnett, Geweke, and Wolfe (1991) and Barnett, Geweke, and Yue (1991). Alternatively, regarding the possibility of nonparametric kernel estimation, see Ullah and Vinod (1988).

Barnett and Yue used Hansen and Singleton's (1982) generalized method-of-moments estimator to estimate the parameters of the Euler equations. Using these parameter estimates and the component data, the estimated Theoretical M1 monetary aggregate $M_s = M(\mathbf{m}_s)$ was computed at each observation. This procedure then was repeated with the M2 data. The components of M2 were clustered into three groups, and asset quantities within the groups were aggregated by simple summation to produce three aggregated components over which we aggregate by the three methods. Using these parameter estimates and the component data, the estimated Theoretical M2 monetary aggregate $M_s = M(\mathbf{m}_s)$ was computed at each observation. Regarding the relevant aggregation procedures, see Barnett, Hinich, and Yue (1991).

At the M1 level, Divisia M1 tracks the estimated Theoretical aggregate rather well. At the M2 level, the growth rates of those two series are usually very close to each other, but diverged from September 1982 through April 1983, with the growth rate of the estimated Theoretical aggregate being consistently higher than that of the Divisia aggregate throughout that brief time period. This phenomenon opened a gap between the plots of the levels of the two series. However, the two paths tracked parallel to each other after the eight months of diverging growth rates, since the growth rates of the two series returned to being very similar after April 1983. We do not know the source of the divergence from September 1982 through April 1983.

The simple-sum aggregate did not track the estimated Theoretical aggregate well at either level of aggregation. In the time domain, the cointegration properties of the three series relative to final targets of policy are investigated in Barnett and Serletis (1990). Again, the Divisia aggregate was found to perform more similarly to the Theoretical aggregate than did the simple-sum aggregate, at each level of aggregation.

4   Conclusions

Barnett and Yue found that the Divisia M1 aggregate tracks the estimated exact Theoretic aggregate more adequately both in levels and in growth rates than does the simple-sum M1 aggregate, throughout their sample period. Using bispectral methods, the dynamic behavior of the two series are explored in Barnett, Hinich, and Yue (1991), who also find that the Divisia and Theoretic M1 aggregates behave similarly.

The aggregation theory developed in Barnett and Yue demonstrates that under rational expectations the Theoretical aggregate can be used either as an indicator or as an intermediate target. If used as an intermediate target, the Theoretical monetary aggregate becomes a state variable in the contingency plans ("feedback rules") solving the economic agent's decision problem, which can be formulated as a recursive Bellman iteration. Hence, if the Theoretical monetary aggregate is used as an intermediate target, its solution process will predictably influence behavior in other markets through the role of the intermediate target as a state variable in economic agents' contingency plans. The more easily computed Divisia index usually tracks the estimated Theoretical monetary aggregate well.

The simple-sum aggregate, on the other hand, plays no direct role in the behavior of any economic agent, regardless of whether or not the aggregate is targeted. Without information on the Theoretical monetary aggregate, economic behavior remains conditional upon information regarding every disaggregated monetary asset's market. That dependency is not altered by the availability of information on any simple-sum monetary aggregate's stochastic process, since the level of a simple-sum aggregate at most can constrain the optimal range of monetary services without rigidly setting that level.

Yet central banks usually target simple-sum monetary aggregates. This paradoxical divergence between the consumer's monetary state variable and the central bank's control variable greatly complicates the Calvo dynamic game. Furthermore, neither of those monetary aggregates appears in the government's budget constraint, but rather the monetary base does, since the monetary base is the tax base for the seigniorage tax.

The literature on the time inconsistency of replanned discretionary monetary policy has emphasized the difficulty of attaining a reputational equilibrium for a central bank, since the economy cannot track the true solution path to the dynamic game unless there is commitment by the central bank to follow that path without replanning. But there is a temptation for the government to replan in order to exploit the current-period inelasticity of supply of the seigniorage tax base, and the consumer knows of that temptation to the government. Still, the time-inconsistency literature assumes there is only one monetary variable in the game: That variable is simultaneously the monetary state variable to the consumer, the monetary control variable to the government, and the seigniorage producing monetary variable in the government budget constraint.

But we have shown that when there are multiple monetary assets in the economy, aggregation does not produce one monetary aggregate that serves all three purposes in the dynamic game. If all monetary assets are outside money, then there are two monetary assets in the game. If any of the monetary assets are inside money, then there are three monetary aggregates, each serving a different purpose. We have demonstrated empirically that the consumer's exact aggregate and the government's monetary control variable differ substantially in behavior. The monetary base, not displayed in our plots, differs substantially from the aggregates displayed in this chapter. Fischer (1980) has shown that time inconsistency can be produced by a divergence between the utility function of the consumer and the utility function of the government. The issue raised here is whether a wedge between the monetary aggregates relevant to the consumer, the fiscal authority, and the monetary authority can similarly produce time inconsistency – or, alternatively, aggravate an already existing problem of time inconsistency – by increasing the difficulty of establishing a reputational equilibrium.

The resulting complications to the dynamic game suggest that establishing the credibility of monetary policy's commitment to the game's true intertemporal solution may be more difficult than previously believed. Cukierman and Meltzer (1986) have argued that ambiguity in monetary policy can be optimal. But their conclusion depends upon the assumption that the ambiguity increases the variance of forecasts without producing bias. The plots supplied by Barnett and Yue suggest that a form of bias-producing ambiguity may exist when simple-sum monetary aggregates are used as intermediate targets. Some relevant tools that might be useful in exploring the issues raised in this chapter are in Mino and Tsutsui (1990). We conclude with the suggestion for further research to untangle the potentially troublesome effects of inconsistent measures of money within an otherwise team dynamic game, when the existence of a single measure is internally inconsistent with the structure of the model.

In the past, research on credibility has been theoretical. But as has been observed by Persson (1988), the issue ultimately is empirical. The results here could be viewed as a first step toward measuring the empirical relevancy of a source of difficulty in establishing monetary policy credibility and reputational equilibrium.

REFERENCES

Alesina, Alberto (1988), "Macroeconomics and Politics," in S. Fischer (ed.), *Macroeconomics Annual*. Cambidge University Press/National Bureau of Economic Research.

Alesina, Alberto, and Guido Tabellini (1988), "Credibility and Politics," *European Economic Review* 32: 542–50.

Arrow, K. J., and F. Hahn (1971), *General Competitive Analysis*. San Francisco: Holden-Day.

Backus, David, and John Driffill (1985), "Inflation and Reputation," *American Economic Review* 75: 530–8.

Barnett, William A. (1980), "Economic Monetary Aggregates: An Application of Index Number and Aggregation Theory," *Journal of Econometrics* 14: 11–48.

(1981), *Consumer Demand and Labor Supply: Goods, Monetary Assets and Time*. Amsterdam: North-Holland.

(1982), "The Optimal Level of Monetary Aggregation," *Journal of Money, Credit, and Banking* 14: 687–710.

(1983), "New Indices of Money Supply and the Flexible Laurent Demand System," *Journal of Business and Economic Statistics* 1: 7–23.

(1987), "The Microeconomic Theory of Monetary Aggregation," in W. A. Barnett and K. J. Singleton (eds.), *New Approaches to Monetary Economics*, Proceedings of the Second International Symposium in Economic Theory and Econometrics. Cambridge: Cambridge University Press.

Barnett, William, Douglas Fisher, and Apostolos Serletis (1992), "Consumer Theory and the Demand for and Measurement of Money," *Journal of Economic Literature* 30: 2086–2119.

Barnett, William, John Geweke, and Michael Wolfe (1991), "Seminonparametric Bayesian Estimation of the Asymptotically Ideal Production Model," *Journal of Econometrics* 49: 5–50.

Barnett, William, John Geweke, and Piyu Yue (1991), "Seminonparametric Bayesian Estimation of the Asymptotically Ideal Model: The AIM Demand System," in W. A. Barnett, G. Tauchen, and J. Powell (eds.), *Nonparametric and Semiparametric Methods in Econometrics and Statistics*. Cambridge: Cambridge University Press.

Barnett, William A., Melvin Hinich, and Piyu Yue (1991), "Monitoring Monetary Aggregates under Risk Aversion," in M. T. Belongia (ed.), *Monetary Policy* on the 75th Anniversary of the Federal Reserve System, Proceedings of the Fourteenth Annual Economic Policy Conference of the Federal Reserve Bank of St. Louis. Dordrecht: Kluwer.

Barnett, William, and Apostolos Serletis (1990), "A Dispersion-Dependency Diagnostic Test for Aggregation Error: with Applications to Monetary Economics and Income Distribution," *Journal of Econometrics* 43: 5–34.

Barnett, William A., and Piyu Yue (1991), "Monetary Aggregation with Risk Aversion," Typescript, Department of Economics, Washington University in St. Louis.

Barro, Robert (1986), "Reputation in a Model of Monetary Policy with Incomplete Information," *Journal of Monetary Economics* 17: 3–20.

Barro, Robert, and David Gordon (1983), "Rules, Discretion and Reputation in a Model of Monetary Policy," *Journal of Monetary Economics* 12: 101–21.

Belongia, Michael, and James Chalfant (1989), "The Changing Empirical Definition of Money: Some Estimates from a Model of the Demand for Money Substitutes," *Journal of Political Economy* 97: 387–98.

Belongia, Michael, and Alec Chrystal (1991), "An Admissible Monetary Aggregate for the United Kingdom," *Review of Economics and Statistics* 73: 497–502.

Calvo, Guillermo A. (1978), "On the Time Consistency of Optimal Policy in a Monetary Economy," *Econometrica* 46: 1411–28.

Cukierman, Alex (1986), "Central Bank Behavior and Credibility: Some Recent Theoretical Developments," *Bulletin of the Federal Reserve Bank of St. Louis* 68: 5–17.

Cukierman, Alex, and Allan Meltzer (1986), "A Theory of Ambiguity, Credibility, and Inflation under Discretion and Asymmetric Information," *Econometrica* 54: 1099–1128.

Fayyad, S. K. (1986), "Monetary Asset Component Grouping and Aggregation: An Inquiry into the Definition of Money," Ph.D. Dissertation, University of Texas, Austin.

Feenstra, Robert C. (1986), "Functional Equivalence between Liquidity Costs and the Utility of Money," *Journal of Monetary Economics* 17: 271–91.

Fischer, Stanley (1980), "Dynamic Inconsistency, Cooperation, and the Benevolent Dissembling Government," *Journal of Economic Dynamics and Control* 2: 93–107.

Grossman, Herschel, and John B. van Huyck (1986), "Seigniorage, Inflation, and Reputation," *Journal of Monetary Economics* 18: 21–31.

Hansen, Lars Peter, and Kenneth J. Singleton (1982), "Generalized Instrumental Variables Estimation of Nonlinear Rational Expectations Models," *Econometrica* 50: 1269–86.

Hurwicz, Leonid (1972), "On Informationally Decentralized Systems," in C. B. McGuire and R. Radner (eds.), *Decision and Organization: A Volume in Honor of Jacob Marschak*. Amsterdam: North-Holland.

Kreps, David M., and Robert Wilson (1982), "Reputation and Imperfect Information," *Journal of Economic Theory* 27: 253–79.

Kydland, F., and E. Prescott (1977), "Rules Rather than Discretion: The Inconsistency of Optimal Plans," *Journal of Political Economy* 85: 473–91.

Mankiw, Gregory (1987), "The Optimal Collection of Seigniorage: Theory and Evidence," *Journal of Monetary Economics* 20: 327–41.

(1990), "A Quick Refresher Course in Macroeconomics," *Journal of Economic Literature* 28: 1645–60.

Mino, Kazuo, and Shunichi Tsutsui (1990), "Reputational Constraint and Signalling Effects in a Monetary Policy Game," *Oxford Economic Papers* 42: 603–19.

Persson, Torsten (1988), "Credibility of Macroeconomic Policy: An Introduction and a Broad Survey," *European Economic Review* 32: 519–32.

Persson, Torsten, and Guido Tabellini (1990), *Macroeconomic Policy, Credibility and Politics.* New York: Harwood.

Phlips, Louis, and Frans Spinnewyn (1982), "Rationality versus Myopia in Dynamic Demand Systems," in R. L. Basmann and G. F. Rhodes (eds.), *Advances in Econometrics.* Greenwich, CT: JAI Press.

Poterba, James M., and Julio J. Rotemberg (1987), "Money in the Utility Function: An Empirical Implementation," in W. Barnett and K. Singleton (eds.), *New Approaches to Monetary Economics,* Proceedings of the Second International Symposium in Economic Theory and Econometrics. Cambridge: Cambridge University Press.

    (1990), "Inflation and Taxation with Optimizing Governments," *Journal of Money, Credit, and Banking* 22: 1–18.

Sargent, Thomas J. (1987), *Dynamic Macroeconomic Theory.* Cambridge, MA: Harvard University Press.

Ullah, A., and H. D. Vinod (1988), "Flexible Production Function Estimation by Nonparametric Kernel Estimators," in G. F. Rhodes and T. B. Fomby (eds.), *Nonparametric and Robust Inference: Advances in Econometrics,* v. 7. Greenwich, CT: JAI Press.

CHAPTER 19

A general equilibrium model with endogenous government behavior

Eric Drissen and Frans van Winden

1   Introduction

In many countries macroeconom(etr)ic models are used for the study of the economy and the evaluation of alternative government policies. These models are criticized, however, from at least two different angles. First of all, Lucas (1976) makes the point that a change in government policy may lead to changes in the behavior of consumers and producers, altering the structure of the model and the values of the estimated parameters. Consequently, models used for the evaluation of government policies should allow for the impact of these policies on the decisions taken by consumers and producers. Second, it has been emphasized in the political economy (public choice) literature that government policies cannot be changed at will; the behavior of public-sector agents is just as endogenous as is the behavior of private-sector agents. As noted by Blinder and Solow (1973) and Crotty (1973), by ignoring this, one runs the risk of a serious specification error and poor forecasts.

The first critique is met by the rapidly expanding literature on (dynamic) general equilibrium models, which are firmly rooted in microeconomic theory. The seminal paper here is Harberger (1962). Harberger analyzed the incidence of a corporate income tax in a neoclassical two-sector model. For solving the model, Harberger used linear approximations of the behavioral equations for consumers and producers, which led to analytical results. However, the system of differential equations thus obtained is appropriate for analyzing only small tax changes. The

This is a revised version of Research Memorandum 9005, University of Amsterdam. Earlier versions were presented at the European Public Choice Meeting in Linz, March 1989, and at the European Meeting of the Econometric Society in Munich, August 1989. The authors are in particular grateful to Lans Bovenberg, Jean-Jacques Laffont, Martin Paldam, Jan Potters, Ben van Velthoven, Jean Waelbroeck, Gerrit de Wit, and an anonymous referee for their stimulating comments. The usual disclaimer applies.

487

investigation of larger changes in taxes was enabled by the introduction of numerical solution methods, based on Scarf's simplicial search algorithm, by Shoven and Whalley (1972, 1973). Unfortunately, the greater flexibility of these models[1] leads to a loss of analytical tractability. In the present context, an additional and more important limitation of these models is that they do not meet the second line of critique that concerns the endogeneity of government behavior. In general equilibrium models, attention is concentrated on the impact of an exogenously imposed government policy on decisions of private-sector agents. Government policy itself is not an outcome of a behavioral model of decision making.

How government policies come into existence can be analyzed in either a normative or a positive way. Normative models that are of relevance here are the optimal taxation models. The positive approach is represented by the so-called political economic models.

In the optimal taxation literature a benevolent government is assumed, one that aims at maximizing social welfare. Seminal papers are Diamond and Mirrlees (1971) on commodity taxation, Mirrlees (1971) on income taxation, and Sheshinski (1972) on linear income taxation. In these papers, a partial equilibrium approach is used, where it is assumed that changes in the tax rates do not alter production prices. This restriction was removed in the general equilibrium model of Feldstein (1973). Feldstein analyzed the general equilibrium effects of a uniform linear income tax in a model where two types of consumers are distinguished, with identical preferences but with a different wage income. In particular, his numerical results suggest that the effects on optimal tax rates of this adjustment are substantial if a capital market and (fixed) tax revenues are taken into consideration.

Although Feldstein takes account of the impact of government policy on private-sector decisions and, through an individualistic welfare function, of private-sector agents' behavior on government decisions, there are some problems with this optimal taxation approach. First, we would like to point at the assumption of identical preferences. As shown analytically in Allen (1982) and numerically in Carruth (1982), results may change significantly if this assumption is dropped. A second issue concerns the way public goods are treated by Feldstein. Although he emphasizes that the level of public expenditures strongly influences optimal tax rates, he does not analyze how government decisions on public expenditures are made. Furthermore, public production is not analyzed. It is only assumed that the production of public goods requires some exogenously

---

[1] For reviews of numerical general equilibrium models, the reader is referred to Fullerton, Henderson, and Shoven (1984) and Shoven and Whalley (1984).

determined amount of money. Finally, Feldstein assumes that public expenditures do not influence utility. Although this assumption may, according to Feldstein, be weakened by treating public expenditures equal to a lump-sum grant, this would mean that public expenditures have the same effect on consumer's utility as private expenditures, which is at least a bit curious. As a third point, it is noticed that Feldstein only obtains numerical solutions. An analytically solvable model is presented in Allen (1982). Although Allen claims that his model is an extension of Feldstein's model, it has a serious limitation in the sense that Allen can only analyze tax changes at the market equilibrium. A more general treatment of consumer and producer behavior using functional forms of greater flexibility is obtained at the cost of a severe and questionable limitation in the range of tax values and tax changes that can be analyzed. Our fourth, and most important, point relates to all optimal taxation models and has to do with the assumption of benevolent government behavior. Whereas (neoclassical) microeconomic theory typically assumes self-interested individuals, the optimal taxation literature assumes that politicians and bureaucrats behave unselfishly. For the development of a positive (explanatory) theory of the interaction between the public and the private sector in an economy – in which we are interested here – this is unsatisfactory. In this respect we will follow the approach advocated in political economic models, where the microeconomic assumption of self-interested behavior is applied to public-sector decision making. To put our own model (to be presented in the next section) into perspective, we shortly discuss three main types of political economic models that are of particular relevance here.

The first type concerns the median-voter model, where government policy is determined by the preferences of the median voter in a majority-voting process in which all individuals are involved. Although very popular for technical modeling reasons, there are a number of limitations to this type of model. First of all, their scope is in fact limited to direct democracies, whereas most (if not all) existing democracies are of the representative kind. Second, the median-voter model in general only applies to situations where a 1-dimensional issue is at stake.[2] Third (and partly for the same reason), when applied to the study of the interaction between the public sector and the private sector, these models typically focus on redistribution policies, neglecting the production and consumption of public goods.[3]

---

[2] Cf. McKelvey (1976).
[3] Cf. Meltzer and Richard (1981). This also applies to the pressure group models of Becker (1983, 1985).

490   Eric Drissen and Frans van Winden

The second main type of political economic models are the macroeconomic models with endogenous government behavior.[4] An important shortcoming of these models is that they do not consider the impact of government policies on the decisions of producers and consumers, which makes them vulnerable to the Lucas critique.

Finally, the third type of models are those that deal with time inconsistency. They are especially of interest here, because in these models both the impact of government policies on private-sector behavior and the influence of private-sector agents on government decisions are considered. This is done by modeling these interactions as a game. In the pioneering contribution of Kydland and Prescott (1977), followed by Barro and Gordon (1983), attention is focused on monetary policies. The government sets the inflation rate using an objective function that involves inflation and (un)employment, while private-sector agents set the wage rate. This model has been extended in several ways: in Cukierman and Meltzer (1986) and Rogoff and Sibert (1988), it is assumed that government maximizes popularity while private agents can influence government decisions by voting under imperfect information; in Alesina (1987), the original model is extended by assuming that there exist two political parties with different attitudes with respect to inflation and unemployment.[5] Our main critique of these models concerns their ad hoc assumptions with respect to the objectives of the government and the private-sector agents; they lack a solid microeconomic foundation.[6] In contrast with these models, Fisher (1980) takes a microeconomic starting point and analyzes the design of fiscal policies by a welfare-maximizing government.[7] We criticized this normative approach with respect to government behavior in our preceding discussion of the optimal taxation literature.

The main goal of this chapter is to analyze the interaction between the public and the private sector in a (closed) economy, and to do so in a way that substantially meets the critique just raised with respect to models that (partially) deal with this research area. To that purpose a general equilibrium model is constructed that (a) builds on a microeconomic foundation regarding the behavior of consumers and producers (including their reactions to government policy changes), (b) is rooted in a positive political economic approach to government behavior that is not restricted to the political setting of a direct democracy, (c) allows for redistribution as well

---

[4] See, e.g., Borooah and Van der Ploeg (1983) and Frey and Schneider (1982).
[5] See Persson and Tabellini (1990, part 1) for further extensions and a review.
[6] Compare the critique in Alesina and Tabellini (1988, p. 548), Driffill (1988, p. 540), Persson (1988, pp. 523, 528–30), and Persson and Tabellini (1990, p. 16).
[7] For extensions and a discussion of the Fisher model, the reader is referred to Persson and Tabellini (1990, part 2).

as the production and consumption of public goods, and (d) is nevertheless analytically solvable.[8] The advantage of an analytically solvable model is that it offers the opportunity to derive comparative static results that hold under (largely) unspecified parameter configurations. Moreover, it generally offers greater tractability. Since there is no such thing as a free lunch, there is a price to be paid; in this case, simple functional forms must be chosen (forms that are nonetheless also used in numerically solved applied general equilibrium models).[9]

The main results can be summarized as follows. In the first place, it appears that changes in government policies are associated with changes in the economy that are in general different from those predicted by the submodel for the private sector, the solution of which is equivalent to that of a traditional general equilibrium model (that is, without endogenous government behavior). Second, the model predicts an undersupply of public goods unless the demand for leisure is zero, in which case the tax-transfer system of the model would effectively turn into one with lump-sum taxation. Third, an increase in political influence of a social group need not always be beneficial to that group. This result follows from the plausible assumption that there is a lack of information regarding the general equilibrium effects of policy changes. Fourth, substitution of a lump-sum taxation system for the tax-transfer system of the model entails a Pareto improvement when lump-sum taxes are determined endogenously. Finally, it is argued that a tax reform involving the enactment of such an (endogenous) lump-sum tax system is not to be expected because of the costs associated with tax reforms and, perhaps more important, the presence of ideological (in particular equity) constraints.

Apart from this introduction, the organization of the paper is as follows. The model is presented in Section 2. Comparative static results are derived and discussed in Section 3. In Section 4, the tax-transfer structure

[8] Compare in this context Zodrow (1988), where a general equilibrium model is constructed in which local government decisions are determined by the preferences of the median voter, while the federal government collects taxes in order to receive an exogenously given amount of revenues. Simulation results are presented for changes in the deductibility of local taxes. Compare, furthermore, Rutherford and Winer (1990). Although their analysis of government behavior is more or less similar to our approach, there are some important differences. First, their general equilibrium framework allows only for numerical solutions; second, they are interested in the operationalization of the model for the study of policy changes, whereas we analyze comparative statics and efficiency effects in an analytical setting.

[9] Another way to keep a general equilibrium model analytically tractable is by linearizing demand and supply functions in terms of prices and tax variables (cf. Keller 1979; Bovenberg and Keller 1983). Although small changes in endowments and parameters will be analyzed in this chapter, linearizing is not adopted here because the endogenization of government behavior explicitly determines the tax values.

analyzed in Sections 2 and 3 is compared with a lump-sum tax system, and tax reform receives some attention. Section 5 concludes.

2   The model

The political economic model for a closed economy that we will develop here consists of two submodels, one for the private sector and one for the public sector. These models will be presented in Sections 2.1 and 2.2, respectively. For each sector, a partial equilibrium solution is determined. For the private sector this equilibrium would be equal to the general equilibrium solution in the case of a traditional general equilibrium model with an exogenous public sector. The general equilibrium solution for the political economic model is presented in the appendix.

In the public economics (optimal taxation) literature it is conventional to assume Stackelberg behavior for the public sector. However, the Stackelberg assumption is appropriate only if a player (the dominant player) acts before the other players or if that player can commit to an announced strategy. Otherwise, the other players will foresee that the dominant player has an incentive to depart from the announced strategy; in these situations, the Stackelberg solution is time-inconsistent. In the game between the private and public sectors, it is typical for the public sector to announce its (fiscal) policy before the private sector acts, but also for the public sector to carry out this announced policy more or less simultaneously with the actions of the private sector. In addition, the public sector can not commit itself to the announced policy, which makes this policy time-inconsistent. Therefore, instead of assuming Stackelberg behavior, it seems more appropriate to formalize the interaction between the public and private sectors in a Nash–Cournot fashion (cf. Blackburn 1987 and Persson and Tabellini 1990).

2.1   The private sector

It is assumed that decisions in the private sector are made by consumers and producers under conditions of atomistic competition. Consumers maximize their utility subject to an income constraint; producers maximize their profits under a given production technology. Consumers and producers take the decisions of public-sector agents as given, while maximizing utility and profits, respectively. An equilibrium in the private sector exists if demand equals supply in all commodity and factor markets. In this section we first model the behavior of producers, and then go into the behavior of consumers. Finally, the conditions for an equilibrium in the private sector are presented.

Production

Producers, running identical firms, are assumed to operate in a competitive market for a single commodity. They maximize profits under a Cobb-Douglas production technology, using capital and labor as inputs.[10] Consequently – using aggregate variables, for convenience – producers are confronted with the following optimization problem:

$$\max_{K_f, L_f} pQ - p_L L_f - p_K K_f \qquad (2.1)$$

subject to

$$\Omega_f L_f^{\delta_f} K_f^{1-\delta_f} = Q, \quad 0 \le \delta_f \le 1, \quad \Omega_f > 0, \qquad (2.2)$$

where L_f and K_f are the labor and capital inputs, p_L and p_K the respective input prices, Ω_f a scaling parameter, δ_f a production elasticity parameter, Q the produced output of the commodity, and p the commodity price.

The optimal input of capital and labor is given by

$$K_f = [(1 - \delta_f)pQ]/p_K; \qquad (2.3)$$

$$L_f = [\delta_f pQ]/p_L. \qquad (2.4)$$

Thus, we get the well-known result that, given constant returns to scale, only the capital-labor ratio is determined by the input prices, whereas the input demand level is determined from the commodity market equilibrium.

Consumption

Consumers are divided into two social groups: capital owners and workers, indexed by $i = c, w$, respectively. The former also run the firms, and are therefore called capitalists/entrepreneurs (or capitalists, for short). The income of workers consists only of labor income, while the income of capitalists consists of both labor and capital income. It is assumed that consumers within a social group have identical preferences; among these groups preferences may differ, however. The utility of a consumer depends on her or his consumption of the private commodity, a public consumption good, and leisure. Consumers maximize utility, subject to a budget and a time constraint; the utility functions are of the Cobb-Douglas type. Thus consumers of each social group solve (again using aggregate variables, for convenience)

$$\max_{D_i, l_i} D_i^{\alpha_{i1}} l_i^{\alpha_{i2}} G^{\alpha_{i3}}, \quad \alpha_{i1} + \alpha_{i2} + \alpha_{i3} = 1, \quad i = c, w, \qquad (2.5)$$

---

[10] Empirical support for this specification can be found in Berndt (1976).

subject to

$$pD_i + p_l l_i = F_i, \quad 0 \le l_i \le E_i, \tag{2.6}$$

where D_i indicates the demand for the private commodity, l_i the amount of leisure, G the amount of the public consumption good, E_i the endowment of labor time, and p_l the shadow price of leisure (equal to $(1-t)p_L$, with t a uniform income tax rate); F_i stands for disposable full income, which equals

$$F_c = (1-t)[p_K K_c + p_L E_c + S_c], \tag{2.7}$$

$$F_w = (1-t)[p_L E_w + S_w], \tag{2.8}$$

where S_i denotes a group-specific transfer, which may be negative. The government has only labor costs $(p_L L_s)$ for the production of a public good G. These costs are covered by the revenues from the uniform income tax. It is assumed that the transfer system is self-financing $(S_c + S_w = 0)$. There is no capital mobility between the private and public sectors. The tax-transfer system as well as the public production process will be discussed in greater detail in Section 2.2.

The demand for the private commodity and leisure (assuming an interior solution) is given by

$$D_i = \tilde{\alpha}_{i1} F_i / p, \quad \tilde{\alpha}_{i1} \equiv \alpha_{i1} / (\alpha_{i1} + \alpha_{i2}), \quad i = c, w; \tag{2.9}$$

$$l_i = \tilde{\alpha}_{i2} F_i / p_l, \quad \tilde{\alpha}_{i2} \equiv \alpha_{i2} / (\alpha_{i1} + \alpha_{i2}), \quad i = c, w. \tag{2.10}$$

Thus, the demand for private commodities and leisure depends on disposable (after-tax) full income, the price of the private commodity, the shadow price of leisure, and the respective relative preference weight.

Using these results, the indirect utility function for a member of a social group can be written as

$$V_i = \alpha_{i0} F_i^{1-\alpha_{i3}} G^{\alpha_{i3}} / (p^{\alpha_{i1}} p_l^{\alpha_{i2}}), \quad \alpha_{i0} \equiv \tilde{\alpha}_{i1}^{\alpha_{i1}} \tilde{\alpha}_{i2}^{\alpha_{i2}}, \quad i = c, w. \tag{2.11}$$

Thus, indirect utility will increase if disposable full income increases, if consumption of the public good increases, or if prices p and p_l decrease.

Conditions for an equilibrium in the private sector

An equilibrium for the private sector is obtained if demand equals supply in all commodity and factor markets.[11] In the model presented in this section, there is one commodity market, a capital market, and a labor market. These markets are at equilibrium if

---

[11] Note that this would be a general equilibrium in case of a traditional general equilibrium model with an exogenous public sector.

$$D_c + D_w = Q, \tag{2.12}$$

$$K_f = K_c, \tag{2.13}$$

$$L_f + L_s = E_c - l_c + E_w - l_w, \tag{2.14}$$

where L_s stands for the amount of labor demanded by the government for producing the public good, and K_c denotes the fixed supply of capital by the capital owners which is rented by the firms.

Taking the wage rate as numéraire ($p_L = 1$) because only relative prices matter, the following expressions can be derived for the commodity price and the price of capital from the equilibrium conditions (2.12) and (2.13) by using equations (2.2), (2.3), (2.4), (2.7), (2.8), and (2.9):

$$p_K = \frac{(1-\delta_f)(1-t)[\bar{\alpha}_{c1}(E_c + S_c) + \bar{\alpha}_{w1}(E_w + S_w)]}{[1 - \bar{\alpha}_{c1}(1-t)(1-\delta_f)]K_c}; \tag{2.15}$$

$$p = \Omega_f^{-1}\delta_f^{-\delta_f}\left[\frac{(1-t)[\bar{\alpha}_{c1}(E_c + S_c) + \bar{\alpha}_{w1}(E_w + S_w)]}{[1 - \bar{\alpha}_{c1}(1-t)(1-\delta_f)]K_c}\right]^{1-\delta_f}. \tag{2.16}$$

Labor market equilibrium follows from Walras' law.

Note that these prices are a function only of exogenous variables and the government policy variables t, S_c, and S_w. Prices do not depend on the public good G because of the separability of the utility function (cf. (2.5)). Since all the remaining endogenous private-sector variables (L_f, K_f, Q, D_i, l_i, V_i) can be written as functions of exogenous variables and the prices p and p_K, they also depend only on exogenous variables and the aforementioned government policy variables. To save space, we leave out the expressions for those variables.

Note from equation (2.15) that the relative price of capital p_K decreases if the tax rate t increases. The reason is that the demand for private goods (D_c and D_w) decreases if the tax rate increases (cf. (2.9)), leading to a lower price of the private good and consequently to a decrease in private production and private demand for labor (Q and L_s, respectively). Because capital is fixed in the private sector, a lower demand for labor decreases the price of capital (cf. (2.3) and (2.4)). The negative effect on the tax base that follows from the fall in capital income is mitigated by the increase in labor supply of capitalists (cf. (2.10)). Whether tax revenues and the public demand for labor will increase is ambiguous.

If S_c decreases and S_w increases by the same amount, as follows from $S_c + S_w = 0$, p_K increases (decreases) if the relative preference for the private commodity is higher (lower) for workers than for capitalists: $\bar{\alpha}_{c1} < \bar{\alpha}_{w1}$ ($\bar{\alpha}_{c1} > \bar{\alpha}_{w1}$). For in that case the decrease in S_c (increase in S_w) causes demand for private commodities and leisure by capitalists (workers) to decrease (increase), while total demand for private commodities will increase and that for leisure will decrease, because $\tilde{\alpha}_{c1} < \tilde{\alpha}_{w1}$ and consequently $\tilde{\alpha}_{c2} > \tilde{\alpha}_{w2}$. The increase in private demand leads to an increase in the commodity price, and this raises private production and private labor demand. The latter increases the relative price of capital, because of the fixed capital input in the private sector. We will return to these results in Section 3, when we discuss the general equilibrium solution of the political economic model.

2.2   The public sector

In the public sector decisions are (formally) made by politicians who, like the private-sector agents, are self-interested. Politicians' behavior is, however, constrained by the structure of the economy and the reactions of other social groups. Important groups are workers in the public sector (bureaucrats) who must carry out the policies decided upon, the political parties that politicians represent, voters, and pressure groups. The reactions (pressure) of these groups force politicians to take account of their interests, to some extent. In modeling the outcome of these different games for the behavior of the public sector, we will use the interest function approach as developed in Van Winden (1983).[12] The central focus in this approach is on the interests of representative individuals of social groups. These interests are formally represented by so-called (elementary) interest functions. In our case these are the indirect utility functions V_i of the workers and the capitalists.[13] The interest function approach implies that the influence of social groups on government behavior can be approximated by assuming that politicians are maximizing a complex (compromise) interest function, which is a weighted representation of the elementary interest functions. The weights reflect the effectiveness with which the groups get their interests promoted by the politicians.[14] In the present context, the interest function is

$$P = V_c^{\mu_c} V_w^{\mu_w}, \quad \mu_c + \mu_w = 1, \tag{2.17}$$

[12] See, for instance, Borooah and Van der Ploeg (1983), Renaud (1989), and Van Velthoven (1989).

[13] For simplicity it is here assumed that public-sector workers (bureaucrats) receive the same wage as private-sector workers, and that their preferences are similar to the workers' preferences. Given these assumptions, we have decided not to distinguish them explicitly as a social group, in order not to overload the notation. The analysis for a separate group of bureaucrats is, however, straightforward.

[14] Apart from pressure this interest representation may come about through multiple positions and mobility; see Van Winden (1983, 1987).

where μ_c and μ_w denote the influence weights (μ_w is implicitly built up by the relative influence weights of workers and bureaucrats).

As mentioned before, a basic characteristic of the interest function approach is that the government focuses on the interests of representative individuals of social groups. This contrasts with the traditional normative approach where the government focuses on the interests of individuals while maximizing social welfare.[15] Furthermore, equation (2.17) differs from a social welfare function in the sense that the latter is typically related to some ethical notion, whereas (2.17) is related to theoretical descriptions of the actual political process.

To indicate the fruitfulness of the formalization from such a positive – behavioral modeling – perspective, it may be useful here to link up our approach with the literature on electoral competition, where attention is focused on the relationship between politicians (candidates) and voters. In particular we refer to Coughlin and Nitzan (1981) and Coughlin (1986). Assuming that candidates from two parties maximize expected plurality and use the (Luce) "binary strict utility model" for the voters' choice probabilities, it turns out that candidate behavior (platforms) will be in line with the maximization of a generalized Nash product as in (2.17), with the weights indicating the (estimated) numerical strength of the different social groups to which the voters belong, if the variances in party choice are identical across voters.[16]

The tax-transfer system consists of two separable segments: a uniform tax rate t; and a group-specific transfer S_i, which may be negative. For simplicity, it will be assumed that the transfer (sub)system is self-financing ($S_c + S_w = 0$). The tax revenues are employed to finance the production of

[15] The importance of focusing on social groups – instead of the pure individual level – for modeling political behavior has recently been stressed by a number of authors; see, e.g., Coughlin, Mueller, and Murrell (1990).

[16] The result that expected plurality–maximizing candidates act in accordance with the maximization of a weighted representation of the utility functions of (representative) voters is also arrived at in Ledyard (1984) and Coughlin et al. (1990), using different models. This literature shows that if the spread is not identical across social groups then it will show up in the influence weights. Note that the weighted-representation-of-utilities formalization would still be appropriate if one allows for the fact that, in the execution of their preferred policies, politicians are confronted with an influential bureaucracy having its own goals (which are here represented by V_w), given that the reasonable assumption is made that the conflicts of interests between politicians and bureaucrats are (largely) resolved in a cooperative way. Suppose that the (generalized) Nash bargaining solution would be a fair approximation of the outcome; then (2.17) could still be used to describe the behavior of the politicians, albeit that the weights μ_i would then reflect the numerical strength of the social groups (c, w) on the one hand, and the bargaining strength of the bureaucrats (increasing μ_w at the cost of μ_c) on the other.

a public good G, using capital K_s and labor L_s as inputs. The relative influence of the social (interest) groups on the tax segment and the redistribution (transfer) segment may be different. In order not to overload the notation, however, it will be assumed that their influence is the same for both segments.

The division of the tax-transfer system into a uniform and group-specific segment is supported by the following two observations. First, following Brennan and Buchanan (1980), the uniform income tax can be interpreted as the (quasi-)constitutionalized part of the system. Since tax systems have some duration, the choice of the system is made behind a "veil of ignorance." The insurance motive – regarding the risk of tax exploitation by the government – thus leads to a uniform tax as a plausible outcome. Day-to-day political decision making, however, determines the actual level of the tax rate. Moreover, it is allowed here that the daily political tug-of-war may lead to special provisions (captured by S_i) affecting the effective tax rate (cf. Becker 1983). In this context – as well as that of the following observation – it is important to note that special provisions, in contrast with the tax rate, "miss the notice of most people."[17] This ignorance with respect to other people's special provisions makes the decisions of an individual independent of differences in these provisions.

The second, somewhat related, observation is that the uniform income tax is the official part (the "flag") of the system urged by the value system (ideology) of a democracy, whereas the transfer part crops up under the force field of the existing political influence structure in society, which also determines the level of the uniform tax rate. In this context the following remarks by Stiglitz (1989, p. 29) are of interest: "In fact, the appearance of equity is often more important than the reality. . . . The seeming public hypocrisy entailed in this kind of behavior may be difficult to understand, but is prevalent in virtually all Western democracies." Lack of information with respect to the precise consequences of government programs seems to play an important role here.[18]

Assuming a Cobb–Douglas production function for the public consumption good, a balanced budget, and a given endowment of capital

---

[17] Tullock (1988, p. 473).

[18] Note that our division of the tax-transfer system is also in line with Musgrave's (1959) distinction between fiscal functions of the government. Major functions are the allocation and the distribution function. Under the allocation function, the government collects taxes for the financing of the production of public goods. This function is represented by the tax segment of our tax-transfer system. The distribution function refers to the adjustment of the distribution of incomes (wealth), which is represented by the redistribution segment of the system. Musgrave's third fiscal function – the stabilization of the economy – is not relevant in a general equilibrium model with full employment.

K_g, the political decision making process can now be represented by the following optimization problem, using equations (2.11) and (2.17):

$$\max_{t,\,L_s,\,S_c,\,S_w} P = \alpha_{c0}^{\mu_c}\alpha_{w0}^{\mu_w}G^{a_3}p^{-a_1}p_l^{-a_2}F_c^{\mu_c(1-\alpha_{c3})}F_w^{\mu_w(1-\alpha_{w3})} \tag{2.18}$$

subject to the following conditions:

$$G = \Omega_s L_s^{\delta_s}K_s^{1-\delta_s}, \quad 0 \le \delta_s \le 1, \quad \Omega_s > 0; \tag{2.19}$$

$$p_L L_s = t[p_K K_c + p_L(E_c - l_c) + S_c] + t[p_L(E_w - l_w) + S_w], \tag{2.20}$$

$$K_s = K_g, \tag{2.21}$$

$$S_c + S_w = 0, \tag{2.22}$$

where $a_j \equiv \mu_c\alpha_{cj} + \mu_w\alpha_{wj}$, and where it is further assumed that public-sector decision makers take the outcomes of the private sector as given (as was assumed for private-sector decision makers vis-à-vis the public sector).

The solution of the preceding problem leads to the following behavioral equations for the public sector:

$$t = \delta_s a_3/[1 - (1-\delta_s)a_3]; \tag{2.23}$$

$$L_s = \delta_s a_3[p_K K_c + p_L(E_c - l_c) + p_L(E_w - l_w)]/\{[1 - (1-\delta_s)a_3]p_L\}; \tag{2.24}$$

$$S_c = [\mu_c(1-\alpha_{c3})/(1-a_3)](p_K K_c + p_L E_c + p_L E_w) \\ - (p_K K_c + p_L E_c); \tag{2.25}$$

$$S_w = -S_c = [\mu_w(1-\alpha_{w3})/(1-a_3)](p_K K_c + p_L E_c + p_L E_w) - p_L E_w. \tag{2.26}$$

It appears that the tax rate depends only on the relative political influence of the social groups (μ_i), their preferences with respect to the public consumption good (α_{i3}), and the labor elasticity of production of the public good (δ_s); it is not influenced by prices or by income distribution. Note that an increase in the influence of a social group does not necessarily lead to a lower tax rate t for this group; this will occur only if it has a lower preference for the public consumption good than does the other group. Of course, the assumption of a uniform tax rate is crucial here. Note, furthermore, that the tax rate is positively related to the labor elasticity of production. This is due to the fact that an increase in δ_s makes labor more productive and capital less productive in the public sector, which leads to a higher labor input and consequently to higher labor costs (note that the wage rate is the numéraire) in the public sector. It then follows immediately from the balanced-budget condition (2.20) that the tax rate will increase.

The demand for labor (and thus the amount of G) depends on the tax rate, the total tax base (earned income), and the wage rate.

Note, with respect to the transfer system (cf. (2.25) and (2.26)), that through this system total full income ($p_K K_c + p_L E_c + p_L E_w$) is redistributed between capitalists and workers, where a group's share in the pie depends on the relative political influence and the preference structure of the group at hand. As is obvious from equations (2.25) and (2.26), the whole full income of a group is transferred away if this group has no political influence ($\mu_i = 0$), or if this group is only interested in the public good ($\alpha_{i3} = 1$). This is due to the nondistortive character of the group-specific transfers and to the fact that the government does not take account of excess burdens when choosing its optimal policy (Nash assumption). Of course, a social group's share of the total full income depends only on the weight of its political influence if all individuals have identical preferences ($\alpha_{cj} = \alpha_{wj}$, $j = 1, 2, 3$).

3   Equilibrium analysis

In this section, the nature of the general equilibrium solution of the political economic model (as presented in the appendix) will be investigated by means of a comparative static analysis. The results are summarized in Tables 1–4 and discussed in Section 3.1, where we focus on the more interesting outcomes. In Section 3.2 we contrast the general equilibrium results with the results of a partial equilibrium (traditional general equilibrium) model.

3.1   Comparative statics

Before presenting the comparative statics results, some preliminary remarks are in order. First – as can be checked from equations (A.1), (A.2), and (A.3), respectively – it turns out that the price of capital p_K, the private commodity price p, and the private output level Q are similarly affected by a change in a parameter or an exogenous variable, except for a change in the private production parameters δ_f and Ω_f or the private capital stock K_c. Second, because in equilibrium capital is fully employed, the effect of a change in an exogenous variable or a parameter on the private (public) demand for labor is of similar sign as its effect on private (public) output, except for a change in the private (public) capital stock (K_c and K_g, respectively) and the private (public) production parameters (δ_f, Ω_f and δ_s, Ω_s, respectively). Third, since $\alpha_{i1} + \alpha_{i2} + \alpha_{i3} = 1$ ($i = c, w$), a change in one α_{ij} implies a simultaneous change in at least one other α_{ij} (for given i). Fourth, because $\mu_c + \mu_w = 1$, the effect of a change in μ_c on an endogenous variable is of equal size, but of opposite sign, in comparison with the effect on this variable of a change in μ_w. Fifth, because

Table 1. *Signs of comparative statics effects of changes in workers' political influence* μ_w

Conditions	Leisure		Prices		Production		Tax	Transfers	
	l_c	l_w	p_K	p	Q	G	t	S_c	S_w
	−	+	±	±	±	±	±	−	+
$\alpha_{cj} = \alpha_{wj}$ $j = 1, 2, 3$	−	+	0	0	0	0	0	−	+
$\alpha_{c1} \leq \alpha_{w1}$ $\alpha_{c3} < \alpha_{w3}$	−	+	±	±	±	+	+	−	+
$\alpha_{c1} \geq \alpha_{w1}$ $\alpha_{c3} > \alpha_{w3}$	−	+	−	−	−	−	−	−	+

Note: The effects of a change in μ_c are of equal size but of opposite sign.

$S_c + S_w = 0$, changes in S_c and S_w, as a consequence of a change in a parameter or an exogenous variable, are of equal size but of opposite sign.

Effects of a change in political influence (μ_c and μ_w)
The most important parameters are, from a political economic point of view, the relative political influence of capitalists (μ_c) and workers (μ_w). The effects of a change in influence depend heavily on the preferences of these social groups with respect to the private and public good (see Table 1). Not surprisingly, if the relative political influence of workers increases (μ_w increases and μ_c decreases), then the transfer for workers (S_w) increases while the transfer for capitalists (S_c) decreases.[19] In case of identical preferences ($\alpha_{cj} = \alpha_{wj}$, $j = 1, 2, 3$) the tax rate t and the production of private and public goods will not change.

An increase in the influence weight of workers will lead to an increase in the tax rate t if and only if workers have a stronger preference for the public good than capitalists ($\alpha_{w3} > \alpha_{c3}$). With increasing μ_w and $\alpha_{w3} > \alpha_{c3}$, the effect on private and public production depends primarily on the preferences of workers and capitalists for private commodities (α_{w1} and α_{c1}, respectively). It turns out that $\alpha_{w1} \geq \alpha_{c1}$ is a sufficient condition for an increase in public production G. However, the change in Q (and thus in p_K and p; see our previous remarks) remains ambiguous. In that case, capitalists have a relatively stronger preference for leisure ($\alpha_{c2} \geq \alpha_{w2}$), and consequently show a stronger labor-supply effect of full income than

[19] Note that these are real variables, expressed in the numéraire.

workers (cf. (2.10)). Thus, if the transfer for capitalists S_c decreases and the transfer for workers S_w increases, the total supply of labor will increase. This extra labor supply may increase the production of private as well as public goods. If it is still assumed that $\alpha_{w3} > \alpha_{c3}$ but that $\alpha_{w1} < \alpha_{c1}$, then the effect of an increase in the political influence of workers on the production of not only the private but also the public good is ambiguous (in contrast with the partial equilibrium result, taking private-sector behavior as given; cf. (2.19) and (2.24)). In that case $\alpha_{c2} < \alpha_{w2}$ may hold, which leads to a decrease in labor supply. Although the tax rate increases, tax revenues – and thereby public production – may decline because of a smaller tax base.

If we now turn to the situation where $\alpha_{w3} < \alpha_{c3}$, then an increase in the political influence of workers still leads to an increase (decrease) in the transfer for workers (capitalists), but the tax rate t will now decrease. Since $\alpha_{w3} < \alpha_{c3}$, an interesting question is whether the production of the public good will decrease if μ_w increases (as suggested by the partial equilibrium result). It turns out that a sufficient condition for a lower production of the public good is that $\alpha_{w1} \leq \alpha_{c1}$. However, if $\alpha_{w1} > \alpha_{c1}$ then it is possible that capitalists have a stronger preference for leisure, $\alpha_{c2} > \alpha_{w2}$, which may lead to a larger supply of labor, and this may result – in spite of a decrease in the tax rate t – in an increase in the tax base and thereby in the production of the public good. With respect to private production, it is noticed that if $\alpha_{w3} < \alpha_{c3}$ then a sufficient condition for a decrease in its level (and, consequently, in the level of p and p_K) when μ_w increases is that $\alpha_{w1} \leq \alpha_{c1}$, in which case labor supply decreases.

In addition to the effects analyzed thus far, we will examine here the effect of a change in relative political influence on the net (of transfer) average tax rate and the utility of a representative individual of a social group. Again using aggregate variables for convenience, the total net tax burden of a (representative) individual of social group i equals

$$T_i = t[\,p_K K_i + p_L(E_i - l_i) + S_i] - S_i, \quad i = c, w, \tag{3.1}$$

whereas the earned income of this individual equals

$$I_i = p_K K_i + p_L(E_i - l_i), \quad i = c, w, \tag{3.2}$$

with $K_w = 0$ (recall that $p_L = 1$). The average tax rate of the individual can now be represented by T_i/I_i. It can be proved that the average tax rate for workers decreases if their political influence increases (this result is independent of the relative preference of workers for public goods).[20] For capitalists this is harder to prove, because of the effects on capital income.

[20] In the proof of this result, account is taken of the condition that $l_w \leq E_w$.

Finally, we indicate the effect of a change in political influence on utility. Surprisingly, it turns out that an increase in the political influence of a social group does not necessarily lead to a higher utility for this group. If all individuals have the same preferences ($\alpha_{cj} = \alpha_{wj}$, $j = 1, 2, 3$), then an increase in political influence always leads to an increase in the utility of a (representative) individual of the group considered, and to a decrease in utility for the other social group. If $\alpha_{cj} \neq \alpha_{wj}$, then an increase in political influence of a social group may lead to a decrease in utility of the members of that group.[21] If, for example, capitalists have a stronger preference for the public good than do workers ($\alpha_{c3} > \alpha_{w3}$), an increase in the political influence of workers (μ_w) leads to a decrease in public production G and, consequently, in the tax rate t. Furthermore, this change in μ_w leads to an increase in the workers' transfer S_w at the cost of an equal decrease in S_c. These effects on the tax rate t and the transfer S_w lead to an increase in workers' full income F_w, and the government expects that the consequent positive effect on workers' utility will compensate the negative effect of the decrease in public production on workers' utility. The government neglects, however, the effect of changes in prices (following from changes in government decisions) on workers' utility (see (2.11)). This is due to the assumption of Nash behavior for the public sector. In particular, the government neglects two important effects: first, the increase in the price of leisure p_l resulting from the decrease in the tax rate t, which has a negative effect on workers' utility. This effect is stronger if capitalists and workers have a stronger preference for the public good and if the labor elasticity of public production δ_s is high, as can be checked from equation (2.23). Second, the government neglects the price effects (p, p_K) that may follow from a change in the demand for leisure. The increase in F_w leads to an increase in the demand for leisure l_w, whereas the effect of an increase in the political influence of workers on the full income of capitalists F_c and, consequently, on the demand for leisure of capitalists l_c is ambiguous. It can be checked, though, that labor supply will decrease ($l_c + l_w$ will increase) if workers and capitalists have identical preferences for private commodities ($\alpha_{c1} = \alpha_{w1}$, implying that $\alpha_{c2} < \alpha_{w2}$). Moreover, it follows that in this situation ($\alpha_{c3} > \alpha_{w3}$ and $\alpha_{c1} = \alpha_{w1}$) the decrease in labor supply is so strong that it not only compensates for the smaller labor demand in the public sector, but also requires the labor demand in the private sector to decrease. The lower labor input in the

---

[21] The result that the utility of workers (capitalists) will decrease if their political influence increases holds, for instance, for the following parameter configuration: $\mu_w = 0.9$, $\mu_c = 0.1$, $\alpha_{w1} = 0.2$, $\alpha_{w2} = 0.1$, $\alpha_{w3} = 0.7$, $\alpha_{c1} = 0.2$, $\alpha_{c2} = 0$, $\alpha_{c3} = 0.8$, $\delta_f = 0.9$, and $\delta_s = 0.9$ ($\mu_w = 0.1$, $\mu_c = 0.9$, $\alpha_{w1} = 0.2$, $\alpha_{w2} = 0$, $\alpha_{w3} = 0.8$, $\alpha_{c1} = 0.2$, $\alpha_{c2} = 0.1$, $\alpha_{c3} = 0.7$, $\delta_f = 0.9$, and $\delta_s = 0.9$).

Table 2. Signs of comparative statics effects of changes in preference weights

Preference weights	Conditions	Leisure		Prices		Production		Tax	Transfers	
		l_c	l_w	p_K	p	Q	G	t	S_c	S_w
Capitalists										
α_{c1} Private commodity		+	+	+	+	+	+	−	+	±
α_{c2} Leisure		+	−	−	−	−	−	−	+	−
α_{c3} Public good		±	+	±	±	±	+	+	±	±
α_{c3} Public good	$d\alpha_{c3} = -d\alpha_{c2}$	−	+	+	+	+	+	+	−	+
Workers										
α_{w1} Private commodity		+	+	+	+	+	+	−	+	+
α_{w2} Leisure		−	±	−	−	−	−	−	±	±
α_{w3} Public good		±	+	±	±	+	+	+	±	±
α_{w3} Public good	$d\alpha_{w3} = -d\alpha_{w2}$	+	−	+	+	+	+	+	±	±

private sector causes the price of private commodities p and the price of capital p_K to decrease. The decrease in the production price has a positive effect on workers' utility, while the decrease in the price of capital has a negative effect on workers' utility, through the lower transfer to workers (see (2.26)) and through an additional decrease in public production, because the tax base decreases. Summarizing, the government neglects the negative effects on workers' utility that follow from an increase in the price of leisure and a decrease in the price of capital, and also the positive effect on workers' utility that follows from a decrease in the price of private commodities. If these negative effects are strong enough, the overall effect of an increase in the political influence of workers on their utility will be negative, as the example in note 21 illustrates. Mutatis mutandis, the same holds for the capitalists.

Effects of a change in preference weights (α_{cj} *and* α_{wj})
The effects of a change in the preference weights concerning private commodity consumption and leisure of capitalists and workers (α_{i1} and α_{i2}) are rather straightforward. Therefore, we will concentrate here on the effects of these parameters on lump-sum transfers and public production (see Table 2). With respect to public production it is noticed that an increase in the preference weight concerning private commodity consumption (α_{i1}) - which in general has an ambiguous effect - has a positive effect on public production if this increase does not lead to a change in the preference weight concerning public good consumption (α_{i3}). Note that in that case the preference weight for leisure decreases, which leads to an increase in the tax base while the tax rate t remains the same. With respect to the effects on group-specific transfers, the asymmetry between the effects of changes in the preference weights α_{c1} and α_{w1} is striking. The reason for this asymmetry is that the amount of the transfer of a social group depends on the political influence-weighted (effective) preference for private commodities (including leisure), represented by $\mu_i(1-\alpha_{i3})/(1-a_3)$, and full income, which equals $p_K K_c + p_L E_c$ for capitalists and $p_L E_w$ for workers (cf. (2.25) and (2.26)). More specifically, it is determined by the difference between $\mu_i(1-\alpha_{i3})/(1-a_3)$ multiplied by aggregate full income $p_K K_c + p_L E_c + p_L E_w$ and the full income of group i. Consequently, capital income $p_K K_c$ differently affects the net share of the pie (aggregate full income) that is transferred to these social groups, which brings forth the asymmetric effects.

As regards the effects of changes in the preference weights for public good consumption (α_{i3}), unambiguous results are obtained only if such a change merely affects the preference for leisure ($d\alpha_{i3} = -d\alpha_{i2}$). In that case all variables are positively (negatively) affected by an increase (decrease) in α_{c3}, except for the transfer to capitalists S_c and capitalists' demand for leisure l_c, for which an opposite effect is obtained. If α_{c3} increases, capitalists are willing to pay more for public goods, which leads to an increase in the tax rate t. The increase in α_{c3} leads, furthermore, to a decrease in the political influence–weighted preference for private commodities $[\mu_c(1 - \alpha_{c3})/(1 - a_3)]$ and, consequently, to a decrease in the transfer S_c and an increase in the transfer S_w, as follows from the redistribution mechanism described in the previous paragraph. The decrease in the transfer S_c to capitalists and their decreased demand for leisure (α_{c2}) lead to a decrease in the demand for leisure by this group. Although workers will show an increased demand for leisure, because of the increase in their transfer S_w, it can be shown that total labor supply will rise in this case.[22] The extra labor supply will, however, not be completely absorbed in the public sector (note that the relative preference for private commodities does not change). The larger labor input in the private sector increases the price of capital, leading to a higher before-tax full income of capitalists ($p_K K_c + E_c$) and consequently to a higher total full income ($p_K K_c + E_c + E_w$). This reinforces the negative effect on the transfer S_c to capitalists, as follows from the aforementioned redistribution mechanism.

In case of an increase (decrease) in workers' preference weight for public good consumption α_{w3} and an equal-sized decrease (increase) in their preference weight for leisure α_{w2}, the effects are similar to those described for capitalists, except for the effect on the transfers which are now ambiguous. This ambiguousness follows because the concomitant decrease in the political influence–weighted preference for private commodities $[\mu_w(1 - \alpha_{w3})/(1 - a_3)]$ has a negative (positive) effect on S_w (S_c), while the increase in capital income $p_K K_c$ has a positive (negative) effect on S_w (S_c).

If the preference weight for private commodity consumption α_{i1} is (also) affected, then the results depend on the configuration of parameter values.

Effects of a change in production parameters (δ_f, δ_s, Ω_f, and Ω_s)

As can be observed from Table 3, a remarkable effect of a change in the labor elasticities of production (δ_f and δ_s) is the differential impact on the two group-specific transfers: an increase (decrease) in δ_f or δ_s leads to a decrease (increase) in the transfer for workers S_w and an increase (decrease) in the transfer for capitalists S_c. The intuition of this result is that an increase (decrease) in one of these elasticities makes labor more (less) scarce

---

[22] Note that price effects have not entered the story yet.

Table 3. *Signs of comparative statics effects of changes in technical coefficients*

Technical coefficients	Leisure		Prices		Production		Tax	Transfers	
	l_c	l_w	p_K	p	Q	G	t	S_c	S_w
δ_f Labor elasticity, private production	−	−	−	±	±	−	0	+	−
δ_s Labor elasticity, public production	−	−	−	−	−	±	+	+	−
Ω_f Scaling, private production	0	0	0	−	+	0	0	0	0
Ω_s Scaling, public production	0	0	0	0	0	+	0	0	0

in relation to capital (cf. equations (A.6) and (A.7)), which leads to a decrease (increase) in the relative input price of capital p_K and in capitalists' before-tax full income $p_K K_c + E_c$. The result then immediately follows from the redistribution mechanism described under the previous heading.

An increase in the labor elasticity of production δ_f stimulates the input of labor in the private sector L_f (cf. (A.6)). By raising the relative price of labor (p_K decreases), it further encourages the supply of labor (cf. (A.5)). Nevertheless, the demand for labor in the public sector L_s, and consequently public output G, will fall in this case because the decrease in p_K negatively affects the tax base (cf. (A.8)). The effect of an increase in δ_f on private output Q is ambiguous, because it makes capital less productive in the private sector ($1 - \delta_f$ decreases). A definite (negative) relationship is obtained, however, if the private capital endowment exceeds the total labor endowment ($K_c > E_c + E_w$); in this situation the decrease in capital productiveness dominates.

The same holds, mutatis mutandis, for the effects of a change in δ_s, the labor elasticity of production in the public sector. Interestingly, although the effect of a change in δ_s on G is ambiguous in general (for the same reasons as in the previous paragraph for the effect of δ_f on Q), the tax rate t is always positively affected, because the consequent increase in L_s leads to higher production costs in the public sector which in turn calls for higher tax revenues.

The results for the production scaling parameters Ω_f and Ω_s are straightforward, given the separability of the utility and complex interest functions. Apart from the negative relationship between Ω_f and the private

Table 4. *Signs of comparative statics effects of changes in labor and capital endowments*

	Leisure		Prices		Production		Tax	Transfers	
Endowments	l_c	l_w	p_K	p	Q	G	t	S_c	S_w
E_c Labor, capitalists	+	+	+	+	+	+	0	−	+
E_w Labor, workers	+	+	+	+	+	+	0	±	±
K_c Private capital	0	0	−	−	+	0	0	0	0
K_g Public capital	0	0	0	0	0	+	0	0	0

commodity price p, changes in the scaling parameters Ω_f and Ω_s only (positively) affect the private and public production levels, respectively.

Effects of a change in labor and capital endowments
(E_c, E_w, K_c, and K_g)
Table 4 shows, not unexpectedly, that an increase in labor endowment will lead to an increase in private and public production. The reason that the effect of such a change on the transfers S_c and S_w is not symmetric for E_c and E_w follows from the same redistribution mechanism as just discussed for the asymmetric effects of changes in the preference parameters α_{c3} and α_{w3}. The effects of changes in capital endowments are straightforward. Apart from the additional negative relationship between K_c and p_K, the effects of changes in K_c and K_g are similar in sign as those referring to the scaling parameters Ω_f and Ω_s, respectively (note that $p_K K_c$ is not affected by a change in K_c; see (A.1)).

In analyzing the effects of a change in labor endowments on endogenous variables, it has thus far been assumed that there is no relation between labor endowments (numerical strength) and political influence. If it is, in contrast, assumed that the numerical strengths of social groups determine the influence weights – which is in line with the aforementioned electoral competition model of Coughlin and Nitzan (1981) – the impact of a change in labor endowments on endogenous variables will alter. As already discussed in Section 2.2, according to the electoral competition model, maximization of expected plurality in a two-party election is in accordance with the maximization of a generalized Nash product if the political influence of a social group equals

$$\mu_i = E_i/(E_c + E_w), \quad i = c, w. \tag{3.3}$$

The relations between the endogenous variables and the labor endowments can now easily be obtained by inserting (3.3) in the equations of the respective endogenous variables as given in Section 2.3. It turns out that the effect of a change in either labor endowment is in general ambiguous for all endogenous variables. If individuals have the same preferences ($\alpha_{cj} = \alpha_{wj}$, $j = 1, 2, 3$) then a change in capitalists' labor endowment has the same effect on the endogenous variables as a change in workers' labor endowment, except for the effect on the group-specific transfers. In this situation, an increase (decrease) in one of the labor endowments leads to an increase (decrease) in both private and public production, while there is no effect on the tax rate, which is in line with intuition. Furthermore, if individuals have equal preferences then a change in capitalists' labor endowment has no effect on the group-specific transfers, while an increase (decrease) in workers' labor endowment leads to an increase (decrease) in workers' transfer and to a decrease (increase) in capitalists' transfer. This asymmetry in the effects on the transfers of changes in capitalists' and workers' labor endowments follows because group-specific transfers depend only on workers' labor endowment and not on capitalists' labor endowment if individuals have the same preferences and if (3.3) holds (cf. (A.10) and (A.11)). The intuition behind this result is as follows. If individuals have identical preferences and political influence according to their number (the latter following from (3.3)), an egalitarian government policy is optimal (compare the optimal policy of a utilitarian government if individuals have identical preferences). Because there is only one wage rate, all individuals earn the same wage income, but capitalists also receive a capital income. To reach the egalitarian solution, the government redistributes only capital income. Consequently, the transfer for capitalists will be negative ($S_c < 0$) while the transfer for workers will be positive ($S_w > 0$), as can be easily checked from equations (A.10) and (A.11). Each individual receives an income equal to

$$p_L + p_K K_c / (E_c + E_w) = [1 - (1 - \delta_s)a_3] / [1 - (1 - \delta_f)a_1 - (1 - \delta_s)a_3],$$

as follows from equation (A.1) and the fact that the wage rate is numéraire. Note that this (after-transfer) income per individual does not depend on the size of the population ($E_c + E_w$), which is due to the transfer system and the linear homogeneity of the production and utility functions. Consequently, an extra individual generates extra income (through an increase in p_K) that is exactly the same as the (after-transfer) income every other individual receives. This extra income consists of labor income, which the new individual receives directly, and of capital income, which the individual receives directly if she is a capitalist and indirectly (through a transfer) if she is a worker. Consequently, a change in the number of capitalists does not affect the transfer from capitalists to workers, while a change in the number of workers does.[23]

An increase in capitalists' (workers') labor endowment has a negative effect on both private and public production if preferences of capitalists (workers) for both private commodities and the public good is very low (α_{c1} and α_{c3} (α_{w1} and α_{w3}) approach zero) and if, in addition, the other social group has a stronger preference for the public good ($\alpha_{w3} > \alpha_{c3}$ and $\alpha_{c3} > \alpha_{w3}$, respectively). Furthermore, in this case the tax rate decreases, the transfer to capitalists increases (decreases), and, consequently, the transfer to workers decreases (increases). In this situation, an increase in the labor endowment of, say, capitalists leads to an increase in their relative political influence, which leads to an increase in capitalists' transfer. Furthermore, because capitalists have in this case a weak preference for the public good, they apply their increased political influence to lead the government to produce less of the public good, which leads to a decrease in government expenditures and consequently to a decrease in the tax rate. Finally, private production decreases, because capitalists use their increased after-tax disposable full income only for extra leisure, whereas workers' after-tax disposable full income decreases, leading to a decrease in their demand for private commodities.

3.2   Comparison with partial equilibrium results

In partial equilibrium (traditional general equilibrium) models, where the values of public-sector variables are exogenously imposed, the effects of changes in the public-sector variables on (private-sector) endogenous variables are analyzed. However, from a political economic point of view, the government cannot freeely choose the shocks in tax variables and public production, as these shocks depend on changes in economic and political variables and parameters. The latter changes also have a direct effect on private-sector variables. As a consequence, if no account is taken of why a tax variable changes, there may be a serious misspecification in the effect of a change in a tax variable on a private-sector variable if this effect is analyzed in a partial equilibrium setting. We will illustrate this claim with some examples.

The partial effect of an increase in the tax rate t on private production Q (and prices p and p_K) is negative (cf. (2.2)). So, one would expect from a partial equilibrium analysis that an increase in the tax rate t leads to a

---

[23] It is assumed here that a change in the number of capitalists does not affect the total capital endowments K_c and K_g.

decrease in private production. If it is now assumed that the increase in the tax rate follows from a decrease in capitalists' preference for leisure (α_{c2}), then private production and the commodity and capital price do not decrease – as would be expected from the relation between these variables and the tax rate – but instead will increase (cf. Table 2 for this general equilibrium effect), because of additional indirect effects through the group-specific transfers and because of the direct effect of a change in the preference weight on private production and the commodity and capital price.[24]

As a second example, consider the expected positive effect of an increase in the transfer to capitalists on private production if $\bar{\alpha}_{c1} > \bar{\alpha}_{w1}$; this follows from substitution of (2.15) and (2.16) into equation (2.3). If the increase in the capitalists' transfer follows from an increase in the labor elasticity of production of the public good (δ_s), the general equilibrium effect of a change in this parameter on private production is negative, as can be checked from Table 3. Thus, again, the partial equilibrium analysis gives false information.

4   Lump-sum taxation and tax reform

In Section 2 it was argued that the tax-transfer system incorporated in the model can be interpreted as an abstract reproduction of existing tax regimes. This view was supported by arguments obtained from Brennan and Buchanan (1980) and Stiglitz (1989). In the present section we will investigate the efficiency of this system.

Let us begin with the efficiency of public production. It can easily be shown that the Samuelson first-best condition for an efficient supply of the public good – demanding that the sum of the marginal rates of substitution (MRS) equals the marginal rate of transformation (MRT) – is only satisfied for the tax-transfer system if individuals of both social groups attach zero weight to the consumption of leisure ($\alpha_{c2} = \alpha_{w2} = 0$).[25] In order to study the efficiency of the tax-transfer system more generally it will be compared with a nondistorting lump-sum tax system. It is shown in

[24] Note that one should also take account of the effect of a change in α_{c2} on private production Q in the traditional general equilibrium case. The analysis of the effect of a simultaneous change in the tax rate t and α_{c2} in a traditional general equilibrium framework differs, however, from the model presented here, because the effect on the tax rate t of a change in α_{c2} is missed in the former framework.

[25] This follows from the equations

$$\text{MRS}_i = -dD_i/dG = [\partial U_i/\partial G]/[\partial U_i/\partial D_i] = (\alpha_{i3}D_i)/(\alpha_{i1}G), \quad i = c, w;$$

$$\text{MRT} = -dQ/dG = (\delta_f QL_s)/(\delta_s GL_f).$$

Section 4.1 that the government provides more of the public good under the latter system than under the former, and that the lump-sum tax system is Pareto superior to the tax-transfer system. The latter result does not, however, carry over to all other tax systems (if no compensation is allowed).[26]

In view of the Pareto superiority of the (endogenous) lump-sum tax system compared with the tax-transfer system, this section concludes with a discussion of the feasibility of tax reform. Two issues are highlighted: the costs of tax reform, and the (quasi-)constitutional and ideological aspects of tax systems.

4.1   Comparison with an endogenous lump-sum tax system

When introducing a new tax system, the government must reconsider the tax payments it will demand from each individual. If taxes are levied by lump-sum taxation, where the lump sums can be different for different social groups, the complex interest function (2.18) for the government changes into

$$P = \alpha_{c0}^{\mu_c} \alpha_{w0}^{\mu_w} G^{a_3} p^{-a_1} p_l^{-a_2}$$

$$\times [p_K K_c + p_L E_c - M_c]^{\mu_c(1-\alpha_{c3})} [p_L E_w - M_w]^{\mu_w(1-\alpha_{w3})}. \qquad (4.1)$$

The optimization problem consequently changes into the maximization of P with respect to the lump sums M_c and M_w, capital input K_s, and labor input L_s, subject to the public production technology (cf. (2.19)), the given public capital endowment (cf. (2.21)), and the budget constraint ($p_L L_s = M_c + M_w$).

The optimal values for the lump-sum taxes and the input of labor are

$$M_c = \frac{\delta_s a_3 + \mu_w(1-\alpha_{w3})}{1-(1-\delta_s)a_3} \cdot (p_K K_c + p_L E_c) - \frac{\mu_c(1-\alpha_{c3})}{1-(1-\delta_s)a_3} \cdot p_L E_w; \qquad (4.2)$$

$$M_w = \frac{\delta_s a_3 + \mu_c(1-\alpha_{c3})}{1-(1-\delta_s)a_3} \cdot p_L E_w - \frac{\mu_w(1-\alpha_{w3})}{1-(1-\delta_s)a_3} \cdot (p_K K_c + p_L E_c); \qquad (4.3)$$

$$L_s = \frac{\delta_s a_3}{1-(1-\delta_s)a_3} \cdot \frac{p_K K_c + p_L E_c + p_L E_w}{p_L}. \qquad (4.4)$$

---

[26] Note that the redistribution of income as specified in the tax-transfer system has no direct excess burden. If, however, capitalists and workers have different preferences with respect to the public good, then income redistribution may have an indirect burden, because it will change the provision of the public good.

Under the lump-sum tax system, (after-tax) full income of capitalists and workers is equal to $F_c \equiv p_K K_c + p_L E_c - M_c$ and $F_w \equiv p_L E_w - M_w$, respectively. It can be shown that these after-tax full incomes are identical under the tax-transfer system and the endogenous lump-sum tax system. This result is due to the separability of the utility and complex interest functions. Because of this assumption, the distribution of aggregate full income $(p_K K_c + p_L E_c + p_L E_w)$ over the after-tax full incomes F_c and F_w and the production factor L_s is fixed and consequently independent of the tax system chosen;[27] that is, if proper account is taken of the shadow prices of these outlays, which are defined here as the per-unit share of aggregate full income that is allocated to these outlays. The structure of the tax system may influence these shadow prices of F_c, F_w, and L_s. If the tax system switches from the tax-transfer system to the lump-sum system, the shadow prices of F_c and F_w are unaffected and equal to 1, because the transfers S_c and S_w in the tax-transfer system operate like M_c and M_w in the lump-sum system. The shadow price of government expenditures differs, however. In the case of a tax-transfer system, the shadow price of L_s can be written as $P_L\{1 + p_L(l_c + l_w)/[p_K K_c + p_L E_c + p_L E_w - p_L(l_c + l_w)]\}$, where the second term is due to the fact that only earned income can be taxed. Under a lump-sum tax system, this second term vanishes.

As can now be calculated from equations (2.9) and (2.12), expenditures for commodities, pD_c and pD_w, and thus total returns from private production pQ, will also be equal under these two tax systems. Furthermore, because the given private capital endowment will again be fully employed, it immediately follows from the linear homogeneity of the production function that the price of capital will be identical under the two tax systems as well (see (2.3)). The same holds, by implication, for private labor input and the private commodity price. The result that the private sector is not affected by the switch from the tax-transfer to the lump-sum system is related to the fact that the tax-transfer system does not affect the price ratio of the labor and capital input in the private sector.

What changes, though, is total labor supply (unless, of course, $\alpha_{c2} = \alpha_{w2} = 0$). If taxes are levied as lump sums, the price of leisure increases and becomes equal to the wage rate. The following relationship between the demand for leisure under the endogenous lump-sum tax system (denoted by l_i^E) and the demand for leisure under the tax-transfer system (l_i) is obtained as

$$l_i^E = l_i[1 - a_3]/[1 - (1 - \delta_s)a_3], \quad i = c, w. \tag{4.5}$$

[27] These fixed fractions are $(1 - \alpha_{c3})\mu_c/[1 - (1 - \delta_s)a_3]$, $(1 - \alpha_{w3})\mu_w/[1 - (1 - \delta_s)a_3]$, and $\delta_s a_3/[1 - (1 - \delta_s)a_3]$ for F_c, F_w, and L_s, respectively.

Because a_3 and δ_s are between 0 and 1, individuals of both social groups will take less leisure under the endogenous lump-sum tax system. As a consequence, total labor supply will increase, which must (in equilibrium) lead to a higher total labor input. Since private labor input does not change, this means that labor input in the public sector is higher in the case of an endogenous lump-sum tax system. Denoting the latter input by L_s^E, the following relationship can be established:

$$L_s^E = [(1 - a_3)/a_1]L_s. \tag{4.6}$$

Because $1 - a_3 = a_1 + a_2$, it follows that $L_s^E > L_s$, unless $a_2 = 0$ (in which case $\alpha_{c2} = \alpha_{w2} = 0$). Consequently, public output G will be higher as well under this tax system, if $a_2 > 0$. It follows from equations (4.5), (4.6), (A.5), and (A.7) that the change in demand for labor in the public sector ($L_s^E - L_s$) equals the increase in labor supply (or decrease in demand for leisure $l_c + l_w - l_c^E - l_w^E$), which is not surprising, because labor input in the private sector does not change. The change in labor supply can be written as $l_c + l_w - l_c^E - l_w^E = t(l_c + l_w)$, which corresponds exactly with the second term in the shadow price of labor input in the public sector under the tax-transfer system, as can be checked with equations (A.1) and (A.5). The distortion (represented by the second term in the shadow price) is due to the fact that leisure is taxed under the tax-transfer system. It vanishes if the tax system switches to a lump-sum system, leading to a shadow price of labor input in the public sector that equals the real price of labor p_L. Consequently, the Samuelson condition for an efficient public output is fulfilled under the lump-sum tax system (recall that under the tax-transfer system this condition is fulfilled only if there is no demand for leisure, i.e., only if $a_2 = 0$). The increase in labor input in the public sector ($L_s^E - L_s$) exactly offsets the distortion.

Summarizing, the main effect in the model of a switch in tax regime from a tax-transfer system to an endogenous lump-sum system is to increase the amount of public output G up to an efficient level; the market sector is not affected.[28] All in all, the change in the tax system influences the utility of individuals in two ways: through an increase of the price of leisure and through an increase in the production of public goods, where the first has a negative effect and the second a positive effect on utility. Comparing the (indirect) utilities under the two tax systems gives

$$V_i^E = \{(1 - a_3)/[1 - (1 - \delta_s)a_3]\}^{\alpha_{i2}}[(1 - a_3)/a_1]^{\delta_s \alpha_{i3}}V_i, \quad i = c, w. \tag{4.7}$$

Since $1 - a_3 = a_1 + a_2$, it follows immediately that the utility of the individuals of both social groups increases if the tax system switches from the

---

[28] The assumption that utility and complex interest functions are separable with respect to the public good is important in this respect.

tax-transfer system to the endogenous lump-sum tax system (unless, again, $a_2 = 0$). Consequently, the lump-sum tax system is Pareto superior to the tax-transfer system.[29]

Finally, we note that the lump-sum tax system is not Pareto superior to all other tax systems. The lump-sum tax system is, for example, not Pareto superior to a tax system consisting only of a uniform tax rate and no group-specific transfers. (The results for this tax system follow immediately from Sections 2.1 and 2.2 if the group-specific transfers are set equal to zero ($S_c = S_w = 0$).) The simple intuition of this result is that if a tax system with a group-specific tax (segment) is in order, then total full income of the members of a social group can be taxed away if this social group has no political influence. If, however, a uniform tax system obtains, then a politically dominant social group cannot tax away the total full income of the other social group without taxing away its own full income. As long as the dominant group attaches a positive preference weight to private commodities and/or leisure, the full income of the other social group will not be taxed away under a uniform tax system.[30] Consequently, the latter group will obtain a higher utility under a uniform tax system than in the case of a tax system with group-specific taxation. If we, in contrast, allow for compensations, then (exogenous) lump sums can be found that Pareto improve the uniform tax system. These lump-sum taxes would not be optimal, however, because some agents could then enhance their utility by influencing these government decisions, as shown by the endogenous lump-sum tax system.

4.2 Tax reform

We have just investigated the relative efficiency of some alternative tax systems, to wit: an endogenous lump-sum tax system, and an (endogenous) uniform income-tax system without group-specific transfers. The endogenous lump-sum tax system appeared to be Pareto superior to the tax-transfer system of the model.

[29] It is noticed here that a change to an equal-yield lump-sum tax system need not be Pareto improving. Under such a system the lump sums are exogenously imposed and set equal to the payments under the tax-transfer system for every individual. By definition, tax revenues are constant, and consequently public production is not affected if the tax system changes. However, now private production and prices change. As shown in an earlier version of this chapter, the change in the tax regime may have a negative effect on the utility of individuals of a social group, which is due to negative price effects that dominate the positive income effects.

[30] Furthermore, note from equations (2.7), (2.8), and (2.10) that under a uniform tax system individuals cannot be forced to supply their full labor endowment.

This may raise the question of the viability of the tax-transfer system. For within the framework of the political economic model, any alternative tax system that leads to a higher maximum for P in equation (2.18) would be preferable to the political decision makers, even if the alternative is not Pareto superior (such as in case of the simple uniform income tax). In answering this question, the following two issues should be addressed: the cost of tax reform, and the interpretations of the tax system referred to in Section 2.2.

As pointed out by Van Velthoven and Van Winden (1991), a change in the tax system demands that the expected change in P make up for the costs involved in a tax reform. These costs are (at least) of two types: first, the one-time set-up costs to the government, due to changes in legislation and administration, which affects the government budget constraint; and second, the one-time adaptation costs to the taxpayers, affecting the individual budget constraint and thereby V_i. One need not go into an explicit analysis to conclude that these costs may thwart a switch to a preferred tax system, such as the endogenous lump-sum tax system.

The other issue concerns the interpretation of the ruling tax regime. In Section 2.2, the tax-transfer system was discussed. It was noticed that the uniform tax segment could be interpreted as the official part of the system. This observation was supported by a (quasi-)constitutional interpretation[31] and an ideological (democratic value system) interpretation. Apart from the cost issue, these two interpretations rule out the more efficient lump-sum tax system as a viable option. As Stiglitz (1989, p. 29) remarks: "the *equity constraint* forces, as it were, an inefficient outcome." Clearly, further research – on such issues as the development of norms and values, and the cost of tax reform – is badly needed here.

For our model it is straightforward to derive a necessary and sufficient condition for this "hypocritical" aspect of the tax system (see Section 2.2) to vanish, which requires that $S_c = S_w = 0$, turning the tax-transfer system into the simple uniform tax system referred to at the end of Section 4.1. As can be checked from equation (A.11), this condition reads

$$\frac{E_w}{E_c + E_w} = \frac{\mu_w(1 - \alpha_{w3})}{1 - a_3} \cdot \left[1 - \frac{(1 - \delta_f)a_1}{1 - (1 - \delta_s)a_3}\right]^{-1}. \tag{4.8}$$

From equation (4.8) it can be inferred that if the social groups have the same preference weights ($\alpha_{cj} = \alpha_{wj}$, $j = 1, 2, 3$) then the political influence of the workers should be smaller than their relative numerical strength, and the more so the lower the labor elasticities of private and/or public

---

[31] This interpretation is supported by the aforementioned one-time costs involved in tax reforms.

production (δ_f, δ_s). If the political influence weights μ_i are equal to the relative numerical strengths of the social groups – as would be the case under an electoral competition model as in Coughlin and Nitzan (1981) – then $S_c < 0$ and $S_w > 0$, implying a redistribution of income from capitalists to workers.[32] The intuition behind this result has already been discussed in Section 3.1.

5   Concluding remarks

In this chapter, we have presented a model that captures both the influence of government policies on private-sector decision making and the influence of private-sector agents on government decision making. For this purpose, a positive model of government behavior was linked to a traditional general equilibrium model. The positive approach to government behavior used here has its roots in the interest function approach presented in Van Winden (1983), and in the stochastic electoral competition model such as presented in Coughlin and Nitzan (1981), which suggest that selfish public-sector workers must take account of the interests of social groups (Van Winden) or voters (Coughlin and Nitzan) while making decisions. With respect to the tax structure, we used a tax-transfer system that consists of a uniform income-tax rate and a group-specific transfer, which differs from the usual uniform linear income-tax system considered in the literature. Theoretical support for this system was given. Another feature of the model concerns the supply by the government sector of a public good, which is an argument in the individuals' utility functions and consequently influences both individuals' and government's decision making. By using relatively simple functional specifications, analytical results could be obtained.

From a comparative static analysis, some counterintuitive results were derived. It was shown, for example, that an increase in political influence of a social group does not necessarily lead to an increase in the utility of the members of this social group, and that an increase in the preference weight of a social group for the public good may have a negative effect on public production. It was furthermore shown that the effects of policy changes determined by traditional general equilibrium models, where government policies are exogenously imposed, may be seriously misleading when used as a prediction of what will actually happen in case of such changes.

---

[32] More generally, denoting the right-hand side of equation (4.8) by RHS,

$$S_c \lesseqgtr 0 \text{ (and thus } S_w \gtreqless 0) \quad \text{if } E_w/(E_c+E_w) \lesseqgtr \text{RHS}.$$

We also compared the tax-transfer system with an (endogenous) lump-sum tax system from an efficiency point of view. The lump-sum tax system leads to an increase in the production of the public good, while private production does not change. The elimination of the distortion in the labor–leisure choice, which occurs under the tax-transfer system, leads to a Pareto improvement. It was argued, however, that the endogenous lump-sum system is not Pareto superior to a simple uniform linear income-tax system (without group-specific lump-sum transfers), because the uniformity of the latter system protects taxpayers from taxing away total (full) income. Finally, in view of the Pareto superiority of the endogenous lump-sum tax system, we discussed the viability of the tax-transfer system. It was argued that (quasi-)constitutional constraints – concerning the costs of tax reform – as well as ideological constraints will hamper the introduction of a full-fledged lump-sum tax system.

Appendix: The general equilibrium solution

In this appendix, the general (Nash–Cournot) equilibrium of the political economic model is presented. We start with the price of capital in the private sector and the private commodity price (recall that the wage rate is used as numéraire; thus, $p_L = 1$). Using equations (2.15), (2.16), (2.23), (2.25), and (2.26) yields

$$p_K = \frac{(1-\delta_f)a_1(E_c+E_w)}{[1-(1-\delta_f)a_1-(1-\delta_s)a_3]K_c}; \tag{A.1}$$

$$p = \Omega_f^{-1}\delta_f^{-\delta_f}\left[\frac{a_1(E_c+E_w)}{[1-(1-\delta_f)a_1-(1-\delta_s)a_3]K_c}\right]^{1-\delta_f}. \tag{A.2}$$

For the private output level, using (2.2)–(2.4), (2.13), and (A.1), we have

$$Q = \Omega_f\left[\frac{\delta_f a_1(E_c+E_w)}{[1-(1-\delta_f)a_1-(1-\delta_s)a_3]}\right]^{\delta_f}\cdot K_c^{1-\delta_f}. \tag{A.3}$$

Using equations (2.7)–(2.9), (2.23), (2.25), (2.26), (A.1), and (A.2), private output demand equals

$$D_i = \mu_i\alpha_{i1}\Omega_f\left[\frac{\delta_f(E_c+E_w)}{[1-(1-\delta_f)a_1-(1-\delta_s)a_3]}\right]^{\delta_f}\left[\frac{K_c}{a_1}\right]^{1-\delta_f}, \quad i=c,w. \tag{A.4}$$

From (A.3) and (A.4) it is easily checked that the equilibrium condition for the product market, $Q = D_c + D_w$, is satisfied.

With respect to the labor market, the expressions for leisure are determined first. Using equations (2.7), (2.8), (2.10), (2.23), (2.25), and (2.26), we obtain

$$l_i = \frac{\mu_i \alpha_{i2}[1-(1-\delta_s)a_3](E_c+E_w)}{(1-a_3)[1-(1-\delta_f)a_1-(1-\delta_s)a_3]}, \quad i=c,w. \tag{A.5}$$

Using equations (2.4), (A.2), and (A.3) for private labor demand, and equations (2.24), (A.1), and (A.5) for public labor demand, it follows that

$$L_f = \frac{\delta_f a_1(E_c+E_w)}{[1-(1-\delta_f)a_1-(1-\delta_s)a_3]}; \tag{A.6}$$

$$L_s = \frac{\delta_s a_1 a_3(E_c+E_w)}{(1-a_3)[1-(1-\delta_f)a_1-(1-\delta_s)a_3]}. \tag{A.7}$$

From equations (A.5), (A.6), and (A.7) it can be checked that the equilibrium condition for the labor market, $E_c - l_c + E_w - l_w = L_f + L_s$, is fulfilled.

From equations (2.19), (2.21), and (A.7), it follows that for the public-sector output level,

$$G = \Omega_s \left[\frac{\delta_s a_1 a_3(E_c+E_w)}{(1-a_3)[1-(1-\delta_f)a_1-(1-\delta_s)a_3]} \right]^{\delta_s} \cdot K_g^{1-\delta_s}. \tag{A.8}$$

For completeness, the income-tax rate is reproduced here:

$$t = \delta_s a_3/[1-(1-\delta_s)a_3]. \tag{A.9}$$

Using equations (2.25), (2.26), and (A.1), the lump-sum transfers to capitalists and workers are, respectively,

$$S_c = \frac{\{\mu_c(1-\alpha_{c3})[1-(1-\delta_s)a_3]-(1-\delta_f)a_1(1-a_3)\}(E_c+E_w)}{(1-a_3)[1-(1-\delta_f)a_1-(1-\delta_s)a_3]}$$
$$-E_c; \tag{A.10}$$

$$S_w = -S_c = \frac{\mu_w(1-\alpha_{w3})[1-(1-\delta_s)a_3](E_c+E_w)}{(1-a_3)[1-(1-\delta_f)a_1-(1-\delta_s)a_3]} - E_w. \tag{A.11}$$

Finally, from equilibrium prices, disposable full income, and the amount of the public good, the indirect utilities can be calculated as

$$V_i = \frac{\alpha_{i0}[\mu_i(1-\alpha_{i3})]^{1-\alpha_{i3}}[a_1]^{\delta_s\alpha_{i3}-(1-\delta_f)\alpha_{i1}}[\delta_s a_3]^{\delta_s\alpha_{i3}}[1-(1-\delta_s)a_3]^{\alpha_{i2}}}{[1-a_3]^{\alpha_{i2}+\delta_s\alpha_{i3}}[1-(1-\delta_f)a_1-(1-\delta_s)a_3]^{[1-(1-\delta_f)\alpha_{i1}-(1-\delta_s)\alpha_{i3}]}}$$
$$\cdot [E_c+E_w]^{[1-(1-\delta_f)\alpha_{i1}-(1-\delta_s)\alpha_{i3}]} K_c^{(1-\delta_f)\alpha_{i1}} K_g^{(1-\delta_s)\alpha_{i3}}[\Omega_f\delta_f^{\delta_f}]^{\alpha_{i1}}\Omega_s^{\alpha_{i3}},$$
$$i=c,w. \tag{A.12}$$

REFERENCES

Alesina, Alberto (1987), "Macroeconomic Policy in a Two-Party System as a Repeated Game," *Quarterly Journal of Economics* 52: 651–78.

Alesina, Alberto, and Guido Tabellini (1988), "Credibility and Politics," *European Economic Review* 32: 542-50.

Allen, Franklin (1982), "Optimal Linear Income Taxation with General Equilibrium Effects on Wages," *Journal of Public Economics* 17: 135-43.

Barro, Robert, and David Gordon (1983), "Rules, Discretion and Reputation in a Model of Monetary Policy," *Journal of Monetary Economics* 12: 101-21.

Becker, Gary (1983), "A Theory of Competition among Pressure Groups for Political Influence," *Quarterly Journal of Economics* 98: 371-400.

   (1985), "Public Policy, Pressure Groups and Dead Weight Costs," *Journal of Public Economics* 28: 329-47.

Berndt, Ernst (1976), "Reconciling Alternative Estimates of the Elasticity of Substitution," *Review of Economics and Statistics* 58: 59-68.

Blackburn, Keith (1987), "Macroeconomic Policy Evaluation and Optimal Control Theory: A Critical Review of Some Recent Developments," *Journal of Economic Surveys* 1: 111-48.

Blinder, Alan, and Robert Solow (1973), "Does Fiscal Policy Matter?" *Journal of Public Economics* 2: 319-37.

Borooah, Vani, and Frederick Van der Ploeg (1983), *Political Aspects of the Economy*. Cambridge: Cambridge University Press.

Bovenberg, Lans, and Wouter Keller (1983), "Non-linearities in Applied General Equilibrium Models," Internal Report, Netherlands Central Bureau of Statistics, Voorburg.

Brennan, Geoffrey, and James Buchanan (1980), *The Power to Tax*. Cambridge: Cambridge University Press.

Carruth, Alan (1982), "On the Role of the Production and Consumption Assumptions for Optimum Taxation," *Journal of Public Economics* 17: 145-55.

Coughlin, Peter (1986), "Elections and Income Redistribution," *Public Choice* 50: 27-91.

Coughlin, Peter, Dennis Mueller, and Peter Murrell (1990), "Electoral Politics, Interest Groups, and the Size of Government," *Economic Inquiry* 28: 682-705.

Coughlin, Peter, and Shmuel Nitzan (1981), "Electoral Outcomes with Probabilistic Voting and Nash Social Welfare Maxima," *Journal of Public Economics* 15: 113-21.

Crotty, James (1973), "Specification Error in Macro-Econometric Models: The Influence of Policy Goals," *American Economic Review* 63: 1025-30.

Cukierman, Alex, and Allan Meltzer (1986), "A Positive Theory of Discretionary Policy, The Cost of Democratic Government and the Benefits of a Constitution," *Economic Inquiry* 24: 367-88.

Diamond, Peter, and James Mirrlees (1971), "Optimal Taxation and Public Production," *American Economic Review* 61: 8-27, 261-78.

Driffill, John (1988), "Macroeconomic Policy Games with Incomplete Information; A Survey," *European Economic Review* 32: 533-41.

Feldstein, Martin (1973), "On the Optimal Progressivity of the Income Tax," *Journal of Public Economics* 2: 357-76.

Fisher, Stanley (1980), "Dynamic Inconsistency, Cooperation and the Benevolent Dissembling Government," *Journal of Economic Dynamics and Control* 2: 93-107.

Frey, Bruno, and Friedrich Schneider (1982), "Politico-Economic Models in Competition with Alternative Models: Which Is Better?" *European Journal of Political Research* 10: 241-54.

Fullerton, Don, Yolanda Henderson, and John Shoven (1984), "A Comparison of Methodologies in Empirical General Equilibrium Models of Taxation," in H. Scarf and J. Shoven (eds.), *Applied General Equilibrium Analysis.* Cambridge: Cambridge University Press.

Harberger, Arnold (1962), "The Incidence of the Corporate Income Tax," *Journal of Political Economy* 70: 215-40.

Keller, Wouter (1979), *Tax Incidence: A General Equilibrium Approach.* 's Gravenhage: Pasmans.

Kydland, Finn, and Edward Prescott (1977), "Rules rather than Discretion: The Inconsistency of Optimal Plans," *Journal of Political Economy* 85: 473-91.

Ledyard, John (1984), "The Pure Theory of Large Two-Candidate Elections," *Public Choice* 44: 7-41.

Lucas, Robert (1976), "Econométric Policy Evaluation: A Critique," in K. Brunner and A. Meltzer (eds.), *The Phillips-Curve and Labor Markets.* Carnegie-Rochester Conferences on Public Policy, v. 1. Amsterdam: North-Holland.

McKelvey, Richard (1976), "Intransitivities in Multidimensional Voting Models and Some Implications for Agenda Control," *Journal of Economic Theory* 12: 472-82.

Meltzer, Allan, and Scott Richard (1981), "A Rational Theory of the Size of Government," *Journal of Political Economy* 89: 914-27.

Mirrlees, James (1971), "An Exploration in the Theory of Optimum Income Taxation," *Review of Economic Studies* 38: 175-208.

Musgrave, Richard (1959), *The Theory of Public Finance: A Study in Public Economy.* New York: McGraw-Hill.

Persson, Torsten (1988), "Credibility and Macroeconomic Policy; An Introduction and a Broad Survey," *European Economic Review* 32: 519-32.

Persson, Torsten, and Guido Tabellini (1990), *Macroeconomic Policy, Credibility and Design.* Chur, Switzerland: Harwood.

Renaud, Paul (1989), *Studies in Applied Political Economic Modeling.* Berlin: Springer.

Rogoff, Kenneth, and Anne Sibert (1988), "Elections and Macroeconomic Policy Cycles," *Review of Economic Studies* 60: 1-16.

Rutherford, Thomas, and Stanley Winer (1990), "Endogenous Policy in a Computational General Equilibrium Framework," Working Paper, University of Western Ontario, London.

Sheshinski, Eytan (1972), "The Optimal Linear Income Tax," *Review of Economic Studies* 39: 297-302.

Shoven, John, and John Whalley (1972), "A General Equilibrium Calculation of the Effects of Differential Taxation of Income from Capital," *Journal of Public Economics* 84: 281-321.

(1973), "General Equilibrium with Taxes: A Computational Procedure and an Existence Proof," *Review of Economic Studies* 60: 475-90.

(1984), "Applied General-Equilibrium Models of Taxation and International Trade: An Introduction and Survey," *Journal of Economic Literature* 22: 1007-51.

Stiglitz, Joseph (1989), "On the Economic Role of the State," in A. Heertje (ed.), *The Economic Role of the State.* Southampton, U.K.: Camelot Press.

Tullock, Gordon (1988), "Future Directions for Rent-Seeking Research," in C. Rowley, R. Tollison, and G. Tullock (eds.), *The Political Economy of Rent-Seeking.* Boston: Kluwer.

Van Velthoven, Ben (1989), *The Endogenization of Government Behaviour in Macroeconomic Models*. Berlin: Springer.

Van Velthoven, Ben, and Frans van Winden (1991), "A Positive Model of Tax Reform," *Public Choice* 72: 61-86.

Van Winden, Frans (1983), *On the Interaction between State and Private Sector*. Amsterdam: North-Holland.

(1987), "Man in the Public Sector," *De Economist* 135: 2-28.

Zodrow, George (1988), "Eliminating State and Local Tax Deductibility: A General Equilibrium Model of Revenue Effects," in H. Rosen (ed.), *Fiscal Federalism: Quantitative Studies*. Chicago: University of Chicago Press.

Printed in the United States
By Bookmasters